# SECRET REPORTS ON NAZI GERMANY

# SECRET REPORTS ON NAZI GERMANY

The Frankfurt School
Contribution to the War Effort

FRANZ NEUMANN
HERBERT MARCUSE
OTTO KIRCHHEIMER

Edited by Raffaele Laudani
With a foreword by Raymond Geuss

PRINCETON UNIVERSITY PRESS
PRINCETON AND OXFORD

Requests for permission to reproduce material from this work should be sent to Permissions, Princeton University Press
Published by Princeton University Press, 41 William Street, Princeton, New Jersey 08540
In the United Kingdom: Princeton University Press, 6 Oxford Street, Woodstock, Oxfordshire OX20 1TW
press.princeton.edu



Library of Congress Cataloging-in-Publication Data

Neumann, Franz, 1904–1974.

Secret reports on Nazi Germany : the Frankfurt School contribution to the war effort / Franz Neumann, Herbert Marcuse, Otto Kirchheimer ; edited by Raffaele Laudani ; with a foreword by Raymond Geuss.
p. cm.
Includes bibliographical references and index.
ISBN 978-0-691-13413-0 (hbk.)
1. Germany—Politics and government—1933–1945. 2. Germany—Politics and government—1945–1990. 3. Germany—Social conditions—1933–1945. 4. Frankfurt school of sociology—Influence. 5. Reconstruction (1939–1951)—Germany. 6. World War, 1939–1945—Economic aspects—Germany. 7. World War, 1939–1945—Economic aspects—Germany. 8. World War, 1939–1945—Germany. I. Marcuse, Herbert, 1898–1979. II. Kirchheimer, Otto. III. Laudani, Raffaele. IV. United States. Office of Strategic Services. Research and Analysis Branch. Central European Section. V. Title.
DD253.N425 2013
940.53'43—dc23 2013003225

British Library Cataloging-in-Publication Data is available

This book is published with the support of the Department of History, Anthropology, and Geography at the University of Bologna

This book has been composed in Baskerville 10 Pro

Printed on acid-free paper. ∞

Printed in the United States of America

1 3 5 7 9 10 8 6 4 2

CONTENTS

# FOREWORD

When Hitler declared war on the United States in the third year of what has come to be called World War II, the US government decided that it needed to have general policies that would be informed by a genuine understanding of who and what its enemy was, what it was trying to do, what strengths and weaknesses it had, and how far it had succeeded in molding Germany, and indeed Continental Europe as a whole, in its preferred image. The conduct of the war required, it was assumed, sober assessment of the real situation and careful thought about the possible long-term outcomes of different policy decisions. In addition, the war needed to be fought with an eye to how it could potentially come, or be brought, to an end; how the process of reconstruction might be managed; and what form a reconstructed Europe might take. To help in formulating such a policy, the US government created a special division, the Research and Analysis Branch (R&A), within its intelligence agency, the Office of Strategic Services (OSS). This research and analysis group tried to recruit as many first-rate minds with wide and appropriate experience as possible, doing so without any special concern for the particular political commitments, national origin, or ideological orthodoxy of those recruited. In the end the analyses this group presented seem to have had some effect on actual policy, although not as much as most of the members of the group would have wished. Many older forms of liberalism had indeed emphasized the inherent value of tolerance and the connection between toleration of intellectual deviancy and success in the pursuit of genuine understanding of the world, but with the onset of the Cold War in the late 1940s, even paying lip service to these ideas came to be thought an expensive luxury that could no longer be afforded. The Research and Analysis Branch was closed in 1949.

In the Anglo-American world of the early twenty-first century, we have become accustomed to a politics of myopic intellectual conformism; of lazy indifference to, and incuriosity about, other people and societies except as potential objects of exploitation or manipulation; of massive governmental deceit; of policy-making by knee-jerk reaction; and of sound bite and television spot as the basic units of political discourse. That in the historical period after George W. Bush and Tony Blair, the above account of the operations in the 1940s of the Research and Analysis Branch of the OSS sounds like the description of an implausible utopia, a never-never land too good to be true, is an indication of how far we have moved on since that time and how much lower expectations about the competence, honesty, and public-spiritedness of governmental agencies have become.

The texts in this volume were written for the R&A division of the OSS between 1943 and 1949. The three main authors, Otto Kirchheimer, Herbert Marcuse, and Franz Neumann, were leftist German-Jewish émigrés who were as united in their concerted attempts to understand National Socialism as clearly and fully as possible as they were in their abhorrence of it. All three rejected the view that National Socialism was a mere historical accident resulting from a unique conjunction of unrepeatable contingent circumstances, but they also rejected the view that it was the expression of some essential, underlying, and invariant properties of German culture or national character. To hold the latter view, they thought, would merely be to take at face value what National Socialism itself preached. Finally, they did not believe in the thesis of a German *Sonderweg*, a special and distinctive path to modernity that represented a "deviation" from the "norms" set by other Western European societies. So National Socialism, in their view, was also not the next step in a long-term path of aberrant development, the origins of which lay in an inaccessible, although historically specific, past. Churchill's interpretation of National Socialism as a new version of "Prussian militarism" may have been a politically effective rhetorical gesture in the Britain of the 1930s, but it was actually, the authors claim, a complete mistake: Prussia in the 1930s always exhibited a lower level of electoral support for the Nazis than other parts of Germany did, and members of the Prussian military aristocracy were most notable by their almost complete absence from the higher echelons of the National Socialist Party; devoted, dyed-in-the-wool Party members and proper "Junkers" always confronted one another with at best deep-seated and very well grounded suspicion and more usually with scarcely veiled mutual loathing. The quasi-feudal structures of pre–World War I Prussia were, for National Socialists, precisely part of the inherited historical rubbish they intended to sweep away. Germany was not to be prussianized, but, on the contrary, Prussia, too, was to be *"gleichgeschaltet" and "verreichlicht,"* to lose its individuality and specific character and become just one more interchangeable cog in the national machine. If one is looking for the sources of German political and military aggression in the twentieth century, Marcuse argues in one of the reports (written together with another young German-Jewish émigré, Felix Gilbert, who later became a distinguished historian), they are to be found not so much in Prussian militarism as in the policies of the German "industrial bourgeoisie" (p. 79). Many very active supporters, including some early and highly substantial financial backers, of National Socialism were captains of industry, who were also clever enough to keep themselves in the background and "camouflage themselves," never accepting any high political office or becoming prominent members of the Party. Many of the reports draw attention to this underlying cause and to the ultimate responsibility of industrialists and business groups for the catastrophes of the 1930s and early '40s. If the intention, as seems likely, was to prevent subsequent denazification procedures (and war crimes trials) from focusing too exclusively on high-profile members of the Party and the military, while allowing equally, if less directly, responsible businessmen and other economic agents to escape scot free, this attempt was by and large a failure. Similarly, the authors warn that the group solidarity of the legal profession will most likely make highly needed denazification of judges especially difficult, as in fact turned out to be the case.

The explicit "medievalism" of some aspects of National Socialist culture was at best superficial window dressing; the reality was that Nazi Germany was one specific kind of highly "modern" mass society. When the philosopher Bernard Williams in a famous passage asserts that it was incoherent to try to live the life of a Teutonic knight in 1930s Nuremberg, he was, of course, correct, but this was not the final judgment to be made on National Socialism. Kirchheimer, Neumann, and Marcuse distinguished as sharply between ideological appearance and reality as most even moderately sophisticated human agents do between official professions of faith and actual intentions. Beneath the Wagnerian posturing was an utterly antitraditional, thoroughly modern cult of ruthless technical efficiency. By 1943 Germany was organized around a system of nonvoluntary cartels and "cartel-like organisations" that was carefully calculated to extract the maximum possible production from the national economy as a whole. This highly integrated and rationalised structure had, and was intended to have, not the slightest resemblance either to a slap-dash collection of medieval guilds that enforced traditional quotas, practices, and norms in individual areas of production or to a "free market" system of unregulated individual entrepreneurs. The cult of technical rationality found its highest exemplar in Albert Speer. In retrospect we can see Speer as perhaps the first in a long line of politically active technocrats that came eventually to include such figures as Robert MacNamara during the Vietnam War and Donald Rumsfeld during the military campaigns in the Gulf and Afghanistan.

If Nazi Germany was an archetypically modern society, responding in a particularly vivid way to imperatives that were not limited in their operation to *Mitteleuropa,* then it was more fruitful also to look for and at the similarities between Hitler's Central Europe, Stalin's Soviet Union, and the Western democracies of Roosevelt, Truman, and Churchill than to focus exclusively on the differences. Kirchheimer, Marcuse, and Neumann thought that National Socialism, Communism, and the capitalist version of liberal democracy were all responses to the same phenomenon: the economic collapse of the late 1920s and early 1930s. US president Herbert Hoover could repeat the orthodox view that the Great Depression was none of the government's business *at all*, because he thought the economy was, and had to continue to be, self regulating. He, however, was virtually the last major politician in the Western world to make any serious attempt to act on this conviction clear-headedly and consistently. When he did act, or rather when he failed to act, it was with disastrous consequences. No European or North American government since the 1930s has been able to get along without a detailed economic and industrial policy that included various regulatory and interventive measures designed to promote at least minimal economic stability, although some have made more or less desperate attempts to deny or obfuscate this fact or to explain it away. The question is not whether politics should or should not set the parameters of economic activity, because in fact, one way or another, it always does that anyway, but what particular form the structuration will take—that is, roughly, who will benefit and who will suffer.

One might think that in addition to the Big Three of Nazism, Stalinism, and capitalist liberal democracy, there was a fourth option and one that formed the object of much speculation for the authors of the texts collected in this volume: "social democracy" as represented in the first instance by the German Social Democrats (SPD). Given the differences in their ideology, party structure, and membership, and the history of their often bloody conflicts with each other, the SPD and the Communists (especially the Communist Party of Germany, the KPD) had to be treated as distinct, and in some ways antagonistic, groups. It is, however, important to recall that the documents in this volume were written during a time in which Roosevelt's "New Deal"—as it were, "social democracy *lite*"—and, after the electoral defeat of Churchill in 1945, Labour's commitment to the welfare state, could reasonably be thought to constitute the continuing framework for capitalist forms of democracy in the modern world. It is thus no real criticism that Neumann, Kircheimer, and Marcuse do not discuss thematically another form of politics and economics that they could in principle easily have imagined, but that would have seemed to them utterly anachronistic: "neo-liberalism," a return to mouthing the pieties of the Hoover era that while actually deploying the considerable resources of modern governments to structure and control the economy in the interests of the rich, gained considerable traction under Reagan and Thatcher in the 1980s. That it eventually failed would not have come as any surprise to the authors of these reports. Doing one thing while professing to do another is, after all, not usually an especially good starting point for conceptual clarity or practical efficiency, although, of course, it might have certain political advantages if one's real intentions or the actual consequences of one's actions are particularly destructive. In fact, as Nietzsche pointed out, those who honestly believe in delusional political programs are in some sense worse off, and potentially more dangerous to themselves and others, than actors who are consciously manipulative and know it, because the latter retain some minimal cognitive grip on reality. The increasingly brittle, and eventually self-destructive, inflexibility of politics in Germany in the 1930s and 1940s was partly the result of the dominance of organizations that prided themselves on excluding opportunists and promoting fanatics. It has often been noted that *fanatisch* was a term of high praise for National Socialists, and fanaticism in general is, after all, a form of honesty, albeit a form that for various reasons is usually not especially attractive to any but the relevant true believers themselves.

The palpable failure in the period after 2007 of the free-market ideologies and policies of radical deregulation that had dominated politics since the time of Thatcher and Reagan may open a space for us to reflect again on customary forms of production, consumption, and exchange; on cherished assumptions about the nature and value of modern western forms of "democracy"; on the meaning and various forms of "freedom"; on the role of the nation-state and of government in an international system increasingly overshadowed by large and powerful corporations and financial institutions; and in general on the relation between politics and economics. In this context these "intelligence reports" from almost seventy years ago, which are focused on the life and death of one historically particularly destructive way of trying to answer these questions, National Socialism, and on the prospects of two other possible answers, Communism and capitalist liberal-democracy, retain a remarkable freshness and relevance.

*Raymond Geuss*

# ACKNOWLEDGMENTS

Many people have contributed to the realization of this volume with advice and suggestions: Carlo Galli, Anna Guagnini, Barry Katz, Ira Katznelson, Mariuccia Salvati, Anna Soci, Nadia Urbinati, Dominique Vidal, and Richard Wolin. My heartfelt thanks go to them, and to the personnel of the National Archives and Records Administration.

*R.L.*

# NOTES ON THE TEXTS

The texts gathered in this volume constitute an ample and important selection of the intelligence reports on Nazi Germany produced over the course of the Second World War and immediately after by Franz Neumann, Herbert Marcuse, and Otto Kirchheimer as analysts in the Central European Section of the Research and Analysis Branch (R&A) of the Office of Strategic Services (OSS). These documents, declassified between 1975 and 1976, are still held in the Civil Archives Division, Legislative and Diplomatic Branch of the US National Archives in College Park, Maryland, Research Group 59; with rare exceptions, all are available on microfilm (R&A Finished Reports).

The texts all have different natures, dimensions, and functions and vary from comments on phenomena of current political events, to the historical and theoretical contextualization of a specific phenomenon, to the production of long and complex reports. All these documents originally circulated in an anonymous form with only a title, publication date, and catalog number. For this reason, the attribution of the single reports is controversial: among the first to work on the OSS's archive materials, Alfons Söllner maintained in his *Zur Archäologie der Demokratie in Deutschland* (2 vols.; Frankfurt am Main: Fischer Verlag, 1986), the impossibility of identifying a specific author for each single report, in virtue of the participation of many analysts in their actual realization. As much as it is certainly true that the reports were the result of teamwork, often with the material participation of many analysts over the various phases of their realization, as new sources unavailable to Söllner show, it is also true that every report was undoubtedly conducted under the precise responsibility of one or more authors charged with coordinating a working group, planning the research, and materially drafting the text. Herbert Marcuse's texts *The Social Democratic Party of Germany*, *Dissolution of the Nazi Party and Its Affiliated Organizations*, and *Policy Towards the Revival of Old Parties and Establishment of New Parties in Germany* are perfect examples: as the author himself explains in a document found in the Marcuse Archive in Frankfurt, most likely written as part of an application for an academic position and now published under the title "Description of Three Major Projects" in H. Marcuse, *Technology, War and Fascism* (ed. D. Kellner [London–New York: Routledge, 1998], pp. 193–98), the three texts were written by Marcuse himself, using various assistance to gather data and to produce the bibliographic information. Not unlike what happens to works published by a publisher or in a review, the final version of the reports was subject to an editorial revision by the R&A Project Committee, then submitted to the author for final approval.

Normally, naming the material author or authors of every single report was possible through consulting other R&A documents —for example, letters, meeting notes, progress reports, or internal memos preserved in the College Park National Archives' Military Records Division, specifically in the Records of the Research and Analysis Branch, Research Group 226, and declassified in 1980. This research was first done by Barry M. Katz for the volume *Foreign Intelligence: Research and Analysis in the Office of Strategic Services 1942–1945* (Cambridge, Mass.: Harvard University Press, 1989), although his indications don't always coincide with the results of the research at the American Archives that I conducted in the preparation of this volume. In any case, I decided to select only texts for which it was possible to identify with reasonable certainty at least one of the three authors responsible for its drafting. The information regarding the texts' authors are provided before each text in a brief editor's note where the document or documents used to trace the author or authors are indicated, together with the catalog number with which the report was originally identified by the OSS. When necessary, other useful information on the context in which the report was published and on possible coauthors has also been provided.

The texts *The German Communist Party*, *The Social Democratic Party of Germany*, *Dissolution of the Nazi Party and Its Affiliated Organizations*, *Leadership Principle and Criminal Responsibility*, *Policy Toward Revival of Old Parties and Establishment of New Parties in Germany*, and *The Revival of Political and Consitutional Life in Germany under Military Government* appeared for the first time in German, anonymous and in certain cases in a partial form, in Söllner's previously cited volume. Excerpts of the reports *Possible Patterns of German Collapse* and *The Attempt on Hitler's Life and Its Consequences* were published in English in the anthology edited by Jürgen Heideking and Christof Mauch, *American Intelligence and the German Resistance to Hitler: A Documentary History* (Boulder: Westview Press, 1998). Here, the reports have been published in their entirety. Only the table of contents and the abstracts that previously appeared at the beginning of the texts have been eliminated, as they do not add any new content. In some cases, a few appendixes that contain statistics or lists of names with little relevance have been omitted, although they are cited in the editor's notes that introduce every report.

Although originally written in English, the texts heavily reflect the German origins of the authors. As Eugene N. Anderson, head of the Central European Section between 1943 and 1945, recalled, the three

German scholars spoke in "broken English," a sort of *lingua franca* further burdened by the "military" stylistic rituals imposed by R&A's direction. Nonetheless, I decided to not alter the texts, limiting editorial interventions merely to the correction of evident typos. In the Notes section, editor's notes are also limited to cases considered really useful for the reader, and in this same section I have inserted page numbers relevant to the text where I felt they would be helpful; these are in brackets. The development of new technologies, particularly the Internet, have in fact profoundly modified the role of the editor, whose quality and reliability are no longer measured by the production of an imposing system of notes but rather by the ability to select useful information from an otherwise almost unlimited surfeit of information, to which the reader now has easy and autonomous access. The editor's introduction and notes to the texts are translated into English by Jason Francis McGimsey.

*R.L.*

# ON THE AUTHORS

## Franz Leopold Neumann

Born in Kattowitz on May 23, 1900, the son of a small Jewish businessman, Franz Neumann studied law, philosophy, and economics in Lipsia—where in 1918 he joined the SPD (Social Democratic Party) and participated in the soldiers' and workers' barricades during the German revolution—and in Rostock and Frankfurt am Main—where, together with Leo Löwenthal, he founded the Socialist Students Society, earning a doctorate in law in 1923 with a thesis on the theory of punishment.

From 1925 to 1927 he worked as law clerk of and assistant to Hugo Sinzheimer, the foremost German Social Democratic labor law theorist and one of the fathers of the Weimer Constitution, and taught at the Trade Unions Academy affiliated with the University of Frankfurt. In 1928 he moved to Berlin, where together with another one of Sinzheimer's former students, Ernst Fraenkel, he worked as an attorney in labor law, representing the construction workers and other unions, and wrote several essays on labor law, cartels, and monopoly economy on the SPD official organ *Die Gesellshaft* while attending Hermann Heller's and Carl Schmitt's seminars at the University of Berlin. In the summer of 1932 he became the leading attorney of the SPD, fighting against restrictions on free speech and against the illegal firing and arrests of workers by the Papen, Schleicher, and Hitler governments.

On May 2, 1933, after the Sturmabtellung (SA), the Nazi storm troopers, assaulted the trade unions offices but before he could be arrested, Neumann fled to London. There he studied with former Frankfurt sociology professor Karl Mannheim and the Marxist theorist Harold Laski at the London School of Economics, earning in 1936 a second doctorate with a thesis titled "The Governance of the Rule of Law: An Investigation into the Relationship between the Political Theories, the Legal System and the Social Background in the Competitive Society." The same year, on Laski's recommendation, he started an association with the Institute of Social Research, promoting its interests and diffusion in England, before moving to the United States. Notwithstanding Laski's support, once in the States Neumann was unable to find a position in the American academic system, instead working mostly as a lawyer for the institute.

His intellectual contribution to institute activity was limited to a couple of essays and a series of lectures on the totalitarian state within the framework of the institute seminars held at Columbia University.

After the publication in 1942 of *Behemoth: The Structure and Practice of National Socialism*, his contribution to the war effort started, first as a consultant to the Board of Economic Warfare, then joining the Research and Analysis Branch of the OSS.

In 1948, after the end of the war and his participation as a member of Justice Robert H. Jackson's team at the Nuremberg Trials, Neumann became professor of political science at Columbia, playing a decisive role in the development of political theory at American universities, while contributing also to the creation of the Free University of Berlin. Then, on September 2, 1954, having become an eminent and highly regarded professor on both shores of the Atlantic, he died in a car accident in Visp, Switzerland. His intellectual production of this period, which has strongly influenced postwar democratic theory in the United States, is now collected in the postmortem volume *The Authoritarian and the Democratic State*, edited by Herbert Marcuse.

## Herbert Marcuse

Born in Berlin on July 19, 1898, Herbert Marcuse was the son of a Jewish businessman, in a family well assimilated into German prewar society. While a student at the Mommsen Gymnasium, Marcuse joined the Wondervogel, one of the many youth movements developing in Germany before World War I, promoting a romantic criticism of the political and social structure of Imperial Germany. The war broke out in 1914, and in 1916 he was drafted into the German Army. Poor eyesight prevented him from being sent out of the country, and he eventually received permission to attend classes at the University of Berlin. The negative effects of the war within German society informed his political conscience: in 1917 he joined the SPD and then the Independent Social Democratic Party founded by Karl Kautsky, but with a strong sympathy for the radicalism of Rosa Luxemburg and Karl Liebknecht' s Spartakusbund, and during the German revolution he participated, as a representative of the soldiers' councils, in the armed defense of Alexanderplatz in Berlin from Freikorps attacks. .

After the kidnapping and murder of Rosa Luxemburg and Karl Liebknecht, strongly disappointed in the SPD, which he considered morally responsible for the murder, and by the dogmatism of the new Communist Party, he resigned all political memberships and returned to his studies at Humboldt University and Freiburg, where in 1922 he completed his doctoral dissertation on the German artist-novel. After completing his doctoral studies, he came back to Berlin, and here, from 1924 to 1929, he worked as a bookseller and publisher in a bookstore, in which his father had helped him to buy a part interest.

In 1929 Marcuse returned to the University of Freiburg to study philosophy. Under the guidance of Martin Heidegger, he worked on a study on *Hegel's Ontology and the Theory of Historicity*, intended to be his *Habilitationsschrift*—the inaugural dissertation required for qualification as a professor—which he then published, in 1932, without Heidegger's consent. During these years, Marcuse produced, in a series of essays published in *Die Gesellschaft*, a first attempt to integrate Heidegger's existentialism within the Marxist theory, a project abandoned after the publication in 1933 of Marx's *Economic and Philosphical Manuscripts of 1844*, of which he wrote one of the first reviews.

After the rise of Nazism, Marcuse emigrated to Switzerland to work, on Edmund Husserl's recommendation, at the Geneva branch of the Institute of Social Research, before moving in 1934 to the United States. During these years, he contributed several essays on the development of the "critical theory of society" to the institute's journal, and in 1941 he published a second book on Hegel: *Reason and Revolution: Hegel and the Rise of Social Theory*.

After the end of World War II and the disbanding of the OSS, Marcuse remained in Washington as an analyst of communist societies for the State Department. Only after the death of his wife, Sophie, in 1950 did he leave the government, after which, thanks to a scholarship from the Rockefeller Foundation, he worked at Columbia (1952–54) and Harvard (1954–55) on a project on soviet communism (*Soviet Marxism*, 1958). In 1955 he married Inge Werner Neumann, the widow of Franz Neumann, and published *Eros and Civilization: A Philosophical Inquiry into Freud*, which inaugurated his academic career.

In 1954 he was appointed professor of philosophy and political science at Brandeis University, where he remained until 1965. After the publication of *One-dimensional Man: Studies in the Ideology of Advanced Industrial Society* (1964), which transformed him as the "father of the student movement," he received an appointment to the University of California in San Diego. His last years are characterized by a rejuvenated political activism and an intensive intellectual production, with works such as *An Essay on Liberation* (1968), *Counterrevolution and Revolt* (1972), and *The Aesthetic Dimension* (1978). His involvement and support of radical protests made him the target of increasing attacks, both from such conservative circles as the American Legion, the Ku Klux Klan, the Republican Party (during his electoral campaign, Governor Ronald Reagan asked for his firing from the University of California) and leftist groups—the Progressive Labor Party and the Weathermen, for example. He died in Stenberg, West Germany, on July 29, 1979.

## Otto Kirchheimer

Otto Kirchheimer was born in Heilbronn, Germany, on November 11, 1905, into a Jewish family. From 1924 to 1928 he studied philosophy and history at Münster, and law and social science at Koln, Berlin, and Bonn, where he graduated in 1928 with a thesis titled "The Socialist and Bolshevik Theory of the State," written under the supervision of Carl Schmitt.

He then worked as a law clerk in Prussian justice administration and as a lecturer in several union schools, while participating actively, with numerous essays, in the leftist critique of the Weimar Republic and SPD politics.

In the summer of 1933, thanks to initial financial support from the London School of Economics, Kirchheimer emigrated to Paris, where he specialized in penal law. Here he started his association with the Institute of Social Research by joining the French branch; then, in the fall of 1937, he joined the US branch in New York as research associate. Until the summer of 1938 his main job for the institute was the revision of Georg Rusche's *Arbeitsmarkt und Strafvollzug*, which was published, with acknowledgment of Kirchheimer's coauthorship, in 1939 under the title *Punishment and Social Structure* and as part of an institute series. Kirchheimer also produced a series of important essays on National Socialism for the institute.

In 1943, when the Institute told Kirchheimer it could no longer support him financially, he accepted a position as visiting lecturer at Wellesley College before joining the OSS first as a part-time consultant and then as a full-time analyst. After the end of World War II, he remained as an analyst at the State Department, where from 1950 to 1955 he served as chief of the Central European Branch of the Office of Intelligence Research.

In 1955 Kirchheimer was appointed professor of political science at the New School for Social Research, and in 1961 he published his magnum opus, *Political Justice*. By 1962 he hadmoved to Columbia University as a professor of government and political science. During these years he developed his theory of "catch-all parties," to describe the increasing tendency of mass political parties to transcend the interests of specific groups of reference to gain the support of the majority of the electorate. He died of a heart attack on November 22, 1965, at Washington's Dulles Airport on the way back to New York.

# INTRODUCTION

1. On a hot summer day during Italy's long 1968, the leader of the French student movement, Daniel Cohn-Bendit (today a member of the European Parliament and distinguished member of the Green Party) frequently interrupted a lecture being given by Herbert Marcuse in the packed Eliseo Theater in Rome, demanding he own up to his scandalous past as a CIA agent during World War II.[1] The accusation —originally circulated in the United States by an anonymous source and later picked up by the European press[2]—was inaccurate: the German philosopher did not in fact have any collaborative relationship with the controversial American agency, much less during the war, when the CIA didn't even exist. Instead, Marcuse had later been under FBI investigation during his period of political notoriety as "father of the student movement" (although, to be truthful, half of the memos connected with that investigation were concerned with protecting him from death threats, especially after 1968). Indirectly, however, the provocation offered by "Danny *le rouge*" contributed to bringing to light a period in Marcuse's life that had previously been neglected. The same was true for other proponents of the so-called Frankfurt School, such as Franz Neumann and Otto Kirchheimer, who also participated in the American war effort as political analysts at the Research and Analysis Branch (R&A) of the Office of Strategic Services (OSS), the first American intelligence agency.[3]

In truth, these thinkers never demonstrated any particular embarrassment in connection with their past government service. Rather, on more than one occasion, they proudly defended their participation as one of the few attempts to make the Frankfurt School's Critical Theory a practical tool in the fight against fascism.[4] Precisely when Max Horkheimer and Theodor Adorno retreated into their Californian exile to write their *Dialectic of Enlightenment*—the Frankfurt School's philosophical urtext, envisioned as a "message in a bottle" for future generations while they faced a present that appeared irremediably evil—the other three Frankfurt scholars produced a formidable number of studies and reports on the "German enemy" that represent the most complex and insightful analyses of Nazi Germany ever put forth by members of the Frankfurt School, as well as an extraordinary historical source for scholars of the Second World War.

The years spent by the three "Frankfurters" in the service of the American government share little of the romanticized life of the secret agent who, immersed in danger, works in the theater of war or the double agent who plots in secret with the enemy; their endeavors much more closely resemble the "labor of the concept" that one associates with a stern German professor.

Directed by the Harvard historian William Langer, the Research and Analysis Branch was in fact the biggest American research institution in the first half of the twentieth century. At its zenith between 1943 and 1945, it included over twelve hundred employees, four hundred of whom were stationed abroad. In many respects, it was the site where post–World War II American social science was born, with protégés of some of the most esteemed American university professors, as well as a large contingent of European intellectual émigrés, in its ranks.[5] To cite only a few such figures: the anthropologist Gregory Bateson, the historian Felix Gilbert, the geographer Richard Hartshorne, the Marxist economists Paul Sweezy and Paul Baran, the economist Walter W. Rostow, future Nobel Prize winner Vassili Leontief, the sociologists Talcott Parsons and Barrington Moore Jr., two-time Pulitzer winner Arthur Schlesinger Jr., the classicist Norman O. Brown, and the Frankfurt School scholars Arkadij Gurland and Friedrich Pollock. These men comprised the "theoretical brain trust" of the American war machine,[6] which, according to its founder, Colonel William "Wild Bill" Donovan, would function as a "final clearinghouse" for the secret services—that is, as a structure that, although not engaged in determining war strategy or tactics, would be able to assemble, organize, analyze, and filter the immense flow of military information directed toward Washington, thanks to the unique capacity of the specialists on hand to interpret the relevant sources.[7] In a global totalitarian war, Donovan was convinced, "intelligence must be total and totalitarian."[8]

2. One may situate the activities of Neumann, Marcuse, and Kirchheimer for the Research and Analysis Branch within the process of "total mobilization" of the American academic and intellectual world that, after the entrance of the United States into the war, pervaded "the classrooms of [its] colleges" and "rustle[d] the thumbed pages of our scholars."[9]

The first of the three German scholars to transfer to Washington was Franz Neumann. After a series of careful investigations by the FBI, he was hired in spring 1942 as chief consultant for the Board of Economic Welfare and later, in August of the same year, as chief economist in the Intelligence Division of the Office of the US Chief of Staff. At the beginning of 1943 he would assume the duties of deputy chief of the Central European Section, the subdivision of R&A charged with analyzing and studying Nazi Germany (as well as Austria and the other Central European countries). He gained these senior positions by virtue of the prestige he acquired after the 1942 publication of *Behemoth: The Structure and*

*Practice of National Socialism*—which was itself the fruit of a memorandum prepared at the request of Assistant Attorney General Thurman W. Arnold and a significant contribution to the American war effort.

In 1941 Marcuse had published *Reason and Revolution: Hegel and the Rise of Social Theory* in the hopes of securing an academic position. Reluctantly abandoning the Institute for Social Research, he joined the Office of War Information (OWI) with the goal of formulating "suggestions on 'how to present the enemy to the American people', in the press, movies, propaganda, etc."[10] In March of 1943 Marcuse joined Neumann in R&A's Central European Section as senior analyst and rapidly established himself as "the leading analyst on Germany."[11]

Kirchheimer, who together with Arkadij Gurland had collaborated with Neumann in 1942 on an important study, *The Fate of Small Business in Nazi Germany*, for the US Senate's Special Committee to Study Problems of American Small Business, worked for a few months as a consultant for the OSS before, in 1944, being welcomed among the members of the Central European Section as a specialist on the German penal and constitutional system.[12]

The government experience of these three members of the Institute for Social Research coincided with a turning point within the Frankfurt School itself. The departure of many of the scholars who had made the school famous marked, in many senses, the end of the Frankfurt School as a theoretically unified movement. One cause of this dissolution was certainly the growing economic difficulties of the Institute for Social Research (directed by Max Horkheimer and hosted since 1937, on New York City's Morningside Heights, by Columbia University).[13] During his negotiations with Washington agencies, on more than one occasion Marcuse earnestly entreated Horkheimer to give him an economic or intellectual reason for renouncing the economic security that his entrance into government service would guarantee him. In the second half of the 1930s, Marcuse strongly contributed to the definition of the program of Critical Theory[14]. For him, then, this experience could be lived in a non-punitive way only if thought along the lines of the contributions that, since the beginning of the war, the institute was trying to provide to the American war effort through the production of memoranda, research projects, and conferences on Nazi Germany.[15] Neumann and Kirchheimer's departures from the institute were somewhat less emotional; indeed, owing to the impossibility of his continuing to support the "costs" of their activities at the institute, Horkheimer was clearly urging them to accept employment offers from the various government agencies in Washington.[16]

As Horkheimer admitted in a letter to Neumann on February 1, 1942,[17] the financial difficulties of the institute were also accompanied by significant theoretical and political divergences that had emerged around the question of the nature and function of National Socialism. The entire group shared the idea that Nazism was in fact part of a wider process of social transformation that included Soviet Communism and liberal democracies in a single paradigm of domination. Nazism was thus part of what Horkheimer and Theodor Adorno would subsequently define in the 1950s as "total socialization," or the process of systemic repression typical of mass society that "strikes the individual, as a presumably mere biological entity, no longer only from outside but in his own interior and makes him a monad of the social totality."[18] The differences consisted in identifying the driving force of the process of totalitarian socialization that Horkheimer, Adorno, and Friedrich Pollock saw in the autonomous movement of politics and technics, to which the economy was now inexorably subordinated. Conversely, for the future analysts of the Research and Analysis Branch, that driving force continued to be of a predominantly economic nature. Horkheimer and Pollock conceived their analysis within the wider theoretical framework of "state capitalism"—that is, as the expression of a qualitatively new social formation, in which, with market autonomy eliminated and the search for private accumulation subordinated to the needs of general planning, the profit motive tended more and more to be replaced by the "motivation of power," and traditional capitalists became *rentiers*.[19] From this perspective, Nazism could certainly be considered a "new order" founded on the "primacy of politics over the economy."[20] Not unlike the theses maintained during the same period by James Burnham, and even previously by the conservative German review *Die Tat*, directed by Ferdinand Fried,[21] Horkheimer's view was that power had assumed a predominantly impersonal nature and was now represented by a new social figure, the manager, in virtue of his superior technical knowledge of the alchemy of organization.[22] Increasingly, capital was administratively regulated by political power, which was itself beholden to the economic dominance of big business, thereby modifying the very composition of social classes.

In *Behemoth*, Neumann had on the contrary defined Nazism as a "non-state," a form of monopolistic-totalitarian capitalism where "ruling groups control the rest of the population directly without the mediation of that rational though coercive apparatus hitherto known as the state."[23] In his eyes, Pollock's thesis concerning state capitalism was a *contradictio in adjecto*, similar in its impracticability to that of the "state of the masses" advanced during the same period by another German émigré, Emil Lederer, who defined fascist dictatorship as "a modern political system which rests on the amorphous masses." This system, in order to guarantee the perpetuation of the dictator's power, had destroyed society's "stratified structure," giving life to a perverse form of "classless society."[24] For Neumann, capitalism under the Nazis hadn't resolved its innate antagonisms, which now operated on a higher level, concealed by the use of a powerful bureaucratic apparatus and the *völkisch* community ideology. In fact, the Nazi regime favored and accentuated the process of monopolistic concentration, reinforcing the power of industrial potentates and weakening the position of the middle and working classes. Thus, while the capitalist system hadn't lost its internal dynamism, and profit was still "the energy that motivated expansion," with the end of market autonomy implied in the monopolization process, a totalitarian political power was now required.

In Kirchheimer and Marcuse's explanation, the Nazis' rise to power was neither the result of a social revolution that qualitatively changed the relationships of production in capitalist society, nor a simple restoration of the *status quo ante* the Weimar Republic. It was, rather, the expression of a shift in the "political compromise" upon which modern German society had up until then been founded. The compromise was no longer between members of parliament and the government, as in classical liberalism, or through agreements between opposed voluntary associations, as in the era of mass democracy (Weimar). German society was now founded upon "pacts" between the heads of dominant groups (big industry, the Nazi Party, and the army), who were united only by the common interest of keeping the regime alive, and whose conflicts were reconciled in the figure of the Führer, "the locus of final compromise," and in his policy of imperialist expansion. The Nazi invective against the "spirit of capitalism" was thus anything but anticapitalist; it was, rather, the expression of the growing obsolescence of competitive capitalism based on individual effort and the rise of an economic power now concentrated in the hands of a few large trusts.[25]

In contast to Horkheimer's perspective, for Neumann, Marcuse, and Kirchheimer economic relations themselves were immediately transformed into political relationships whereby the state was the "executive organ" of the economy that organized and coordinated the entire nation for imperialist economic expansion. The advantages that were derived for big economic groups from the immediate identification of the state with dominant economic interests rendered their lack of independence acceptable. In particular, Nazism eliminated the typical characteristics of the liberal era—the monopoly on the legitimate use of force, the universality of the law, the state as a system of rational administration—all of the overlap between politics and society. At the same time, Nazism's politicization of the private sphere could qualify the Third Reich as a "state of the masses," where all forces and individual interests were "submerged into an emotional human mass, skillfully manipulated by the regime" and united only by the common instinct of self-preservation. This politicization, however, did not result in even a perverse form of a classless society. Like every capitalist society, National Socialism was constituted around two opposed social classes, "the small number of those who control the productive process and the bulk of the population which, directly or indirectly, is dependent upon the former." Its specificity consisted in having streamlined the process of social differentiation, repressing all intermediate agencies and groups, which resulted in the *de facto* expansion of the base of exploitation. In this sense, it represented "the specifically German adaptation of society to the requirements of large scale industry" that with liberal democracies and Soviet communism shared the affirmation of a new form of rationality. This was the "technical rationality" that "functions according to the standards of efficiency and precision. At the same time, however, it severed itself from everything related to the humane needs and wants of individuals; it is entirely adapted to the requirements of an all-embracing apparatus of domination."[26]

3. The three German scholars had very different backgrounds. Neumann was a student of Hugo Sinzheimer and Harold Laski; until the publication of *Behemoth*, he had practiced as a lawyer for the Social Democratic Party (SPD) and various union organizations. Marcuse was a philosopher who had studied under Heidegger, with brief political experience in his youth during the November Revolution of 1918–19, from which he developed his own approach to Marxism and an implacable antipathy for German Social Democracy, responsible, in his opinion, for the failure of the revolution. Kirchheimer was a student of Carl Schmitt, with brief experience as a Prussian penal administration secretary and a disinclination for activist politics. Despite these varied experiences, they came to Washington united by a solid bond of friendship, which extended even to their respective families. Above all, they were united by a shared methodology and theoretical perspective, cemented over the years of their collaboration with the Institute for Social Research.

However, in Washington Neumann, Marcuse, and Kirchheimer found a working environment that was profoundly different from the institute and a cultural terrain that was undoubtedly less favorable for practicing "critical theory." Despite the three German scholars' clearly Marxist orientation, however, their difficulties were not of a predominantly political or ideological nature. Until the advent of the Cold War, the American administration's priority was to make the best possible use of the talents of the leading specialists available for the war effort. For example, Paul Sweezy—who was already well known before the war as a brilliant student of Schumpeter with a clearly Marxist orientation—was hired by General Donovan for R&A's Economic Division without any concern whatsoever for the young radical's Communism. Donovan only wanted to make sure, for reasons of expediency, that Sweezy wouldn't take part in violent demonstrations and that he wasn't against the political use of explosives or the like.[27] The same went for Neumann, whose Socialist political orientation was noted by government officials well before his joining the OSS.[28] What's more, today we know that, at least for a short time, Neumann acted as a KGB informant during his service with the OSS with the code name "Ruff," providing the Soviets with top secret materials (e.g., those used to write the report on the attempts against Hitler's life—published here—and which were denied to his colleagues at the R&A's London branch).[29] And Neumann's collaboration with KGB was possibly known to the American secret services through "Venona," a system of decoding the encrypted messages of Soviet espionage agencies, without any accusations of treason or conspiracy against him having arisen.[30]

Much more troubling for the three German scholars were the "ethnic" prejudices in the OSS against European émigrés. This prejudice was evident in the decision to assign supervisory duties to American WASPs, thus preventing the alien "enemies" from assuming administrative responsibility in subdivisions like the Central European Section—even when, as in Neumann's case, their superior abilities were universally acknowledged.[31]

Still, what had the greatest impact on Critical Theory was R&A's bureaucratic organization, which manifested itself in a series of internal directives that obsessively demanded a policy of scientific objectivity and neutrality throughout the war. The purpose of the directives was to prevent the authors from influencing readers with personal opinions, to the point that terminology in the drafting of reports was regulated down to the last minute detail.[32] This positivist obsession was driven by the Project Committee, the R&A office charged with approving every report written and its subsequent distribution (the main recipients being the "operative" units of the OSS, the American and British military hierarchies, the White House, and the various departments of Roosevelt's administration). The Project Committee was directed by the "orthodox" geographer Richard Hartshorne, for whom "Proust, Joyce or Gertrude Stein would all be equally out of place in R&A" because "intelligence reports find their literary merit in terseness and clarity rather than in expressive description."[33] On more than one occasion the circulation of the Central European Section's reports was blocked because they were considered beneath R&A's expected standards of "mature and objective scientific research."[34]

To avoid undermining the very presuppositions of a theory that aimed at being "critical" and that had begun precisely with the refusal of a positivist conception of scientific research as the "mere duplication of the real in thought," those in the Frankfurt group found themselves forced to reconfigure the inner logic of their research activities. They abandoned philosophical and theoretical categories for an analysis that was apparently more descriptive but that was, in reality, spurred by specific questions or strictly political or military phenomena. This approach resulted in their work at times assuming even more critical contours, thereby provoking veritable political "battles" inside the American administration—which they nearly always lost.

Their access to a number of "unconventional" sources, such as secret intelligence materials and reports from individual theaters of war, press reviews, telephone taps, war prisoner interrogations, as well as the entire resources of the Library of Congress, provided a more consistent empirical base for the group's research in comparison with the parameters at the Institute for Social Research. A typical example of this new working method for Critical Theory was Marcuse's report *German Social Stratification*. Marcuse was by far the most speculative Frankfurt School member in Washington, yet here we can see the "classic" thesis of the tripartite division of Nazi sovereignty argued in *Behemoth* supported by a statistical and factual base that allowed the precise definition of German class structure. Marcuse was thus able to debunk once and for all claims concerning the end of class divisions under Nazism.[35]

By adapting Critical Theory to the American cultural and bureaucratic machine, the Frankfurt group was rapidly able to impose their own "intellectual guidance" on the Central European Section, which despite being staffed by over forty analysts of different cultural and political backgrounds, ended up producing a cohesive interpretation of the Nazi "enemy" with a clear Frankfurt imprint. "The ablest persons to be found have been appointed," we read, for example, in a memoir prepared by Eugene N. Anderson, head of the Central European Section between 1943 and 1945 and the main sponsor of the Frankfurt group in the OSS.

> But in selecting personnel . . . have stressed the ability to do cooperative research. . . . The policy of mutual criticism and assistance has been consistently maintained. . . . Whenever a topic is assigned, all the analysts able to contribute anything on the subject, whether material or ideas, have sat in conference with the analyst responsible for the topic and have offered their information and knowledge. . . . Much credit in this respect is owing to Dr. Neumann and Dr. Marcuse, who both believe in and practice this approach to their work."[36]

Amazed, Anderson noted the relative ease with which the Frankfurt group was able to imprint upon the entire section their own research strategies. In this way, the three German scholars managed to reconcile their intellectual agenda with the "productivist" exigencies of the American intellectual-military establishment. In a letter to Horkheimer sent shortly after his joining the OSS, Marcuse wrote ironically, for example, of having received the grade "excellent" in the evaluation that, periodically, in consummate military style, all of the R&A analysts received.[37]

During the "endless" weekly meetings, shrouded in a blanket of smoke, the "excellent" Marcuse distinguished himself with his philosophic digressions, which apparently only Neumann could contain, and with his capacity to discover the authors of anonymous reports and memoranda in virtue "of his knowledge of dialectics."[38] As John Herz, who was Kirchheimer's closest collaborator at the time, recalls, "It was as if the left-Hegelian *Weltgeist* had taken up temporary residence in the Central European Section of the OSS."[39]

4. The Frankfurt group's arrival at the Central European Section coincided with a decisive moment in World War II, immediately after the Nazis' defeat in Stalingrad and Tunisia, when the American (and German) military and political hierarchies became convinced of an ultimate Allied victory. On more than one occasion, the section was thus called upon to comment on the "possible patterns of German collapse" and to identify the likely partners and interlocutors following the regime's fall. Along the same lines as the understanding of Nazism they developed before entering into government service, the Frankfurt group immediately warned the American authorities of the impossibility of operating with the same logic used following the defeat of the Second Empire in 1918. In that case the German military dictatorship had acted "exclusively at the top and never succeeded in gaining thorough control over the organizations and lives of the German people." Germany's military setbacks thus had provoked a decline of German "morale" that opened the way for a transition of political power "quietly, while hostilities were still in progress, and well in advance of the so-called revolution."[40] Still, Nazi totalitarianism presented a qualitatively different scenario: society had been "completely pulverized into its individual atoms which are then organized and manipulated from the top-down," "well-trained" to "want . . . 'peace, bread, and security', not politics" and to recognize "private sorrows, food, shelter, safety for themselves and their children" as its only priorities in a repressive context where "fear and distrust prevents them from articulating even these private sorrows." Apathy, fatigue, and distrust were therefore the fundamental characteristics of the German people, who, though wounded by the setbacks of war, had not been fundamentally transformed.[41] From the point of view of psychological warfare—which, the Frankfurters explained, shouldn't be "concerned with what people feel and think about their governments but rather to what extent these feelings and thoughts will and can affect their behavior within the framework of the enemy society"[42]—"morale" seemed wholly inconsequential. Rather, from this perspective, Nazism had truly managed to build a "nearly foolproof" society: if, in fact, "in a free society, the feelings of individuals are likely to be political facts of the highest importance," in a totalitarian regime like Nazi Germany they

were merely "a minor vulnerability" that could be used by the regime to its own advantage.[43] As the Allied bombing raids had also demonstrated, despite the important results reached on a strictly military level, on a social and political level they risked pushing the German people even closer to the Nazi government, perceived "as the only bastion against personal and national destruction."[44] Nazism had managed "to reduce the importance of individual feelings to a minimum" and transform even a coward into the most courageous fighter. "An entrepreneur," Marcuse commented provocatively,

> for instance, may dislike the Nazis; he may be convinced that they will lose the war. He may ardently desire peace and may even be willing to accept unconditional surrender. His morale may thus be said to be 'low.' What is the effect of his low morale on the operation of his armament factory? A worker may be a defeatist or even a revolutionist. Will he work less and can he work less? A soldier may not want to fight. Will his will have a chance of asserting itself?"[45]

In all three cases, distancing oneself from the regime would have been imprudent and irrational in a Hobbesian sense, because it would have meant putting one's own life seriously at risk. In such a repressive context, where morals had become "a democratic luxury," the "ordinary methods of psychological warfare" became totally inadequate. The Allies could only counter the totalitarian order "by smashing the structure for the management of morale," that is, destroying the Nazi system itself and the social and institutional structures of which it was the expression.

For the same reason, the Frankfurt group was suspicious of identifying the "heart of [Nazi] Germany" in "Prussian militarism" and its "destruction" as the main objective of the Allied forces. This strategic perspective reproduced, on a military level, the widely held idea, deep rooted in the United States, that there was a common antidemocratic path in Germany's history "from the romantics to Hitler."[46] To the Frankfurt group, this meant not grasping the "modern" nature of National Socialism, with serious consequences for effectively concluding the war. "Industrial concentration and the totalitarian integration of Germany into the imperialistic war economy," Marcuse and Felix Gilbert explained in their October 23, 1943, report published here, "have led to a new distribution of power in which political control rests solely with the new Nazi Party hierarchy and its industrialist military and petty bourgeois."[47] The transformation of the German Reich into a totalitarian political regime subject to centralized terroristic control had in fact rendered necessary the dissolution of Prussia as an autonomous political and administrative unit and, more generally, the dismantling of the "social and political complex" that guaranteed the Prussian Junker political predominance over all of Germany. The Junkers were tied to the Nazi regime only in virtue of the economic control of the large holdings in the occupied eastern territories, conceded to them as "compensation" for their political marginalization. Identifying Nazi Germany with "Prussian militarism" was misleading also from an ideological point of view. As Marcuse had already clarified in a report sent to the American governmental authorities before joining the OSS, the "new German mentality" was in fact much closer to the philosophy of efficiency and success typical of "western" bourgeois democracies than to the old German *Kultur* and conservative and semifeudal Prussian authoritarianism.[48] The Nazi regime embraced a "democratic" ideology founded on "the standards to technocratic efficiency regardless of traditional status and privileges." This was also true for the German army, the traditional center of the Junkers' political and social power, where the ruling logic was incompatible with the "obedience of corpses" of the old Prussian army. "The strength of the Nazi army" (again in the Marcuse-Gilbert report *The Significance of Prussian Militarism for Nazi Imperialism*) "depends to a great extent on the striking power of highly specialized small units having high technological and organizational efficiency," units that require "a technical training which is entirely alien to the tradition of the Prussian nobility, and . . . an organizational coordination unsuitable to the caste spirit of the *Junkers*."[49] Winston Churchill's reiteration of the old proverb of the struggle against the "Teutonic urge for domination," to which even the American political hierarchies seemed sensitive, thus risked leaving an "escape route" open for the ones truly responsible for Nazi oppression and aggression. This view of Prussian militarism also risked putting the Soviets in a privileged position as negotiators for conservative German circles hostile to Hitler's regime, since the Soviets —through the support of the League of German Officers and the National Committee for a Free Germany—seemed to have grasped the growing marginalization of the Prussian tradition in favor of industrial and financial structures.

However, Neumann and Marcuse discounted the possibilities of negotiating peace with some sectors of the German elite or arranging for an internal overthrow of the regime through traditional conservative circles, two prospects that a few American military and political groups had, at least for a time, anticipated. With the nominations of Heinrich Himmler to the Reich's Ministry of the Interior and Albert Speer as the "dictator of the German Economy" (August–September 1943), it became clear to the Americans that the Nazi leadership was determined "to fight the war to the bitter end and not to allow the emergence of a Badoglio government,"[50] and that the party intended to force different components of the Nazi's "compromise" to "stand together" through the application of totalitarian terror "to the limit." It is from this perspective—that is, in response to the shifting internal balance in the Nazis' "compromise," to the party's advantage—that Neumann interprets the failed assassination of Hitler on July 20, 1944. Written just two days after the attempt on Hitler's life, Neumann's analysis is that the German General Staff had in fact maintained its own identity throughout the course of the regime, even though it was full of faithful Nazis. With Himmler's promotion to internal dictator, the military authorities saw their control over the army seriously threatened by the SS and feared the loss of the only institutional tool that could play any role in "managing" a defeat with their own allies (industrial tycoons, bankers, the Junkers, and high-ranking officials).[51] Unlike the situation in 1918, military hierarchies could no longer count on "a Social Democratic leadership which would entrust demobilization and reorganization of the Army to the old Officers' Corps, encourage the establishment of a Free Corps, and protect the *Reichswehr* from parliamentary control."[52]

More generally, the Frankfurt group excluded the possibility of "a smooth transfer of political power from a totalitarian dictatorship to an organized political opposition . . . because the very essence of totalitarian dictatorship is the absence of organized opposition."[53] In such a scenario, the only real ally of the "United Nations" (i.e., the Allies) could be, in their opinion, the underground movement. However, not having the forces to autonomously conduct a movement of liberation from Nazism, the underground needed the "support of the United Nations"—that is, the military defeat and occupation of Germany by Allied powers.

5. By request of the Civil Affairs Division of the War Department, from the end of 1943 and for all of 1944 the Central European Section worked, under Neumann's direction, on the *Handbook on Nazi Germany* and, above all, on the *Civil Affairs Guides*, an important series of reports (in total over forty guides were planned, of which more than thirty were effectively realized) on political, economic, legal, and administrative problems that the military government would have to face in the first phases of occupation. The War Department's intention was to limit these proposals to furnishing "recommendations" to military government personnel working in liberated zones, without any pretense of an immediate political effect. Kircheimer, who was now working full time for Neumann and his Central European Section group, was responsible for the main guides on legal and administrative issues. Neumann and the group turned these guides into a tool to lobby the American administration, which was then occupied with internal discussions on how to treat the enemy at the end of the conflict. The Central European Section group transformed the proposals into an articulated program for the democratic reconstruction of the country. At the political and institutional level, the group recommended "competing political parties, civil

liberties and protection for small property holders." At an economic and social level, the recommendation included socialist measures, such as "the nationalization of key industries with the full exercise of democratic rights and liberties."[54]

In the American administration's internal debate, from the outset the Central European Section opposed the so-called Morgenthau Plan, which recommended the territorial dismembering of Germany and the destruction of its industrial base. Instead, it proposed an alternative centered around "the removal from German society of the causes of aggression." As Neumann explained in the October 11, 1944, report, *The Treatment of Germany*, the destruction of Germany's industrial base risked provoking serious internal social and economic tensions, both consigning the occupying forces to a long-term commitment as well as threatening "the post-war economic recovery of Europe" and its "pacification."[55] Similarly, the destruction of Germany as a political entity would have also created competing spheres of influence, or, even worse, "the consequence would be that the control over the policing of Germany would fall to the USSR," better situated than the United States and the UK to undertake "the investment of a considerable force for a long period," necessary in the case of a division of German territory imposed from above and lacking meaningful popular support.

The Frankfurt group held that "the task of governing [postwar] Germany is tremendous" and could not be simply resolved via the political and economic destruction of the country.[56] In their opinion, a *tabula rasa* policy was also impracticable from a strictly legal and administrative point of view. As Kirchheimer explained, "year by year," an endless stream of laws, decrees, and ordinances which have affected and transformed life and institutions in Germany to such an extent that the immediate wholesale abrogation of this legislation, though not without psychological benefit, would lead to chaotic conditions."[57] Both from the point of view of the "imperatives" of the military security of the United Nations as well as the ideals that they sought to promote, the only possible policy would consequently "include the gradual restoration to the German people of the liberties necessary for the reconstruction of their society in a democratic form."[58] In fact, without appealing to "indigenous personnel," it was impossible to aim for truly eliminating the "roots" of Nazism: "For security reasons alone," explained Kirchheimer, "the extent of the administrative functions to be carried out by Military Government will not be comparable with the scope of similar functions performed during the first two years of the military occupation of the Rhineland" at the end of the First World War.[59] In that case, the functions of the military government were limited to "contacts with a German government which was still intact and functioning outside the zone of occupation, and to a mild form of supervision of this government's regional and local machinery in the zone of occupation." Considering the forms and modalities of Nazi domination, as well as the war's impact on the German economic and social system, the military government would instead be forced to assume such vast administrative responsibilities that it couldn't avoid relying on German personnel.[60] This meant, from an organizational point of view, maintaining the formal framework of many German agencies, including, for example, the centralized control systems of raw materials, industry, and transportation in the European countries occupied by the Nazis,[61] while putting them under the political control and supervision of the military government.

The proposal to collaborate with the German people did not imply in any way a lenient treatment of the enemy. "Reasons of political morality," Neumann specified in his "tactical" memorandum against the Morgenthau Plan, "further require that the German people must share the responsibility for Nazism and its train of aggressiveness and atrocities. No matter how many Germans have rejected the works and ideology of Hitlerism . . . measures must be devised, therefore, which will impose upon Germany certain liabilities and responsibilities to be borne by the German people."[62] Similarly, a series of long-term punitive "impositions" needed to be immediately established, including the permanent interdiction of a standing army and a prohibition against arms production. However, for the Frankfurt group, the occupying force's intransigence should be mainly directed through a radical policy of denazification that extended beyond merely purging the Nazi political and military leadership. The denazification policy should also undermine Nazism's "economic base," which had been promoted and sustained by elements external to the party, and which, over the years, came to pervade "all spheres of public and private life."[63] In a series of proposals coordinated by Marcuse, the Central European Section presented a list of 1,800 businessmen and officials who belonged to seemingly "neutral" economic institutions outside of the Nazi Party's ranks but who were "essential for the rise and maintenance of Nazism." These figures under the Nazi regime "exert[ed] considerable direct influence over economic controls" and so should be added to the approximately 220,000 "active Nazis" to be immediately put into preventive custody.[64]

"The most thoroughgoing possible elimination of Nazi and militaristic influences from German life"[65] could not, however, be limited to the aforementioned measures. It also presupposed a profound transformation of Germany's social structure "through a process of democratic evolution from below." An integral part of the military government's denazification program thus had to support the rebirth of a party and union system typical of liberal democracies, without, however, succumbing to the liberal democratic "repressive tolerance" that hypocritically claimed being impartial and neutral: "The principle of equal treatment of all political parties," Marcuse claimed in the report *Policy Toward Revival of Old Parties and Establishment of New Parties in Germany*, "will not be immediately applicable in post-war Germany." Treating nationalist rightwing groups the same as anti-Nazi groups and not grasping the fundamental distinction that exists "between acts of violence perpetrated by Nazis and those committed by anti-Nazis and directed against known terrorists and henchmen of the Nazi regime" would be tantamount in his opinion "to perpetuating the greatest threat to the security of the occupying forces and to the restoration of a peaceful order."[66] Denazification, therefore, had to be partisan and selective, distinguishing the real "anti-Nazis"—those who had demonstrated their active opposition not only to a few incidental aspects of the regime but also to its social, political, and ideological structure—from simple "non-Nazis" and, above all, from figures like the industrialist Fritz Thyssen, who "may again become an ardent supporter of a new aggressive militaristic policy if he deems it profitable for his business interests" or from reactionary circles and "National Bolshevism," which resented only the plebeian character of the regime but which were hostile to truly democratic policy. A mere willingness to cooperate with the occupying forces couldn't be considered a sufficient element to establish "anti-Nazi activity," since, foreseeably, many people "will seek the favor of the occupation authorities in order to retain the position they held under the Nazi system." This was true above all in the case of industrialists or bankers. Such figures "increased their power during the Hitler period" by participating in "the spoliation of the occupied territories, the 'Aryanization' of property, etc." They would nevertheless be ready to offer their services to the occupying authorities "in order to avoid identification with Nazi policies" by claiming to have "served" their country exclusively as businessmen without having held political office under Nazism.[67]

For the Frankfurt group, sincere cooperation was only possible with leftist anti-Nazi opposition (in which, as proof of a perspective that was still very dependent on the political framework inherited from the Weimar period, the Catholic *Zentrum* was also included). The immediate interests of leftwing opposition, in the opinion of the Frankfurt group, coincided with the security necessary to the military government. "The security of the occupying forces," Marcuse explained, "requires the immediate restoration of law and order, but the establishment of law and order is conditioned upon the elimination of Nazism, which can be accomplished only through the indigenous political opposition in Germany itself, . . . the greatest potential instrument for the destruction of German aggression."[68] In addition, activists from the anti-Nazi opposition could serve as a reserve army to partly fill the vacuum left by the necessary purging of the German administrative and legal machine, without blocking its functioning. "In the operation of modern administration," Neumann wrote, "the role of the trained civil servant . . . is quite frequently exaggerated." The anti-Nazi activists' lack of technical knowledge was undoubtedly compensated for by the "vast political and social experience" and "trust" that they had among the population. In a certain sense, their "technical" incompetence could work to break the "*esprit de corps* of the German bureaucracy" that, ever since the Weimar Republic, was "one of the greatest obstacles to the penetration of democratic elements into the judicial and administrative bureaucracies."[69]

This was particularly true of the working class parties and movements that were the vital core of the clandestine anti-Nazi movement. According to Marcuse, these working class parties represented the country's only internal forces able to "transform a non-political community solidarity into political solidarity" and, hence, "light the spark which can transform apathy and hatred and weariness into action."[70] In fact, in the context of military occupation, the communist movement would reorganize itself around a "minimal program" of collaboration with the country's democratic forces and the socialist movement would return to its traditional liberal democratic reformist orientation.[71] The same was true for unions that, according to Neumann, "were likely to provide effective support for the occupation forces" if they were reconstituted on a truly democratic basis. In his opinion, "the most complete repudiation of Nazism and the most direct and complete avowal of democratic principles" was contained in the defense of union "freedom to organize."[72]

6. Although the Central European Section's recommendations were accepted by the military government's authorities on more than one occasion—for example, the proclamation of the dissolution of the Nazi party prepared by Marcuse as an appendix to the guide dedicated to this topic largely corresponds to the decree actually mandated by the military government[73]—Neumann and his group perceived their contribution to the democratic reconstruction of Germany as a failure. For the most part, the American political authorities preferred to follow a different path from the one suggested by the Frankfurt group. The American authorities had established a privileged relationship with the Christian-democratic center, whose ideological flexibility made that party a perfect "rallying ground for all forces seeking to stabilize Central European society by preventing both a social revolution as well as a new form of German imperialism."[74] For the Frankfurt group, this American policy meant that the "revolution through legal means" that was to be the denazification and democratic reconstruction of Germany was deprived of the progressive political energy that the working class's anti-Nazi opposition purportedly provided and was reduced to the "social democratic compromise" that inspired the "comfortable, smooth, reasonable, democratic unfreedom" later criticized by Marcuse in the 1960s.[75] As John

Herz commented in an essay emblematically entitled *The Fiasco of Denazification*: "Denazification, which began with a bang, has since died with a whimper, [since] it opened the way toward renewed control of German public, social, economic and cultural life by forces which only partially and temporarily had been deprived of the influence they had exerted under the Nazi régime."[76]

Only slightly more successful was the dossier that the Frankfurt group furnished for the preparation and conduct of the Nuremberg Trials. Even before the United States established an official position regarding war crimes perpetuated by the Axis Powers, Neumann had in fact prepared a report, *Problems Concerning the Treatment of War Criminals*,which General Donovan immediately sent to the assistant secretary of war, John J. McCloy, accompanied by a note that described it emphatically as the study that definitively clarified the problem of how to face the question of war crimes.[77] Owing to his reservations concerning the possibility of prosecuting more politically complex war crimes like the persecution of the Jews (later redefined as "crime against humanity"), or of the Nazis' political opponents in an international court, Neumann contemplated establishing an inter-ally "political agency" that could "apply generally recognized principles and standards of criminal law" with full discretion (i.e., without necessarily having to be based on a specific legal system). Neumann's report provided multiple criteria for "implementing" the principles enshrined in the *Statement on Atrocities* signed by the Allies in Moscow on October 30, 1943—which, in a comment on December 10 of the same year, both Kirchheimer and Herz had generally approved.[78] In particular, Neuman's report insisted on establishing a clear theoretical framework through which the controversial question of assessing individual responsibility for Nazi criminals could be addressed. Anticipating what would be the main defense for Adolf Eichmann and many other Nazi officials, Neumann recognized obedience to "imperative" higher orders as one of the possible weak points in the Allied policy in prosecuting war criminals. Western legal systems, including the American one, acknowledged the legitimacy of such a defensive strategy. On the other hand, in an authoritarian system like Nazism, where "individual resistance against orders" was "more dangerous and consequently less to be expected than elsewhere," refusing the admissibility of such a defense wasn't practicable. The solution, then, was to be found in whether or not the defendant had voluntarily adhered to the Nazi Party or one of its affiliated organizations while engaging in crimes such as shooting hostages, the forced deportation or dispossession of civilian populations, ill treatment of prisoners of war, collective reprisals, and, above all, as in Eichmann's case, the annihilation of Jews or political opponents . In this case, in fact, the defendant's "full knowledge" of the practices and functioning of the Nazi regime could be assumed, "and [he] can therefore not avoid his share of responsibility."[79] Instead, the question of criminal responsibility could be resolved by appealing to the very foundations of the Nazi legal structure and, specifically, to the *Führerprinzip*. In the Nazis' own theoretical interpretation the *Führerprinzip* implied a concept of responsibility that was wider than that normally accepted in Western legal systems, extending all the way to include the objective responsibility of the commander for the acts of his subordinates even when they are not the result of any specific order. In this way, the Nazis themselves could be considered "objective enemies," depersonalized, impersonal criminals, identifiable as such in virtue of their voluntary and sincere participation in a regime that was intrinsically hostile to democracy.[80] In fact, both Kirchheimer and Herz, who were appointed by Neumann to give this innovative theory of criminal responsibility a systematic form, explain:

> In reversing these standards and in making the Nazi leaders responsible for what *we* [i.e. Western democracies, italics in original] consider as war crimes, they would indeed have to answer for what has actually been done in accordance with their own standards and policies. The 'law' according to which the Nazi leaders have acted was in reality the absence of any legal limitation and since their actions have been in contradiction to what an over-whelming majority of peoples and nations consider as fundamental standards of law and decency, the application of these standards to them seems to imply not the absence of but the vindication of justice."[81]

As a result of these and other preparatory reports,[82] Neumann (who in the meanwhile had been promoted to acting chief of the Central European Section),[83] was called to London as head of a specific OSS research group on "war crimes,"[84] with the responsibility of assembling all the available information on Nazi efforts to seize the power in Germany and extend its domination all over Europe, in order to be used for the trial.[85] . He was assigned to the team of Justice Robert H. Jackson, who in May 1945 had been named as chief prosecutor for the American part of the International Military Tribunal of Nuremburg. By May 30, 1945, Neumann and his group had already made a great quantity of materials and evidence available to Justice Jackson's office, including twenty-five trial briefs, a list of the main war criminals, and a "trial run" of the case against Göring.[86] Traces of this preparatory work are evident in the four counts presented at the main trial, for which Neumann had written a provisional draft;[87] The Frankfurt group's influence is especially notable for the idea of a "common plan" of imperial aggression and control, which is described in detail in Marcuse's long introductory text to the series of reports he coordinated for *Nazi Plans For Dominating Germany and Europe*."[88] The idea of including "domestic crimes" against the Jews and other civilian groups among those normally recognized as war crimes was part of the Frankfurt group's central contributions to the prosecution's strategy.[89]

However, where the Frankfurt group's influence was most evident—and most controversial—was in the part of the trial devoted to the Holocaust. In fact, Neumann has recently been accused of having been responsible for its general underestimation.[90]

From the beginning of the OSS's involvement, the author of *Behemoth* was able to impose on the organization an interpretation of anti-Semitism as the "spearhead" of the universal Nazi terror: "The slaughter or the expulsion of the scapegoat, however," Neumann explains in the May 1943 report that begins this volume,

> marks in mythology the end of a process, while the persecution of the Jews, as practiced by National Socialists, is only the prologue of more horrible things to come. The expropriation of the Jews, for instance, is followed by that of the Poles, Czechs, Dutchmen, Frenchmen, anti-Nazi Germans, and middle classes. Not only Jews are put in concentration camps but pacifists, conservatives, Socialists, Catholics, Protestants, Free Thinkers, and members of the occupied peoples. Not only Jews fall under the executioner's ax but countless others of many races, nationalities, beliefs, and religions."[91]

The Jews were particularly useful in this role "as guinea pigs in testing a method of repression" because they were strong enough to justify "in the eyes of the peoples" their being made "the supreme foe" but not so strong as to force the Nazis to be "involved in a serious struggle with a powerful enemy."

From its initial articulation in *Behemoth*,[92] this interpretation of the Nazi anti-Semitism was criticized within the Frankfurt School itself. Leo Löwenthal, who had already started collaborating with the Office of War Information at the beginning of the war and who worked with Horkheimer and Adorno in drafting the chapter on the "Elements of Anti-Semitism" in the *Dialectic of Enlightenment*, in a long letter to Marcuse on June 29, 1943, stressed his perplexities about Neumann's "spearhead" theory, which had described the "final solution" as a preparatory phenomenon. Lowenthal was instead partial to the traditional "scapegoat" theory, which identified Nazi anti-Semitism as a "diversion" that blamed all manner of political ills on the Jews. Lacking a real bureaucratic tradition and resistant to being assimilated into the German ideological sphere, the Jews had become the representatives of "bourgeois bad conscience" and the capitalist past founded on competition and free enterprise. The Jews thereby channeled both the hatred of those sectors of the bourgeoisie that flourished on bureaucratization as well as those of less privileged strata that tended to be destroyed by the processes of economic concentration.[93] Marcuse had also adopted this approach, and he privately stressed to Horkheimer the need to revise the "spearhead" theory in light of the developments in Nazi anti-Semitism. "The function of this anti-Semitism," he wrote,

> is apparently more and more in the perpetuation of an already established pattern of domination in the character of men. Note that in the German propaganda, the Jew has now become an 'internal' being, which lives in Gentiles as well as Jews, and which is not conquered even with the annihilation of the 'real' Jews. If we look at the character traits and qualities which the Nazis designate as the Jewish elements in the Gentiles, we do not find the so-called typical Jewish traits (or at least not primarily), but traits which are regarded as definitely Christian and 'human.' They are furthermore the traits which stand most decidedly against repression in all its forms."[94]

Despite these internal debates, the "spearhead" theory was employed in the reports on anti-Semitism prepared by the Central European Section for the Nuremburg Trials: "It is the purpose of the Prosecution," we find for example in the report *The Criminal Conspiracy Against the Jews*, drafted by Charles Irwing Dwork (director of R&A's Jewish Desk) in collaboration with the Institute of Jewish Studies in New York in the series dedicated to the Nazi plans for dominating Germany and Europe, "to demonstrate the existence of a common plan or enterprise of the German Government, the Nazi Party and the German military, industrial, and financial leaders to achieve world domination by war. The destruction of the Jewish people as a whole, although an end in itself, was at the same time linked to and closely tied up with this aim of world conquest."[95] As a result, the "spearhead" theory was directly adopted by Justice Jackson in the Nuremburg Trials: "Anti-Semitism," he explained in his opening address,

> also has been aptly credited with being a 'spearhead of terror.' The ghetto was the laboratory for testing repressive measures. Jewish property was the first to be expropriated, but the custom grew and included similar measures against Anti-Nazi Germans, Poles, Czechs, Frenchmen, and Belgians. Extermination of the Jews enabled the Nazis to bring a practiced hand to similar measures against Poles, Serbs, and Greeks. The plight of the Jew was a constant threat to opposition or discontent among other elements of Europe's population—pacifists, conservatives, commu-

nists, Catholics, Protestants, socialist. It was, in fact, a threat to every dissenting opinion and to every non-Nazi's life."[96]

Inserting the annihilation of the Jewish people into a more general "plan" of repressive domination of the world didn't, however, presuppose in any way for the Frankfurt group an underestimation of its centrality in the ideology and practice of National Socialism, much less conceal evidence of extermination from the Nuremburg Trials.[97] As Arthur Schlesinger Jr. recently reminded us, figures of Jewish origin like Neumann, Kirchheimer and Marcuse, all of whom lost many close family members in the Nazi lagers, were "the last people inclined to ignore or discount reports of a Final Solution."[98] In a context where the "Jewish question" had still not become an independent variable in American foreign relations and where, above all, the very concept of "genocide" had still not been affirmed, it was in large part thanks to Neumann's research team's documentation that kept "the fate of Europe's Jews from disappearing entirely from the American military and diplomatic agenda."[99] Neumann's team also helped to ensure that the International Military Tribunal had access to much of the evidence of the criminal conspiracy against the Jews, including an official estimate of at least 5,700,000 deaths.[100] From their perspective, however, the struggle against Nazi anti-Semitism had to minimize the specificity of the Jews' fate and to affirm the principle that their treatment be equal to that of the other German citizens.[101] For the same reason, denouncing Nazi crimes could only be extraneous to the attempts to "essentialize" the Holocaust that would later become typical of Zionist politics.

7. In any case, the honeymoon between the Frankfurt group and Justice Jackson—if there ever was one, considering the reciprocal diffidence that characterized their relationship from the start—soon ended. Neumann resigned in protest as head of the research team on war crimes just days after the official opening of the main trial. Shortly thereafter he also resigned from the American administration in order to dedicate himself to the construction of new political science departments at Columbia University and the Free University of Berlin (thus ending up contributing, despite himself, to the progressive Americanization of postwar German political philosophy). As Vice Prosecutor Telford Taylor admitted in his memoirs of the Nuremburg Trials, on more than one occasion Jackson ignored, with no apparent reason, the contribution of Neumann's group in the decisive phases of selecting the defendants to formally bring to trial.[102] This went above all for the inquiry concerning the so-called "economic cause," from which Neumann's group was totally excluded, despite having prepared a series of studies that unequivocally

showed the German industrialists' collusion in the perpetuation of Nazi war crimes and that included a list of sixty-five leading businessmen implicated in the criminal policies of the Nazi regime.[103] The Frankfurt group's disappointment in seeing its struggle against the German enemy deprived yet again of one of its essential elements was expressed by Marcuse in a 1978 interview with Jürgen Habermas: "Those whom we had listed first as 'economic war criminals' were very quickly back in the decisive positions of responsibility in the German economy. It would be very easy to name names here."[104]

The Frankfurt group's marginalization in Justice Jackson's team was coupled with a more general marginalization of the OSS, which itself was closed by President Truman shortly thereafter, in October 1945. As an example of their progressive marginalization, following the end of the U.S-USSR collaboration, the strategic importance of which the Frankfurt group had insisted upon numerous times, Marcuse and Kirchheimer were transferred to the State Department. "You will have heard," writes Marcuse bitterly in a letter to Max Horkheimer on April 6, 1946, "that the State Department's Research and Intelligence Division has come under fierce attack for alleged communist tendencies. With this justification the Appropriations Committee has, for the time being, rejected new funding. Now the general horse-trading over the usual compromise begins, but quite possibly the Division will be dissolved on June 30. Actually I wouldn't exactly be sad were that to happen."[105] Marcuse's predictions proved to be accurate: at the end of April, the Research and Analysis Branch that the State Department had inherited from the OSS was terminated. The department hierarchy, under pressure from conservative circles in the American administration, was in fact convinced that the intelligence group was led by a series of people from the OSS with "strong Soviet leanings" and who, from an ideological point of view, were "far to the left of the views held by the President and his Secretary of State," and who desired "a socialized America in a world commonwealth of Communist and Socialist states dedicated to peace through collective security, political, economic, and social reform; and the redistribution of national wealth on a global basis."[106] Unable to leave Washington due to his wife, Sophie's, serious illness,[107] Marcuse (like Kirchheimer) was thus part of that "staff of Jewish scribblers" that, facing the new Cold War mentality and under continuous surveillance by the House Committee on Un-American Activities (HUAC), languished for several years at the State Department in an atmosphere similar to Kafka's *The Castle*, where "one never knew who would answer the telephone or even whether it would be answered at all," and where everyone was continually frustrated in their efforts to counteract these anticommunist tendencies.[108]

It was in this political climate, already fully pervaded by Cold War divisions, that, in August of 1949, Marcuse oversaw the long and detailed State Department report, *The Potentials of World Communism*, which concludes this volume. In his introductory presentation, he explains the consequences of the fact that, contrary to Marx's Communism had been victorious in the Soviet Union, an underdeveloped and isolated country. These two facts constituted an obstacle to the global development of Communism and instead favored a forced, step-by-step industrialization of Soviet society. Even if Western Communist parties were not yet totally discredited among proletarian strata, and thus still maintained a certain degree of autonomy from Soviet leadership, the social base and the possibility of development of these parties were undermined by a series of policies. The Marshall Plan, the American containment doctrine, and the first attempts at systematic commercial relations between the East and West contributed to stabilizing the system and helped diminish the support that Western Communist parties had found outside of their membership circles immediately after the war. There were objective limits to the rise of European Communist parties that anticipated their "integration"—as indicated by their embrace of a nonrevolutionary "minimal program"—within the democratic framework of Western liberalism.[109] In the "Western zones" of occupied Germany the political force of the Communists had declined to the point of being "insignificant." In the case of a new economic crisis it was more probable that disadvantaged sectors of the population sided with neo-Nazi movements, as the anti-Semitic residues still very much present in the occupied zones demonstrated. Hence, for Marcuse, a Communist threat was nonexistent; instead, the truly antidemocratic tendencies in Germany lay in the unnatural, prolonged occupation of Germany's post-Nazi political order that could otherwise have favored transversal alliances between many different subjects and groups around the question of "national liberation."[110]

Here, too, Marcuse's "recommendations" fell on deaf ears. As Kirchheimer would explain a few years later in *Political Justice*—his 1961 magnum opus in which the traces of R&A's activities are evident—"every political regime has its foes or in due time creates them."[111] The "free world" had already created its new enemy. It had, however, also created its own internal criticism: in fact, a short time later, having left government service, Marcuse would revive the analysis of the German enemy in order to reproach the bad conscience of Western democracies, which equated the "totalitarian" tendencies of Nazism and Soviet Communism, thus transforming the very liberty they claimed to defend into a "powerful instrument of domination" of society and the world.[112]

# Part I

# THE ANALYSIS OF THE ENEMY

# 1

## Franz Neumann

## *ANTI-SEMITISM: SPEARHEAD OF UNIVERSAL TERROR*

(May 18, 1943)

Editor's note: R&A 1113.9. This text was published in the internal newsletter of the OSS's Research and Analysis Branch (*Psychological Warfare Weekly Roundup* no. 9, May 18–May 24, 1943, section II). Neumann's authorship is explicitly indicated on page 17.

Classification: Secret

In one of the recent issues of *Das Reich*, Dr. Goebbels pledges the extermination of the Jews in the East. The *Voelkischer Beobachter* in a recent issue equally threatens the complete extermination of the Jews in Poland. The *New York Herald Tribune* of May 15, 1943, reports the complete liquidation of the Warsaw ghetto, and a large number of reports indicate that the threats are being realized.

1. This most recent stage in the long process of the extermination of the Jews makes it mandatory to re-examine the function of anti-Semitism within the framework of the Nazi system. Anti-Semitism has been, from the very foundation of the Nazi Party, the most constant single ideology of the Nazi Party. No other element has so constantly figured in the forefront of Nazi ideologies and Nazi activities. We may, indeed, say that anti-Semitism is the sole ideology that can possibly cement the Nazi Party, and it is this unique function of anti-Semitism that gives it its peculiar character.

The understanding of anti-Semitism is impaired by the widely accepted scapegoat theory according to which the Jews are used as scapegoats for all evils of society. The slaughter or the expulsion of the scapegoat, however, marks in mythology the end of a process, while the persecution of the Jews, as practiced by National Socialists, is only the prologue of more horrible things to come. The expropriation of the Jews, for instance, is followed by that of the Poles, Czechs, Dutchmen, Frenchmen, anti-Nazi Germans, and middle classes. Not only Jews are put in concentration camps but pacifists, conservatives, Socialists, Catholics, Protestants, Free Thinkers, and members of the occupied peoples. Not only Jews fall under the executioner's ax but countless others of many races, nationalities, beliefs, and religions. Anti-Semitism is thus the spearhead of terror. The Jews are used as guinea pigs in testing a method of repression. It is, however, only the Jews who can possibly play this role. National Socialism, which has allegedly abolished the class struggle, needs an enemy who, by his very existence, can integrate the antagonistic groups within this society. This foe must not be too weak. If he were too weak, one could not justify in the eyes of the peoples to make him the supreme foe. He must clearly not be too strong because otherwise the Nazis would become involved in a serious struggle with a powerful enemy. It is for this reason that the Catholic Church has not been raised to the rank of the supreme foe. It is the Jews who admirably fill the role being neither too strong nor too weak.

It follows that in this anti-Semitic ideology and practice the extermination of the Jews is only the means to the attainment of the ultimate objective, namely, the destruction of free institutions, beliefs, and groups. We may call this theory of anti-Semitism the spearhead theory of anti-Semitism.

2. While anti-Semitism has thus been a constant and consistent policy of National Socialism, its manifestations have changed considerably from 1933 to 1943. It is these changes in anti-Semitic policies which allow us to gain an insight not so much in the fate of the Jews but rather in the structure of the Nazi system.

The first manifestation of an all-out anti-Semitism was April 1, 1933, the day of the anti-Jewish boycott.[1] This period of anti-Semitism may be called the SA anti-Semitism. At that time it was the lower middle classes, the scum of the proletariat, and many professionals—lawyers and doctors—who either actively participated in, or at least rejoiced at, this outburst of anti-Semitic activity. It is known that the boycott was prematurely broken off at the insistence of Schacht[2] and of the Anglo-American powers, and that the economic disadvantages resulting from this anti-Semitism far outweighed the advantages accruing from the satisfaction of base instincts. It is thus the regard for public opinion and the hope for economic collaboration with England and America which prevented the outbreak of a full-fledged Jewish persecution in 1933. The Nazis had tested foreign opinion, found it unfavorable, and abandoned their attempt.

3. The succeeding period up to November 1938 is one of a cold, calculated, legalized persecution of the Jews in Germany, a step by step enactment of anti-Jewish legislation. The situation changed in November 1938

when, under the impact of the assassination of vom Rath[3], a pogrom was staged and the complete exclusion of the Jews from German economic and social life was carried out. To understand the anti-Jewish activities during this period, it will be necessary to find out whether or not the pogrom was a spontaneous popular reaction or a skillfully organized and manipulated manoeuvre. Each and every correspondent who had occasion to observe the pogrom agrees that there was no spontaneity in the anti-Semitic manifestations. Every single report that has since come out of Germany affirms the view that spontaneous anti-Semitism is unknown in Germany today and that anti-Semitic manifestations are manipulated from above.

There is a second factor which supports this thesis. The anti-Semitic legislation of November and December 1938 which excluded the Jews from economic life was carefully prepared in advance. A decree of April 26, 1938, had already compelled the Jews to "register and evaluate their total domestic and foreign properties" and an executive decree of the same date forbade them to acquire any industrial, agrarian, or forestry enterprise.

The fact that as early as the spring of 1938 registration of Jewish property was ordered makes it clear that the decrees of November and December 1938 were planned long in advance and that the death of vom Rath merely served as a pretext for unleashing the concentrated fury of the regime.

4. There still remains the question why the period between the spring of 1938 and December 1938 was chosen for the enactment of the radical anti-Jewish legislation. Two factors explain the selection of that period. On February 4, 1938, Hitler assumed the supreme army command. On March 13, 1938, Austria was united with Germany. On May 20, 1938, the construction of the Western Wall was started[4]. On September 12, 1938, at the Party conference at Nuremberg Hitler initiated the destruction of Czechoslovakia. The year 1938 is thus the year in which for the first time the power of resistance of the democracies against Nazi Germany was put to the most severe test. It is in this connection that the radical anti-Semitic legislation must be understood.

But there is a second consideration. Early in 1939 the two decrees for the combing out of handicraft and retail were enacted and the government thus, for the first time officially, proclaimed the exclusion of considerable sectors of the middle classes from an independent economic existence. The economic exclusion of the Jews had thus been merely a prologue of the blow directed against the independent middle class.

5. The physical extermination of the Jews in the spring of 1943 takes place in similar circumstances. The Labor Mobilization Act of January 27, 1943, has again deprived hundreds of thousands of middle class men

of their independence. The political situation is as difficult as it can possibly be imagined. The antagonisms within German society are only concealed by an all comprehensive terrorist machine. The denunciation of bolshevism, socialism, democracy, liberalism, capitalism as Jewish, together with the planned extermination of the Jews, has the following functions:

1. Dr. Werner Best[5] has, in 1942, clearly defined the function of anti-Semitism for consumption abroad. A country, he said, that surrenders to anti-Semitism has thereby already surrendered its liberal tradition. It has thus abandoned its bulwark against totalitarianism and is on its way of becoming a totalitarian society.
2. Domestically, anti-Semitism is still the testing ground for universal terrorist methods directed against all those groups and institutions that are not fully subservient to the Nazi system.
3. Persecution of the Jews, which is practiced at the order of the Nazis by ever larger strata of the German people, involves these strata in a collective guilt. The compulsion to commit so vast a crime as the physical extermination of the Eastern Jews makes the German army, the civil service and large masses perpetrators and accessories in the crime and makes it therefore impossible for them to leave the Nazi boat. It is, I believe, safe to assume that the new wave of anti-Semitism is also intended to make separate peace negotiations by non-Nazi members of the ruling class impossible. The Nazis want them, each and every one of them, to be stained by the crime that is now being committed.

*Use*: The above remarks must prevent us from making anti - anti-propaganda. It would be futile to refute the anti-Semitic propaganda of the Nazis since this propaganda is probably not believed. It would be dangerous to praise the Jews for their contributions to civilization or for their patriotic attitude or for their anti-Nazi activities.

Anti-Semitic propaganda should be treated as has been indicated above.

# 2

HERBERT MARCUSE

## *POSSIBLE POLITICAL CHANGES IN NAZI GERMANY IN THE NEAR FUTURE*

(AUGUST 10,1943)

Editor's note: R&A 1034. Marcuse's authorship is indicated in *Political Intelligence Report* no. 21, section I.1 (R&A 1113.21).

Classification: Secret

1. It is certain that the German ruling groups have come to realize that the war is militarily lost. There may be Nazi groups which would like to die honorably rather than live in what they regard as shame and which, for this reason, would want to resort to desperate military measures, such as an all-out bombardment of England or an attack on the Middle East through Turkey. This is extremely unlikely. Quite apart from the fact that Germany's military capabilities are probably not adequate to car-ryout such measures of despair, they would certainly meet the determined resistance of the military, the industrialists, and the Junkers, who know that desperate measures would not only destroy Germany's military might but would also lead to their own complete destruction.

2. If military measures thus do not offer an escape from certain military defeat, the only hope of Germany lies in the field of politics. It may not be an exaggeration to maintain that the political aspects of the war will henceforth lead to overshadow military operations, which would lead inexorably to the ultimate destruction of Germany's military machine. The problem therefore arises what political activities the German government is going to pursue in order to avoid utter political and military defeat. Two lines of strategy are open to the Germans. The one is to exploit political and social differences in each of the enemy countries, to utilize soft spots in each enemy country to undermine their morale and to help pro-German or anti-war elements into power. Germany must realize that this is a hopeless endeavor. As to England, such hopes had to be abandoned at a very early stage of the war. In the Nazi anti-

American strategy, hope was pinned on the election of a president who could be counted upon to conclude an early peace. But time is now too short to wait for the American elections, and it is certain that in their hearts the Nazis know that 1944 will again frustrate their expectations. The creation of the National Liberation Movement and the National Liberation Army under General Vlassov,[1] the attempt to split the Ukrainians from the Russians have met with but little success and any hope to undermine the Russian home front will thus have to be abandoned. This does not mean that the Nazis will abandon their propaganda in this field. They will undoubtedly continue it for domestic consumption, but it is safe to assume that they realize the hopelessness of this kind of political strategy.

3. There thus remains the second strategic approach, namely to split the United Nations and to unite a negotiated peace with one or the other, either with Russia or with the Western Powers. This they may hope to achieve by demonstrating to the Western Powers, the danger of the Bolshevization of Europe and to Russia, the danger of an Allied intervention against Soviet Russia.

The German leadership, however, realizes that both Russia and the Western Powers have committed themselves not to deal with Hitler and the Nazi Party. As a consequence, the German ruling groups *are faced with the problem of finding a constitutional arrangement that would satisfy either Soviet Russia or the Allied Powers without actually destroying the basic features of the Nazi system.* It is in this light that the news from Berlin[2] and Madrid must be evaluated. The Berlin report states that important discussions of a military and political nature have taken place at Hitler's headquarters and that Goering, Ribbentrop, Speer, Himmler, Goebbels and Bormann of the Nazi Party and Keitel, Doenitz, Milch, Jeschonnek, Zeitzler and Jodl of the military participated. The Japanese ambassador to Berlin was present and was received in the presence of Keitel and Ribbentrop.

The Madrid report indicates that a triumvirate, composed of Keitel, Doenitz and Goering, has taken charge of all military and political affairs and that "powers of enormous magnitude" have been centered in the hands of Reichsmarshal Goering.

4. It may be assumed that the latter report is essentially true. *It would constitute, in the first place, an attempt to coordinate fully all military, political and economic activities by subordinating everything to the final consideration of defending the German-controlled Fortress.*

It implies that Hitler recedes for the time being into the background and that the Nazi Party is transformed into an organ of this triumvirate. This triumvirate may be said to constitute a compromise between the armed forces and the Nazi Party. Goering, it must be remembered, is the only outstanding Nazi political figure who has no official post within the Nazi Party. He is a simple Party member—to be sure with great influence in the Party—but he is not a functionary of the Party or of any of its auxiliary organizations. He is above all not a Reichsleiter of the Party and may thus be said to be more useful than any other Nazi leader to an army leadership willing to sue for peace. It is known in addition that through the Goering Combine, Goering has mobilized the support of powerful industrial and financial leaders and that he has made it possible for them to participate in the economic spoliation of occupied Europe.

The factual subordination of the Nazi Party to the triumvirate has been made, no doubt, to alleviate the grumbling of the army and the people about the prerogatives and privileges enjoyed by the Party.[3]

5. It may also have been intended that the triumvirate would be more acceptable to the United Nations than the system prevailing before. But the personnel of the triumvirate has been so closely connected with the Nazi Party that the United Nations will undoubtedly reject it as a bargaining partner. Keitel and Doenitz are far more men of Hitler than of the armed forces. Goering's name will be associated forever with the unleashing of air attacks on Great Britain, with the destruction of Rotterdam and Warsaw and with the economic spoliation of occupied Europe. He, as Hitler's Delegate for the Four Year Plan, was and is responsible for this exploitation.[4]

It is even very unlikely that the triumvirate believes itself acceptable to the United Nations, the less so since Hitler and the Nazi Party are retained.

6. The establishment of this triumvirate must be considered merely as a first step to further constitutional changes. *The aim of future steps will be to create a system of government which would allow certain political changes with a minimum of social and political disturbance and without changing the basis of the Nazi system.* The essential question is, of course, the retention of the Nazi Party in one or the other form. It is certain that all groups among the ruling classes realize that without a totalitarian party the home front cannot be organized and revolution cannot be prevented.[5] The revolution of 1918 demonstrated to the German army that it is incapable of providing leadership for the home front. Unless there exists a monolithic political party which wipes out opposition, incorporates every German into the totalitarian machine and makes him a willing or unwilling cog in the wheel of totalitarianism, solid support by the home front cannot be expected. The abolition of the Nazi Party therefore would be tantamount to the abdication not only of the Nazi leadership

but to the complete disintegration of the German home front, no matter whether revolutionary impulses are strong or weak. Even if revolutionary spontaneity should be non-existent within the German people, the lack of a totalitarian "Menschenführung" would inevitably give rise to revolts, to disintegration, desertions, refusals to work and to fight. The German army's recognition of its need for the Nazi Party was reported in the dispatch from Madrid announcing the triumvirate.[6] It must therefore be expected that a political reorganization of Germany under the auspices of the ruling groups will continue the Nazi Party as a means of *Menschenführung*, of manipulating the masses. But it will certainly entail a change in the status of the Nazi Party within the framework of the German state.

7. The understanding of the forthcoming changes will be facilitated by a brief discussion of the present-day structure of German political institutions. The most remarkable phenomenon is the fact that there have been but few changes in the composition of the Nazi hierarchy since 1934. With the exception of the emasculation of the SA and the assassination of Roehm, all Nazi hierarchs who held power in 1934 hold it now.[7] This is in sharp contrast to Italian Fascism where almost every year witnessed a change in leadership. But Italian Fascism had at least two institutions where political decisions could be discussed and possibly made, the Grand Council of Fascism and the Monarch with his advisers.

The Nazi constitutional system, if such word is allowed, is, in contrast, characterized by its complete formlessness, that is by an utter lack of supreme political institutions where leaders can meet, discuss and formulate plans. This shapelessness is the outcome of the merger of the offices of the president and the chancellor after Hindenburg's death. Since then the idea of the leadership state has been developed.[8] Apart from Hitler as leader, there is no supreme institution. The Reich Cabinet is not a policy making body. The Privy Cabinet Council, which is presided over by Freiherr von Neurath, is without functions. The Reichstag is overwhelmingly composed of Party officials appointed by Hitler's deputy. The Ministerial Council for the Defense of the Reich is not a representative body.

There is also no institutionalization within the Party. There are Reichsleiter in charge of the various functional departments. There are Gauleiter in charge of the major regional divisions of the Party, but there is no supreme Party institution apart from Hitler himself. Many Nazi leaders, especially Alfred Rosenberg,[9] have proposed the creation of a National Socialist Order as the supreme organ of the Reich for policymaking and regulating Hitler's succession. Such proposals have not been accepted with favor by Hitler who was apparently afraid that an institutionalization of political leadership in Germany could be used as an instrument against him. He has preferred to deal with specific leaders for specific problems, to call in party, army, or industrial leaders at his pleasure, and to discuss with them whenever he felt such discussion to be necessary.

8. This lack of institutionalization becomes especially apparent when we study the Enabling Act of March 24, 1933. The Reichstag then delegated to the Reich Cabinet the authority to enact national laws which may deviate from the constitution in so far as they do not affect the position of the Reichsrat or the powers of the president. The Reichsrat has been abolished, and the office of the president has been abolished and merged with that of the chancellor. The Enabling Act expired, after previous prolongations, on May 10, 1943. The Nazis forgot to renew it in time and the Reichstag which had originally passed it did not renew it at all. Instead a Hitler *Erlass* (edict) was issued[10] which simply declared that the powers contained in the Enabling Act would in the future be exercised as before, with the proviso that a confirmation of the legislation may be sought from the *Grossdeutsche* Reichstag.

The constitution of Nazi Germany is thus summed up in the single sentence that all powers reside in Hitler and that he can do what he pleases. This is indeed what Nazi constitutional lawyers accept as the given fact.

9. The second principle of the Nazi system is the supremacy of the Party over the state, by which the Nazis understand the civil service and the army.[11] According to their view, the Party is "the bearer of the political will of the state." Recent measures in the political field, especially the institution of the Reich Defense Commissars and their war economy staffs, have translated this doctrine into a political reality and have given the Gauleiter supreme power over many activities on the home front.

*These two facts*—the shapelessness of the German political system and the supremacy of the Party—*make it impossible for the Nazi system—with or without the triumvirate—to hope for acceptance by, or to bargain successfully with the Western Powers or Russia.* Unless institutional arrangements are made that allow a gradual transformation in the political system, preserving the Party organization behind a new facade and without ensuing chaos and collapse of the home front, no such negotiated peace is obtainable to them.

Second, such institutional arrangements must be made when Germany is still militarily strong. Only then can Germany offer something and only then can it maintain, at least for a time, a running political and economic system.

10. The appointment of the triumvirate must therefore be considered as a first step toward future political changes of much greater significance. We envisage these changes as follows. It is likely that the Reichstag will be convened. It is likely further that the offices of presidency and chancellorship will be divorced and that Hitler will assume the functions of a president while a chancellor, either a military man or a high civil servant or an outstanding banker or industrialist, will assume the functions of a chancellor. The Reichstag may also create a new institution; it may, for instance, re-establish the Reichsrat as a kind of senate or upper house composed of military, civil servants, industrialists, bankers, agrarians, and probably Catholics, and Protestant clergymen. Free elections for a new Reichstag are unlikely and even impossible since this would presuppose the restitution of some kind of civil rights which the system cannot tolerate or it would collapse due to internal disorder.

With the creation of such a Reichsrat or upper house an institution will then exist where political decisions can be discussed or even made. The Reichsrat may then appoint a new cabinet composed primarily of military and technicians (industrial and administrative). The Nazi Party will not be dissolved but will be purged and will be transformed into an organ of the state so that the relation between Party and State will be reversed.

This cabinet with its chancellor will then sue for peace. It has two bargaining points: Hitler as president and a still powerful military machine. It will offer as consideration for some kind of acceptable peace the resignation of Hitler. Hitler may then be persuaded to step down addressing the German people in a lachrymose speech in which he explains what he sacrifices himself for the sake of the German people.

The peace offer of the new German cabinet will aim to divide the United Nation by a separate peace with either the Western Powers or with Russia (see page 00 above). If the Western Powers and Russia have not agreed upon a German policy toward Germany by the time that the Germans attempt such a peace *manoeuvre*, the *manoeuvre* may succeed in dividing the United Nations.

If the new German government should first seek a separate peace with the Western Powers (bulwarking their offer with the threat of a separate peace with Russia), the success or failure of the *manoeuvre* will be determined in part by the intervening developments in Italy. It is easy to foresee that if Italy should give birth to revolutionary Communist or Socialist movements threatening to overthrow the established structure of society, the receptivity of the Western Powers to such a constitutional arrangement in Germany may be considerably enhanced. Should the Western Powers be taken in by such a Nazi *manoeuvre*, they would thereby forfeit all influence upon German liberals and German workers, the impact of Russia on Germany would increase by leaps and bounds and the Free Germany Manifesto would become a political reality of the first order.

Gauleiter Wagner's speech to the Party workers in Baden and Alsace may be considered as a psychological preparation for this. Wagner is reputed to have said: "to have Mussolini disappear for awhile is good. Enough mischief will then be created by Red roughnecks so that the neutrals will get the wind up." He remarked that Communism is not wanted by anyone and ended by saying: "In this way we will also get the Church with us which is another good thing. The Church can still get a good peace from us."

It is of course not certain that such a reconstituted German government will sue for peace from the Allied Powers. It is as possible that it will approach Soviet Russia. The Free Germany Manifesto with its insistence on a strong German government and a strong army leaves ample leeway to the Russians to accept such proposal. The exhaustion of Russia by the war and the war weariness of the Russian people may provide a powerful stimulus to the acceptance of a German peace proposal under these conditions, the more so if the new German government should be composed of representatives who are adherents of the eastern orientation of German foreign policy.[12] The military consequences for the Western Powers of a separate Russo-German peace are obvious. The masses of the German people would feel a great relief, and the democratic opposition to Nazism would suffer a defeat from which it is not likely to recover.

# 3

Herbert Marcuse

## *CHANGES IN THE REICH GOVERNMENT*

(August 20, 1943)

Editor's note: R&A 1130. Marcuse's authorship is indicated in "Political Intelligence Report," no. 23, section I.A.1 (R&A 1113.23).

Classification: Free

The Fuehrer has relieved Freiherr Constantin von Neurath, Reich Protector of Bohemia and Moravia, from his office at his request.

The Fuehrer has appointed Dr. Wilhelm Frick, Reichsminister of the Interior, to be Reich Protector of Bohemia and Moravia and has relieved him from the offices of Reichminister [*sic*] and Prussian Minister of the Interior and of his office of Delegate-General for the Reich Administration. Freiherr von Neurath and Dr. Frick continue to be Reichsministers.

The Fuehrer has placed "en disponibilité" Hans Pfundtner, the principal Under Secretary of State in the Reich Ministry of the Interior at his own request.

The Fuehrer has appointed Heinrich Himmler to be Reichsminister and Prussian Minister of Interior and Delegate General for Reich Administration.

The Reich Labor Service no longer falls within the competence of the Reichsminister of Interior. The Leader of the Reich Labor Service as Head of the Supreme Reich Authority is immediately responsible to the Fuehrer. Konstantin Hierl, Leader of the Reich Labor Service, has been given the title, rank, and functions of a Reichminister [*sic*] by the Fuehrer.

In consequence of the appointment of a new Reich Protector, the mission given to Daluege, Colonel General of the S.S. and Police, to deputise and take charge of the functions of Reich Protector has come to end.

The Fuehrer has appointed Karl Hermann Frank, Under Secretary of State with the Reich Protector of Bohemia and Moravis, to be Minister of State, ranking equal with Reichsministers.[1]

## Himmler's New Powers

Himmler's appointment to the Reich Ministry of the Interior is the most important change in the Nazi regime since the Roehm purge of 1934. While it may shift the balance of power within the inner circle of Nazi leaders, it must be regarded as the decision of this inner circle as a whole, bound by the conviction that their only hope for survival depends upon standing together. The appointment tightens and extends the control of the SS and Police formations over all branches of the home front. The "Traditionalistic" strata of the Civil Service (of the ministerial, provincial, and local bureaucracy) which for some time have seen their influence reduced as contrasted with that of the Nazi forces, are further weakened. The Gestapo chief takes over the entire internal administration of the Reich,[2] which is thus merged with the terroristic apparatus of the Nazi party. Himmler's appointment may portend a large-scale purge of the administrative bureaucracy.

This interpretation is confirmed by the retirement of Hans Pfundtner as "Leading Secretary of State" in the Ministry of Interior. Although a member of the Nazi party, Pfundtner is a civil servant of the traditional type, having entered the bureaucracy before 1914. His retirement leaves as senior Secretary of State in the ministry Wilhelm Stuckart, who is an SS Group Leader and has played an important role in the administration of both incorporated and occupied areas.

The appointment of Himmler as Reich Minister of the Interior testifies to growing internal difficulties and to the determination of the regime to go to the limit in applying the totalitarian terror. The opposition will now be ferreted out and destroyed even more ruthlessly than before. As far as the underground movement is concerned, this will mean little change. The increase in Himmler's powers seems to be primarily directed against the "conservative" groups in the Civil Service, against opposition among the middle classes and intellectuals, and against those business circles which may be inclined to favor an understanding with the Western Powers. In the balance of power within the Nazi inner circle Himmler's elevation may be interpreted as a defeat for Goering, who, among the Nazis, is reputed to have the strongest connection with these business groups. The retirement of von Neurath, long regarded as a link between the Nazi regime and conservative forces in Germany and the west, looks in the same direction.

Frictions between Himmler and the Armed Forces have often been played up. It is doubtful whether his new position constitutes a triumph of the SS over the Army. The Army Command must be vitally interested in "securing" the home front, and Himmler is certainly the man to prevent a "stab in the back" as long as it can be prevented by terror. On the other hand, as indicated elsewhere in this report, the removal of Hierl and the Reich Labor Service from the Ministry of Interior to the position of an independent agency immediately subordinate to Hitler may be attributed to the unwillingness of the Armed Forces to subordinate their auxiliary, the Labor Service, to Himmler.[3]

At the moment when the air is filled with rumors of peace feelers and of German hopes for a compromise peace, the Nazis place at the head of the Reich administration the very man with whom no peace and no compromise whatsoever seem to be possible. In the eyes of the world, Himmler stands for the Nazi terror and the Nazi racial policy in their most brutal and aggressive forms. His elevation does not finally destroy the possibility of further political changes in Germany as were outlined by the Central European Section in its special report of August 14, 1943, "Possible Political Changes in Nazi Germany in the Near Future."[4] But for the moment the advancement of Himmler means that the Nazis attach more importance to the most rigid control of the home front than to any hope for a compromise. Within Germany, Himmler's elevation must crush hopes for the creation of an atmosphere more favorable to a negotiated peace and for the readiness of the regime to bring about the conditions for such a peace. It is tantamount to a Nazi declaration of determination to fight to the bitter end under the leadership of the Nazi Party.

It seems natural to draw an analogy between Himmler's appointment and the appointment of Scorza in April of this year;[5] also Scorza's appointment was intended to tighten the grip of the party over the Italian people when a critical situation was approaching. Yet such comparison would be misleading. Scorza had played no important role in Italian politics for many years: the hope connected with his appointment was that a newcomer, a man with fresh energies and new ideas, would be able to revive the spirit of the people and to vitalize party institutions. Himmler has been an important figure in German politics ever since the Nazis came to power; he is well entrenched in the German administration and his appointment means that well-functioning and efficient organizations like the Gestapo and the SS which have been powerful factors in German politics for a long while, will be freed from the last obstacles and restraints and exercise full control. Himmler's appointment is not so much an attempt at a new departure, as Scorza's appointment was, but the logical end of a long-prepared development.

State and party positions now held by Himmler:

a) *State*:
   1) Reich and Prussian minister of the Interior*
   2) Commissioner General for Reich Administration in the Ministerial Council for the Defense of the Reich*
   * New position.

3) Chief of the German Police
4) Reich Commissar for the Strengthening of German Folkdom
5) Member of the Reichstag
6) Member of the Prussian State Council (*Staatsrat*)

b) *Party*:
1) Reich Leader of the SS
2) *Reichsleiter* of the NSDAP
3) Delegate of the NSDAP for all Questions of Folkdom or Race

## Himmler and Germany's Eastern Policy

Although organizationally the Ministry of the Interior has no competence over the former Russian territories now occupied by Germany and no change has been reported in the functions exercised by Himmler in this area, Himmler has contacts with the East through his position as Reichs Leader of the SS and Chief of German Police and as Reichskommisar for the Security of German Nationality (*Reichskommisar fuer die Festigung deutschen Volkstums*). He is the exponent of a definite policy in regard to the treatment of the eastern peoples, and it can be taken for certain that, in making Himmler Minister of the Interior, the possible effect of his appointment on the development of German-Russian relations, will have been taken into account.

In contrast to Rosenberg, the head of the Reich Ministry for the Occupied Eastern Territories, who favors a certain autonomy for the eastern peoples, Himmler is the representative of a policy of absolute intransigence. He has always insisted upon the extermination of the intellectuals and rejected any native autonomy whatsoever; he has favored the concentration of all governmental authority in the hands of the Reich Germans and the transfer of land and property to them, in short the complete and permanent exploitation of the Eastern territories and their peoples by Germans for Germany. The Eastern territories are the field on which Himmler's racial policy has been most thoroughly tested and carried out. Furthermore it should be mentioned that these areas have been used by Himmler to strengthen the ties of the SS with big business and with the Junkers, since he has been able to award them large estates there. To Himmler the future of Germany is bound up with German domination over the Eastern regions. Himmler's SS and police have acted in the Eastern areas in accordance with these ideas and the Soviet radio has been full of reports of their atrocities. From this point of view, Himmler's appointment seems to preclude Nazi reconciliation with Russia.

However, it should not be overlooked that Himmler's idea of German expansion allows for a certain flexibility. On the one hand, it means an attempt to extend German control as far to the East as possible; this is indicated by the fact that the *Volksdeutsche* in the Ukraine have been granted German citizenship by a special decree, and yet there has been virtually no re-settlement of them to other areas—an action reserved in all other cases to territories incorporated or to be incorporated. On the other hand, Himmler as the Reichkommisar for the Security of the German Nationality has devoted himself to building up a German wall in the annexed Polish territories and in Lithuania; this wall is the minimum bastion, securing the existence of the German *Volk*.

If it is not possible to maintain German control over the wider Eastern regions, then the Nazis might try to use these regions for bargaining in a separate peace move, and fall back to the German wall.

Himmler's new position consolidates his control over the *Volksgenosse* in the whole eastern area, for the Ministry of the Interior is competent for citizenship and nationality, and for Maintenance of *Germandom* in Frontier Areas. Whatever policy seems feasible or necessary, the Germans in the East are ready to his hand for its execution. A man who unites ruthlessness and opportunism as Himmler does is ideally fitted for the handling of a situation in which developments in various directions are possible.

## Changes Regarding the Reich Labor Service

The Reich Labor Service is the organization for the compulsory labor which every German boy and girl has to devote to the Reich at the age of 17. It thus has nothing to-do with the general administration of labor. Since the restoration of conscription in Germany, the Labor Service has been regarded as preparatory to the period of military service. During the war, the Labor Service has become an auxiliary of the Armed Forces, its units performing tasks of repair and construction all along the German fronts.

The Reich Labor Leader of the Labor Service, Konstantin Hierl, is an old career officer, who joined the Nazis in the twenties. Although the Labor Service nominally had been in the Ministry of the Interior since the mid-thirties, Hierl having the rank of State Secretary, actually both had been independent of the ministry and of the control of Frick as minister. The elevation of Hierl's office to an independent agency, immediately responsible to Hitler, thus means hardly any change in Hierl's powers and his relations to other Reich authorities. It may, however, indicate that the Armed Forces, which today have the most immediate interest in the Labor Service, do not wish it to appear as in any way connected with, or subordinated to, Himmler as Minister of the Interior.

## The Changes in the Protectorate

The facts affecting the Protectorate in this administrative shuffle are:

1. Neurath, who has held only an honorary title since 1941, completely severs connections with the Protectorate.
2. Daluege, who has never been able to give full time to the Protectorate, is freed to devote all his time to his other tasks.
3. Frank, who has been one of the most powerful men in the Protectorate, receives a higher rank and retains his previous important position.
4. A new personality enters the picture through the appointment of Frick as Reichsprotektor.

## Comments

1. The position of Reichsprotektor has been given increased importance by the appointment of an active, full-time holder, and by breaking with the previous equivocal situation of having an inactive Reichsprotektor "on leave," with a succession of temporary Acting Reichsprotektors who at the same time retained other important positions in the Reich (Heydrich was Chief of the Security Police, Daluege Chief of the Order Police).

This emphasizes the crucial importance of the Protectorate to the Reich, and indicates that the Reich intends to maintain control over the Protectorate to the bitter end.

The Protectorate is important to the Reich from three points of view:

First, and by far the most important, its steadily increasing *economic* value to the German war machine. The Protectorate's industrial production is of *absolute* value to Germany. In 1941 Germany took goods valued at over a billion and a half Reichsmarks from the Protectorate, and the total has increased very considerably since then. Its *relative* value is steadily increasing; every time a factory in western Germany is bombed out, its sister plants in the Protectorate become that much more vitally important, since this area is still out of reach of steady raids.

Second, the Protectorate is of *military* importance. Reliable reports indicate that Germany is steadily fortifying the Slovak-Moravian frontier, which constitutes the shortest natural line of defense for the Reich proper in the East. (In 1939 German writers pointed out that the incorporation of the Protectorate had actually shortened the total *length* of Germany's frontiers while increasing its total *area*.)

Third, the Protectorate has *ideological* importance. Along with the Sudetenland and Austria, its retention is one of the cornerstones of German domestic propaganda. Should Germany be forced to evacuate territory acquired by purely military conquest, its loss could be more easily justified to the German people than the loss of these three sectors which German propaganda claims were not incorporated through conquest, but through at least a semblance of voluntary, "legal" action.

2. Although the Protectorate has thus gained in importance within the Reich through the new appointments, its *internal situation* will probably be little changed. German policy toward the Czechs has had a dual face from the very beginning. The vital importance of Czech industrial production has obliged Germany to make every effort to keep Czech workers on the job and more or less satisfied with their position. The principal effort of German policy has therefore been propagandistic, an attempt to convince the Czechs that it is to their best interests to cooperate voluntarily with the Reich. Coupled with this has been ruthless terror against those who fail to be convinced. The terror, however, has for the most part been secondary, except for certain periods when a major crack-down seemed necessary. These terror waves have usually coincided with outside events unfavorable to Germany, such as the failure to conquer Russia in the fall of 1941, the Allied landings in North Africa in November 1942, etc., which raised the hopes of the Czechs. It is probable that the Russian victories in the East and the Allied conquest of Sicily will also arouse new resistance in the Protectorate, and that there will therefore be a new wave of executions in the near future. The promotion of Karl Hermann Frank, who is SS and Police Leader in the Protectorate and who has always been associated with the application of terroristic measures, shows that this aspect of German policy will not be neglected in future, although at the same time the appointment of Frick as Reichsprotektor probably indicates that the dual emphasis on voluntary collaboration plus terror will also continue. Frick is not an SS man and has not been publicly responsible for terrorism, although as an old-line Nazi he will certainly not hesitate to approve its use wherever necessary. It is likely that Frick, with his many years of administrative experience, will concentrate on the technical administrative coordination of the Protectorate, leaving the policing of the population to his chief aide, Frank.

3. The promotion of Frank will be considered by the Czech population as a renewed insult. Frank, who is the most cordially hated man in the Protectorate, is an old Sudeten German leader, for years one of the most rabid anti-Czech propagandists of the Henlein party[6]. The mere fact of his appointment in 1939 was a calculated insult to the Czechs, for he is the negation of everything for which democratic Czechoslovakia stood: he is violently anti-intellectual, sneeringly anti-democratic, and a believer in iron-handed terrorism.

4. The departure of Neurath is of little immediate importance to the Protectorate, for he has had nothing to do with it since 1941. It has minor import in that it represents a formal abandonment of the former German attempt to make the incorporation of the Protectorate palatable to the non-Nazi powers. Neurath's appointment in March 1939, when the outside world was still horrified at the implications of the German occupation, indicated that Germany hoped to appease the Czechs and avoid heavy-handed measures, and his two-year tenure of office actually bore this out in many respects. Although the iron hand was definitely applied in September 1941, with the appointment of Reinhard Heydrich as Acting Reichsprotaktor, Neurath nevertheless retained the title of Reichsprotektor and was held, so to speak, is reserve for possible future use. Now that he is definitely replaced by a full-fledged Nazi, all pretense is abandoned.

## Appendix

### Himmler as Commissioner General for Reich Administration

The position of Commissioner General for Reich Administration means membership in the Ministerial Council for the Defense of the Reich, whose other members are Göring, Keital, Funk, Bormann, and Lammers. This council was created at the outbreak of the war with the dual purpose of relieving Hitler of any but the most crucial decisions and of concentrating the highest policy-making, especially legislative power in a small body which in practice replaced the Reich cabinet. In this body of six, Reich Minister of the Interior Frick, as "Commissioner General for Reich Administration," represented the entire field of state administration in the broader sense, including also justice, education, and church affairs.

Since the establishment of the Defense Council, general laws have usually been enacted in the form of decrees by the Defense Council, while laws referring to administrative affairs have often been issued by Frick as Commissioner for Administration in conjunction with two of his colleagues on the Council. His position thus implied large legislative powers. Although Himmler had already been deputy to Frick as Commissioner for Administration and as such had frequently signed decrees, he has now fully replaced Frick and thus holds his share in legislative power within his own right.

### Himmler as Minister of the Interior

The Interior Ministry has functions in the realm of legislation as well as administration. One of the main legislative functions of the Interior

Ministry is the preparation of all laws in the following main spheres: the constitutional structure of the Reich, including the relation between Reich and the states, and the relation between the state and other public bodies, such as the party and its affiliations; the organization of all administration, including that of the states and their sub-divisions, the provinces, districts, counties, etc. (this means the establishment of new authorities, their jurisdiction, changes in their powers or areas, abolition of administrative agencies, etc.); citizenship and nationality; government of cities and other municipalities; and the civil service and the status and privileges of civil servants. Moreover, since the first instance of an increase in Reich territory, that of the incorporation of the Saar, it has been the task of the Interior Ministry to prepare the laws and other measures relating to these incorporations, including the "co-ordination" of their administration with that of the Reich, and this even in cases where, as in the Protectorate and the Government General, the respective territory is not entirely assimilated to the Reich. In a sense, the Interior Ministry of the Reich has assumed the functions of an Interior Ministry of the "New Order." This, however, does not refer to the occupied Russian territories where a separate Reich ministry has been put in charge.

Besides preparing legislation, the Interior Ministry is in charge of the execution of all laws concerning general interior administration. This sphere is much larger than that of interior ministries in other countries. It comprises all levels of government down to local government, where "self-government" has ceased to exist.

Side by side with the right to give orders and to supervise the activities of all agencies of interior administration, the minister's executive powers include appointment, promotion, and dismissal of many officials and functionaries, while in other cases it means the right to propose such decisions to the Fuehrer. Thus, for the larger cities, the interior minister practically appoints the mayors and other leading agents.

With respect to one of the most important executive branches traditionally belonging to German interior administration, the police, the appointment of Himmler as minister does not, of course, add much to the powers he already had as "Reich Leader of SS and Chief of the German Police." Although this position was formally in the Interior Ministry, Himmler actually was not under Frick's orders but exercised his police powers independently. Taking over the ministry will, however, give him added power to use the whole of the administrative machinery in the interest of police functions and also facilitate the preparation of legislation in police matters in a way more to the liking of the Gestapo.

Regarding general administration, the appointment of Himmler may foreshadow a general re-shuffling, or even purge, of the administration. It may announce a "Nazification" of the civil service even more complete than had already been the case, since, under Frick, technical efficiency had sometimes prevailed over special assiduity in the service of the party. It might even mean that the influence of certain party branches will have to give way to that of the SS, whenever this body wants such influence or power. In short, it may indicate the complete "co-ordination" of the administrative executive with the Gestapo. As such, it may bring the terror machinery of the regime closer to the population, which, while strengthening the hold of the regime over the people, may also enlarge the gap between the regime and all those who still considered the Gestapo as an "extraordinary" weapon of the state, and not as its general instrument of "day to day" administration.

# 4

Franz Neumann and Paul Sweezy

## *SPEER'S APPOINTMENT AS DICTATOR OF THE GERMAN ECONOMY*

(September 13,1943)

Editor's note: R&A 1194. The authorship of the two writers is indicated in a letter by the head of the Central European Section, Eugene N. Anderson, to Carl E. Schorske on September 10, 1943 (RG 226, entry 59, box 1, folder: Project Committee Correspondence).

Classification: Restricted

Paul Marlor Sweezy (1910–2004) was an American economist. After graduating in 1931 with a degree in economics from Harvard University, he studied for a year with Harold Laski at the London School of Economics before returning to Harvard as Joseph Schumpeter's assistant. In 1937 he obtained his PhD with his thesis "Monopoly and Competition in the English Coal Trade, 1550–1850." In 1942 he enlisted in the US Army and worked until 1945 in the Economic Division of the Research and Analysis Branch of the OSS. In 1949, together with Leo Hubermann, he founded the independent Marxist journal *Monthly News* that, in the 1960s, would have a strong influence on the so-called New Left and Third World social movements. His works include *Theory of Capitalist Development* (London: Dobson, 1946) and (with P. A. Baran) *Monopoly Capital: An Essay on the American Economic and Social Order* (New York: Monthly Review, 1966).

### 1. The Hitler Decree

a. On September 2, 1943, Hitler issued the following decrees:

The contingencies of war necessitate the further concentration and unification of the control and organization of the war economy, in order to utilize even more effectively than hitherto the economic strength of the German people for war purposes.

Total productive capacity and manpower will in the future have to be used to an even greater extent and more intensively to achieve an increase of armament production. To this end, German war production has to be directed from one place, according to uniform directives.

A decree by the Fuehrer of Sept. 2, 1943, concerning concentration of the war economy puts the Reich Minister for Armaments and Munitions in control of total German production for the duration of the war, while the Reich Minister of Economics will be responsible for the general economic policy, for supplying the population with consumption goods, for money and credit policy, for foreign trade questions within the framework of the foreign trade policy of the Reich, and for the financing of the economy, as well as for production.

The authority of the Reich Minister of Economics in these spheres has been extended. To insure the execution of these tasks the Reich Marshal of the Greater German Reich in his capacity as Delegate for the Four Year Plan has appointed the Reich Minister of Economics Dr. Walther Funk to be a member of the Central Planning Board.

Simultaneously, the Reich Marshal has extended the authority of Reich Minister Speer in his capacity as Commissioner General in the Four Year Plan for Armament Tasks to the whole war production.

The Reich Marshal has ordered the setting-up of a Planning Office with a Commissioner General for Armament Tasks and War Production. This measure brings into line various planning authorities of the war industry.

The jurisdiction of the Reich Marshal of the Creator German Reich, in his capacity as Delegate for the Four Year Plan, is not affected by this new arrangement. Nor is the competence of the Reich Minister for Foreign Affairs for the foreign trade policy of the Reich and for preparing and conducting foreign trade negotiations affected.

b. A radio speech by Dr. W. Heitmueller[1] interpreted the decree in the following manner. The appointment of Speer is "the beginning of greater simplification and a tightening of Germany's war economy." "It is understood that" . . . Speer "by the forming of Main Committees will exploit for an increase of production all the reserves." "Contrary to the methods. . . . which in their broad lines had been drawn up by Dr. Hjalmar Schacht. . . . Speer will not be restricted to problems of raw material production and the distribution of orders. . . . but will decisively influence production." The commentator stresses that Speer's "unbureaucratic methods" have released "technical energies" and that the "exchange of experiences, the concentration of orders with the most efficient works" and rationalization have brought the armament industries under Speer to "a remarkably high standard." He added that the new distribution of power between Funk and Speer did not come as a surprise.

The self-government of industry, the raw material control agencies and the whole apparatus thus far under Funk will come under Speer.

Funk in turn has received greater powers over credit policy and will have the "supreme authority for all credit institutions." The details, in this respect, have not yet been published.

The Central Planning Committee of Göring as Hitler's Delegate for the Four Year Plan, consisting so far of Paul Koerner, Field Marshal Milch and Speer, has been enlarged by adding Funk to it.

c. Another broadcast[2] stresses that "total productive capacity and manpower will, in the future, have to be used even to a greater extent and more intensively to achieve an increase of armament production." It is for this reason that the German war economy has to be directed from one place—that is, the Speer Ministry. The broadcast also mentions that Speer as Commissioner General for the Armament Tasks in the Four Year Plan Office has received additional power and that Göring, apart from the Central Planning Board, has established a Planning Office with the Commissioner General for Armament Tasks in order to coordinate the various planning agencies.

d. Two measures have already been enacted by Speer. The first[3] orders the reorganization of the manufacture of certain component parts for war material, especially those made of textiles, paper, tin, wood, and soldering work. This work will have in the future to be done primarily at home in order to enable married women to work at home instead of in factories. This measure, the decree says, will not only save time but insure the continuity of work during air raids.

Another decree[4] establishes a ministerial committee for standardization for the purpose of coordinating the many agencies engaged in the rationalization and standardization of the German economy.

## 2. The Careers of Funk and Speer

Walther Funk was born in 1890, studied economics and became in 1916, after having changed jobs frequently, financial editor of the *Berliner Boersenzeitung*. This newspaper belongs to General Jochim von Stuelpnagel, brother of General Otto v. S., Military Commander in France. The Stuelpnagels are, so to speak, liaison officers between the industrial and military hierarchies.[5] They own a considerable part of the Waldhof Cellulose Trust and many other industrial corporations. Funk, during the World War, was the spokesman of Pan Germans and annexationists and was a very articulate labor baiter and hater of socialism. In 1920, he married into a wealthy family of manufacturers.

In 1930, he became economic adviser of the Nazi Party and, after Hitler's access to power, joined the Ministry of Propaganda as Goebbels' chief aide. He succeeded Schacht as Minister and Reichsbank president and has, throughout his career under National Socialism, defended private capitalism.

Albert Speer was born in 1905 and is an architect by profession. He joined the Nazi Party early and soon became Hitler's favorite builder. He was put in charge of all Party buildings and was made Inspector General for the Reconstruction of the Capital, directly responsible to Hitler. He succeeded Reich Minister Fritz Todt to all positions held by Todt. He is a close friend of Hitler whose mania for architecture is well known. Speer has often sung the praise of private initiative in economic life.

Funk is thus a normal reactionary labor baiter who has joined the Party in order to promote his interests as well as those of the groups behind him. Speer is what may be considered a genuine Nazi enjoying the full confidence of Hitler. He has worked closely with German heavy industry and may be considered a technocratic monomaniac.

## 3. The Relative Position of Funk, Speer, Göring and Certain Commissioners in the German War Economy

a. Funk heretofore held the following positions. He was, since the outbreak of the war, Commissioner General for the Economy. As such he was placed in charge not only of the Ministry of Economics but also of the Ministry for Food and Agriculture, the Office of the Reich Forest Master and the Ministry of Labor. In addition, he held and still holds the president of the Reichsbank and is, in this capacity, directly responsible to Hitler. Exempt from his jurisdiction were the Ministries of Finance and Transportation which the Germans considered primarily as "technical" as opposed to "policy making ministries." Funk's power derives primarily from his full control of the Ministry of Economics. The Ministry operates through its bureaucratic organs and through the self-government of industry. The bureaucratic organs consist primarily of the Ministry proper, the Regional Economic Offices (*Landeswirtschaftaemter*), and the Local Economic Offices (*Wirtschaftaemter*). The regional organization of the Ministry of Economics was created with the outbreak of the war and is primarily concerned with the rationing of consumers' goods.

The jurisdiction of Funk was a twofold one. He was responsible for the whole civilian sector of the economy. But he was also in charge of planning production and of raw material control. The system of raw material control was revised in the winter of 1942 by the creation of so-called Spheres of Steering (*Lenkungsbereiche*). Twenty-two such Spheres of Steering were established. They are directed either by National Commissioners who are mostly businessmen, or by the managers of the Economic Groups, or by the *Reichsvereinigungen*, the national compulsory peak cartels created in the spring of 1942 and controlled by the big combines. The directors of the twenty-two Steering Spheres used for the execution of their tasks the *Reichsstellen* (the National Boards for raw material control), many cartels (as *Verteilungsstellen* - Distributing Agencies), and many Groups as *Bewirtschaftungsstellen* (Rationing Agencies) or *Auftragslenkungestellen* (Order Allocation Agencies).

From the spring of 1942 on, raw material control shifted to an ever greater degree from civil servants to the self-government of industry, that is, the Groups and cartels.

By his control of raw material allocation Funk exercised an influence which far exceeded his control of the civilian sector of the economy.

b. Speer's rise dates from the spring of 1942 when, under the impact of defeat in Russia, a reorganization of the German economy was undertaken. From that time on, the Ministry for Armaments and Munitions expanded rapidly and created a bureaucratic and a self-governing apparatus, thus competing with and duplicating the Ministry of Economic Affairs and incorporating the Armament Office (*Ruestungsamt*) of the War Economy and Armament Office of the Supreme Command of the Armed Forces.

I. The Ministry of Armament and Munitions is composed as follows:

a. the *Zentralant* (Central Office)—chief: Paul Pleiger of the Goering Combine and president of the *Reichsvereinigung* "Goal";[6]
b. the *Technisches Amt* (Technological Office)—chief: Mayer Liebel;[7]
c. the *Ruestungslieferungsamt* (Office for Delivery of Combat Material)—chief: State Councillor Dr. Schieber of the synthetic fiber industry and deputy leader of the National Group "Industry";
d. the *Amt fuer Ruestungsausbau* (Office for Expansion of Armament Production)—chief: Dr. Voss of the Goering combine.

This office operates—as will be shown below—also through field offices;

e. the *Amt fuer Energieplanung* (Office for the Planning of Power)[8]—chief: Schulze-Fielitz, Secretary of State in the Ministry. The office is composed of 13 members coming from all important producers of electric power. It coordinates the work of the Inspector General for Water and Power and of the corresponding Main Committees, deals with the coordination of supply of electricity and gas for the whole war economy and operates through *Energieingenieure* (power engineers).

f. the *Buero Transportordnung*[9] (Office for Regulating Transport) is engaged in rationalizing transportation. Under it are *Transporthaupt-kommissionen* (Transport Main Commissions) to avoid long-distance and unnecessary hauls for specific industries.

II. The Ministry operates also through special deputies who are charged with the solution of specific problems. Two such deputies are known to exist:

a. On October 10, 1942, Speer appointed Government Councillor (ret.) F. Kirstein his Deputy for Inland Navigation for the purpose of coordinating the civilian and military demands with regard to the annexed and occupied territories. The appointment was made by Speer in his dual position: as Minister for Armaments and Munitions and as Commissioner General for Armament Tasks under the Four Year Plan.

b. Krupp director Houdremont is his deputy for metal substitutes.

III. The Speer ministry has organized a number of corporations to which certain important functions have been delegated. This constitutes an entirely new approach to the solution of the difficulties with which the Nazi war economy is faced. The shares of these corporations are either partly or wholly held by private industry. The following corporations can be identified:

a. The *Ruestungskontor*. Limited Liability Company. The chairman of the corporation is the *Generalreferent* in the Ministry, Dr. Nettlage, who still is a member of the directorate of the Commerzbank. This corporation is a central clearing office for the allocation of steel to armament producers.

b. The *Generatorkraft* AG, with a capital of 9 million marks. Half of the capital is owned by the *Ruestungskontor*; the other is owned by private timber industry.[10] The function of this corporation is to finance the transformation of liquid-driven vehicles into producer-gas vehicles.

c. The Ministry is also responsible for the establishment of the *Heeres-Ruestungskredit AG*, by the *Deutsche Industriebank* for the administration of long-term credits to manufacturers of army equipment[11].

d. The *Arbeitsgemeinschaft Ruestungshandel* (Working Community in the Armaments Trade)[12] covering all trade groups interested in deliveries to the armaments industry, and charged with the same general tasks as the autonomous organs of industry previously existing.

IV. As important as the central organization of the Ministry are the regional agents through which it operates, namely:

a. *Wehrkreisbeauftragte* (Army District Deputies) for each army district, consequently also in occupied Europe. They are to see to it that the Committees and Rings fulfill their tasks, that technical progress is made available to the armament factories. The Army District Deputies use for the executions of their tasks the Gau office for technology of the Nazi organization.[13]

b. The Office for Expansion of Armament Production maintains *Aussenstellen* (field offices) for each district.

c. Transport Deputies of the Ministry are appointed with the Economic Groups and for Trade Groups to disentangle the transport problem.[14]

d. The Power Engineers have already been mentioned.

e. *Baubevollmaechtigte* (Building Construction Deputies) are strictly speaking the regional agents of Speer in his capacity as Commissioner General for Building Construction. They serve, however, at the same time, as the regional agents of the Speer Ministry for all matters concerning building construction.

f. The most important regional agents of the Speer Ministry are, however, the Armament Inspectors and the Armament Commandos. The Armament Inspectors are also the chairmen of the Armament Commissions which coordinate armament production in the regional level.

The above organs of the Ministry may be called the "bureaucratic" pillar of the Ministry. The departments, the corporations, the regional agencies are direct bureaucratic organs, unbureaucratic as their form may be.

doubtful whether the Price Commissioner will be subordinated to him. There is thus no question that Speer emerges as the key figure in the German war economy and that he controls the whole war production including raw material control, labor control, rationalization and standardization, transportation raw material allocation, and that the whole apparatus of the Ministry of Economics, of the Four Year Plan Office, and of his own Ministry are at his disposal.

Speer's appointment thus parallels that of Himmler as Minister of the Interior. Just as Himmler, who already factually controlled the Ministry of the Interior, has now been put in charge of all domestic affairs (with the exclusion of economic controls) including the Ministry of the Interior, the Ministry for Church Affairs, the Ministry of Education and the Ministry of Justice, in the same way Speer's factually predominant position now found legal recognition.

The elevation of Speer does not indicate a corresponding loss of Goering's power. Though Goering may have lost direct control of the whole or parts of the Four Year Plan Office, he still retains his position as Hitler's Delegate for the Four-Year-Plan. In addition, his henchmen (Roehnert, Pleiger, Voss, Schieber) occupy predominant positions in the Armament Council and the Speer Ministry.

## 5. The Causes of the Decree and Impending Organizational Changes

The decree is a consequence of a steadily deteriorating economy which is suffering heavily from defeats in the field, from serial bombardment and from the less of economic resources in the East and the South. The major factor is probably the dislocation of German industry produced by air attacks. Heretofore, economic decisions had to be reached by compromises between Funk, Speer and the Four Year Plan Office. Such time-consuming procedure is no longer possible. Utmost speed is required in deciding whether or not an industry should be transferred, plants should be closed down, machinery should be shifted, labor should be moved. Heretofore, the Speer Ministry had to go to the directors of the 22 Spheres of Steering for the raw materials necessary for armament production. The National Commissioners in turn had to consult with the various organs set up by the Economic Groups for the purpose of deciding whether or not such allocation could be made. This method is no longer applicable when decisions have to be made almost instantaneously. In the situation in which Germany finds herself today, speed is more important than rational discussion. Acquired rights and property titles cannot be permitted to hinder the speedy execution of measures that leadership regards necessary. The consequence is that the self-government of German industry under the Ministry of Economics, that is the National Economic Chamber, the 7 National Groups, the Economic Groups, Trade Groups and Sub Trade Groups, may either disappear or cease to perform any function for the duration of the war. A partial integration of Groups and Main Committees has already been achieved by appointing, in a number of cases, chairmen of Main Committees to the leadership of Economic Groups.

It will mean that the Speer Ministry will actually assume the direction of raw material control, planning of production, closing down of plants, shifting of machinery, allocation of labor, all standardization and rationalization measures. There is little doubt that these powers will be ruthlessly used in the interest of maintaining arms production. No longer does a separate authority responsible for the civilian economy exist; as a consequence the level of consumption will unquestionably be curtailed to a minimum.

It is, of course, impossible for the new organization to increase arms production. It may, however, prevent too sharp a decline. Not much, however, can be expected. The conscious policy of concentration may have to be partly abandoned and closed marginal plants may have to be reopened. This may become necessary as a consequence of the destruction of efficient producers and the impossibility of expanding facilities of other efficient producers. This will, of course, require more labor and the heavy strain on manpower will thus be increased. The report on page 00 that home work will be encouraged for the manufacture of certain component parts, confirms this view. The above-mentioned report indicates that the Main Committees with their regional organization will be primarily the agents through which the Ministry will operate.

At the regional level, the dualism between the Armament Commissions headed by the Armament Inspector and the War Economic Staffs (*Kriegswirtsschaftstaebe*) headed by the Gauleiter in their capacity as National Defense Commissars may disappear. It is likely that the War Economic Staffs will be either dissolved or put under the Armament Commissions whereas, heretofore, the War Economic Staffs were above the Armament Commissions. In any case, the influence of the Speer Ministry will also become predominant at the regional level.

## 6. The Probable Attitude of Industry

The new measure will deepen the antagonism between industry and the Nazi Party. The full concentration of powers in the hands of Speer and Himmler respectively is an expression of the determination of the Nazi leadership to fight the war to the bitter end and not to allow the emergence of a Badoglio government. The Nazi leadership realizes, of course, that hope for military victory is rapidly declining. It knows that the United Nations will not make peace with them, but that the enemy may enter into negotiations with industrialists, generals, and high civil servants. The Nazi leadership is thus in complete isolation and one of the purposes of the decree is to overcome this isolation by making the industrial leadership a willing or unwilling partner in the struggle to the death.

It has been indicated above that the Ministry of Armament and Munitions does not operate through civil servants but almost exclusively through engineers and construction men. This has been interpreted by many observers to mean that the very structure of the Ministry of Armament and Munitions is "anti-capitalistic" and that the exclusion of bankers, economists, jurists and corporation administrators indicates the hostility of National Socialism to big business and the system of capitalist economy. This is not true. Wilhelm Zangen, President of the Mannesmann Combine, Leader of the National Group Industry and Funk's Deputy for Rationalization of the Economy, had a statistical analysis made of the composition of the directorates of 35 industrial corporations in the Ruhr district. The result was that the 143 members composing the managing boards (*Vorstaende*) were composed as follows: 85 technicians, 47 businessmen and 11 jurists, so that the technicians constitute a huge majority in the managing boards of the most powerful industrial corporations. This is in accordance with the practice of the German industrial ruling class. First generation capitalists usually send one of their sons to a university to study economics and the other son to a *Technische Hochschule* to study engineering or chemistry so that the two sons then can run the inherited corporation technically and financially. All the 15 chiefs of the Main Committees are managers or owners of the most powerful corporations.

The Main Committee No. 1 (*Wehrmacht und Allgemeines Gera*—Armed Forces and General Equipment)—the most important one—is headed by Wilhelm Zangen. The Main Committee *Triebwerke* (Engines) is headed by William Werner of the Auto-union. The Main Committee *Schienehfahrzeuge* (Rail Vehicles) is headed by Degenkolb of the Flick Combine. The Main Committee Machinery is headed by A. Tix of the Bochumer Verein. The Main Committee Shipbuilding is headed by State Councillor Rudolph Blohm, owner of the famous shipyards, Blohm and Voss. The Main Committee Armed Vehicles and Tractors is headed by Dr. Walter Rohland of Krupp. All of the sub-committees established by the Main Committees are headed by representatives of the most powerful Combine owners or directors. There is thus no question but that the whole Speer Ministry, the department chiefs, the various special delegates and the Main Committees are run by representatives of the most powerful and the most reactionary strata of German industry.

The Armament Council (*Ruestungsrat*) which coordinates the Main Committees and is the advisory body of the Speer Ministry is, besides, composed of five high officers (Milch, Fromm, Witzoll, Thomes, Loeb) and eight industrialists (Buecher—General Electric; Poensgen and Voegler—Steel trust; Roehnert and Pleiger—Goering Combine; Roechling—Roechling Combine and president of the *Reichsvereinigung* "Iron"; Zangen—Mannesmann; and Kessler—Siemens.

Thus there seems to be a deliberate policy of the Nazi leadership aimed at overcoming the isolation in which it finds itself. By transferring the most important functions in the economy (closing down, shifting of plants, shifting of labor and so on) to representatives of big business, the resentment engendered by the hopelessness of the situation will be directed as much against big business as against the Nazi leadership. Big business is also compelled to assume responsibility for the economic conduct of the war whether it wants such responsibility or not.

It is of course true that the power and financial position, the spoils of Germanization, Aryanization, and concentration of capital have up to America's entrance into the war appeared as compensation for the risks involved in Germany's adventurous policy. But German big business leadership is undoubtedly highly intelligent, has a large number of international connections, and realizes the hopelessness of the situation. There is no question but that it desires a way out. The raw appointment, while it appears to make this problem more complicated and more difficult of solution, must stimulate the industrialists to redouble their efforts to discover an avenue of escape.

# 5

HERBERT MARCUSE AND FELIX GILBERT

# *THE SIGNIFICANCE OF PRUSSIAN MILITARISM FOR NAZI IMPERIALISM: POTENTIAL TENSIONS IN UNITED NATIONS PSYCHOLOGICAL WARFARE*

(OCTOBER 20,1943)

Editor's note: R&A 1281. Herbert Marcuse and Felix Gilbert's authorship is indicated in a letter, dated September 24, 1943, from Eugene N. Anderson, head of the Central European Section of the Research and Analysis Branch, to Carl E. Schorske (RG 226, entry 59, box 1: Projects Committee Correspondence), where authorization is requested for a study on the destruction of Prussian militarism.

Classification: Restricted

Felix Gilbert (1905–91) was a German historian of Jewish origin who became a naturalized American citizen. A student of Frederick Meinecke, he is noted for his studies on Renaissance Europe (including *Machiavelli and Guicciardini: Politics and History in Sixteenth-Century Florence* [Princeton: Princeton University Press, 1965]). After having emigrated to the United States, beginning in 1943 he worked with Neumann and Marcuse at the Central European Section, before transfering to the OSS's London offices in the summer of 1944.

## Introduction

The destruction of Prussian militarism is today a crucial problem for United Nations Psychological Warfare against Germany. Roosevelt and Churchill have, in almost identical statements, declared that the annihilation of Prussian militarism is a capital war aim. Churchill elaborated this as follows:

> The core of Germany is Prussia. There is the source of the recurring pestilence. . . . I am sure the British, American and Russian peoples, who have suffered measureless waste, peril and bloodshed twice in a quarter of a century through the Teutonic urge for domination, will this time take steps to put it beyond the power of Prussia or all Germany to come at them again. Nazi tyranny and Prussian militarism are the two main elements in German life which must be absolutely destroyed.[1]

About the same time as Churchill's speech, a Union of German officers was founded in Moscow which includes high ranking Prussian militarists among its leaders. Over the Moscow radio they appeal to the German officers and men to overthrow the Nazi tyranny and to sue for an immediate peace. Russia seems to be convinced, if Germany's military situation continues to deteriorate, that she can use the Prussian officers for inducing the German army to turn against the Hitler regime and start a political revolution in Germany.

This propaganda from Moscow seems to be based on interpretation of the social and political structure of present day Germany which does not conform to that of the Western Powers. The Swedish press has already declared that Roosevelt's and Churchill's statements might be construed as political countermove against the National Free Germany Committee.[2] Grave conflicts in Psychological Warfare and in actual policy might be the consequence of this divergence. Under these circumstances, it is appropriate to evaluate the actual role of Prussia and Prussian militarism in the rise and in the possible defeat of the Nazi system.

The problems to be discussed are: Is Prussia still the "core of Germany"? Is Prussian militarism chiefly responsible for Nazi oppression and aggression? The following analysis attempts to show the Nazi regime has brought about profound changes in the distribution of social and political power in Germany. In the course of these changes, Prussia as a political unit has been dissolved, the Prussian nobility has lost its powerful position, and the forces that make for imperialist aggression are not typically Prussian but are rather the interests of German heavy industry located in Western and Central Germany and in Upper Silesia, (2) the militarists, (3) the nationalistic elements of the middle classes and the intellectuals, (4) government leaders trying to harmonize bitter conflicts between the social and economic groups by way of nationalistic aggression.

In view of these facts, and because the definition of war guilt and responsibility is one of the most decisive factors in our PW against Germany, the singling out of Prussian militarism as "one of the two main elements in German life which must be absolutely destroyed" is perhaps an inadequate expression of our war aim. It may leave an avenue of escape for the aggressive forces not covered by this term; it may be interpreted as implying the separation of Prussia or East Prussia from the Reich,—a plan which would not eliminate the source of German aggression and besides would create a strong and irreconcilable *irredenta*.

*

The term *Prussian militarism* refers to a definite social and political complex in German society. This complex contains roughly the following elements:

a) geographical: the Prussian territories east of the Elbe
b) economic: the large agrarian estates which characterize the economic structure of this region
c) social: the owners of these estates as a specially privileged class, the Prussian *Junkers*. This class has exercised its political influence either directly (as the most powerful land owners in the Reich), or, through its sons in the high officer corps of the German army and the higher ranks of the Civil Service.
d) ideological: a semi-feudal authoritarianism, resulting from the manifold personal, political, and administrative powers vested in the owners of the large estates.[3]

## Prussia under the Empire

The spectacular rise of Prussia to the rank of a great power in the 18th century was achieved in opposition and struggle against Reich and Emperor. Eighteenth-century Prussia, chiefly extending over Eastern "colonial" territories, was hardly regarded as a German state. Only at the end of the Napoleonic wars, through the Congress of Vienna, which enriched Prussia with the highly developed and densely populated Rhineland, did Prussia become central in German life.

The failure of the revolution of 1848 and the reactionary regime of the fifties were of decisive importance for the establishment of Prussian influence in German life. In defeating the liberal movement, the Junkers assured the continued existence of Prussia as well as their own dominant position in the Hohenzollern monarchy. It became certain that they would agree to the foundation of a German national state only if they felt that their continued existence and power would be guaranteed in the new Reich.

This Prussian influence in the Reich was assured in three different ways:

1) By retaining an electoral law in Prussia which made a conservative majority in the Prussian parliament certain (*Dreiklassenwahlrecht*), the Prussian conservatives continued to be the rulers of the Prussian state. They determined the general line of policy, and the entire higher administration of Prussia was reserved to members of their class, or to persons of whose conservative outlook they had made sure.
2) The constitution of the Reich assured dominant Prussian governmental influence (a) by establishing personal union between the Prussian Prime Minister and the Reichschancellor; (b) by the number of votes in the *Bundesrat* which the Prussian government had at its disposal.
3) The Junkers retained control of the army. No Reich army was created, but—with exception of the armies of Bavaria, Wuertemberg, and Saxony, which remained independent units—the troops of the German states were incorporated into the Prussian army. Thus the direction of military affairs was not in the hands of a Reichsministry, but rather in those of a Prussian government official—the Prussian War Minister. Moreover, the Prussian officer corps was protected from political interference by the fact that the key military institutions—the General Staff and the Military Cabinet, which determined selection and promotion of officers—were directly subordinated to the Emperor.
4) The economic strength of the Junkers did not keep step with their political power. The industrialization of German life led to the rise of new classes and groups which threatened the privileged position of the Junkers. To be sure, their political influence was strong enough to prevent the bourgeoisie from ushering in a new form of social life. Germany remained a semi-feudal state. The acceptance of the higher bourgeoisie into the ruling group remained dependent on their adherence to conservative standards. Moreover, through the institution of the *Reserveoffizier*, the way of life of large parts of the German bourgeoisie came to be patterned on the ideals, the code of honors, the behavior of the Prussian Junker.

Nevertheless, the political position of the Junkers was gradually undermined by the deterioration of their economic position. Strong international competition for agricultural products threatened the German market. Because of the poor soil of the Junker estates, their transformation into profitable competitive enterprises would have required considerable investment of capital, but the Junker estates were overvaluated to such an extent that they could not obtain the capital necessary for such transformation. They had therefore increasingly to rely on protective tariffs which they could get only by entering into a political alliance with German heavy industry. The two diverging interests agreed on a compromise by which industry consented to the protective tariffs, while the Junkers supported the expansionist foreign policy of heavy industry. *The imperialist policy of the German Empire was chiefly the policy of the industrial bourgeoisie* supported by militarist, intellectuals, and middle class nationalists. The National Liberal Party, the staunchest supporter of this policy, was representative of industrial interests. In the two great organizations propagandizing for German imperialism—the German Colonial Society and the German Navy League—the leading members were not Prussian Junkers but industrialists and academicians and publicists.

The simultaneous existence of such mutually hostile groups as the semi-feudal landowners, industrialists and other capitalists, the salaried middle classes, artisans, and industrial workers in a country so recently unified led politicians and even the government to use nationalistic aggression as a means of overcoming these internal conflicts.

## Prussia under the Republic

The political position of the Prussian Junkers declined under the Weimar Republic. The constitutional guarantees which the Junkers had enjoyed in the Bismarckian Reich were annulled. Although Prussia was not dissolved, as originally planned in 1918, she became a parliamentary democracy based on universal suffrage, and the conservatives lost their ruling position. Throughout the whole period of the Weimar Republic, Prussia was ruled by a leftist government; even in the election of 1933, the percentage of Nazi votes in Prussia was smaller than in any other German state. Although having lost all constitutional hold on governmental machinery, the Junkers continued to exert strong influence as a pressure group, through the army, and through their alliance with industry.

1) Because the new republican regime felt forced to make off the existing administrative apparatus (a monopoly of the conservatives during the Empire), a strong conservative element remained in the higher civil administration; since the old imperial civil servants continued in influential positions, they were able entirely to obstruct the democratization and republicanization of the civil administration.

2) The Prussian nobility remained firmly entrenched in the Officer Corps of the Republican *Reichswehr*. When the *Reichswehr* was founded, former Prussian officers remained in key positions, and since the *Reichswehr* of the Republic was a small professional army, these officers could apply a highly selective system in the choice of the officer corps, and could pattern the requirements in such a way that the Prussian Junker

remained a decisive element. In 1932, 27.15% of German officers were nobles, vastly more than the percentage of nobles among the Reich population would warrant. However, the strength of the nobles in the higher army leadership and in the traditional army branches was much stronger than it was in the newer technical arms which became increasingly important.

3) The position of the conservatives in bureaucracy and army was reinforced by the election of Hindenburg as president in 1925, for he became a powerful advocate of these groups.

4) The alliance between large landowners and industry grew more intimate. The competitive position of the large Eastern estates on the international market continued to deteriorate, and the Junkers had more than ever to rely on outside protection. German industry was most willing to support the demands of the Junkers who were its best customers for agricultural machines, and for artificial nitrogen (a domestic monopoly of the German Dye Trust,[4] which at that time had already fallen in line with the policy of heavy industry). Industrial pressure groups and parties backed the granting of *Osthilfe*,[5] which protected the Junkers from open bankruptcy. Although the Junkers regained considerable influence, the fact that the conservative party had, since 1928, come under the leadership of Alfred Hugenberg[6] (connected with the *Vereinigte Stahlwerke* and with *Krupp*, shows the extent of Junker dependency on the power of big industry.

## Prussia under the Nazi Regime

The Nazis completed the process of eliminating the Prussian Junkers as a decisive political power. This was necessitated by several factors:

a) the transformation of the Reich into a centralized totalitarian state under unified terroristic control led to the abolition of Prussia as a political unit. All Prussian ministries (except the Finance Ministry) have been merged with the Reich ministries. The Prussian provinces have been reduced to *Gaue* on an equal administrative footing with political units all over the Reich. (See appendix)

b) the requirements of the war economy compelled the Nazis to develop German industry to full capacity regardless of market profits. The economic structure of Germany was reorganized in its entirety in the interests of the industrial sector.

c) Simultaneously, the political power (direct and indirect) of big industry increased steadily. The amalgamation of the "self-government of business" with governmental agencies and institutions reveals the extent to which the Nazi state is shaped by the interests of the large industrial and financial concerns.

d) This state has adopted a new ideology oriented to the standards to technocratic efficiency regardless of traditional status and privileges. The Nazi state functions through the organization and manipulation of masses and machines. All these features conflict with the semi-feudal conservative authoritarianism of the Prussian Junkers. To this must be added the anti-Christian tendencies of the Nazi ideology which also are antipathetic to them.

e) The initial petty bourgeois and equalitarian character of Nazi popular support demanded a type of social and governmental regime hostile to the Junker tradition.

This resulted in the practical disappearance of the Prussian Junkers from the policy making level: A study of the top ranks of the Nazi hierarchy (The *Reich Cabinett*, the *Reich Statthalter*, the N.S.D.A.P. *Reich Leiter* and *Gauleiter*, and some other top officials) with respect to the ratio of Prussians and Prussian Junkers, shows that only ten out of eighty-six are of Prussian origin (from territories East of the Elbe), while not a single Prussian Junker is among them. Moreover, with the exception of two (Daluege and Lohse), all Prussian Nazi officials are of minor political importance. The vast majority of really powerful Nazi leaders come from the Rhineland, Bavaria, Central Germany, and Austria.

Among the higher ranks of the S.S. (*Oberst* and *Obergruppen-führer*), only five out of sixty-four leaders belong to the nobility, and three of these come from Western and Southern Germany.

The position of the Prussian Junker in the German army deserves special discussion. In the Armed Forces High Command (OKW), there is not a single member of the nobility. However, this is not the case if we examine the commanders of army groups; among the seven commanders of army groups, only one does not belong to a noble family. In the higher ranks of the Officer Corps, the proportion of nobility is still rather large. Among generals (and above), about 40% belong to the nobility, among major generals about 25%, among brigadier generals about 16%. It is not surprising that, owing to the dominant position of the Prussian Junkers in the *Reichswehr*, the German army still has a strong aristocratic element. But it is also characteristic of recent developments that this element declines rapidly in the lower grades, so that at present the share of the nobility in the Officer Corps is far below the 27.5% of *Reichswehr* days, a percentage much more in proportion to the ration of nobility to the rest of the German population.

Two other factors should be considered: in the foregoing figures, no distinction is made between Prussian nobility and German nobility in general, and close examination of the aristocratic names in the German army shows that the portion of South German and Austrian nobility is very great. Moreover, these figures refer only to the German army; neither the Air Corps nor the Waffen SS has been taken into consideration. Since these branches are of rather recent origin, and demand technical knowledge or abilities not typical of the Prussian Junker, the share of the nobility in these branches has been very small, and has never gone beyond 10% even in the highest ranks. The requirements of modern warfare undoubtedly led to a democratization of the army, to new relations between officers and men, and to a decline of the Prussian "spirit."

The strength of the Nazi army depends to a great extent on the striking power of highly specialized small units having high technological and organizational efficiency. Leadership of such units calls for a technical training which is entirely alien to the tradition of the Prussian nobility, and for an organizational coordination unsuitable to the caste spirit of the Junkers. The strict discipline of these units lies in the cohesion of technical teams rather than in the *Kadavergehorsam* of the old Prussian army.[7] Here too, the technocratic morale of industrial super-organizations has replaced the semi-feudal ideology of Prussianism.

On the policy making level of the German higher Civil Service (as far as it is not identical with the military hierarchy), *i.e.*, among the Under Secretaries of State, the chiefs of the Main Departments of the Reich Ministries, and the Presidents of the *Oberlandesgerichter* we find only three who may be considered as Prussian Junkers. Even in the *Reich Food Estate* (*Reichsnahrstand*), the Nazi overall organization for German agriculture, the leadership does not rest with the Junkers. The list of the administrative and political officials includes only a few noble names; here, too, control is exercised by Nazi bureaucrats and by the new Nazi "peasant elite."

The great exception is the German Diplomatic Corps. Here, the influence of the traditional Prussian nobility is still very strong. Yet it should not be forgotten that the traditional character of the German Foreign Service is intentionally retained by the Nazis in order to have at their disposal negotiators for potential compromise.

All this does not mean that the policy of the Nazis has been adverse to the economic and social position of the Junkers. On the contrary, they have been protected in many ways: the *Fideikommisse* (right of entail) have been maintained, the advantages of the Hereditary Estate Law[8] have been made available to them, they have been supplied with foreign slave labor, and the process of agricultural centralization has continued. Moreover, some Junkers have been rewarded with large estates in the occupied Eastern territories. These economic privileges, however, do not invalidate the fact that the Junkers have lost their political predominance. Industrial concentration and the totalitarian integration of Germany into the imperialistic war economy have led to a new distribution of power in which political control rests solely with the new Nazi Party, hierarchy and its industrialist military and petty bourgeois.

## Prussian Militarists in the Union of German Officers in Moscow

The Prussian militarists retain, however, a dominant position in the higher brackets of the German army, and it is by virtue of this position that they constitute a special target for PW: A military *coup d'état* against the Hitler regime is unquestionably one of the possible form of German collapse. In this event, Prussian Junkers officers would probably be among the leaders of such an army revolt, and the question arises whether and to what extent our PW should be prepared to utilize the tension between the old Prussian officer corps and the Nazis. The Russians have already done so. The *Union of German Officers*, recently established in Moscow and affiliated with the National Free Germany Committee, numbers among its leaders many Prussian aristocrats. Indeed, it seems that the Russians have taken great pains to include in the Union as many members of the old Prussian nobility as possible, men with names suggesting that very Prussian militarism denounced by Roosevelt and Churchill as the arch enemy.

The president of the Officers' Union is General of Artillery Walter von Seydlitz of the oldest Silesian nobility; his family dates back to the 13th century. Vice presidents are (among others) Lieutenant General Maximilian Alexander Moritz Wilhelm Edler von Daniels-Spangenberg, Knight of the Order of St. John, and Colonel van Huven. Among the members of the Union who have also been included in the National Free Germany Committee are Major Egbert von Frankenberg und Proschlitz, whose family goes back to 1200, and Isenhardus von Knobelsdorff-Brenkenhoff, of old Saxon nobility going back to 1203.

The accumulation of such names cannot be accidental—the less so since it was preceded by the nomination to the Vice Presidency of the Free Germany Committee of Count von Einsiedel, a great grandson of Bismarck. The Russians certainly wanted to impress the higher ranks of the German army, but perhaps they also wanted to demonstrate their determination, if no agreement with the Western Powers can be reached, to go ahead with their own policy towards Germany.

The immediate goal of this policy is to win over certain anti-Nazi cliques in the Army Officer Corps who may some day (if the German defeats continue) be able to overthrow the Hitler regime. From this point of view, the choice of the leaders of the German Officers' Union was a shrewd one.

General von Seydlitz and Lieutenant-General Edler von Daniels are considered to be officers of high military accomplishment. A reliable source reports that they have tried at pistol's point to compel General von Paulus to withdraw from Stalingrad contrary to Hitler's orders before the last opportunity to do so had passed. The officers of the Union are said to be highly esteemed by their colleagues on the Eastern front, and they may already have established contacts with German officers now leading troops against the Russians. Soviet propaganda may thus be able to make good use of the activities of the Union. Its effects in Germany cannot yet be assessed, but unquestionably its broadcasts are listened to—Paul Schmidt mentioned them in one of his official press conferences, and the Bern correspondent of *Nya Dagligt Allehanda* reported that the appeal of the Officers' Union circulated so swiftly in Germany and carried so much interest that Himmler is considering the strictest countermeasures—even the confiscation of private radio sets.

The Russians apparently believe that the tensions between the "Prussian" and the Nazi circles in the Army command are strong enough to dissolve the cohesion of the Wehrmacht when defeat seems to be inevitable. If this should happen before the British and American troops have approached the inner core of the European Fortress, the Russians would have considerably strengthened their bargaining position in the shaping of post-war Europe.

What are the other implications of this PW policy? We must face the possibility that, if the situation on the Eastern front continues to deteriorate, the dissenting groups in the army command may actually turn against the Hitler regime and stage a successful *coup d'etat*. The revolting generals could not set up a government of their own without some kind of popular support, and they will have to ally themselves with groups and programs capable of providing them with such support. Now there is—apart from the ruling Nazi hierarchy—only one group that seems to be excluded from such alliance according to the program of the Officers' Union, namely, the "heads of the financial and industrial concerns," the present leaders of German industry. Next to the Nazis, they have been most consistently singled out as the "organizers" of the Nazi crimes and their "associates" in them.[9] This means that the Russians will probably strive for a reorganization of former industry, (perhaps for some form of nationalization), and that they have reason to believe that the military leaders whom they have won over will not stand in the way of such reorganization. In other words, the Russians consider the present setup of German industry as the actual source of German aggression, and they think that, with the destruction of this source, Prussian militarism has lost its danger.

## Appendix: Prussia's Present Status in the Governmental and Administrative Organization of the Reich

Prior to 1933, Prussian and the other *Laender* (which were the constituent units of the German Reich) were still politically and administratively important. They had comparatively large law-making powers of their own, and as to executive powers, they retained the crucial departments of police and of general interior administration. Through the institution of the Federal Council (*Reichsrat*), moreover, the *Laender* directly influenced Reich policies, especially in the realm of legislation. Prussia, in particular, was important because it comprised more than half of the Reich's population and territory.

National Socialism, in a little over a year after its rise to power, abolished the traditional federal structure of the Reich, making it a strictly centralized state. Although the *Laender* retained the outward appearance of constituent units as to name, boundaries, and, in most cases, governmental institutions, they actually lost their autonomy and became mere administrative sub-divisions of the Reich. This was achieved by putting them under the direction of a Reich-appointed official, the Reich Governor (*Reichsstatthalter*), who takes his directives from, and is under the supervision of, the Reich Government, and transmits its instructions to the *Land* government (still so-called) or to the regional *Land* authorities. The abolition of the Federal Council and various *Laender* parliaments put an end to their legislative activities or influences. In the field of the executive, moreover, police and interior administration—besides many other branches of executive government—were taken away from the *Laender* and handed over to the Reich.

In the case of Prussia, this process of disintegration has gone even further. Prussia was beheaded by the Nazis and dissected into its component parts. This has been achieved by merging the top of its government with Reich authorities, and by making its main sub-divisions, the Provinces, administrative units directly under the Reich government. The "Prussianization" of the Reich after 1871 has thus ended in the *Verreichlichung* of Prussia.

All Prussian ministries, with the exception of Finance, have been merged with the corresponding Reich ministries which, in addition to their activities concerning the whole of the Reich, exercise those functions for Prussia which in the case of the other *Laender* are still left to the *Laender* ministries. Although Goering, to whom Hitler has delegated his powers as Reich Governor of Prussia, retains in addition the title of Prussian "Minister President," this means rather less than being Governor or Minister President in another *Land*. Since, with the one exception mentioned, ministries no longer exist, directives are given by the Reich agencies directly to the respective middle or lower authorities. There would be no point in, *e.g.*, the Reich Labor Ministry's asking Goering to transmit a directive to regional Labor Offices, because there is no longer a separate Prussian Labor Ministry coordinating labor matters for Prussia. It also would make Goering appear as a subordinate to the various Reich ministries, a situation which he would not be likely to put himself in.

Real regional government, (that part of government and administration which, under Reich auspices, is exercised in the case of the other *Laender* by the *Laender* governments), lies with Prussia in the Provinces. Here, the Provincial Presidents (*Oberpraesidenten*), [most of whom are *Gauleiter*], fulfill those functions which in the other *Laender* and the *Reichsgaue*, are entrusted to the Reich Governors. They are "commissars" of the central Reich government, who must see to it that Reich policies are executed in their regions, and that regional government and administration proceeds in accordance with Reich directives. The center of gravity for regional administration has thus shifted from Prussia as a whole to the Prussian Provinces, and there is not much which is left to Prussia as a unit.

What remains of centralized activities is the following: Goering, as Minister President, exercises some of the powers which are left to other Reich Governors and *Land* governments: *e.g.*, the issuing of those decrees which the Reich Government wants Prussia also to decree; the appointment of certain classes of officials; the exercise, in certain cases, of the right of pardon. Otherwise his functions are largely ceremonial. Thus, he appoints, convenes, and presides over the Prussian State Council (*Staatsrat*), a body of Nazi dignitaries and other "conspicuous" persons which was supposed to "advise" Goering upon his Prussian functions, but actually has not been convened since the outbreak of the war and, before that met only to listen to music or an occasional address by one of its members.

Prussia still has retained certain autonomy in financial matters. It has its own budget and levies certain taxes, mainly taxes on real estate. These functions are exercised under the direction of the Prussian Ministry of Finance, which also controls a number of public enterprises, as for instance, the Prussian State Bank and certain mining enterprises.

Another example of Prussia's decline is the fact that almost all territories formerly belonging to the Reich which were re-incorporated since 1935, and which, prior to 1918, had been Prussian were not given back to Prussia but were made units of the Reich (*Reichsgaue*). While Prussia regained only Polish Upper Silesia and parts of *Ostpreussen*, the formerly

Prussian provinces of Posen and *Westpreussen* and the formerly Prussian parts of the Saar territory were not restored to Prussia. Thus it appears that the present political and administrative unit known as Prussia is less important than at any other time in its history, even less important than other subdivisions of the Reich—Bavaria, Saxony, etc.

# 6

HERBERT MARCUSE

# *GERMAN SOCIAL STRATIFICATION*

(NOVEMBER 26, 1943)

Editor's note: R&A 1547. Marcuse's authorship is indicated in a letter dated December 8, 1943, and sent from the Central European Section to the secretary's office of the Projects Committee to communicate the delivery of the report (RG 226, entry 60, box 1, folder: Projects Committee Correspondence). The original document has been lost. Only a few microfilm copies, in very bad condition and including various illegible words, are still in the archives.

Classification: Restricted

## I. Ruling Groups

### A. The Five Ruling Groups

Since the abolition of all popular representation, the political decisions in Germany have been reached by compromises between the leadership of the Nazi Party, the Army, the ministerial bureaucracy, and the representatives of certain powerful business groups. The economic groups have usually kept in the background, although their voice in the fundamental decisions of policy-making was just as strong as, and perhaps even stronger than, that of the government (state and Party). They must, therefore, be included among the ruling groups.

The ruling groups are defined by their participation in policy-making, foreign as well as internal. By the same token, they are responsible for the actions of the Nazi regime, and they are the chief beneficiaries of its policy; their status and power have definitely increased under Nazism. One may distinguish five such groups:

1. *The Leadership of the Nazi Party and Affiliated Organizations*
   a. The Reich Leaders (*Reichsleiter*) of the Nazi Party

b. The Gau Leaders (*Gauleiter*) and their staff
c. The leadership of the German Labor Front
d. The leadership of the Hitler Youth and other affiliated organizations
e. The leadership of the SS down to the Group Leaders
f. The few Nazi big-wigs who do not hold any high Party position but rather government positions (such as Goering)

2. *The Top Strata of the Governmental and Political Bureaucracy*
   a. The Reich Ministers, the Undersecretaries of State, Ministerial Councillors, etc.
   b. The Reich Commissars, General Commissioners under the Four Years Plan, etc., the Trustees of Labor
   c. The *Oberpraesidenten*, *Regierungspraesidenten*, etc.
   d. The Presidents, Judges, and Prosecutors of the Higher Courts, of the Peoples Courts, the *Reichserbhofgericht*, etc.

3. *The High Command of the Wehrmacht and its Representatives in 2 (a, b) and 4*

4. *The Leadership of Big Business*
   a. Especially the owners, managers, and directors of the large industrial and financial concerns
   b. The leadership of the "self-government" of industry: the Reich Groups, *Reichsvereinigungen*, Economic Chambers, etc.
   c. The leading engineers, technicians, and experts, particularly in the Main Committees (*Hauptauschuesse*) and Industry Rings.

5. *The Landed Aristocracy*
   a. The owners of the great estates, especially in Northern and Eastern Germany.
   b. The new "peasant elite," perhaps best represented by the *Bauern-fuehrer* in the Reich Food Estate.

### B. Numerical Strength

Group 1:
a. About 40 (including the Party Chancellory and the *Reichs-Organizationsleitung*)
b. 43 Gau Leaders, each with a staff of approximately 30-40; 822 Kreis leaders
c. About 65 in the Central Office; 45 *Gauobmaenner*, 822 *Kreisobmaenner*

d. About 50 for each (Hitler Youth, Reich Labor Service, S.A., N.S. Motor Corps, N.S. Flying Corps); altogether about 250

e. About 125 Oberts-, Ober-, and *Gruppenfuehrer* about [*illegible number*] *Brigadefuehrer*

(a-e). *Total* about 2,200 excluding the District (Kreis) level
*Total* about 3,850 including the District (Kreis) level

Group 2:

a. About 180

b. About 60 Reich Commissioners and Commissars
About 23 Trustees of Labor
About 42 Chiefs of *Gau* Labor Exchanges

c. 12 *Oberpraesidenten*, 52 *Regierungspraesidenten* and Police Directors, 199 *Landraete*, 105 *Polizeipraesidenten*[1]

d. 32 *Oberlandengerichte* and *Generalstaatsansralte*, about 200 *Landgerichte*

e. About 15 Lord Mayors of cities with 500,000 and more inhabitants

(a-e). *Total* about 1,550

Group 3:[2]

| | |
|---|---|
| 15 Field Marshals<br>19 Colonel Generals<br>172 Generals<br>470 Lieutenant Generals | ARMY |
| 4 Field Marshals<br>8 Colonel Generals<br>61 Generals<br>78 Lieutenant Generals | AIR FORCE |
| 2 *Grossadmirale*<br>3 *Generaladmirale*<br>17 Admirals<br>25 Vice Admirals<br>43 Counter Admirals | NAVY |
| 917 | |
| 1,375 Major Generals (Army)<br>175 Major Generals (Air Force) | |

Group 4 a, b: Fairly accurate estimates are impossible. In 1932 Theodor Geiger estimated the number of the leaders of the *unpersoenliche Grossunternehmungen* (large joint stock corporations) at 15,000.[3] Today, their number is probably much smaller, due to the process of concentration and rationalization under the Nazi system.

The following figures may give some indication of the numerical strength of this stratum:

NUMBER OF ESTABLISHMENTS EMPLOYING MORE THAN 200 PERSONS (1933)[4]

| *Number Employed Per Establishment* | *Industry* | *Trade Communication Transportation* |
|---|---|---|
| 201–1,000 | 3,983 | 1,748 |
| 100–5,000 | 498 | 118 |
| 500 and over | 18 | 3 |

The center of this stratum must be sought in the last two categories. If it is assumed that the top management consists of 20 persons for each establishment, one arrives at a figure of 12,740.

After 1933, the number of enterprises employing more than 5,000 workers has greatly increased; at the same time, they have been concentrated in fewer hands. Today the actual ruling core of group 4 comprises probably not more than 1,000 persons.

Group 5:

a. If one assumes as a qualification for membership in the landed aristocracy the ownership of agricultural estates of 500 hectares and over, one arrives at a figure of 6,726 (counting one owner for each estate). The actual ruling groups of the landed aristocracy, however, are the owners of much larger estates. The number of agricultural estates of 1,000 and more hectares was 2,807 in 1933.[5] No statistical breakdown of this figure is available.

   Walter Darré, the first Nazi Minister of Agriculture, wrote in 1936 that 412 Junkers owned as much land as 1,000,000 peasants.

b. The center of the Nazi peasant "elite" is probably constituted by the Peasant Leaders. In 1942–3, there were 30 Regional Leaders and about 700 District Peasant Leaders.[6]

## C. Basis of Superior Position

These five groups are closely interconnected economically as well as politically. To a great extent there is even an identity of personnel, particularly between the members of groups 1, 4 and 5. A totalitarian society implies centralization of control and the abolition of the basic distinctions between society and the state. Consequently, (a) economic power tends to become political power, and (b) political power is increasingly strengthened by economic power.

1. Groups 1 and 4.

   a. Economic power becomes political power:
      i. German industrialists and financiers hold key positions in the government of the Reich.
      ii. The Reich government has entrusted the peak business organizations with the performance of functions which in a totalitarian state involve far reaching political decisions (planning of production, allocation of raw materials and government orders, exploitation of the occupied countries).
      iii. Lending business men are rewarded with high ranks in the SS, thus sharing the political privileges of this organization.

   b. Political power is strengthened by economic power:
      i. High ranking members of the Nazi Party and its affiliated organizations function in the boards of the large industrial and financial enterprises.
      ii. The Party and its affiliated organizations operate giant business enterprises of their own (for example, the enterprises of the German Labor Front and of the Wilhelm Gustoff Foundation). In some fields, Party-dominated enterprises hold a virtual monopoly (e.g., the Franz Sher publishing house).
      iii. The gigantic Hermann Goering Combine is in fact controlled by big-wigs of the Nazi Party.

In group 4 must be included the leading engineers and technicians in industry whose power has been steadily increased under the Nazi regime. The *Hauptausschuesse* (Main Committees) and *Industrieringe* (Industrial Rings), which constitute the key organizations for the nationalization of the German war economy, are exclusively composed of engineers and technicians. A German statistical analysis shows that out of 143 members of the managing boards of 35 industrial corporations in the Ruhr District, 85 are technicians.[7] They exercise more than merely technological or economic power; owing to the totalitarian merger of economic and political power, they plan an important part in the perpetuation of the Nazi system (formulation and application of Nazi methods for intensified exploitation of labor, etc.).

This "technocratic" stratum will certainly dissociate itself from the Nazi ideology after the breakdown of the Hitler regime and will offer collaboration with the United Nations. It should not be forgotten, however, that, by tradition, education, and training, those leading engineers are tied up with the expansionist interests of German heavy industry,[8] which has always been hostile to a democratic reorganization.

2. Group 2 and 3. The Army (as also the Nazi Party and its armed organizations) is a most powerful political factor if only by virtue of its size and strength. Despite the totalitarian centralization of control, the gigantic terroristic administrative and military machines of the Nazi state operate under their own weight and impair the freedom of political action of the ruling groups. The independence of these terroristic, administrative, and military machines, however, has its definite limitations. The apparatus is tied to the existence of a strong national government which is capable of asserting Germany's independence, keeping the monopolistic economy going, and "coordinating" the labor force. Without such a government, the apparatus in its prevailing structure and composition would either have no function or could be reduced considerably. It is this identity of interests which binds the German Army and Civil Service to a nationalistic and anti-democratic government. The "neutrality" of the conservative Army circles and of the Civil Service is to a large degree deceptive.

Apart from these general considerations, the Army and the Civil Service have most concrete ties with the highest economic group (4). In the Armament council, five generals sit together with eight industrialists. In addition, personnel connections are established by the inclusion of high Army officers and Civil Servants in the boards of the key economic enterprises.

3. Group 5. The power of the landed aristocracy has unquestionably decreased under the Nazi regime in favor of the industrial sector of the economy. Their members, however, hold many leading positions in the SS, and the Army High Command is still to a great extent composed of members of the old nobility. The Nazi regime has left untouched the vast Entail Estates in Eastern Germany; it has granted some of their owners the privileges of the Hereditary Estate Law, and the SS has rewarded them with giant new estates in the occupied Eastern territories.[9] Other landed aristocrats have strengthened and expanded their traditional connection with big business.

To summarize, the privileged position of the ruling groups of Nazi Germany still rests on the old foundations—economic and political power (the latter defined by control over the terroristic, military, and administrative machine). The general trend, however, is that political power is increasingly amalgamated with and even dependent on economic power. This trend is caused by the following facts:

a. The Nazi regime was set up in order to cope effectively with the internal conflicts which had assumed an ever more threatening form under the Weimar Republic (between big and small business, capital and labor, between the "new" and "old" industries). Also to conquer the "living space" necessary for the functioning and the expansion of the highly monopolized economy.
b. This was conditioned on the establishment of a war economy which was bound to rationalize the entire economy under the leadership of the most efficient and advanced industrial enterprises.
c. At the same time, the efficient control of labor, which was one of the most urgent goals of the Nazi regime, could best be accomplished through the mechanisms of economic control.

But the concentration of economic power was accompanied by a continual strengthening of the terroristic apparatus which was necessary for keeping the subjected population in line. By the sheer weight of this apparatus, its masters have acquired a position of power which overshadows that of the industrial and financial leadership. The latter, for the most part, has kept skillfully in the background and refrained from too conspicuous political exposure. This may make it easy for them to dissociate themselves from the Nazi regime after its final defeat.

### D. Changes in the Composition of the Ruling Groups Since the Weimar Republic

The fundamental change in the forms of political control which marked the transition from the Weimar Republic to the Nazi state was not accompanied by an equally fundamental change in the type of the ruling groups. To be sure, the Leadership of the Nazi Party and affiliated organizations is a newcomer, and the High Command of the *Wehrmacht* has greatly extended its influence.

Moreover, within the Leadership of Big Business the process of concentration has eliminated from the ruling stratum a large number of formerly decisive industrial and financial interests and has unified the formerly conflicting tendencies within this group. The core of the leadership of big business and the Landed Aristocracy and, to a lesser extent, the "export" personnel of the Governmental and Judicial Bureaucracy, has remained, however, unchanged. It is true that the leadership of big business contained quite a few industrialists and bankers who stood for a more liberal and democratic policy, but they were almost exclusively connected with the light industries which were rapidly losing out against heavy industry. Their political influence was steadily declining with the decline of their economic position. The only large German trust which, at the end of the Weimar Republic, could still be considered as antagonistic to the Nazi regime, the *I. G. Farbenindustrie*, came into the Nazi camp shortly after 1933.

One large group has definitely been excluded from the ranks of the ruling groups by the Nazi regime, namely, the labor bureaucracy. Through its representatives in the trade unions and in the Parliaments, labor was a strong partner in the compromises which shaped the policy of the Weimar Republic. In the Nazi state, labor is no longer represented on the policy-making level. The German Labor Front is not a new form of the old trade unions, but rather an over-all organization of employers and employees, in which the latter have a voice only in questions of minor factory conditions and of efficiency improvement. The leadership of the German Labor Front does not represent labor, but the governmental and Party bureaucracy.

The disappearance of labor from the policy-making level illustrates the extent to which the ruling groups have tightened their control in the Nazi state. One may say that, under the Weimar Republic, the political decisions were the result of a compromise between the ruling and the ruled, whereas, under the Nazi regime, they result from a compromise among the ruling groups. This change has also brought about the decline in the political weight of another social group which had played an important part in the Republic and whose function was perhaps best represented by the role of the Center Party. This party (Catholic, but not requiring a profession of that faith from its members) included representatives from all social strata, but it drew its chief strength from the Catholic workers and trade unions (especially in Eastern and Southern Germany), the clergy and the free professions. Owing to the fact that the Center Party frequently held the balance between the ruling and the ruled groups in the parliamentary system, the Center Party had managed to hold a key position which lost its foundation under the Nazi regime.

## E. Cliques and Class Consciousness

Within the five ruling groups, there are numerous cliques, [*illegible*] a community of specific interests which range all the way from the "rackets" or competing gangs to differences in industrial policies. [*We must*] limit ourselves to a few examples:

1. *Cliques within the Party*: They are based chiefly on different business [*illegible*] and/or different tactics of securing and strengthening the present power position as much as possible. The following may be mentioned:
   a. the Goering clique (strongly affiliated with heavy industry)

b. the [*illegible*] clique (which has recently fortified its ties with the landed aristocracy, without neglecting big business and finance, particularly in the exploitation of the Eastern territories)
c. the "radical" clique (inclined to revive the National Bolshevist tendencies in the Party, mainly in the old SA)

In addition, there are many cliques grouped around personal jealousies and hatreds.

2. *Cliques within the Army Command*:
   a. the "conservative" ("old Prussian") clique against the Nazi officers
   b. the school of "Eastern orientation" against that of "Western orientation"

1. *Cliques within big business*:
   a. competition and collusion among the large concerns, although regimented by the war economy, still produce the traditional antagonisms.
   b. the old established enterprises against the Nazi undertakings (Hermann Goering Combine; Bank of German Labor, etc.)
   c. finance against industrial capital, especially the problem of the financing of armament orders. Nazi industrialists have increased their control over the banks.

All these cliques readily unite as soon as their basic interest is threatened, namely, their grip on the economic and political apparatus of Germany. The Nazi regime has tremendously strengthened the class consciousness of Germany's ruling groups; the establishment of this regime was in itself the expression of a united and strengthened class consciousness. These groups agreed on the setting up of a totalitarian regime and submitted to stern regimentation of their affairs because they saw no other way of disciplining labor and carrying through a streamlined imperialistic policy. At the same time, they submitted to a series of pseudo-democratic measures, destined to create the illusion of a *Volksgemeinschaft* (racial community). Many conspicuous privileges have been abolished in order to retain the basic and essential privileges of economic and political power.

[*illegible*] before the war, many privileges of comfort and luxury had been [*illegible*] to the rich, while certain elegant places, hotels, [*illegible*] were thrown open to loyal Nazi workers. The war has of course [*strengthened*] this trend. The ruling groups must keep their privileges out of the public eye. It is reported that well-dressed people are frequently [*illegible*] at on the streets and subways in German cities, and that widespread resentment exists against rich [*illegible*].

## III. RULED GROUPS

### A. Numerical Strength of Social Groups[10]

On the basis of Geiger's classification, more than 90% of the gainfully employed persons in Germany would belong to the ruled groups, without any political representation, without any participation in the policy-making decisions—mere objects of totalitarian regimentation. This vast [*illegible*], however, comprises the beneficiaries and practitioners as well as the victims of the Nazi terror: the rank and file of the SS and the hundreds of thousands of Nazi officials in the Party and its affiliate organizations, the profiteers of "aryanization," Germanization, and Nazification among the middle classes, and the reactionary [*illegible*] in the Civil Service.

### B. General Trend

The following fundamental changes in the composition of the ruled groups here occurred under the Nazi system: the process of rationalization, necessitated by the war economy, has completely undermined the position of the old middle classes (small and medium business, artisans). Even if their numerical strength has not considerably decreased, their economic and political status has become one of total dependency. Economically they are now dependent on the organizations of big business, which have made them their outlets, subsidiaries, or agents. The retail trade has been decimated by the closing down of shops in the process of total mobilization (for figures see below under D). Between 300,000 and 500,000 have been mobilized as industrial workers. Politically, they are not represented on the policy-making level; the Leadership of the Economy Group Retail Trade, for example, is dominated by the large commercial interests.

While their economic basis is thus gradually disappearing, the old middle classes have not ceased to form a clearly defined social group. They have kept their own mentality and reactions which are equally remote from those of the new middle classes and the working classes. They still regard their shop and their trade as part and parcel of their personality, and the proletariat as their worst enemy. Among all the strata of the German population (with the possible exception of the farmers) they have been the least changed by the totalitarian forms of life under the

Nazi state. Privacy under law and order still comprises their supreme value. They are anti-Nazi in so far as the Nazis have ruined their business, dissolved family life, and alienated the young generation by the activities of the Hitler Youth, the SA, etc. They are violently anti-bolshevist and thoroughly nationalistic.

## C. Labor

The process of division within the working population, already in progress under the Weimar Republic, has become a fundamental element of Nazi labor policy. As a result, the working population now appears to be split into at least four social groups:

a. a numerically and politically strong labor aristocracy, consisting of the various officials and [*Vertragesmaenner*] of the Labor Front in the plants, the "sub-leaders," [*illegible*], etc.
b. the members of the highest paid groups in the efficiency wage system, from whose ranks group a is partly recruited,
c. the bulk of skilled and semi-skilled German workers,
d. the unskilled and lowest-paid groups, including the majority of female labor.

These groupings apparently follow the line of strictly technological distinctions (higher skill, higher efficiency, higher wages), but they have very definite political implications. Under the Nazi regime, whose labor policy is in its entirety directed to mass domination and manipulation, performance above average efficiency means spontaneous participation in this policy; in other words, political and ideological reliability.

The higher wage is not only the reward for the more efficient performance but also for collaboration with the ruling groups. For this reason, group (a) and a large part of group (b) must be considered as a Nazified stratum.

It will be relatively easy to identify groups (a) and (b), which constitute the Nazi-infiltrated stratum of labor. The Nazis themselves have distinguished the members of this stratum, and the workers in the respective factories will well remember them. They appeared as the officials of the Labor Front, and, more important, as the "shock troops" (*Aktivisten*) of the plants, the holders of Work Efficiency [*books*], the participants in the Works Proposal Scheme, who advanced valuable suggestions for the streamlining of Nazi production and control.

Another significant change in the structure of the German labor force is the shift in the age and sex factors. The bulk of the working population [*illegible*] consists of age groups over 45, and the proportion of female labor has greatly increased.

Not less significant is the change in the living conditions of the German workers. While it may be assumed that, up to the very last, the workers will be far better fed than the "normal consumer," their feeding has seriously deteriorated in consequence of the air raids and the migration of industry. At the end of the war, a large part of Germany's working population will be housed in camps and barracks, close to the plants, and separated from their families.

To what extent have these changes affected Germany's working class as a social group?

During the first years of the Nazi regime, the creation of full employment constituted a powerful bond between the regime and the vast majority of the working population. The political opposition was either annihilated or driven underground. A specially privileged stratum of politically reliable workers (supervisors, foremen, sub-leaders, officials of the Labor Front) were established in every plant; the rest were kept in line by the omnipresent Nazi organization, which isolated the workers in the individual plants and even in the different shops in the plant, and brought them together only in closely supervised mass undertakings ("Strength through Joy").

The political consciousness characteristic of the German workers was thus destroyed, and the majority of the working class became dependable and obedient attendants of the Nazi machine.

This attitude persisted and was even stimulated during the first years of the war as long as the victories of the German armies seemed to prove the efficiency and strength of the Nazi system. However, the situation changed under the impact of the increasing strain of work (efficiency wage system), and the general deterioration of German war potential.

The steady increase in female labor and in the higher age-groups (which had received their political training prior to and under the Weimar Republic) fostered apathy and dissatisfaction. However, the terroristic apparatus of the Nazi machine and the disillusionment of the oppressed population prevented the rise of a political opposition—this was confined to the small underground groups and to acts of isolated sabotage.

At the end of the war, German labor will probably be united only in these ways: the desire to obtain peace for a fairly modest security of work and living; the preservation of Germany's national independence, which they have always regarded as a prerequisite for social progress and democratic reconstruction. The former political tendencies which have split the German workers will probably be resurrected in a new form as soon as civil liberties are restored, but notwithstanding these political differences, German Labor is the strongest and largest democratic force in Germany. The only serious obstacle to full-fledged collaboration will be the suspicion of a dismemberment of the Reich, of its enslavement, and its reduction to semi-colonial status.

## D. Artisans and Trade

The Nazi regime has made great efforts to preserve the artisans as a social group, partly for ideological reasons, partly (and more important) in the interest of race domination. The Nazis wanted to maintain and to strengthen in this group a class consciousness different from that of the wage proletariat, toward which the economic position of the artisans tended to develop. The treatment of the artisans as an independent social group (for example, the revival of certain features of the old guild system) thus served to split further the ruled masses.

The German artisan has always been characterized by a strong pride in the work of his hands, in the individuality of his shop, in the personal relationship between him and the customer for whom he worked. These traits made him hostile to capitalistic industrialization: many artisans were loyal members of the Social Democratic Party. There, however, they formed a rather conservative stratum. Their tradition and patriarchal order in their shop rendered them antagonistic to revolutionary changes and to internationalism. The German artisan has a definite aversion to anything that is "foreign"; in this sense, he is nationalistic. But he knows that he will not profit from a policy of imperialistic expansion (which is bound to increase the power of big industry); a positive policy may not find it difficult to win him over for democratic reconstruction.

The number of artisan enterprises in the German economy is still very great, notwithstanding the combing-out process. In 1933, the number of industrial and commercial enterprises employing only 1–5 persons was 3,256,906 (amounting to 91.9% of all industrial and commercial establishments).[11]

Since 1933, special regulations were applied to the classification of an enterprise as an "artisan establishment." In 1939, there were 1,567,472 artisan enterprises in greater Germany (including Austria and Sudetenland) employing 5,197,922 persons, representing 31.5% of all persons employed in industrial establishments.[12]

For trade, statistical figures are available only for the time prior to the great closing-down process. In 1939, 3,023,094 persons were employed in commercial establishments in great Germany (2,750,063 in the old territory). About two thirds of these were employed in retail trade. Only the figures for 1933 are available: 852,728 retail establishments employed 1,937,441 persons.[13] Of the total number of establishments, only 0.2% were department stores, and only 0.4% were five and ten-cent stores.

The requirements of the war economy necessitated an ever increasing curtailment of consumer's goods and a rapid rationalization of establishments. By August 1, 1941, 6.4% of all retail shops had already been closed down. The Total Mobilization Decree of January 1943 will have affected about one-third of all remaining shops.[14] Moreover, numerous small shops throughout Germany have been merged into so-called "sales co-operatives" (*Kriegsverkaufsgemeinschaften*).

The same process has also victimized the small industrial enterprises. The urgent need for saving manpower and material and for increasing output accelerated a standardization and rationalization of work which concentrated production in the technically best-adapted large enterprises. One small plant after the other thus was absorbed by the great industrial concerns and combines.

The end of the war will find these strata of the old middle classes uprooted and dissolved—part as industrial workers or home laborers, part as employees of the large industrial and commercial enterprises, part as impoverished shop-keepers and artisans. They have certainly been disappointed and disillusioned by the Nazi regime, but—apart from the Social Democrats among them—they have no native democratic and liberal philosophy. They (together with the lower ranks of the Civil Service) provided the Nazi movement with its the most loyal followers, and their declining social status (between the rising bureaucracy of big business and the organized masses of the wage [*council ?*]) makes their ranks a breeding ground for violent resentments. Anti-Semitism is widespread among them, as is nationalism and distrust of "foreigners."

## E. Civil Servants

Numerical Strength:[15]

| | | |
|---|---|---|
| 1933 (including the Saar) | 1,481,000 | 2.3% of total population |
| 1939 (old territory) | 1,818,000 | 2.6% " |
| 1939 (including Austria and Sudetenland) | 2,000,000 | 2.6% " |

The top stratum of the Civil Service (the higher ministerial and judicial bureaucracy) belongs to the ruling groups in Germany. Here, we are concerned with that vast majority of Civil Servants who perform non-political, technical-administrative functions. They comprise the minor employees of the governmental bureaucracy and of the provincial and municipal administration, postal and railroad employees, etc. In 1933, their numerical distribution was as follows:[16]

| | |
|---|---|
| a. Reich Postal Service | 224,916 |
| b. Reich Railways | 275,874 |
| c. Federal, provincial, municipal administration; administration of justice | 425,928 |
| d. Schools, etc. | 259,235 |
| | 1,125,953 |

With the exception of a relatively small number of Civil Servants included in (c), these strata are usually regarded as performing non-political functions. For the German Civil Services however, the distinction between political and non-political functions is a very indefinite one. The German Civil Service has always been not only an administrative but also an authoritarian bureaucracy: by tradition, training, and attitude, the Civil Servant was the bearer of an authority which placed him above the rank and file of the population. His "*Amt*," the function which he performed, reared to him something unquestionable, ordained from above, a part of an almost mystical "law and order." With the higher strata of the Civil Service, this attitude was the expression of a definite caste consciousness. With the lower strata, particularly in group (a) and (b), the authoritarian attitude had almost completely disappeared by the time of the Weimar Republic; many of their members were old Social Democrats.

The Weimar Republic did not succeed, however, in democratizing the bulk of the groups (c) and (d). The ministerial bureaucracy maintained its apparently neutral attitude towards the political form of government, but this neutrality was conditioned upon the incapacity or unwillingness of the government to reorganize the authoritarian bureaucracy in a genuinely democratic way. It may be expected that the ministerial bureaucracy will show the same neutrality after the downfall of the Nazi government: they will style themselves as strictly administrative experts who are ready to collaborate with any regime that promises to maintain "law and order."

The same holds true for a great part of the Civil Servants in group (d). Chauvinism, authoritarianism, and hostility to democratic forms is widespread among both, the academic and the non-academic strata. The elementary-school teachers furnished a relatively large percentage of the membership of the Nazi Party, and many university teachers made themselves the spokesmen of Nazi philosophy. It is noteworthy that resistance against the latter came from the old conservative rather than from the liberal or neutral university circles. They objected to the barbarian and terroristic features of National Socialism in the name of German "culture," but, by the same token, they will be most hostile to any foreign interference with German life, and their anti-democratic philosophy has certainly been strengthened by the failure of the Weimar Republic.

The German Civil Service was a highly organized group. The *Deutscher Beamtenbund*, a politically "neutral" organization, comprised 1,019,902 members at the end of 1930; the Socialdemocratic *Algemeiner Deutscher Beamtenbund*, only 175,050.

F. Salary Earners

Numerical Strength:[17]

| | |
|---|---|
| 1933 | 4,032,345 |
| 1939 (old territory) | 4,663,773 |
| 1939 (including Austria and Sudetenland) | 6,269,662 |

*Distribution*

| | *1933* | *1939 (old)* | *1939 (new)* |
|---|---|---|---|
| Industry | 1,300,818 | 1,651,566 | 1,846,255 |
| Trade, Communication, Transportation, etc. | 1,784,161 | 1,750,782 | 1,974, [*illegible*]78 |
| Public and Professional Service | 831,048 | 1,167,442 | 1,338,57 [*illegible*] |
| Forestry, Agriculture | 97,878 | 75,267 | 89,550 |
| Domestic Service | 18,[*illegible*] | 18,716 | 20,600 |

The numerical strength of this stratum, which forms the core of the so-called new middle class, has increased during the last twenty years, as has its social prestige and consciousness. From the old middle classes, the salary earners are distinguished by a greater degree of security and dependency, from the wage earners by a definite anti-proletarian class consciousness and by a widespread identification with the interest and attitude of their employer.

The salaried employees are not, however, a politically unified group. Of the organized salary earners, 26.8% belonged to the Socialist unions, 34.1% to the Christian-National unions, and 22.6% to the Democratic unions (figures for 1931). The Socialdemocratic *Allgemeiner Freier Angestelltenbund* (Afa) had 486,000 members (1931), the (predominantly nationalistic) *Gesamtverband Deutscher Angestellten Gewerkschaften* 593,000 (1933), the *Gewerkschaftsbund der Angestellen* (predominantly democratic) 335,428 (1931).[2] The nationalistic union was thus the strongest among the employee unions; its main organization, the *Deutschnationaler Han-*

*dlungsgehilfen Verband*, officially anti-Semitic, was the most active pressure group; it had its own representatives in the Reichstag, and it became the stronghold of Nazism among the salary earners.

## G. Free Professions

Numerical Strength:

| | *1933*[18] | *1939*[19] *(old Reich territory excl. Saar)* |
|---|---|---|
| a. Churches, religious institutions | 165,072 | 180,565 |
| b. Artists, writers, editors | 23,368 | 22,177 |
| c. Lawyers, economic councillors, etc. | 191,035 | 112,382 |
| d. Physicians, dentists, nurses, etc. | 401,418 | 401,939 |
| e. Theater, film, radio, etc. | 163,134 | 134,467 |

Groups (b) and (c) have been thoroughly Nazified, but the active Nazis among them can be easily identified since they have been conspicuously honored by the Regime and since their activity has become well known throughout Germany. The other groups may be considered as politically neutral; their status has considerably declined under the Nazi system, and the majority will go along with the democratic forces.

The clergy will be treated in a separate chapter.

## H. Peasants

Numerical Strength:[20]

| | *1925* | *1939 (old territory)* |
|---|---|---|
| Gainfully employed in agriculture and forestry | 9,763 | 8,934 |
| Dependents | | 3,331 |
| TOTAL | 14,434 | 12,265 |
| Owners, managers, etc. | | 1,985,142 |
| Unpaid family workers | | 4,772,278 |
| Wage earners | | 2,111,029 |

*1933*

| *Size in hectares* | *Number of Enterprises in Ownership of Land*[21] |
|---|---|
| 0.51–1 | 307,154 |
| 1–2 | 429,253 |
| 2–5 | 743,271 |
| 5–10 | 597,972 |
| 10–20 | 436,071 |
| 20–50 | 256,892 |
| 50–100 | 51,424 |
| 100–200 | 14,971 |
| 200–500 | 9,349 |

The greatest number of small agricultural enterprises (under 20 hectares) is found in Bavaria, the Rhineland, Wuerttemberg, Brandenburg, Westphalia, Baden, and Hannover.[22]

The most important change that took place during the last decade is the decline in the farm population. The latter constituted 22.8% of the total population in 1925, but only 17.7% in 1939. Since then, the decline has continued: a German estimate of August 1943 gives a figure of 16%.[23] This tendency expresses the critical condition of German agriculture. At least since 1925, agricultural prices were below the world market, and agricultural labor was greatly undervaluated. The subsidies were to a large extent turned into benefits for the bigger estates, many small peasants were dispossessed, and a process of agricultural concentration was taking place. The Nazis did not succeed in stopping this process.

Part II

# PATTERNS OF COLLAPSE

# 7

## Franz Neumann

## *GERMAN MORALE AFTER TUNISIA*

(June 25,1943)

Editor's note: R&A 933. This was an OSS report published in the form of a pamphlet for internal use. An introductory note points out that the text is "based on a memorandum from the Research and Analysis Branch." Most probably, this was the memo titled "The Nazi Defeat in Tunisia, the Coming Invasion of Europe, and Our PW," sent by William Langer to General Donovan on 17 May 1943, because in his opinion it was "particularly interesting" (which would also explain the reason for its redrafting, unlike most of the reports R&A produced, into the form of an essay). Neumann's authorship is indicated in *Political Intelligence Report* (R&A 1113.6-8, section I.A.I), and in a letter, dated May 14, 1943, from H. Deutsch to William Langer (RG 226, entry 38, box 5).

Classification: Secret

The United Nations have received many reports in recent weeks of a marked deterioration in German "morale." The defeat in Tunisia, according to these reports, has driven home the lesson of Stalingrad and dissipated finally the myth of Nazi invincibility, even for the Nazis. German propaganda is now having to concern itself seriously for the first time with the possibility of defeat. Tales of unrest, of war weariness, even of open opposition are appearing on every hand. For some observers, these items add up to a familiar pattern of impending collapse. The question now becomes urgent whether, in fact, the United Nations have any ground for expecting Germany to repeat the debacle of 1918.

### (a) Morale in a Totalitarian State

The reports from Germany are probably basically correct. Yet the inferences drawn from them about the precarious state of German morale may produce unjustified optimism. The interpretation is too often based on the fallacious assumption that the feelings of the people play much the same role in the totalitarian states as they do in the democracies.

The essential question must be, not how the people feel, but what effect their feelings have on the workings of the government: the problem is thus intimately bound up with the whole organization of society. In a free society, the feelings of individuals are likely to be political facts of the highest importance. But in an army, on the other hand, the object of organization is to reduce the importance of individual feelings to a minimum, and it is possible to devise sanction and controls which will make a coward fight with bravery.

A totalitarian state is in this respect much more on the model of an army. A good deal of the Nazi genius has gone to constructing a society which, from the point of view of morale, is as nearly foolproof as possible. The sum of Nazi institutional and social arrangements is designed to render individual feelings negligible—to force the industrialist to produce, the worker to work, the soldier to fight, no matter how much they may hate the regime and desire to end the war.

Morale is thus a Nazi expendable. Where in democratic nations loss of faith in the government, disunity, defeatism may be expressed by political acts dangerous to the prosecution of the war, in a totalitarian country they constitute by themselves only a minor vulnerability; they may be managed by the regime, even turned to its own purposes. Totalitarian "morale" cannot be effectively attacked by the ordinary methods of psychological warfare. It can be attacked only by smashing the structure for the management of morale—which means by smashing the Nazi system itself.

## (b) The Impact of Tunisia

The management of morale, though simple enough so long as the basic structure remains intact, still requires a constant adaptation of methods to circumstances. The downhill slide, started by Stalingrad and pushed along by Tunisia, has placed in jeopardy the favorite Nazi theme of victory through *Blitzkrieg*. Not since Crete has the German offensive spirit produced a decisive triumph; and now, with both victory and *Blitzkrieg* appearing increasingly remote, it is becoming necessary for the Nazis to jettison the whole propaganda line.

The de-glorification of the offensive is well under way. Military commentators, especially General Dittmar, emphasize the value of the "strategy of waiting," and argue that a United Nations offensive today would be a sign of weakness, as a German offensive was in 1918. *Festung Europa* has been built up as the moral equivalent of *Blitzkrieg* to a degree which has convinced some observers that the Nazis are acquiring a Maginot complex of their own.[1] Yet propaganda so long based on the infallibility of attack cannot be reversed without creating some misgivings among the German people.

Even more dangerous to the traditional Nazi propaganda pattern has been the gradual emergence of a possibility hitherto denied: defeat. "In spite of the reverses of the first winter of the war with Russia," remarks the Swiss weekly *Die Weltwoche*, "the ominous word 'defeat' was never used—but after Stalingrad, the use of the word could no longer be avoided." Tunisia considerably advanced the discussion of what would happen in case of defeat. The mounting urgency with which such questions will be raised makes it likely that Nazi methods for managing morale are in a crucial stage of transition. But it does not mean that the morale itself is in danger of collapse.

## (c) Strength through Fear

Though fear of defeat may demoralize a nation, it may also nerve it to its ultimate exertions. The Nazis are hard at work capitalizing on the positive aspects of the changed situation. Party orators and writers, by drawing a grim picture of the consequences of collapse, have succeeded in strengthening the will-to-resist of people who were beginning to falter. Kaufman's pamphlet advocating the sterilization of the German people, the anti-German writings of Vansittart, Filipowicz, Kingsbury Smith and other Allied commentators,[2] are extensively circulated in order to remind all Germans that they are in the Nazi boat. While it is not clear that many Germans believe that the British and Americans actually propose to carry out extreme plans of annihilation, they none the less see little hope in United Nations victory, and they are perfectly willing to believe the Russians capable of any degree of inhumanity.

From the start, the Nazis have understood that their system of control rested on keeping people in a perpetual state of tension. Their essential governing technique has been to give people the choice between submitting themselves to the system or rebelling against it; to make that the only choice; and constantly to confront them with that choice, so that a succession of decisions results in moral and psychological commitments of ever mounting strength.

For years, anti-Semitism has served the purpose of forcing all Germans either to identify themselves with Nazism or pay the price of dissent. The recent stepping-up of anti-Semitism, in connection with the general terrorist campaign against all home front dissidents, whether intellectuals, dispossessed shopkeepers or grumbling aristocrats, is in large part a campaign to renew the national act of faith: Germans must again decide between accepting the guilt of the regime or openly resisting it, and the act of acceptance increases the widespread conviction that all Germans must stand or fall with Adolf Hitler. Robert Ley's recent statement to the Party is being extended to the nation: "Every National Socialist has burned his bridges on entering the Party. And even if those veteran National Socialists had wanted to return to the old world, it would no longer be possible. . . . There is no retreat."

## (d) Centers of Resistance

The Nazi apparatus of control, the conviction that all Germans are in the same boat, the long record of Nazi success, have all made "bad morale" impotent and inconsequential. Yet, once liberated, "bad morale" may well produce revolution. There is increasing evidence that among certain groups in the population the internal strains of Nazism have encouraged the growth of "bad morale" to a degree where it provides important targets for United Nations PW operations.

It seems likely, for example, that labor's basic antagonism to the regime, so long concealed by Nazi victories, has grown to a point where it may now be exploited. Absenteeism has become a major problem. In some basic industries the eight-hour day has been restored. Nazi orators have begun again to concentrate on the socialist side of National Socialism. Goebbels, Sauckel, Ley and the left wing of the Party seem to have been given license to revive the revolutionary, anti-capitalist appeal which played so large a part in the Party's rise.

The Munich trials disclosed another growing source of opposition in the intellectuals, a fact tacitly confirmed by Goebbels when he devoted the whole of a recent article in *Das Reich* to denouncing them. The church groups, Lutheran and Catholic, and the dispossessed sections of the middle classes form other nuclei of potential opposition.

## (e) Revolutionary Prospects

Yet the Nazi system may keep this opposition merely potential for a long time. Even among the working classes there is no serious labor trouble, only war weariness. The rising hatred of the regime in these various groups may interfere hardly at all with their performances in the Nazi war effort.

The task for United Nations PW is to convert this war weariness, this covert and thwarted unrest, into actual opposition. The only way in which this discontent may be released in a form which will exert pressure on the state is by destroying physically the system whose controls have so successfully eliminated morale as a crucial factor.

In so far as air raids break up existing institutional arrangements and force survivors into spontaneous, self-help groups, they are creating mediums for the expression of morale. In so far as sabotage weakens the system of control, it encourages activity outside the totalitarian organization. Even propaganda may keep hopes alive; and if it could provide a decent alternative for resisting groups, it might go far in undermining the Nazi doctrine of everybody in the same boat. But in last analysis only invasion and the destruction of the *Wehrmacht* can be expected to crack the Nazi system to a point where morale may operate as a political factor.

Most Germans are still caught in the Nazi trap. Whatever their personal desires or fears, they must continue doing the Nazi job: the only alternative is the concentration camp or the executioner's ax. As parts of the Nazi system crumble, opportunities are created for forms of spontaneous organization which may give morale a chance to affect the state. But this can in no lasting sense be accomplished by anything less than an invasion of Europe. Until the invasion is forthcoming, it will be highly unwise to gamble on a repetition of 1918. Hitler learned that lesson well. His system is designed, above most other things, to prevent that moment of history, at least, from repeating itself.

# 8

## Herbert Marcuse

## (assisted by Franz Neumann and Hans Meyerhoff)

# *MORALE IN GERMANY*

(September 16,1943)

Editor's note: R&A 1214. Marcuse's authorship (assisted by Neumann and Meyerhoff) is indicated in "Political Intelligence Report," n. 26, section III.D.4 (R&A 1113.26).

Classification: Secret

Hans Meyerhoff (1914–65) was a philosopher and political activist against the Vietnam war. Of Jewish origin, he emigrated to the United States in 1934 after the enactment of the law that impeded the enrollment of Jews in the university. After having obtained his PhD in philosophy from UCLA, he joined the Research and Analysis Branch of the OSS and then, after its closing, was transfered to the State Department, like Marcuse. In 1948 he moved to UCLA's Department of Philosophy, where he would remain until his death, in November 1965, in an automobile accident. In 1968, on the occasion of the First Annual Hans Meyerhoff Memorial Lecture, Marcuse presented a lecture titled "Beyond One-Dimensional Man" (now in Herbert Marcuse, *Towards a Critical Theory of Society* (edited D. Kellner, [London–New York: Routledge, 2001], pp. 107–20), where he defined Meyerhoff as "his best friend."

1. PW operations are not concerned with what people feel and think about their governments but rather to what extent these feelings and thoughts will and can affect their behavior within the framework of the enemy society. The answer to this question cannot be sought in what is understood by "morale" but rather in the sum total of the enemy's institutional and social arrangements. An entrepreneur, for instance, may

dislike the Nazis; he may be convinced that they will lose the war. He may ardently desire peace and may even be willing to accept unconditional surrender. His morale may thus be said to be "low." What is the effect of his low morale on the operation of his armament factory? A worker may be a defeatist or even a revolutionist. Will he work less and can he work less? A soldier may not want to fight. Will his will have a chance of asserting itself?

Let us take the last instance first. The organization of the army may be such that even a cowardly soldier may be compelled to fight magnificently. If he does not, he may face death by the hand of the Field Gendarmerie. If he does, however, he has a chance of survival. The institutional arrangements may thus be such that the soldier can choose only between certain death at the hand of his own Field Police or possible survival in combat.

The entrepreneur in Germany is enmeshed in a network of authoritarian organizations such as Chambers, compulsory trade associations (Groups), technical committees, armament commissions and so on. The Nazi Gauleiters and the Armament Inspectors watch and control him. He has to produce if he wants to survive.

The worker is exposed to controls so tight as no other group in society. To revolt against the controls means either death or the concentration camp.

2. The last example leads us to a general statement concerning morale in a totalitarian society. The essence of modern factory organization consists in devising a pattern of control which would prevent a drop in productivity even if the worker abhors the work which he performs. The conveyor belt system introduces an outside force into the process of production. The speed of work is no longer determined by the morale of the worker but by a technical mechanism. The worker who does not like the speed can merely quit.

This, however, is exactly what he cannot do in Germany. And not only the worker cannot do it, but nobody can drop out unless he is willing to risk life or freedom.

The system of National Socialism has been devised for the very purpose of making a repetition of 1918 impossible—that is, to make morale dispensable. Morale, so to speak, has become a democratic luxury.

3. If we were to forget this simple truth, we should have to assume that Germany is already in a state of collapse. Report after report indicates that the people have lost faith in victory and that the fighting spirit is seriously impaired. Says one article on "Rumors and Criticisms": "If one were to believe the rumors and loose talk which can be picked up in the streets, it would make us all despair of our future fate, because, accord-

ing to them, we have already lost the war anyway."[1] The Party's prestige has suffered seriously; it is uniformly criticized and despised. "Above all, they criticize the Party and its work."[2] Embarrassing questions are repeated: "Where are our political leaders; we don't see any uniforms."[3] Productivity declines due to deliberate slow-downs and sabotage; fraternization between German and foreign workers is becoming common as reported even by the *New York Times*.[4] Even middle class people attend opposition meetings and the Socialist and Communist underground is gaining strength.[5]

All this is most likely true. The question is to what extent does it affect the Nazi pattern of government and society which seeks to dispense with the morale factor in its operations?

A very intelligent P/W captured in Sicily with the Hermann Goering Division stated the German morale problem in an admirable way. "The Hermann Goering Division fought well as long as it was together. But when it was split up in groups of 40 men or less, the attitude changed."[6] This statement confirms our thesis: so long as the organizational framework is more or less intact, bad morale will not impair the fighting and productive efficiency of Germany. The paramount question is, therefore: is the apparatus still intact? The answer must be given separately for the various strata of German society.

4. Two measures have recently been taken to insure the full control of the Nazi party over society: The appointment of Himmler as Minister of the Interior and as Delegate General for the Administration of the Reich,[7] and that of Speer as virtual dictator of the German war economy.[8]

The two appointments concentrate all powers over the domestic life of the German people in the hands of two reliable Nazis. This, however, is but one aspect of the organizational changes. Both—Himmler and Speer—are closely cooperating with the most reactionary strata of German society; the Junkers and heavy industry. Himmler has consistently used his power as Commissioner General for the Strengthening of German *Folkdom* in the East to enrich members of the German nobility. He has handed over to them estate after estate in occupied Poland, Russia, and the Balkan states.[9] Speer employs in his Ministry for Armaments and Munitions exclusively members of the Goering Combine and of the corporations in heavy industry.

These moves do not necessarily express an identity of policy of the Nazi party, the Junkers, and heavy industry. Junkers, industrial leaders, and the Nazis realize that the war is lost and that the only alternative to a crushing defeat with ensuing loss of wealth and power is a separate peace with either Russia or the western powers. But the Nazi leadership also realizes that neither Russia nor the western powers are willing to negotiate with them but that avenues of escape may still be open to the army leadership and its allied Junkers and industrialists.

The two appointments and the policies of Himmler and Speer thus in turn tend to close the avenues for the generals, Junkers and industrialists. They make the three groups of the German ruling classes, willing or unwilling, accessories of the Nazi party leadership. They intend to make a German Badoglio spirit infinitely more difficult, the more so because in contrast to Italy, there is in Germany no institution comparable to the Grand Council of Fascism or the monarchy. The very shapelessness of the Nazi constitutional system—if such term can be applied to Germany—makes it extremely difficult for Junkers, generals and industrialists to articulate their opposition and to translate their feelings into policies and actions[10].

We may, therefore, say that in spite of differences between the views of the Nazi leadership on the one hand and the generals, Junkers and industrialists on the other, the control of the Nazi leadership over these groups in the ruling class today is as strong as ever before. There is at present no likelihood of the emergence of a politically powerful opposition within the ruling classes, except if manipulated by the Nazi leadership itself. These reactionary elite groups, however, might combine into anti-Party front in order to save themselves, if a further deterioration of the military situation should so strengthen genuine democratic elements inside the country as to threaten seriously the present control pattern for their own and the party's interests.

5. While the control apparatus over the ruling groups is thus powerful, it has considerably weakened in so far as middle class and labor are concerned. The following outstanding facts deserve to be mentioned.

Air raids have destroyed the belief in the inviolability of German territory and have, for the first time since the wars of liberation, made Germany a battleground. Their effects have broken the conveyer belt pattern of Nazi control at many places. According to a Swiss traveler, a new collectivist spirit has been created during and after air raids as a result of the general misery in which thousands have lost their possessions. This community spirit is not only restricted to the momentary situation but extends into the future—that is, the period of reconstruction after positive defeat. Civilian air raid victims are reported as saying that they "will have to pool everything and start afresh in common as the Russians did."[11] This is also confirmed by a recent report of the Berlin correspondent of *Stockholm Tidningen* which mentions the "increasing material proletarianization caused by the air war" and the measures of "pure Communism" (*sic!*) or "practical Christianity" adopted for their alleviation.[12]

Though this community spirit supports for the time being the Nazi system, it is almost certain that it carries within it the germs of the Nazi system's destruction. This new morale element is alien to Nazi regimentation for it may produce an attitude of national or social cohesion within activities without party symbols and organization. It also tends to allay fears of Russia, one of the most characteristic fears which the Nazis have successfully exploited so far.

Misery, defeat, air raids, destruction of property—they all have contributed to the detestation in which the Nazi party is held. The party begins to show serious deficiencies in its main task of mass manipulation. Evacuation programs suffer from the inadequacy of party functionaries; transfer of large masses of people often removes them from immediate control of local party bosses, accentuates regional and class conflicts, helps the spread of subversive rumors, and impairs the effectiveness of the official Nazi propaganda line promising safety and retaliation.[13] Other factors support this point even more substantially: The order of the SA leadership to SA men to wear SA uniforms and badges as often as possible, especially after air raids. Repeated exhortations to this end testify to the unwillingness of the SA men to expose themselves to contempt, hatred, and possible assault. Purges are carried out within the party. This is candidly admitted by the leadership of the NSKK (National Socialist Motor Corps). "Corps Leader Krauss," a senior group leader writes, "has ordered a purge within our organization. Anyone lukewarm or tolerating a defeatist attitude must go. It is better to have fewer men in our ranks but all of them fanatics. We must keep our knives sharpened. It is better for us to be feared than to be ignored." Or, as the *Hamburger Fremdenblatt* threatened recently: "The time has come, like 1934, when the chaff must be separated from the wheat."[14] The statement coming from the NSKK is of great significance because this party organization is an elite formation of a semi-military character serving with the army and the Organization Todt as a corps of supply.

Hitler's September speech, finally, though making a serious effort at a matter-of-fact analysis of the present political and military situation, did not hold out any definite concrete promises of victory. The only hope he invoked was that Providence is, as usual, working for Germany. But the Germans have also been accustomed by their military leaders to believe that God is always on the side of the stronger battalions, as Frederick the Great once said, and they realize that the United Nations have the stronger battalions.

Thus the ideological, social and political apparatus of the Nazi party, under the severe losses of the people, is no longer intact. But the crucial question remains to what extent these "breaks" in the control pattern of the Nazi system can be enlarged and exploited for successful political action against the regime.

6. There is now no doubt that the majority of the masses are not Nazis. But that does not imply that they are anti-Nazis. As our P/W put it, "The number of convinced anti-Nazis is small, but so is the number of convinced Nazis." In spite of the inadequacies of their control, the Nazi leadership has probably little to fear from the masses of the people. Apathy, weariness and distrust are the outstanding characteristics of the masses. There is general agreement in all P/W reports on the point that what people want is "peace, bread, and security," not politics. The domestication of the German masses has gone far. Private sorrows, food, shelter, safety for themselves and their children is what they care about most. Fear and distrust prevents them from articulating even these private sorrows. Thus weariness, distrust and domestication play directly into the hands of the Nazi leadership which needs less coercive measures and a smaller terroristic machinery than it would need if the masses were politically active or even awake. This compensates, to a considerable extent, for whatever signs of strain state and party machinery show under the present political and military situation.

Political opposition thus rests with the underground inside and outside the Nazi party. It is the underground which, with the assistance of the United Nations, may transform a non-political community solidarity into political solidarity. It alone can light the spark which can transform apathy and hatred and weariness into action.

# 9

Franz Neumann, Herbert Marcuse,
and Felix Gilbert

## *POSSIBLE PATTERNS OF GERMAN COLLAPSE*

(September 21, 1943)

Editor's note: R&A 1483. The identity of the three authors is indicated in "Political Intelligence Report," n. 34, section I.2. (R&A 1113.34), as well as in a successive report dated December 4, 1943, and titled *The Process of German Collapse* (R&A 1487), that is evidently an integration and update to the report published here. There is also a previous report from 1943 titled *German Situation in 1918 and 1943* that, in a letter to Sinclair Armstrong (OSS London) dated January 17, 1944, Neumann cites as his own (RG 226, entry 146, box 84, folder 98).

Classification: Secret

### 1. Introduction: The Pattern of 1918

It will be useful to preface this analysis of present prospects facing Germany with a brief survey of the patterns of collapse in 1918.

The breakdown of resistance in 1918 was in the first instance a military phenomenon, though its course and outcome were determined by the social, economic, and political structure of the German nation as a whole. The high command recognized as early as August 13 that the war was definitely lost. The defection of Germany's allies, which began in September, merely hastened the process of defeat. In October, after a few inept and futile peace feelers, the high command was forced to ask for armistice terms.

The decline in Germany's military position from August to November was accompanied by a shift in the locale of political power. Since 1916, when Hindenburg and Ludendorff took over the high command, political power had rested in a military dictatorship which was allied to the interests of big business. So long as there seemed to be a reasonable prospect of military success the opposition to this arrangement was largely passive. War weariness and longing for peace were growing among the masses, but their political representatives, the Social Democrats, the Centrum and the Progressives, were unable or unwilling to make a serious bid for power until the political prestige of the high command was fatally compromised by the imminent prospect of defeat. Even then it is more accurate to say that political power was abandoned by the military dictatorship than that it was seized by parties in the Reichstag. The decisive step was the appointment of the ministry of Prince Max early in October; Germany for the first time had a genuine parliamentary regime. The real shift in the locale of political power thus came about quietly, while hostilities were still in progress, and well in advance of the so-called revolution.

It is important to understand the conditions which gave rise to this special pattern of development. The military dictatorship in 1916 had little in common with the present-day totalitarian dictatorship. It was imposed upon the political structure of the pre-war Reich and had to work through established agencies and channels. It operated exclusively at the top and never succeeded in gaining thorough control over the organizations and lives of the German people.

Why did power fall into the hands of a democratic parliamentary coalition? The reason is twofold: both the temper of the German people and the existing organizational structure of political life favored this outcome. On the one hand, the German people were sick of the war with its appalling bloodshed and undernourishment; and they were for the most part under the influence of a democratic ideology. On the other hand, there were in existence well-organized democratic parties which were in a position to represent the wishes of the people for peace and constitutional reform. No other serious contenders for power existed. The conservatives were compromised by their reactionary policies and the revolutionary parties were sectarian.

The situation in the summer of 1918 can be summarized in the following way. The German people had had their fill of war and autocracy; they had never tried democracy, and believed in its possibilities. Then defeat became certain, the high command lost power which shifted almost automatically to the non-revolutionary democratic parties.

## 2.Possible Patterns of Collapse in 1944

### I. The Differences between 1918 and Today

In its military and economic aspects the present position of Germany offers both parallels and contrasts to that of 1918. But on the political side there is hardly anything in common between now and then.

Military defeat for Germany seems just as certain now as it must have in the summer of 1918. But her enemies are still a long way from the homeland at present; there is more defensive space in which to maneuver now than there was in 1918. This relative advantage is partly offset by the vastly greater importance of air war today, which reaches into the heart of the Reich. The people are better fed than they were in 1918, but again air raids are an offsetting factor. War weariness must be felt on a scale at least comparable to 1918. Thus in 1943 a war-weary German people is faced with defeat, perhaps less immediately but no less certainly than in 1918.

Politically, however, the situation today is utterly different from 1918. The Nazi dictatorship is entirely different from the military dictatorship of the last war: unlike the latter it is a totalitarian dictatorship used in the sense that society has been completely pulverized into its individual atoms which are then organized and manipulated from the top down, not from the bottom up. No voluntary organization—except the churches—are left above ground; any attempt to form them or to express discontent is met with ruthless terror.

It is, of course, true that there has been close agreement between the Nazis and Germany's traditional ruling groups, and the former have increasingly penetrated into the latter, so that many big industrialists and some generals today were upstart Nazi politicians a few years ago. But the process of integrating the Nazis into the ruling class is a long way from complete; the group still has a separate and recognizable identity. As long as the regime was enjoying successes this separateness was not particularly important, and it even had its advantages. The Nazi movement provided a social escalator for the recruitment of talent from the lower middle class; in the event of complete merger with the ruling groups the old hardening of class lines would set in again. But in times of adversity, the distinctive position occupied by the Nazi governing clique has a special importance which it is essential to understand. In the eyes of people all over the world, both inside and outside Germany, the Nazi leadership, including those industrialists, bankers, civil servants and generals who have openly sided with it, bear the responsibility for the war and all that it has brought with it. As long as things were going well for Germany, this meant disapproval from outside and approval from within. But now that things are going badly and Germany is faced with the prospect of defeat, the Nazi group is becoming the object of nearly universal popular detestation. They are the one group which can have no hope of salvaging anything from the approaching debacle. And this means, as a matter of course, that whatever their services to Germany's ruling class may have been in the past they are rapidly becoming a liability and a menace at present time.

If the Nazis nevertheless remain in power the reasons are easy to understand. So long as the system of totalitarian control over every aspect of German life remains intact, there is no possibility for a popular opposition to crystallize. And the army leaders, who are the only ones having disposition of sufficiently powerful force to challenge the Nazi position, would run the risk of annihilation if they should attempt an ouster move. The Nazis have, especially in the Gestapo and the SS, forces with which to fight back. If an open conflict would develop, the door would be open to revolt from within and invasion from without. Clearly the army leaders and the industrialists, with whom they would undoubtedly be allied, must act with extreme caution in any plan to kick the Nazis out, and it may even be that they will be permanently paralysed by the dilemma facing them.

In 1918 the absence of totalitarian controls and the presence of political parties made the transfer of political power relatively simple and bloodless. No such conditions exist today.

In addition to the organizational aspect of the problem, there are other differences between the popular opposition of today. Then, workers, liberals, and Catholics were under the influence of democratic ideology; it seems unlikely that this will be so a second time. The Weimar Republic was in itself a bitter experience for many of the masses. The working class and what remains of the lower middle class is likely to emerge from this war in a "never again" frame of mind. It is, of course, possible that the German people will be too exhausted and battered to play an active role for some time after the close of hostilities, but when their influence is felt again it will probably be much more revolutionary than the democratic opposition of 1918.

Further political differences between 1918 and 1943, in the sense of differences in outlook and motivation among various classes of the population, are traceable to the different character of the opposition coalitions then and now. In 1918 it was France, England, and the United States, countries with essentially similar social structures, which were all fighting for the same straightforward goal: to stop Germany's drive for greatly increased world political and economic power, and to weaken Germany so that she would not soon be in a position to try again. Today it is England, the United States, and Soviet Russia. England and the United States, again similarly constituted and similarly motivated, are working with socialist Russia for a common immediate military aim. But Russia may have more far-reaching goals than checking Germany's renewed drive for world conquest: she may be looking forward to the social and economic reconstruction of Germany. Alongside an immediate community of interest, there may thus be a long-run diversity of interest between the two major parts of the anti-German coalition. This fact naturally has powerful repercussions inside Germany. The same factors were present in Germany after the Russian revolution in 1917–18, but because of the greater attractive power of democratic ideology and the weakness of the young Soviet republic they were not yet of decisive importance.

So far as the Nazis are concerned there is not much difference between Germany's eastern and western enemies, a fact which finds formal expression in the Anglo-Russian alliance binding the two parties not to enter into negotiations with the "Hitlerite government."

For army leaders and industrialists, however, the situation is different. They would certainly like to be on the winning side against Britain and the United States, but they are not sentimentalists and will hardly be inclined to fight to the death in a losing cause. As between the western powers and Russia from the economic and social angle, they must necessarily prefer the former, and since victory is out of the question, they may work for the defeat which is least dangerous to their own material interests, a defeat which will permit the preservation of private capitalism. The army leaders and industrialists may therefore try to ensure the dominance of Anglo-American over Russian influence in the reconstruction of Europe. This may give them a chance to play the role of junior partner to British and American businessmen in the rehabilitation of world economy. This objective does not exclude the possibility that these interests can try to cooperate politically with the U.S.S.R. in order to improve their bargaining position.

For the potential popular opposition in Germany, the character of the enemy coalition is also likely to have a profound significance. If the United States and Britain continue to show themselves hostile to or fearful of popular forces, it is possible that, despite undoubted anti-Russian feelings in the middle and lower classes, a German popular movements may be strongly pro-Russian in its orientation. The reason is very simple: that the Russians have nothing to fear and everything to gain from the fullest possible development of a radical popular movement.

To sum up: today the political situation in Germany is radically different from 1918. A smooth transfer of political power from a totalitarian dictatorship to an organized political opposition is out of the question because the very essence of totalitarian dictatorship is the absence of organized opposition. And as long as the totalitarian controls remain intact the army must hesitate to intervene for fear of precipitating a crisis which would involve the disruption of both home and fighting fronts. It is in this setting that we must attempt to trace the possible courses of German collapse.

## II. Pattern of Collapse

a. Against this background, the following possibilities of collapse may be envisaged.

*If the United Nations remain united—that is, if Germany's political warfare aimed at splitting them and at concluding a negotiated peace with either Russia or the Western Powers is unsuccessful, the following alternative courses will remain open.*

1. The Nazi leadership may determine to retain control to the very end. There are certain indications that the Nazis are preparing for this eventuality. The concentration of all power over the domestic fields in the hands of Himmler and Speer, the reactivation of the SA indicate the resolution of the Nazi leadership not to allow the emergence of a non-Nazi government. By doing this, the Nazis will become fully isolated and lose completely any hold over the masses and traditional ruling groups. Then power could be maintained only by more terror. Wholesale execution of potential oppositionists must then be expected. It is also likely that the Nazi leadership will then resort on a large scale to the scorched earth policy in occupied Europe. Each withdrawal will be accompanied by wholesale destruction.

The defeat will then leave an utterly exhausted European continent. Industries, if not already blasted by air attacks, will be destroyed by the SS. The transportation system will be disrupted. The administrative machinery will have collapsed. Farmers will hoard, workers will refuse to work.There will then certainly occur a series of social upheavals. But these upheavals are likely to have the character of social convulsions. No group may have the strength to organize Germany politically and socially prior to the entry of foreign troops.

Military Government in such a situation will be faced with stupendous tasks. It will have to run state and society. It will have to organize the country from scratch. It may only find assistance at the municipal level. Exhaustion and destruction will then have to transform the German people into mere objects of rule.

Military Government in such a situation will have to protect Germany from the wrath of her neighbors. The more intense the terrorization of occupied Europe becomes the deeper will be the hatred of everything German. Military Government will have to prevent unorganized vengeance.

2. The Nazi leadership, realizing that the game is lost, may resort to a shadow government. Hitler may be pushed into the presidency of Germany and a government composed of generals, industrialists, high civil servants, may be put into power by the Nazis. Such a government might accept unconditional surrender, and dissolve the Nazi party with the understanding that the essentials of the Nazi system be preserved. Given those conditions, the SS will go underground and establish a cadre SS

organization, penetrating any political movement that may emerge. Especially, it may try to penetrate left wing groups.

Under these conditions, political movements will arise in opposition to the outwardly conservative government. These movements are likely to have revolutionary aims. The revolution may start with a simple strike in a big factory. The government may be unable to cope with this situation. The strike may spread. The oppressive machinery may not be adequate to cope with it. Though the revolutionary movement may be restricted to relatively small groups, it may assume major proportions. It may aim at a social revolution.

Always assuming that the United Nations are still united, this movement could be directed toward a democratic socialism by the joint efforts of the United Nations. It is the timing of military government which will then be important. Every major social transition is bloody in its beginnings. If Germany is occupied during the initial stage of this revolution, the occupying army may be compelled to oppose the revolution and to side with the shadow government, in order to restore law and order whether this shadow government is recognized by them or not. This will create hostility to the United Nations, and, if Russia should cooperate, will wipe out Russia's esteem. It will strengthen nationalism, and national socialism, and will reinforce the clandestine Nazi movement.

If, to use Mr. Churchill's words, Germany is "left to stew in her own justice" prior to military occupation, thereby tolerating the growth of a revolutionary movement, a possibility, maybe even a likelihood, exists that the period of violence will be short and a national and democratic government may be established. The government will, of course, be weak, and its powers will be challenged by internal opposition and hostility from occupied Europe.

3. A conservative anti-Nazi government composed of generals, industrialists and high civil servants may be established in opposition to the Nazis, possibly by a *coup d'état*. Such a *coup d'état* will lead to the arrest of Hitler and other Nazi leaders; it may rescind the anti-Jewish legislation; restore the freedom of the churches and invite persons like Dr. Kass[1], the last parliamentary leader of the Catholic Centre Party, and Niemoeller to enter the government.[2]

In this way, the political opposition in Germany would be split. Large masses of the people who are merely war-weary will be satisfied with any kind of government that ends the war and restores some kind of dignity. The stability of such government will, however, depend entirely upon the attitude of the United Nations.

For there is no question that revolutionary movements will arise again, even though they may lack mass support from peasants, middle class, and even that of sections of the workers. The conservative government will certainly be unable to cope with this revolutionary trend. The [*illegible*], primarily of a Nazi character, will have them broken down and fanatic Nazis and the SS in especial may join the revolutionary forces.

Military occupation in such a situation will face the most difficult problems: to side with the conservative government; to side with the revolutionary forces; not to recognize either. Non-recognition of the revolutionary forces implies, however, fighting against them.

b. *If the United Nations are split, the following possible courses of collapse may be envisaged.*

The split of the United Nations cannot be utilized by the Nazis themselves. Russia and the Western Powers are committed not to deal with a Nazi government. If the Nazis want to profit from disunity they must ostensibly disappear. The Nazis may determine to stay (see a-1), but this may be considered unlikely, because of the determined opposition of the traditional ruling groups.

1. A Camouflaged Nazi government may be instituted by the Nazis. The composition of this government will depend on whether it is to deal with Russia or with the Western Powers. If it is to deal with Russia, representatives of the "Eastern Orientation" of German society will be put into power, that is, generals of the Seeckt school,[3] diplomats of the Brockdorff-Rantzau school,[4] high civil servants, and some industrialists. If Russia were to conclude an armistice with these groups, such a government may appeal to national-bolshevist trends with the Communist Party and the Nazi Party and thus try to get mass support. In this case the German Communist Party will play the role that is dictated to it by Russia. If such a separate peace with Russia should be concluded, democratic and socialist forces in Germany will receive a blow from which they are not likely to recover.

It has been suggested that a separate peace with Germany might be concluded if Germany's defensive powers relative to Russia's military strength should turn out to be so great as to threaten the Russians with a complete internal economic exhaustion. Having the prospect of a separate peace with Russia before them, army leaders would find their hand greatly strengthened, and they might succeed in removing the Nazis and stabilizing their rule. If they then turned all of Germany's strength against Western powers, the character of the war would be entirely changed, and it is not profitable to attempt to predict its course or outcome at the present time.

On the whole, however, this appears to be a rather remote possibility. Given growing pressure in Germany from the west and south, there is little reason to suppose that Russia's staying power is less than Germany's. Russia would probably not have much to gain from a separate peace since, with Germany in the defensive, the tempo of activity on the eastern front is already almost entirely in the control of the Russians. If they want a pause they can have it without a separate peace, and in any case they could not demobilize while the war is still going on. Finally, they have much to lose from a separate peace: it would create the only situation in which it would be politically feasible for Germany to bargain with Britain and the United States as well as with the USSR. In view of the small possible gains and the great risks which would be involved, it seems very unlikely that the Russians will be tempted to negotiate with an undefeated and conservative German regime. Nevertheless the possibility cannot be ruled out *a priori*.

2. The Nazi shadow government may then be set up to deal with the Western Power. It will be composed of generals from the school of General Max Hoffmann,[5] of diplomats from the Stresemann school,[6] and of bankers and industrialists with international connections (of the Schacht and I.G. Farben type).[7] Such government will be popular among the traditional ruling groups but will lack mass support. It will set about arranging the most favorable form of capitulation which would undoubtedly mean maneuvering to insure dominance of Anglo-American as against Russian influence in the armistice and peace settlements. During this phase the outbreak of popular discontent and revolutionary movements should be expected.

It is unlikely that such government will find support among the Western Powers because of the risks involved. It would be directed opposed to Russia which would not only threaten intervention but would activate communist-revolutionary propaganda to such a degree that the whole European continent may be shaken in its foundations.

A Nazi shadow government with the two possibilities of dealing either with Russia or with the Western Powers may be excluded from consideration.

3. A *coup d'état* may, however, be staged by the traditional ruling classes if the probability of a separate peace with either Russia or the Western Powers appears likely.

A genuine conservative government to deal with Anglo-Americans will have considerable popular support in its initial phase. It will retain this support as long as the material conditions of Germany have not deteriorated. If this happens (and it is likely to happen) the strong undercurrent of hatred of Anglo-American imperialism will merge with the anti-capitalist sentiments, and the support which the opposition will undoubtedly receive from Russia will merge into a powerful revolutionary movement with a strong national Bolshevist flavor. Military government will, under these circumstances, be extremely precarious.

4. A genuine conservative government to deal with Russia will have powerful support from the officer corps, considerable support from parts of German industry and strong popular support. This popular support will be readily forthcoming, because the fear of Russia will be relieved and the left wing labor groups will realize that middle Russia's support of such government will be merely an expedient of temporary nature, a conservative pro-Anglo-American government will be there to stay because of Anglo-American support.

c. *The Possibilities of a Revolution*

There is, of course, always present the possibility of a revolution in Germany regardless of the unity or disunity of the United Nations.

1918 has taught us, however, that a revolution directed against a system of control not broadly based socially and in which the autonomous political and social organizations were still intact must be hopeless until the control system itself was already in a state of decomposition. The Bolshevik revolution had demonstrated that it is only possible to overthrow a government that does not exercise efficiently the means of coercion and social control.

The situation in Germany is, however, much more unfavorable to a revolution than was the case in 1918. The Nazis have learned from 1918. The nearer military defeat comes, the stronger the controls become. Moreover, the traditional ruling classes are much more afraid of a revolution in 1944 than they were in 1918. They could—and did, then—successfully rely on the trade unions to prevent the transformation of a political and constitutional upheaval into a social revolution. Without the trade unions and the Social Democratic Party, 1918 might have given birth to a socialist revolution.

This bulwark no longer exists. A revolution today will certainly take a much more radical turn than it did in 1918. The traditional ruling class will, for this reason, stick to the Nazi Party in its attempt to ward off a revolution, pinning their hopes on a *coup d'état* and on support from all or some of the United Nations.

The objective conditions thus do not favor a revolution. The subjective aspects, however, show an extremely ambivalent character. The atomization of German society has confined articulate opposition to small sectarian groups, probably localized and thus without national cohesion and organization. On the other hand, the mood of the essential part of the workers and of many intellectuals, farmers and middle class men is certainly much more radical than ever before in German history.

Can one expect the small revolutionary groups in Germany to assume political leadership of the discontented masses prior to Germany's military defeat or the removal of the Nazi Party rule under the above-mentioned conditions? The answer is no. Strong as the longing of the masses and the determination of the underground groups may be, the controls are too tight. The revolutionary groups can play an active role only if a non-Nazi government (indigenous military dictatorship, etc.) exists.

To sum up:

a. If the United Nations are united:

1. The Nazis determine to stay to the very end.

   Consequences:
      Utter internal collapse
      Scorched earth policy by the Nazis
      External threats
      Social convulsion
      No indigenous political movement powerful enough
   A real possibility.

2. A Nazi shadow government

   Consequences:
      The SS goes underground
      Revolutionary movements toward democratic socialism
      The importance of timing of military occupation
   A real possibility.

3. A conservative *coup d'état*

   Consequences:
      Greater stability
      Revolutionary movements with smaller mass basis
   A possibility.

b. The United Nations are split:

1. The Nazis determine to stay

   Consequences: see n° 1
   Little possibility.

2. A Nazi shadow government to deal with Russia

   Consequences: Considerable support from sectors of the traditional ruling classes and masses
   Unlikely to be accepted by Russia.

3. A Nazi shadow government to deal with Western Powers

   Consequences:
   Support from the traditional ruling classes
   Partial initial mass support
   Later; intensified revolutionary movements
   Unlikely to be accepted.[8]

4. A *coup d'état* conservative government to deal with the Western Powers.

   Consequences:
   Considerable initial popular support
   Growth of revolutionary movement with deterioration of social and economic conditions.
   Real possibility.

5. A *coup d'état* conservative government to deal with Russia

   Consequences: Considerable popular support; transition into Socialist government with Russia's support
   Real possibility.

c. The possibility of a Revolution apart from the alternatives under (a) and (b):

No real possibility.

# 10

Franz Neumann

## *THE SOCIAL AND POLITICAL EFFECTS OF AIR RAIDS ON THE GERMAN PEOPLE: A PRELIMINARY SURVEY*

(June 9, 1944)

Editor's note: R&A 1546. Neumann's authorship is indicated in a letter from Eugene Anderson to Carl Schorske dated November 17, 1943 (RG 226, entry 60, box 1: Projects Committee Correspondence).

Classification: Confidential

### I. The Raids

#### A. Extent of Impact

The strategic aerial bombing of Germany has been increased to such an extent during the last twelve months that approximately 65,000 people are now bombed out of their homes each week. The number of unusable and destroyed houses in April 1944 totaled 1,600,000 in the Reich and the protected areas. A large number of the great industrial centers of Germany, such as Berlin, Hamburg, Bremen, the Ruhr district, Rostock, Hannover, Leipzig, Frankfurt a/M, Mannheim-Ludwigshafen, Stuttgart, Brunswick, Augsburg, Nürnberg, München, Kassel, Wiener-Neustadt, etc., have been severely damaged. In several of these cities it has been estimated that between 50 and 80 percent of the houses have been destroyed or badly damaged. In the first phase of the Battle of Berlin—from 18 November 1943 to 15 February 1944—the official report states that at least 326 factories of which 103 were of vital importance to the German war effort, were either destroyed or damaged.[1]

The manpower cost of air-raid defense and post-raid restoration constitutes a significant drain on labor resources, but the extent of this is difficult to estimate. Industrial output has probably dropped 10 to 15 percent owing to the raids.[2] In certain key industries, like ballbearings and fighter planes, the decrease of monthly output was estimated to be about 50 and 70 percent, respectively, by April 1944.[3] Likewise, the shortage of consumer goods has become acute.

About 20 million of the civilian population have been directly exposed to air-raids. Accommodations had to be provided for some 5,400,000 people, including children evacuated as a precautionary measure. Approximately 5 million have inadequate housing or no housing whatsoever. Reliable estimates as of 1 January 1944 place the number of dead to be at least 100,000.[4]

In considering the direct and indirect effects of the bombings on German morale, one must bear in mind that only a limited sector of the population is exposed to them and that heavy attacks are followed by extended periods of relative quiet during which the population has time to recuperate.

## B. Strains on the ARP[5] System

Over 30 different organizations are concerned with air-raid activities in Germany. In August 1943 it was estimated that more than a million members of military and para-military organizations plus approximately nine million civilians were engaged in one or another phase of air-raid precautions.[6]

The Aircraft Reporting Service (*Flugmeldedienst*) was controlled by the Air Forces until 31 May 1942 and the household ARP organization and warden service were under the general supervision of the Air Minister, Hermann Goering. The mobile part of the municipal and defense service (fire-fighting, first-air service), which had been closely associated with the police, was then transferred to the control of Himmler, the Reich SS leader and Head of the German Police. This organization was named Air Raid Protection Police (*Luftschutz-Polizei*).[7] The change, which considerably strengthened the Gestapo chief's power over the home front, was made in response to signs of weakness in the control of the civilian population after the first big raids on Cologne. Failure to prevent raids was to be counteracted by terror.

A Reich decree of August 1942, which applies to most large towns, makes it compulsory for all citizens from fifteen to seventy years of age, except invalids, cripples and those with special responsibilities, to assist in the Self Protection Service (*Blockschutz*; *Selbstschutz*). Its main task is to extinguish minor fires or to keep larger conflagrations in check until the fire brigade or Party Fire Brigade Commandos (*Feuereinsatzkommandos*) can come to their assistance.

Military authorities decide whether a factory is to be defended by AA,[8] and, if so, a battery is installed and the guns are manned by the employees. In view of the intensified air warfare the *Deutsche Nachrichten Bureau* announced on 22 April 1944 that heavier demands on members of the staff in factories for stand-by service would have to be made. The new regulation provides for the following duty periods every months:

> Boys of 15 years, up to four times;
> Boys between the age of 16 and 18, up to eight times;
> Male staff over 18, up to ten times;
> Girls between 15 and 18, up to four times;
> Female staff over 18, up to eight times.

Exceptions are made for expectant mothers, women with small children, wives of seriously injured men, etc. No difference is made between officials, employees, and workers.[9]

The general picture of civilian cooperation with organized ARP services is not one which indicates any widespread apathy or disaffection. It is natural that the German population is anxious to protect its property and personal belongings wherever possible. However, reports of warnings against slackers who "as soon as the air is thick" take their luggage and disappear into a bomb-proof shelter"[10] are not at all uncommon in the German press. Eyewitnesses report that in big apartment buildings the Self Protection Service is of no practical value as the tenants simply save what they can and abandon the place to the flames.

As a method of improving cooperation the Party has engaged in elaborate propaganda campaigns designed to label civilians engaged in Air Raid Protection as "front line fighters." They have been granted the same compensation rights as soldiers and several thousand have been decorated. Extra food allowances are given to ARP workers who are engaged for periods of more than 24 hours.[11] Persons who evade ARP duty by unauthorized flight from town during air raids run the risk of losing compensation for their property if it is destroyed in an air raids, "because they can be accused of neglecting their duty to avert or reduce the damage."[12]

More serious are the shortages or ARP facilities which have developed as the weight of Allied bombing increased. To overcome these difficulties all fire-brigades of Germany have been completely motorized; when large-scale attacks occur, the fire-brigades of neighboring towns are called on for assistance. These strains are only local in character and no inference of impending national collapse of the ARP system can be drawn.

## II. Recovery from the Raids

### A. Emergency Relief Measures

The impact of the raid momentarily disrupts the functioning of the city as a co-ordinated unit, but immediately after the all-clear signal, a complicated array of Party, government and army officials begins to operate, and within a few days cities which have suffered average raids are functioning again. Even after heavy raids a real bottom organization soon emerges.

The task of supplying immediate emergency food and lodging falls to such party organizations as the NS People's Welfare Organization (*NS Volkswohlfahrt*), the German Labor Front (*Deutsche Arbeitsfront*), the National Socialist Motor Corps (*NS Kraftfahr-Korps*), and the German Red Cross (*Deutsche Rote Kreuz*). The Technical Emergency Corps (*Technische Nothilfe*) and the Todt Organization[13] clear debris and effect demolition. Additional labor is supplied by Army units stationed in Germany, the National Labor Service (*Reichsarbeitsdienst*), the Debris Removal Corps (*Aufräumungstruppe*), the Building Repair Corps (*Bauhilfstruppe)*, and other agencies.[14] Within a few days the administrative controls for the readjustment of commerce, housing, communication and transportation begins to take effect.

1. *Commerce*. The legal grounds for the new administrative measures which must be taken are based on a decree of the Minister of Economics of 5 June 1943 and a ruling of the National Trade Group of 11 June 1943 creating the Emergency Staffs (*Einsatzstäbe*) of Trade.[15] These staffs prepare the accumulation of reserves and establish additional storage capacities (*Ausweichlager*)—often outside the city limits—and traveling stores (*Fliegende Verkaufsstellen*) in conjunction with the Economic and Food offices. They register the stocks of retail and wholesale trade, survey air-raid damage, and report it to the Regional Economic Offices. They are also authorized to install bombed-out merchants in the premises of others, and to assign merchants to trade in specific commodities if necessary.[16]

While there have been no acute shortages in basic food requirements, the replacement of clothing and household goods had met with insuperable difficulties. To facilitate the sale of available stocks to bombed-out persons purchase permits stamped "F1"(*Fliegerbeschädigter*) are issued. The inability of other civilians to obtain goods for which they have ration stamps has led to considerable discontent. Open criticism is, however, seldom voiced in public for fear of the police.

For the protection of depositors, regulations have been issued which make it possible for depositors whose bank has been bombed to continue banking in unbombed banks.

2. *Housing and Communal Feeding*. At the outbreak of war in 1939 Germany had a housing shortage of at least 1,500,000 dwellings. The number of households exceeds the number of dwelling by 12 percent. The war further aggravated the housing situation, particularly in industrial and strategic areas, where in several instances from 50 to 80% of the dwellings have either been destroyed or severely damaged (see Section I, Extent of Damage).

Under the authority of the Reich Compensation Law (*Reichsleistungsgesetz*) of 1 September 1939 and a series of subsequent laws[17] bombed-out persons are in most cases quickly provided with temporary shelter, however undesirable. The chief methods employed are forced billeting in all available unbombed dwellings in the area; evacuation; transformation of attics, offices and stores into dwellings; and construction of a limited number of temporary barrack-like houses. The bombed-out persons are encouraged to build their own emergency homes with material available locally (clay, rubble, timber from destroyed houses) or with prefabricated parts. The state pays a premium of RM. 1700 for each finished edifice conforming to prescribed dimensions (20 to 22 sq. m.). Some 40,000 prefabricated dwellings were reported to have been built in the last quarter of 1943 and the construction of another 100,000 is foreseen for 1944.[18] Industrial enterprises may release 5 percent of their staff or suitable foreign workers for the building of emergency houses if the remaining workers make good the time lost by working overtime. In order to speed up the construction of dwellings, 40,000 German workers are reported to have been removed from eastern districts, together with 100,000 war prisoners, to be used for such work.[19] In spite of all these measures the shortage in housing cannot be overcome.

As a result of the evacuation of women with small children, the destruction of homes, and the shortage of cooking ranges, communal feeding has grown to unprecedented proportions. Some 12 million German workers and civilians and 14 million foreigners now obtain their meals from camp kitchens or in workers' canteens.[20] Restaurants are overcrowded, and in several cities permits are issued to workers and civilians essential to the war entitling them to preferred treatment during rush hours. Home life seems to be almost completely disrupted in heavily bombed cities.

3. *Communications and Transportation*. The permanent reestablishment of communications and transportation facilities presents the most difficult problem. Aside from the effect of damaged transportation on overall industrial production, Reich officials have the problem of establishing transportation facilities adequate to distribute essential incoming supplies of food and the problem of maintaining some portion of the public utilities system. The work is largely accomplished by the Technical Emergency Aid (*Technische Nothilfe*) supported by battalions of prisoners of war, civilians, and in some areas by units of the Todt Organization. Despite the difficulties involved, it is significant to note that in Hamburg during the first week in Sept. 1943 (about two weeks after the last big raid) electricity, gas, and water were being supplied in an adequate fashion, trucks were bolstering the transport system, although the mail was still disrupted.[21]

*4. Recreation.* All eyewitness reports maintain that among the first services to be reestablished are the cinema and the theater. The need for such facilities to afford relief from strain is obvious. Party officials display a great deal of interest in this phase of restoration, and pressure is applied to mobilize the resources of the Reich Chamber of Theaters.[22] In the summer of 1943, the head of the Artists' Section, announced in *Artistenwelt* the determination to proceed ruthlessly against artists who break their contracts in the air raid emergency districts and issued an official announcement stressing that air raid emergency districts are given preference in any case.[23]

The overall picture of post-raid rehabilitation seems to be one of a rather high level of efficiency in reestablishing the basic social and economic organization of the bombed-out cities.

## III. Problems of Evacuation

As of 1 January 1944, it was estimated that about 5 million individuals had been evacuated from bombed-out or bomb-threatened areas. Originally all evacuations from bombed districts were assigned to a specific Gau elsewhere in the Reich, which was designated as a reception area. As bombings increased and as precautionary evacuation was instituted, other Gaue in addition to the original reception areas were assigned. Finally, the bombing of reception areas made it necessay further to modifiy the procedure. Currently, evacuees are sent either to one of several specific regions of reception in other parts of the Reich (including occupied areas) or to unbombed parts of the Gau.[24] Disorderly flight after particularly intense bombings has occurred. The general effect of this pattern forced by increased and deeper bombings has been to bring the evacuation problems to all parts of the Reich.

Administration of the evacuation is [*illegible word*] in the NSV[25] and its subdivision Camping Program for Evacuated Children (*Erweiterte Kinderlandverschickung, KLV*) under Arthur Axmann; it handles all precautionary evacuation of children. The Labor Front cooperates with the NSV in providing relief to the evacuees. A person may not be evacuated from his home locality unless he has procured a departure certificate from the local NSV office.

## IV. The Party's Propaganda Reply

### A. Treatment of Air Raids in Domestic Press and Radio

The disastrous development of the air war in the last two years has forced the Nazi propagandists to adopt a mainly defensive attitude in the treatment of air raids. The basic concerns of the Nazi propaganda up to the beginning of 1944 have been:

1. To counter belief among some Germans that the Nazis started the war.
2. To deflect dissatisfaction because the Nazis are not providing more countermeasures.
3. To combat the impression that German war production is seriously affected by the raids.

To effect these objectives the Nazis have a number of themes which were used, dropped, and reused. The most important of these were:

1. To stress the positive aspects of bombings, i.e. emergence of community feelings, civilian heroism.
2. To express sympathy with suffering victims; in particular not to withhold recognition of civilian sacrifice and not to minimize the losses sustained by individuals.
3. To praise the teamwork of the various branches of German defense—civilian and military.
4. To expose the enemy air war as evidence of barbarism, and as immoral. (terror theme)
5. To declare the air war strategically futile
   a) It is no shortcut to victory.
   b) It does not break the enemy, physically, morally, or military, but strengthens him.
   c) It inflicts heavy losses in men and material on the attacker.
6. To declare Germany equal to the challenge.
7. To assure Germans that Germany would take revenge.
8. To promise rehabilitation after victory—but only then.

Faced with the belief in some quarters that bombing of civilians in the Reich was caused by Germany's prior employment of air warfare, Nazi propaganda devoted considerable energy to prove historically that England alone was responsible for initiating air war against civilians. This line was also meant to deflect hostilities caused by the misery of bombings from the Nazis to the enemy. Promises of retaliation, which figured prominently in the press in the latter part of 1943, were welcomed only by a minority of the German population, who saw therein a possibility of ending the raids. The failure to supply adequate countermeasures resulted in criticism which was met by praising the work done by party members and by decorations awarded to ARP workers. The people were also assured that the leaders were not at all indifferent to their hardships. On 23 March 1943 and on 1 January 1944 Hitler went out of his way to extend sympathy to the bombed-out persons. Growing war weariness and demands for peace were countered by a campaign which painted the consequences of defeat in the most lurid colors: bolshevism in Germany, inflation, forced labor for the German people, mass sterilization of Germans, etc. People were exhorted to have faith in the miraculous power of the Fuehrer—in some mysterious way he would find a way out of seemingly insurmountable difficulties.

The irrational, negative approach probably deepened widespread apathy and despair on the part of the civilian population, making them still more painfully aware of their utter helplessness. Symptoms of deteriorating morale among occupational troops, which reflected the change in civilian morale, were particularly undesirable in view of the threatened Allied invasion. The resumption of the air war on London finally gave Nazi propaganda an opportunity to adopt a more positive attitude. The period of passive resistance was over, they declared, and Germany could not hope to win the war if she remained on the defensive. The Luftwaffe, far from being knocked out, was on the offensive again; according to press and radio it was winning victory after victory. London was being successfully attacked and the number of Allied planes destroyed by the Luftwaffe was tremendous. The idea that Allied attacks were terror raids was no longer stressed. Instead the attacks were dramatized as air battles in which German superior skill and striking power was proved again and again.[26] A new group of air heroes was created—aviators who were reported to have shot down from 50 to 250 Allied planes. The effect of bombings on industrial plants was minimized or even ignored "in order not to give valuable information to the enemy." The failure of the invasion to materialize in April induced the propagandists to revert again to the terror and futility themes. The air war had failed to break German morale, the Luftwaffe could not be knocked out of the skies, the attacks on industrial centers had cost more than they had accomplished, and the latest attacks on communication centers would prove a great failure.

### B. Compensation and Promises of Post War Reconstruction

In September 1943 the Nazis placed compensation for home front air raid casualties on the same level with front line casualties. The Reich Minister of Finance ruled that all regulations and directives so far issued in favor of the dependents of men killed in action—including children's assistance, income tax, and death duties—shall equally apply to the dependents of fatal air raid casualties among the civilian population.[27] Already a comprehensive code of compensation had been evolved for wages, rents, and property lost through air raids. Reports seem to indicate that the compensation system works effectively to the end of supplying relief for immediate extreme hardships. But the problem of reconstruction of the vast property damage can only be met by measures which will take effect in the post-war period.

The Nazis have not hesitated to incorporate such promises into their propaganda. Speer, by an edict of Hitler,[28] was made an Inspector-General for the Building of the Reich Capital. He is responsible for the planning of the reconstruction of towns designated by Hitler as worthy of speedy reconstruction; he will "make all decisions in questions of town building." Detailed "blueprints," which assume a German victory, appear frequently in the press. Typical is an article in the *Leipziger Neuste Nachrichten* entitled "How Long Will It Take Us to Rebuild" by President of the German Institute for Economic Research Prof. Dr. Ernst Wagemann.[29] Wagemann reaches the conclusion that if the entire nation concentrated on that task, all the damage that the RAF could conceivably inflict throughout the war could be repaired within a decade. With the issues of survival for the Nazi Party being decided at the front and in the air, such promises are relatively easy to make.

## V. Social and Political Effects

### A. Social

1. *Further impoverishment of the middle classes.* With respect to physical destruction and loss of property, the middle classes have probably been the hardest hit. The workers, who did not have much property to lose, are in many cases housed in barracks at the outskirts of the cities; the rural population is relatively secure from heavy raids, and the wealthy classes are better equipped and better protected. The middle classes had already lost most heavily by the closing-down of non-essential shops and offices by the process of economic concentration; now they experience the destruction of their homes and the dissolution of their families. It is not surprising that the Nazi regime takes great pains to placate these groups by the most lavish promises for the future. The air war has led to a decentralization of plant facilities which, in the Nazi propaganda, is being presented as a breaking-up of the large combines and as a restoration of small and medium enterprises. However, the increasing need for craftsmen and artisans to repair raid damages apparently testifies to the strengthened position of these lower middle class professions in the Nazi economic system.

2. *Isolation of the workers from the other strata of the population.* In the large cities, which have been most frequently exposed to air raids, large parts of the population except the workers essential to the war, have been evacuated or have evacuated themselves. This isolates and distinguishes

the workers in a particular way, which may have far-reaching implications for further developments:

a) It must almost inevitably strengthen the class consciousness of the workers, who, as a specific social group, constitute the shock troops of the home front. As much, they are visibly and daily exposed to special dangers and are stimulated by special privileges (higher and extra rations, efficiency rewards, etc.). This class consciousness in itself is by no means a revolutionary one: for the time being at least, it rather strengthens the tie with the Nazi regime which has so far been able to take care of the immediate needs of the workers. However, the same tendencies which make for the workers' acceptance of the Nazi regime as long as it is capable of keeping the machinery going may quickly turn into radical opposition when the machinery has broken down. Then, the distinction and isolation of the workers from the other strata of the population may become a cohesive force to overcome the atomizing tendencies of Nazi mass domination; this would make the workers a more or less homogeneous group in the fight for social reconstruction.
b) The foreign workers have been exposed to the same isolation. Although they are separated from the German workers as far as possible in their housing, leisure, and working conditions, they inevitably belong to the distinct group of non-evacuees who form the active core of the home front. There are many indications that despite constant supervision and the difficulties of language, fraternization between German and foreign workers takes place. The extent of such fraternization should not be overstressed: it is probably first of all an entirely unpolitical matter of help and pity. Here too, the significance of this tendency lies in its future potentialities. Simple human solidarity might turn into a political weapon when the Nazi controls are destroyed.

3. *Increasing antagonisms between the rural and urban population.* The continuous air raids increase the antagonisms between the rural and urban population on three different grounds:

a) Difference in the standard of living. Although the vast majority of the German peasants lived far below the standard of the urban middle classes and even of a large part of the industrial workers, the peasants have apparently succeeded in retaining for themselves more and better food than the urban population.

b) Greater security of the rural population.

c) Tension between hosts and evacuees. The steady influx of bombed-out city dwellers, who frequently look down on the peasant's way of life and his relative security, has certainly increased the peasant's animosity against the city people.

4. *Strengthening of the regional differences within the Reich.* They are closely connected with the antagonisms discussed in the previous section (#3). The bombed-out people have frequently been evacuated to reception areas where the population differs widely from the "guests" in temperament, religion, social composition, etc. This would for example be the case if Rhinelanders were evacuated to East Prussia or the Warthegau, or Hamburgers to Bavaria and Austria. It must be emphasized again that these differences are not of a political nature and do not warrant any assumptions as to the strength of future separatist tendencies in Germany.

5. *Further disintegration of the family and of control over youth.* Wholesale evacuation and migration has naturally led to a separation of husband and wife, parents and children. Even when the family stays together the exigencies of air raids make effective control over youth extremely difficult: reports on juvenile delinquents are becoming increasingly numerous. On the other hand, the same exigencies provide new ways and forms of occupying youth and thus binding it to the Nazi control apparatus (auxiliary police, relief and fire squads, etc.). In the last analyses, however, the effects of the air war probably tend to increase the difficulties in the control over youth because the essential services which the juveniles perform and the authority which they exercise during and immediately after the raids may strengthen their self-consciousness and their will to greater freedom.

*Administrative dislocation.* Disruptions in the system of transportation and communication, of utilities, rationing etc. occur after almost every large scale air raid. Housing of the bombed-out people is encountering increasingly difficulty. Disruption of banking service is frequently reported. With a few exceptions, however, the Nazi administration has been able to restore very quickly all these services on an emergency basis sufficiently strong for the maintenance of the whole administrative system. Some government offices have apparently been removed from Berlin (probably to Silesia and suburbs of Berlin) but this has not seriously affected the functioning of the governmental machinery.

## B. Political

*1. Increasing dependence of the population on the Nazi Party as an agency of relief and protection.* While it is universally recognized that the obvious inability of the Nazi regime to prevent or even to protect Germany effectively against the intensified air war must inevitably undermine the regime's reputation among the German people, another much less evident but perhaps not less effective tendency has not yet been sufficiently emphasized—that the civilian population is becoming even more dependent of the functioning of the Nazi relief organizations. As a Swiss paper recently put it:[30]

> The bombings have played into the hands of the Gestapo in a way, as the people are deprived of food, clothing and homes, so that their naked existence is dependent on the mercy of the party and the organs of government which control the very necessities of life. This applies chiefly to the cities, and the cities are mothers of all revolution.

The Party was quick to take advantage of this situation: it has apparently extended the functions and services of the relief agencies which look after the most urgent needs of the affected people. The officials and institutions which were first of all organs of terroristic political control thus assume the appearance of organs of humanitarian help and protection (the *Blockwart* of the Nazi Party, for example, takes over the renewal and distribution of ration cards). Without these agencies, the population would suffer utter distress and ultimate destruction.

2. *Dislocation of labor and police controls.* The destruction of files, records, offices, etc. by air raids facilitates the evasion of the strict labor controls prevalent in Nazi Germany. Numerous reports state that workers do not show up at their working places, that they fail to register if their places of employment have been destroyed, that they move without authorization to other regions.

The same holds true for the system of police controls. In many cases, the Gestapo files have been destroyed, and "suspicious" people could turn up in other places and get new identity cards, presenting themselves as bombed-out workers.

The Nazi regime has so far been able to cope with these dislocations, chiefly because of the tight and comprehensive rationing scheme, which makes any free movement of the population almost impossible.

The frequent "economic crimes" which are reported as taking place during and after air raids, especially by foreign workers (looting, stealing, etc.) may sooner or later become a political factor. Even now, individual acts of revenge against Nazis, SS men, etc. are allegedly being perpetrated. Such reports have come from Berlin and Munich.

3. *Advantages and disadvantages for anti-Nazi opposition.* With respect to the anti-Nazi opposition, the air war seems to have an ambiguous effect. On the one hand, there can be no doubt that the opportunities for perpetrating acts of sabotage and for evading Gestapo control are greatly increased. On the other hand, the dislocations in the system of control also work in disfavor of the opposition. The migration of factories and of personnel disrupts the organization of the opposition: new contacts have to be made, new surroundings to be exploited, etc. The question which of the two conflicting tendencies will prevail cannot yet be answered; it may be significant, however, that so far no large scale sabotage and unrest during and after air raids have been reliably reported.

4. *Resentment against the privileged elite.* The resentment of the affected population seems primarily to be directed against the prominent Nazis. They are not only better protected but they apparently also enjoy other privileges. Reports such as the following are typical.[31]

The fact that only people close to the Party can obtain transportation for their belongings and ship them out of Berlin causes bitter resentment. Nobody else can obtain trucks or wagons because they have all been requisitioned by the authorities. The whole population of Berlin is sitting in a mousetrap.

This attitude does not contradict the tendency discussed in # 6. The population apparently makes a definite distinction between the Party as an indispensable institution of daily life and the parasites who are a disgrace to the Party as well as to the home front.

5. *Changes in the attitude towards property.* Much has been made of reports stating that large parts of the German population are turning under the impact of the air war towards communism. It is said that a general leveling of the population is taking place, that many people lose respect for private property and that they would not mind too much if the whole institution should be abolished altogether. Many of these reports must be discarded as German propaganda spread to increase the fear of a bolshevized Europe after the defeat of Nazism. It is unquestionably true that a process of equalization is going on between the middle classes and the industrial workers, but nothing indicates that it works in favor of communist tendencies. As far as the middle classes are concerned, the loss of property has only strengthened the desire to regain it; they see in communism a form of life that would perpetuate their losses. As regards the workers, numerous reports indicate that a majority is still averse to all experiments which would necessarily involve civil war and a new

dictatorship. Even in so far as they are inclined to accept communism as a post-war solution, they want a decidedly non-bolshevist society, perhaps one which combines the nationalization of key industries with the full exercise of democratic rights and liberties.

There is no justification for the assumption that the air war has fundamentally changed the traditional attitude towards property prevalent among the majority of the German population.

## C. General Conclusions

Manifold as the effects of the air raids on the German population may be, they have one common characteristic—they tend to absorb all political issues into personal issues, on the national as well as individual level. The impact of the raids on the personal life of the individuals is so great that it obliterates all problems which go beyond the immediate questions of mere survival. For the time being at least, this attitude amounts to an obliteration of the social and political antagonisms which continue to exist within the Nazi "people's community." The conflicts of interests between capital and labor, between the landed aristocracy and the peasants, between the authoritarian and the democratic forces, are suspended under the necessities of the daily struggle for the mere maintenance of life, a struggle in which the Nazi government and the Nazi Party take an effective leadership. Several reports on prisoner of war interrogations draw attention to a significant change in the attitude towards the Nazi regime: the latter is increasingly regarded, not as a definite political or social system, but as the legitimate national government of the Reich which is alone capable of protecting the individuals and the nation from complete annihilation.[32] This "unpolitical" attitude was found even among non-Nazis and anti-Nazis.[33] It is to a great extent the combined result of the air war and of the lack of any specification of the unconditional surrender formula which makes the present government of the Reich appear as the only bastion against personal and national destruction.

At the same time, there seems to be no wide-spread feeling of increased hatred against the British and American "terror raiders." This does not mean that the population puts the blame for the air war on the Nazi regime: only a very small minority seems to realize that "area bombing" was started by the Luftwaffe. It is rather the general political apathy which makes the population suffer the air raids as one of the inevitable implications of total war. It would only be natural that the German people should be inclined to differentiate between the Western Powers on the one hand and the Russians on the other; the latter so far have not started area bombing of Germany. Some reports state that such a distinction is actually being made, and that the "prestige" of the Russians is increasing. However, this tendency (which is certainly confined to a very small part of the population) seems to be effectively counteracted by the terrible fear of bolshevism which holds the vast majority of the German people in its grip and which is continuously exploited by Nazi propaganda.

Most of the social and political effects of air raids discussed above seem to play into the hands of the Nazi regime and to strengthen the cohesion of the home front. The counter-tendencies are being neutralized by the evergrowing importance of the Nazi control apparatus for the maintenance of the life of the population. If this apparatus breaks down and is no longer capable of sustaining the bare life of the population, the forces which now make for the cohesion of the home front and for the stiffening of its resistance will have lost their basis. The complete disintegration of the home front may then be expected to occur almost overnight.

# 11

## Franz Neumann

## *THE ATTEMPT ON HITLER'S LIFE AND ITS CONSEQUENCES*

(July 27, 1944)

Editor's note: R&A 2387. Neumann's authorship is indicated by himself in a letter to Chandler Morse dated August 3, 1944 (RG 226, entry 146, box 84, folder 98). A previous version of the report from July 24, titled *Effects on the Attempted Coup d'Etat on the Stability of the German Regime* (R&A 2383), cites a memorandum of July 22 titled "The German Coup d'Etat."

Three appendixes that listed the main retired German generals from 1938, the highest ranking reserve officers, and the high officers have been omitted.

Classification: Secret

### I. The Background

#### A. Principles for the Evaluation of German Morale

An understanding of the political significance of the latest attempt on Hitler's life may be aided greatly by a recapitulation of principles for the evaluation of German morale. These principles have been evolved in a series of papers[1] and may be summarized as follows:

1. The ruling group in Germany is made up of four segments: Party hierarchy, Army leadership, industrial and financial leaders, and high civil servants.
2. In the course of the war, the political power of the industrial leadership and of the civil servants has diminished to such a degree that they can assert themselves only by attempting to influence either Party or Army.

3. Therefore, the Party and Army leaderships are the politically important factors of the ruling group.
4. Though the Army leadership is permeated by reliable Nazis, it still preserves an identity of its own.
5. Since the ruling group itself must make the political decisions its morale is determined by its own evaluation of the total political situation.
6. The morale of the subordinate strata is not conditioned by their thinking and feelings but rather by the institutional controls of Nazi society which compel the subordinate strata to work and fight no matter what may be their attitudes toward war and Nazism.
7. There is no potentially powerful revolutionary movement from below, although underground organizations of considerable strength do exist. These can become active only if a *coup d'état* paves the way for the destruction of the Nazi controls.
8. Such a *coup* could not be expected before the invasion. It can come only if the Army leadership fears the loss of the German Army, which it needs as the instrument for domestic control and political bargaining with foreign powers.

## B. Party and Army

The retention of the generals' control over the Army is the key to the understanding of the plot. Without an army which is independent of the Nazi Party, the Army leadership and its allies—industrialists, bankers, Junkers, and high civil servants—cannot possibly play a role during the collapse and the post-war period. The Army leadership cannot count again upon a Social Democratic leadership which would entrust demobilization and reorganization of the Army to the old Officers' Corps, encourage the establishment of a Free Corps, and protect the *Reichswehr* from parliamentary control. If the generals lose Army control this time, they will be unable to exert any influence upon domestic developments or foreign policy.

It may be objected that these expectations of the generals are utterly without foundation, in view of the declared policy of the United Nations to destroy the German Army and to demobilize Germany. It is true that the United Nations have stated formally this to be their policy. But there is little doubt that the German generals hope and will continue to hope[2] until the opposite is clearly demonstrated to them, that they can create differences between the USSR and the Western Powers and thereby retain at least the remnants of their instrument. With regard to the USSR, they see some hope in the Free Germany Committee and the German Officers' Union. They also may remember Stalin's statement of 21 October 1942, when he said that he desired only the destruction of the "Hitlerite army." The Army undoubtedly will continue to hope to bring about some understanding between Germany and the Western Powers against "the danger of Bolshevism," which it will present as the major danger to Europe.

Futile as these hopes may turn out to be, it is likely they influence and determine the outlook of the generals, just as they shaped the policies of Hindenburg, Gröner, Seeckt, Reinhardt, and Schleicher in the fateful days of 1918 and 1919.

The antagonism between Army and Party is of long standing. It first manifested itself on 30 June 1934, when Hitler purged Röhm and his group, which desired, broadly speaking, to transform the Army into an affiliate of the Party. On 30 June 1934, therefore, the Party was purged in order to maintain the organizational autonomy of the Army. In 1944, the Army was purged in order to save the Party. If Hitler had not purged the Party in 1934, the Army would have become a Party formation; but if he had tried to do so, the Officers' Corps would have tried to overthrow him even then. Thus 1934 was the decisive year for the Nazi Party, a year that sealed the fate of Nazism as a revolutionary movement.

But the same purge that preserved the Army's organizational independence led to its political decline. The purge was not confined to Röhm and his followers, but also included the two generals who had done most to preserve the army under the Weimar Republic—von Schleicher and von Bredow. The Army leadership accepted this development and thereby subordinated itself to National Socialism. Step by step the influence of the conservative Officers' Corps was undermined, and subservient Army leaders took charge.

While this change tended to subordinate the Army politically, a new antagonism arose over the question of strategy. This difference was clearly brought out in a speech by Colonel General Ludwig Beck delivered in 1935 on the 125th anniversary celebration of the Military Academy.[3]

"It is the imperative demand that military questions should be traced back in their inner coherence to their origins in systematic intellectual labor, penetrating the problem step by step. That demand must be fulfilled, today more than ever before, by every one who desires to lead. Only its fulfillment can give the necessary basis for the responsibility, independence and initiative of the leader.

"Such systematic thought must be carefully learned and exercised. To that end above all these years at the Academy are meant to contribute. Nothing could be more dangerous than to follow sudden inspirations, however intelligent or brilliant they may appear, without pursuing them to the logical conclusions, or to indulge in wishful thinking, however sincere our purposes. We need officers capable of systematically following the path of logical argument with disciplined intellect to its conclusion, strong enough in character and nerve, to execute what the intellect dictates.

"The *coup d'oeil*, the so-called lightning-like grasp of a momentary situation, formerly so highly praised, can certainly continue to be of importance in many situations in land warfare. In general, however, it must be considered of less importance, at least in the higher regions of leadership, than an understanding of the situation matured out of an intellectual penetration endeavoring to exhaust all possibilities. . . ."

This speech reveals, perhaps better than the history of the various campaigns, the profound differences in the strategic approach of the conservative generals and of Hitler. It is undoubtedly Hitler's strategy on the Eastern Front that has led to the annihilation of the German field army. This must have created an ever-growing antagonism between the Party and the generals, exemplified by the retirement of many leading generals and supported by a huge number of intelligence reports (see also below page 000).

The attempt on Hitler's life can be understood best if it is assumed that the Army leadership is primarily concerned with the preservation of the Army as its instrument. Such a situation now prevails. The field army is exposed to annihilation on the battlefield. Every general officer likely has realized since 6 June 1944 that nothing can prevent military defeat.[4]

All that will remain to the army leadership is the Home (Reserve) Army. But the *New York Times* published on 20 July, one day before the attempted assassination, the statement that Himmler was to be appointed dictator of the Home Front and head of the Reserve Army, with the power to appoint and dismiss generals. Such a measure, which was decided upon long before the attempt on Hitler and thus was well known to the army officers, threatened to deprive the Army leadership of its control of the Home Army, consequently leaving the leadership without any bargaining power.

It is against this background—threatened annihilation of the field army in battle and loss of control of the Home Army by subordination to the SS—that the attempted *coup* may be analyzed.

## II. Analysis of the Attempt

### A. Friction between the SS and the Army

The impending transfer of the Home Army to Himmler explains the timing of the attempt. Indications of this are contained in Hitler's speech of 2 July 1944, delivered at the funeral of General Dietl, and Goebbels' article in *Das Reich* of 7 July, in which it was stated that the only danger to the Nazi regime lay in the home front. There were many more signs of the growing antagonism between the Party and its SS and the Army, apart from the basic strategic differences. The Army allegedly had tried to establish "security posts" in bombed towns throughout Germany in order to counteract SS domination;[5] General von Falkenhausen and Colonel General Friedrich Dollmann were replaced by SS officers,[6] and the SS and SA apparently were destined to play the lion's part in Hitler's "People's war" at the hour of military defeat.[7]

Mounting instances of acute friction and counteraction between Army and SS commanders end, not infrequently, with the recall or the death of Army generals.[8] The reckless employment of SS troops, attributed to Army generals, particularly to Rundstedt,[9] was said to have resulted in demands by the SS for a greater, if not the dominant, share in military leadership.[10] Distrust by the SS of Army officers and demands for their dismissal were grounded in instances of defeatism among Army generals.

The *coup* also coincided with what appears to be the collapse of a German plan of defense, apparently a slow withdrawal from the East and firm resistance in the West, with the West maintaining strategic priority for the time being. Dittmar indicates that this strategy has been revised owing to the "unexpectedly rapid Soviet advance," so that to some extent the center of gravity thus once more will be shifted to the East. According to secret reports,[11] a number of divisions from the strategic reserves have now been sent East, and more are promised.

It is quite possible that this newest change in strategy was unacceptable to those Army circles which have retained sufficient independence of judgment to recognize the handwriting on the wall.[12]

Their action may be motivated by recognition that further sacrifice of troops entailed in this strategy would end in the complete destruction of German manpower, and of the German armies in particular. But it was the impending appointment of Himmler as dictator of the home front that forced the conspirators' hand.

### B. The Peace Feelers of the Beck Group

It is also known that a group of Army generals attempted to establish contact with the Allies in order to negotiate a separate peace. It was clear, even at that time, that this peace feeler was made either with the connivance of the SS Security Service or that the Security Service was at least acquainted with it,[13] and allowed the generals to approach the Allies in order to get full knowledge of all the ramifications of the plot. It also may have been the threatened exposure of their activities which compelled the plotters to act. This is likely in view of the fact that Suendermann's statement to the foreign press seems to imply that General Beck was shot before the attempt on Hitler was made.[14]

## C. The Identity of the Plotters

It is much more difficult to determine the identity of the plotters and their backers. The Nazi spokesmen endeavored to create the impression that only a small clique of inconspicuous officers"[15] had made the attempt. Göring[16] narrows it down to "a miserable clique of former generals who had to be ousted . . . because of a leadership as cowardly as it was incompetent."

Very soon, however, emphasis was shifted from retired to active generals. The statement from Berlin to the European press admitted that active officers "holding important positions in the reserve"[17] were not only concerned in, but had actually inspired, the plot. Colonel General Heinz Guderian, the new Chief of Staff, finally laid the responsibility to a "few officers, some of them on the retired list,"[18] thereby admitting the majority were active officers. Goebbels finally laid responsibility[19] for the leadership of the plot on a colonel general, retired many years ago (apparently Beck), and another colonel general removed from the Eastern Front because of cowardice.[20]

The reasons for this change in emphasis are not hard to discover. The death or execution of active officers could not be hidden and had to be justified. As a consequence, their participation in the plot had to be established. According to German statements, therefore, the plot was confined exclusively to officers, namely, retired generals and members of the Home Command.

If Zeitzler really was among the plotters, he may have been planted there by the Nazis.[21] This would explain his temporary dismissal. To the list of those who were probably purged may be added the name of General Georg Thomas, Chief of the War Economy and Armament Office of the Supreme Command of the Armed Forces. Up to the time of Speer's ascendancy, Thomas was the key controller of the Nazi economy. Since 1942 he has continually lost power to Speer and his Armament Office was incorporated into the Speer Ministry, while Thomas himself has been made subject to Speer's orders. Thomas is the outstanding liaison officer between the Army and the leading industrialists.

Appendix I gives a list of the leading German generals who have been retired since 1938, Appendix II contains the names of the major officers in the Home Command.[22] There is little doubt that General Beck participated in the preparation of the *Putsch*, although it is doubtful that he plotted the assassination of Hitler. Deputy Press Chief Suendermann's speech to the Foreign Press[23] seems to imply that he was shot before the attempt was made.

There is no hint in German statements that civilians were in any way involved in the *Putsch* and the attempted assassination. And yet this appears likely. The aim of the *Putsch* was not only the assassination of Hitler, but also the assumption of governmental powers by the plotters in order to surrender to the Western Powers. If this is assumed to be true—and available intelligence supports this conclusion[24]—civilians must have participated in the preparation of the *Putsch*. Without the active cooperation of leading civil servants, and possibly of industrialists, the generals could not have assumed control of the huge governmental machinery that is necessary to install a new national government. The fact that the Germans have not admitted the participation of civilians may mean either they are not cognizant of this (which is doubtful), or they are reluctant to admit the extent of the opposition to the regime. In addition, by mentioning only generals in connection with the plot, the Nazis made it possible to shift the burden of the defeat on the Eastern Front from Hitler's strategy to treason by Army officers. This point will be elaborated later.

### D. The Political Character of the Conspiratorial Group

The members of the conspiratorial group did not represent a positive political program for Germany save on one point: surrender to the Western powers in order to save the Army. They clearly counted upon what they consider "natural affinities" between Germany and Western culture and society, fear of Russia, in spite of all declarations to the contrary, and aversion to a German revolution which may spread and infect Europe. The group thus "gambled on what they conceived to be latent intentions of the Western Powers and the 'hidden' antagonism between the Western Powers. . . ." The group was "favorably disposed to the military occupation of Germany by the Western Powers."[25]

The group was probably drawn from those favoring the so-called Western Orientation of German foreign policy,[26] which was formulated most clearly by the late General Max Hoffmann[27] as against those favoring an Eastern Orientation (the late von Seeckt, von Brockdorff-Rantzau, von Kuhlmann, and a large number of active generals).

But apart from its hope to sell itself to the West for what it believes to be the ultimately necessary war against the USSR, the group represented nothing except bankrupt generals, nationalist intellectuals, and (possibly) nationalistic Social Democrats and civil servants. This by no means implies that the group would not have found backing if it had succeeded in its *Putsch*. The desire for peace is believed to be so intense in Germany that any group, no matter how compromised, would have found almost universal acclaim if it succeeded in ending the war, though its power would have vanished rapidly once peace was declared. The extermination of the group thus does not impede the political regeneration of Germany.

## III. The Consequences of the Attempt

### A. The Purge of Opposition Leaders

No matter how narrow the basis of the plot may have been, there is little doubt that it will be the occasion for a large-scale purge of generals, former political leaders, and possibly of industrialists, bankers and high civil servants. One statement in the Goebbels speech of 26 July 1944[28] indicates that there is to be a wholesale purge. Goebbels, when reporting his instructions to the Commander of the Berlin Guard Batallion, Major Remer, added: "Immediately after the end of my speech officers and soldiers take up their machine pistols and rifles to *get them ready to settle accounts*."[29] Intensified attempts to exterminate the active or potential opposition were reported for some weeks prior to the attempt. These purges, of course, never were publicized. The generals' plot provides the opportunity of carrying out large-scale purges which could not possibly be hidden from the German people, but which can now not only be brought into the open but even given a convincing and rational justification.

Though it is likely that the purge will affect equally the members of the Western and Eastern orientation within the Officers' Corps, the influence of the Easterners undoubtedly will increase. This is due to two factors. The Eastern orientation has many more adherents, especially in view of the influence of the late General von Seeckt. Besides, in the Free Germany Committee and the German Officers' Union, the Easterners already possess a rather strong organization abroad, staffed with well-known officers. This fact, together with the possible rise of Communist movements in the post-hostilities period (see below), is likely to cause an Eastern orientation of important strata in the German people unless the post-hostilities policy of the USSR is held primarily responsible for the deprivations of Germany.

To some extent, the pattern of 30 June 1934 likely will be repeated. The 1934 pattern means that the Nazi leadership will publicly admit only a very limited purge while it actually will attempt to exterminate all those who could possibly organize resistance. The purge by no means will necessarily be confined to army officers and the potential revolutionary opposition[30].

There are, of course, very good reasons why the Nazi leadership cannot possibly admit that the plot has broad ramifications. To do so would be to admit the instability of the regime, and thus, while Germany is enduring one military defeat after another, to invite mutinies and desertion. The tightness of domestic-controls will prevent the people from learning the extent of the purge (years passed before the seriousness of the 1934 purge was known in Germany—if it is known even now).

Each local incident of the purge thus can remain isolated and justifiable, and the picture presented by the Nazis (a plot confined to a few) may thus be believed.

## B. The Success of the Purge

Has opposition, actual and potential, now been purged effectively? This question cannot be answered with certainty, since two major factors are unknown: the strength of the opposition and the extent of the purge. But it is safe to assume that the rise of a new opposition within the Army leadership has been made much more difficult, while the joining of industrialists and high bureaucrats is now unlikely in view of the fear that the purge is likely to create among this group. Even those who have considered joining a *Putsch* are now likely to submit declarations of loyalty. They will probably avoid even the slightest indication of a conspiratorial spirit.

On the other hand, it is impossible to annihilate the potential opposition without crippling the army, state, and industrial machines in so doing. There can be no doubt that the high Officer Corps and many high civil servants and industrialists are overwhelmingly conservative, though their great majority is non-political in the sense that it merely obeys the orders of a duly constituted central authority. Had the coup been successful, the bulk of the high Officer Corps, civil servants and industrialists would have been likely to follow the new leadership. As the situation now stands, this potential reservoir of opposition has been deprived of a leadership which alone would have been capable of transforming oppositional feelings into concerted action.

At the same time, it must be kept in mind that without a previously successful army *coup*, no successful revolution from below could have been expected.

## C. The Effects on Army Morale

The outcome of the *coup* and purge is the tightening of Nazi controls over the armed forces, which probably will now lose their identity and become, so to speak, an affiliate of the Nazi Party. Symbolic of this is the imposition of the Nazi salute on the armed forces. The Reserve Army seems destined to be thoroughly Nazified. It was, in the *Wehrkreise* (corps areas), commanded by older and often re-activated generals who were strongly imbued with the traditional spirit of conservatism[31] and constituted the most powerfully entrenched army bureaucracy. They likely are to be removed and probably will be replaced by the Higher SS and Police Leaders whose jurisdiction tallies with that of the *Wehrkreise*.

What will the reaction of the remaining officers be? It is most likely that they will continue to fight—with the one reservation mentioned below.

There are a number of reasons for this:

The first is inherent in the pattern of army organization and in the army tradition. Rebellion of the army against civil authority is, of course, the exception. Very few officers have the courage to risk their lives in this way, the great majority fights as long as a central authority exists and orders it to fight. The central authority not only exists but is now outwardly stronger than before. Considerations of pure self-interest must not be forgotten. German officers have increasingly become civil servants eager for promotion and anxious for pensions.

The second question is whether field commanders will surrender with their army units before the military situation compels them to do so. This appears unlikely. This view is based on the case of General Hoffmeister, recently captured by the Russian army. It seems clear that Hoffmeister had either some kind of contact with the Free Germany Committee and the German Officers' Union at Moscow or was acquainted previously with the aims of the Moscow organization. It is evident from his broadcast to the German army in the East that he was genuinely critical of Hitler's strategy and was in complete opposition to his leadership. And yet his broadcast reveals, clearly,[32] that in spite of his probable contact with the Seydlitz group,[33] and in spite of his opposition to the personal strategy of Hitler, he fought until the military situation compelled his surrender. Military honor and tradition thus will make it unlikely that generals will surrender except under military necessity.

But the *coup* and the purge are most likely to influence their estimate as to what "military necessity" is. Prior to the *coup*, the generals fought bitterly because the whole army leadership appeared united in the determination to fight to the finish. Now it is being demonstrated to them that Germany's outstanding military leaders—whose patriotism, experience, and skill are beyond doubt—have abandoned hope and have admitted that nothing, save a miracle, can avert complete military disaster for Germany. They may now come to believe that their own contribution to the fight matters little, and they may now interpret the term "military necessity" rather liberally and surrender without putting up a last-ditch fight.

It is difficult to judge whether the morale of the Army has been adversely affected, or will be impaired within the near future. The common soldier may actually experience a certain upswing. He may even believe that the defeat in the East was due to treason rather than faulty German strategy and Russian superiority. If this is his reaction, then he will be compelled to revise his views if he is ordered to withdraw further.

In the Officers' Corps, the number of Nazis among the junior officers is very high, but is fairly small in the upper ranks. The *coup* and purge unquestionably will impair morale. The uncertainty about the ramifications of the plot is likely to create distrust among the Officers' Corps; fear of denunciation will grow, and initiative will be further crippled because responsible commanders will shrink from any strategic and tactical decision not approved by the Party, lest it be attributed to a treasonable spirit.

There are, however, no indications as yet that the fighting spirit has been impaired, though the Nazis tend to create this impression. Lt. Gen. Dittmar's talk[34] attributes the defeat in the East at least partly to treason. "We are," he said, "far from wanting to deduce the development of the situation in the East *only*[35] from detrimental influences exerted by the traitors . . . For that their circle was too small and its import on the whole organization of the army not great enough." The dilemma of Nazi propaganda is clearly revealed here. Part of the blame for the defeats is shifted from Hitler's strategy to the plotters, but the whole responsibility cannot be attributed to them without admitting wide and deep ramifications of the plot.

## D. Consequences for the Home Front

The direct consequence of the abortive *coup* is the full concentration of all powers in the hands of the triumvirate of Himmler, Göring, and Goebbels as manifested by Hitler's edict of 26 July 1944.[36] Further labor mobilization will deprive the civilian population of even the barest conveniences, will make it impossible to replace even the most primitive objects destroyed by air warfare. Many administrative offices are likely to be closed, the Economic Groups may be dissolved, and sole responsibility for war production may be given to Speer's Committees and Rings. This is probable in view of the praise which Goebbels heaped on Speer.[37] The ascendance of the *Gauleiter* over the traditional administrative agencies may culminate in the complete abolition of many administrative bodies. It is likely that *Kreisleiter* will become mayors and *Landräte*, and such offices as that of the provincial presidents may be replaced simply by the *Gau* administration.

Though Goring and Goebbels appear to share power with Himmler, they are, in reality, his subordinates and it will be their duty merely to implement his decisions on policy.

Will Himmler aim at nationalization of the means of production? Will he try to institute a system of National Communism in order to stimulate production? This appears unlikely. Himmler and the SS long since have ceased to attack industrialists. The Speer organization and the Goring combine are permeated with SS leaders who have close links with business.[38] Robert Ley referred to the plotters as "German counts," "criminal members of the nobility" and to the "reaction"[39] but made no mention of industrialists and bankers. Besides, it would be disastrous to undertake a large-scale program of economic reorganization at a time when every ounce of manufactured war material counts. All that can be expected, therefore, is a radical elimination of many administrative control agencies. Large-scale expropriations can only be expected as a last desperate attempt to organize a *levée en masse* for which the enthusiastic approval of the worker would be needed.

## E. The Pattern of German Collapse

The *coup* and purge are likely to change the pattern of collapse. This aspect exceeds the scope of this paper and therefore will be treated very briefly:

It has heretofore been assumed[40] that fighting is not likely to take place on German soil because generals leading a successful *Putsch* would depose the Nazi leadership and sue for peace. This now appears less likely. It can now be assumed that the Nazi leadership is committed to a fight to the finish and will not hesitate to make Germany a battlefield. But it is doubtful whether this will be possible.

It is questionable that the Nazi leadership will be successful in achieving its three major tasks:

To prepare and execute an orderly retreat;
To keep the masses of workers from striking;
To prevent the surrender of army corps commanders with their armies once this state of the war is reached.

Tentatively, the following development may be envisaged when German territory is invaded in the West and East, or if in the East, large-scale inroads are made on German territory, strikes are likely to break out.

It is doubtful that they can be suppressed. These strikes may not be revolutionary, but merely defeatist. The armies will try either to hurry home or, if obstacles exist, surrender without centralized command. There will then be no central authority unless the Nazi government itself surrenders and Germany will be in a state of chaos.

The consequences of the abortive coup may well be the rise of National Bolshevist movements in the post-hostilities period.[41] The problem which the Nationalist movement faced in 1918 and 1919 will arise again. To the genuine Nationalist youth in Germany, the solution of the problem after the defeat of National Socialism will be very different from what it was after 1918. The Nationalist groups may point to the enormous internal and external strength of the USSR. They may attribute this strength to the fact that the bourgeoisie has been eliminated in Russia and that, while the Nazis talk about the People's community, the Russians have established it by the extermination of their own industrialists, bankers, Junkers and middle classes. These groups, therefore, may attempt to ally themselves with the German working classes, hoping to swing them in a Nationalistic direction. They may strive to bring about a reconciliation of Nationalism and Communism and orient their policy towards an understanding with Russia, hoping that with Russia's backing Germany can be restored to the position of a great power.

# Part III

# POLITICAL OPPOSITION

# 12

FRANZ NEUMANN

# *THE FREE GERMANY MANIFESTO AND THE GERMAN PEOPLE*

(AUGUST 6, 1943)

Editor's note: R&A 1033. Neumann's authorship is indicated in a letter, dated August 10, 1943, from Sherman Kent, head of the Europe-Africa Division of the Research and Analysis Branch, to Eugene Anderson (RG 226, entry 37, box 2).

Classification: Secret

The Manifesto by the National Committee of Free Germany[1] is, if considered divorced from its political surroundings, a document of no prime political significance. Statements on Post-War Germany have been issued by many refugee groups, all of them unimportant. Three facts make this manifesto significant:

1. the backing it apparently received from Soviet Russia;[2]
2. the revolutionary implication of the manifesto;
3. its appeal to the desire for national self-preservation.

## The Content of the Manifesto

1. The content of the Manifesto is at first sight not much different from that of the Weimar Constitution of 1919, in spite of the fact that the Manifesto declares that it "will have nothing in common with the helpless Weimar regime." It desires a "strong" government, a "strong democratic power," the "annulment of all laws based on national and racial hatred . . . of all measures of the Hitlerite authorities directed against freedom and human dignity, and the restoration of religious freedom. This means the reactivation of Articles 109 (equality before the law), 114, 115, 117, 118 (freedom of the person, of the home, of communications, of opinion), and Article 135 (of religion). It demands the "restoration and extension of the political rights and social gains of the working

people," formerly contained in Articles 159 (freedom of trade union organizations), 165 (cooperation of labor organizations in the administration of the economy), 161 (maintenance of health and capability to work). The Manifesto promises the restoration of the freedom of economy, trade and handicraft; the guaranteed right to labor and to own lawfully acquired property— almost direct quotations from Article 153 (freedom of property), 152 (freedom of trade and industry), 164 (protection of the independent middle classes), 157 (labor power stands under the special protection of the Reich). The Manifesto is thus almost literally a summary of Part Two of the Weimar Constitution entitled "Fundamental Rights and Duties of the Germans," while the basic idea of Part One "Structure and Task of the Reich" is but scantily treated, since there is no mention of parliamentary organs.

2. The Manifesto, however, may have today a much greater significance than the Weimar Constitution ever had in its time.

a) The appeal to democratic memories and principles could by itself hardly have any effect in Germany. P/W interrogations show that only the politically conscious anti-Nazis criticize the regime on social and political grounds. The young generation knows nothing about democracy,[3] and the older one is probably still reminiscent of the impotence and failure of the Weimar Republic. The importance of the Manifesto consists in the fact that it shows the democratic revolution as a way to terminate the war *without losing national unity and independence*. The Manifesto goes beyond the Unconditional Surrender by implying the preservation of Germany's national unity and sovereignty after the abolition of the Hitler system. In doing so, the Manifesto avoids the gravest mistake of our PW against Germany, namely, the failure to show the German people a way of terminating the war and overthrowing the Nazi regime without surrendering its national independence to a foreign conqueror. The Manifesto makes an ingenious use of our failure by telling the Germans that, if they continue to submit to Hitler, they will be inevitably defeated by our growing military power: "Hitler then will be overthrown only by the force of the coalition armies. But this will signify the end of our national independence and of our state existence, the dismemberment of our fatherland." If, on the other hand, the German people does not wait until the Wehrmacht is beaten, if the German army keeps its arms and turns them against the Nazi regime, it will, in beating Hitler, at the same time beat the enemies: the United Nations would not invade a democratic Germany which has eradicated the Nazi system. The fight against

Hitler is thus presented as a fight for Germany's national self-preservation, as a war of social *and national* liberation.

b) The democratic appeal of the Manifesto is, however, not only tied up with the longing for national self-preservation, but also with the desire for far-reaching social changes. Every vestige of Marxism is carefully avoided, but the Manifesto has nevertheless definite revolutionary implications, which obtain additional weight through the Communist signers of the document. These implications are revealed in the sentences on the "confiscation of property of those responsible for the war and of the war profiteers," on the punishment of the instigators, ringleaders, and accomplices "behind the scene," in the appeal to the "working men and women on all fronts," in the exhortation to organize "fighting groups at the enterprises, in the villages, in the labor camps, in the universities." They are furthermore indicated by the explicit statement that the future German democracy "will have nothing in common with the helpless Weimar regime."

c) The Manifesto thus combines the national and the revolutionary appeal on a democratic basis, thereby utilizing the strongest interests and desires prevalent among the potential anti-Nazi opposition.

3. In doing so, the Manifesto directs itself to the following groups:

a) the workers, especially the politically trained older workers who will have no difficulties in recognizing the revolutionary content in the nationalistic form,

b) the small peasants, who have become increasingly resentful of the totalitarian regimentation of agriculture,

c) those strata of the middle classes which have been proletarized in the process of total mobilization,

d) a large part of the intelligentsia,

e) the common soldiers,

f) certain high army circles which are favoring an understanding with Russia rather than with the Western powers (in this group might be included the so-called "left wing" of the Nazi leadership and the SS).

There can be no doubt that these groups cannot form the basis for a future democratic government in Germany. The diverging interests of the workers, the middle classes, the officer corps, and the "left-wing" Nazi leadership cannot be united after the breakdown of the Nazi system any more than under the Weimar Republic. Consequently, the Manifesto refrains from any too explicit revival of the Popular Front conception and limits the "united front" to the task of overthrowing the Nazi regime. With this limitation, however, the Manifesto and the policy suggested by it is bound to have a considerable effect on all the beforementioned groups, chiefly on account of its emphasis on national self-preservation.

The appeal to national self-preservation is by no means an appeal to imperialistic or nationalistic tendencies. The protest against dismemberment of the old Reich (the Manifesto proclaims the renunciation of all conquests) and the insistence on national unity and sovereignty will be readily accepted even by the Socialist and Communist opposition. The Marxian tradition is probably still alive among the older generation of German workers, and in this tradition, national independence is one of the preconditions of social progress. The German people—like all civilized people—regard this right as an integral part of the right to shape its own destiny. The idea of national independence arose with the idea of democracy, and precisely the democratic forces have most strongly insisted on its realization. The United States and Great Britain have been considered in Germany as the model countries where democracy and national unity have been achieved. We can hardly blame the democratic forces in Germany for adhering to an ideal which we ourselves have realized and promoted. If this ideal is taken over and implemented by the genuine anti-Nazi opposition, there is no danger of its being abused for imperialistic aggression. Imperialistic nationalism is the characteristic of certain social groups whose interests are dependent on aggressive expansion (mainly the monopolistic strata of German industry, the Junkers and militarists); it is not to them that the Manifesto appeals; it rather calls for their "punishment" as the war profiteers and instigators.

4. There is one aspect of the Manifesto, however, which sounds a different appeal. It is directed not only to the German people but also to the British and American statesmen, challenging them to come out with a declaration of post-war policy toward Europe. If an understanding between the Western powers and Russia cannot be reached, the "Free Germany" movement may become an instrument for power politics. The Manifesto contains a clear indication of that, in appealing to those army and party circles which may prefer a German-Russian coalition to British-American occupation. If the United Nations do not succeed in allying themselves with the genuinely anti-Nazi opposition in Germany, if they do not give the German people the chance of social as well as political reconstruction as a free democratic nation, then the Manifesto might easily become the first attempt to create a "National-Bolshevik" regime in Germany. For that it could revitalize a significant political trend on the Left as well as on the Right in Germany.

## The National Bolshevist Tradition

National Bolshevism has two origins, one in the Communist Party, the other in the nationalistic organizations, especially the Free Corps. The first used nationalism as a means to seduce the nationalist youth into the communist camps, the second to draw communists into the nationalistic ranks.

### 1. National Bolshevism in the Communist Party

a) National Bolshevist trends became apparent at the time of the discussion of the Versailles Treaty. On May 13, 1919, the Comintern issued a manifesto entitled "Down with the Versailles Treaty."[4] The CP leadership, especially Paul Levi and Karl Radek,[5] were compelled to attack the already existing trends towards National Bolshevism which became especially apparent in the Hamburg CP.[6] Under Paul Levi's influence the ultra-Left (the National Bolsheviks and Syndicalists) was compelled to leave the party as an aftermath to the second illegally held party conference of the CP. Under his influence participation in the elections was decided and direct revolutionary action as advocated by the Hamburg group was rejected. The ultra Left opposition under the leadership of Laufenberg and Wolfheim formed the KAPD (Communist Workers Party of Germany) and soon lost influence completely. The eliminated radicals found, however, entrance into the CP when the party became what was then called a "revolutionary mass party." Though it is not our task to show the many changes through which the policy of the CP passed, a few incidents must be mentioned.

b) The National Bolshevist trends became predominant in 1923, a year characterized by two major events: the occupation of the Ruhr and the inflation. The slogan of the CP then was "Beat Poincare on the Ruhr and Cuno on the Spree."[7] The fight of the CP was thus directed against French imperialism and the cabinet of Chancellor Cuno, who was undoubtedly a representative of German shipping and industrial interests. Actually, however, the CP directed its attack almost exclusively against France and supported the passive resistance of the German people. This was in line with Soviet Russia's foreign policy after the conclusion of the Rapallo treaty with Germany.[8] Soviet Russia considered England and France as the protagonists of anti-Russian interventionism. The Comintern as well as the Central Executive Committee of the Russian CP thus protested against the Reich occupation.[9] It is during that time that within the Communist Party the idea arose that Germany was a suppressed country and that consequently the Communists must assume the leadership in the struggle for national liberation. The CP deputy Dengel stated while surveying the political situation in 1923 in the 11th Party Congress of 1927 that a just war of national liberation would have been possible in 1923.[10] In the course of the inflation, political and social antagonisms deepened in Germany. The petty bourgeois wavered, according to Communist conceptions, between Fascist and Communist sympathies.[11]

The CP believed that the time of a new revolution had arrived, and from the summer of 1923 on it became the rallying point of all discontented masses. Thousands entered the Communist Party. It is in these circumstances that the National Bolshevist theory and tactics were adopted. Rakosi praised it in 1923.[12] Radek delivered a speech at the occasion of Schlageter's execution by the French.[13] It is worthwhile remembering that Schlageter is one of the Nazis' most celebrated national heroes. Radek said: "The history of this martyr of German nationalism shall not be clothed in silence nor shall it be settled with an alighting phrase . . . Schlageter, the courageous soldier of the counter-revolution, deserves honor in a manly and honorable fashion by us soldiers of the revolution. . . . Only an alliance with the German working classes can liberate Germany from the yoke of imperialism."[14]

Radek's speech became the starting point for the National Bolshevist campaign. Count Reventlow was invited to write in the *Rote Fahrus*. Lower CP officials went so far as to publish posters adorned with the Soviet star and the swastika and invited Nazis to speak in Communist meetings. Ruth Fischer, then a member of the Executive Committee of the CP, addressed the nationalist students in Berlin in the following way: "The German Reich . . . can be saved only if you, gentlemen of the German racial groups, recognize that you must fight jointly with the masses organized in the CP." She continued, "Whoever attacks Jewish capital . . . is already a class fighter even if he doesn't know it. . . . Crush the Jewish capitalists, hang them on the lampposts, trample them." She ended by saying, "French imperialism is now the greatest danger in the world. France is a country of reaction. The German people can drive French capital from the Ruhr only in an alliance with Russia."[15] The campaign had no success and the National Bolshevist line was dropped. It did not become a predominant feature of Communist policy until the very end of the Weimar Republic.

c) The elections of 1930 showed the growth of National Socialism, and the Communist Party desperately sought for a new political line which would allow them to counteract the growing influence of the National Socialist Party on the masses. The leadership went to Heinz Neumann, the most irresponsible Communist leader. Neumann directed the attack of the Communist Party almost exclusively against the Social Democrats who were labeled as "Social Fascists." Slogans like "Drive the Social Fascists from their positions in the plants and factories," "Beat the Social Fascists" were formulated. Thaelmann himself said, "Without being victorious in the fight against the social democracies, we shall not be able to beat Fascism."[16] The Executive Committee of the CP adopted as late as September 1932 an anti-Socialdemocratic resolution.[17]

At the same time the National Bolshevist line was rejuvenated under the auspices of Heinz Neumann. He addressed a Goebbels meeting in Berlin in the following way: "Young Socialists! Brave fighters for the nation! The Communists do not desire fraternal strife with the National Socialists."[18] This time the Communists were successful to some extent. Lieutenant Scheringer, whom the Supreme Court had sentenced to imprisonment for National Socialist activities within the army, was converted to Communism primarily under the influence of his fellow prisoner, the Communist Captain, Ludwig Renn.[19] A number of other officers, especially of the Free Corps Bund Oberland, also joined the CP.

The election manifesto of the Communist Party published on August 24, 1930, begins with the following words: "We shall tear up the thievish Versailles "Peace Treaty" and the Young Plan which enslaved Germany. We shall annul all international debts and reparation payments." The manifesto ends with the words, "Down with the Young Plan! Down with the government of the capitalists and Junkers! Down with Fascism and social democracy! Long live the dictatorship of the Proletariat! Long live Soviet Germany!" The manifesto insists on the socialization of heavy industry, banks, large estates and big traders and officers, and on a union of all toiling masses on the basis of the broadest possible soviet democracy.

In his speech before the Executive Committee of the CP, April and May 1931, the then Party leader Thaelmann declared that the whole tradition of the CP was permeated by its fight against Versailles. He reminded the listeners of the policy of the Spartakus union and of the Ruhr struggle of 1923 and he did not concede a contradiction between the struggle for national liberation and proletarian internationalism.[20]

In February 1932 at the meeting of the Central Committee Thaelmann reiterated the position of the Communist Party in the following manner: "We are the sole party in Germany which really and with the greatest determination fights against the policy of fulfillment. . . . National liberation cannot be divorced from the social liberation of the toiling people, that is from the overthrow of capitalism. . . . One cannot fight against the Versailles system if one engages in violent baiting of the only government in the world which did not sign the shameful Versailles treaty. . . . The Hitler party will become the direct ally of Pilsudski's Poland which with her policy of the Polish Corridor and in Upper Silesia where she enslaves and tortures German workers and peasants. . . . One cannot fight against the Versailles Treaty and the Young slavery without unfurling the banner of proletariat internationalism."[21]

d) This National Bolshevist approach was superseded by the doctrine of the "people's revolution" shortly before Hitler's access to power. This doctrine is outwardly incompatible with the old Bolshevist theory that revolutions are prepared by small groups of determined professional revolutionaries. The doctrine of the people's revolution, however, must be considered as a forerunner of the Manifesto of the Free Germany Committee. This doctrine was proclaimed for the first time in 1931. "The Communist Party . . . must organize the people's revolution against Fascism and economic castigation—that is its historic task."[22] The program of the people's revolution, so another manifesto said, "will bring liberty to the toiling peasants."[23]

The crowning tactical step of the people's revolution doctrine was the Referendum in the summer of 1931 for the dissolution of the Prussian Diet with the aim of overthrowing the social democratic government of Braun and Severing. Though the Communist Party originally opposed the initiative sponsored by Nazis, Nationalists, and the Steel Helmet.[24] Heinz Neumann succeeded in bringing the Communist Party behind the National opposition. Remmele, his second in command,[25] supported Neumann. Thaelmann against his better insight was compelled to defend the inglorious Referendum.

Only in October 1932 did the Thaelmann group begin to attack the National Bolshevist line and the doctrine of the people's revolution.[26]

e) The Russians have killed almost all the advocates of this National Bolshevik line—Heinz Neumann, Remmele, Max Hoelz—and have thus shown, from 1933 to 1941, to have definitely rejected the National Bolshevik theory. Only in November 1932 was there a mass manifestation of Bolshevik and Nazi solidarity. The Berlin Transport Workers struck. The Social Democratic Trade Union outlawed the strike but the National Socialist Workers Cell Organisation (N.S.B.O.) together with the Red Trade Union Opposition, carried the strike, supported it and succeeded in organizing sympathy of almost the whole Berlin population.

f) It follows from the above that the Communist Party has frequently attempted to exploit the nationalist traditions and longings among huge groups of the German people, especially among the army and the intellectuals. It was unsuccessful from 1919 to 1933 because the Nationalists preferred to join the Nazi Party which, due to its predominantly nationalistic appeal, appeared to be a much more effective guardian of nationalistic aspirations. But the Nazi Party is in a state of disintegration and its power will decline with the decline of Germany's military fortunes. It is not impossible that this collapse of the Nazi Party may enable the Communist Party to organize better than ever before the genuine nationalistic passion inherent in the German youth, the German intelligentsia and the professional soldiers and officers.

## 2. National Bolshevik Trends in the Nazi Movement

a) National Bolshevik trends are not represented in the present Nazi leadership. It can even be said without exaggeration that Hitler established his total control over the Party primarily by the ruthless elimination of those who adhered to this doctrine that appeared to him the greatest impediment to the seizure, maintenance, and strengthening of the Party's control over the German Reich. It has elsewhere been pointed out[27] that the turning point in the strategy of the Nazi Party was the fiasco of the Munich Putsch of 1923. The failure of this attempted overthrow of the established government by means of violence taught Hitler a lesson which he never forgot, the lesson, namely, that the Nazi Party can come to power only with the assistance of the most powerful ruling groups in Germany through Parliamentary processes. The subsequent history of National Socialism has amply demonstrated his conviction that he can retain power only by letting the ruling groups share in the spoils of peaceful and warlike exploitation of the German masses as well as those of occupied Europe. This insight led Hitler to a ruthless war against those who advocated some kind of a National Bolshevist program.

b) It is commonly believed that Goebbels and Ley are the two spokesmen of the so-called radical wing in the Nazi Party, a wing that would not hesitate to resort to Socialist and even Bolshevist measures if the power of the Nazi Party could thereby be maintained.

It is quite true that when Goebbels started his career within the Nazi Party he joined forces with Gregor Strasser, the leader of the Political Organization of the Party. Jointly with Gregor Strasser, Goebbels created and edited a semi-monthly periodical "Nationalsozialistische Briefe" (National Socialist Letters), not designed for public consumption. The first issue appeared on October 1, 1925, and the slogan was the "Reconciliation of Socialism with the East." The program of this group was formulated by Goebbels in the middle of 1925 in an article in the *Voelkischer Beobachter*,[28] where the following statement appeared: "The future lies with the dictatorships of the Socialist idea." The Strasser-Goebbels group attacked Rosenberg's anti-Russian and anti-Semitic conceptions. It demanded eastern orientation of the Nazi Party, opposition to American and English imperialism and assistance to Russia's fight against this imperialism. Germany's place was on the side of Russia, Turkey, China, India, in short on the side of all those people which are hostile to Versailles. Russia therefore is the natural ally of Germany and it is nobody's concern how Russia is internally governed.

These views were supported by Gregor Strasser's brother, Otto Strasser, and by Count Reventlow, who belonged to the *Deutsch Voelkische Freiheitspartei*, which had formed an alliance with the Nazi Party in March 1923.

c) The occasion for dealing the first blow to the National Bolshevist trend within the party was the Communist sponsored referendum for the expropriation of the princely houses. On February 14, 1925, Hitler called a meeting of the party leaders to Bamberg. The northern Gaue were represented only by Gregor Strasser and Goebbels. Hitler succeeded, in spite of Strasser's opposition to commit the party to wholesale opposition to the Communist initiative by depicting it as Jewish engineered. Goebbels used this occasion to desert Strasser and to swing over entirely to Hitler's side. From that day on Goebbels as well as Ley have consistently followed Hitler's directives and that day created the deadly enmity between Goebbels and the Strasser brothers which led ultimately to Gregor Strasser's assassination on June 30, 1934. The *Arbeitsgemeinschaft* of the northern Gaue was dissolved.

d) The fight between the two wings, especially between the Strasser group and the Hitler majority, is well known. While Gregor Strasser finally accepted the leadership of Hitler, his brother Otto Strasser did not. He founded the "Fighting Community of Revolutionary National Socialists," later called Black Front, and submitted to the German public "Fourteen Theses of the German Revolution."[29] These theses, though outwardly socialistic, do not contain any foreign political program except the demand for the unification of all Germans and the destruction of the Versailles Treaty. Otto Strasser has, however, exposed his foreign political views in his book "Structure of German Socialism" to which his famous discussion with Hitler is appended[30].

The handing over of the trade unions to Ley's Labor Front instead of to the NSBO; the elimination of Roehm; the decline of the SA,—all these are steps in the eradication of the so called "socialist," that is National-Bolshevik wing of the Nazi Party.

The National Bolshevist doctrine had a deep fascination especially for nationalistic intellectuals. The most articulate post-war nationalist, Moeller van den Bruck, espouses these ideas in his *Das Dritte Reich*, (3rd edition, Hamburg, 1931), and in his lesser known but possibly more important book *Das Recht der Jungen Voelker*.[31] The only novelist of repute that National Socialism has produced, Ernst Jünger[32] must be considered as the pathbreaker of National Bolshevism.[33]

The collapse of the Nazi system will again bring to the fore National Bolshevik trends that have heretofore been suppressed by the Nazi leaders.

The problem which the Nationalist movement faced in 1918 and 1919 will arise again. To the genuine Nationalist youth in Germany the solution of the problem after the defeat of National Socialism will be very different from what it has been after 1918. The Nationalist groups may point to the enormous internal and external strength of Bolshevik Russia. They may attribute this strength to the fact that the bourgeoisie has been eliminated in Russia and that, while the Nazis talk about the people's community, the Russians have established it by the extermination of their own industrialists, bankers, Junkers and middle classes. These groups, therefore, may attempt to ally themselves with the German working classes, hoping to swing them into Nationalistic directions. They will strive to bring about a reconciliation of Nationalism and Bolshevism and they will orient their policy towards an understanding with Russia, hoping that with Russia's backing Germany can be restored to the position of a great power.

To sum up: although the National Bolshevik leadership in the Communist as well as in the National Socialist Party has been exterminated, a situation may well arise in which National Bolshevik ideas may again receive a powerful stimulus. Such a situation will occur if, after the breakdown of the Nazi regime, conditions are imposed upon Germany which will destroy her unity and independence as a nation. In this case, the German nationalists may succeed in exploiting the sentiments and desires of the German masses for a National Bolshevik policy. It is reported that, in anticipation of such a situation, important Nazi groups, especially among the SS, are already infiltrating into the Communist centers of resistance.

## III. The Attitude toward Russia

1. Apart from the National Bolshevik tradition predominant in the radical Communist movement and among the nationalistic organizations, there is a very powerful pro-Russian trend which is quite independent of the internal structure of Russia. It is well known that for the conservatives the re-insurance treaty between Germany and Russia concluded between Bismarck and Schouvaloff[34] on June 18, 1887,[35] was the cornerstone of the conservative foreign policy and that the conservative opposition never forgave William II not to have renewed the re-insurance treaty.

At the end of the World War 1914–1918 three foreign political trends became apparent in Germany, the Eastern orientation, the Western orientation and the so-called Bridge theory. For the easterners, friendly relations with Russia were to enable Germany to get rid of the Versailles Treaty and to establish herself as a great power. To the westerners, the entrance of Germany in the concert of Western Powers was to provide the same result. The adherents of the third theory conceived Germany as a bridge between eastern and western Europe and hoped by careful juggling between the East and the West, by playing off Russia against France and England, to achieve concession after concession.

2. The western orientation stems from Frederich List.[36] It found its most powerful expression in the writings of General Hoffmann.[37] According

to Hoffman, the basic fact which the great powers in the world have to face is the crisis of industrialism intensified by Russia's elimination from the world economy and Bolshevism's fight against the fundamental interests of capitalistic society. The solution therefore is the destruction of Bolshevism and the re-integration of Russia into a world economy based on world economic collaboration and political integration of Germany, Great Britain, and France.[38] Hoffmann desired to this end the financial and economic cooperation of the United States. It is this thesis which went into Hitler's *Mein Kampf* and into Alfred Rosenberg's mythology. It amounted to the suggestion of establishing a huge world trust directed against Soviet Russia.

3. This western school was, however, violently opposed by the army leadership and by a number of industrialists and diplomats.

The position of the German army towards foreign policy has been formulated with utmost clarity in General von Seeckt's book, *Germany between East and West*.[39]Seeckt considers the west, especially France, to be Germany's natural enemy. He therefore advocates collaboration with Russia in spite of all differences in internal systems and ideologies. There are, he says, "no antagonisms between Germany and Russia based on geography, history, and race." Russian State Socialism is "a purely internal affair." He advocates that German business expands into Russia and that it becomes "indispensable and liked in Russia." Bolshevism, he adds, is a "purely Russian product." "Bolshevism in Russia will not break down if we dissolve the treaties of Rapallo and Berlin; but we shall then have an enemy on our border whose impact on our internal situation will not be less . . . Our attitude towards Bolshevism has nothing to do with the possibility of economic and political cooperation." He is afraid of Germany's isolation and he believes that Germany will have to face two enemies if her political relations with Russia are not friendly. "We address German politicians: Keep me the back free."

There are many more of such proponents.[40] It is well known that Count von Brockdorff-Rantzau passionately desired the alliance with Russia in order to fight the Treaty of Versailles and resigned office when he did not succeed in convincing the Weimar coalition, Social Democrats, Catholics and Democrats. Baron von Maltzahn, the head of the eastern department in the German Foreign Office, was a well known partisan of Seeckt and Brockdorff-Rantzau. Other German diplomats shared this view such as the well known Richard von Kuehlmann.[41]

The geo-politicians, whose influence on German foreign policy is, however, greatly over-estimated, were in favor of Russian-German collaboration, and Karl Haushofer has, during the German-Russian nonaggression pact, reformulated the idea of the joint organization of the Russian-German space.[42]

4. It was the Social Democrats and the Liberals who sought to incorporate Germany into the concert of the Western Powers without alienating Soviet Russia. It is characteristic, however, that this policy could be carried out only during the time when the Weimar Republic appeared to be stabilized. Streseman[43] repudiated "the thesis that German foreign policy must have either a western or an eastern orientation." Erich Koch-Weser, the spokesman of the German Democratic Party,[44] took Streseman's position and insisted that Germany's task is "to be the bridge between the east and the west." He expressly repudiated the eastern orientation. "It is impossible for Germany to carry out a policy of resistance against the west trusting in Russian assistance. Today Russia is not up to such a task. Should we be drawn, however, into a war between Russia and the Western Powers, a Russian victory may bring us freedom against the West but the inundation and subjugation by Bolshevism." The third conception of Germany's foreign policy, the bridge thesis, is today probably that doctrine which has the least support since liberalism in Germany, never powerful in history, has today but little appeal. It is known that Streseman lacked support even by his own party and that his major support came from the Social Democratic party.

If the United Nations do not come out with a united policy Germany will again be compelled to choose between the east and the west. The eastern orientation has always been strong among the high officer corps and among the conservatives, but even groups in heavy industry which considered England to be the main competitor were striving for friendly relations with Russia.[45]

## V. The Strength of Communism and of Other Anti-Nazi Groups

1. The last free Reichstag elections in Germany were held on November 6, 1932.

The result was:

| | | |
|---|---|---|
| | ( NSDAP | 196 deputies |
| Right | ( Nationalists | 52 |
| | ( German Peoples Party | 11 |
| | ( Bavarian Peoples Party | 20 |
| Center | ( Center Party | 70 |
| | ( Democratic Party | 2 |
| | ( Social Democrats | 121 |
| Left | ( Communists | 100 |

The elections of March 5, 1933, were no longer free. Terror had already started. The whole Communist and Socialdemocratic press was banned, and many communist deputies were either in SA barracks or in exile. Still the elections showed the following picture:

| | | |
|---|---|---|
| | ( NSDAP | 288 |
| Right | ( Nationalists | 52 |
| | ( German Peoples Party | 2 |
| | ( Bavarian Peoples Party | 18 |
| Center | ( Center Party | 74 |
| | ( Democratic Party | 5 |
| | ( Social Democrats | 120 |
| Left | ( Communists | 81 |

2. The number of communist voters in the last six months of the Weimar Republic was thus around six million. This figure is, however, highly deceptive, since the communist vote was subject to great fluctuations and corresponded in no way to the actual strength of the Party proper. Official communist estimates of party membership[46] were as follows:

1919—90,000
1920—50,000 (KAPD—38,000)
1921—78,000
1922—380,000
1923—267,000
1924—180,000
1927—150,000
1928—130,000
1930—120,000
1931—200,000
1932—320,000[47]

The CP has thus never been able to organize a considerable part of the working classes. The influence of the CP, however, went far beyond the membership, especially when the late Kurt Muenzenberg was put in charge of CP propaganda and covered Germany with a network of transmission-belt organizations.

3. The membership of the SPD vacillated around 1,000,000,[48] but the SPD could count on the support of the Free (Socialdemocratic) Trade Unions[49]. The Social Democratic Party, however, was in reality weak. It held no attraction for the youth. In 1930, the age composition of the SPD was:

| | |
|---|---|
| 25 years and under | 7.82 percent |
| 26–30 years | 10.34 " |
| 31–40 " | 26.47 " |
| 41–50 " | 27.28 " |
| 51–60 " | 19.57 " |
| 60–70 " | 7.16 " |
| over 70 " | 1.34 "[50] |

The CP, on the other hand, had a great attraction for the youth and communist youth organisations (apart from the religious ones) were the only ones that allowed to the youth a broad enough field for activities.

4. There are other considerable differences. The dissolution of the SPD and of the trade unions came as an unexpected blow to the leadership, which had done nothing to prepare for underground activities. The Executive Committee of the SPD had even refused to entertain such ideas as late as March 1933, while the Trade Union leadership tried to make peace with the new Nazi rulers.[51] The CP, on the other hand, at once started its underground activities for which it was trained many years ago and for which it had skilled Russian assistance.

Under the Nazi regime, the fates of the Social Democracy and of the CP were utterly different. The Social Democratic membership displayed considerable resistance against the pressure of Nazism. No SPD and no union leader of repute has joined the Nazis,[52] and the older ranks of the memberships were almost immune to the lure of Nazism.

5. Some Communists, however, joined the Nazi movement, especially members of the RFB, the Red Front Fighting League,[53] which was shot through with gangsters. On the other hand, the underground CP organization was the most active underground movement.

Ps/W interrogations indicate:

a. that the CP underground still is the most important organization;
b. that the Communist Youth Organization is still the most active youth underground;
c. that, however, Gestapo agents have found entrance into the CP underground[54].

While the CP thus is the best organized and strongest underground group in Germany, the appeal of Russian Communism has not increased and may even have decreased.

6. The esteem for Communism among the German workers rose considerably during the Spanish Civil War—a crucial period in Europe; it declined sharply during the German-Russian non-aggression pact, and climbed steeply with the decline of Germany's military fortunes on her Eastern Front.

These pro-Soviet sentiments are, however, counteracted by two basic factors: the low esteem in which the CP leadership is held,[55] and the fear of Russian domination over Germany. This fear is probably the most important single psychological factor inside of Germany. It has two causes:

1. the feeling of guilt; and
2. the fear of economic reparations.

Nazi terror in occupied territories aims not only at intimidating the opposition but at making all Germans participate in the commission of terror acts so as to create a collective feeling of guilt and collective responsibility for crime.[56] The Nazis have largely succeeded in this and Ps/W interrogation abounds in statements that the Germans fight supremely well in Russia because they are afraid of retribution for their crimes.

They are also afraid of the post-war period. "Enjoy the War, Peace will be terrible" is a famous German slogan. This applies to the relations with Russia even more than to those with the Allies. The destruction wrought in occupied Russia must be paid some day by Germany. How can it be paid—so they may argue—except by German slave labor if Germany's industrial equipment should be badly damaged by air attacks?

The Manifesto tries to allay these fears.

7. The SP and Trade Union leaderships are probably the most discredited leaderships of any German democratic organization. The SPD and the trade unions wielded power—the CP not. The SPD ruled Prussia until July 20, 1932; it continually boasted of its strength.[57] It was the only great party fully committed to the defense of the Republic. The Weimar Republic may even be considered *the* creation of the SPD. And yet it failed completely to adopt its policy to the new requirements.

This does not mean that the democratic spirit is dead. The idea of a democratic socialism exists, and may now be stronger than it ever was.[58] There certainly will have arisen a new leadership among the many localized groups in Germany not burdened by the failure of the old leadership.

The SPD and trade union influence in Germany must not be underestimated for another reason, though the SPD groups may be much less organized than the CP. The age composition of the SP may even prove to be advantageous today. Of 28,000,000 workers and salaried employees employed today approximately 11,200,000 are foreign workers, which leaves approximately 17,000,000 Germans. Of these, at least 11,000,000 are women, which leaves only 6,000,000 male Germans. Among these, the huge majority are 40 years and over; that would cover the age groups 31–50 years mentioned on p. 30, that is, those age groups which are most strongly imbued by the Social Democratic tradition. But numerical strength is not identical with real strength. The Communist groups in Germany are certainly small, probably not exceeding 30,000—40,000. But their thorough indoctrination, their tight organization and the backing that they may obtain from Russia—all this makes them the potential leaders in the period of military and political collapse. Spontaneous uprisings are of great importance, but spontaniety evaporates if it is not channelled into an organization and a definite policy. Today, the Communist groups are potential leaders of the spontaneous opposition in Germany. This idea which has been insisted upon by the Central European Section time and again is confirmed by Ps/W interrogations.

The fear of Soviet Russia will then be subordinated to the desire to remain an independent nation and to assure to the Germans an adequate standard of living, political, social and economic security.

8. Many of the industrialists must realize that a victory of Great Britain and the United States may mean the end of Germany's industrial expansion and may even lead to a considerable contraction of economic activities. High officers may realize that with the economic isolation of Germany her military destruction is indissolubly bound up. Without an expanding economy modern armies cannot be maintained. The army may again become a small professional army without adequate combat weapons. Industrialists and high officers, however, may be convinced that Russia may not desire a Communist Germany for reasons which cannot be discussed here but that an alliance with Russia may give to German industry considerable opportunities for expansion. The officers' corps may convince itself that Russia may desire a strong Germany against possible intervention by France, England and America. If England and America should support Poland's claims for Germany's Eastern provinces, these groups will still more be driven into the camp of Russia hoping to avert the dismemberment of Germany by placing themselves wholly at Russia's disposal.

It follows from the above that there is no pro-Russian sentiment among the large masses of the people, that Communist sympathizers, Social Democrats and Catholics and liberals would prefer leadership by the Allied powers than submission to Russia, provided that this leadership does not destroy Germany's national unity and independence.

There is much less resistance to cooperation with Soviet Russia among groups of German industries and the high officers' corps.

In default of such leadership all groups with the possible exception of practicing Catholics and Junkers, will try to establish cooperation with Soviet Russia basing their policy on the strong National Bolshevik trends within Communism and National Socialism and on the traditional pro-Russian orientation among powerful groups of the German ruling classes.

# 13

HERBERT MARCUSE

## *THE GERMAN COMMUNIST PARTY*

(JULY 10, 1944)

Editor's note: R&A 1550. In this case it was not possible to find solid proof as to the authorship of the text. Barry Katz, in his *Foreign Intelligence*, explicitly attributes it to Marcuse, although without providing specific evidence. This attribution, however, seems plausible: it was a habitual practice in the Central European Section to entrust Marcuse with reports and analyses on left-wing opposition parties. Beyond that, there is a letter dated November 25, 1943, from Francis T. Williamson (who assisted Marcuse more than a few times in the preparation of reports under his responsibility—e.g., R&A 1655.4 and 1655.5, published in this volume) to William B. Kip., in which Williamson asks for a copy of the article "Der Weg der KPD" by W. Rist, published in *Neue Blatter der Sozialismus*, saying that he was interested in documents on the Communist Party in general, and particularly on its organization, finances, and the anagraphic composition of its members (all themes that are effectively presented in the report published here).

The original text was accompanied by four appendixes—here omitted—that contain, respectively, (1) a table of the votes obtained by the Communist Party in the federal elections from 1924 and 1933; (2) a list of the organizational districts of the German Communist Party; (3) a list of the most important Communist newspapers before 1933; and (4) a list of the main Communist leaders in exile.

Classification: Secret

### Introduction

Prior to 1933, the German Communist Party was an important force in the German political system and one of the three largest political parties.

Since its dissolution in 1933 by the Nazis, the party has continued to exist, both inside and outside Germany, retaining the loyalty of many of its former members and possibly gaining recruits by its opposition to the Hitler regime. At present, the Communist Party is the only pre-1933 party which has formulated a systematic program and developed tactics to exploit the conditions which it anticipates will exist in Germany. The inherent strength of the Communist movement in Germany, its cooperation with military groups in the Free German movement, and the play of international forces give the Communists an advantage over other existing political groups in Germany.

The following paper attempts to show the historical position of the Communist Party in German politics, its present strength, and the plans by which it hopes to become a political force in post-war Germany.

## I. The Origins of the German Communist Party

### A. The Social Democrats and the Communists

The two chief leftist political parties of Germany—the Communists and the Social Democrats—prior to their suppression by the Nazis, had long competed for the support of the working class and adopted divergent policies to fulfill their conception of the best protection of labor interests. In terms of origin, objectives and methods, the two parties were in sharp opposition during the Weimar period. Their divergence on all issues was a constant factor in German politics.

Before the first World War, most of German labor had been represented politically by the Social Democratic Party, operating within the ideological framework of the Second International to achieve the creation of a socialist society. The party exercised pressure in the German parliamentary system by electing representatives to national and local political bodies. Its prominent position in German politics was assured by the increasing number of people who voted for the Social Democratic platform because they wished either to see the fulfillment of the socialist goal or to register their lack of confidence in Imperial policy. Behind the party deputies in the Reichstag there developed a great structure of trade unions and other associations which sought to increase the numerical strength of the party and establish it as the effective representative of labor interests. By 1912 the Social Democratic Party had succeeded in becoming the largest single party in the Reichstag.

Within the frame of reference of pre-1914 Europe, the methods of the Social Democratic Party were revolutionary. While decrying direct action the party was dedicated to the overthrow of capitalism and the establishment of a socialist state as described in Marxian philosophy. There was increasing evidence after the turn of the century, however, that "revisionism" in Marxian thought had become the official ideology and that the historic goals were to be sought only by political action and pressure. A division began in the party— the "radical left" demanding revolutionary methods and the official leadership continuing to insist on reformist programs and the orthodox tactics followed by political parties operating under the Imperial constitution.

For many years the Social Democrats had voted consistently against armaments budgets as a means of opposing the Imperial Government. Their support of the Kaiser and the war in 1914 supplied the reason for the defection of the "radical left." In 1916, the Independent Social Democratic Party (USPD) broke away and attempted to unite the anti-war elements of the old party by advocating a negotiated peace and renunciation of all conquests. The USPD, however, did not express the revolutionary sentiments held by groups in the labor movements of all European powers in the later years of the war. These groups in Germany gradually coalesced as the *Spartakus-Bund*, the parent organization of the Communist Party.

## B. The Spartacists

Under the leadership of Rosa Luxemburg, Karl Liebknecht, Franz Mehring and others, the Spartacists denounced the Social Democrats as betrayers of the working class and the USPD as "petty bourgeois pacifists" who would not fight for their objectives. The doctrines of the Spartacists were revolutionary. They refused to support the war or capitalist society and refused to work with any party actually supporting the war or the *status quo*.

The founding of the Spartacist movement coincides in time with the development of anti-war and revolutionary groups in other European states. But the Spartacist leaders did not approve the ideological developments which culminated in the formation of Communist International. They participated in the conferences at Zimmerwald and Kienthal, but rejected Lenin's theses concerning the International and the methods and duties of Bolshevist parties. The Spartacists believed, on the contrary, that revolution should be spontaneous. They feared that the Bolshevist theory of the role of the party would stifle the revolutionary enthusiasm and democratic action of the masses. However, the inspiration of the successful revolution in Russia was too great and the leaders were forced by pressure within the Spartacist League to join the Third International and change the name of the organization to *Kommunistische Partei Deutschlands* (KPD).

## C. The KPD and the Weimar Republic

While both Communists and Social Democrats derived their motivation from Marxist philosophy and stated their objectives in terms of working class interests, the gulf between them was increasingly widened by the course of social and ideological change in the post-war world. The Communists were committed to the policy of the revolutionary dictatorship of the proletariat. Their tactics were determined not only by political expediency, but also by the changes in the party line of the Third International. The Social Democrats, on the other hand, became one of the main champions of the Weimar Republic, assuming a direct responsibility for the maintenance of the Republic and the post-war social order. Political responsibility laid a heavy hand on the Social Democratic Party. Bureaucratic controls increased in party administration and vested interests were acquired in the maintenance of national and local political forms. To many contemporary observers, the historic aims of the party were compromised. The Social Democrats represented the skilled workers and many elements of the petty bourgeoisie who feared revolutionary conditions and the attempt to form a new society. But the Communists increasingly represented the social groups most adversely affected by the inflation and the growth of unemployment. They had no fear of the revolution, because they had no property or status to be destroyed.

The Communist uprisings of 1919 intensified this violent relationship. Against the advice of their leaders, the Spartacists engaged in insurrections early in 1919 throughout Germany. The Social Democratic Minister of Defense called on the militaristic and nationalistic Free Corps to suppress the disorders. In the course of the suppression Rosa Luxemburg and Karl Liebknecht were shot "while trying to escape."

After 1919, the relations between the two parties were subject to many strains. Conflicting objectives in the labor movement and in German foreign policy were vital factors. The Social Democrat political power rested in large part upon their control of the German trade unions. Realizing that no party advocating labor interests could gain power without union support, the Communists tried to win this support. Competitive unions with revolutionary objectives were founded but did not attract mass support, and attempts to infiltrate into established unions did not result in KPD control of any one union. The Communists were forced to accept second place in the struggle to dominate German labor.

In the field of foreign policy, the Social Democratic Party accepted the peace treaty in 1919 and worked consistently to have Germany fulfill the terms of the settlement; support was given the League of Nations and efforts to secure peace and disarmament. The Communists, however, refused to accept the Versailles Treaty and generally opposed the efforts to orient German foreign policy within the western European security framework. As a member of the International, the KPD opposed any diplomatic policy which could be construed as directed against the USSR.

On all issues of foreign and domestic policy, the Communists and Social Democrats could be expected to occupy hostile positions. The Social Democrats attempted to support the Weimar Republic and achieve socialism by means of democratic action. The ultimate objective of the Communists was the establishment of socialism by means of revolutionary dictatorship. This brought the Communists into violent conflict with the Social Democrats and the whole system of Weimar.[1]

## II. The Framework of the KPD

### A. Membership

The KPD operated as one of the major political parties in the German parliamentary system, and drew support in the elections from many who were not members. At the same time it was a revolutionary organization, with a controlled membership recruited from persons accepting the ideology and direction of the Third International. The KPD had neither a large nor a stable enrolled membership. The Social Democrats had a consistent dues-paying membership of approximately one million; the KPD usually averaged about one-fifth that number.

A significant feature of the party membership was the high rate of fluctuation. In specific years increases may be attributed to social and political conditions existing within Germany, as the inflation in 1923 and unemployment after 1929.[2] According to the official figures, one-third of the members left the party each year. In the Berlin area, the annual rate of fluctuation reached 40 percent. The core of the party was a devoted and consistent group, comprising about four to five percent of the total membership which had been in the party for ten years or more.[3] The rate of fluctuation also may be explained in terms of the party's propaganda and its organizational requirements. The KPD made use of the current political situations in Germany to issue appeals to workers, unemployed and intellectuals who were critical of the *status quo*. The appeals attracted a large floating membership, but enrollment in the party involved responsibilities and risks which only the convinced revolutionaries were willing to accept for a long period of time. Party membership brought financial burdens, meetings, demonstrations, and organization work which did not find a wide or consistent appeal.[4]

The KPD fundamentally was a working-class party. After 1930, membership was drawn increasingly from the unemployed, and by 1932 the party estimated that three-fifths of its members were without work. An important element in the membership was the skilled worker, particularly in the building and metal trades. Many other party members were employed as transport workers, miners, and longshoremen.

The KPD was composed of younger elements of the German population than those found in the Social Democratic Party—or any of the conservative parties. The largest single age group was 25–45. In 1930 the average age of the KPD Reichstag deputies was 38 years in contrast to the average of 50 for the Social Democrats and 47 for the entire Reichstag. The membership of the KPD was predominately male; it had the lowest percentage of female voters of any political party in Germany.

## B. Organization

Until 1926 KPD organization was based on residential units called "groups of ten," which were the product of revolutionary traditionalism. The need for party reorganization was recognized in the period of stabilization when the basic appeals for revolution failed to attract or hold a consistent party membership. In 1925–6, the KPD adopted a functional organization based on the existence of "cells" or "nuclei," and grouped on a hierarchical principle into a centrally-controlled party. The function of the cells was to direct the work of members and to spread Communist influence by attempting to gain control of associations.

The chief emphasis was placed on the occupational cells (*Betriebszelle*), which were founded in various enterprises, such as factories. Since party members were usually articulate and aggressive, they were able to exercise an influence out of proportion to their numerical strength. The existence of factory cells was based on the theory that the proletarian revolution depended on the strength of the Communists in factories and associations rather than in formal parliamentary groupings. The duty of the factory cells was to advance the cause of revolution by seeking to control the trade unions and works' councils, but the risks involved in the opposition of the owners and the trade unions caused many members of the nuclei to remain passive.

In addition to the factory cells, the KPD had a residential form of organization in the street cell to include people not qualified for membership in the occupational groups. Although thousands of street cells were formed, they were not as active as the factory cells. Communist officials charged that their members were passive and permitted the officials to do the required work. The International report of 1931 complained that fewer than 40 percent of the members of street cells attended meetings and only half of these participated in group discussions. The street cells became increasingly important with the growth of unemployment, but, in the Communist view, the tactical importance of the street cell was less than that of the factory nuclei.[5]

The use of cells to establish leadership among the workers and capture the control of existing associations was hindered by the relative weakness of the cells in the large factories. The KPD groups were concentrated in the smaller factories, their strongest position being in plants employing between one hundred and five hundred workers. The secretary of the International, Piatnitzky, stated that as a general rule the Communist influence was less in the larger factories. The figures for 1926 show that the nuclei in 75 percent of the factories in the Berlin-Brandenburg district consisted of one party member[6]. Factory cells were weakened by the decline in the percentage of employed factory members. The party ideal was a revolutionary organization of industrial workers, and in 1928 the ideal was approximated with 62 percent of the members employed in factories. The increase in unemployment after 1928 and the influx of other occupational groups, however, brought a rapid decline in this percentage, which dropped to 22 percent in 1931.[7]

The factory and street cells provided the base for the hierarchical organization of the KPD. The hierarchy followed the lines of the German electoral system to allow Communist participation in national and local elections. Both types of cell were combined into local groups (*Ortsgruppe*) and sections, each under the direction of a secretary and a committee representing the various units. In urban areas, the sections were grouped into municipal organizations, which in turn were united into districts (*Bezirke*) with a secretary, committee, and regional congress.

The highest organization of the party was the Central Committee in Berlin. The Committee was divided into a political bureau, organization office, and a secretariat, each office having full powers which could be annulled only by a plenary session of the committee. After the reorganization of the party in 1925–6, the Central Committee exercised complete control over the local party branches. The most important body was the "Polit-Bureau" which informed the lower cadres of policy changes and removed all oppositional elements. Only speakers chosen by the Polit-Bureau were permitted to explain party policy. Editorial committees of the party press and members of the regional committees also were chosen by the Bureau.

The principle of "democratic centralism" in party organization implied strict hierarchical control. Democratic action was possible in the early days of the party and local units were able to exercise pressure on the formation of ideology and tactics. But reorganization brought concentration of control, vested in the Polit-Bureau and the Central Committee, and with it the Committee lost its independence—because complete control of the KPD by the Third International was the result.

The numerous offices in the hierarchical organization tended to create a party bureaucracy. The officials were poorly paid, but generally were intensely loyal to the party and its aims. Communists elected to public office were required to turn their salaries over to the KPD treasury and received a party salary instead. The bureaucracy was important in supplying the continuing factor in the fluctuating membership.

## C. The KPD and Trade Unionism

The KPD policy towards trade unionism was determined by tactical changes in the Red International of Trade Unions (Profintern). After the German revolution, Communist unions were founded to compete with the Social Democrats. These unions (*Rote Gewerkschafts Internationale* or RGI) , directed for many years by Paul Merker, included organizations for miners, metal workers, building construction and transport workers, but they did not succeed in attracting any considerable number of German workers.[8] Changes in tactics in 1925–6 (see below p. 000) stressing the united front and infiltration of Communists into existing proletarian associations led to the abandonment of the RGI and severance of all connections with the Profintern. Party members were instructed to enter the free unions, establish cells and strive for control of the local factory council. But they did not achieve their objective; although strong in specific unions, they did not gain control of any single union. The slogan, "Join the Unions," was replaced soon after 1926 by a new slogan, "Create Revolutionary Opposition," a policy which culminated in the founding of the RGO (*Rote Gewerkschafts Opposition*) under the leadership of Paul Merker. The RGO consisted originally of party members expelled from trade unions for their radical tactics, but it welcomed any worker who subscribed to the Communist program. Merker's plan was to develop the dual unions to compete with free unions in the works' council elections. Unions were established in the greatest areas of Communist strength (metal workers, transport and building). However, according to party statistics, its membership was 250,000 in contrast to the five million members in the Social Democratic unions. The greatest strength of the RGO was in Berlin and the Ruhr.

## D. Affiliated Bodies

The KPD possessed a number of affiliated groups which attempted to spread Communist influence and create a mass support among the German people. One of the most important was the Communist youth movement (*Kommunistische Jugendverband* or KJVD), affiliated with the Communist Youth International in Moscow. The organization of the KJVD paralleled the hierarchical structure of the party and contained approximately 30,000 members. Cells were founded in factories, schools, sports associations, and similar institutions.[9] Outstanding members were sent to party schools for training in party tactics and dialectics. The young Communists also had a fighting organization called *Rote Jugendfront* (RJF) which was affiliated with the *Rote Frontkämpfer Bund* (see below). It was a paramilitary organization containing 22,000 members at the time of its dissolution in 1929. The rate of fluctuation in the youth organizations was greater than in the party, averaging as high as 50 percent a year.[10]

The fighting organization of the party was the *Rote Frontkämpfer Bund* (RFB) containing approximately 150,000 men who engaged in the political tactics of street fighting. The RFB was founded in Halle in 1924. Spreading to other cities, it soon developed a central organization which controlled the membership by military discipline. A specialized unit known as the *Rote Marine* operated in the coastal cities. The RFB operated as a preparatory school for party membership in addition to serving as the paramilitary force in protecting the party interests. It was declared illegal in Prussia in 1929 and later in the entire Reich by the Social Democratic government, but continued to operate as an illegal body.[11]

Numerous other organizations existed under KPD direction and control. One of the distinctive organizations was *Rote Hilfe*, which provided legal aid for those accused of political crime and assisted families of men killed in the street fighting. *Rote Hilfe* had about a half million members and published its own newspapers and periodicals, as *Der Rote Helfer* and *Tribunal*. The chief woman's organization of the KPD was the *Rote Frauen und Mädchen Bund*, organized and directed for many years by Klara Zetkin. The party also formed many functional and occupational groups (as unemployed councils, sports associations, singing societies, chess clubs) and specific action committees (as Committee for the Defense of the Scottsboro Boys). In 1930, the various party organizations were united into the *Kampfbund gegen den Faschismus* under Hermann Remmele. The *Kampfbund* contained thirty-two affiliated organizations and approximately 100,000 members. Its periodical was *Die Fanfare*.

## E. The Communist Press

One of the most important means of KPD propaganda was the party press. Numerous papers were owned and operated by the party's holding company, *Peuvag A–G*, throughout Germany. The leading paper was *Rote Fahne* in Berlin which was the organ of the Central Committee and carried official pronouncements. In addition to the papers in the major cities, the party issued *Kopfblätter* in the smaller towns which were identical with one of the leading papers, appearing either with a local title or a page of local news. Factory papers and flysheets were published by the KPD cells and were sold either at low cost or distributed free. The chief affiliated groups likewise published their own papers.

In terms of circulation the party had an important propaganda arm in the semi-official press owned and operated by Willy Münzenburg and the *Kosmos-Verlag* and with a circulation more than double that of the official party press. The chain included such important papers and periodicals as *Welt am Abend* (Berlin), *Berlin am Morgen, Neue Montagszeitung, Unsere Zeit* and *Arbeiter Illustrierte*.[12]

## III. The Contest for Votes

The growth of the political power of the KPD shows a continuous development except in the Reichstag election of December 1924. From small beginnings the party increased its popular support until 1932 when it polled nearly six million votes. The following table shows the growth of the Communist vote in the national elections as compared with that of the Social Democrats:

| | *KPD vote* | *KPD seats in Reichstag* | *KDP percent of total vote* | *Social Dem percent of total* |
|---|---|---|---|---|
| June, 1920 | 441,800 | 4 | 1.7% | 21.6 |
| May, 1924 | 3,693,100 | 62 | 12.6 | 20.5 |
| Dec. 1924 | 2,708,300 | 45 | 9.0 | 26.0 |
| May, 1928 | 3,263,400 | 54 | 10.6 | 29.8 |
| Sept. 1930 | 4,590,200 | 77 | 13.1 | 24.5 |
| July, 1932 | 5,369,700 | 89 | 14.6 | 21.6 |
| Nov. 1932 | 5,980,600 | 100 | 16.9 | 20.4 |
| March, 1933 | 4,848,100 | 81 | 12.3 | 18.3 |

Even in the Nazi-coerced election of 1933, the KPD polled nearly five million votes. Its losses in this election, however, were greater than those of the Social Democrats.

The main strength of the party vote was centered in the metropolitan and industrial districts, as Communism did not gain a foothold among the peasants and the residents of small towns. The popular vote was concentrated in Berlin and the densely-populated areas of western and northwestern Germany. The Communists were particularly strong in Berlin, where the party drew 38 percent of the popular vote in the 1932 elections.[13] As early as 1924, the KPD had replaced the Social Democratic party as the expression of left-wing opinion in Merseburg and Düsseldorf. In addition to these districts, the KPD outvoted the Social Democrats after 1930 in the following *Wahlkreise*: Berlin, Potsdam I and II, Oppeln, Westfalen Nord and Süd, Köln-Aachen, and Baden. These districts, with the exception of Baden, were centers of industrial activity and were vitally affected by the depression and unemployment after 1930.

The popular strength of the KPD was registered in Reichstag and presidential elections rather than in local contests. The Communists never equalled the Social Democratic vote in state elections, although the party had a strong representation in the *Landtage* of Prussia, Saxony, Hamburg, and Bremen. The KPD found its strength only when it could raise broad national issues or advocate plans for revolutionary change of the entire social order.

## IV. Ideology and Tactics

During the Weimar period, the ideology and tactics of the KPD were marked by numerous major changes. The KPD played a dual role in German politics. It essentially was an organization applying the Marxist-Leninist philosophy of revolution to the German situation and was a faithful member of the Third International. At the same time it was a German political party, subject to local pressures and interests which did not necessarily find an exact expression in the ideology emanating from the Soviet Union. The KPD always was faced with the problem of equating these two forces. The efforts led the KPD to advocate many contrasting types of political action, as shown by the various stages of the party's ideological development.

### A. The Spartacists[14]

In the German revolution of 1918–1919, the one group with a definite revolutionary program was the Spartacist League. It was composed of representatives of many shades of revolutionary opinion in the German working-class and the left-wing of the Social Democrats who were resolved that the result of the revolution should not be the establishment of a bourgeois republic. The leaders of the Spartacists were experienced and trained in the German labor movement and for many years had expressed the revolutionary opposition to the policy of the Social Democrats. They denounced the Majority Socialists as guilty of "social patriotism and chauvinism" and the Independent Socialists as "petty bourgeois pacifists." The Spartacist ideology, which began to take shape in the Spartacist Letter of 1915, held that a revolution was necessary, but that it should be the spontaneous expression of the revolutionary enthusiasm of the masses and not the work of a few professionals. Rosa Luxemburg and Karl Liebknecht regarded the Soldiers and Workers Councils of 1918–1919 not only as the democratic expression of the revolutionary will, but as representing the armed power of the workers. The association of the Spartacists and the councils in 1919 aroused the opposition of the Social Democrats as well as the conservatives, who feared the "Bolshevization" of Germany. As a result, the Free Corps responded to Gustav Noske's appeal in 1919 to suppress the

Spartacist disorders, during which the Spartacist leaders were killed. This action widened the gulf between the Spartacists and the Republic, and the newly-formed KPD resolved to abstain from any participation in the parliamentary elections on the grounds that elections would only postpone the revolution. The German delegation to the Second World Congress of the Communist International argued that if elections could be prevented by force, the proletarian revolution would follow. They asserted that Communists should wage a "permanent offensive" against capitalism and its political institutions.

The Spartacist leaders advocated a democratic organization of the party in which all groups would participate in the formation of policy. They opposed the Leninist theory of the party as the "vanguard of the proletariat" and the International as the director of worker's revolutions. The Spartacist form of organization remained in the KPD until the "Bolshevization of the party" in 1925–6; then the Spartacist viewpoint on organization and tactics was denounced as "Luxemburgism" and its advocates expelled from the party.

## B. The Defensive Period, 1919–23

After the crushing of the Spartacist uprisings throughout Germany by the Free Corps, the KPD renounced the offensive theory and in October 1919 decided to participate in the parliamentary system. This action was the work of Paul Levi, a former Social Democrat with long experience in German labor politics. Levi was faced with the problem of the growing dependence of the party on the Comintern for its ideological line and political tactics. Although he agreed with the resolution of the International in 1921 renouncing the theory of immanent revolution and ordering the KPD to recognize the "defensive" nature of the struggle for proletarian liberation, Levi found it increasingly hard to be relatively independent of Comintern control.

The issue of control was raised in 1920 when the left-wing of the Independent Social Democratic Party (USPD) joined the Communists. The program drawn up for the admittance of the USPD, known as the "Twenty-One Conditions," called for the elimination of reformists from party posts and trade unions, a continuous fight against "imperialism," obedience to the International, and complete support of the USSR. Levi opposed this line but was forced to accept, and after criticizing the strike activity of Communist unions in 1921 he was removed from the Central Committee. After that time, no one remained on the Committee who did not agree implicitly with the decisions of the International.

The defensive policy not only recognized the political realities in Germany but reflected primarily the change in the policy of the USSR from War Communism to the New Economic Policy. Between 1920 and 1923, the KPD showed a tendency to cooperate with other political groups. After the removal of Levi, the leadership was in the hands of Heinrich Brandler, August Thalheimer, Jacob Walcher and Paul Frölich, who represented a conciliatory attitude towards the Social Democrats.

## C. The Revival of Activism 1923

The internal and external situation of 1923 gave the KPD an opportunity to revive its revolutionary tactics. The inflation had reached its high point, creating a situation among the German people which easily found expression in violent action. Occupation of the Ruhr gave the KPD an opportunity to denounce the capitalist powers of Western Europe and assume the role of the defenders of German national sovereignty. Many left-wing elements in the party agitated for revolutionary action in 1923, but on orders from Moscow the Central Committee refused to permit insurrections. Under the reformist leadership of Brandler, the KPD forbade mention of "the dictatorship of the proletariat" or socialist revolution.

In October 1923 the Comintern changed its policy to order the KPD to lead the revolution which it believed to be impending. Communist deputies entered the Social Democratic cabinets in Saxony and Thuringia, and preparations were made for insurrections in Berlin and Hamburg. The Central Committee, however, recognized that the KPD was not prepared to lead a revolution, and on advice from Moscow the plans were cancelled, although couriers failed to reach Hamburg in time to prevent an abortive insurrection. The Reichswehr dispersed the governments of Saxony and Thuringia. The policy of the Committee embittered many party members and strengthened the left-wing in its opposition to the reformism of Brandler. At the party congress in Frankfurt in 1924, the left-wing gained a majority and a new leadership emerged, including Ruth Fischer, Arkadi Maslow, and the leader of the Hamburg insurrection, Ernst Thälmann.

The outstanding ideological development in 1923 was the adoption of the theory of National Bolshevism by many elements in the KPD.[15] National Bolshevism was a product of the war and revolution. It began to take definite shape in the work of two Hamburg Communists, Heinrich Laufenberg and Fritz Wolfheim, whose brochure, *Grundlinien proletarischer Politik*, published in 1915, denounced the parliamentary methods of the Social Democrats and held that the proletariat could influence foreign and domestic policy only through the army. Many followers of Laufenberg and Wolfheim joined the Spartacist movement, but after a conflict with the party machine they formed a splinter group called the Communist Workers Party (KAPD). The chief center of National Bolshevist activity was Hamburg, where in 1922 the *Bund für Volk, Freiheit und Vaterland* was founded. Similar groups were established in Berlin and Munich.

Until 1923, National Bolshevism was condemned by Lenin and the KPD as "infantile leftism." The exponents of the theory attempted to form a working alliance with bourgeois groups and army officers to combine the aims of peace system destruction and German revolution into a single policy. Their policy was based on close relations with Soviet Russia in a common front against the policy of the western European states and the bourgeois German government. The National Bolshevist appeals found wide acceptance among army officers and the Free Corps who were advocating an eastern orientation in German foreign policy as well as in Communist circles. These divergent groups found a common ground in the National Bolshevist acceptance of Russian aid in the fight against the peace settlement and the Weimar government, the opposition to which was so strong in nationalist circles that they were willing to accept an anti-capitalist revolution as an alternative to Social Democratic rule and foreign controls.

When the French occupied the Ruhr in 1923 many Communists engaged in militant opposition along with the Free Corps. A group led by Heinz Neumann (later a member of the Central Committee) cooperated with the Free Corps in fighting the separatist movement in the Rhineland. Sensing the nationalistic reaction in Germany at the time, the Central Committee in Berlin reversed its stand on National Bolshevism and began to advocate some of its basic conceptions. A new slogan was coined—"Beat Poincaré on the Rhine and Cuno on the Spree."

Karl Radek, who had published a pamphlet, *Gegen den Nationalbolshewismus*, in 1921, declared in a stirring speech at the time of the execution of the Free Corps leader and early Nazi martyr, Leo Schlageter, that Communists must cooperate with nationalists in destroying the exploitation of Germany by foreign capitalists. Klara Zetkin declared that since the proletariat had no fatherland it would have to conquer Germany. The editors of *Rote Fahne* asked the reactionary aristocrat, Count Reventlow, to contribute an article on his plan for a Russo-German alliance and war against France. Nazi speakers were invited to address Communist gatherings. Posters appeared linking the swastika and the Soviet star: Ruth Fischer declared that Jewish capitalism must be destroyed.

### D. The Return to Gradualism

With the French withdrawal from the Ruhr and the stabilization of currency, KPD appeals for revolution found no wide acceptance. The popular vote of the party suffered a serious decline in 1924, and membership in the party and trade unions decreased to the lowest point since 1920.

The failure of Communist tactics in 1923, and the new orientation in the internal policy of the Soviet Union, led to a change in KPD policy.

The chief result of the tactics of 1923 was the emergence of a "left-wing" leadership, which included Ruth Fischer, Arkadi Maslow and Ernst Thälmann. After 1924 some of these leaders were expelled (e.g., Ruth Fischer) and a leadership was established which followed the directions of the International. The struggle within the KPD paralleled the Stalin-Trotzky contest for power in the Soviet Union. The process of expelling the leftist elements in the KPD involved the entire reorganization of the party and the establishment of the absolute power of the Central Committee. The power granted to the Polit-Bureau was assurance that opposition would not be permitted to arise in the future.

The object of KPD tactics in this period of stabilization was the extension of its mass influence by the creation of various organizations (see above p. 000) and expansion of the so-called *Einheitsfront*. The competitive Communist trade unions were abandoned and members were urged to enter the free unions to establish cells. Party members infiltrated into existing associations and attempted to gain control.

Although the KPD dropped its activist program at this time, it did not cease opposing the Social Democratic Party. The *Rot Frontkämpfer Bund*, under the nominal leadership of Thälmann, fought the Socialists on the streets until the organization finally was dissolved by the Prussian Government in 1929. In this period, the chief factor affecting Communist relations with the Weimar government was the problem of foreign policy. The party held, as did Soviet diplomacy, that the western orientation in Stresemann's foreign policy and the security system revolving around the Locarno Treaties was a threat to the Soviet Union.[16] In 1927, Stresemann accepted, for Germany, a seat in the Council of the League of Nations. At the party congress in the same year, each member of the KPD was required to take an oath to support the USSR. National Bolshevist ideas were revived in the election of 1928, and the KPD served as the party of protest against the internal economic policy of the Republic and the western orientation in its foreign policy. While the party increased its vote in these elections, it did not recover the losses suffered after 1923.

### E. "The Third Period"

In 1928, the Third International proclaimed the end of the period of stabilization and the beginning of *the "third period" which would mark the downfall of capitalism.* A new policy was adopted by the party at its congress in 1929, which was executed by the surviving leaders of 1923 - Thälmann, Remmele, and Neumann. It was directed specifically against the

Social Democrats, and to gain support the KPD revived the National Bolshevist line. The trade union policy was changed to permit the establishment of the RGO (see above p. 000) to compete with the Social Democratic unions.

The Communist leaders viewed the depression as being the fulfillment of their prophecies and the creator of a revolutionary situation. Official policy was affected by the growing number of unemployed, who not only doubled the membership of the party but also created a reservoir of revolutionary material. The Nazis and the KPD competed for the political support of the unemployed, leading to a radicalized program which served to widen the gulf between the Communists and the great mass of Social Democratic workers. The KPD list of enemies read "Capitalists, Fascists, Social Democrats." The term "Social Fascist" was used by the KPD to stigmatize the Social Democrats as "the deadly enemy of the working class."[17]

One of the important concepts in KPD ideology during the depression was the "people's revolution." Formulated in the Comintern, it was based on the necessity for a united front to combat Fascism, but one which was formed "from below" rather than by the leadership of a "bureaucratic" (i.e., Social Democratic) party. The united front was to be created by bringing the mass organizations of the German workers under a revolutionary leadership, setting up cadres of "political functionaries" in all factories, separating the Social Democratic workers from their leadership, and liquidating the mass influence of the Social Democratic party.[18] To achieve this objective, the KPD sponsored the formation of unemployed councils throughout Germany "to mobilize the masses of workers on the basis of their everyday struggles for its KPD political aims."[19] The miscellaneous party organizations were combined into the *Kampfbund gegen den Faschismus* (see above p. 000). The KPD thus agreed to participate in a united front if Communists were placed in key positions, an attitude exemplified by the statement of Ossip Piatnitzky, secretary of the Third International, that Social Democratic workers should be brought into such united front organizations as strike committees, "but, of course, not in such numbers as would put them in a majority."[20]

The party leaders found National Bolshevism to be useful in their fight against the Social Democrats. Taking advantage of the nationalist reaction to the peace terms, the KPD attempted to turn the popular opposition to the Versailles Treaty and the Young Plan to a pro-Soviet attitude by showing that the USSR was the only major state in Europe which had not accepted the peace settlement. The party program of 1930, entitled "Program for the National and Social Liberation of the German People" denounced the "thieving" Treaty of Versailles and denounced the Social Democrats as "traitors" for accepting it.[21] Thälmann argued that the record of the KPD in the opposition to the peace settlement gave the party the "right to march at the head of the national struggle for liberation."[22] A year later he declared that "only a workers' and peasants' republic in alliance with the Soviet Union could break the chains of national oppression."[23] He reconciled the support of nationalism with the internationalist basis of Communist theory by saying that "one cannot fight against the Versailles Treaty and Young slavery without unfurling the banner of internationalism."[24]

In following this policy, the KPD supported the referendum to dissolve the Prussian Government in 1931 on the grounds that the Social Democrats had betrayed the workers. Support was given to the Berlin transit strike called by the Nazis in 1932. In the same year Heinz Neumann explained the principles of National Bolshevism to a meeting sponsored by Goebbels. In fact, National Bolshevism attracted a number of officers and nationalists to membership in the KPD, such as Ludwig Renn (Arnold Vieth von Golsenau), Captain Beppo Römer (former chief of staff of the *Oberland Bund*), Bodo Uhse, Bruno von Saloman, Graf Stenbock-Fermor, and others.

Thus, in the period from 1919 to 1932, the KPD made many changes in public policy, ranging from "putschism" to regular parliamentary activity, and from internationalism to nationalism.

## V. The KPD Since 1933

Since its dissolution by the Nazis in 1933, the KPD has maintained an underground in Germany and the official structure of the party leadership abroad. The Central Committee moved to Moscow and many prominent members of the hierarchy escaped from Germany to carry on party work in various parts of the world. Party congresses were held in Czechoslovakia and Belgium after 1933, but with the general imposition of legal sanctions against Communist activity, the German movement centered in Moscow, London and Mexico City. In theory, the party leaders exercise control over underground members in Germany, but it is impossible to ascertain the effectiveness of that control. There is evidence, however, that the party underground knows of the changes in the official line and apparently approves the new directions in Communist policy.

The ideology and tactics of the party since 1933, like that of other Communist parties, followed the changes decreed by the Comintern. United front tactics were adopted in 1934 and German Communists supported the united front both in France and Spain. In 1939, the KPD supported the Soviet-German Non-Aggression Pact and denounced the Anglo-German war as "imperialistic." After the dissolution of the Comintern the KPD renounced the immediate goal of a proletarian revolution.

## A. The Communist Underground in Germany

The theory underlying the Communist underground in the period following the dissolution of the party was that the Nazi regime soon would collapse and be succeeded by a Communist state. For this reason, the KPD maintained its rigid, complex organization in the underground and insisted on mass propaganda. Party members infiltrated into Nazi formations and associations in order to take control when the collapse of National Socialism occurred. The party was able to engage in considerable illegal activity, but the underground was particularly vulnerable to Gestapo penetration. Heavy losses were suffered in the middle and lower cadres of party officials who remained. During the period of the German-Soviet Non-Aggression Pact (1939–41) Communist illegal activity practically disappeared, but was revived after the attack on the Soviet Union.[25]

The available intelligence indicates that since 1941 the Communist underground has increased its strength and activity and at present is the best organized and most effective opposition group in Germany. It is impossible, however, to judge its exact strength and distribution or the extent to which it may attract popular support. According to fragmentary reports, the underground is grouped in cells containing very few members whose chief duty is to maintain contact with each other.[26] Various camouflaged groups also may exist, but the important tactical unit is the cell. While there is no precise information on the composition of the cells, there are indications that they consist of a few older Communists, younger workers raised in Communist families, and recruits drawn from dissatisfied members of the Hitler Youth.[27] There also are indications that students are participating.

In spite of police controls which prevent organized and widespread opposition, the Communist cells have many opportunities for activity against the Nazis. Those in the factories can sabotage the Nazi war production, or persuade other workers to slow down their work. Sabotage can be affected, however, only on a small scale, and in view of the risks involved, the Communists have not advocated any extensive resistance. The cells also can be important in spreading defeatist attitudes through leaflets, illegal papers, and political discussion. The reports from Germany indicate that the Communists have engaged in this type of activity rather than direct sabotage. At various times, particularly in 1941 at the time of the outbreak of the war against the Soviet Union, and in 1943 during the great German reverses, the Gestapo has made wholesale arrests of "Communists" in attempting to eradicate both the actual and potential leadership of the underground. A new wave of arrests began in April 1944 following the speech of Gauleiter Wernicke complaining that low morale and rumors in Germany could be traced to listening to the Moscow and London radio.

The changing military position of Germany has increased the possibilities for illegal action. The increased duties of the security forces in the air war has tended to relax controls. While it is easy to overestimate the extent of opposition activity in Germany, demonstrations against the regime nevertheless have taken place. The peace demonstration in Hamburg following the air attacks in the fall of 1943 and the sporadic strikes in Western and Central Germany are examples. These situations give the KPD cells an opportunity to extend their influence and to establish leadership in anti-Nazi activity. The air war has made it possible for people to disappear or change their identity, and many "enemies of the state" have been able to continue their activity because of the destruction of records.[28]

There have been only general reports about the extent and distribution of the Communist underground. It apparently is concentrated in the traditional areas of party strength—Berlin and the industrial centers of Western and Central Germany. Specific groups have been identified as the *Navajos*, a Communist group which operates within the Hitler Youth,[29] the *Kommunistisches Jugend, Deutsche Friedens Bewegung*, and *Anti-Faschische Aktion*, which is concentrated in Berlin and the Rhineland. It is reported that in Wedding, the former great center of Communist strength, the Nazis have not been able to eradicate the Communist loyalties which are particularly strong among the construction workers and railwaymen. Other reports state that the *Internationale Arbeiter Hilfe* and *Rote Frontkämpfer Bund* continue to exist in illegal form. The Communists insist on the existence of independent cells as the best guarantee against police suppression.

Efforts have been made to keep the cells informed of the party work in Germany as a whole. An illegal paper called *Kader-Information* not only provides direction for the work of the cells, but also makes it possible for them to follow the party line.

### B. The Party Structure Abroad

In 1933 and after, many prominent officials of the KPD fled from Germany to establish centers of party activity abroad. In the 1930's, these centers were Czechoslovakia and France whence party officials, taking their orders from the Central Committee in Moscow, could direct underground activity in Germany. After the fall of Czechoslovakia and France, the party centers were moved to London and Mexico City.

The Central Committee of the KPD is located in Moscow. The leader of the party is Wilhelm Pieck, a member of the Committee since the days of Rosa Luxemburg, who was elected chairman at the Party Congress in Brussels (1935) to serve as long as Thälmann remains a prisoner of the Nazis. Associated with him are prominent Communists such as Walter Ulbricht, Erich Weinert, Friedrich Wolff and others who represent the highest surviving brackets of the party hierarchy. The Central Committee in Moscow apparently exercises the same rigid control over the party as it did before 1933.

In London there are approximately 350 registered members under the leadership of Wilhelm Koenen, a member of the Committee since 1920. Associated with him are many prominent Communists such as Karl Becker, Johann Fladung, and Hans Kahle. The London unit has been active in extending its influence among other groups and attempting to build an *Einheitsfront* in accordance with the current tactics of the party. The most significant achievement was the founding of the *Freie Deutsche Kulturbund* (1939), containing around 1,500 members, to preserve and develop the culture of a free and democratic Germany. The *Kulturbund* has followed the changes in the Communist line since 1939. Other organizations in which KPD members occupy prominent or leading positions are the *Freie Deutsche Hochschule, Freie Deutache Jugend*, Allies Inside Germany Council, and the War Aid Committee of German Refugee Women.

The KPD group in Mexico City is led by Ludwig Renn (Arnold Vieth von Golsenau), a prominent author and soldier whom the German Communists regard as "the military theorist of the KPD." The leading political theorist in Mexico City is Paul Merker. Other prominent members in Mexico City are Bodo Uhse, Anna Seghers, Ladizlo Radvanny (Johann Schmidt), Àndre Simon, and Erich Jungmann.

The KPD cannot function as a legal party in the United States, however, its influence is felt through "front" organizations, such as the German-American Emergency Conference, Joint Anti-Fascist Relief Committee, and the German-American Cultural League. The group in the United States and the few German Communists scattered in the Latin-American countries and Canada are under the direction of the organization in Mexico City. Small KPD groups exist in Sweden and South Africa.

## C. The Ideology of the KPD Since 1933

The policy of the KPD at present stands in marked contrast to the revolutionary program advocated by the party during the Weimar Republic. Yet, the policy is the result of the logical development of Communist tactics during the past ten years and reflects the new directions made necessary by the dissolution of the Comintern in 1943. Apparently the party discipline has been maintained, for the statements of policy made by prominent leaders in the emigration and the political attitudes of the underground follow the same pattern.

A distinct change in Communist tactics took place in the Brussels Congress of 1934. Resolutions adopted at that time declared that the "Program for the Social and National Emancipation of Germany (1930)

. . . . is now out of date" (see above pp. 000–00). The party justified its programs of 1930 and 1932 by saying that they served to unmask the "nationalist demagogy" of the Nazis. The Communist goal of 1935, however, still was oriented in national terms, calling for the complete annullment of the Versailles Treaty, the union of all territories taken from Germany by force into a "Free Germany," and close relations with the Soviet Union. The methods proposed to achieve this end were democratic—the establishment of political parties in Germany and freedom of political action, the right of association for workers and farmers, civil liberties, and the purging of Nazis from the army and state administration. The party made known its willingness to cooperate with Social Democrats, Centerists, dissident Nazis, or any group willing to fight against the Nazi regime.[30] Since the Brussels Congress, the KPD has continually stressed the nationalist theme as well.

The party broadcasts from Moscow since 1941 have characterized the Nazis as enemies of the German people and called for a revolt against Hitler to insure an "integral, individual, independent Germany, equal among equals."[31] Bismarck has been quoted frequently by the broadcasts to the effect that Germany and the Soviet Union must cooperate if both are to survive, and they have repeatedly warned that unless a popular revolt overthrows Hitler, the German army will be destroyed and Germany will face destruction.[32] Appeals have been sent in the name of the party to soldiers in the German army to lay down their arms and organize as they did in 1918 with "peasants, middle classes and all enemies of war . . . under workers' leadership. The soldiers must realize that they are fighting against the great socialist state and demand the end of the war."[33]

The Communist objective of a "Free Democratic Germany" in which the people are free to choose the regime they want is pictured as the spontaneous and democratic demand of the German people. This line has been stressed by German Communists throughout the world in the publicity given to the conference of the German Peace Movement (*Deutsche Friedens Bewegung*), held "in a Rhenish city" in December 1942. The meeting was publicized in the Communist press of the United States and Mexico in January 1943, and provided the incentive for many steps in Communist tactics—the statement of policy by Paul Merker in his pamphlet *Was Wird aus Deutschland*, the growth of the Free German movement, and the appeals by the Austrian Communist, Ernst Fischer, from Moscow for the formation of a similar movement in Austria.[34] The widely-publicized Rhineland program was drawn up by a conference said to include many types of people. According to Communist press reports it consisted of professional men, workers, a Catholic priest, small business men, a *Wehrmacht* captain, Nazi opposition groups, Social Democrats, Communists, German nationalists, peasants, Centerists, representatives of illegal trade unions, all united into a "National German Front."[35] Their duty is to organize a struggle within Germany against the Nazi regime for "only the mounting activity of the Germans themselves . . . can save Germany from a most terrible fate." The United Nations were urged to give publicity to the manifesto of the conference in radio programs and leaflets to encourage "our Allies inside Germany" to revolt. In this way, said the manifesto, a just peace can be concluded "guaranteeing Germany's independence and national existence." The continuation of the war, it declared, would turn Germany into a theater of operations and "the harder will be the terms of peace . . . a second Versailles."

The ten-point program outlined the steps for the overthrow of Hitlerism and the establishment of a "national democratic peace government" by a constituent assembly on the basis of equal and direct suffrage and the secret ballot. The program called for the immediate end of military operations, renunciation of all conquests, liquidation of the Nazi regime, disbandment of the SS and Gestapo, and punishment of war criminals. The economic program included the abrogation of all Nazi economic laws and the creation of a new system based on the constitutional protection of private property and freedom of development for small and medium enterprises. The workers were promised jobs, fair wages, the eight-hour day and the right to rest. A foreign policy of "collaboration with all peoples and states" was promised for the new Germany—a Germany which "will not be a weak and defenseless state; it will be a strong state backed by the unity and freedom of the people."

The advocacy of the creation of a broad national front has been utilized in Communist tactics in other countries, as Italy, Hungary and Austria. The stress on nationalism and democratic methods is the logical development of the Brussels program. The Rhineland manifesto did not single out any social group for special consideration, such as the workers, but proposed a program which could be supported by many groups which the KPD formerly opposed. The Communists have renounced their plans for a "Soviet Germany." They also say that they do not wish to reestablish the type of government and social system found in the Weimar Republic but advocate a new type of democracy which would seek to protect the German national interest and not the interests of any particular social class.

The available intelligence concerning the political orientation within Germany indicates that many members of the Communist underground share the view of the Rhineland manifesto and the refugee party organization in seeking a new direction. A distinction should be drawn in the German underground between the "old" and the "new" opposition. The "old" opposition consists largely of older people who had adult political experience before 1933 and seek to revive the forms and attitudes of the old political parties. The "new" opposition seeks to create new political forms and groups, motivated by the slogan "No repetition of Weimar." Although traces of the pre-1933 ideology may remain among the older Communist families, the activist members of the underground represent the viewpoint of the new opposition.[36] The reports from Germany and the interrogation of prisoners agree that the Communists do not want the reconstruction of the "Bolshevist" viewpoints and organization of the past. Instead they want a "German Communism" with the benevolent protection of the USSR, providing the means for the achievement of the Communist objectives while preserving the freedom of action which the party enjoyed under the Weimar government.[37] Prisoner-of-war party members who have been interrogated agree with a former underground organizer that the German Communists want a "liberal, democratic Communism" which does not advocate extremist measures.[38]

The party in Germany nevertheless has continued to be subject to the same type of split and factionalism which marked its history in the Weimar Republic. Many Communists are reported to disagree with the official party line of *Volksfront* democracy and moderate demands. These so-called "new Communists" refuse to abandon the ideal of proletarian dictatorship or to compromise their internationalist approach. They vigorously denounce the party tactics of cooperating with the generals in the Free Germany Committee (see below p. 000). The "new Communists" represent a left opposition to the official line and probably will bear the label of "Trotzkyites" in the future.[39] Another group, followers of the late Heinz Neumann, agree with the official party line in accepting the aid of the generals and in establishing an alliance with the Soviet Union, but wish to combine these moves with a revolution in Germany. This group is the chief exponent of National Bolshevism, which Heinz Neumann advocated from 1923 to 1933, but is not an opposition group as there are no irreconcilable differences between it and the official party line.

## VI. The Communist Party and the Free German Movement

The most important factor affecting both the current policy and the future of the Communist party is the development of the Free German movement. In the National Committee of Free Germany in Moscow, the Communists have found partners for a "united front" to replace the usual organizations and parties of the working-class. The formation and operation of Free German movements outside of Moscow is the work of Communist refugees. Although the original purpose of the Committee may have been psychological warfare against the Nazis, it has found surprising strength among German exiles. Numerous favorable repercussions to its propaganda have been reported in Germany.

The Free German Committee in Moscow, formed in July 1943, is a combination of Communist party members, anti-Nazis without political affiliation, officers and soldiers of the German army, and Nazis who foresee the possibility of German defeat. It invites to membership any individual or group desiring the overthrow of the Nazi regime and establishment of a free, democratic Germany. As a result, many interests and social groups are represented on the Committee, now under the leadership of Erich Weinert, a Communist writer. The head of its important affiliate, the Officers Union, is General von Seydlitz, defeated at Stalingrad and an advocate of the Eastern orientation in the German army. These two men together direct regular broadcasts to Germany and supervise the extension of Free German organization among the prisoners in Russia.

The objective of the National Committee is the overthrow of Hitler, ending of the war, and negotiation of peace after renunciation of all Nazi conquests. The creation of a national government is promised which will be formed by "a fight for freedom by all classes of the German people" and army groups remaining faithful to the Fatherland. The Committee demands the punishment, and the confiscation of the property, of war criminals and the annulment of all Nazi laws which have an adverse effect on human dignity and freedom. It promises an economy based on freedom of opportunity and the sanctity of private property, with a social organization which would guarantee civil liberties and the right of association. The new government, they say, must be strong enough to win the peace and restore Germany's equal rights in international affairs.[40]

In a broadcast from Moscow on 20 January 1944, Oberleutnant Gerlach said that the Committee might be considered "Utopian." "You may wonder," he stated, "whether a Communist could unite for a common struggle with a German nationalist, or even a National Socialist . . . or even a general."[41] The Committee, however; is not Utopian, for it is based on historic precedents in German politics and on a realistic political orientation which may find a wide social basis in post-war Germany.

The relationship between the Communist party and the National Committee involves a consideration both of the origin and the structure of the movement. It was formed after many prisoner-of-war conferences in the Soviet Union dating from October 1941. The first such conference drew up a program which called for German military defeat and the overthrow of the Hitler regime. It was written in a form highly reminiscent of the 1930 Communist program for national and social liberation. The conference was made up of privates and non-commissioned officers. Walter Ulbricht of the Central Committee of the German Communist party became the representative of the party in a praesidium to be formed by other prisoner conferences. This action was repeated in other camps by privates and non-commissioned officers and was followed in March

1942 by the Conference of Junior Officers. In April, *Pravda* announced that 805 prisoners had signed an appeal urging the German people and army to overthrow Hitler.

The National Committee was formed on 11–12 July 1943 by the representatives of the prisoner conferences and the German Communists. The manifesto was signed by eleven officers none of whom was above the rank of major, eight soldiers, and eight prominent members of the German Communist party. The number of Communist sympathizers among the soldiers and officers is not known, although the privates were workers in Germany and one of them was a prominent organizer of illegal trade unions. The Officers Union, formed on 11 September 1943 under the chairmanship of von Seydlitz, issued a statement which agreed in principle with the manifesto of the National Committee. After hearing Committee members explain their views, the officers decided to join it and von Seydlitz was made co-chairman with Weinert. Other officials of the Officers Union were incorporated into the leadership of the National Committee.

In places other than Moscow, the formation of Free German Committees has been the work of exiled German Communists. Early in 1943, prior to the establishment of the National Committee in Moscow, *Freies Deutschland* was inaugurated in Mexico City by Ludwig Renn and Paul Merker. The movement grew rapidly and by September 1943, the Mexican group had succeeded in uniting anti-Nazi groups in fourteen countries in the Western Hemisphere into the Latin-American Committee of Free Germans (*Comite Latine Americano de Alemans Libres*). The German Communists in Mexico exercise a control over the subsidiary organizations and have been active in disseminating Communist objectives. Renn stated that agreement on the Free German program has "entailed concessions and sacrifices of some of the basic beliefs of all parties represented," but the necessary accommodations have been made in the articles of the publication *Freies Deutschland* to bring the views of the Communist leaders into line with the program of the National Committee in Moscow. Renn denied that the Latin-American Committee is affiliated with the Moscow Committee, but is "in accord with the declarations of their program."

The Free German Committee in London was formed on 25 September 1943 after a long correspondence with the Mexican group on policies and methods. Due to the strong representation of Social Democrats in London, however, the Communists have made little headway in attracting non-Communists to support their objectives. The Committee was formed largely through the efforts of Wilhelm Koenen, a member of the Central Committee of the KPD since 1920, and Hugo Graef, prominent as a Communist trade union organizer since 1919. The president of the Committee is Dr. R. R. Kuczynski who has long been known as a Communist sympathizer. In addition to the Communists, the original Committee included two Social Democrats, Karl Rawitzki and Frau Schreiber-Krieger, who joined despite the orders of their party; W. von Siemsen of the *Nationale Volkspartei*; August Weber, president of the *Staatspartei* and several others with no definite political affiliation. Later another Social Democrat, Viktor Schiff (former editor of *Vorwärts*) and a Catholic priest, Father Taussig, joined.[42] The objectives of the London Committee as stated in a policy leaflet distributed 11 November 1943 include the building of a "National Freedom Front" to fight Hitler to be formed along the same lines advocated by the Rhineland Peace Manifesto. The Committee also wished to collaborate in Allied written and spoken propaganda to Germany and ultimately to establish "an independent propaganda from Free Germans to Germans." Koenen's offer to help the BBC in the formulation of its German programs, however, was not accepted.

Communists in Stockholm also established a Free German group which received the support of Fritz Tarnow and his circle of trade unionists. It is opposed by the official German Social Democratic Party in Sweden. Unlike the groups in Mexico City and London, the Stockholm group could find a basis of agreement only as a cultural society and not as a group with political objectives. The Committee, founded by Max Hodann in November 1943, was replaced 20 January 1944 by the Free German Cultural Society, also headed by Hodann.[43] The issue on which the first organization was destroyed was a resolution calling on all Germans to support the restoration and physical reconstruction of the Soviet Union after the war even if it involved the shipment of German labor. Those who opposed the resolution were denounced by the Communists as "saboteurs" of the Allied war effort.[44] The Cultural Society avoids such issues and concentrates on lectures and discussions on German science and literature.

There are reports that a Free German committee has been founded in Helsinki by Germans who wished to be evacuated but were refused permission by the German ambassador. The Helsinki group is said to consist of members of the *Deutsche-Verein* who several years ago opposed the formation of the Nazi-controlled *Deutsche Kolonie Verein*. The formation of a Free German committee in Switzerland also has been reported.

Communists in the Free German movement have found it necessary to change their line in order to accommodate the developments in the discussion of the terms of peace to be imposed on Germany. In London, several members of the Committee have resigned in protest over the issue of Communist control and the nature of the peace they advocate, while in Moscow and Mexico City the Free German propaganda has been altered to agree with the anticipated tenor of the peace terms.

The chief issue now is the problem of German territorial losses and war guilt. The earlier distinctions between the Nazis and the German people in Free German propaganda have broken down, and the Communists in London and Mexico City state that "the German people as a whole must bear the consequences of Nazi domination."[45] There is no indication by the Moscow Committee that the issue of war guilt has been broadened to include all the Germans, but von Seydlitz is one of the few who continues to draw the distinction by blaming the SS for the atrocities committed during the war.[46] Since the Mexican group often has been used to express new lines in official policy, the Communists on the Moscow Committee may adopt the ideas of Merker and the London group.

The problem of the transfer of territory has brought to light a major split in the London Committee. The demands made by the Union of Polish Patriots in Moscow for the transfer of East Prussia and Upper Silesia to Poland found a favorable response in Communist circles, although such action conflicts with the aims of the Free German movement, as stated in 1943, to protect the German nation against a hard peace. Even as late as 3 February 1944, the London Committee passed a resolution against the advice of the Communist members urging the maintenance of German territorial integrity "within the 1933 frontiers." The change in the Communist line, as well as in Free German propaganda, began to take shape after the Teheran Conference. After the publicity given to the demands of the Union of Polish Patriots, the Communists openly approved the transfer of German territory. In London, a resolution was introduced by the Communist members calling specifically for the cession of East Prussia, but it was not brought to a vote because of the opposition of the non-Communist members. Nevertheless, the March issue of *Freie Tribüne*, the Committee's official paper, stated that the guarantee against future German aggressions required the cession of land to Poland. An article refuting this viewpoint was refused by the editors on the grounds that any criticism of the decisions of the Teheran Conference would endanger the "world alliance." Again in May, the *Tribüne* repeated the demands for the transfer of East Prussia, characterizing as "leftist" anyone who endorsed the application of the Atlantic Charter to Germany. Several members of the Committee submitted their resignation, leaving the Committee almost entirely Communist except for the two Social Democrats who were among the original members. Those who resigned were Viktor Schiff (Social Democrat), Father Taussig (Catholic), Leopold Ullstein (*Staatspartei*), August Weber (*Staatspartei*), Fritz Wolff, Heinrich Fraenkel, Artur Liebert, and Frau Imgard Litten.

The Communists in Mexico City likewise modified the conceptions which marked the early stages of the Free German movement. At the same time that the Union of Polish Patriots was demanding German territory, Merker's articles in *Freies Deutschland* intimated that since the German people were guilty they must make reparation for the crimes of the Nazis. Merker supported the Polish territorial demands in February 1944 on the grounds that a Poland with close relations to the Soviet Union must be built up as a security measure in Eastern Europe. He argued that Lenin's condemnation of the forceable transfer of territory did not rule out the necessity for granting "free" nations access to the sea. By their refusal to agree to the proposed territorial changes, Merker said that the Social Democrats were helping the destruction of Germany and thus could be classed with Lord Vansittart as "enemies of the German people."[47]

## VII. The Possible Future Role of the Communist Party

The future of the Communist party in Germany depends on such unknown factors as the nature of German defeat, the conditions which exist after the close of hostilities, and the possibilities of the adoption of its program by large numbers of the German people. The party has devised tactics based on the conditions and forces which it anticipates will exist.

An important basis for consideration of the future role of the KPD is the strength and activity of its underground. The Communists apparently have the best organized and most effective underground in Germany. Its cells are organized on a local basis in various places, particularly in the factories, and their illegal activity has given them a measure of prestige among anti-Nazi Germans. At the present time, the Communist underground opposes widespread activity and sabotage because of the fear of detection and suppression. As the military situation of Germany deteriorates and internal controls weaken, the underground may be able to play an important role either in the overthrow of Hitler or the liquidation of the Nazi regime under military occupation. The tactics proposed by the Communists and the Free German Committees would give the party's underground a vantage point for the creation of political leadership. In December 1943 the National Committee advocated the formation of "combat committees" in factories, Nazi organizations and formations, and the army for the purpose of organizing the people against Hitler. Their plan called for a "passive resistance" against the Nazis rather than an open revolt. The appeal on 11 June 1944 called for "people's committees" in all urban and rural areas to wage a "national struggle," but did not advocate an open revolt against the Nazis.[48] The existence of Communist cells which are active in the anti-Nazi struggle would make them important as leaders of people's committees and as nuclei around which local political association could be made following the Nazi collapse.

Since the beginning of 1944 the Free German movement has been active within Germany and in the army in preparing a revolt against Hitler. Representatives of the National Committee are present as "front delegates" in combat zones on the Eastern front to discuss politics with any prisoner who cares to consult them.[49] According to Weinert, "hundreds of thousands" of prisoners have subscribed to the Free German manifesto. Regular broadcasts are beamed to Germany and loud speakers have been installed on the front; many reports from Germany indicate the effectiveness of this propaganda in undermining popular support of the Nazis. Free German leaflets are distributed among German troops on the Eastern front, as well as in Italy and France and among the civilian population in Germany. It is reported that "soldiers' committees" have been formed among the German troops in France, publishing regular newspapers as *Soldat im Weste, Soldat am Mittelmeer (Organ der Soldaten Organisation in Frankreich*) and *Volk und Vaterland*. Although the regular appearance of the publications indicates they may be produced by the French underground, they repeat the arguments of the National Committee and quote its principal members.[50] The Free German activities have been widely distributed, but reactions among the soldiers cannot be measured at this time, except for specific denunciations by prisoners who have heard of the movement and question its patriotic motives. Apparently the Free German propaganda has made little impression as yet on the average soldier, although it may be involved in the current high rate of desertion. Its importance lies in the effect on higher officers, civil servants, and the Communists within Germany.

The Communist tactics call for definite action by the party in the period of military occupation. In 1943, the Communist groups inside Germany and in the Free German movement decided to oppose military occupation by subversive action.[51] After the question of the peace conditions was settled at the Teheran Conference, the line was changed and the occupation forces are now hailed as "armies of liberation." The current tactics are based on the assumption that the period of military occupation will be a transitional phase between the liquidation of the Nazi regime and the establishment of a new German political life.

The party foresees the liquidation of the Nazis "and the big capitalists behind them," but stresses that it must not take any responsibility for the "blood bath" which may result from popular wrath against the Nazis. There is to be no interference with farmers or middle classes who will play an important part in the *Volksfront* democracy. The party assumes a tripartite division will be made of Germany for military occupation and proposes that agitation be carried on in the British and American zones against military occupation but not to the point of endangering relations between the Allies. The agitation is to emphasize that better living conditions and greater political liberty exist in the Soviet zone of occupation. The party is to give every assistance to the Soviet occupation forces and attempt to gain recruits.[52] Although these tactics may be changed by the course of events prior to the defeat and occupation of Germany, they represent the manner in which the party hopes to establish its position as a political force. The future of the party depends on the extent to which these tactics can be applied to the German and international situation and the support they draw from the German population.

The Communists operating through the Free German Committee propose a social order which is designed to appeal to many groups of people. The program for the transitional period does not endanger the vested interests of any group except the Nazis and war criminals. It is based on the assumption, which has been expressed by Communist writers, that after the war the German people will not accept extremist political solutions such as the party advocated before 1933. The basic recurrent theme in the intelligence from Germany is that the German people are "tired" and not interested in political activity, thus giving an advantage to activist political groups such as the Communists.

Both the Free German and Communist programs are devised to appeal to a defeated population. In stressing German nationalistic history as an important basis of their ideology, the Communists apparently hope to provide compensations for defeat and a foundation for the reconstruction of German power in Europe. The nationalistic appeals centering on the incidents of close relations with Russia as a source of military strength, as the Tauroggen Alliance of 1812[53] and the Bismarckian diplomacy, may find a response in the powerful army circles in Germany which advocate an eastern orientation. These groups may cooperate with the Communists as they have in the past and now do in the National Committee.

The potential appeal of the Free German-Communist program may be widened by the growing prestige of the Soviet Union in Germany. There have been many indications that a number of German civilians and soldiers refuse to accept Goebbels' propaganda picture of Russia as a backward, illiterate and barbarian country. While fear of "Bolshevism" and Russian occupation is still the dominant theme in the prisoner-of-war interrogations, there is a tendency on the part of many soldiers to disregard the official propaganda and recognize the military and cultural achievements of the Soviet Union.[54] Within Germany there has been a distinct change of feeling in regard to the Russian workers and prisoners who have won the sympathy of many Germans in local areas, while others say that the Russians do not make war on civilians by bombing the

German cities.[55] The Nazi officials say that Russians are the best of the foreign workers.

The Communists believe that their future in Germany is assured by the benevolent attitude of the Soviet Union. They assume that the party will be revived in the Soviet zone of occupation, and by its important political role will gain the recruits necessary to make it a major German party. If the party is revived in the Soviet zone, it will do so in what was previously the weakest area of Communist strength, and will add to the party strength in western and central Germany. The Communist party continues to be the most faithful exponent of Soviet policy in Germany. Although the Free German Committee has not been officially recognized by the Soviet Union except as a means of psychological warfare, and the Soviet authorities may not have a high opinion of German Communists,[56] the party can be expected to give unquestioning support to any policy which the Soviet Union may adopt towards Germany. In this sense, the Soviet Union may utilize the party in the implementation of its German policy just as it has in psychological warfare against the Nazis. If this occurs, the Communist party will have the advantage of external support which no other German political group now possesses.

Against the possibilities of a Communist revival in Germany are certain factors which may limit its political power after the war. The recent change in Communist line to support the hard peace, involving transfer of territory, reparations and the use of German labor for Soviet reconstruction, may affect its political strength in Germany. The Communists in this case followed the trends in Soviet policy at the expense of their earlier plans of protecting the integrity of Germany and drawing the distinction between Nazis and the German people in assessing guilt for the war. The political position in Germany of groups supporting a hard peace will depend largely on currents which develop during the defeat and occupation.

Another possible limitation lies in the relation of the party to the German labor movement and possible groupings of other political parties which may emerge. The renunciation of Socialist objectives, the institution of a program which caters to middle class interests, and cooperation with ex-Nazis and militarists, may serve to alienate the Communist party from working class support except for those members who would support the party under any conditions. In no way has the Social Democratic underground cooperated with the Communists, and in spite of the talk of unified trade unions, the historical differences between the two parties still persist. The Communist denunciation of the Social Democrats as "one-sided" because of their concentration on workers' interests may indicate that they have decided to solve the problem of numerical inferiority by seeking the support of other groups. The relations of the party to the labor movement cannot be ascertained until the program of the Social Democrats materializes. If the Communist party should be unable to control the majority of the workers in Germany, it is conceivable that it may again adopt National Bolshevism in order to attract the support of nationalistic groups. Indications of this trend may be seen in the German Officers Union in Moscow and its relations with the Communist members of the Free German Committee. If this, in turn, alienates mass support in the working-class, the Communist party may develop as a professional political group which uses various combinations of political interests to achieve power, depending for its ultimate strength on its real or supposed connection with the Soviet Union.

There is no reason to believe that the Free German movement will survive the period in which it serves the immediate ends of the Communist party, and without Communist participation, the National Committee would lack any mass support. The nature of Communist strategy implies that the Free German movement is regarded by the Communists as a transitional measure to operate during the defeat and period of military occupation. The policy of the party after that time is part of the problem of the future of Communist parties throughout the world.

# 14

Herbert Marcuse

# *THE SOCIAL DEMOCRATIC PARTY OF GERMANY*

(September 1, 1945)

Editor's note: R&A 1549. Marcuse's authorship is indicated in a memorandum sent on July 23, 1945, from Richard Hartshorne, head of the Projects Committee, to William Langer (RG 226, entry 1, box 3). Confirmation is also found in H. Marcuse, "Description of Three Major Projects," in his own *Technology, War and Fascism*, on pages 193–98.

The report was the object of a fierce disagreement between the Central European Section and the Projects Committee, which explains the delay with which the report was approved and circulated in contrast to other reports on German opposition groups. According to the Project Committee, the report didn't meet R&A's standards of "mature and objective scholarship" (see the July 14, 1945, letter from Richard Hartshorne to Sherman Kent and Carl Schorske and the reply from Langer to Hartshorne's memorandum of July 23, 1945 [RG 226, entry 37, box 5, folder: Project Committee Correspondence]).

The original text contained three appendixes, here omitted, that showed the results of the 1921–33 federal elections, the socialist groups in exile, and a list of the main German Social Democratic leaders in the first years of allied occupation.

Classification: Confidential

## I. Introduction

Among the German political parties that may be revived after the destruction of the Nazi regime, the Social Democratic Party of Germany (*Sozialdemokratische Partei Deutschlands*—SPD) is likely to play an important role. Dating from the earliest years of the German Empire, the SPD has maintained a tradition as the strongest, and prior to 1917 the only, labor party in Germany. All indications are that the Nazi regime, while successful in abolishing the Party's organization and in killing off or imprisoning many of its leaders, has not succeeded in destroying the allegiance of much of the old Social Democratic membership. This conclusion becomes more manifest as testimony accumulates from German prisoners of war and German civilians in occupied Germany. It may therefore be assumed that the SPD will be revived at an early stage of the post-war political development in Germany.

In order to evaluate the prospective strength of the SPD in the post-war period and the problems with which the Allies would be confronted were the SPD to be revived, it is necessary to survey the traditional Social Democratic organization and policy in several major aspects.

## II. Origin, Composition, and Strength of the SPD

### A. Origin

The German Social Democratic Party was the result of the fusion of two workers' organizations: the *Allgemeiner Deutscher Arbeiter-Verein* (founded in 1863 by Ferdinand Lassalle) and the *Sozialdemokratische Arbeiterpartei* (founded in 1869 by Wilhelm Liebknecht and August Bebel). The two parties joined in 1875 into the *Sozialistische Arbeiterpartei Deutschlands*, which soon thereafter called itself *Sozialdemokratische Partei Deutschlands* (SPD).

These origins of the Party determined to a great extent the traditional dualism of its policy. The Lassallean conception of abolishing class conflicts through gradual peaceful reform with the help of the state clashed with the Marxian conception of establishing a classless society through the revolutionary overthrow of the capitalist system. Under the monarchy, adherents of the two conceptions could be reconciled without serious internal conflict since they agreed that the establishment of a democracy with free, equal, and universal suffrage would be the most favorable condition for attaining their respective goals. However, after the establishment of such a democracy in 1919 the policy of gradual reform and of revolutionary class struggle could no longer be reconciled. The SPD, in becoming the dominant party in the German state, came to identify the prosecution of its cause with the maintenance of this state and of the society which formed its basis. The Party followed the policy of democratic gradual reform, while the Marxian ideology was relegated to the theoretical sphere.

## B. Composition and Strength

The SPD was founded and organized as a workers' party and remained such throughout its history. The program of the party congress at Gorlitz (1921), the first such meeting after the overthrow of the monarchy and the establishment of a parliamentary republic, declared the Party's goal as the organization of "all manual and intellectual workers who depend on the yield of their own labor." Despite this extension of the term "workers" to include small craftsmen, small businessmen, intellectuals, etc., regarded by more radical Marxists as "petty bourgeois," the masses of industrial workers continued to constitute the chief strength of the party. According to an estimate made in 1926 by a Communist source, 75–80 percent of the SPD votes for the Reichstag elections were "proletarian votes" and the ratio of workers and "petty bourgeois" in the Party membership was given as 60 to 40.[1] That much of its strength was consequently from urban areas is shown by statistics compiled by an SPD source in 1925, which reveal that the SPD obtained more than one-third of its votes in sixty-three Reich cities with over 60,000 inhabitants.[2] The Party never succeeded in gaining a permanent foothold among the rural population, although it showed considerable voting strength in the predominantly agrarian election districts of Mecklenburg and Schleswig-Holstein. No essential change in this distribution seems to have occurred during the last six years of the Weimar Republic.

The numerical strength of the SPD within the German working population is indicated by the following figures:

| *Number of wage earners in Germany*[3] | *(in thousands)* | |
|---|---|---|
| | *1925* | *1933* |
| Wage earners and dependents | 28,390 | 29,326 |
| Wage earners | 16,035 | 16,168 |
| *Voting strength of the two major labor parties* | *(in thousands)* | |
| | *Dec. 1924* | *March, 1933* |
| Social Democrats | 7,881 | 7,182 |
| Communists | 2,709 | 4,848 |
| *Party membership figures* | *(in thousands)* | |
| | *1925* | *1931* |
| Social Democrats[4] | 845 | 1,000 |
| Communists[5] | 180 (1924) | 200 |

Out of the 16 million wage earners in these years, it is apparent that only 1 to 1.2 million were organized in the two leading labor parties. However, the actual strength of the SPD was greatly increased by its close affiliation with the trade unions. The *Allgemeiner Deutscher Gewerkschaftsbund*, the Social Democratic peak organization of trade unions, showed the following strength:[6]

| | |
|---|---|
| 1914 | 2,076,000 members |
| 1919 | 5,479,000 " |
| 1924 | 4,618,000 " |
| 1928 | 4,653,000 " |

These figures, of course, cannot be considered equivalent to those of the SPD membership, although more than 50 percent of the Party members were also trade unionists. However, identity of personnel existed to a great extent on the top layers of the Party and trade union bureaucracy, and the SPD worked closely with the free trade unions in all decisive political and economic questions.

From 1912 to 1930, the SPD was the strongest single party in the Reichstag and in the various State Diets. The Party furnished the Reich Chancellor (Prime Minister) from 1919 to 1920 and from 1928 to 1930; it participated in the government of the Weimar Republic from 1918 to 1923 and from 1928 to 1930. In other words, during the republican period it was represented in ten of the twenty-one cabinets.

### C. Regional Strength

The regional strength of the SPD was greatest in the following areas: Magdeburg, South Hanover-Braunschweig, Mecklenburg, Hamburg, Liegnitz, and Schleswig-Holstein. In these districts, the Party obtained in 1929 between 31 and 37 percent of all votes cast. The following large cities showed the greatest SPD strength: Magdeburg, Hanover, Altona, Dresden, Leipzig, Chemnitz, Nuremberg, Kassel, and Bielefeld.[7]

The Social Democratic influence was especially great in regional and local government. In 1929, one of the peak years in its history, the Party held the following offices:[8]

4,278 *Kreistag* Deputies (sub-provincial bodies)
419 Provincial Deputies
353 Aldermen (*Besoldete Stadträte*)
947 Lord Mayors and Mayors
9,057 Deputies of the Municipal Diets (*Stadtverordnete*)
1,109 Village Presidents (*Gemeindevorsteher*)

## D. Spheres of Influence and Activity

SPD, like most German parties, made an effort to extend its influence and activity beyond the political field to almost all spheres of life. Affiliated with the Party were:[9] a youth organization (*Sozialistische Arbeiterjugend* with a membership in 1929 of 55,800); numerous sport associations (combined membership in 1929: 1,284,737); educational institutions (*Arbeiterhochschulen, Kulturbund*, etc.); and consumer co-operatives (*Konsumverbände*). In addition, the Party controlled a large chain of newspapers and periodicals, publishing firms, and through the affiliated trade unions had influence in a housing and building concern (*Dewag A.G.*), insurance companies, and the *Bank der Arbeiter, Angestellten und Beamten, AG* (capital stock in 1929: 12 million RM.).

## E. Secessions from the SPD

From 1875 to the First World War, the SPD was the only German labor party and had managed to maintain its unity. During the First World War, the split of the German labor movement into a conservative-democratic and into a revolutionary wing was foreshadowed by two major dissensions over the Party's support of the war. In 1915, Karl Liebknecht, Rosa Luxemburg, and Leo Jogiches founded the Spartacus League (*Spartakusbund*), the predecessor of the German Communist Party (established in January 1919). In March 1916, another group within the SPD refused to endorse the Party's support of the war, seceded from the majority of the SPD delegates in the Reichstag, and founded, within the Party framework, the Social Democratic Workers Community (the *Sozialdemokratische Arbeitsgemeinschaft*) which, in 1917, separated from the Party and constituted itself the Independent Social Democratic Party. The Independents obtained twenty-two seats in the National Assembly of 1919 and eighty-four seats in the Reichstag of 1920 (as against one hundred sixty-five and one hundred and two Social Democrats on each occasion). Despite their initial strength, however, the Independents were not capable of maintaining a middle course between the conservative-democratic policy of the SPD and the revolutionary policy of the Communists. The Independents were united only in their opposition to the war policy of the SPD; the combination of reformist and revolutionary elements could not be maintained for any length of time after this unifying issue ceased to exist. As early as 1920, the Independents split, and the majority joined the Communist Party. The minority returned to the SPD in 1922 and became the nucleus of the left wing of the SPD, criticizing the Party's policy at congresses, at meetings, and in the press, without going into political action against the Party bureaucracy. The opposition expressed itself in favor of a more orthodox Marxian policy, a more militant attitude toward the right, and cooperation with the Communists. The main strength of the opposition was in Saxony, Silesia (Breslau), and Thuringia. In 1931, its leaders seceded from the SPD and founded the Socialist Workers Party, but it never mustered sufficient strength to swing or even to influence the Social Democratic policy. The Communist Party remained the only real competitor of the SPD within the German labor movement, and the bitter rivalry between the two parties lasted without interruption throughout the history of the Weimar Republic.

## III. The Policies of the SPD

### A. Political Policy

The SPD was, according to its program, committed to the abolition of the capitalist system, to the "transformation of the instruments of labor into the common property," and thus to the "establishment of a socialist society."[10] However, the SPD considered the democratic form of government the prerequisite for the attainment of its economic and political goals. The Party has adhered to this conception against an over-growing opposition, which appeared first within the Party itself. Since 1917, the SPD has upheld its views in contrast to the newer, more radical labor parties which advocated a speedy transition to a soviet system in Germany. The Party programs[11] are quite definite on this point:

> "The social problem cannot be separated from the political problem; the solution of the former is conditional on the solution of the latter and is possible only in a democratic state." (Eisenach, 1869).
>
> "The Socialist Workers' Party of Germany demands as the foundation of the state: universal, equal, and direct suffrage with secret and obligatory vote for all citizens. . . ." (Gotha, 1875).[12]
>
> "The SPD regards the democratic republic as the historically irrevocable form of the state and every attack against it as an *attentat* against the vital rights of the people." (Görlitz, 1921).
>
> "The democratic republic is the most favorable ground for the liberation of the working class and thereby for the realization of socialism. The SPD therefore protects the republic and fights for its development." (Heidelberg, 1925).

With the establishment of the Weimar Republic, the adherence to the democratic form of government came into conflict with the adherence to the socialist goal. In the Weimar democracy, the labor parties (SPD,

Independents, and Communists) did not obtain a popular and parliamentary majority. Under these circumstances, the SPD had only two possibilities of political action: it could either join the radical left (Independents and Communists) in a revolutionary class struggle for socialism against the "bourgeois" parties, or it could cooperate with the latter within the framework of the capitalistic-democratic state. From the beginning of the Weimar period, the SPD chose the second course: it placed adherence to the democratic form of government before attainment of the socialist goal by revolutionary means. On 9 November 1918, the very day of the revolution in Berlin, the Party Executive of the SPD rejected the demand of the Independent Socialists that the "entire executive, legislative, and judicial power should rest exclusively with the elected delegates of the entire working population and of the soldiers." The demand was rejected because, to the SPD, it meant "the dictatorship of a part of a class which is not backed by the majority of the population." The demand, the Party Executive declared, thus "contradicts our democratic principles."[13]

The SPD entered immediately an alliance with the Army and the industrial leadership against the revolutionary movements on the left. On 10 November 1918, the Social Democratic leader Fritz Ebert concluded an agreement with Hindenburg in which he promised the support of the SPD for the Army's fight against Bolshevism. Five days later, the Social Democratic trade union leaders concluded an agreement with the industrial leadership for peaceful cooperation.[14] The foundation was thus laid for democratic collaboration with the "bourgeois parties" in order to maintain a government with a workable parliamentary majority. Consequently, the SPD participated in national coalition governments with the German Democratic Party, the Centrum, the Bavarian People's Party, and the German Peoples' Party; and it tolerated the purely "bourgeois" government of Brüning. The general policy of the SPD toward participation in coalition government was stated in a resolution of the Party Congress at Kiel (1927), which declared that "the participation of the SPD in the Reich Government depends solely on examination of the question as to whether the strength of the SPD . . . assures, in a given situation, the attainment of certain definite goals which are in the interest of the labor movement, and the prevention of certain reactionary laws."[15]

The SPD had thus become part of a government and of a state which was sustained by an alliance between the Social Democrats on the one hand and the political representatives of the Army, the industrial leadership, the Catholic Center, the liberal middle classes on the other. For the SPD, this alliance meant the abandonment of revolutionary socialist tactics and maintenance of the labor movement within the framework of legalism and parliamentarism. This policy led to the violent conflict between the Social Democrats and Communists. In a manifesto of 18 December 1918, the Communist Spartacus League had declared:[16]

> "It is sheer madness to believe that the capitalists would comply with the verdict of a parliament, a national assembly, that they would renounce ownership, profit, and the privilege of exploitation. . . . The struggle for socialism is the greatest civil war in history, and the proletarian revolution must prepare the necessary weapons for this civil war and learn to use it. . . ."

Accordingly, the manifesto demanded "the abolition of all parliaments and municipal councils, and the transfer of their functions to workers and soldiers councils and their committees and organs."

This Communist program, formulated and strengthened under the impact of the Bolshevist revolution, was in irreconcilable contradiction to the Social-Democratic conception of a parliamentary-democratic development into socialism. From this time forward, the SPD had to uphold the Weimar Republic not only against the monarchists and other enemies on the right, but also against a considerable part of the labor movement itself. The examples of this struggle quickly multiplied. In the fight against the leftist opposition, the SPD relied to a great extent upon the Reichswehr. In January 1919, Gustav Noske, the Social-Democratic "Peoples' Commissar" for Army and Navy, mobilized the Garde Regiments under Colonel Wilhelm Reinhard, who beat down the Communist-led uprising in Berlin. Its leaders, Karl Liebknecht and Rosa Luxemburg, "were murdered on the way to prison,"[17]

In April-May 1919, Johannes Hoffmann, the Social-Democratic Prime Minister of Bavaria, asked for the dispatch of troops from the other parts of the Reich in order to remove the government of Workers and Soldiers Councils in Bavaria. The request was granted and the "Peoples' Republic" was liquidated. Subsequently, troops were used for removing leftist governments in Saxony, Thuringia, Bremen, Braunschweig, and Hamburg.

Since the SPD regarded itself as a part of the existing state rather than as the opposition to this state, the Party was also led to discard one of the most powerful weapons of the oppositional labor movement, namely, the political strike. Only once did the Party endorse the use of the general strike—against the monarchist Kapp putsch in 1920—and this strike was sponsored by the government itself.[18] Under the influence of the trade union bureaucracy, which was closely allied with the Party leadership, the strike became more and more an instrument for the attainment of limited economic objectives. The trade unions saw in the political strike a threat to their position and their vested interests in the prevailing state, and the Party eventually recognized this conception.[19] The trade union periodical *Die Arbeit*, which was edited by Theodor Leipart, the President of the *Allgemeiner Deutscher Gewerkschaftsbund*, declared in 1925 that the SPD could become and remain a government party only if "the trade unions in the future renounce revolutionary methods and confine their activity to the economic field. Only under these conditions will the bourgeois classes grant them that confidence without which the labor government could never again rule." The trade unions, the journal said, have "to draw the consequences from the fact that they have become the organs of a government party (*regierungsfähige Partei*)." As a matter of fact, strikes, both political and economic, actually declined from 3,682 in 1919 to 433 in 1931 and 634 in 1932.[20]

During the fourteen years of the Weimar Republic, the SPD adhered so consistently to the rules of legality and to the policy of combating the radicalization of the labor movement that even in the face of the Nazi counter-revolution it did not resort to traditional revolutionary means against open violence from the right. In 1932, when Franz von Papen evicted the legally elected Prussian government of Otto Braun, the SPD merely appealed to the Constitutional Court. In January 1933, a few weeks before Hitler's ascent to power, Hilferding wrote[21] that the decline of Fascism had already set in, and that, in the prevailing situation, the Social Democrats must fight the decisive struggle against the Communists. On these grounds, he rejected the proposal for a united front with the Communist Party. Subsequently, no appeal for a general strike against the installation of the Hitler regime was made, although the SPD deputies voted unanimously against the Enabling Bill in the meeting of the Reichstag on 16 March 1933.

## B. Economic Policy

The conception of the Social Democratic Party as a "part of the State" also determined the economic policy of the SPD and led to a redefinition of the socialist goal. From the very beginning, the Party conceived the transition from capitalism to socialism in terms of a process under the guidance of the state. Governmental legislation rather than revolutionary action should, according to this conception, bring about this transition. The heritage of Lassalle becomes manifest in the formulation of the Gotha program:

> "The Socialist Workers Party of Germany demands, in order to pave the way for the solution of the social problem, the establishment of socialist productive cooperatives (*Produktionsgenossenschaften*) with the help of the state under the democratic control of the working population."

Under the Weimar Republic, the economic policy of the SPD applied the legalistic-parliamentary conception of gradual reform to the economic field. Described as "economic democracy" (*Wirtschaftsdemokratie*), it represented, in practice, the supplanting of the Marxian doctrine of the revolutionary abolition of the existing economic system by legislative measures for the improvement of the existing economic system. The Social Democrats thought that "economic democracy" would come about through an increase in the state-controlled sector of the economy over the private sector. Labor, as represented by the Free Trade Unions, would gain, it was believed, an ever more influential position in this process. In accordance with this conception, the SPD advocated "control by the Reich of the capitalist possession of the means of production,"[22] but rejected all radical socialization measures "from below" and all revolutionary action, by the workers themselves, in the plants and shops.

The Party stuck to this policy of attaining its goals through the orderly process of legislation. As early as March 1919, when public sentiment for immediate socialization reached its peak, the Social Democratic Minister for Economics, Rudolf Wissel, declared in the National Assembly that, against the "threat of anarchy . . . the Reich government unanimously considers it its duty to open for the socialist efforts a legal field of activity through legislation." Otto Hue, the leader of the miners' union, followed up by stating that "wild socializations in individual plants are the opposite of socialism."[23]

The legislation proposed by the Social Democratic government was not socialism. The "socialization law" submitted in 1919 by the Scheidemann cabinet stated, in accordance with the above-mentioned principles, that the Reich is entitled to bring into the collective economy (*Gemeinwirtschaft*) certain enterprises which are suited for socialization, but the proposed legislation was confined to the governmental regulation of the coal industry.[24] He emphasized that this measure was not nationalization because the government sought "to avoid the detrimental effects of bureaucratization."[25] The abortive nature of these moves was epitomized by the career of a parliamentary "committee for socialization," which was supposed to examine the possibilities for the nationalization of certain branches of the economy; the committee met in December 1918, but dissolved itself in April 1919 without achieving any results.[26]

The Party's identification with the prevailing economic tendencies went so far that the theoreticians of the SPD regarded even the growth of the big monopolistic concerns as a positive factor in the strengthening of "economic democracy." They held that "within the organizations of the entrepreneurs, decisions affecting economic welfare were being made which can no longer remain within the private sphere but which must become a matter of the community."[27] This conception was carried to its logical conclusion by Rudolf Hilferding in the Party Congress at Kiel (1927). He interpreted "organized capitalism" as socialism:

> "Organized capitalism thus means in reality that, in principle, the capitalist principle of free competition is being replaced by the socialist principle of planned production."[28]

If this is the case, he stated, the contrast is no longer between capitalism on the one hand and socialism on the other but between "capitalist organization of the economy on the one hand and state organization of the economy on the other," and the task is to "transform the capitalistically organized economy into an economy directed by the democratic state."

The policy of economic democracy furthermore required that the SPD concentrate its strength on the fight for extended social legislation within the capitalist system. The SPD and the trade unions attained their greatest achievements in this field: they sponsored a stable system of collective bargaining, obtained the recognition of workers' representation in the plants, and established a most comprehensive system of social welfare and insurance. Almost equally great were the improvements which the SPD achieved through its numerous key positions in municipal and county administration. However, these achievements blinded the Party against the danger which threatened the economic foundations of the Weimar democracy.

In the face of the rapidly progressing concentration and rationalization of German industry, the SPD retained its belief in the gradual transition from organized capitalism into a socialist economy. Even during the crisis of 1929–1932, when the number of unemployed rose from 1,260,000 to 7,603,000, the SPD developed no economic policy of its own but supported or tolerated the subventionary and deflationary measures of the Brüning government, which brought increased tax burdens to the middle and lower classes, decreases in wages, and heavy cuts in the expenditures for social legislation.

The concentration of SPD policy on social and economic legislation within the framework of the democratic-capitalistic state led to a steady increase in the influence of trade union interests over the Party. The trade unions not only implemented the economic policy of the Party, but they also took the leadership on the road to economic class collaboration.

The pattern for economic collaboration between the Social Democratic trade unions and the entrepreneurs was set by the foundation of the *Zentralarbeitsgemeinschaft der industriellen und gewerblichen Arbeitgeber Deutschlands* on 15 November 1918. Most instrumental in this organization were, on the part of the entrepreneurs, the industrialists Hugo Stinnes, von Siemens, and Borsig, and, on the part of the workers, the trade union leaders Karl Legien and Siegfried Aufhäuser. In the contract, which was then drawn up, it was stipulated that wages and labor conditions should be regulated by collective agreement between the employers' and employees' organizations, that workers' committees together with the entrepreneur should supervise the fulfillment of these agreements in the plants, and that the employers should withdraw their support of the so-called "yellow dog" unions and recognize only the free, Christian, and democratic unions.[29] Recognition of the trade unions, together with the main stipulations of this private agreement, were later incorporated into the Weimar constitution (Articles 159 and 165). The trade unions endorsed (and perhaps even determined) the policy of peaceful collaboration with the capitalist parties and organizations. The Trade Union Congress of 1927 adopted the tenets of "economic democracy."

The principle of neutrality toward the various political parties, which was accepted by the Trade Union Congresses of 1919 and 1922, strengthened the collaborationist policy. It culminated in the declaration, on 9 April 1933, of Theodor Leipart and Peter Grassmann, the chairmen of the Free Trade Unions, in which they dissolved their connections with the Social Democratic Party and announced their intention to collaborate with the Hitler regime, provided that the trade union organization remained intact.[30] The offer was rejected, and the trade unions were abolished on 2 May 1933.

## C. Foreign Policy: Attitude toward War and Rearmament

The SPD has always emphasized its international ties with the labor movement in other countries. Since the liberation of the working class was considered an international social problem, the SPD operated as a member of the Socialist Workers' International. The SPD played a leading role in the Second International and German Social Democrats became its chief theoreticians.

In accordance with the principles of international socialism, the Congress of the International at Stuttgart (1907) adopted a resolution which committed the various sections of the association to do everything in their power to prevent the outbreak of war. If, however, war did break out, the socialist parties were to utilize the event for the destruction of the capitalist system. This resolution was never effectively implemented, because the internationalism of the Social Democrats was combined with and often superseded by a strongly positive attitude toward national interests. This was particularly manifest in Germany, where national unification and social and political progress on the national level were regarded by the SPD as a pre-condition for the development of the labor movement. This conception determined the policy of the Party toward war; the Party backed the national war effort insofar as it was a "defensive" war waged against enemies who were more "reactionary" than the German State.

The definition of a "defensive war" was, of course, open to interpretation. Even prior to 1914, a strong wing of the SPD under the leadership of August Bebel supported the military preparations of the Empire. In August 1914, the Party voted for the war budget in the Reichstag, although fourteen members dissented in caucus. From that time on, however, the opposition against the Party's war policy increased within the SPD and led, in 1916–1917, to the secession of the Independents and the Spartacists. In 1917, the SPD endorsed a parliamentary resolution calling for peace without annexations and conquests. Subsequently, the Party played an ambiguous role in the discussions which preceded the acceptance of Wilson's Fourteen Points and the abdication of the Kaiser.[31] Two Party members, Scheidemann and Gustav Bauer, joined the Imperial Government early in October 1918, and Scheidemann and Ebert tried to save the monarchy as long as possible.[32] At the same time, the Party made itself the spokesman for the widespread sentiment in favor of the Kaiser's removal.

The Party's legalistic tradition, nevertheless, made the SPD reluctant to assume the leadership of the German revolution; on 9 November 1918, for example, Ebert violently reproached Scheidemann for having proclaimed the republic; "You have no right to proclaim a republic. What Germany is to be, a republic or anything else, is for the Constituent Assembly to decide."[33] On the following day, the Ebert-Hindenburg agreement for the maintenance of law and order and for the common fight against bolshevism was concluded.[34] This agreement set the pattern for the liaison between the SPD and the Reichswehr. The SPD supported the building up of a republican Reichswehr for two basic reasons:[35] (a) the maintenance of law and order and the domestic struggle against bolshevism were best assured by a well equipped military force; and (b) the SPD's efforts to strengthen Germany's national unity and independence and its opposition to unilateral disarmament required an army. By the same token, the SPD Ministers in the Marx Cabinet (1928) endorsed, with the approval of the Party, the appropriation for the battle cruiser "A," an appropriation against which the SPD had waged the preceding election campaign,[36] and the great majority of the SPD delegates in the Reichstag merely abstained from voting against the appropriation for a second cruiser in 1931.[37]

The SPD had, under protest, accepted the Treaty of Versailles and endorsed the League of Nations and the principle of international arbitration. Throughout the period of the Weimar Republic, the SPD supported the conception (best represented by the foreign policy of Gustav Stresemann) of Germany as the "mediator between Western Europe and Russia."[38] It encouraged, furthermore, efforts to establish friendly relations with Soviet Russia as well as with the Western Powers. At the same time, however, the Party maintained its negative attitude toward the

Soviet system. This attitude, which had contributed to the secession from the Party of the Independent Socialists, the Spartacists, and the Socialist Workers Party, remained basically unchanged in the subsequent years.

### D. The Appeal of the SPD

The distribution of votes and the membership figures of the labor parties and trade unions show that the majority of the organized workers voted Social Democratic up to the very end of 1933. This fact suggests that the majority of the organized workers in Germany endorsed the policy of the SPD and its trade unions as against the Communist policy. The statement, however, needs qualification. Even if the rank and file had not wanted to endorse the policy of the Party, they would have had hardly any means for effectively expressing their opposition. Mass demonstrations and mass strikes, it is clear, depended for their success largely on the support of the Party and trade union apparatus, and this apparatus was firmly controlled by the bureaucracy. Democracy did not operate on the top layers of the Party and trade union bureaucracy, which laid down their collaborationist policy fairly independently. The Social Democratic bureaucracy thus sustained the loyalty of the laboring population which, in turn, recreated and sustained the power of the bureaucracy.

If the majority of the laborers continued to vote for the SPD and to follow its orders, it was probably because they saw in the SPD the only force capable of stemming the reactionary tide and of maintaining the social and political achievements of the Weimar Republic. This conclusion was probably strengthened as the months passed. By 1924, after the liquidation of the last leftist governments in Central Germany, the strength of the German Democratic Party had dwindled, and in the Center Party the left wing (under the leadership of Joseph Wirth) was losing out to the rightist elements which prepared the coalition with the Nationalist Party (1925). The Social Democratic Party was thus the only mass party which, in the public mind, was unequivocally identified with the democratic republic. Therefore, its eventual failure to save this republic from the Nazi counter-revolution must have compromised the Party even more than its failure to carry out the promised social and economic changes. This fact is important for the evaluation of the future prospects of the SPD and its strength among the German population.

## IV. The SPD in Exile

The Hitler regime destroyed the entire apparatus of the SPD, removed its members from all important public positions, threw many of its militant members and leaders into concentration camps, and liquidated unknown numbers of them. Most of the top leaders went into exile. Until the outbreak of the war, fairly regular contacts were maintained between the exiles and their Party friends in Germany; during the war, these contacts all but stopped. In Germany, most of the older members of the SPD and the trade unions remained loyal to their former organization. Small groups of trusted friends tried to get together regularly, but no centrally organized Social Democratic "underground" movement existed. Some Social Democrats apparently succeeded in obtaining and keeping positions as members of Confidential Councils (*Vertrauensräte*) of the Labor Front (DAF) in the plants, where they tried to promote the interests of their comrades.

In the concentration camps, the Social Democrats (as well as the other militant political prisoners) succeeded in preserving and developing their political convictions and ideas. The anti-fascist united front, which came into the open during and after the breakdown of the Nazi regime, was to a great extent prepared and formed in the concentration camps. Perhaps the most significant document testifying to the political efforts of the Socialist prisoners is the *Buchenwald Manifesto* of Democratic Socialists, signed by Hermann Brill and dated 13 April 1945. The Manifesto regards the transformation of Germany into a socialist society as the precondition for the elimination of Nazism and militarism.

> "Convinced that the ultimate cause of this most horrible of all wars lies in the predatory nature of the capitalist economy, of finance-capitalistic imperialism, and in the moral and political deterioration of the tatterdemalion protelariat produced by both of them, we demand that the crises of society be terminated by a socialist economy. Germany's economic reconstruction is possible only on a socialist foundation. The rebuilding of our destroyed cities as private-capitalistic business is just as impossible as the reconstruction of industry out of the pockets of the tax payers."

The Manifesto guarantees the protection and development of peasant property, but demands the expropriation of the large estates and their collective (*gemeinwirtschaftliche*) utilization.

These tasks are to be carried through within the framework of a democratic "people's republic" with the cooperation of all anti-fascist forces. The Manifesto envisages the establishment of a democratic republic through the immediate formation of anti-fascist "people's committees," to be called together into a German People's Congress on the Reich level. A unified trade union organization, "independent of the state," is to be established. Radical elimination of all Nazi personnel, and abolition of all Nazi laws, institutions, and organizations is demanded. The

Manifesto acknowledges the German people's obligation for rehabilitation, professes to direct all efforts toward the prevention of future wars, and states two presuppositions for Germany's reentry into a peaceful federation of European nations: (1) German-French and German-Polish understanding (*Verständigung*), and (a) Germany's entrance into the "Anglo-Saxon culture" (*Kulturkreis*).

The Manifesto, written in the terroristic isolation of the concentration camps, is distinguished from the later declarations of the German Socialistists by its political sharpness and radicalism. At the same time, it shows a marked emphasis on "western orientation,"[39] characteristic of a very large part of German Socialists now in the western zones, and the strong adherence to democratic processes and anti-fascist cooperation which has become the present predominant feature of the post-Nazi German labor movement.

As to the exiled SPD groups, there is almost general agreement that the SPD should be reformed and rejuvenated, but the suggestions include few if any essential changes of the old line. Common to most is the call for a single unified labor party and trade union organization. It has been emphasized, however, that the Communists can be accepted only if they abandon "all direct or indirect dependence on the USSR." In point of fact, among the exiled groups only Fritz Tarnow's *Arbeitskreis* in Stockholm and the Social Democrats in the New York Council for a Democratic Germany worked together with the Communists. The Union of German Socialist Organizations in London includes the SPD, the *Sozialistische Arbeiterpartei*, *Neu Beginnen*, and the *Internationaler Sozialistischer Kampfbund*, but not the Communists. The Social Democratic Party Executive and its followers voice strong opposition to the Soviet policy in Eastern Europe, which in their opinion threatens to bolshevize Germany. There appears, at present, little chance of an agreement between the exiled SPD leadership and the Communists, in spite of the fact that the Communist line implies the abandonment of the class struggle and the adoption of democratic procedures for post-Hitler Germany.

The exiled SPD leadership itself reiterates its adherence to democratic principles and procedures. It proclaims as its political goal for Germany a "social democracy" and a "democratic republic," based on all genuinely anti-Nazi groups and parties. The revived party would try to win over not only the workers, but also the small middle classes and peasants and the free professions. Religion is again designated as "a private affair," and freedom of worship is demanded. The cooperation of the Church is solicited. The Party appears again to be aiming toward the socialization of private-capitalistic property and the abolition of classes, but, for the period after the downfall of the Hitler regime, it is suggested that only "the essential utility services" and the Nazi enterprises be brought under "public administration." It is furthermore emphasized that in "all factories, etc. . . . the workers, together with the technical and clerical employees, must secure for themselves a controlling influence in the factory administration, without prejudice to a later central ruling on the property rights in factories, etc."[40]

With regard to the peace settlement, the exiled Social Democrats maintain a strict distinction between Nazis and anti-Nazis and insist that the majority of the German workers has always been opposed to Nazism. Consequently, they seek to have punitive measures restricted to the Nazis. A partition of Germany is rejected. The cession of large German territories to Poland is violently attacked, as are the use of German workers as "slave labor" in any form, and the program of de-industrialization of Germany. With the development of Soviet policy in Germany, the tone of the exiled old-line SPD leadership has become even more hostile to the Soviets and the Communists.

The exiled SPD leadership's chances of playing a role in post-Hitler Germany will be discussed in the last chapter.

## V. Developments in the SPD Since the Occupation of Germany

### A. In the Western Zones

Although the ban on organized political activity in the western zones has now been lifted, the SPD in these sectors has not yet been officially reconstituted. The Party's reemergence may be expected soon: groups of SPD leaders and members appeared everywhere after the breakdown of the Nazi controls, and preparations for the formal reestablishment of the Party are reported to be far advanced. But, in accordance with Anglo-American policy, the SPD—like all other parties—will at first be allowed to organize only on a local level, a fact which may give a headstart to the SPD in the Soviet zone, where it is being centrally organized and integrated.

1. *Participation in MG.* Meanwhile, SPD functionaries and Party regulars have furnished a large number of anti-Nazi appointees to Allied Military Government positions. In September 1945 Social Democrats in the western zones were strongly represented on all levels of the administration. On an over-all basis, indeed, the SDP in this area has acquired more posts of all kinds than any other party. Its strength is plainly concentrated in city administration, which since the SPD has always been representative primarily of the urban working classes is understandable. The Catholic Center Party follows the SPD as a weak second.[41]

2. *Program.* As yet the Social Democrats in the western zone have not developed any specific program. When they do—as they doubtless will

in the near future—its objectives will probably include nationalization of large-scale industry, thorough elimination of Nazism, and restoration of a democratic, parliamentary system. This, at least, can reasonably be inferred from the Social Democratic programs which have been coming out of the Soviet occupation zone and other European countries.

3. *Leadership*. In the western zone, the SPD has an opportunity to develop with more independence than its counterpart in the east is likely to enjoy. The Party may attempt to take up where it left off in 1933, without basic changes in either leadership or policy. For example, one SPD leader, Wilhelm Knothe, who now holds an influential position through his editorship of the *Frankfurter Rundschau*, reacted favorably to a suggestion that exiled Weimar leaders such as Ollenhauer, Stampfer, and Aufhäuser be returned to power as soon as possible.[42] Kurt Schumacher, at present one of the most active SPD leaders in the western zone, has reportedly invited the exiled SPD leaders in London to attend a conference near Hanover.[43]

Attempts to revive the Party under the old leadership, however, are likely to meet strong opposition even in the western zone. Such intelligence as is available suggests that those who wish to reconstitute the Party under a new leadership and with a new policy command much more popular support than "old-line" advocates. On the other hand, the various dissident groups which broke off from the SPD prior to and after the Nazi regime do not appear to have won any significant following in Germany. No activities of the *Neu Beginnen* movement have been reported. Representatives of the ISK (*Internationaler Sozialistischer Kampfbund*) and of the SAP (Socialist Workers Party) are reported busy in Bremen. Frankfurt, Hamburg and some other cities, but the chances of these groups developing as independent parties seem to be negligible.

4. *Relations with the KPD*. Although in the western zone SPD circles are free to give vent to anti-Communist sentiments, and have often availed themselves of the privilege, cooperation between KPD and SPD individuals or groups operating under Military Government has frequently been secured. The most notable instances have been the various "Antifa" organizations, informal committees led chiefly by Communists, but with strong SPD participation, which sprang up in several places shortly after and even prior to the entrance of Allied troops.[44]

According to American observers, Social Democrats in their sector tend to fall into two clearly defined groups. Members of the first regard the Communists as moderate persons with views close to their own; they speak occasionally of the formation of a single working-class party, a project that is being sponsored by the Communists in the Soviet zone. They assert that the former split between the working-class parties was an important factor enabling Hitler to carry out the counter-revolution. To prevent its recurrence and to achieve certain social and economic objectives they would be willing to collaborate with the Communists and the USSR.

Other Social Democrats profess to fear a red revolution in Germany under Soviet and Communist auspices. They still regard the Communists as agents of Soviet imperialism and as the spearheads of a totalitarian system that threatens to overcome most of Europe. To date, there is not enough information to show which point of view commands the greater strength.

## B. In the Soviet Zone

The Social Democratic Party in the Soviet zone was formed almost immediately after Marshal Zhukov's order of 10 June 1945 was issued permitting political parties to exist provided they registered with the Soviet authorities. On 19 June 1945 it joined an anti-fascist front with the Communists, and nearly a month later, on 14 July, all five parties in the Soviet zone formed a United Front of Anti-Fascist Democratic Parties, with a broad program demanding freedom of thought and destruction of militaristic ideology. Within the Front, apparently, the several parties are to retain their organizational independence and at least some freedom of action.

1. *Program.* Though the SPD in the Soviet zone subscribes to this Front platform, it has also a program of its own, which it laid down in a manifesto in the first issue of its own newspaper, *Das Volk*, on 7 July. In economic matters this program placed its greatest stress on reconstructing the German economy in order to prevent unemployment and starvation. It also demanded important changes in the structure and organization of the German economy—nationalization of banks, insurance companies, natural resources, mines, and the power industry, and assurance that in the future there shall be no unearned income from the land.[45]

Further demands included the participation of trade unions, works councils, and consumers' cooperatives in the organization of the economy. Whether this meant giving the unions managerial functions is not altogether clear. But the program stated that the Free German Trade Union League should set up special organs, staffed with well qualified persons, for this "Herculean" task. Entrepreneurs are to be regarded, according to the SPD program, as trustees of the plant given them to manage, and must not become exploiters, dictators, or wage cutters. Salaried employees and workers are to be considered co-workers with equal rights—a demand which may lead to trouble in defining the lines of authority within the plant and in establishing discipline. The SPD program pointed out, on the other hand, that because of the destruction of the German economy and its low state of productivity the workers will have to be content for some time with low returns, and that an organized struggle between employer and employee interest groups for a share in the total output is out of the question.[46]

2. *Relations with the KPD*. The issuance of this manifesto provided one indication of the SPD's determination to retain its identity. Confirmation came in an interview granted the well-known Soviet journalist, Karl Hoffmann, by the Party's Central Committee. Spokesmen for it stated that after mature consideration they and their Communist friends had come to the conclusion that the time had not yet arrived organically to unite the two parties.[47] That the Party remains anxious to cooperate with the KPD, however, is evident from recent issues of *Das Volk*. Nearly every one of these has stressed the necessity for harmonious relationships with the Communist Party.

3. *Leadership*. This desire for closer working relations with the KPD in the task of thoroughly reorganizing German society has been a large factor motivating the SPD in the Soviet zone in its rejection of the Party's exiled leaders, who are felt to be basically anti-Soviet. In its interview with Hoffmann, the Central Committee said:

> "We in Berlin have no knowledge concerning the position taken by the former Social Democratic Leaders outside the country. . . . We cannot be identified with them. . . . Only we have the right to speak in the name of the Social Democratic Party of Germany."[48]

The three present co-chairmen of the SPD are Max Fechner, Erich W. Gniffke, and Otto Grotewohl. Fechner is a rather colorless Party functionary, formerly an editor of an SPD publication dealing with municipal problems and an ex-employee of the Executive Committee. Gniffke has remained virtually unknown to most of the membership. Grotewohl, on the other hand, is a colorful and energetic man, now active in trade union as well as Party matters. At one time a member of the Independent Social Democratic Party, he later returned to the SPD. In an article in the first issue of *Das Volk*, 7 July 1945, he asserted, "The cares of the bare struggle for existence on the part of the German people unite us with all antifascist groups and parties. . . . What unites us is stronger than what separates us."[49]

In the new executive committee (*Zentralausschuss*) the most important members are apparently Gustav Dahrendorf and Otto Meier, the editor of *Das Volk*. Slightly behind them comes Josef Orlopp, former trade unionist and now on the Berlin town council. Dahrendorf, who held no position of leadership in the SPD until 1933, made perhaps the most significant speech which has yet come out of the Party. At a meeting in Berlin of the Communist, Social Democratic, Center, and Democratic Parties, on 12 June 1945, Dahrendorf stated: "The new Social Democratic Party has no connection with the political practice of the old SPD . . . nor does the new SPD have any connection with the policies of the emigres. . . . The program of the Communist Party finds our frank and unreserved support. We are ready to stand on this ground; we are ready for the common task."[50]

As for Otto Meier, under his direction *Das Volk* has followed a policy of playing up anti-fascist unity which differs little from that found in the Communist press. By some persons acquainted with his previous record he is regarded as an opportunist.

Orlopp's importance appears to stem more from his position as a Berlin Council member in charge of trade than from any intellectual contributions of party policy. His rather technical speech on the occasion of the introduction of new trade measures gave the impression that he was sympathetic to the plight under the Nazis of the small shopkeepers and similar lower middle-class groups and anxious to assist the genuine anti-Nazis among them[51].

Together with Dahrendorf, Meier, and Orlopp on the Party Central Committee are a number of party regulars—Karl Germer, Bernhard Göring, Hermann Harnisch, Helmuth Lehmann, Karl Litke, Fritz Neubecker, Hermann Schlimme, and Richard Weimann. Some of them, like Göring and Schlimme, formerly leading men in the German labor movement, have been fairly active in the reconstruction of the trade unions. Their occasional public statements indicate that they do not share fully the enthusiasm of the top Party leaders for close relations with the Communists. But they are distinctly secondary in importance within the Party. Moreover, opposition to the ex-Nazis and to many of the ruling groups in Germany, with some pressure from the Soviets, should hold together the Communists and the Social Democrats in this zone for some time to come.

### C. SPD Policy on Specific Problems

1. *Trade unions.* As has been pointed out in the earlier chapters, much of the strength of the SPD derived from its close connection with the trade union movement, and its "gradualism" was consonant with the unions' strategy of day-to-day improvement of the worker's lot. SPD leaders in both zones, therefore, are exerting every effort to restore the unions to some semblance of their former power.

In the western zones, at the present time, trade unions are severely restricted in their activities: they are not yet entitled to bargain over wages and working hours and they must keep away from politics. If they wish to organize on a larger basis than the individual plant, their requests have to be approved by USFET headquarters, and—officially at least—they will not be permitted to organize beyond the *Kreis* level. In actuality, however, trade union preparations for integration on a provincial or state level seem to be well in progress, particularly in Bavaria.

Trade union programs so far published have been—with the exception of their demands for thorough de-Nazification—entirely unpolitical; they profess, indeed, strict neutrality toward all political parties and emphasize labor-management collaboration in the immediate tasks of economic reconstruction, continuing in this the tradition of pre-Hitler German trade unionism. Their most important deviation from this tradition has been the apparently general endorsement of a unified single trade union organization, to include the formerly independent Christian and democratic trade unions and the Communist units. The chances of this proposal being actually carried out are raised, certainly, by the fact that at the moment the attention of the trade unions is being directed almost wholly to the immediate problems, with matters of policies being played down and even "outlawed."

SPD "regulars" seem to be taking leading roles in the reviving trade unions. They are reported strongly to favor a powerful central executive which would appoint all major officials and leave to be elected only those at the lowest shop steward level.[52] Similar intimations of authoritarianism in the new trade union movement can be found in the tendency to institute compulsory membership.[53]

In the Soviet zone, a single, unified trade union organization has already been established in Berlin on an industry-wide basis, and a newly-formed preparatory trade union committee has demanded the extension of this organization to the entire province of Brandenburg[54]. Similar organizations have been formed or are in process of formation in other cities and regions throughout the Soviet zone. The SPD has everywhere endorsed these movements.

2. *De-Nazification*. A constant complaint in Social Democratic circles has been that under the Anglo-American administration de-Nazification is proceeding too slowly. The Social Democrats strongly resent the pressure allegedly put upon the western occupying authorities by some conservative and Centrist groups to maintain in positions of even limited responsibility and power those Nazis who claimed they joined the Party under compulsion. The bulk of the Social Democratic Party membership, according to most reports, remained anti-Nazi, whether actively or passively, throughout the Hitlerian rule; many of them, without any doubt, suffered persecution, imprisonment, and torture. Thus they naturally favor stern treatment of Nazis.

It should be noted, moreover, that anti-Nazism has become one form through which the struggle for political power between rightist and leftist groups has continued under a system in which a more overt struggle is rendered impossible by the presence of the occupying powers. To the extent that the Social Democrats and leftist groups are able to classify their rightist opponents as Nazis, or Nazi sympathizers, and to force the military government authorities to take action against them, their objective of winning power at a later date has been made easier to attain. The fact, on the other hand, that many rightist groups, particularly the industrialists, avoided open identification with the aims and practices of the Nazi Party has shown the left the limits of usefulness of this approach, and has suggested that the fundamental problem of the reconstruction of German society cannot be reached by de-Nazification alone.

3. *Reparations*. SPD leaders have generally accepted the necessity of Germany's paying reparations and have not sought to evade the responsibility of their fulfillment. The SPD is, however, likely to oppose any attempt to shift the burden of reparations onto the working classes, remembering that reparations policy after 1918 resulted in the impoverishment of German labor and the revival and extension of the power of the industrialists. The SPD and its followers will be the more anxious to prevent the recurrence of such a development since most of these industrial magnates are identified in their eyes with Nazism; preferential treatment of them would be the very negation of the de-Nazification the SPD is urging.

While not opposing the use of German labor for the rehabilitation of formerly occupied territories, the SPD violently objects to the employment of German workers as "slave labor," without the enjoyment of the elementary guarantees and rights of contracted labor.

4. *De-industrialization*. Since de-industrialization of Germany would deprive the SPD of most of its working-class base, the Party is likely to oppose this measure with whatever strength it can command. Party leaders are likely to argue that German industry can serve the peaceful reconstruction of Europe, provided control over it is taken out of the hands of the industrialists. In the Soviet zone, however, from which the Soviets have already removed a considerable quantity of industrial machinery, the newly reconstituted SPD has uttered no public protest. This may safely be ascribed more to its fear of the consequences of such a statement than to any complacency over the prospect of a "pastoralized" Germany.

5. *Nationalization*. Nationalization, at least of the key industries and of credit, is again on the Social Democratic program as in pre-Nazi days. This plank would seem to make the SPD program more radical than the Communist, for the latter is focused on the destruction only of the "fascist" trusts and monopolies, and stresses more strongly than the SPD manifesto, the necessity of private initiative. Both parties agree in promising the protection and preservation of small individual property.

However, such long-range fundamental principles of social reconstruction have at present, under military occupation, little relevance for the actual policy of the German labor parties. Nor should it be expected that differences over the extent of nationalization will provide much of a problem. Confined to certain "fascist" types of enterprises, nationalization today would have the endorsement not only of the SPD and KPD but even of the left wing of the middle-class parties. The decisive social and political conflicts will probably arise, not over the question of whether, as the SPD program urges, *all* key industries should be nationalized, but over the form which nationalization should take—that is, whether or not it should be made the lever of socialization through the transferral of the nationalized enterprises from state control to management by the organized workers. Neither the Social Democrats nor the Communists have raised this controversial point.

In the eastern zone, the Soviets are reported to be following a policy of turning over to local government control such enterprises as have been confiscated from persons who profited from the Nazi regime, or which were abandoned by their owners. The SPD may advocate a similar procedure in the western zones.

6. *Agrarian policy*. The Social Democrats as well as the Communists demand the division of the large estates, especially those belonging to Nazis and pro-Nazis. In addition the Social Democrats advocate consumers' associations and cooperatives.

7. *Separatism*. The vast majority of Social Democrats both in Germany and in exile appears opposed to separatist movements such as have appeared in the Rhineland and in Bavaria. They profess fear that the separation of these territories would enable their industrialists to escape the consequences of defeat. A second and equally important reason for SPD opposition is the Party's anxiety lest separation lead to reactionary local dictatorships under Catholic auspices. A final reason—one which does not come to the surface readily in SPD discussions of the problem today, but which has played an important role in the past—is the belief that a strong though peaceably inclined Germany offers the greatest guarantee of security for the German working class.

8. *Partition*. Former SPD leaders in New York and elsewhere have reacted violently to the territorial truncation of Germany. Social Democrats in Germany itself have made no statements on this aspect of Potsdam—probably because by this time they realize that they are in a position to do little or nothing about this question, and have accordingly resigned themselves. This is apt to be the attitude particularly of SPD leaders in the Soviet zone. The issue, however, may in the future decisively affect the relationships between the SPD and the Communist Party. And if it should appear that these territorial exactions are the forerunners of a general partition of Germany, the SPD, though it may reconcile itself to the loss of certain lands in the east, will almost certainly express its opposition with whatever means it possesses.

9. *Religion*. Social Democrats in the western as well as eastern zones are welcoming the cooperation of liberal Catholic and Protestant groups

for de-Nazification and immediate reconstruction. They reiterate the Party's designation of religion as an individual and private affair. At the same time, many SPD functionaries have expressed fear of the alleged reactionary aims of the upper ranks of both the Protestant and Catholic clergy, and have opposed the extension of their political influence.

## VI. The Prospects of the SPD

Evaluation of the prospects of the SPD depends to a great extent on how long the present united anti-fascist front in Germany will continue. This united front is today held together by three main ties: the common effort to eliminate Nazism, the necessity of restoring indispensable social and economic services, and the restrictions imposed upon the full development of political life. These factors have compelled the parties constituting the front to pare down their political programs to a certain common denominator and to lay aside their traditional differences. But the united front may be expected to dissolve with the completion of the first phase of de-Nazification and with the fuller development of political life.

This seems, indeed, already to be taking place in the western zone, where many of the anti-fascist committees are apparently breaking up into their former political components and the old social and political conflicts characteristic of modern Germany are reemerging.[55] In short, as the process of de-Nazification has stripped the Hitlerian layers from the structure of German society, its pre-Nazi shape has begun to appear once more. Closely expressive of German society of this former period—divided against itself—were the political parties, which, representing specific social groups, worked for the most part at cross purposes.

The parties now making up the united front are essentially these same old parties, with the exception of the extreme Right (which was too openly identified with Nazism to be revived at this stage). Functioning at present in one or more zones are the Liberal Democratic Party (formerly the left wing of the German People's Party and the German Democratic Party), the Christian Democratic Union (formerly the Center Party), the SPD, and the Communist Party—two labor and two "bourgeois" parties. There are, as has been noted, no fundamental conflicts in the present programs of these parties, but, as the positive reconstruction of Germany's society and economy gets under way, the traditional conflicts are likely to reemerge over such issues as nationalization, radical agrarian reform, the extent of labor's participation in the actual management of the economy, the final settlement of Germany's frontiers, and the distribution of the burden of reparations. Indications are that, on all these issues, the bourgeois parties will try to counter every effort to push reconstruction to a point where it would threaten the position of the former upper classes. In the face of such action, the united front would dissolve into separate labor and "bourgeois" blocs.[56]

Once the dissolution of the united front has begun, evaluation of the prospects of the SPD part of the labor bloc must be highly tentative. So much depends on factors which cannot accurately be forecast, such as the development of military government policies, the intentions of the USSR, economic conditions in Germany, etc. The chances of either a united labor party or a common labor policy do not, however, appear very great.

This conclusion is supported by several recent developments. For example, the Communist-sponsored suggestion of an organizational union of the parties has been rejected by the SPD in the Soviet zone—at least for the time being.[57] The Communists are not now pressing the issue.[58] In the western zone, furthermore, the Allied policy of discouraging a united democratic front may strengthen the efforts to keep independent parties. The Social Democrats themselves contribute a factor militating against a united labor party. It is likely that the traditional anti-Communist sentiment of a large majority of the SPD members, which was subdued during the period of de-Nazification and immediate reconstruction, will again come into play. This sentiment, moreover, has been buttressed by the fact that the Communists are largely identified with some features of Soviet policy in Germany (de-industrialization, removal of plant equipment, the truncation of Germany in the east), which are disliked by a great part of the German population otherwise sympathetic to the Communists.

At the same time there are also indications that even in the Soviet zone, the popular strength of the Communists is declining.[59] This development may have repercussions on the situation in the western zone, where the Social Democrats are showing considerable strength, not only in the administration, but also in the factories.[60] They profit doubly: by their large recruitment for positions under Military Government, and by the identification of the Communists with the Soviet occupation measures.

It may be tentatively assumed, therefore, that, in the western zone, the prospects for the reestablishment of the SPD as a large noncommunist labor party (including leftist elements of the middle classes and the intelligentsia) are rather favorable. Although the post-Nazi SPD is likely to resemble strongly the pre-Nazi party in composition and policy, its leadership will chiefly be new. The fact that the SPD is greatly compromised by its failure to resist effectively the rise of the Nazi movement will require large-scale jettison on the top layer—despite some sentiment in favor of the exiled leaders.

The favorable prospects for the SPD depend, however, on the continued operation of two chief factors: the identification of the Communists with present unpopular Soviet occupation policies in Germany, and the cooperation between Military Government and the Social Democrats in the western zone. Any change in either situation will unfavorably affect the prospects of the SPD. If economic and political reconstruction should procede more effectively in the Soviet than in the western zone, Communist strength is bound to increase at the expense of the SPD. Under such circumstances, the close identification of the Social Democrats with Military Government administration in the western zone would appear as a liability rather than as an asset.

The SPD, moreover, faces a possible internal threat. It is possible that after the break-up of the anti-fascist organizations and following the fuller development of political life, the SPD in the western zone may be confronted with a split among both its leadership and the rank and file. The split is most likely to occur over the issue of continued collaboration with the Communists. It may be recalled that prior to 1933, the Party leadership had little difficulty in restoring Party unity against the rather weak opposition of leftist schismatics. Now, however, with the powerful party machine gone and the central leadership destroyed, the prospects for the growth of this opposition seem to be much better. The split seems to be foreshadowed by the reported antagonisms between the "old men" (longtime party functionaries with an anti-Communist record) and the younger, more militant socialists[61]. If the leftist dissidents should secede from the Party, however, they would be more likely to join the Communist Party than to form independent splinter groups, since the history of such groups has scarcely proved encouraging.

In the Soviet zone, the development of the SPD into an independent mass party seems improbable. Thus far, the SPD there has fully and consistently endorsed the Communist program and policy, and there is no evidence that this relationship will change in the near future. The SPD in the Soviet zone is likely to continue as a separate organization, and has emphatically reiterated its claim to become once again "a spokesman of the German working class,"[62] but this status undoubtedly will be conditional upon the SPD's willingness to continue its cooperation with the Communist Party.

Part IV

# DENAZIFICATION AND MILITARY GOVERNMENT

# 15

Otto Kirchheimer

## *THE ABROGATION OF NAZI LAWS IN THE EARLY PERIOD OF MG*

(no date, presumably end of March 1944)

Editor's note: R&A 1655.7. The original typescript is not dated, and on the cover there is an annotation that reads: "Preliminary draft not yet approved by the Editorial Committee on Civil Affairs Studies." In a letter dated January 18, 1944, from Eugene Anderson to Carl Schorske, R&A's Central European Section asked for authorization from the Project Committee to realize, by request of General John H. Hilldring, director of the Civil Affairs Division of the War Department, a report to be titled *The Abrogation of Nazi Laws in the Early Period of MG [Military Government]*, with a planned deadline of May 1, 1944. The drafter of the report is indicated as Franz Neumann, with the assistance of Otto Kirchheimer and John Herz. However, successive internal documents indicate Kirchheimer as the author (RG 226, entry 44, box 2, folder: Status of Reports). We can presume, then, that Neumann had left the responsibility to Kirchheimer, who, in the meantime, had affirmed himself as the main legal analyst of the Central European Section.

Regarding the date, a list of works in progress in the Civil Affairs Guides dated April 4, 1944, indicates the report as already being finished, while the list for April 18 shows that the report was ready for approval by the Editorial Committee. Thus we can assume that the report was finished by the end of March 1944.

Classification: Confidential

### I. Analysis of the Problem

This Guide deals with the immediate measures in the field of Nazi legislation and judicial administration which the MG Administration may desire to take directly upon occupying German territory or very early in the first stage of occupation. Less urgent measures will be treated in various Guides dealing with the respective fields of criminal law and procedure, family law, civil law, etc.

While it is sometimes suggested that all legislation enacted by the Nazis should be considered unconstitutional and therefore invalid, there are in practice serious objections to such a drastic policy. The Nazi regime, whether constitutionally or not, has issued year by year an endless stream of laws, decrees, and ordinances which have affected and transformed life and institutions in Germany to such an extent that the immediate wholesale abrogation of this legislation, though not without psychological benefit, would lead to chaotic conditions. Moreover, a piece of German legislation is not necessarily objectionable simply because it has been issued by Nazi authorities. Many regulations issued by whatever authority are of technical character, such as the rules concerning the installation and supervision of boilers. Moreover, Nazi legislation frequently amounts simply to a consolidation or codification of previous statutes.

There are, however, a number of provisions which are incompatible with either the requirements of military security and public order or with the ideals for which the United Nations stand. In respect to such laws and institutions immediate abolition will be desirable.

The principle that laws incompatible with public order and safety may be invalidated by the occupying powers has been accepted for a long time and has been incorporated into the Hague Convention governing military occupation. In addition, the Moscow Three-Power Declaration concerning Fascism has corroborated this doctrine that laws may be invalidated because of their incompatibility with occupying powers' basic concepts of "public order." According to this statement, Allied policy should be based upon "the fundamental principle that Fascism and all its evil influence and configuration shall be completely destroyed and that the (Italian) people shall be given every opportunity to establish governmental and other institutions based upon democratic principles."

There are three major groups of laws which would appear to contradict basic concepts of public order prevailing among the Allies and the immediate abrogation of which will therefore be necessary. These groups comprise:

1. Laws, and other legislative rules, which contradict the principle of the equality of all citizens before the law. Under this heading would come all acts embodying racial discrimination, acts discriminating against political opponents, and, by analogy, acts unreasonably discriminating against foreigners residing in Germany, such as foreign workers. The principle of racial and similar discrimination has been the very basis of Nazi ideology and has formed the political and propagandist entering-

wedge for Nazi propaganda all over the world. Allowing any part of this legislation to continue, if only for a brief transition period, would compromise the occupying powers not only in their own public opinion but also in the eyes of all non-Nazi Germans, and might lead to disturbances and confusion. Under this heading would likewise fall the judicial institutions and procedures set up for the special purpose of persecuting political opponents of Nazism.

2. The second group consists of measures wholly abrogating or restricting fundamental rights of freedom of individuals or social groups. Since the basis for the abrogation by Nazism of these freedoms has been the establishment of the Nazi Party and its organizations and institutions, the elimination of the institutional aspects of Nazism will constitute the first and most elementary measure to be undertaken in this field. In the wording of the Moscow Declaration regarding Italy, "all institutions and organizations created by the Fascist regime shall be suppressed," and "all Fascist and pro-Fascist elements shall be removed from the administration and from institutions and organizations of a public character." However, the first question, that of the elimination of the Party and its organizations, will be taken up in a special Guide on "The Elimination of Nazism," while the second problem, that of the de-Nazification of public administration, etc., will be dealt with in a special Guide on "General Problems of Administration."

Measures to be dealt with here concern the abolition of restrictions upon the traditional "freedoms." Again in the words of the Moscow Declaration on Italy, "freedom of speech, of religious worship, of political belief, of press and of public meeting shall be restored in full measure to the people, who shall also be entitled to form anti-Fascist political groups." Measures concerning the release of political prisoners of the regime, both in prisons and concentration camps, would likewise come under this category. While measures of the first category (legal discrimination) would have to be abolished *in toto*, those of the second group (abrogation of freedoms) would have to be carefully scrutinized in order to determine those provisions which can be abrogated immediately and those whose abrogation will have to be accompanied by the simultaneous enactment of a new body of administrative law and regulations. But the most objectionable measures in this field cannot well await the building up of a new administrative machinery. Again, as in the case of the discriminatory legislation, certain parts of Nazi legislation concerning freedom have been so closely connected with the fundamental theories and policies of Nazism that for MG to preside over their enforcement, however briefly, would be impossible. A substantial part of the German people would oppose their continued enforcement and a general state of insecurity might ensue during which no one would know exactly which laws were in force.

3. There are certain legislative measures which do not fit into the categories either of discriminatory laws or of laws restricting freedom, but the immediate abrogation of which would likewise appear to be imperative. For example, the continued validity of any of the acts concerning Nazi symbols (Swastika, uniforms, etc.) would not only endanger the security of the occupying forces but would also be in total disagreement with Allied principles. Likewise, the enforcement of Nazi eugenic legislation, although not endangering the security of the Allies, would seem undesirable even during transitional period since it has been one of the mainstays of Nazi ideology and propaganda.

4. Another group of measures where immediate action seems imperative concerns the de-Nazification of the judiciary and the ensuing necessity of suspending the activities of the courts for a certain period.

It would appear at first glance that the fate of the judiciary is not of immediate concern. It could be argued that the abolition of special courts and jurisdictions for the prosecution of political opponents would eliminate the most objectionable parts of the judicial system and its most undesirable elements, and that other reforms of the judiciary could therefore well be left to a later stage of MG Administration. This, however, would overlook the role which the judiciary has played in German politics since 1918. For instance, without the active abetting of the German judiciary, Germany's illegal rearmament effort starting in the early twenties with the organization of the "Black-Reichswehr," and the hiding away of munitions and armaments from the Allied control commissions, would have encountered great difficulties. Moreover, without the discrimination between nationalist and Leftist political opposition on the part of the judiciary, the various nationalist groups, including the Nazis, could never have been able to build up terroristic organizations undisturbed by official interference. The attitude of the judiciary, particularly of the criminal courts in "political" cases, was always the symbol of "official" reaction towards the group in question. Thus the judiciary constituted one of the chief benefactors of groups thriving upon aggressive nationalist policies.

Under the Third Reich the judiciary, although increasingly deprived of its political influence, has become increasingly "coordinated" with the Nazi regime both in its functions and in its personnel. The new masters did not leave the judiciary any latitude for using their own political judgement in deciding cases and any remaining "neutrals" among the judiciary have been weeded out during the repeated and vigorous purges of the judiciary which have been undertaken since early 1942. It would, therefore, be a mistake to base a favorable judgment of the judiciary on the few cases of opposition to the Nazi regime or of resistance to certain measures which occurred during the early stages of the regime, and thus to rely on any large amount of neutral or even anti-Nazi feeling in the judiciary.

Continuance of most of the members of this judiciary in office, even if under probation and MG supervision, would contribute neither to Allied security nor to the re-establishment of the confidence of the German people and might encourage continued Nazi activities. Besides, a considerable number of German judicial personnel have been used for the administration of occupied European territories and are now returning to their previous positions. Since most of them may be subject to prosecution as war criminals, MG could not possibly delegate judicial authority to them even for a very brief transitional period.

It might seem sufficient to suspend only judges who have functioned as criminal judges, or who were members of the Special Courts (*Sondergerichte*), and the People's Court. But such a distinction does not seem practicable. Since 1937 the assignment of duties to judges has come under the direct supervision of the Ministry of Justice, and care has been taken to rotate the assignments. Thus each judge at one time or another has had to function in criminal cases. Moreover, in the smaller local courts there has been no division of functions between civil and criminal assignments. Also, in most cases the Special Courts did not function as separate courts but were simply criminal divisions of the District Courts (*Landgerichte*) sitting as Special Courts.

For all these reasons, it seems necessary that all the 12–13,000 judges and public prosecutors be suspended from office until each of them has been thoroughly investigated. This means that the activities of the courts must be suspended for a certain period.

Under the impact of war conditions the Nazis were obliged to suspend in 1943 most of the functions of the courts concerning civil cases. Therefore, a system of suspension extending to the civil activities of the courts for a short period would mean but little change for the population. Suggestions for the solution of ensuing problems and difficulties will be found in a later part of this Guide.

## II. Recommendations

### A. General

The preceding pages have already indicated the necessity of four major groups of measures to be taken immediately by MG in relation to Nazi legislation and judicial institutions: first, the abrogation of "discriminatory" laws; second, the abrogation of laws restricting fundamental liberties; third, the abrogation of certain other laws intimately connected with

Nazi ideology and Nazi policies; and, fourth, the immediate reform of the judicial system. In order to implement four general recommendations it now becomes necessary to consider the details of the measures to be taken, in respect to both substance and form.

It might be suggested, at least with respect to the first two groups, that laws and decrees could be declared invalid by reference to broad categories and without a detailed enumeration. This method, however, would open the way to all kinds of uncertainties and differences of interpretation. The enumeration of at least the major legislative acts in the respective fields is therefore necessary. In the Appendix to this Guide, there will be found a list of laws and decrees which, it is suggested, should be specifically referred to in the proclamation invalidating Nazi legislation. While this list contains, as far as possible, an exhaustive enumeration of the laws and decrees, it does not contain executive orders issued on the basis of a law or decree, or intra-administrative instructions and regulations resting on them, because it is assumed that such enactments become invalid automatically with the abrogation of the main law or decree. On the other hand, wherever this seems possible, there should be added to the detailed enumeration a general clause to cover gaps which might otherwise invalidate the abrogations.

### B. Abrogation of Discriminatory Legislation

Discrimination against groups and individuals has been at the basis of Nazi thought and Nazi practice; both start from the assumption of the inequality of races. Even within the "higher" racial group, the right of an elite to rule without restrictions over the mass of the population is implicit. The abrogation of Nazi laws in this field means the re-establishment of the principle of equality before the law as traditionally held in democratic societies. Re-establishment of this principle requires measures in connection with several groups of Nazi laws, e.g., the so-called "Aryan" legislation, the legislation discriminating unduly against foreign workers, and similar measures. It is worth considering whether the new penal regulations to be issued by MG should not provide imprisonment or fines or both, for those who foment race hatred as well as those members or personnel of public agencies, private persons of corporations who commit acts of discrimination on the basis of race or creed.

1. *Aryan Legislation*. It is recommended that all Nazi legislation discriminating against "non-Aryans" (defined negatively as persons of non-German blood; defined positively as Jews or as Jewish-mixed blood) be immediately abolished; special regulations are necessary concerning citizenship. Nazi measures against non-Aryans have never been enacted in one general statute but have been invoked in a process extending over

several years. It is necessary, therefore, to revoke all kinds of legislative enactments in this field—from laws in the realm of citizenship to laws or decrees concerning economic disqualifications. A complete list of laws and decrees to be rescinded will be found in the Appendix. A few words, however, need to be added here in order to explain certain problems.

In 1935, through the so-called Nuremberg laws, a new concept of citizenship was enacted. The new laws introduced a distinction between "subjects" and full "citizens," but the distinction was made only in order to deprive so-called "non-Aryans," as defined by this law, of the rights traditionally deriving from citizenship—access to public offices, to the professions, etc. This law, therefore, must be retroactively rescinded. In principle, citizenship questions should be solved on the basis of the citizenship law of 1913, which is still in force. Questions concerning loss of citizenship should be treated as if this law had never been modified by the law of 1935. At the same time, the individual and general measures of expatriation which have been carried through by the German Government after 1933 should be declared invalid. As, however, many of those who have lost German citizenship after 1933 have left Germany and in the meantime have acquired citizenship or declared their intention to become citizens in other countries, the validity of this retroactive revocation of German laws and orders should be restricted to residents of Germany. This does not exclude other persons living outside Germany from filing an application to recover their citizenship after returning to Germany. But automatic restoration might at present unnecessarily harm the position of former Germans, who voluntarily or otherwise are residing abroad. As regards the acquisition of German citizenship on the basis of Nazi laws either by individual order or general decree, no revocation is recommended. Most of the persons here affected are the so-called "Racial Germans," South Tyrolians, Baltic Germans, etc., who were repatriated under Nazism. Since a large number of them had been, or had become, ardent Nazis, their former countries will hardly welcome them back, and they will thus have to stay in Germany, whether individually they prefer this solution or not.

Under Nazi legislation and practice, Gypsies, as well as Jews, were the only important groups discriminated against as "non-Aryans." Therefore, measures similar to those mentioned above, which apply to this group, should likewise be abrogated.

2. *Discriminatory Legislation against Foreign Workers.* It is recommended that all legislation discriminating against foreign workers in Germany be immediately abolished.

The Nazis, since the outbreak of the war, have deported millions of foreign civilians to Germany and forced them to work for their war machine. Since the repatriation of these foreign workers will have to be effected gradually, it is necessary to eliminate immediately any legal discrimination under which they have been put by Nazi legislation—restrictions with respect to free movement, marriage restrictions, wage discrimination etc.

## C. Abrogation of Special Privileges

It is recommended that legislation be immediately abolished concerning special employment-privileges of former members of the armed forces and the police in the German civil service.

The legislation of most countries contains provisions for special employment-privileges of former members of the army and police. German legislation has probably gone farther in this direction than any other national legislation. It has always been a German principle to reserve clerical and other minor positions in the civil service for former soldiers and policemen. The Third Reich, while continuing this tradition, added the category of Party members, in particular "old fighters," providing for them various preferences with respect to the length of required training period, the required examinations, or generally the availability of openings to them. While obviously the immediate abrogation of these privileges will work hardship in individual cases, it should nevertheless be enforced. The very fact that the authorities in Germany had always to rely on army and police veterans to fill their middle and lower ranks contributed much to the rigidity and authoritarianism of German government. In addition, during the ten years of Nazi domination the police and SS have been packed with the toughest and most reliable Party members. To maintain the employment privilege of police veterans would be tantamount to filling up the administrative ranks with the very people whose elimination from public positions should be one of the foremost aims of MG. To maintain the privilege for all ex-service men would practically prohibit MG from using its discretion in replacing the Nazified civil service with persons of its choice. As all openings and waiting-lists would be swamped with war veterans the public employment of those persons who spent the war in prisons and concentration camps would be automatically excluded. Of course, disabled and partially employable war veterans must be taken care of, but this should be a problem of general social welfare legislation, and the difficult problem of recruiting a new civil service should not be complicated by this additional burden.

## D. Non-Discrimination in Criminal Law and Procedures

It is recommended that there be abolished immediately such special courts as the People's Court and the *Sondergerichte*, as well as all legislation referring to their jurisdiction. It is further recommended that laws be rescinded which put "racial" crimes under penalty.

The Nazis have established an elaborate system of special courts in order to deal with political crimes and political opponents or, in a particular ruthless manner, with certain other types of crimes. The various types of courts and procedures have been described in sections 2E and 2 of the Civil Affairs Handbook on Germany. The People's Court and the Special Courts (*Sondergerichte*) erected at the ordinary criminal courts should be immediately abolished. Military courts as well as special SS and Police Courts will be eliminated automatically with the demobilization of the armed forces and the abolition of the SS. No ordinary court should be permitted to apply any of the special laws which are applied by the courts martial and the SS courts.

With regard to criminal law, Nazism has profoundly changed the whole system, completely obliterating the protection of the accused in order ruthlessly to assert state authority. While MG must carry through a number of fundamental changes in the second stage of occupation, only a few reforms would seem immediately necessary because, in spite of the proposed suspension of all court activity in the first period, their mere existence in the statute-book would give rise to misunderstanding. Thus the crime of "race defilement," part of the Nuremberg race legislation, should be revoked immediately, together with similar criminal laws concerning racialism. It should further be immediately proclaimed that the crimes of treason and high treason, major weapons in the hands of Nazism in its persecution of political opponents, will lapse automatically during the occupation and will be replaced by the ordinances concerning the security of the occupying forces. It is an established principle of international law that during occupation the sovereignity of the occupied country is replaced by that of the occupying powers.

### E. General Clause Concerning the Elimination of Discrimination

It is recommended that, in addition to the enumerated abrogations, a general rule be proclaimed which forbids the application of discriminatory laws and regulations.

The principle of discrimination against certain groups and individuals and of consequent inequality before the law has permeated Nazi legislation and its application so completely that a general clause forbidding the application of any such rule or regulation not already expressly repudiated would appear desirable. Such a clause would state that the application of any statute or other legislative rule or any regulation, instruction or other administrative rule, or any part of a law or regulation, which provides for, or refers to, discriminatory treatment of individuals or groups not warranted by ordinary and traditionally accepted standards of justice on the part of any-authorities, judicial or administrative, is forbidden. This would mean, for instance, that financial authorities, now advised to apply discriminatory standards with regard to taxation to "Aryans" and "non-Aryans," or Party members and non-Party members, or foreign workers and German workers, would not be allowed to continue this policy. On the other hand, higher income taxes for higher income levels would, of course, not constitute "undue" discrimination.

## III. Abolition of Legislation Restricting Political and Civil Liberties

Ten years of Nazi rule have made a shambles of the liberties of the people. Regimentation has been practiced in all fields, and the hand of the state and Party has lain heavily on everybody not conforming to official patterns. Because MG has no desire to perpetuate its rule, it should be pledged to a program of speedy restoration of liberties. Government cannot be turned over to native German authorities as long as MG must fear that the government would revert to the hands of a bellicose and rapacious minority. This experiment can be undertaken only when the German people have gained some experience once more in the full development of social and cultural patterns of their own. Therefore it should be one of MG's earliest steps to grant the German people as much political and individual liberty as is compatible with the security of MG, and with the energetic suppression of all attempts to indulge openly or in veiled manner in Nazi activities.

### A. Political Activities

It is recommended that the laws concerning the outlawry of political parties and the monopoly of the Nazi Party be immediately abrogated.

The legal monopoly of political organization enjoyed by the Nazi Party rests on the Act against the Reconstitution of Political Parties of 14 July 1933 and the Act for the Safeguarding of the Unity of Party and State of 1 December 1933. The immediate abolition of these laws opens the way to the reconstitution of political parties. But the right to form associations of political and economic character cannot be an unlimited one. Obviously the NSDAP as well as all its affiliated organizations and any possible front or "ersatz" organization must be dissolved, and it is one of the foremost tasks of MG to see to it that they are not reconstituted under any disguise. The elimination of the Nazi Party and its affiliated organizations, however, is more a problem of abolishing institutions than one of invalidating legislation and will be treated in a special Guide on the Elimination of Nazism.

The Nazis had established a monopoly of organization in the realm of labor by giving the German Labor Front the status of the sole organization in this field (Decree of 24 October 1934). The abolition of this monopoly is also one of the first tasks of MG in the interest of the re-establishment of political freedom. While trade unions will thus be given the same freedom of organization as the political parties, an exception must be made, first for any organization which may appear as a continuation of the Nazi Labor Front or similar Nazi organization, and second for the German Nationalist Business Employees Association (*Deutschnationaler Handlungsgehilfenverband*). This association, which was closely connected with the German Nationalist Party, heavily contributed to the development of Nazism among business employees and can, for this reason, be assumed to constitute a possible refuge for disguised Nazis. While the outlawing of the Labor Front constitutes an immediate measure to be taken by MG, details on the re-establishment of free trade unions will be dealt with in a special Guide on Labor Problems.

### B. Social, Economic, and Cultural Activities

It is recommended that there be restored, with certain restrictions, freedom of association and freedom of assembly. It is further recommended that freedom of opinion be restored by abrogating the Editor's Act and the laws underlying the Nazi Chamber of Culture. The freedom of the Protestant Church should be restored through the abrogation of the Law concerning the Constitution of the Protestant Church. This would not be necessary for the Catholic Church; relations between Church and State have been governed by the Concordat of 1933 which, being a bilateral treaty, could not be unilaterally changed at any rate.

Under Nazism, the previously existing freedom to form associations in the field of social, economic, and cultural activities was restricted, since the Decree for the Protection of People and State of 28 February 1933 subjected this right to administrative control and supervision. Henceforth cultural and sports organizations as well as associations in the field of trade and commerce, e.g., employers organizations, should be permitted, although during the transitional period, care must be taken that these organizations are not replicas of the extinguished Nazi organizations utilizing the old personnel. In order to achieve this aim, these organizations should be required to register their by-laws, officers, employees, and members, as well as periodical financial statements, with MG authorities.

In the transitional period it also would be advisable to introduce a system of permits for meetings, at least for meetings to be attended by more than a certain number of persons. The granting of permits should belong to the discretion of local MG, since the individual decisions will largely depend on local circumstances.

But the re-establishment of freedom of cultural activities is not completed with the restoration of the freedom to form organizations of all kinds in this field. It is intimately connected with the establishment of freedom of opinion in the realm of the press, radio broadcasting, movies, theater and other artistic activities, and religious freedom of the Churches. Since Nazism, in most of these fields, has abolished freedom by the simple means of compulsory membership of all participants in such activities in Nazi institutions with a monopoly of organization, the restoration of freedom of opinion is closely connected with the elimination of these institutions.[1]

There are, however, in this field, certain laws whose immediate abolition is imperative.

1. *Press*. Since 1933 publishing of any kind of printed material (books, periodicals, newspapers, etc.) has been dependent on the author's as well as the publisher's membership in the strictly controlled Culture Chamber. With the abolition of the Culture Chamber and the transformation of its affiliated organization, freedom of expressing one's opinion in writing will be reestablished in principle. The exercise of the profession of newspaper editor (including editors of political periodicals) has further been made dependent on admission to the Reich Union of the German Press which could be refused at the discretion of the Nazi leadership of this association. Although the Editor's Act (*Schriftleitergesetz*) of 4 October 1933 should be abolished, the publishing of newspapers and political periodicals should come under MG supervision in order to prevent Nazi or pro-Nazi elements from gaining or maintaining influence over public opinion. No editor-in-chief or deputy chief of a German newspaper between 1933 and the occupation should be permitted any journalistic activity. Moreover the publisher and editor-in-chief of any newspaper or political periodical should be required to have a license from MG authorities, to be given only after close scrutiny; he must be held responsible for the policy of his paper. Any additional pre-censorship should be discarded, but MG, of course, will have the right to confiscate and forbid publications if their content endangers public safety and the right to punish or discipline the editor or author.[2]

2. *Church*. In a long struggle the Nazi regime tried to establish close control over Church affairs. For this purpose, a Reich Ministry for Church Affairs was established. The Protestant Church was officially centralized as a Reich Church with a Reich Bishop at its head. Controversies among Protestant groups were to be decided by a specially created office in the Church Ministry, thus excluding recourse to ordinary courts. The law concerning the Constitution of the German Protestant

Church of 14 July 1933, which sought to centralize the Protestant Church under Nazi control and which even the Nazis were not able to fully apply, should be abolished. As the Church Ministry, together with its special office for the decision of church conflicts, should likewise be abolished, authority within the Protestant Church will revert to the still existing constituent parts, the *Landeskirchen*.

The relation between Catholic Church and the state in Germany is based on a Concordat of 1933 between the Holy See and the Reich, and can therefore not be abrogated or changed unilaterally. Relations concerning the Catholic Church will therefore continue to be governed by the Concordat.

Laws restricting the right of churches and religious groups to make collections should be abolished.

(For all details concerning the future status of the Churches, see special Guide on Churches.)

## IV. Abolition of Legislation Possessing a Particularly Strong Nazi Character

There are certain parts of Nazi legislation the immediate elimination of which is not so much a security measure as a step to abrogate "the evil configuration of Fascism" symbolized by such laws.

### A. Abolition of Nazi Symbolism

It is recommended that laws, decrees, and other regulations dealing with political symbols be immediately abrogated. Political symbols, such as flags, colors, uniforms, songs, slogans, have always played a considerable role in German political life and have been cleverly used by the Nazis to influence the emotions of large masses of people and to instill successfully an almost mystical sense of loyalty to such Nazi symbols as the Swastika, the various colored shirts, etc. Therefore, it is of importance that the use of these symbols, whether as signs of state authority or as symbols of a creed and a party, be immediately outlawed and suppressed by MG authorities. At the same time, MG must make sure that no substitute symbols make their appearance. Whether new symbols are merely "ersatz" symbols of a continuing Nazi movement will need to be inferred not so much from any outward likeness or similarity with the original symbol but rather from the intention of the users. On the other hand, legitimate groups and parties should have the right to use or create symbols of their own choosing without interference on the part of MG. The creation of a new official flag and other official symbols should be left to the reconstituted German authorities.

In this field, however, rules of all kinds are too abundant to be abrogated by exhaustive enumeration. Therefore, in addition to a list of certain major enactments in the field, a general provision should be issued forbidding the use of Nazi symbols and the application of any law or other rule which refers to such symbolism. A general clause such as the one suggested would with one stroke eliminate all flags and uniforms, official songs and slogans, but also of festivals and holidays introduced by Nazism, names given to cities, literary contests and art prizes, and so on.

### B. Eugenic Legislation

It is recommended that there be abolished immediately the Nazi legislation concerning sterilization as well as the legislative rule concerning castration of certain criminals.

Nazi ideas in the field of "race biology" have produced the Law for the Prevention of Hereditarily Diseased Offspring of 14 July 1933, which provided for the sterilization of persons with more or less well-defined hereditary diseases. The law has been extensively applied under Nazism and charges of grave abuses have been made against it. The law, which thus is considered as a typical example of Nazi legislation, should therefore be immediately abrogated, without prejudice to any future eugenic legislation which the German people may venture to adopt.

Besides sterilization ordered by special "Eugenic Courts," the Nazis introduced castration as a special punishment for certain sexual crimes, to be meted out by the criminal courts. This is a type of punishment which is to be considered as "cruel and unusual" and should not be allowed under the authority of MG.

### C. Labor Legislation

It is recommended that the basic Act for the Regulation of National Labor be immediately abrogated.

While the re-organization of labor law constitutes a matter not to be dealt with in the period immediately following the occupation, but rather in the next stage, details will be treated in the special Guide on Labor. There is however, in the realm of labor legislation, one statute which, because of its "symbolic" character, should be abrogated immediately:

> the Act for the Ordering of National Labor (*Gesetz zur Ordnung der nationalen Arbeit*) of 20 January 1934. This law contains the basic principles of Nazi regulation of labor, including such institutions as "leadership" of the enterprise and "followers," labor trustees, Councils of Trust, etc. Since it has been made symbolic of the Nazi spirit in the realm of labor, its immediate elimination is advisable.

## V. De-Nazification of the Judiciary

### A. Reorganization of the Judiciary

It is recommended that German judges and public prosecutors be superceded for a period of two months. It is further recommended that immediately upon the start of the occupation, the investigation of the record of the suspended personnel and the recruitment of new members of the judiciary be initiated. No new appointment to a judicial or prosecutor's position should be made without public hearing, and appointment should only be made on a provisional basis.

As has been pointed out in "Analysis of the Problem," the removal of all members of the German judiciary from office seems necessary both in the interest of the security of the occupying forces and in the interest of the elimination of Nazism. "Member of the German judiciary" may be defined as every civil servant who is employed under the authority of the Reich Ministry of Justice and fulfills the prerequisite of becoming a judge (*Befähigung zum Richteramt*), i.e., not only actual judges but also public prosecutors, substitute-judges (*Assessor*), and law candidates (*Referendare*). New appointments, to be made by MG during the two-month period of suspension of courts, should proceed on the basis of petitions to be submitted by those desiring to be appointed or re-employed. All those who fulfill the prerequisites of becoming a judge, i.e., judges, prosecutors, and attorneys-at-law, should be entitled to submit petitions. This means that there would be two main groups from which to select judicial personnel: first, those among the dismissed persons found to be reliable, and second, trustworthy members of the bar. Should these two groups prove insufficient, MG might consider persons who appear specially qualified without having the required professional qualifications. It should however be remembered that this would be likely to meet with more resistance on the part of the legal profession than any merely political step.

With the submission of a petition, the personal files of the petitioner as well as any professional act (e.g., lawyers' briefs, judges' decisions) of the petitioner will become part of the record to be scrutinized. Furthermore, no decision should be made by MG authorities without previous public hearing to be held in the communities where the officials have been recently employed. The public should be allowed to take part in these proceedings. However, care should be taken to avoid personal controversies.

The suggested proceedings seem to be complicated and time-consuming, it should be kept in mind that there are now about 13,000 judges and prosecutors in "Greater Germany." Considering that MG will have to deal with pre-1938 Germany only, and that many proceedings will belong to the jurisdiction of MG, not more than 9–10,000 positions will need to be filled. Assuming that one MG official will be able to deal with seven cases a day, twenty officials would be able to carry through the reorganization within two and a half months.

In case of re-employment of a suspended official, MG should be free to employ him in whatever position deemed suitable without regard to his former rank and position. Considering the importance and responsibility of the job, moreover, appointments should be revocable in case he proves unreliable.

### B. Suspension of Court Activities

It is suggested that all German courts be closed for a short period. For the same period, legal transactions which according to German law require authentication by a notary public or a similar public formality should be forbidden, and any transaction made in violation of this rule should be considered null and void. Also, for this period, the effect of the Statue of Limitations should be suspended.

Closing of the courts is necessary in order to give MG a chance to reorganize the judiciary and because of the necessity speedily to revise certain parts of German legislation. It would, for example, be awkward to have pending divorce cases decided on the basis of Nazi marriage law under the authority of MG. If courts are closed, all criminal and civil proceedings must be suspended. While pending or new criminal investigations can either be taken over by MG or be postponed, civil law cases will be suspended entirely. This means that during this period not only no new suits will be accepted and no pending ones will be carried through, but also that the legal transactions mentioned above are prohibited in order to prevent Nazis from making transactions intended to secure immovable or movable properties against possible attachment. Thus, during this period, no new entries can be effected in the land register (*Grundbush*) kept by the local courts, no inheritance certificates (*Erbscheine*) can be issued, no entries can be made in the trade register (*Handelsregister*), etc.

In order to protect the legal rights and claims of persons who are affected by the closing of the courts, it should be proclaimed that according to articles 69 of the German Penal Law Code as well as article 203 of the Civil Law Code the effect of the Statute of Limitations is suspended for the period during which the courts are suspended.

### C. Release of Prisoners

All inmates of concentration camps or similar detention camps, who are not detained by virtue of a judicial sentence, should be released immediately.

Inmates of prisons should be released if their crime is either a political crime or has been committed for political reasons.

Reduction of excessive sentences for other crimes and, quite generally, the review of other sentences should constitute part of a general amnesty for all but serious crimes to be proclaimed as soon as possible.

1. The liberation of political inmates of concentration camps should be one of the urgent immediate concerns of MG authorities. Concentration camps are the epitome of all that is shameful in Nazism, and the camps should be immediately investigated and closed. However, it must be kept in mind that besides political opponents, Jews, etc., the regime has also used the concentration camps to detain certain categories of criminals deemed particularly reprehensible, such as "dangerous habitual criminals" and black-market operators. Insofar as such persons found there are detained without trial or have already served their sentences in prison and are merely being detained in concentration camp in addition, they should be released as in the case of political prisoners, since there would be no legal basis for detaining them further in prisons. As the facilities of existing concentration camps will be needed for the detention of the large numbers of active Nazis and similar categories of persons to be detained by MG for reasons of security, a speedy dissolution of the Nazi camps seems imperative.

2. One of the most urgent measures, which large parts of the German public will expect the new authorities working under MG supervision to resort to immediately, is the liberation of those political prisoners who have been convicted by Nazi courts. For this purpose a line must be drawn between those convicted for political crimes and "ordinary crimes": those which are intrinsically political, such as treason, desertion, mutiny, etc., and, second, those which, although ordinarily non-political, may assume political character by being motivated politically, as, e.g., murder committed for political reasons, or arson, perjury, libel, under the same circumstances. The task of MG is, however, complicated by the fact that many offenses which under ordinary circumstances would appear as non-political, have assumed political color under the conditions of Nazism. There is, for example, a combination of both individual motives and desires to revolt or protest against the regime in such "crimes" as "breach of labor contract," "absenteeism," and similar acts. In doubtful cases, it should be the policy of the new German authorities working under MG supervision to decide in favor of the respective prisoner in all such cases. Relief for a large percentage of all convicts will be brought by the proclamation of a general amnesty, which will remit or considerably scale down sentences. The working out of such a measure, however, will require one or two months, and the release of political prisoners should not be retarded by waiting for this amnesty[3].

## Appendix: List of Nazi Laws Requiring Abrogation

| | *Page*[4] |
|---|---|
| *Citizenship:* | |
| 1. Gesetz über den Widerruf von Einbürgerungen und die Aberkennung der deutschen Staatsangehdrigkeit, 7-14-1933 (Statute on Revocation of Citizenship and Expatriation) | |
| Version of 7-10-1935 | 1015 |
| 2. Verordnung zur Durchführung des Gesetzes über den Widerruf von Einbürgerungen und die Aberkennung der deutschen Staatsangehörigkeit, 7-26-1933 (Dec. 1. Ex. Decree for Execution of Statute on Revocation of Citizenship and Expatriation) | 480 |
| 3. Reichsbuergergesetz 9-12-1935 (Statute on Reich Citizenship) | 1146 |
| 4. Erste Verordnung zum Reichsburgergesetz, 11-14-1935 (First Decree on the Statute on Reich Citizenship) | 1333 |
| 5. Zweite Verordnung zum Reichsburgergesetz, 12-21-1935 (Second Decree on the Statute on Reich Citizenship) | 1524 |
| Special provisions required to supplement the abrogation of Nos. 3, 4, and 5: | |
| a. Expatriated persons who are in German territory when these decrees are abrogated shall re-acquire German citizenship as of the date of this abrogation. | |
| b. Expatriated persons who are outside German territory at this time may apply for re-naturalization. | |
| c. In general, the acquisition and the loss of German citizenship shall be regulated by the Staatsangehörigkeitsgesetz of 7-22-1913 (RGB1. 1913 I p. 583). However, paragraph 1 of the Verordnung uber die deutsche Staatsangehörigkeit of 2-5-1934 (RGB1. 1934 I p. 85) remains in force: there shall be no "Landes-Staatsangehörigkeit." | |
| *Discrimination* | |
| *a. against "Non-Aryans":* | |
| 1. Gesetz über die Zulassung zur Anwaltschaft, 4-7-1933 (Statute on Admission to the Bar) paragraphs 1 and 2 | 188 |
| 2. Verordnung über dis Zulassung von Aerzten zur Tätigkeit bei den Krankenkassen, 4-22-1933 (Decree on the Admis- | |

| | Page[4] |
|---|---|
| sion of Physicians to Public Social Insurance Institutions) paragraph 22 | 222 |
| 3. Gesetz gegen die Überfüllung deutscher Schulen und Hochschulen, 4-25-1933 (Statute for the Elimination of Overcrowding in German Schools and Universities) paragraph 4 | 225 |
| 4. Gesetz über die Zulassung von Steuerberatern, 5-6-1933 (Statute on the Admission of Tax Consultants) Article I | 257 |
| 5. Gesetz zum Schutz des deutschen Blutes und der deutschen Ehre, 9-15-1935 (Statute for the Protection of German Blood and Honor) | 1146 |
| 6. Reichsärzteordnung, 12-13-1935 (Federal Physicians' Statute) paragraph 3 (2) No. 5 | 1433 |
| 7. Reichstierärzteordnung, 4-6-1935 (Federal Veterinarians' Statute) paragraph 3 (2) No. 5 | 347 |
| 8. Deutsches Beamtengesetz, 1-26-1937 (German Civil Service Act) paragraph 25 | 39 |
| 9. Bestallungsordnung für Apotheker, 10-8-1937 (Law on the Licensing of Pharmacists) section I, paragraph 2 | 1116 |
| 10. Gesetz über die Rechtsverhältnisse der judischen Kultusvereinigungen, 3-28-1938 (Statute on the Legal Status of Jewish Religious Communities) | 338 |
| 11. Verordnung gegen die Unterstützung der Tarnung jüdischer Gewerbebetriebe, 4-22-1938 (Decree against Furthering the Concealment of the Jewish Character of Commercial Enterprises) | 404 |
| 12. Gesetz zur Vereinheitlichung des Rechts der Eheschliessung und der Ehescheidung im Lande Oesterreich und im übrigen Reichsgebiet, 7-6-1938 (Law on the Unification of Marriage and Divorce Proceedings in Austria and all other parts of Germany) paragraph 4 | 807 |
| Special provision required to supplement the abrogation of No. 12: Divorce and annulment suits pending at the time of this abrogation shall be suspended for a period of three months. | |
| 13. Gesetz über die Zulassung zur Patentanwaltschaft, 9-4-1938 (Law on the Admission of Patent Lawyers) Article III, section I, paragraph 3 | 1150 |

| | Page[4] |
|---|---|
| 14. Verordnung zur Ausschaltung der Juden aus dem deutschen Wirtschaftsleben, 11-12-1938 (Decree on the Elimination of Jews from German Economic Life) | 1580 |
| 15. Verordnung über den Einsatz des jüdischen Vermögens, 12-3-1938 (Decree on the Utilization of Jewish Assets) | 1709 |
| 16. Gesetz ueber Mietsverhaeltnisse mit Juden, 4-30-1939 (Law on Leases with Jews) | 864 |
| 17. Polizeiverordnung zur Kenntzeichnung der Juden, 9-1-1941 (Police Decree on Badges for Jews) | 547 |
| 18. Verordnung ueber die Beschäftigung von Juden, 10-3-1941 (Decree on Employment of Jews) | 675 |

*b. against Foreigners and Foreign Workers:*

| | |
|---|---|
| 1. Verordnung über die Behandlung von Ausländern, 9-5-1939 (Decree on the Treatment of Foreigners) | 1667 |
| 2. Reichstarifordnung fuer polnische landwirtschaftliche Arbeitakräfte, 1-8-1940 (Federal Regulation on Wage and Labor Conditions of Polish Workers) (quoted in Birkenholz and Siebert, *Der ausländische Arbeiter in Deutschland*, p. 813) | |
| 3. Verordnung über die Behandlung von Vermögen der Angehörigen des ehemaligen polnischen Staates, 9-17-1940 (Decree on the Disposition of the Assets of Citizens of the Former Polish State) | 1270 |
| 4. Anordnung des Reichsarbeitsministers über die Behandlung polnischer Beschäftigter, 10-5-1941 (Order of the Reich Labor Minister on the Treatment of Polish Employees) (quoted in Birkenholz and Siebert, *Der ausländische Arbeiter in Deutschland*, p. 705) | |
| 5. Verordnung ueber die Besteuerung und die arbeitsrechtliche Behandlung der Arbeitskräfte aus den neu besetzten Ostgebieten, 1-20-1942 (Decree on Taxation and Labor Conditions of Laborers from the Newly Occupied Eastern Territories) | 41 |
| 6. Erlass des Reichsministers der Finanzen betreffend Steuer der Arbeitskräfte aus den neubesetzten Ostgebieten, 2-25-1942 (Order of the Reich Minister of Finance Concerning Taxes or Laborers from the Newly Occupied Eastern Territories) (quoted in Birkenholz and Siebert, *Der ausländische Arbeiter in Deutschland*, p. 968) | |

| | *Page*[4] |
|---|---|
| 7. Anordnung über die Beschäftigung von Zigeunern, 3-13-1942 (Order on the Employment of Gypsies) | 138 |
| 8. Verordnung über die Einsatzbedingungen der Ostarbeiter, 6-30-1942 (Decree on the Conditions of Employment of Eastern Workers) | 419 |
| Special provision required to supplement the abrogation of Numbers a.1 to 18 and b.1 to 9: No authority or other organization chartered or licensed by public authorities shall issue or apply any law, decree, police ordinance regulation or by-law which discriminates against an individual or groups of individuals for reasons of race, religion or nationality. | |

*Preferences for Members and Veterans of Party, Police, and Armed Forces:*

| | |
|---|---|
| 1. Gesetz über die Schutzpolizei der Länder, 7-17-1922 (Statute on the Protective Police of the States) paragraph 2 | 597 |
| 2. Wehrmachtsversorgungsgesetz, 8-4-1921 (Law on Preferential Treatment and Pensions Granted to Former Army Members) paragraph 30 | |
| Version of 9-19-1925 | 349 |
| 3. Gesetz über die Versorgung der Kämpfer für die nationale Erhebung, 2-27-1934 (Law on Preferential Treatment and Pensions for the Fighters for the National Revolution) | 133 |
| 4. Wehrgesetz, 5-21-1935 (Law on the Organization of the Army) paragraph 32 | 609 |
| 5. Verordnung ueber Fürsorge für Soldaten und Arbeitsmänner, 9-30-1936 (Decree on the Care of Soldiers and Workers) | 865 |
| 6. Runderlass des Reichs- und Preussischen Ministers des Innern, 4-2-1937 (Circular of the Prussian Ministry of Interior) (published in *Reichsministerialblatt der Inneren Verwaltung*, vol. 1937, p. 515) | |
| 7. Wehrmachtsfürsorge und Versorgungsgesetz, 8-26-1938 (Law on the Care and Pensioning of Former Army Members) paragraphs 37 to 45, and 201 | 1077 |
| Version of 8-20-1940 | 1162 |
| 8. Gesetz über die Versorgung der Militärpersonen und ihrer Hinterbliebenen bei Dienstbeschadigung (Reichsversorgungsgesetz), 5-12-1920 (Law on the Pensioning of Military Personnel and Their Survivors in the Event of Injuries Suffered in the Line of Duty) paragraph 33 | 989 |

| | *Page*[4] |
|---|---|
| 7. Gesetz über die Hitlerjugend, 12-1-1936 (Law on Hitler Youth) | 995 |
| *b. Cultural Activities:* | |
| 1. Reichskulturkammergesetz, 9-22-1933 (Law on the Reich Culture Chamber) | 661 |
| 2. Gesetz ueber die Einrichtung einer vorlaufigen Filmkammer, 7-14-1933 (Law on the Organization of a Provisional Film Chamber) | 483 |
| 3. Schriftleitergesetz, 10-4-1933 (Act on Editors | 713 |
| 4. Lichtspielgesetz, 2-16-1934 (Act on Moving Pictures) | 95 |
| 5. Theatergesetz, 5-15-1934 (Act on Theaters | 411 |
| c. *Church Activities*: | |
| 1. Gesetz über die Verfassung der Deutschen Evangelischen Kirche, 7-14-1933 (Law on the Constitution of the German Protestant Church) | 471 |
| 2. Gesetz zur Regelung der offentlichen Sammlungen und sammlungsähnlichen Veranstaltungen, 11-5-1934 (Law Regulating Public Collections) paragraph 5 to be abrogated with regard to churches. Churches shall be unrestricted in their collection activitie | 1086 |
| 3. Gesetz zur Sicherung der Deutschen Evangelischen Kirche, 9-24-1935 (Law Guaranteeing the Existence of the German Protestant Church) | 1178 |
| *Nazi Ideology:* | |
| *a. Symbols:* | |
| 1. Erlass ueber das Setzen der Hakenkreuzflagge auf Kauffahrteischiffen, 4-29-1933 (Edict on Hoisting the Swastika on Merchant Vessels) | 244 |
| 2. Gesetz zum Schutz der National Symbole, 5-19-1933 (Law for the Protection of the National Symbol) | 285 |
| 3. Gesetz gegen heimtueckische Angriffe auf Staat und Partei und zum Schutze der Parteiuniformen 12-20-1934 (Law Against Malicious Attacks against State and Party and for the Protection of the Nazi Uniform) | 1269 |
| 4. Reichsflaggengesetz, 9-15-1935 (Reich Flag Law) | 1145 |

| | Page[4] |
|---|---|
| 5. Verordung ueber die Hoheitszeichen des Reiches, 11-5-1935 (Decree on Official Reich Symbols) | 1287 |
| 6. Erlass ueber die Reichssiegel, 3-7-1936 (Edict on the Reich Seal | 147 |
| Special provision required to supplement the abrogation of Nos. a. 1 to 6. The display of the Swastika flag or the wearing of Swastika or NSDAP party symbols is forbidden. | |

*b. Eugenics:*

| | |
|---|---|
| 1. Gesetz zur Verhutung erbkranken Nachwuchses, 7-14-1933 (Law on the Prevention of Hereditarily Diseased Offspring) | 529 |
| 2. Strafgesetzbuch (Penal Code) paragraphs 42 a. no. 5 and 42 k. | |
| Version of Gesetz gegen gefährliche Gewohnheftsverbrecher, 11-24-1933 (Law against Dangerous Habitual Criminals) | 995 |
| 3. Gesetz zum Schutz der Erbgesundheit des deutschen Volkes 10-18-1935 (Law for the Protection of the Hereditary Good Health of the German People) paragraph ld | 1246 |

*c. Labor:*

| | |
|---|---|
| 1. Gesetz zur Ordnung der Arbeit in oeffentlichen Verwaltungen und Betrieben 3-23-1934 (Law on the Organization of Labor in Public Administration and Enterprises) | 220 |
| 2. Gesetz zur Ordnung der nationalen Arbeit 1-20-1934 (Law for the Regulation of National Labor) | 34 |
| Version of 11-30-1934 | 1193 |

# 16

Herbert Marcuse

# *DISSOLUTION OF THE NAZI PARTY AND ITS AFFILIATED ORGANIZATIONS*

(July 22, 1944)

Editor's note: R&A 1655.5. Marcuse's authorship is indicated in a letter from Eugene Anderson to Carl Schorske on January 19, 1944 (RG 226, entry 60, box 1: Projects Committee Correspondence). Information on the discussions that preceded the report's approval are found in RG 226, entry 44, box 3, folder III.B. Another confirmation is also found in Marcuse, *Description of Three Major Projects*.

Of the seven appendixes that accompany the report, only the first is published here. It contains a draft proposal for the proclamation of the dissolution of the National Socialist Party that, in fact, corresponds to the decree passed by the AMGOT (MG Law no. 5), now in *Documents on Germany Under Occupation, 1945–1954* (ed. B. Ruhm von Oppen [London–New York: Oxford University Press, 1955], pp. 9–13). There is also a supplement from March 1945 (R&A 1655.5A), *The Dissolution of the Nazi Party and Its Affiliated Organizations: De-nazification of Important Business Concerns in Germany*, that has not been republished here because there are no precise indications as to who the author is.The report was published as War Department Pamphlet 31-110.

Classification: Confidential

## I. Analysis of the Problem

### A. General

When the Allies march into Germany, they will probably find the Nazi regime in a state of disintegration. Some of the agencies and institutions of Nazism may still be functioning, especially those which performed primarily "technical" functions (local administration, relief and welfare organizations), but the key positions of political control and terror will have been abandoned. The Nazi officials who held these positions will have fled or be in hiding; the less known and less conspicuous representatives of the Nazi Party and Government will have discarded all outward signs of their former position and will pose as ordinary citizens.

The suspension of the Nazi control apparatus is likely to cause widespread unrest, upheavals, and dislocation of the necessary services. The anti-Nazi opposition, persecuted and terrorized for years, may come into the open, and acts of spontaneous revenge and retribution may be numerous. The occupying authorities are committed to safeguarding the security of the Allied Forces and to maintaining public law and order, and they are also committed to the destruction of Nazism. The achievement of the first purpose depends to a great extent on the achievement of the second. The quicker and the more thoroughly the elimination of Nazism is accomplished, the quicker and better will security, law and order be established. It is precisely the interest of the security of the occupying forces, and of restoring law and order, that calls for leniency towards the spontaneous acts of the anti-Nazi opposition,[1] and for harshness towards all Nazi elements. Nazism can in the last analysis be eliminated only through an internal political movement in Germany.

The first step in this undertaking would be the dissolution of the National Socialist Party and of its affiliate and controlled organizations, and the removal and apprehension of all officials who participated in the formulation of policy or had considerable responsibility in carrying it out. It might seem that the dissolution of the Nazi Party and the apprehension of its chiefs would at one stroke break the hold of Nazism over the German people. But Nazism was not confined to the activities and institutions of the Nazi Party: in one way or another, every sphere of public and private life was shaped by the Nazi system. The system was promoted and supported by elements outside the Nazi Party (for example, some top groups in business, the landed aristocracy, and the military). Many Fascists have cleverly avoided open identification with the policies of the regime and have not held any position in the Party and its affiliated organizations.

The occupation authorities are, therefore, faced with a twofold task:

1) the dissolution of the Nazi Party and its affiliated and controlled organizations, and the apprehension of the policy-making Nazi officials;
2) the surveillance or apprehension of "active Nazis" who are not identified by their position in the Nazi Party or Government.

B. Components of the Nazi Party

The Nazi Party comprises the following formations and associations:

*Gliederungen* (*Formations*):

SA (Sturm Abteilungen; Storm Troops).

SS (Schutz Staffeln).

Nationalsozialistischos Kraftfahrkorps (NSKK; National Socialist Motor Corps).

Hitler Jugend (HJ; Hitler Youth), including Bund Deutscher Mädchen (BDN; League of German Girls).

Nationalsozialistischer Deutscher Studentenbund (NSD-StB; National Socialist German Students' League).

Nationalsozialistisches Fliegerkorps (NSFK; National Socialist Flying Corps).[2]

Nationalsozialistischer Deutscher Dozentenbund (NSDoB; National Socialist German Association of University Instructors).

Nationalsozialistiche Frauenschaft (NSF; National Socialist Women's Association).

*Angeschlossene Verbände* (affiliated organizations):

Deutsche Arbeitsfront (DAF; German Labor Front).

National sozialistische Volkswohlfahrt (NSV; National Socialist Public Welfare Organization).

Nationalsozialistischer Deutscher Aertzebund (National Socialist German Medical Association).

Nationalsozialistischer Rechtswahrerbund (National Socialist Association of the Guardians of the Law).

Nationalsozialistischer Lehrerbund (NSLK; National Socialist Teachers' Association).[3]

Nationalsozialistische Kriegsopferversorgung (NSKOV; National Socialist Organization for War Victims).

Reichsbund der Deutschen Beamten (RDB; Reich Association of German Officials).

Nationalsozialistischer Bund Deutscher Technik (National Socialist Association of German Technology).

*Betreute Organizationen* (supervised organizations):

Deutsche Studentenschaft (German Students' League).

Nationalsoziatistischer Altherrenbund (National Socialist Alumni Association).

Deutsches Frauenwerk (German Women's Work).

Deutscher Gemeindetag (Association of Municipal Governments).

Nationalsozialistischer Reichsbund für Leibesübungen (National Socialist Sport Association).

Reichsbund Deutsche Familie (Reich Association of German Families).
Nationalsozialistischer Reichsbund Deutscher Schwestern (National Socialist Association of German Nurses).
Reichskolonialbund (Reich Colonial League).
Nationalsozialistischer Reichskriegerbund (National Socialist Veterans' Association).[4]

*Mixed Organizations of State and Party:*[5]
Reichsarbeitsdiens (Reich Labor Service).
Organisation Todt (OT; Organization Todt).
Baustab Speer (Organization Speer).
Technische Nothilfe (TN; Technical Emergency Corps).
Reichsnährstand (Reich Food Estate).

## II. Recommendations

### A. Dissolution of the Nazi Party

As soon as possible after the occupation, a proclamation should be issued announcing the dissolution of the Nazi Party and its affiliated, supervised, and mixed organizations (including those listed above).[6]

The entire property of these organizations should be taken into custody by the occupying authorities (see CA Guide, *Property of the Nazi Party, Its Affiliates, Members, and Supporters).* A draft of the text of such a proclamation is appended.

Institutions and organizations which, although not officially formations or affiliates of the Nazi Party, are products of the Nazi spirit and have become identified in the public mind with Nazism, should likewise be dissolved. For example:

Volksbund für das Deutschtum im Ausland (VDA).
Deutsches Auslands Institut (DAI).
Verband Deutscher Vereine im Ausland (VDVA).
Kameradschaft USA.
Ibero-Amerikanisches Institut.
Dentscher Fichte Bund.
Weltdienst.
Reichskulturkammer.

### B. Apprehension and Detention of Nazi Officials

The security of the occupying forces and the maintenance of public law and order require that those Nazi officials who, by virtue of their position, have had command over the Nazi terror apparatus and its manifold branches should be apprehended and detained. This principle applies to Party as well as government officials, and also to officials of mixed organizations. These officials fall under one or several of the categories listed below, totaling approximately 222,000.

In reality, the number of people to be seized by the occupation authorities will be considerably smaller. Some of the categories are necessarily overlapping. Moreover, many of the designated persons will be in the armed forces, and many may not be located. It may be assumed that the Nazis have made extensive preparations for the event of defeat, and that all possibilities for disguise and concealment will be utilized. The latter will be particularly easy for the lesser-known officials, and their apprehension will be possible only through the help of the local population.

Lists of the officials to be apprehended should be drawn up prior to the occupation, and photographs should be secured whenever possible. Notices with stipulations on rewards and punishments should be distributed in Germany at the earliest possible moment. Fear of reprisals and nationalistic feelings, however, will be strong among the German population and will deter many people from giving information to the occupation authorities. The most active support is likely to come from the political and ideological anti-Nazi opposition, which may be expected to deal with the Nazis in its own way. This may frequently lead to spontaneous acts of revenge. When occupation authorities have to detain the perpetrators of such acts in the interest of security and order, they should make extensive use of their right to pardon. If native German anti-Nazi courts should be established, they should be given jurisdiction over these people.

Among the Nazi officials to be apprehended will be many war criminals, who must be treated according to inter-allied agreements. Final disposition of all other seized Nazis should be left to future decision.

The detained Nazis could be kept in the concentration camps wherever the prisons are filled.

| | *Approximate number* |
|---|---|
| 1. Ministers and Under Secretaries of State (*Staatsekretäre*) | 40 |
| 2. The officials of the Reich Propaganda Ministry and its regional branches, the heads of its subsidiary agencies | 300 |
| 3. All high officials (from Ministerial Councillor up) in Speer's Reich Ministry for Armaments and Production, and the chairmen of the *Hauptausschüsse* and *Ringe* in the same ministry | 70 |
| 4. Heads of other Supreme Reich Authorities (Commissars, Inspectors, Division Chiefs in the Four-Year-Plan Office, etc.) | 30 |

| | Approximate number |
|---|---|
| 5. Heads of certain Reich institutions such as the *Reichsbank*, the Reich Office for Social Insurance, the Supreme Administrative Tribunal, the Reich Health Office, Supreme Court Martial | 20 |
| 6. All members of the People's Court (incl. lay members and attorneys) and Special Courts | 300 |
| 7. All Reich Governors and Provincial Presidents (most of them are *Gauleiter*) | 30 |
| 8. All members of *Land* governments | 30 |
| 9. All District Presidents (*Regierungspräsidenten* | 40 |
| 10. Mayors of cities over one hundred thousand inhabitants and all Lord Mayors | 90 |
| 11. All Reich Labor Trustees | 40 |
| 12. All Attorney Generals (*Generalstaatsanwälte*) | 30 |
| 13. All District Attorneys (*Oberstaatsanwälte*) | 200 |
| 14. All County Presidents (*Landräte*) | 700 |
| 15. All members of the present German *Reichstag* and of the *Preussische Staatsrat* (most of them are already covered by other categories)[7] | |
| 16. All officials of the Reich Food Estate (*Reichsnährstand* from the *Kreisbauernführer* up) | 800 |
| 17. The leadership of the National Economic Chamber (*Reichswirtschaftskammer*) | 10 |
| The chairmen or presidents (and their deputies) of the (7) National Groups (*Reichsgruppen*) | 14 |
| The chairmen or presidents (and their deputies) of the (6) National Transportation Groups | 12 |
| The chairmen or presidents of the (about 60) Economic Groups under the National Groups | 60 |
| The chairmen or presidents of the (42) Gau Economic Chambers and the (18) affiliated Economic Chambers | 60 |
| 18. All *Wehrwirtschaftsführer*[8] | 150 |
| 19. All political functionaries of the NSDAP in the *Reich-*, *Gau-*, and *Kreis* administration | 40,000 |
| 20. All Local Group Leaders (*Ortsgruppenleiter*) of the NSDAP | 27,900 |

| | *Approximate number* |
|---|---|
| 21. The officers of the SS and SA from the *Untersturmführer* (incl.) up[9] | 46,000 |
| The non-commissioned officers of these organizations from the *Scharführer* (incl.) up | 33,000 |
| All full time (paid and honorary) employees of these organizations who are not covered by the preceding categories | 1,000 |
| 22. The officials of the German Labor Front in the *Reichs-* and *Gau-* administration | 300 |
| 23. The political Shock Troops and the members of the Plant Brigades (*Werkscharen*) in the factories | 15,000 |
| 24. All officials and employees of the *Gestapo* and the Security Service | 10,000 |
| 25. The teachers and the administrative personnel of the Party Schools, and training schools, *Ordensburgen*, etc. | 20,000 |
| 26. The officers of the NS Motor Transportation Corps (NSKK) | 200 |
| 27. The officers of the Reich Labor Service (*Reichsarbeitsdienst*) | 250 |
| 28. The officers of the Technical Emergency Corps (*Technische Nothilfe*) | 150 |
| 29. The officials (male and female) of the Hitler Youth League from the *Bann* (*Bannmädelführer)* up | 10,000 |
| 30. The national and Gau officials of the German Students' League (*Deutscher Studentenbund*) and of the NS University Instructors' League (NSDOB) | 200 |
| 31. The chiefs of the German military and civil administration in the occupied countries and territories | 3,000 |
| 32. The NS Party officials corresponding to No. 2, and 17–30 in the occupied countries and territories | 30,000 |
| About | 222,026 |

Special measures should be taken to prevent the persons listed under Nos. 31 and 32 (many of whom fall under the category of war criminals) from crossing the border into Germany.

(The personnel of the *Wafen-SS*, of the *Organisation Todt*, and of the NS Flying Corps is considered as part of the German *Wehrmacht* and not included in this list.)

## C. Identification of "Active Nazis" Other Than Those Identified by Their Official Position

The dissolution of the Nazi Party and the apprehension of the responsible Party and government officials is only the first step towards the elimination of Nazism from German society. Many of the most active Nazis are not covered by the categories discussed above, and many social and economic institutions which were essential for the rise and maintenance of Nazism are apparently "neutral" institutions outside the range of the Nazi Party.[10]

The detection of active Nazis not identified by their official position is difficult and can eventually be made only with the help of the local population. Persons who, during the period of Nazism, participated in the following activities are suspect:

1. Denunciation of political opponents to the Nazi regime, and/or contribution to their seizure.
2. Instigation or perpetration of acts of violence and brutality for political reasons against political and religious opponents of the Nazi regime, against foreign and German workers, Jews, prisoners of war, etc.
3. Dissemination of Nazi ideology (in the case of teachers, writers, editors, publishers, actors, doctors, lawyers, etc.: beyond their professional duties).
4. Willing reception of honors from the Nazi Party.
5. Acceptance of transfer of real property, securities, or other property of substantial value incident to the spoliation of the occupied countries, the program of "Aryanization," and the confiscation of property of political opponents, Jews, *Volksschädlinge*, etc.

In addition, the following categories of persons must be considered as suspect unless and until their good faith is established:

6. The political representatives of the German Labor Front (in addition to those mentioned in Nos. 22 and 23 on p. 000) in the plants, shops, and offices (subleaders, *Betriebsobmänner*, etc.). It must be emphasized, however, that in some cases non-Nazis and even anti-Nazis may have accepted such functions in order to cover up their oppositional attitude.
7. Members who joined the Nazi Party prior to 1933.

While the last category and to a lesser degree the sixth are based upon exact and objective criteria, the first five involve criteria which admit of considerable latitude of interpretation and whose use should ordinarily require extensive investigation if serious abuses are not to result. These criteria, or similar ones that may occur to anti-Nazis, can according be applied in the identification of active Nazis only through consultation with the local population best acquainted with the facts of Nazi behavior.

Experience has demonstrated the insufficiency of two widely used methods, namely, identification through locally prominent personalities (the priest, the judge, the mayor, etc.), and anonymous denunciations. The local civic leaders, even if they have not been Party members and active Nazis, have been closely connected with the Nazis by social and political ties; in many cases these people may not only be reluctant to denounce the real Nazis but may even protect and defend them against denunciations from other quarters. Church leaders who have not compromised themselves by supporting the Nazi regime may be a much more objective source of information. However owing to their unpolitical attitude, they may have a much too narrow conception of "active Nazis," and they may be inclined to focus their attention only on people who have interfered with the Church. Anonymous denunciations will be very frequent, and the occupation authorities can hardly avoid following them up in many cases, but they should not be used as the main source of information or as the basis for the final decision. For the element of personal revenge is likely to prevail in such denunciations, and may also be used by the Nazis themselves in order to cover up their own past activities.

Accurate identification can best be made by the anti-Nazis who have known the respective persons at work. It is recommended that the occupation authorities establish as soon as possible contact with the local anti-Nazis opposition for that purpose.

All persons falling under the seven categories should be carefully scrutinized. Not all of them must be dangerous Nazis at the time of the occupation; many of them may have changed their mind and become sincere non-Nazis. At the same time, these categories certainly include the most vicious and brutal type of active Nazi. Treatment will therefore depend on the outcome of the investigation of the individual case and will accordingly range all the way from imprisonment or detention to surveillance and loss of office.

Since such an investigation, however, will necessarily involve long-term procedures, measures should be taken at once to prevent active Nazis and active Nazi supporters from continuing in or assuming important public functions. The following is suggested:

Pending the required investigation, all persons belonging to the following categories should be prohibited from exercising any important public function.[11]

1. In addition to the officials included in the list on pages 000 and 000, all other paid and unpaid (honorary) officials of the Nazi Party and its affiliated and supervised organizations.
2. Active members of the Nazi Party and the SS, SA, and other paramilitary Party organizations and all those members of the Nazi Party who hold political rather than technical jobs.
3. In addition to the government and business personnel included in the list on pages 000 and 000, all persons who have faithfully served the Nazi regime in leading positions in the government or leading positions in the organization of the economy.

The same categories should be prohibited from exercising their franchise if elections should take place.

In selecting personnel for any kind of function, and in preparing elections of any kind, the occupation authorities should call for sworn statements concerning the applicant's status as to Nos. 1 to 3 above. Severe punishment should be stipulated for false information.

## Appendix A. Proklamation Betreffend Die Aufiösung Der National Sozialistischen Deutschen Arbeiterpartei

Die Nationalsozialistische Deutsche Arbeiterpartei, N. V. Nüachen, und alle angesschlossenen und betreuten Gliederungen und Verbände werden heirmit aufgeloest.

Den Mitgliedern der Nationalsozialistischen Deutschen Arbaiterpartei, die öffentlichen Vertretungen angehören oder das Reich, die Länder, Provinzen, Gemeinden oder Gemeindeverbände in öffentlichen oder privaten Unternnamungen vertreton, ist die Ausübung ihter Fungtionen untersagt.

Das Vermögen der Nationalsozialistischen Deutschen Arbeiterpartei, und der ihr angeschlossenan Gliederungen und Verbände wird von der allierten Militärverwaltung in Verwahrung genommen, die es bis auf weiteres als Treuhänder verwaltet.

Die alliierte Militärverwaltung erlässt die notwendigen Ausfährungsvorschriften.

Die Proklamation tritt mit ihrer Verkündung in Kraft.

### Proclamation Concerning the Dissolution of the National Socialist German Workers' Party

The Nationalsozialistische Deutsche Arbeiterpartei, N. V., München, the formations thereof, and all associations affiliated therewith or supervised thereby are hereby dissolved.

All members of the National Socialist German Workers' Party who are members of any public representative body or who represent the Reich or states, provinces, communities, or associations of communities in any undertaking, whether public or private, are hereby prohibited from exercising their function of office.

The Allied Military Government hereby takes over the property of the National Socialist German Workers' Party, formations thereof, and affiliations therewith, to be for the present administered in trust.

All decrees necessary and proper to the carrying out of this Proclamation will be issued by the Allied Military Government.

Effective upon publication.

# 17

Franz Neumann

# *GERMAN CARTELS AND CARTEL-LIKE ORGANIZATIONS*

(n.d.)

Editor's note: There is an undated typescript in the archives of the Research and Analysis Branch with the title "German Cartels and Cartel-Like Organizations," with the annotation: "Preliminary draft not yet approved by the Editorial Committee on Civil Affairs Studies" (RG 226, entry 44, box 4). In a prospectus on works in progress in the Civil Affairs guides of April 13, 1944, Neumann is indicated as the author of the report, which was assigned the provisional catalog number R&A 1655.30; the number, however, is not present on the typescript.

The report is accompanied by three appendixes—here omitted—with the texts of decrees on cartels from 1923, 1930, and 1933.

Classification: Confidential

## Analysis of the Problem

### I. Introduction

The fundamental fact of German industrial organization is the preeminence of the large vertical combines. Cartels and other associations of business, which blanket the German economy almost completely, have been used by the combines as means for the domination of industry and are in part a reflection of the degree of concentration of German industry.

The prototypes of the combines are those within so-called heavy industry. Single *Konzerne* control extensive mining properties, coking plants, iron and steel works, heavy engineering works, and often inland transportation, expecially inland navigation companies. They dominate the Rhine-Ruhr region, the middle German industrial region, and upper Silesia. The growth of the combines has been furthered under National Socialism by the Aryanization of Jewish businesses, the Germanization of foreign enterprises, and the elimination of small and medium-size firms. Cartels and other "self-governing" organizations of German business have served even before the Nazis as the instruments though which the small number of powerful combines have imposed their will upon industry at large and thereby stabilized the conditions under which business is conducted.

Clearly, therefore, the enormous concentration of capital represented in the combines constitute the major characteristic of German business organization with which planning for the reconstruction of the German economy, by whomever undertaken, must contend. The cartel, and its various special forms under the Nazis, may be regarded as a secondary manifestation of the condition in which a relatively few firms control so large a part of German capital and production. Even if it were somehow possible to eliminate cartels through vigorous enforcement of an anti-trust program, effective restraints of trade would nevertheless persist in the fields where combines predominate due to their tacit appreciation of a common interest in concerted behavior.

Above and beyond the objective conditions which promote cartellization in German industry is the ingrained propensity of German businessmen to act within the framework of industry-wide organizations and to seek the intervention of such organizations in reducing competition and stabilizing market relationships. This pattern of business behavior in Germany has never really been tainted with illegality and has not had to assume the sub-rosa forms which have appeared elsewhere as a consequence of anti-trust enforcement. In fact, government sanction has been repeatedly granted to associations of German business, both in law and in the practice of successive governments in dealing with such organizations as points of contact with entire industries.

It is important that its policy towards cartels be formulated by AMG in the light of these central facts: that the problem of cartels is a secondary manifestation of the monopolistic control of German industry—the primary factor is the power of industrial combines; and that the cartel form of organization is a business institution deeply rooted in the German economy.

## II. The Role of Cartels and Cartel-Like Organizations in Germany

### A. Pre-Nazi Position

1. *Cartels.* Long before the Nazis came into power, cartels played a large role in the German economy. Though adequate and precise statistical indications of the extent of cartellization in Germany are not available,

it has been estimated that, by the middle thirties, practically all domestically produced industrial raw materials and semi-finished goods and more than half of finished goods output were cartellized.

Cartels have been defined as "contractual associations of legally independent enterprises in the same or similar fields of business formed with the intent, effect, or potentiality of influencing the market by means of regulation of competition." There are many forms of such associations but the principal types are the price cartel, the quota cartel and the cartel for the geographical division of markets. Effective price cartellization is under certain circumstances also achieved through indirect agreements such as those entered into by condition cartels which regulate terms of sale, or by calculation cartels which fix methods of cost determination. There is, of course, wide variation among cartels in the range of products covered, the proportion of the industry included, and the tightness of the controls imposed. The most effectively organized cartel, combining most of the forms mentioned above, is the association with a joint sales agency or syndicate. Though small and inefficient enterprises were sometimes kept alive under the protections of cartel agreements, the basic cartel policies were set by the big combines which were in control by virtue of their larger voting power based on the quota.

The pre-Nazi cartels were voluntary organizations of businessmen except for a few special cases in which compulsory organizations were set up by special Parliamentary enactment. The so-called Coal Socialization Law of 1919, for example, provided for compulsory membership in regional syndicates, headed by a national cartel and established as the supreme organ of the coal industry a Reich Coal Council composed of mine owners, workers, technicians, and representatives of the State, the coal merchants, and the consumers. About the same time a similar compulsory organization was established by statute in the potash industry. But with a few such statutory exceptions, firms possessed the legal right to join or not to join cartels, and under the rather liberal provisions of the 1923 Law, could often withdraw from membership in cartels when it seemed in their interest to do so. As a result of the encroachment of outsiders, periodic outcroppings of competition occurred, and striving for quotas together with the threat of withdrawal made difficult the maintenance and smooth working of cartel agreements in a number of fields.

Almost from the inception of this form of private market control it was recognized by the courts as a legal exercise of freedom of contract. In a suit brought by a cartel in 1888 against a member who had violated the agreement by exceeding his production and sales quota, the Bavarian Supreme Court, in upholding the cartel, stated that it was "incumbent upon prudent businessmen belonging to a branch of industry which is suffering from a depression to get together and enter into agreements regulating the ways and means of operating their industry with a view to promoting recovery." Implicit in many subsequent court decisions was the view that cartels somehow represent a higher form of economic organization than the "primitive" system of free entrepreneurs competing in an open market. This view was even reflected in the opinions of economists and lawyers who participated in the ambitious and comparatively liberal *Enquetausschuss* of the late twenties (the German counterpart of the T.N.E.C.).[1] They held that it was not the purpose of cartel law to protect the principle of free competition as against market organizations. The Committee would not even go so far as to report favorably upon a suggestion that registration of all cartels be made compulsory and that a permanent commission be established for supervising and investigating all cartellization.

There were occasions, however, when public sentiment became aroused against cartels and monopoly to a point where the government was forced to take formal steps. These concessions came as a result of major economic calamities such as the inflation of the early twenties and the depression of the early thirties.

The inflation wiped out substantial sectors of the independent middle class and enriched monopoly business at the expense of workers and small producers. As a result the first and most sweeping of the pre-Nazi decrees subjecting cartels to control was adopted in 1923. The decree established a cartel tribunal with jurisdiction in all disputes between a cartel and the Government, among cartel members, and between cartels and outsiders. The Reich Minister of Economics could sue before the cartel tribunal for the dissolution of a cartel or any particular clause if an agreement "or any particular mode of its observance shall endanger the economic life of the community." The tribunal, on motion of the Minister of Economics, could also sue any other combination in restraint of trade in order to permit a party to withdraw from the agreement if any conditions of sale or method of fixing prices "endangered the economic life or the good of the community." In addition, boycotts and similar measures could be executed against cartel members or outsiders only with the consent of the president of the cartel tribunal. The Cartel Decree of 1923 thus vested broad powers in the government to void existing agreements and to enjoin cartels from carrying out certain practices. Yet the key provisions of the decree remained on the books as mere statutory grants of power which were never invoked in practice.

In response to pressures that arose during the depression of 1930, the government took official note of the fact that recovery was hampered by the price system of cartels and issued another decree which enhanced its statutory powers to control cartels. The power to dissolve cartels or to nullify particular clauses of agreements was vested directly in the Reich

Cabinet without the necessity of intermediate recourse to the special tribunal. The tribunal retained its jurisdiction in cases of boycotts and in suits arising from breach of the cartel contract.

These statutes represented considerable grants of power to the Weimar government, and if vigorously exercised, might have served to bring cartels under control or at least to prevent their worst abuses. However, little initiative or energy was displayed by the State in the application of the laws, and, except for the dissolution of the lignite cartel which represented a special case, no significant results can be adduced. It would be accurate to say that private organizations of business under Weimar almost never had to submit to real external state regulation of competition and seldom reckoned with the possibility of state interference in setting basic marketing policies.

The powerful domestic German cartels (and through them the big German combines) were the dominant factors in international cartels in most of European industry. This was especially true of chemicals, iron and steel, electrical equipment and radio, to mention only a few of the more important cases. Through such agreements, German industry was able to exercise monopoly control over large sectors of non-German industry—restricting output, controlling prices and technology.

2. *Inter-Cartel Organization.* Inter-cartel organizations in the pre-Nazi period existed on a flexible and voluntary basis culminating in the powerful *Reichsverband der deutschen Industrie.* The R.D.I. was composed of many layers of trade associations, cartels, powerful individual intrepreneurs, or even territorial pressure groups. But the key affiliates were the so-called *Fachverbände* which were embraced in 23 *Fachgruppe* or main industrial groups and which in turn were composed of many lower and smaller units within a particular industry. It was through this organization that business exerted its political pressure in the national sphere and the R.D.I. came to be regarded as the official spokesman of German industry.

The *Reichsverband* provided a number of services for its members in matters of broad economic policy such as foreign trade, finance and reparations. One of the most important services was provided by its cartel department which functioned as an advisory and coordinating agency for all cartels, furnishing legal advice, formulating master cartel agreements, and adapting the propaganda machine to general cartel marketing policy. The prestige and influence of the cartel department in national affairs was tremendous.

It should be noted that in a number of cases the *Fachverband* or voluntary trade association behaved like a cartel—fixing prices and assigning production quotas. But in general the *Fachverband* had a broader coverage than individual cartels, and concentrated its activities on servicing functions and lobbying for the industry.

3. *The Regional Organization of Business.* Traditionally the local Chambers of Industry and Commerce in Germany represented a kind of pool of all business experience in a given region. They antedate the Weimar Republic. Before the reorganization of 1942 this territorial basis of business organization was a reasonable and efficient method for the performance of certain important services for all business in the area. Officials of the Chambers were elected by the members on the basis of equality (one vote per member, irrespective of size of firm). Membership was compulsory and moderate dues were collected like taxes. The Chambers were under the general supervision of the Ministry of Economics.

The functions traditionally performed by the Chambers have not been essentially restrictive in their character. They provided information on taxation and raw materials. They served as pressure groups in municipalities, and in general played a considerable role in the regional life of the community. In particular the Chambers provided a voice to the smaller businessmen and to industries of local importance.

In addition to the 111 Chambers of Industry and Commerce, there were 71 Chambers of Handicraft, with much the same characteristics.

### B. Development under the Nazis

1. *General Policy.* The main content of Nazi policy toward cartels and cartel-like organizations is twofold: the strengthening of the power of cartels over their individual members, and the strengthening of state control over cartels. In addition to granting to cartels various disciplinary powers over their members, and to the state powers over cartels, this policy has been implemented through: (a) consolidation of cartels and other associations of business; (b) enforcement of compulsory membership and the leadership principle; (c) the use of private business associations as organs for administering governmental functions; and (d) denial to cartels, under the pressure of war, of the chief marketing functions formerly performed.

a. *Consolidation of Cartels.* The consolidation of cartels under the Nazis may be viewed as part of the general policy of reducing the number of private business entities with which government must deal. This desire for closer control over private organizations took the form not only of the elimination of small-scale individual firms, but also had its impact in the "rationalization" of associations of business. Thus, many of the 2300 cartels, which it is estimated formerly existed, have been dissolved and incorporated into larger units. It is expected that when the process is completed only about 500 cartels, mostly of a national character, will remain. A similar process has taken place with respect to the Chambers or regional business organizations where 42 *Gau* Economic Chambers now replace approximately 180 former Chambers of Industry and Commerce and Chambers of Handicraft.

The reduction in the number of cartels was due in part to direct action taken under the authority of the "Cartel Combing-Out Decree" and in part was a natural consequence of the establishment and fostering of the "self-governing" organization known as the *Gruppe*. (See below p. 000) Originally the intention was for the groups to concern themselves with administrative functions while the cartels confined their operations to marketing activities. Gradually, as the marketing functions of cartels disappeared as a result of full utilization of capacity, the functional distinction between the two sets of organizations also disappeared, and many cartels were dissolved in favor of the broader groups. The highest stage in this development was reached in the merger between cartel and group in the form of *Reichsvereinigungen* or national peak cartels such as those in coal and iron. (See below p. 000.)

b. *Compulsory Membership and the Leadership Principle*. These policies were widely introduced further to enhance state control over "self-governing" business organizations as well as to increase the powers of those organizations over their members. Just a few months after the Nazis came into power a Compulsory Cartellization Decree was issued which vested in the Minister of Economics the power to create compulsory cartels and to order any entrepreneur to join existing cartels. This represented a considerable departure from pre-Nazi practice when compulsory cartellization was resorted to on rare occasions and could be brought about only after long discussion and by Parliamentary enactment. Under the authority of the Compulsory Cartellization Statute the Nazi government has created a number of new compulsory cartels and in hundreds of cases has decreed compulsory attachments to existing cartels. Compulsory membership has also been a feature of the new Nazi "self-governing" business organizations such as the groups (national groups, economic groups, trade groups, etc.) and the *Reichsvereinigungen*.

In the Chambers membership had always been compulsory. But the Nazis abolished the former system whereby officials of the Chambers were democratically elected on the basis of one vote per member and substituted the *leadership principle*. Thus, the essential feature of the only business associations where the smaller businessman could exercise some influence was abolished. In the Chambers, party reliability was the ruling criterion for the selection of managers. In the rest of the new business organizations the leadership principle was also universally imposed. In practice what this meant was the appointment of leading businessmen from the biggest concerns provided they were also acceptable in terms of Party reliability. In the case of Main Committees and Industrial Rings, technical and engineering competence was an additional requirement for appointments.

c. *Cartels as Agents of Government*. The main rationale of the various devices used by the Nazis to subject business associations to rigid control was not so much the desire to control or supervise their private activities. That was the basis for Weimar policy with respect to cartels. Under the Nazis, existing "self-governing" organizations have been used and new ones set up as part of a positive policy making such organizations conscious agents of state-planned production and distribution.

In all the intricate procedures connected with wartime procurement, production control and raw material allocation, the cartels, groups or specially created "self-governing" business organizations have served as the point of contact between a central government control agency and the individual firms. Orders of the chief procurement agencies such as the Army, Ministry of Transport, etc., are allocated to individual firms by Main Committees (See below p. 000) which are newly established associations of firms producing identical products. There are Main Committees covering each important category of finished war goods. In addition the Nazis have established Industrial Rings which are organizations of producers using common components such as ball bearings. The Rings, which in their membership cut across the Main Committees, are responsible for assisting in the allocation of key industrial components. In addition, the Main Committees and Rings have chief responsibility for the standardization and rationalization of production and the combing out of inefficient plants.

Besides these organizations specifically set up as agents for production planning and control, the cartels and groups have also been delegated important functions in this sphere. Individual firms do not contact the *Reichsstellen* (the central raw materials allocating offices) directly for their raw materials. Instead the firm goes to its *Bewirtschaftungsstelle* which serves as the intermediary between it and all the *Reichsstellen* from which it requires raw materials. The *Bewirtschaftungsstelle* is usually a cartel or economic or trade group. Moreover, the *Reichsstelle*, as the central office for the allocating of a single raw material, does not have the personnel or the administrative machinery for making specific allocations. It, therefore, has been forced to rely upon *Verteilungsstellen* which again are in almost all cases cartels or groups. The activities of the *Reichsstellen* proper are confined to broader policy and overall decisions. Yet in several cases even the *Reichsstelle* itself is an economic group. This is the case in the machine industry, the electrical engineering industry, and the precision and optical instrument industry, where the diversified and technical nature of the products give rise to such complex problems that an organization from within the industry must be relied upon even for the primary decisions.

The cartels, groups, and *Reichsvereinigungen* also play an important role in the regulation of prices and sales margins; the latter two organizations aid in the setting of foreign trade policy and in the spoliation of occupied Europe. On the regional level their activities are integrated with those of the Chambers, which assist the Main Committees and the groups in the subcontracting of orders, and serve as the key regional agency in foreign trade and exchange control.

The delegation of key governmental powers to private business organizations has served at the same time to strengthen the influence of such groups over their members and to expedite the organization of the German economy in the interests of the war machine. It is important to remember in this connection, however, that except for a few special instances, the power to set basic policy has continued to reside in the higher echelons of government, especially the Speer Ministry and to a lesser extent in the Ministry of Economics and its *Reichstellen*; the cartels and cartel-like groups serve as technical agents in the implementation of these policies.

d. *Denial to Cartels of Marketing Functions.* As early as 1934 price fixing by cartels was made subject to governmental approval. At present new price agreements cannot be made nor existing cartel prices changed except with the consent of the Reich Price Commissioner. Moreover, cartels and syndicates must register existing price agreements at the beginning of each year. Thus one of the keystones of the cartel's control of the market has been made subject to government surveillance.

The other major feature of the cartel's market control, namely, the quota, has also disappeared. With the attainment of full employment in 1936, it gave way to the allocation of production among cartels members in accordance with technical criteria of capacity and efficiency. Official recognition of this condition was embodied in an appeal by the leader of the National Group Industry requesting the abolition of quotas in cartels and syndicates. The appeal has the force of an order and violations are subject to severe punishment. The larger firms have naturally benefited most from this situation, especially since it meant the end of the system whereby producers who did not reach their quotas were indemnified from fines paid into the cartel treasury by members who exceeded their quotas.

The denial to the cartels of their power to control the market was, of course, neither motivated by the desire, nor did it have the effect, of enforcing competition in German industry or reducing the power of the large combines relative to smaller-scale business. If anything, as pointed out above, it had the opposite effect. The sole purpose of these restraints was to prevent inflation and maximize production in the interests of the war economy by making the government ultimately responsible for the key marketing decisions.

2. *The Organizations.* The implementation of Nazi policy with respect to cartel-like organizations can be appreciated in more specific terms by an examination of the status of each type of organization.

a. *Cartels*. The present status of cartels can best be viewed in terms of the legislation passed by the Nazis dealing with this type of organizations. The following is a brief statement of the most important laws:

1) The Statute of 15 July 1933. The power of the Reich Minister of Economics to dissolve cartels or void particular clauses now lies wholly within his discretion. Resort to suit before the cartel tribunal[2] is no longer necessary. Thus, the most important provision of the Emergency Decree of 1930 (See above p. 000) is made a permanent feature of cartel control. The measure enhances government control over cartels by excluding judicial and semi-judicial considerations, guaranteeing quick decisions and insuring secrecy of proceedings. Another provision liberalizes the possibility of boycotting cartel members or outsiders who fail to adhere to the cartel's price policy, thus strengthening cartel control over an industry.
2) Another Statute of 15 July 1933 introduced compulsory cartellization by simple decree. The Minister of Economics has the power to create compulsory cartels, to order any entrepreneur to join an existing cartel, to regulate the capacity of existing plants and to prohibit the establishment of new plants. This law made possible complete and effective cartellization of industries such as cement, where for years producers were precariously organized and constantly involved in bitter fights with outsiders who threatened their positions.
3) The Decree of 5 September 1934 further strengthened the power of cartels against members and outsiders. The filing of a motion with the cartel tribunal, whether by members or by outsiders, against intended boycotting measures no longer had suspensive effect.
4) The Decree of 23 November 1940 codified the various rulings of the Price Commissioner with regard to the price fixing activities of the cartels. Price cartels and resale-price maintenance schemes can be made or changed only if the consent of the Price Commissioner has been secured. Cartels must register the existing price agreements at the beginning of each year. Bidding agreements for public orders are valid only with the consent of the Price Commissioner.
5) The Decree of 20 November 1942. This decree vests the most sweeping powers with the Minister of Economics. It authorizes him to interfere according to his discretion not only with the cartels but also with any entrepreneur, and to issue to all enterprises that "influence the market" general or individual

orders, to make the conclusion of cartel agreements dependent upon his consent, and to change existing cartel agreements.

6) The Decree of 27 October 1942. On the basis of this so-called "Cartel Combing-Out Decree," the Minister of Economics engaged in a streamlining of the whole cartel structure. According to official German statements, only 500 out of 2300 cartels will ultimately remain, but the remaining cartels will mostly have a national character.
7) The Appeal of the National Group Industry in February 1943 abolishing cartel quotas. This appeal has the force of law.
8) The Decree of 20 May 1943. This gave the Groups the right to engage in marketing activities wherever cartels had been dissolved, unless they were incorporated into bigger ones.

The net effect of these regulations is that, while the power of cartels increased immeasurably, the controlling power of government over the cartels is so sweeping that the government can do anything it desires to undertake.

The cartels under the Nazi system are, of course, no longer private marketing organizations, but have become administrative organs for the execution of State policies. In this respect they are difficult to separate functionally from the Groups, which were specifically set up as such. In fact, almost any of the activities generally undertaken by the groups (See below p. 000) are in some industries carried out by the cartels and in almost all cases with the assistance of cartels. Without the integration of the cartels into the administrative apparatus a considerably greater number of government administrators would be required for the execution of state policies.

b. *The Groups*. The *Gruppen* are the basic unit for the functional "self-government" of industry. The Act of 27 November 1934 and the supplementary executive decree provided that all businessmen, even public enterprises, must be members of a group. The whole economy, exclusive of transportation[3] and agriculture, is divided into seven National Groups (*Reichsgruppen*): (1) industry, (2) trade, (3) banking, (4) insurance, (5) power, (6) tourist industry, (7) handcraft. The National Groups are subdivided into Economic Groups (*Wirtschaftsgruppen*), among them 31 in industry, 4 in trade, 6 in banking, and so on. The Economic Groups are subdivided into Branch Groups (*Fachgruppen*) and in some cases further divided into sub-Branch Groups (*Fachuntergruppen*). The groups stand formally under the jurisdiction of the Reich Ministry of Economics, but since September 1943 control over them actually resides with Speer's Ministry for Armaments and War Production. The following chart may clarify the structure of the groups.

| *Funk's Ministry of Economics* | | | | *Speer's Ministry for Armaments and War Production* | | |
|---|---|---|---|---|---|---|
| National Group Handicraft | National Group Power | National Group Insurance | National Group Industry | National Group Trade | National Group Banking | National Group Insurance |
| \| | \| | \| | \| | \| | \| | \| |
| \| | \| | \| | 31 | 4 | 6 | 2 |
| Economic Groups | Economic Groups | Economic Groups | Economic Groups | Economic Groups | Economic Groups | Economic Groups |
| | | | Branch Groups (several hundred) | | | |

The Economic Groups, and more specifically those within the National Group Industry, are the key units in the entire structure. The Economic Groups levy the contributions and finance the National Groups above them and the Branch Groups and Sub-Branch Groups below them. The following is a list of the Economic Groups within the National Group Industry.

1. Mining
2. Iron Producing
3. Metals
4. Foundries
5. Fuel
6. Iron and Steel Construction
7. Machines
8. Vehicles
9. Aircraft
10. Electrical Equipment
11. Precision and Optical Instruments
12. Finishing and Other Branches of the Iron Industry
13. Iron, Steel, and Sheet Metal
14. Metalwares
15. Stone and Earth
16. Building
17. Timber Processing
18. Glass
19. Ceramic

20. Sawmills
21. Chemicals
22. Paper etc.
23. Printing
24. Paper Processing
25. Leather
26. Textiles
27. Clothing
28. Foodstuffs
29. Breweries
30. Sugar
31. Alcohol

The new groups set up by the Nazis correspond to the old trade associations under the Weimar Republic. Thus, the National Group Industry is coextensive with the *Reichsverband der deutschen Industrie* and the Economic Groups correspond to the *Fachverbände* under Weimar. In fact, most of the executive decrees by which groups have been set up have simply transformed the previously existing trade associations into the new groups. The Nazis, however, incorporated two new and important features: compulsory membership and the leadership principle. The leaders of the national groups are appointed by the Minister of Economics; the leaders of the lower organizational units are also appointed from above. Each leader of an Economic Group is assisted by a presidential council composed of the most important businessmen in the field, but the actual management of the Group rests with full-time managers who, in many cases, have been taken over from the old trade associations.

As stated above, the original intention was for the groups, as compulsory organizations, to concern themselves with administrative functions delegated to them by the state, whereas the cartels were to confine themselves to marketing activities. Despite a number of formal attempts via statute and decree to maintain a functional dichotomy between the private cartels and the public groups, the distinction has largely disappeared as a result of economic developments. For one thing, as full utilization of capacity was approached, the quota setting function of cartels naturally receded in significance; and the authority of the Price Commissioner considerably restricted their autonomous pricing activities. As their marketing functions diminished, many of the cartels were dissolved in favor of the groups, and in such cases whatever marketing activities remained could in accordance with the decree of 20 May 1943 be taken over by the groups. There is also considerable interlocking personnel among the leaders and managers of the more important cartels and the groups. An attempt was made by the government to dissociate the top personnel of the groups from that of the cartels but nothing seems to have come of it. Just as in the more powerful cartels, the roster of group leaders reads like a Who's Who of concentrated industry. In some industries the formal right of the groups to supervise the cartels has been used to solidify the position of the larger combines.

So far as the actual functions of the groups are concerned, they are in some cases performed by the groups themselves and in others delegated to cartels. In general, they play a large role in raw material allocation, in a few instances actually assuming the duties of the *Reichsstellen* or raw material allocating boards. In other cases groups have been made *Bewirtschaftungsstellen* and as such stand between the producer and the raw material allocating organs. Some groups and cartels have also been made *Auftragslenkungsstellen* or order distributing agencies.

In addition to these tasks and the usual services that trade associations render their members, the Groups fulfill a large number of supplementary functions. They have a considerable part in foreign trade policy; they assist in the spoliation of occupied Europe, and thus maintain their agencies abroad; they advise the Price Commissioner in the regulation of prices and profits. They operate both as national organizations and on the regional level. On this level they are integrated with the Chambers, the Armaments Commissions established by the Speer Ministry, and the War Economy Staffs established by the Gauleiter.

c. *Reichsvereinigungen*. The *Reichsvereinigungen* represent the highest stage in the development of the merger between cartel and group. They were established in 1941 and 1942 as compulsory national peak cartels operating under the leadership principle. *Reichsvereinigungen* exist in the following fields: coal, iron, chemical fibers, hemp and textile processing. There are, in addition, a number of national cartels with functions similar to those of the *Reichsvereinigungen*, such as the National Shoe Association (*Gemeinschaft Schuhe*), the Iron Rope Works Association, the Forestry Association, and the like.

The *Reichsvereinigungen* are a combination of cartels, groups, and in many cases, of a raw material allocating and order distributing agency. Unlike the cartels and groups, however, they have no counterpart in the pre-Nazi period. They were created to coordinate all "self-governing" organization and industrial entrepreneurs operating in the above-mentioned industries, and they are designed to assist the German government in the spoliation of occupied Europe. They are, thus, marketing associations, trade association, rationalization agencies, and foreign trade agencies in one. The *Reichsvereinigungen* for iron, chemical fibers, hemp, and textile finishing have also been assigned by the Price Commissioner the task of fixing the prices of the commodities which they control. The Price Commissioner retains only a supervisory function over the price-fixing policy.

Though nominally under the authority of the Ministry of Economics, they now actually function under the complete domination of Speer.

d. *Chambers*. A drastic revision in the whole territorial set-up was made in 1942 when the 42 *Gau* Economic Chambers were instituted causing the virtual elimination of the old territorial organization embodied in the Chambers of Industry and Commerce. The Nazi character of the new organizations is manifested by the fact that the district of the *Gau* Economic Chambers corresponds to that of the Party *Gau*. Also the leadership principle was introduced, the presidents and vice-presidents of the Chambers being appointed by the Ministry of Economics after consultation with the Party *Gauleiter*. All meetings of the *Gau* Economic Chamber must be attended by the *Gau* Economic Advisor of the Party. Thus, the rather uniquely democratic features of the pre-Nazi chambers have completely disappeared.

The functions of the chambers are very far-reaching indeed. They generally assist their members to find their way through the maze of government regulation, whether it be taxation or price control or raw material allocation or labor control. But they have also been delegated certain specific tasks. They assist in the distribution of orders within the territory of the *Gau* Economic Chamber. Prime contractors, especially, have to use the Chambers for the selection of sub-contractors. The *Gau* Economic Chambers act as the district foreign trade offices of the Ministry of Economics. It is here that licenses and permits for export, import, and foreign currency transactions have to be cleared. Chambers are combing-out agencies for retailers and artisans under the Four-Year Plan decree. They decide which businessmen have to abandon their businesses and what indemnification has to be paid to them.

In the pre-Nazi period there existed no body which integrated the regional and industry-wide organizations of German business. The Reich Economic Chamber has been set up as such an organ. Its members are the National Groups and the *Gau* Economic Chambers. The primary task of the Reich Economic Chamber is to act as the supreme disciplinary court (*Ehrengerichtshof*) for all entrepreneurs belonging to chambers and groups. It can issue warnings or impose fines on anyone who violates the standards of behavior of a "decent" German businessman, or can declare such a person incapable of filling posts within the chambers or groups.

e. *Main Committees and Industrial Rings*. While cartels, chambers and groups are either continuations or adaptations of traditional German forms of business organization, the Main Committees (*Hauptausschüsse*) and Industrial Rings (*Industrioringe*) were established *de novo* under the Nazis. They were set up as a consequence of the shortcomings of the economic control system which were becoming apparent during the winter of 1941–42 under the impact of the defeat suffered on the Russian front. With the shattering of hopes for a short war came the realization that it was no longer possible to rely on accumulated stocks for raw materials and military equipment, and that heavy military wastage rates would impose a tremendous burden of replacement on Germany's industrial resources. The Committees and Rings were set up as perhaps the most important of a series of measures designed to squeeze the utmost out of the productive system.

Just as the cartels, chambers, and especially the groups might be regarded as the "self-governing" sector of industry through which the Ministry of Economics operates, so may the Committees and Rings be considered the "self-governing" organs of Speer's Ministry of Armaments and War Production. While groups, however, are set up by industrial branches (metals, fuel, ceramic), the Committees are set up along product lines (tanks, engines, bearings, etc.). Main Committees are composed of manufactures of major identical end-products, whereas an Industrial Ring comprises industrial enterprises which are users of given important components. Both Main Committees and Industrial Rings are composed exclusively of engineers and construction men drawn from the most important industrial corporations. In Germany it is common for directors and other top business managers to possess at the same time technical training and education, and it is this type of person who predominates in the Committees and Rings. At present there seem to be 15 such Main Committees and three Industrial Rings.

Their overall task is the rationalization and standardization of industrial production. Under the stress of air and land war, however, their tasks have considerably increased, a development which has been accompanied by a decline in the power of the groups and chambers. In the field of military equipment the Committees and Rings have become virtually claimant agencies for raw materials, thus replacing the several branches of the armed forces. They also are the agents for allocating government military orders to prime contractors since they possess the requisite technical information combined with an inside knowledge of the industry. They are now the agents who decide upon the closing down and, in many cases, about the transfer of industrial plants, and can exercise authority in both raw material and labor allocations. The Committees and Rings operate both nationally and regionally. The regional organization is directed by so-called Armaments Chairmen; one for each corps area (*Wehrkreis*).

## Recommendations

### I. General Approach

The proposals advanced in this section stem from the preceding analysis of the present and past position of cartels and other associations of business in Germany and the orientation suggested by the general objectives and prospective scope of AMG control.

The purpose of Military Government has been defined as the consummation of the defeat of our enemies, politically and economically as well as militarily, in such a manner as to facilitate the emergence of a democratic indigenous German Government. The period of Military Government is to be brief and its personnel rather strictly limited in number. Basic changes and long-range reform of Germany's economic structure must be ruled out as the job of AMG and left to the German people themselves acting through a new Government. AMG must largely confine its own activities to the fulfillment of its major objectives: the most thoroughgoing possible elimination of Nazi and militaristic influences from German life, and the general supervision of the Germany economy to secure that minimum level of efficiency required to prevent gross privation in Germany and secure for the United Nations commodities essential to the relief of liberated Europe.

### A. De-Nazification

As indicated above, the prime characteristic of Nazi policy was to subject cartels and other business associations to State control through the establishment of new organizations, the consolidation of existing organizations, and the introduction of compulsory membership and leadership principles. The principal aim of AMG, therefore, is the elimination of the new organizations (wherever their functions are redundant) and the coercive measures applied to the traditional associations. This policy must be accompanied by the ousting and detention of all active Nazis, and continued control to insure that Nazi influence is not restored through the election of Nazis or the infiltration of Nazism through persons under their direction. Cartels must be prevented from serving as disguises for Nazi political organizations or covert means of sabotaging other policies which AMG may choose to adopt, such as an anti-combine program. This could be done by requiring all business associations to register with AMG their by-laws, officers, employees and members, as well as periodic financial statements.

It is contended that AMG ought to go further and forbid cartels outright. This policy is urged for two reasons:

1. The unique opportunity afforded by the military collapse, it is claimed, should be utilized to foster whatever tendencies toward competition and free enterprise exist in Germany. If cartels are not to be completely outlawed, at the very least their activities should be strictly controlled to prevent their engaging in conventional restrictive marketing practices.

2. The elimination of cartels would strike a blow at the power of industrialists who, it is contended, have been guilty as a class of fostering Nazism and militarism in Germany.

This policy must be rejected on the following grounds:

1. AMG will not be in a position to enforce competition in Germany. Not only will it be lacking in staff for such a job, but effective enforcement of the program in the German courts would be impossible. The Weimar Republic was well equipped with broad legislative powers to control, restrain, or even to dissolve cartels, if only the will to invoke the power and to see the litigation through had been present. The Nazis, to be sure, did in a sense achieve effective control of cartel organizations, but it was directed to war purposes and was achieved only under the compulsion of an apparatus of terror.
2. The right of association cannot be taken from businessmen as a class without applying the same policy to other groups. Except for Nazi groups, AMG must promote rather than suppress freedom of association in order to facilitate the growth of a political organization leading to the establishment of a domestic indigenous German Government.
3. The political power of industrialists resides essentially in their wealth and control of large corporations. To some extent cartels have been used as instruments through which this power has been exercised, but any program to eliminate the fundamental economic foundations of German aggression would involve profound changes in the entire structure of individual and corporate property in Germany. Should an anti-combine program be adopted by AMG, then steps should be taken to prevent cartels from being used to sabotage or circumvent such a policy.

### B. Administration

The part played by cartels and economic groups as administrative agencies for Government economic policy has been stressed. To the extent that materials-allocations programs are adopted in particular fields, compulsory cartels and economic groups will have to be retained. But many functions connected with central procurement and the need to get the utmost efficiency out of the economy will have disappeared with the termination of the war. The general state of extreme shortage which is characteristic of wartime will give way to one of great slack, and most areas of production may be left to function in response to market mechanisms. There will, however, probably be a small number of fields in which central production-planning and raw-material control will continue to be needed. These are fields in which Germany's domestic production threatens to be short relative to her own essential needs, or where it may be necessary to divert such a large amount of German supplies to provide for the needs of other parts of Europe that a shortage within Germany is possible. In such cases, compulsory cartels or economic groups should be retained, but their Nazi leaders should be removed and replaced by managers chosen by free election.

## II. Specific Recommendations

### A. Cartels

With one exception, none of the basic decrees affecting cartels should be abolished at the outset. The exception is the decree of 5 September 1934 which strengthens the powers of cartels against members and outsiders. The rest should be retained, since they provide AMG with comprehensive powers over the existing cartel system - powers which may be used by AMG for the execution of any economic policy which may be established. On the basis of this legislation, AMG, acting through the Ministry of Economics or directly, may dissolve cartels, make transfers within the existing cartel structure, control cartel prices, and prohibit any uneconomic restrictions on prices and production.

The compulsory features of cartels should be withdrawn except for those particular industries in which AMG adopts a production and allocation program for which a cartel may serve as an agent of control. A proclamation should be issued granting to all members of cartels the right to withdraw within two months. In order to establish more firmly the freedom to withdraw from cartel agreements, it should be provided that thereafter the life of specific cartel agreements be limited to one year whereupon they may be renewed. Contracts drawn up for longer periods of time than one year should not be enforceable in the courts. It is expected that this guarantee of the right of firms to sever cartel connections will result in many entrepreneurs seeking to regain their economic liberty. In a number of fields cartels are artificial creations and would disintegrate as soon as the protection of the government were withdrawn. It should be added in this connection that, should AMG adopt a price regulation policy and use cartels as adjuncts of control, there will for this reason alone be no necessity for constituting compulsory cartels. In fact, there are definite advantages in a situation in which outsiders are permitted to petition a Price Commissioner for lower price schedules.

AMG should require the registration of all cartels including their directors, employees, members, and periodic financial statements. It should exercise veto power over all such organizations as may be found to be cloaks for Nazi groups or means for the circumvention of any other program which AMG chooses to adopt such as, for example, an anti-combine program.

B. Groups

The Groups in general should be abolished except for particular ones which AMG might choose to retain as administrative organs if a production or allocation program is adopted in a given field. Although the Groups have a certain historical continuity with the previously existing trade associations, they are in their present form Nazi creations, having been set up under the leadership principle to assist in the mobilization of the economy for war. No bar other than registration should be placed in the way of the reconstitution of voluntary trade associations such as those which existed under the Republic.

C. Reichsvereinigungen

The *Reichsvereinigungen* should be dissolved. As explained elsewhere, they are organs for the coordination of all entrepreneurs and semi-governmental organizations in their respective fields. They are utterly unacceptable since they have played a leading role in the exploitation of occupied Europe.

D. The Chambers

After a thoroughgoing de-Nazification of its leadership, the present system of Chambers should be retained.

The Chambers would represent a valuable and immediately available point of contact between all business in a given area and Military Government. Any general regulations or orders of AMG could be communicated and explained to businessmen through the facilities of the Chambers. AMG would find particularly useful the experience of the Chambers in allocating orders within their districts and in directly assisting businessmen in foreign-trade and foreign-exchange licensing.

These responsibilities can continue to be vested in the Chambers only after a purge of their management. All Chamber presidents, managers, and a majority of the members of the presidential councils are at present trusted Nazi businessmen. Unless they, as well as all other active Nazis, are removed, AMG will be confronted with a situation of continual sabotage of its orders. It should not be difficult to find a reliable businessman in a given locality, possibly a former Chamber manager, who could temporarily take charge of the Chamber. As soon as military security permits, elections should be held in accordance with the pre-Nazi statutes covering the Chamber system. At the very outset, however, it might be well for political reasons to change the name "*Gau* Economic Chamber" simply to "Economic Chamber." Of course, should an acceptable indigenous German government desire to completely abolish the present Chamber system and revert to the old territorial set-up, they will be free to do so. But that is not a task which AMG should undertake.

There will of course be no need to retain the Reich Economic Chamber in view of its functions as the chief disciplinary agency for both Groups and Chambers.

### E. Main Committees and Industrial Rings

The Main Committees and Rings should be dissolved. They owe their origin to the desire of the Speer Ministry to have full technical control over the production apparatus of Germany.

It is expected that the functions which the Main Committees and Rings performed under the Nazi system will be redundant under AMG. Should it happen, however, that the economic policies which AMG pursues in Germany require considerable rationalization of industry, concentration of plants, transfer of industries, etc. there exist other agencies well equipped to assist in these tasks. Each trade association (and under Nazism each Economic and Trade Group) possesses a so-called "Standardization Committee"(*Normenauschuss*). These Committees have issued and still issue standardization and rationalization orders which the Minister of Economics can declare valid for all members of the industry. They could, if necessary, continue to be used under AMG.

# 18

HERBERT MARCUSE

# *POLICY TOWARD REVIVAL OF OLD PARTIES AND ESTABLISHMENT OF NEW PARTIES IN GERMANY*

(JULY 22, 1944)

Editor's note: R&A 1655.1. The authorship of Marcuse is indicated in various documents, including a letter of December 10, 1943, from Eugene Anderson to Carl Schorske (RG 226, entry 60, box 1: Projects Committee Correspondence). Confirmation is also found in Marcuse's *Description of Three Major Projects.*

The report was published as War Department Pamphlet 31-116.

Classification: Confidential

## Foreword

This Guide deals with policy toward political parties in post-war Germany exclusively from the point of view of the security of the occupying forces and the elimination of Nazism. Consequently, the prospective parties are evaluated according to their probable attitude toward these two objectives of Allied military government. Recommendations are made on the basis of these objectives only.

It is assumed, however, that the elimination of Nazism, as one of the purposes of military occupation, includes the gradual restoration to the German people of the liberties necessary for the reconstruction of their society in a democratic form, which alone can eliminate the roots of Nazism in Germany. Accordingly, the parties and organizations which may be expected to oppose a democratic reconstruction of Germany are considered in relation to a possible revival of Nazism.

## 1. Analysis of the Problem

### A. Introduction

The military occupation of Germany will probably find the Nazi state in full disintegration. The Nazi control apparatus will be disrupted at decisive points, and the long-terrorized population will respond with acts of spontaneous violence and revenge. Political parties and groupings are likely to spring up almost immediately after the breakdown of the Nazi controls, chiefly on the local and regional levels. The underground movement will come into the open and wage its own war for the elimination of Nazism. The labor parties and trade unions will revive. Against these anti-Nazi forces, the Nazis will try to rally their reserves, which probably have been especially trained for such a situation.

The occupation authorities will thus be faced with a difficult problem: the security of the occupying forces requires the immediate restoration of law and order, but the establishment of law and order is conditioned upon the elimination of Nazism, which can be accomplished only through the indigenous political opposition in Germany itself. This opposition will be the greatest potential instrument for the destruction of German aggression. It is well to recall that one of the reasons for the failure of an enduring peaceful reconstruction of German society after the First World War was the lack of recognition and support on the part of the occupation authorities of the new democratic forces and institutions which had arisen during the revolution. The French occupation authorities, for example, considering that the new soldiers and workers councils were contrary to public order, decided that they could not be recognized and insisted on their dissolution. The French also objected to elections for new municipal councils.[1] The consequences were that anti-democratic forces in the civil service and in the industrial leadership were encouraged and strengthened.

At the end of the present war the importance of indigenous political movements for the disarmanent and pacification of Germany will be even greater than in 1918, for, this time, no firmly established and organized democratic force will exist in Germany. It will have to be built up on new ground. There will at first be no well-trained and disciplined organizations (like the free trade unions) whose apparatus could be used for the peaceful reconstruction of Germany. Whatever is left of their former strength will be split into small groups with little or no connection on the national levels, and frequently with conflicting aims and strategies.

Political life will probably be revived first on the local level. With the disintegration of the Nazi controls, and perhaps before Allied occupation, small groups will spring up which will try to remove or replace the

Nazi machinery in the villages, towns, city sections, plants, barracks, etc. Their activities will center on the most immediate local issues: keeping the factories and services going, seizing political opponents, setting up a new administration. In some cases, they will have taken over the factories or the local administration, and will present themselves to the occupation officers as the legitimate new German authorities.

These groups may be expected to develop rather quickly along more or less definite political lines and will tend to become integrated into national parties. As they do so, there will emerge a general pattern of political organization corresponding to the prevailing structure of German society.

During the period of the Weimar Republic, German political life was determined chiefly by three social groups (1) Heavy industry, the agrarian aristocracy, and the military; (2) labor; and, (3) the Center, a Catholic integration of members from all social groups, holding the balance between Right and Left. The old middle classes (small and medium business, retail trade, artisans) were by themselves no longer a decisive political factor. The same holds true for the peasants, who voted mostly for the Right and the Center until a large part of them went into the Nazi camp.

The chief political parties corresponded closely to the three major groups mentioned above:

1. The German National People's Party (*Deutschnationale Volkspartei*) and the German People's Party (*Deutsche Volkspartei*).
2. The Social Democratic Party and the Communist Party.
3. The Center Party and the Bavarian People's Party (*Bayerische Volkspartei*).

The Nazi regime has abolished these and all other parties with the exception of the Nazi Party, but it did not essentially change the social stratification of which the German party system was a reflection. Heavy industry and the landed aristocracy, on the one hand, and labor on the other hand, still form the chief groups of German society. Between them, the middle classes, already declining during the period of the Weimer Republic, have been further weakened through the closing down of nonessential business and through the concentration of the war economy in the large enterprises. The sector formerly covered by the Center Party will probably show increased strength and attract many who see in a balance between Right and Left the best possible solution. The interests and policies of the two main social groups conflicted with each other throughout the period of the Weimer Republic; the Nazi regime has achieved a temporary integration through the creation of full employment and of a totalitarian terroristic apparatus, but this integration will dissolve as soon as these factors will no longer persist. It may, therefore, be expected that the revived political life of Germany will, in its main lines, follow the old-established pattern: the party systems will revolve around the two poles on the Right and the Left.

It cannot be assumed, of course, that the traditional parties will reappear in their old forms. Some of them will probably change their names, slogans, and programs; they will adapt themselves to the conditions of defeat and military occupation. These conditions will require that some parties adopt minimum programs and that others work under total or partial camouflage or go underground. All parties will probably represent themselves as anti-Nazi as believing in the democratic form of government, and as willing to cooperate with the occupation forces for the establishment of peaceful order. In some cases, however, this will be a mere facade behind which the real political issues will be fought out.

The main issue will probably be the preservation or the reestablishment, at the earliest possible moment, of Germany's national independence and unity as against control by foreign powers, separatistic tendencies, and outside attempts at the dismemberment of the Reich. All forms of forced labor would be violently fought by all parties, and a strong desire for national integrity and independence will be prevalent among the leftist parties. The latter issue will be tied up with the efforts for a social reconstruction of Germany directed toward breaking the power of the Junkers and industrial imperialists and securing full employment within the framework of a peaceful economy. Social and economic reorganization will be demanded by the labor parties and the liberal groups among the middle classes, with the more conservative parties opposing. The conflict will take place within the framework of the issues of national honor and independence, and with anti-Nazi and democratic slogans.

The acceptance of anti-Nazi and democratic ideologies will, as mentioned above, in some cases be a mere form of camouflage. This tendency to camouflage will present a most difficult problem to the occupation authorities. The security of the occupying forces requires that the groups hostile to the Allies and to the democratic reconstruction of Germany be discovered and eliminated from political life, because it is in these groups that the active Nazis will continue their activity.

The following sections will attempt to anticipate the various possible forms of camouflage and to suggest methods for identifying those elements which constitute the gravest threat to the security of the occupying forces and to the restoration of law and order.

## B. Revival of Nationalistic Rightist Parties

Under the Weimar Republic, the Rightist parties were represented chiefly by the *Deutschnationale Volkspartei* and the influential right wing of the *Deutsche Volkspartei*. They were directed by the interests of heavy industry, of the landed nobility, and of the officer corps. These groups have been ardent supporters of the Nazi regime, and they may be expected to continue to work against a thoroughly democratic reconstruction of German society. It is precisely because of their well-known antidemocratic program that the parties of the Right will probably not be revived under their old names and slogans. They may reappear as national democratic parties, and their program may be centered on what they will picture as a struggle against the Bolshevization of Germany and a fight for Germany's cultural tradition, freedom of enterprise, the elimination of politics from the administration of public life, the independence of the judiciary, and Christian principles in the state. Their real aim, however, is likely to be the maintenance of the privileged position of the old ruling groups, and, for this reason, they will oppose any movement that may endanger their hold over Germany's political, military, and economic machinery. Genuine fear of Russia and of Communism and leftist movements may induce them to offer to the Western Powers cooperation against what they will term the forces of anarchy and communism that they will try to utilize any support which they may possibly receive for pursuing their selfish interests. These can eventually be safeguarded only by an authoritarian regime which does away with popular control and representation, suppresses civil liberties, and prepares for a new German bid for world conquest. The Nazis will therefore again choose to work within these parties, whose policy must thus, in the last analysis, involve hostility to the Allied cause. If the leadership of such parties offers collaboration to the Allies, it will do so in order to secure its position against the forces of democracy and to foster disunity among the United Nations. Under cover, the Rightist leadership will probably continue to support extremely nationalistic and authoritarian ideologies and activities.

The open leadership of such parties will perhaps lie in the lands of prominent civil servants and businessmen who have not conspicuously identified themselves with the Nazi regime, of intellectuals and religious leaders with a conservative background, and possibly of generals dismissed by Hitler. Some former democrats and Center men may be included. The rank and file will be drawn chiefly from demobilized officers and from the middle classes (small and medium business, retailers, salaried employees, and civil servants), and many adherents of the Nazi regime will be among them.

### C. Camouflaged Nationalistic Grouping

1. *Business and professional organizations.* Rightist antidemocratic forces may deem it appropriate — during the period of military government — to refrain from any open political activity and appeals and, instead, pursue their interests through "neutral" professional and technical or-

ganizations (associations of trade and industry, of engineers and technicians, etc.). This form of camouflage would be the more promising since the antidemocratic elements within the German business community have always maintained close liaison with the governmental bureaucracy on the regional as well as national level. Under the Nazi regime, the "self-administration of business" has become an integral part of the machinery of political control, and the engineers have been made into political functionaries by entrusting them with the technical and ideological training of the employees as dependable Nazis. By virtue of this tradition, the professional organizations in Germany are powerful potential pressure groups which can easily transform economic, technical, and administrative problems into political issues which may engender internal conflicts detrimental to law and order. Moreover, the conditions which are likely to prevail in Germany at the end of the war may facilitate such activity. The destruction of plant facilities, the scarcity of certain raw materials, and the urgent need for the replacement of machinery may offer opportunities for disrupting necessary services, hampering the reconversion of production, and precipitating labor unrest.

2. *Sport, educational, and cultural organizations:* The immediate subversive potentialities of educational and cultural organizations are very limited: They lend themselves chiefly to the transmission and dissemination of ideologies which cannot be propagated openly. The elements of Nazi ideology which are most likely to be preserved after the war are nationalism and anti-Semitism. Nationalism will inevitably be strengthened by the mere fact of military occupation by the victors. Nationalism will also be prevalent among the Leftist parties insofar as they will see in Germany's national independence a prerequisite for the democratic reconstruction. The nationalism of the Right, however, will be of a very different tinge; it will be colored with antidemocratic authoritarian tendencies and with a strong emphasis on the racist symbols and contents of German culture. Anti-Semitism can easily be combined with this education program by propagating the teachings of such "great Germans" as Luther, Fichte, and Treitschke.

Sport organizations will readily lend themselves to premilitary training if their leadership falls again into the hands of former nationalists and Nazis.

## D. The Revival of Labor Parties

For the reasons stated above, the traditional groupings are likely to reappear: German labor will probably again gravitate around the two chief parties representing the conservative and the radical tendencies of the workers' movement, namely, the Social Democratic and the Communist Parties. Their programs and policies, however, may differ from those which they pursued under the Weimar Republic.

1. *The Communist Party.* The policy of the Communist Party is likely to be guided by the conception that Nazism in Germany will be followed by a period of political democracy which will give the Party an opportunity to gain new mass support and to organize the workers for possible future seizure of power. Thus for the time being the Communist Party may abandon the struggle for the dictatorship of the proletariat and work within the framework of democratic measures and appeals. The Communist Party will probably strive for a united front of all anti-Fascist forces in Germany, perhaps even including dissenting groups on the extreme Right (anti-Nazi conservatives), and will utilize the widespread nationalistic sentiments by presenting Germany's national liberation as a prerequisite of her social liberation. While some elements of the Nazi Party, the SS, and the SA may seek to join forces with the Communists, it is more likely that any union of Rightist and Leftist radicals will be consummated, not in the Communist Party, but in small dissenting groups outside the Party. (See D. 3.) The Communist Party will probably press demands for the punishment and expropriation of Nazi profiteers and war criminals, seeking to give these measures a very broad interpretation and to use them as a preparation for far-reaching social and economic changes.

The Socialist revolution will remain the final aim of the Communist Party, but, under the conditions of military government, a "minimum program" will probably be worked out, postponing the achievement of the final aim and avoiding, as much as possible, conflicts with the occupation authorities. The participation of Russia in the occupation of Germany is likely to strengthen this "collaborationist" trend.

The Communist Party will probably be most active on the local and regional levels in questions of administration, reorganization of plant management, fixing of working conditions, relief, seizure of active Nazis, etc. This emphasis will hold true, of course, for all political parties under a zonal system of military government organization on the national level will be extremely difficult, if not impossible. In the case of the Communist Party, however, the emphasis on the local and regional levels will be more than a temporary adjustment to external conditions. The Communist Party will continue to operate under strictly centralized control, but it may be expected to work chiefly through small, tightly organized groups in the plants, offices, shops, residential blocks, etc., which promise the Communist Party a more direct foothold among the working population than do over all organizations such as the trade unions; this strategy will naturally concentrate the policy of the Communist Party on the local and regional levels. The Communists would thus probably propagate shop and factory councils as the truly democratic form of labor representation.

This Communist orientation of labor policies on the local rather than the national level, on workers' councils rather than on trade unions, together with a definite orientation towards Soviet Russia, will perhaps be the most important difference between the Communist and the Social Democratic groupings in post-war Germany.

2. *Social-Democrats.* The Social-Democratic Party, throughout the period of the Weimar Republic, advocated what it termed political and social democracy. Its leaders in the Government and in the trade unions accepted the prevailing social and economic system as the framework for their activities. They strove for a better position of labor within this state and society, and they opposed a revolutionary overthrow of capitalism and a dictatorship of the proletariat. The Social Democratic leadership fought bitterly the radical policy of the Communists and helped to quell all uprisings against the prevailing form of society. It may be expected that after the war the Social-Democratic Party (which apparently still has a loyal following in Germany) will appear again as a party of reform rather than revolution. However, the party may come out for the gradual socialization of heavy industry and credit on a national scale, and for the expropriation of the estates of the *Junkers*. Moreover, the Party will probably maintain its long-standing hostility against the Russian system and the Russian policy.

It is doubtful that competition with the Communist Party will drive the Social-Democratic Party to revolutionary radicalism. The bulk of the Party's membership had been recruited from the older workers (age groups 31–60): these are likely to constitute again its main strength, and their foremost desire will be for peace and a maximum of social stability. Moreover, the Social-Democratic Party has been closely affiliated with the trade unions, which, by their whole structure, have been bound to a policy of collaboration between management and labor. The question whether the Social-Democratic Party will again be able to find the support of the majority of the German working population is hard to answer. The fear of Bolshevism prevalent among the masses will probably operate to the disadvantage of the Communist Party but will not necessarily work in favor of the Social-Democratic Party. Large numbers of the German workers apparently blame the appeasement policies of the Social-Democrats under the Weimar Republic for the rise of Nazism and may oppose their return to power. The attempt to reestablish the Social-Democratic trade unions may engender bitter conflicts with the more radical shop councils which may be expected to spring up after the break-down of the Nazi controls.

3. *Other labor parties.* During the period of the Weimar Republic, numerous Leftist "splinter" parties were formed. Most of them were secessionists from the Social-Democratic or from the Communist Party; one was syndicalistic. They differed from one another chiefly over questions of revolutionary tactics, each of them claiming to represent the true Marxian-Leninist principles.

It is impossible, of course, to anticipate the programs and policy of such Leftist opposition groups after the war. It may be expected, however, that a defectionist Communist opposition may again arise. It would be likely to place chief emphasis on the class struggle in Germany and would press for immediate measures of socialization.

On the other hand, if the Leftist splinter groups do not find support among the masses of the working population, they may accept the co-operation of the radical elements in the Nazi movement. If this should be the case, they might follow a "National-Bolshevist" line; that is, they might subordinate propaganda for the socialist revolution to that for Germany's national liberation from the foreign conqueror, advocating an alliance with Russia as a counterweight against the Western Powers. The threat to military government implied in such a program would be considerably neutralized, however, by the fact that these groups are not likely to find a mass following. No leftist group outside the Communist and Social-Democratic parties has ever succeeded in gaining a strong foothold among the German masses.

## E. Democratic Middle-Class Parties

It may be expected that attempts will be made to unite all middle groups of German society in a democratic program equally opposed to neo-totalitarian tendencies of the Right and revolutionary tendencies of the Left. Such a program would be likely to call for a democratic form of government similar to that of the Weimar Republic, for the repeal of all Nazi laws, for restoration of civil liberties (including the right of collective bargaining), and for the guarantee of free enterprise and private property. The program would probably call, however, for state regulation of the economy and for elaborate public works.

A party of the sort indicated above would appeal chiefly to small and medium business, artisans, and salaried employees. By virtue of their social position (which has been gradually undermined by the trend toward monopoly in heavy industry and by accelerated concentration of economic power in large enterprises), these groups are averse to any radical change of the social system which would endanger the remnants of their independence. Under the Weimar Republic, the majority of the middle classes (with the exception of the liberal professions) saw a threat to their position chiefly in the growing influence of labor; they tended to follow therefore the reactionary parties of the Right.

After 1919 the German Democratic Party (later the German State Party), the only nonlabor and nonconfessional democratic party under the Republic, never succeeded in winning over large portions of the middle classes; the party remained politically insignificant and was dominated by a few liberal businessmen and intellectuals.

The only significant party representing the business interests of the middle classes under the Weimar Republic was the *Reichspartei des Deutschen Mittelstandes* or the *Wirtschaftspartei* (German Middle-Class Party), which obtained 1,363,000 votes in the parliamentary elections of 1930. Despite its apparently "professional" character, the party was decidedly nationalistic, antidemocratic, and authoritarian. The program of 1926 called for a revision of the Weimar Constitution by making the government largely independent of popular vote, for increase of the voting age to 24, and also for the restoration of the German colonies and of frontiers adequate to needs of German expansion.

It may be expected that after the war the middle classes, because of their deteriorated economic and social position, may again easily succumb to nationalistic appeals. On the other hand, the totalitarian experiment has been discredited, and the new middle-class party may become the rallying point for many elements of the German population outside the ranks of labor who see in democratic reorganization the only means of returning to peaceful business and security. These elements would be found chiefly among the free professions, small manufacturers, retailers, and artisans.

## F. The Center Party

The German Center Party will probably be revived along its traditional lines. The Party, which accepted the republican form of government throughout the history of the Weimar Republic, was a nonconfessional Catholic party, recruiting its membership mainly from the Catholic population, comprising large numbers of the clergy, the workers and the peasants, the nobility, and the liberal professions. The chief strength of the Center Party was in the predominantly Catholic territories of Western and Southern Germany (the Bavarian leadership seceded from the Party in 1920 because of objection to the centralistic policy and founded the Bavarian People's Party, which, however, followed the Center Party in all decisive questions).

The fact that the Center Party is held together by religious philosophy rather than by a definite political program makes its policy extremely flexible; it can accept any government that recognizes the basic principles of Catholic social philosophy—private property, collaboration between capital and labor, Christian education, the family. The Party was antifascist, but it was even more anticommunist. Moreover, it would not be likely to support a democracy which would threaten the Party's existence. The Centrist Franz von Papen in just such circumstances (1932–33) played an essential part in destroying the Weimar democracy; an influential circle in the Party represented especially by the last leader of its parliamentary group, Dr. Kaas, had collaborated closely with the antidemocratic Rightist parties since 1918.

The post-war situation may give the Center Party a key position in the political set-up. The Party may become the rallying ground for all forces that try to stabilize Central European society by preventing a social revolution as well as a new form of German imperialism. A Catholic bloc consisting of a Bavarian-Austrian federation may appear a convenient instrument for breaking the predominance of Prussia in Germany, and the Catholic Center Party, with its strong anti-Prussian tendencies, might be inclined to support such a policy.

Should the Center Party actually follow such a line it would be likely to precipitate political conflict, for the vast majority of the German population would probably oppose a policy which might lead to the partition of the Reich. The Germans will be vitally interested in the preservation of the country's national unity; even in the most bitterly anti-Prussian states, such as Bavaria, the anti-Prussian feelings will probably not go so far as to support separatism. (See I. G below.)

Two other possible policies of the post-war Center Party may be envisaged. The party might again, as it did under the leadership of Joseph Wirth (1920–22), join with the Right wing of labor and with other prospective liberal groupings into one democratic bloc against the radical Left and Right. Or, the party might enlarge its religious basis in order to take in all the forces of "law and order." The downfall of the Hitler regime may bring a strong religious revival in Germany; vast strata of the population are likely to be tired of politics, and they may drift to the Center Party because it would appear less political than the other German parties. Despite such an enlargement of the political basis, however, the Catholic Church will probably continue to be the driving power behind the Center Party and will probably continue to direct the Party in the interest of the Church.

## G. Separatist Parties

It has already been mentioned that, after the war, forces outside Germany may endeavor to prevent a renewal of German imperialism by breaking up the centralized structure of the Reich or even by dismembering the Reich. Within Germany, this movement may to some extent be supported by those who wish to strengthen the *Länder* at the expense of Prussia; in other words, by the movement to make Germany a confederation of independent states rather than a centralized federal structure. After the First World War such a movement appeared in Bavaria and in the Rhineland. In the latter territory, it assumed definite secessionist forms: the independent Rhineland would have been more or less dependent on France.

A zonal division of military government will tend to make the national integration of the various parties extremely difficult if not impossible. Under such a division party activities would be regionally restricted and would reflect regional forces and interests. Distinction must be made, however, between parties striving for regional independence within the framework of the Reich (particularist parties) and parties aiming at secession from the Reich (separatist parties).

It is unlikely that any particularist party in Germany will be able to unite the various social forces and interests of one German state into a particularist program. The political differences characteristic of German society will reappear on the state or regional level and will tend to make the particularist party the spokesman of particular interests within the respective state or territory. These will probably be the interests of some business and agricultural groups which may hope to serve their purpose better by allying themselves with non-German countries, and they will be opposed by the majority of the working and middle-class population. The economic structure of Germany is such that none of the German *Länder* can maintain real independence of the Reich or of an adjoining foreign nation for any length of time; consequently, the particularist parties in Germany since the foundation of the Reich have been either insignificant or have confined themselves to safeguarding certain state interests within the Reich (as did the Bavarian People's Party).

These limits of German participation also apply, to a much greater degree, to *separatism*. The only example of an actual separatist movement in recent German history is the party of the Rhenish Republic after the First World War. The party tried to utilize the religious differences between the Catholic population of the Rhineland and Prussia to establish an independent Rhenish Republic. The party was only able to maintain its existence with the support of the French army of occupation: the Rhenish Republic was a failure from the very beginning.

The situation may not be essentially different at the end of this war. The resentment against the Nazi regime has certainly strengthened anti-Prussianism, especially in Bavaria, but this attitude probably does not reflect a desire to secede from the Reich. With the occupation of Germany by the Allied Powers, the desire to preserve national unity is likely to outweigh resentment against Prussian predominance. This will probably hold true even for Bavaria. The proposal that there be a Bavarian-Austrian federation may be supported in Southern Bavaria, but the Protestant population of Northern Bavaria is likely to be hostile to the proposal—so much so that it probably could only be imposed by force. The separatist movement would have still less chance in the Rhineland; it could become an indigenous movement only where there is a strong minority or a majority of non-German population within the Reich.

## II. Recommendations

### A. General

The security of the occupying forces and the maintenance of public law and order call for certain general measures to be applied to all political parties and groupings:

1. Prohibition of all weapons and instruments of violence.
2. Prohibition of all auxiliary guards attached to a particular political party or group (*Sanischutz, Bürgerwehr*, etc.).
3. Prohibition of all activities that may hamper the seizure and trial of war criminals and the elimination of active Nazis from political life.
4. Prohibition of all propaganda and activities that incite acts of violence against the occupying forces and against the democratic forces in Germany.
5. Prohibition of all parties, groupings, assemblies, and institutions that continue to advocate Nazi practices and ideologies.

The principle of equal treatment of all political parties will not be immediately applicable in post-war Germany. The Nazis and their supporters will probably endeavor to continue their activities under the camouflage of new slogans and groupings. To treat these equally with the anti-Nazi groupings (for example, to grant them equal protection from interference by hostile parties) would be tantamount to perpetuating the greatest threat to the security of the occupying forces and to the restoration of a peaceful order. Crimes and misdemeanors must, of course, be brought to justice. The Military Government authorities could well exercise their right to pardon in cases of anti-Nazi activities based on purely political motives. But this right should be carefully exercised in such a way as not to encourage indiscriminate vengeance and violence. As soon as German courts can be reconstituted and cleansed of Nazi elements, the prosecution of Nazis should be confined to them.

### B. Attitude toward Nationalistic Rightist Parties

Since it is these parties which will provide the best place of refuge for those seeking to continue Nazi policies, they will need to be carefully supervised by the occupation authorities. Their program in itself may not warrant any interference for it will be skillfully couched in unpolitical if not democratic terms and will even be camouflaged by attempts to collaborate with the Allies. During the first period of the occupation, the neo-Nazis within these nationalistic parties will work chiefly behind the scenes: collecting funds, establishing liaison among the various reactionary circles, and trying to secure certain key positions in the administration, gathering and training reliable followers ready to strike when the moment comes.

In these circumstances it would be detrimental to the security of the occupying forces to permit these elements firmly to entrench themselves in post-war Germany. The following ways of preventing such an entrenchment are open to the occupying authorities:

1. Prohibition of all parties and groupings that are dominated by former active Nazis, Nazi collaborationists, and Nazi sympathizers. These include all prominent members of the former *Deutschnationale Volkspartei* and of the Right Wing of the *Deutsche Volkspartei*, the *Stahlhelm*, the *Kyffhäuserbund*, and other veterans' organizations.
2. Cutting off of all financial support coming from persons mentioned under No. 1.
3. Refusal to assent to the installation of any former Nazi or Nazi collaborator in any higher position in the administration, the judiciary, the educational system, welfare organizations etc., whether by election or appointment.

### C. Attitude toward Camouflaged Nationalistic Pressure Groups

Among the camouflaged political groupings it is the business and professional organizations that are likely to be the most difficult to control and therefore the most dangerous associations. Generally, the suggestions formulated above (B) are also applicable to these organizations. Their chief activity, however, will be in the field of business and economic administration rather than politics. Under the conditions of defeat and occupation, economic problems and business matters can be easily used for political sabotage. In discussing such questions as shut-down of plant facilities, lock-outs, reconversion of production, fixing of work-conditions, the occupation authorities should therefore insist that all parties directly concerned (including trade unionists and other local anti-Nazis) be present and have an opportunity to be heard.

With respect to the cultural, educational, and sport associations, close supervision and control will be necessary. Nationalistic and antidemocratic indoctrination can be camouflaged so well and in such seemingly harmless forms that, for supervision and control, the occupation authorities will probably have to rely to a great extent on the vigilance of the indigenous anti-Nazi forces. Direct interference on the part of the occupation authorities in cultural and educational activities is likely to lead to more resentment and more opposition than any other form of control.

The best results can probably be achieved by a strengthening of the liberal forces in Germany itself (building up of a democratic school system, democratic youth organizations, trade-union activities, etc.)

The formation of para-military organizations will need to be prevented in any case. After the First World War, the Allies permitted and even supported the establishment of such organizations as an auxiliary police supposedly to fight communism and anarchy. A pretext was thus given for building up the nuclei of the new German army, and many of the later Nazi leaders distinguished themselves as leaders of the Free Corps. The same pretext would be welcomed and seized upon again. It is therefore recommended that the occupation authorities do not delegate their responsibility for the maintenance of public law and order to any German agency other than a reorganized and denazified police. (See the Civil Affairs Guide on the Police.)

## D. Attitude toward Labor Parties

1. *Communists.* If, as may be expected, the Communist Party abandons under military government the propaganda for an immediate transition to socialism and for the dictatorship of the proletariat, the Party will probably be ready to collaborate with the occupation authorities on all questions concerning the elimination of Nazism and of active Nazis from civil life. Because the Communists have maintained an organized underground opposition throughout the Nazi period, they may provide valuable information on camouflaged Nazis and Nazi activities.

Since the Communist Party's fight for the elimination of Nazism will probably be concentrated on the plants and shops, it may lead to disruptions of necessary services (through strikes, occupation of factories, etc.), and acts of violence may occur. In punishing such acts, the mode and degree of punishment should be based upon a distinction between acts of violence perpetrated by Nazis and those committed by anti-Nazis and directed against known terrorists and henchmen of the Nazi regime.

2. *Social-Democrats.* The Social-Democratic Party may be expected to revive along its traditional line of advocating liberal democracy. The Social-Democrats will probably be willing to collaborate with the occupation authorities while pursuing a policy of gradual social reform. Cooperation with former Nazis is improbable. However, a renewal of the violent struggle between the Social-Democratic and the Communist wing of the German labor movement may be expected, a struggle which may lead to bloodshed and widespread internal disorder. In this situation, recommendations 3 and 4 may be found applicable.

3. *Other labor parties.* If Nazis should filter into splinter groups on the extreme Left a policy of suppressing groups under Nazi domination or influence might become applicable.

### E. Attitude toward Other Parties

No specific recommendations seem to be necessary with regard to possible democratic middle-class parties and to the Center Party. These parties will in all likelihood cooperate with the occupation authorities, will adhere to the rules of peaceful democratic processes, and will refrain from terror and violence.

Separatist parties would be likely to offer a more difficult problem. There is hardly a region in the Reich where a separatist movement would have the support of the majority of the population. Such a movement could probably succeed only with the armed support of the occupying powers. In the eyes of the German people, the separatists would thus become agents of a foreign power, and such a situation would be likely to lead to civil war.

# 19

Otto Kirchheimer

# *GENERAL PRINCIPLES OF ADMINISTRATION AND CIVIL SERVICE IN GERMANY*

(July 22,1944)

Editor's note: R&A 1655.12. A letter dated January 18, 1944, from Eugene Anderson to Carl Schorske points to Franz Neumann as the person in charge of realizing a report, with this catalog number, titled *MG and General Principles of Administration*. However, in all successive documentation the author is named as Otto Kirchheimer. In particular, a prospectus on works in progress from the Civil Affairs Guides gives Kirchheimer the task of combining in a single report the above-mentioned *MG and General Principles of Administration* and the successive *Adjustment of the National Level of German Administration to the Needs of MG* (R&A 1655.13), with the title *German Central Administration and Civil Service* (RG 226, entry 44, box 2, folder: Status of Reports). It is therefore probable that Kirchheimer was given the responsibility to realize the report that was originally assigned to Neumann.

Published as War Department Pamphlet 31-133.

The original document is accompanied by three appendixes—here omitted—containing lists of the nominations and percentages of public functionaries during Nazism.

Classification: Confidential

## I. Analysis of the Problem

### A. The Administrative Problems Facing Military Government

The administrative tasks of Military Government will be of greatest magnitude and importance and surpass by far those which fell to the Interallied High Command after the signing of the armistice in November 1918.

First, the territory to be administered by Military Government will be many times the size of the zone occupied under the clauses of the Compiègne armistice. Second, as in 1918, the occupation forces will be of various nationalities, but coordination will be more difficult than in 1918. Third, the defeat of Germany implies the defeat of Nazism as a political and social system. Given the forms and means of domination applied in Germany within the last ten years, and considering the impact of the war on the German social and economic system, it can be safely assumed that the German administrative machine will have suffered a much graver disruption than in 1918. A large proportion of public utilities and transportation and housing facilities will have been destroyed; medical installations and supplies will be deficient. The demobilization of the German army, the repatriation of more than 10,000,000 foreign laborers and prisoners of war, and the reconversion of German industry to the production of consumer goods present weighty problems to those concerned with the operation of the German administration in the immediate post-war period.

For security reasons alone, the extent of the administrative functions to be carried out by Military Government will not be comparable with the scope of similar functions performed during the first two years of the military occupation of the Rhineland. This was restricted to contacts with a German government which was still intact and functioning outside the zone of occupation, and to a mild form of supervision of this government's regional and local machinery in the zone of occupation.

Today Military Government administration must be prepared to assume much greater responsibilities in regard to German territory and population. However, Military Government cannot itself carry out the tasks of administration except in marginal cases (disarmament). In general, it must confine itself to giving the directives and to supervising their execution. Therefore, national administrative units and German personnel are needed from the very beginning. Yet the central German agencies, as they now stand, could not be profitably integrated into the new administration, because they will have to be adapted to the administrative organization to be set up by Military Government. Closely connected with the question of adapting German agencies to the needs of military government is the question of personnel policy. The thorough permeation of the German administration by Nazis creates tremendous difficulties for the satisfactory handling of the personnel problem.

## B. Characteristics of the Present-Day Administration

The German administrative organization, though under the supreme authority of Hitler, has in recent years been dominated by two features: the emergence of the Ministerial Council for the Defense of the Reich as supreme governmental authority, and the cropping up of numerous special commissioners, who are appointed whenever regular agencies fail or new urgent tasks arise.

The Defense Council has taken over legislative and coordinating functions. This council is composed of Göring as Chairman, Himmler as Commissioner of Administration, Funk as Commissioner of Economics, Keitel as Commander of the Armed Forces, Borman as Chief of the Party Chancellery, and Minister Lammers (the head of the Reich Chancellery) as executive secretary. Thus the other ministries were transformed into executive organs of the Ministerial Council. Many of the ministries have lost part of their functions to special commissioners (Delegates, Commissioner General, Inspector General) who are personal appointees of Hitler and are personally responsible to him. The regional administration, which previously had some measure of autonomy, has been made completely subordinate to the central authorities. Reich Governors and, as far as they still exist, State Governments as well, are merely executive agents of the central authorities. Beside these agencies of general administration, there are several branches of special administration which are entirely federalized and whose regional agencies are, therefore, directly under the respective ministries. Thus regional administration is partly general administration, coordinated by the Provincial Presidents in Prussia and the Reich Governors in the other States. It is also partly special administration, such as Justice, Labor, and Communications; these are handled by special Reich agencies.

In order to appraise the nature of the specific tasks facing Germany's future administration, some features which are responsible for the unwieldy character of the German administration should be mentioned. To some extent even before the rise of the Third Reich, but with increasing frequency since 1933, new administrative functions were not handed over to the old cadres which united all services on the Provincial or the State level. Germany's administrative landscape is dotted with special administrations integrated with the old units very loosely, or not at all. Furthermore, the traditional political units, the States, became more and more meaningless, but a new principle for the distribution of functions was still not available. Another factor which contributes to the complexity of the administrative machinery is not peculiar to Germany alone. It concerns the relation of the administration to private enterprise. Although the administration exercises a group of supervisory functions over private economy and has a somewhat vague and confused responsibility for the functioning of the economic system as a whole, its control nevertheless is almost never exercised directly. It operates through the so-called Self-administrations of Industry, which, for their part, have assumed many public functions. However, no redefinition of the relationship between administration and private economy has taken place in

Germany. If the Nazi political system binding together the administrative bureaucracy and the self-administration of industry should break down, the ensuing separation of government and industry will create new administrative problems.

### C. The Fate of the German Central Agencies

A partial solution of the German administrative confusion may be found in the suspension of a number of unnecessary special administrations and in the merging of the remaining ones with other agencies to be continued. If a central German administration should be maintained in one form or another, only those central agencies should be allowed to function which correspond to actual social needs. For the same needs, indeed, it might actually become necessary to establish some new German central agency in order to implement Military Government policies. But even if all central German agencies should be totally discarded, the various agencies often had local branches; a decision on the highest level seems imperative as to which of them should be closed down entirely and which of them should be transferred to agencies which will continue to function on the regional or local level.

Three major groups of central agencies and of branches thereof can be totally abolished. The first group consists of those agencies which have been created to disseminate Nazi ideology, as for example, the Ministry for Popular Enlightenment and Propaganda. The second comprises those agencies which in any event will be completely superseded by the occupation authorities, such as the Foreign Office, the High Command of the Armed Forces, the Presidential Chancellery, and the Reich Chancellery. The third group comprises these agencies which were created in order to prepare and carry on the war and to coordinate political and economic life in Germany—the office of the Delegate for the Four-Year Plan, and the office of the Reich Leader of the SS and Chief of the German Police.

### D. Relation between German and Military Government Agencies

The relationship between German and Military Government agencies will depend upon the degree of Military Government participation in internal German affairs.

On whatever level German administration may continue to function, it will do so satisfactorily only after a thorough purge of its Nazis. In order to be effective, such a purge must be carried out according to uniform directives. A subagency of the Allied central occupation authority and endowed with power over the personnel policies of all agencies having German personnel might best be able to achieve the necessary unification of personnel policies.[1] Furthermore, whatever may be the extent to which German officials and agencies continue to take part in the administration on the national or zonal level, final responsibility during military government will rest exclusively with Military Government. All executive power should be concentrated in Military Government for German officials (or advisory bodies) should not exercise responsibility for policies whose elaboration would lie almost exclusively in the hands of Military Government officials. The responsibility for the forms and manner of execution may to some degree be left to native officials and groups, but they should not be associated in the responsibility for policy-making.

The different zones agreed upon by the Allied powers will not form a uniform administrative whole; every zone contains side by side with the former smaller states some Prussian provinces or parts of provinces which do not have all the administrative divisions usual in a state government. The offices of the Prussian Provincial President and of the Prussian District President have a strictly regional character. The question arises as to whether a native German administration should be set up in the zone through the consolidation of the different provincial agencies with the ministries of the states. This seems inadvisable. Setting up a German zonal agency would result in duplication and a top heavy administrative structure; it would also cause a great deal of administrative waste because the concentration of executive tasks in the Military Government agency would leave the higher German zonal authorities without important functions of their own. Military Government may therefore have to find other methods to achieve some measure of coordination of the German agencies throughout the zone. Military Government may assume responsibility for transmitting all orders to the German authorities on the regional level, e. g. the Provincial Presidents, the District Presidents, and the Ministries of the smaller states. If such a procedure seems too cumbersome, Military Government may decide to make the provincial administration at the seat of the zonal commander into a sort of transmitting agency. The zonal commander would thus be able to channel his orders to the various regional authorities through a single German agency. If, for example, the seat of the Zonal Commander were in Hanover, he could designate the Provincial President in Hanover as his transmitting agent for questions of general administration. The same would correspondingly apply to a *Reichsbahn* Division Management or to a Gau Labor Exchange. The transmitting agency, however, would not acquire the function of a German Zonal authority. It would be confined merely to the technical functions of a transmitting agent; executive authority would rest exclusively with Zonal Military Government.

## E. Civil Service

Although in the period of occupation the responsibility for Germany's administration will lie primarily in the hands of Military Government, it would be impossible to think of replacing the whole range of German administration by Military Government personnel. If there should be a native German government to which a number of functions could be delegated at the beginning, the problems would be simplified. Although in this case the recruitment of the German Civil Service would be in the hands of the native government, the range of questions which will come up is nearly identical with that which would arise in the absence of a native government.

In 1933, before the increase in the number of bureaucracies, and although the tasks of war preparation and war economy had been started, the number of Federal, State, and municipal civil servants, in the public services (*Öffentliche Dienste*) was 661,449.[2] The number of the academically trained civil servants working in all branches of public administration was 77,172. Even assuming that the great majority of the nonacademically trained civil servants can be retained in office, it would seriously tax Military Government to find a substitute for every academically trained civil servant. Therefore, principles should be established according to which the reorganization and the purge of the German administration should be carried out.

## F. The Nazis and the Civil Service

The influx of new officials varied according to the importance of the respective offices and branches of administration. It was more marked in the general internal administration than in more specialized fields like transportation or social security. In 1942, for example, 81.9 percent of all higher officials attached to the general internal administration on the State, Provincial, District, and County levels were Nazi appointees. The fact is, especially in the first three years of Nazi domination, that appointment by the Nazi government was not tantamount to the appointee's being an active member of the Nazi Party. Only gradually was the membership card made a prerequisite for entry into public office. However, if official pressure forced most officeholders to acquire *pro forma* membership in the Party, mere membership alone would not be a sufficient indication of the unfitness of the official for the job. Many an official whose duties were of a more technical nature, like the officials of a Water Construction Office (*Wasserbauamt*), may, even after becoming a member of the Nazi Party, have confined himself within the limits of his official duties, and restricted his participation in Nazi affairs to the minimum required to keep his position. In some cases, however, a "specialist" may have been an ardent Nazi, although the vast majority of the fifty thousand members of the Nazy Party among the civil servants before 1933 came from the intermediate ranks of the Civil Service, not from its lower and higher ranks. On the other hand, those officials who worked in the field of the general internal administration, even if they were hold-overs from the Republican regime, became identified in the eyes of the public with the Nazi regime, whose policy they were forced to represent and carry out.

A study which has been made on the subject of the recruitment of Prussian County Presidents (*Landräte*), the chief representatives of the government in rural counties, shows that after nine years of Nazi domination, only one-fifth of them were pre-Hitler appointees. About half the new appointees joined the party before 1933; about 42 percent of the new appointees were nonprofessionals, the majority of whom came from the ranks of the Nazi Party bureaucracy. Those older County Presidents who survived the Hitler regime and those professionals who owed their positions to the Nazi government had to give strong and repeated proofs of loyalty and had to take a prominent part in Nazi Party activities in order to keep their jobs. The example of the County Presidents shows to what degree the ranks of the political bureaucracy have become penetrated by Nazism.[3] Anyone who participated in the formulation of policy or who had considerable responsibility in the carrying out of political decisions might be considered a political civil servant to be removed by Military Government. Under the Republic and under the Third Reich the Civil Service Act has contained a list of "Political Civil Servants" who were liable to instantaneous removal from office according to the Civil Service Act. The concept of Political Civil Servant as derived from our definition would be much broader. In addition to a great number of the closer collaborators of the Political Civil Servants as enumerated in the Civil Service Act, as well as the Mayors and the Presidents and Vice Presidents of the technical branches of the administration, it might include everyone who has been an "active" Nazi. It may be assumed that between seven thousand and eight thousand higher officials will have to be dismissed during the early stages of occupation. However, as a number of the positions need no longer be filled, and as some would be taken over by Military Government, the immediate replacement need would not be as high as the number of dismissals.[4]

## G. The Problem of Civil Service Replacements

The gaps in the German administration caused by an extensive purge cannot be filled by Military Government officials because of insufficient trained personnel. However, it would not be good policy to defer the arduous task of selecting new German personnel. This would be especially true in the event that a native German government quickly comes into power. During a transitional period, many administrative tasks would remain undone, yet experience has shown that the life of society goes on even if the traditional administrative machinery ceases to function normally. In principle, it might seem possible to fill the administrative vacuum by replacing the higher officials by the middle ranks of officialdom. Versed in the daily routine, they could carry on under the supervision of Military Government the tasks which had been previously handled by academically trained officials. However, given the peculiar German situation, such a solution cannot be recommended. Generally speaking, the clerical service contained a greater proportion of convinced Nazis than did upper levels; this was especially true of the higher clerical ranks. These officials, occupying a rank intermediate between the clerical staff and the academically trained officials, did not develop a trade-union mentality to any considerable degree. Their special outlook, which kept them apart from the lower ranks, made them an easy prey for the Nazi ideology. That may be one of the reasons why the Nazis were able to restrict the purge of this category to far fewer officials than those dismissed in the high category. Only 2.33 percent of the higher clerical, clerical, and custodial ranks were purged or demoted in Prussia as against 15.5 percent of the high officials. Therefore, only in exceptional cases should an official of the clerical or higher clerical service take the place of a high official.

It thus becomes necessary to consider the problem whether replacements can be obtained outside the present ranks of the German Civil Service. One source of replacements may be found among the civil servants who were dismissed or demoted by the Nazis. Although their number would by no means be sufficient, their employment would be useful both for psychological and for service reasons. It would serve notice on the population that the Nazi hold on the Civil Service has been definitely broken. At the same time they would provide a nucleus of civil servants who are not only absolutely trustworthy but thoroughly familiar with the conditions and practices of the service. Furthermore, new civil servants may be recruited from the opposition groups. One might consider the employment of members of opposition groups wherever feasible, even if they lack the necessary training for the positions. Their wide range of political and social experience and the trust which the population places in them would amply compensate for their lack of formal training. A reservoir of administrative knowledge may also be found in the members of municipal assemblies and state diets of the pre-Hitler period, although many of them may be too old to be of any great service.

If a policy of replacement of unreliable civil servants by energetic members of the opposition groups is actively pursued, there may be a chance that the narrow *esprit de corps* of the German bureaucracy, which proved strong enough to neutralize the few outsiders appointed during the Weimar Republic, might be broken. The new elements would face their task with much greater confidence if they are assured that they have full Military Government support in their endeavor to ferret out saboteurs and hidden attempts to continue Nazi policies and organizations. Military Government officials might find themselves confronted with various methods of passive resistance like showdowns and all sorts of intentional "misunderstandings," which might be difficult to cope with in the absence of a loyal group of German collaborators. If the new elements should again be dominated by the old guard, a "united front" of a nationalist civil service might become the focus of all the forces wishing to oppose the foreign conqueror. Much therefore depends on a democratic reconstitution of the German Civil Service. One of the ways in which its structure might be democratized may be the granting of the right for most classes of civil servants to organize on trade-union lines.

## II. Recommendations

### A. Policy towards German Agencies

The following list should be regarded as illustrative rather than definitive. Agencies and divisions established in order to exploit occupied countries have not been specifically mentioned but should of course be dissolved.

1. *Agencies automatically superseded by agencies of the occupying power.*
   - *a.* Presidential Chancellery of the Führer.
   - *b.* Reich Chancellery.
   - *c.* High Command of the Armed Forces.

     Insofar as disarmament and demobilization come under the authority of the High Command, they should be transferred to the respective political and administrative agencies.
   - *d.* Reich Air Ministry.

     For disarmament and demobilization see 1–c.
   - *e.* Reich Weather Bureau and the German Marine Observatory.

     It should come under the jurisdiction of the transportation authorities. Civil aviation should come under the jurisdiction of the transportation authorities. Questions of international aviation, as far as Germany is concerned, should be handled by the Allied political authorities.

*f.* Reich Ministry of Foreign Affairs.

The remaining tasks should be transferred to the political authorities.

2. *Agencies to be dissolved because they disseminate Nazi ideology.*
   *a.* Reich Ministry of National Enlightenment and Propaganda, including the Reich Chamber of Culture. Censorship activities should be transferred to the office of the political authorities.
   *b.* Reich Ministry of Church Affairs.
   *c.* Academy of German Law under the supervision of the Ministry of Justice.
   *d.* Reich Ministry of Food and Agriculture: Main Department 10: Conservation of Germandom.
   *e.* Agencies under the supervision of Reich Ministry of Science, Education, and National Culture, e.g.: Institute of History of New Germany.

3. *Agencies for war preparation and for coordination of political or economic life.*

   Some agencies of this character should be dissolved in any case; others should be dissolved only in case Military Government finds it unnecessary to use them for prosecution of its policies in Germany: if they are dissolved their functions will in certain cases have to be transferred to other agencies.

   Still others, though they should be retained as a whole, will require reorganization involving in some instances a closing down of certain sections.

   *a. Agencies Which Must Be Dissolved.*
   1) Reich Commissioner for Strengthening of the German Folkdom.
   2) Youth Leader of the German Reich.
   3) Commissioner General for the Allocation of Labor.

   *b. Agencies to Be Dissolved Unless Found Necessary for Prosecution of Military Government Policies.*
   1) Offices of the Delegate for the Four-Year Plan and of its sections and its Commissioners General.

      The activities of the Reich Commissioner for Price Control should be transferred to the economic authorities.

      The activities of the Section "Currency" should be transferred to the finance authorities.

      The activities of the Section "Forests" should be transferred to the agricultural authorities.
   2) Inspector General for the German Highway System.

The functions of the section L, "Reich Highways", should be transferred to the transportation authorities.

3) Inspector General for Water and Power.

The functions of the section "Water and Power Division Economy" should be transferred to the central German authority for transport.

The functions of the section "Power Economy" should be transferred to the economic authorities.

4) Inspector General for Building Activities.

Functions to be transferred to health and social welfare authorities (to be mentioned below).

5) Inspector General for Motor Transport.

6) Reich Commissioner for Ocean Shipping.

Functions to be transferred to the transportation authorities.

7) Reich Commissioner for Housing.

Functions to be transferred to health and social welfare authorities (see below).

8) Reich Ministry of Armaments and Munitions.

9) Office of Large Space Planning.

10) Reich Forestry Office.

The functions of the Reich Forestry Office should be transferred to the agricultural authorities.

11) Delegate General for Sanitation and Health Service.

Functions to be transferred to health and social welfare authorities (see below).

c. *Agencies to Be Reorganized.*

1) Ministry of the Interior.

The following sections of the Ministry of the Interior should be closed down immediately:

a) Reich Leader of the SS and Chief of the German Police.
b) Reich Labor Leader of the Labor Service.
c) Department I, except for Constitution, Legislation, Administration.
d) Department of "Civil Defense and Occupied Territories."
e) Department IV "Maintenance of Germandom in Frontier Areas."
f) Department VIII "Sport."
g) Reich Genealogical Office.
h) Reich Chamber of Physicians.
i) Reich Chamber of Veterinarians.
j) Reich Chamber of Pharmacists.
k) Reich Office of Sports.
l) Reich Academy of Physical Exercise.

m) Technical Corps for Public Emergencies.
n) Office for the Cultivation of the German Language.

The following offices should be made independent of the supervision of the Reich Ministry of the Interior or its successor:

a) Commissioner for Voluntary Nursing.
b) Central Information Office for War Losses and War Graves.
c) German Local Government Assembly.
d) Reich Archives.
e) German Red Cross.

The activities of the following agencies and divisions of the Ministry of the Interior should come under the jurisdiction of the health and social welfare authorities.

a) Reich Health Office.
b) German Institute for Youth Aid.
c) Department III Veterinary Affairs.
d) Department IV Public Health.

2) Ministry of Justice.

The following agencies working under the supervision of the Ministry of Justice should be abolished:

a) People's Court and Special Courts (*Sondergerichte*).
b) Reich Chamber of Attorneys.
c) Reich Notary Chamber.
d) Reich Chamber of Patent Attorneys.

The abolition of these agencies should not be construed as a prohibition of the revival of free professional associations in the respective fields. Care, however, must be taken that Nazi influence is excluded from these free organizations.

3) Ministry of Food and Agriculture.

The following agencies working under the supervision of the Reich Ministry of Food and Agriculture should be abolished:

a) Reich Hereditary Farm Court.
b) Reich Board of Resettlement.
c) Reich Food Estate.
d) Ministry of Labor.

The following divisions and subdivisions of the Ministry of Labor should be transferred to the agency responsible for housing and social welfare:

a) From the Department II b: Social Welfare.
b) Department IV: land settlement, housing, and city planning.

*4. Remaining German central agencies.*

After the suspension of the agencies mentioned above the structure of the remaining German central agencies would have the following pattern:

1) Finance.
2) Justice.
3) Economic Affairs.
4) Food and Agriculture.
5) Labor.
6) Education.
7) Post.
8) Transportation.
9) Health and Social Welfare.
10) Interior.

This pattern may be used, if it is decided to retain German central agencies, but the pattern might also be useful for the establishing of administrative Military Government agencies on the zonal level.

A word seems necessary to explain the presence of a special health and social welfare agency. No central German welfare administration existed. Such functions have been handled by the various State welfare departments and local agencies. Federal functions such as housing or unemployment relief were handled by the Reich Ministry of Labor. Some of the public health functions were centralized in the Reich Ministry of the Interior. In the post-war period the specific health and welfare problems will increase considerably. A great part of the German people will have to rely on one or another form of public assistance—outright dole, assistance for disabled war veterans, or temporary shelter. These welfare problems should be dealt with separately from the wage, bargaining, and work problems of those who are gainfully employed and which will come under the jurisdiction of the Labor Department. While close collaboration between both departments is required, the specific welfare, relief, health, and housing responsibilities should, nevertheless, receive the attention of a separate department. At the same time, the Health and Welfare Department would be utilized by the demobilization section to carry through many of its administrative acts. Therefore the Health Department of the Ministry of Interior, Department IV, should become one of the main departments of a new Housing and Social Welfare Agency. So also should Department IV of the Ministry of Labor, which centers around housing, and part of its Department II b, which would form the nucleus of the social welfare division of the new agency. If war veterans' care should be put on a straight welfare basis, it should likewise be included in the new agency. If, however, legal claims of veterans should be maintained, it should remain within the Labor Agency. Social insurance, although many of its aspects are connected with social welfare problems, is more closely related to the wage structure of gainfully employed workers. Its transfer to a social welfare agency, indicating a weakening of the legal position of the insured, would meet vehement political opposition and should therefore not be considered. The Reich Health Office and the German Institute of Youth Aid should come under the supervision of the Housing and Social Welfare Agency.

*5. Personnel Problems*

If central German agencies should be allowed to function under the supervision of joint Military Government, a certain freedom of action might conceivably be granted to their German personnel. Most positions within the agencies would continue to be filled by Germans, as few Military Government officials would have the necessary technical experience to perform these functions satisfactorily. It may even be preferable to name reliable German officials as heads of the central agencies. In reality, the agencies would in this case form the initial nucleus for a future German government. They would, of course, work under general directives of joint Military Government and be subject to its orders. This arrangement may lead to serious frictions. The German under-secretaries and their staffs will in all probability be blamed by their compatriots for orders actually issuing from "Headquarters Staff." Such a state of affairs, however, is best remedied by the speedy reconstitution of a full-fledged German government responsible to the German people.

Responsibility for administration on the zonal and regional level should rest with Military Government officials by the very nature of their work. These Military Government officials are, of course, solely responsible in turn to the Allied central authority. German officials will be excluded from participation in political decisions, but in regard to administrative functions their professional knowledge should be used to full advantage. However, no division of authority between Military Government and German officials should be contemplated. Where German Officials are employed, they should function subordinate to the responsible Military Government official. Military Government, however, will hold power only on a temporary basis. Therefore, the question as to the relation between a Military Government position and any rights which the official may possibly derive by virtue of earlier employment in Civil Service is to be left to the decision of a reconstituted German government. The personnel should be used wherever its services are most profitable for Military Government. In the higher ranks, however, the previous German ratings should be binding neither for the employment of the official nor for his salary.

Military Government should refrain from automatically confirming German officials in their positions. A great number of German central agencies will have to be closed with the result that automatic confirmation would lead to overstaffing. It would make it more difficult to dismiss officials or to transfer them to other agencies. Any order issued at the start of military occupation concerning the duty of officials to continue work at their assigned jobs should therefore draw attention to the purely provisional character of such a measure. Only those higher officials qualified by their specialized professional knowledge and their absolute political reliability should be confirmed by Military Government. No position whatsoever should go to any official on any level of the service who was a Nazi Party member before 1 February 1933, or to any official who has participated in formulating or carrying out political decisions and whose office and functions have become identified by public opinion with Nazi policies.

Members of resistance groups (trade unionists, intellectual and church opposition) should be given preference over members of the Civil Service in responsible nontechnical jobs.

As it does not seem desirable to create special committees to advise Military Government, the assignment of members of resistance groups to important administrative positions would minimize the danger of Military Government losing contact with the population. Even if such employment of "outsiders" should be a source of friction, the value of such a step for Military Government as well as for the members of resistance groups would justify such an undertaking.

From the very beginning, the German population should be given a chance to collaborate in the choice of German officials to be used by Military Government on every level of the administration.

The fate of the ministerial bureaucracy will vary according to whether or not there is a central Military Government for the whole of Germany. If there is, a part of the central bureaucracy may be utilized, although the principles given above will automatically exclude many of its members from reemployment. Special attention should be given to the difference between technical and political functions. The Finance, Transportation, or Labor Ministries will offer more candidates likely to fulfill the Military Government's conditions of employment than the Interior or Justice Departments. Yet the dissolution of the numerous central agencies will give Military Government sufficient material from which to pick the candidates for specialized employment. On the other hand, if there should be only a zonal Military Government, the central agencies will have to be suspended altogether. The function of their officials should automatically cease with the suspension. Otherwise, central German agencies would continue to function in the absence of a central Military Government agency. All central functions being transferred to zonal Military Government, no native zonal German Military Government machinery would exist and Military Government with its various departments would have to assume the functions of all central agencies. It does not seem probable that zonal Military Government could absorb a great number of the members of the central bureaucracy. As zonal Military Government must concentrate on the problems of a comparatively small number of regions, it seems more advisable to consider the employment of officials domiciled in these regions, as they are not only in possession of the necessary technical knowledge, but are also conversant with the special problems of those regions.[5] No employment privileges for public service should be granted to former members of the police, the professional army and uninjured war veterans. Military Government will have full freedom in recruiting the German professional staff from the best available material.[6]

No pension should be granted to those who have not been reemployed by Military Government. Whatever the hardships which may be imposed on some of them, it would seem unjustified to grant former officials preferential treatment in the form of pensions. A special decision should be made in each case when an official asks to be pensioned while working under Military Government. Each case should be decided on its merits, that is, by taking into consideration the achievements and the political attitude shown by the official during his employment with Military Government. The right of Military Government to decide each request on its own merits will be a powerful influence for keeping the older officials in line during the Military Government period. It should, however, be made clear from the outset that the ultimate decision on all pension rights will lie in the hands of the next constitutional German government and that Military Government measures are valid only during the period of Military Government.

The purge and reform of the German Civil Service will necessitate changes in Civil Service legislation.[7] Most of the provisions of the German Civil Service Act of 26 January 1937,[8] which has replaced most of the State Civil Service regulations in force under the Weimar Republic, are of a merely technical nature, as are the numerous executory decrees and rules appended to this act. But the law establishes a number of principles based on and permeated by the Nazi ideology; these should be annulled. The principles to be abrogated may be put in the following categories:

1) Provisions which establish a duty of loyalty towards the Fuehrer and the National Socialist State.[9]
2) Provisions granting the party authorities certain rights in connection with Civil Service appointments or dismissals,[10] or making party membership a prerequisite for Civil Service appointments,[11] or granting preferences and special privileges to party members.[12]
3) Provisions legalizing discrimination on racial grounds.[13]

# 20

Otto Kirchheimer

# *ADMINISTRATION OF GERMAN CRIMINAL JUSTICE UNDER MILITARY GOVERNMENT*

(July 29,1944)

Editor's note: R&A 1655.8C. Kirchheimer's authorship is indicated in varous documents, including a prospectus on works in progress from the Civil Affairs Guides (RG 226, entry 44, box 2: Status of Reports). Originally, the report was assigned the title *Adaptation of Penal Law.*

The report is concluded with an appendix, here omitted, that lists the laws and decrees to abrogate.

Published as War Department Pamphlet 31-108.

Classification: Confidential

## I. Analysis of the Problem

### A. Introduction

German criminal law, as it stands today, conflicts in many respects not only with the theories and practices for which German criminal law had previously stood but also with the theories which, in Anglo-American countries, are traditionally connected with the functions of criminal law. This conflict alone does not suffice to impose upon Military Government a duty to revise or revoke criminal legislation. Every country has the right to formulate its own policy on the balance between the rights of the individual and those of the community at large. This freedom of action has been recognized in international law in the rule that an occupant should retain local laws, customs, and institutions of government insofar as they are consonant with the purposes of military government (Article 43 of the Hague Convention on the Rules of Land Warfare, FM 27-10, Par. 282; see also FM 27-20, Par. 285). The United States has accepted this rule, as is shown in the existing directive to retain such laws (FM 27-5, Par. 9h). The thorough overhauling which the whole system of German criminal law is thought to require is, therefore, a problem whose solution may be left to the German people, and is not a matter of concern for Military Government until it is explicitly directed to take such action.

Recognition of, and respect for, such freedom of action in the German people does not, however, imply that Military Government has no liberty to act in criminal matters. In contrast to these provisions, which would seem to indicate a duty to retain the existing system, Military Government has been charged, both under international law (Article 43 of The Hague, *supra*) and under policy directives already in existence (FM 27-5, Par. 12b), with the maintenance of law and order in the areas subject to its jurisdiction. In addition, Military Government has been directed, as far as the situation permits, to annul laws which are discriminatory on the basis of race, color, creed, or political opinion and, at all events, to respect such discriminatory practices only if they do not "outrage civilized concepts" (FM 27-5, Par. 12n). The problem for Military Government will, therefore, resolve itself into two issues: first, how far, in view of the military situation, Military Government may find it possible to retain any or all of the existing system of criminal law; second, what additions, if any, must be made to satisfy the requirements of military occupation and to fulfill the purposes and policies of the United States.

This Guide will, consequently, concern itself only with those changes in the German criminal system which are necessary not only for the security of the occupying army and the orderly development of German political and social life, but also for the execution of the policies and purposes of the United Nations. It will not consider in detail the abolition of the purge of Nazi courts or of racial legislation, problems which are considered in other Guides.

## B. Nazi Changes in Criminal Law

Prior to 1933 German criminal legislation and practice was one of the highly respected systems of criminal law. While there had been no systematic codification since the 1870's, progressive legislation had maintained and developed the standards set in the early codes. These codes sought to establish legal security and protection against arbitrary procedures both for the offender and for the community. This tradition was continued under the Weimar Republic. Criminal law and procedures were to some extent influenced by progressive reforms. The political pressures, which finally brought about the break-down of the parliamentary machine prevented the introduction of a new and consolidated code of criminal law and restricted the legislative contribution of the last 2 years of the Republic to emergency decrees formulating new provisions in the simplification of criminal procedure and new devices in the fight against political extremism.[1]

The Third Reich departed abruptly from the philosophies and practices which had hitherto governed the development of German criminal law. It saw in criminal law a major opportunity to create weapons for throttling resistance to its policies. It fused the political enemy with the ordinary criminal. The Nazis took the position that the transgressor was an archenemy of society—an enemy to be ruthlessly destroyed. They were at great pains to make abundantly clear the abyss separating their policy, which was aimed at the extermination of the criminal element, from that of the Weimar Republic, which was characterized as "weak and inefficient" humanitarism. To this purpose the whole body of regulations on substantive law, criminal procedure, and execution of punishment was thoroughly purged and amended.

## C. Substantive Law

In pursuance of these goals, the Nazi regime effected many alterations, both theoretical and practical, in the framework of substantive criminal law. In the field of criminal theory, the National Socialist contribution glossed over the objective elements in the definition of a criminal act and sought to wipe out all distinction between criminal attempt and consummated act.[2] However, the importance of these shifts in traditional theory vanish before the flood of legislative changes.

1. *General criminal legislation under the Nazi regime.* In order to achieve its political objectives and to maintain an impregnable position for its administration, the Third Reich gradually brought the substantive side of criminal law into harmony with its philosophies. This operation at times required recasting of the definition of crimes and allied matters. In a number of cases minor changes in specific fields were deemed sufficient.

a. *Political crimes.* Since 1932, a never-ending stream of legislation concerning crimes against public order introduced new crimes, redefined and widened the scope of old ones, or increased the punishment for such crimes.[3] Concerned in the first instance with the fortification of its place within the German political system, the Nazi regime early introduced statutes which banned the formation of new parties,[4] suppressed and penalized the activity of the existing opposition, and imposed heavy punishment for attacks upon the Party[5] and for political terrorism.[6]

The legislation concerning treason was changed several times by enlarging its scope and by increasing the penalties.[7]

b. *Basic changes in the criminal code.* These changes in the direction of the German criminal code did not suffice to produce the results which the Nazi regime required. It became necessary to cut deeply through the existing code provisions and to redraft their details.

i. *Article 2.* Article 2 of the Criminal Code had originally forbidden the analogous application of penal rules. It formulated a rule designed to serve the same purpose as that served in Anglo-American law by the axiom "No punishment without a law." As changed in 1935 by the Nazis, this article now permits punishment, even though there is no statutory violation squarely in point, by permitting the invocation of an existing law, provided that the fundamental purpose of the invoked statute could be applied by analogy to the case in hand, and further, that the "sound feelings of the people" required it. The latter ground, pregnant with possibilities for subjective reasoning, appeared increasingly as basis of decision.

ii. *Pre-war changes in the criminal code.* In addition to the expanded definition of treason, already mentioned, other changes in the criminal code were found necessary in order to synchronize it with the requirements of Nazi policy.

No less vital than the need for protection afforded by a changed definition of political crime was the adjustment found necessary in such cases as the provisions on habitual offenders,[8] duels, breach of trust,[9] corrupt practices of civil servants,[10] and offenses against the security of communications.[11] It was also found expedient to frame special provisions on highway robbery with the use of auto traps.[12]

In many instances the change involved an increase in penalties for existing crimes[13] or the application of a penalty on a retroactive basis.[14] The latter amounts directly to a violation of the well-known legal axiom "No punishment without law."

iii. *Changes in the criminal code necessitated by the war.* The preparation for war and the outbreak of war itself served as the motive for additional changes in German criminal law. The decree against the enemies of the people[15] and the decree against perpetration of crimes of violence,[16] with their broad definitions and their wide range of death penalties, became the cornerstone of criminal jurisprudence in wartime.

Specific legislative provisions were found necessary to regulate espionage, guerrilla warfare, and similar issues.[17] It was also felt necessary promptly to impose penalties for damages to munitions, interference with important enterprises, participation in antimilitary organizations,[18] and relations with war prisoners.[19] As the war progressed, it was considered expedient to issue regulations protecting the collection of winter clothing for the soldiers at the front,[20] imposing penalties for the theft of food from the fields,[21] and for the protection of marriage, family, and maternity.[22]

*iv. Penalties.* The introduction of new crimes and shifts in the definition of the essential elements of familiar crimes were not the only devices by which the Nazis sought to make criminal law a weapon of their political purposes. One of the chief alterations made by the Nazis in the German criminal code has been the introduction of severe penalties, designed to force conformity with the Nazi pattern.

As has been pointed out, the change often involved only an increase in penalties for existing crimes.

Two further examples of this technique are the introduction of the penalty of castration and the increased use of death penalty.

Castration was introduced as a penalty in 1933, when an all-embracing program of measures of security against habitual criminals considered dangerous was launched.[23]

Before 1933, the death penalty was restricted to a very few crimes, such as murder in the first degree, white slavery, and the use of high explosives with foreseeable results. The use of the death penalty had, in fact, been hotly disputed during the Weimar Republic. With the rise of Nazism, and especially since the beginning of the war, there has been a tendency to use the death penalty extensively.[24] Since 1940 it has been imposed in those cases in which hitherto the punishment had been long or medium terms of imprisonment of hard labor.

*v. Juvenile cases.* The Third Reich codified its numerous provisions in the field of criminal law as to juvenile offenders in November 1943. Previously, the Nazi regime had given special attention to the juvenile problem, following in many instances the pattern which depression and then the war brought to the rest of the world. It partly continued progressive features of earlier legislation and partly returned to earlier repressive measures.[25]

The Nazis have varied the rule that a child under 14 years of age should not be held criminally responsible for his criminal acts by lowering the age limit to 12 years. The juvenile courts have jurisdiction over children up to 18 years of age, but it should be pointed out that it lies within the discretion of the prosecutor to refuse the benefit of trial before juvenile courts to youths between 16 and 18 years of age, whom he considers "dangerous criminals."

## D. Procedural Law

As in the case of substantive criminal law, the Nazi regime has found it possible to make criminal procedure the servant of its policies without the introduction of an entire new code. In sharp contrast to the Anglo-American policy of protecting personal freedom in criminal litigation, the position of the defendant in Nazi criminal procedure has steadily deteriorated. This has resulted not only from the changes wrought in procedure itself but also from the new social and political climate. It is apparent in many aspects of criminal procedure, but only a few such problems need now be brought to Military Government's attention.

1. **Preventive detention.**—One of the chief instruments used in securing obedience to Nazi dictates has been the abuse of preventive detention (*Untersuchungshaft*) orders. This terms covers only detention in jail pending trial. The pre-Nazi code surrounded its use with provisions safeguarding the individual. The so-called Lex Hoefle was enacted as a result of the fact that a Reich Minister committed suicide while undergoing a prolonged period of preventive detention.[26] This statute required hearings on the question of the desirability and necessity of maintaining a preventive detention. It was annulled by a statute of 24 April 1934.[27] Not content with removing these safeguards, by one of the provisions of the statute of 28 June 1935[28] the Nazis considerably expanded the reasons for which preventive detention could be ordered. They directed that public sentiment caused by the offence should be considered in weighing the necessity of a preventive detention order. The removal of the requirements for hearings and the introduction of subjective considerations in the need opened the way for the issuance, and the continuance in operation, of arbitrary preventive detention orders.

2. **Right to representation**. The right of the defendant, at this and other stages of criminal litigation, to representation by counsel has been recognized by German criminal procedure. In contrast to the Anglo-American stress upon the right to have counsel, in the majority of cases in which appearance by a defense lawyer is not made mandatory by criminal procedure the defendant in a German criminal trial has customarily had no attorney because of the cost of retaining counsel. With the change from liberal constitutionalism to the concept of a racial community, the field of action for defense counsel has been reduced both in fact and in law.

Under the Third Reich, practice before the People's Court was allowed only to those lawyers who, upon special tests, were found politically reliable. In the practice before other courts, the supervision of all lawyers by the Party, the NS Lawyers' Organization, and the courts was considered sufficient guarantee of the lawyers' "correct behavior." Thus, for all practical purposes, the defense lawyer, when he exists, has become an auxiliary of the state rather than the representative of the defendant.

In addition to this shift in the conception of the function of the defense counsel, statutes enacted since the outbreak of the war have reduced the number of cases in which representation by counsel is mandatory.

3. **Right to bring a case to trial**. Exposed to the new drastic procedure of preventive detention and practically divested of an efficient representative, the defendant is further handicapped by his inability under German procedure to take active steps in his own defense. The statute of 28 June 1935[29] and subsequent emergency decrees, abolished, among other things, the preliminary judicial investigation (*Voruntersuchung*), which had been mandatory in cases in which there was no appeal on the facts.[30] The position of the state's attorney has been considerably strengthened since the courts are now only in very exceptional cases in a position to reject the state attorney's request to bring a case to trial.

This shift in practice cannot be ascribed to hostility to the decisions made by the courts, for they had exercised their right to reject the prosecutor's request for trial sparingly. It is to be explained probably by the fact that the existence of this right delayed the clearing of the docket, because its exercise was based upon the presumption that the court was familiar with the whole record of the case, and not merely with the indictment or information.

4. **Right to introduce evidence**. The rules of evidence, familiar to Anglo-American lawyers, have no counterpart on German criminal procedure, in which the judge directs the trial and freely weighs the evidence offered.[31] For Military Government purposes, the most important innovation as to criminal evidence is the rule that a court may refuse to hear evidence. Paragraph 24 of the decree of 1 September 1939 provided that a court may reject a motion to hear evidence if it deems that evidence unnecessary. Added to the other impediments placed in the way of the presentation of the defendant's case, such as the statute requiring special permission before Nazi officials could be called to give evidence,[32] this rules makes a formidable contribution to the silencing of the defense.

5. **Right to appeal and to ask new trial**. Under pre-Nazi procedure, all decisions of the local courts were subject to two appeals, the first of which was heard in the district court and could lead to complete retrial. This procedure was criticized as productive of delay, especially in its requirement of complete retrial. A decree of 14 June 1932[33] had rectified this in part by sending more important cases directly to the criminal division of the district court, which sat with three professional judges and

two lay judges. It allowed an appeal but not complete retrial on appeal. Homicide cases and certain other cases continued to go to the assize courts.

This improved procedure did not satisfy Nazi purposes. In order to guarantee the unification of its repressive agencies, the Third Reich gradually abolished criminal appeals by the defendant. The statute of 28 June 1935,[34] among other things, discouraged appeals by the defendant by abolishing the rule that the defendant could never make his position worse through an appeal, thereafter the defendant's right to appeal was progressively curtailed.[35]

Further, in designing the new courts which were to give special force and vitality to its program, the Third Reich was careful to hold that their decisions should not be subject to review.

The next step was the creation of an elaborate new procedure exclusively reserved for the State's request for review of decisions. This concept is foreign to Anglo-American legal thinking, which tends to confine the right of appeal in criminal cases to the defendant, and only rarely gives the state an appeal and then only on questions of law. The requests for such review are addressed to the special "senates" of the Supreme Court, and later to those of the appeal courts, and amounted to request for new trial, the desired new sentence being clearly indicated in the request.[36]

5. **Basis of decision**. While there has been no change in the letter of the rule that decisions as to guilt and punishment are by vote of a two-thirds majority of the court, the spirit of the rule has been nullified by the "leadership principle" in the courts. The "leadership principle" as applied to courts refers to the ideology which requires the associate judges to accept the guidance of the president of their panel.

## E. Problems of Jurisdiction

Under the Third Reich the setup of the criminal courts has undergone a profound change. Criminal courts for special categories of persons have replaced the ordinary run of law courts.[37] Even there, where the old law courts still have jurisdiction, their criminal functions have been largely shifted to specially picked divisions of the courts, which in turn are called special courts. Lay judges, a familiar device in German courts, were gradually eliminated and completely discarded in 1939. The reestablishment of special military jurisdictions necessitated the reintroduction of rules for court-martial procedures.[38] They were streamlined for the exigencies of war in the wartime procedural rules of 1938-39.[39] The substantive military penal code was thoroughly revamped and a new version was published in 1940.[40] With the deterioration of the German political and military situation, the system of penalties in the military penal code was revised, and very recently the most severe penalties were laid down.[41]

While the changes in the criminal code referred primarily to the suppression of crime within the Reich, successful military campaigns and the desire to control the population of occupied areas made it necessary to consider changes in the concept of territorial jurisdiction. It was held expedient to include within the jurisdiction of courts inside the Reich the punishment of offenses committed outside the Reich. To this end, the decree of 6 May 1940 materially widened the jurisdiction enjoyed by German courts over crimes committed in other countries.[42]

## F. Problems of Administration

For purposes of administration, the German system of criminal justice falls into two parts: first, the functions of the prosecutor in preparing and initiating litigation; second, the functions of the court.

1. **Prosecutors.**[43] In the pre-Nazi period the prosecutor or state's attorney was in a key position as he was in charge of the investigation of offenses and initiated criminal litigation. The Third Reich has changed this in many respects and reproduced criminal prosecutions to a basis of arbitrary and selective action. Criminal investigation has become an independent police function. Statutes have cut down the prosecutor's discretion as to the offenses to be tried, often transferring the decision to the Minister of Justice. Amnesties containing *nolle prosequitur* clauses granting wide exemptions from prosecution, together with the impossibility of prosecuting Nazi supporters, have prevented an independent policy of prosecution. The centralization of criminal investigation in the police has reduced the prosecutor to a kind of secondary transmitting agent, acting only when the police for reasons of propaganda elect not to deal summarily with cases.

2. **Courts.** The Nazi regime has brought the courts into line with its policies not only through purge of personnel but also through increasing the administrative duties in which the court presidents act on the order of, and as the representative of, the Minister of Justice.[44] The assignment of the judges is now made by the court president alone, acting for the Minister of Justice. Judges are also subject to reassignment during the fiscal year for any reason, and are bound to accept any type of assignment within the jurisdiction of the Minister of Justice. The fact that court presidents were increasingly transformed into top administrators, bound to execute the Ministry's wishes, suggestions, and orders through their "corps of judges," has become especially evident during the latter years of the Nazi regime.

## II. Recommendations

### A. Military Government's Approach to Criminal Law

At first glance, it may seem sufficient to give the state's attorney new instructions as to what kind of criminal prosecution to initiate, to replace the death penalty as introduced by the Nazis by milder forms of punishment, and, generally, to recognize in the judge a wide discretion in fixing penalties. Thus a liberalization of punishment would be achieved, while the task of reforming the law itself would be left to the German people. Such a policy would not suffice, because Nazi legislation has changed the whole framework of criminal law and created entirely new concepts. On the other hand, a complete abrogation of the criminal legislation of the Third Reich cannot be considered, as such a project of reform is no concern of Military Government's. The issue resolves itself finally into a problem of abrogation of those features wholly objectionable. A system of limited abrogation is particularly [*missing word in the original text*] in keeping with Military Government's functions as it will reduce the number of acts of the occupant which may require validation by the German state.

It is therefore recommended that, in the absence of explicit directives to the contrary, Military Government approach the problem of criminal law on the assumption that the revision of the criminal system is an issue for the German people and that Military Government should make only such changes as are necessitated by requirements of military security, Military Government's obligation to maintain law and order, and its duty to implement the policies and purposes of the United Nations.

The effect of this recommendation, as well as of the more specific recommendations which follow, is to leave a residue of some rather loose redefinitions of old crimes and definitions of new crimes introduced by the Nazis, together with the bulk of the narrowly defined rules of the code of 1871. The German courts worked with an antiquated system before Hitler came to power and will presumably be able to go on with a purged code and subsidiary statutes, until reforms can be completed by those immediately concerned.

### B. Substantive Law

#### 1. General Criminal Legislation under the Nazi Regime

a. *Political crimes.* One of the first problems confronting Military Government is the treatment to be given the Nazi definitions of treason and public order.

The ties of allegiance between Military Government and the individual within the occupied areas are not identical with those existing between the individual and the German Government, and thus would not justify Military Government's retention of the statutory provisions on treason even if their philosophies were acceptable to Military Government. Their revision is essentially a problem for the German people. However, this is not an impediment to Military Government's regulation of the performance of the duties of allegiance which the population of the occupied areas owes it or its penalizing of the breach thereof (FM 27-10, Pars. 205, 350.)[45]

The duties imposed upon Military Government as to the maintenance of law and order and the protection of the occupying forces under international law and the terms of existing directives (see above p. 000 ff) likewise authorize Military Government to pursue an equally independent line of action in questions of public order.

It is therefore recommended that Military Government declare suspended the operation of German regulations on public order and political terrorism, and place in effect its own proclamations on the subject. It is suggested that Military Government restrict the jurisdiction of German criminal courts to the application of those public order and security statutes and code provisions which were on the statute books before the Papen regime took power (31 May 1932).

Paragraphs 80 to 104 of the Criminal Code, which deal with treason, should be suspended. The following provisions on public order associated with special statutes or decrees should be specifically abrogated:

1. Presidential Decree of 4 February 1933 (Protection of German People)—*RGB1.*, I, 35.
2. Par. 4 of the Presidential Decree of 28 February 1933 (Protection of People and Country—*RGB1.*, I, 83)
3. Statute of 4 April 1933 (Defense Against Political Terrorism)—*RGB1.*, I, 163.
4. Statute of 19 May 1933 (Protection of National Symbols)—*RGB1.*, I, 285.
5. Statute of 14 June 1933 (Formation of New Parties)—*RGB1.*, I, 398.
6. Statute of 13 October 1933 (Guarantee of Internal Peace)—*RGB1.*, I, 723.
7. Statute of 20 December 1934 (Surreptitious Attacks on State and Party and Protection of Party Uniform)—*RGB1.*, I, 1269.
8. Statute of 7 April 1937 (Protection of NSDAP Labels)—*RGB1.*, I, 442.

There may be other laws or decrees enacted or promulgated prior to 30 January 1933, that encroach upon civil and political liberties and therefore require invalidation., this may be accomplished either by suspension of such laws or by military proclamation stating contrary regulation. To this category belong the following decrees:

1. Presidential Decree of 3 May 1932 (Dissolution of Communist Atheist Organizations).[46]
2. Presidential Decree of 9 August 1932 (Political Terrorism).[47]
3. Presidential Decree of 19 December 1932 (Maintenance of Internal Peace).[48]

b. *Basic changes in the criminal code.* The revisions which Military Government will need to make in other fields of criminal law are not as simply ascertained. In some instances Military Government may desire to retain a portion of the Nazi legislation.

i. *Article 2.* From the point of view of psychological effect and political reaction, no more vital decision will be made by Military Government in the field of German criminal law than its decision as to Article 2 of the Criminal Code (see above p. 000). Even in the early period of the Nazi regime, this Nazi revision served as a continuing remainder of the fact that the nonexistence of legislation squarely covering the offense in question was no ground for acquittal. Legislation of this type has already been condemned by an international tribunal.[49] It is therefore recommended that Military Government abrogate the Nazi version of Article 2 and restore the version under which the German criminal system had previously operated.

ii. *Pre-war changes in the criminal code.* Military government may find it advisable to eliminate those changes in the Penal Code and special statutes introduced by the Nazis to facilitate the execution of their oppressive policies and the preparation for war. It is therefore recommended that Military Government abrogate the following statutes:

Statute of 26 May 1933 (changes in the code—RGB1., I, 295;
Statute of 28 June 1935 (changes in the code)—RGB1., I, 839;
Statute of 2 July 1936 (changes in the code)—RGB1., I, 532;
Statute of 22 June 1938 (highway robbery with auto traps)—RGB1., I, 651.

The abrogation should be absolute except for the following substantive provisions[50] which Military Government may desire to retain:

1. The provisions as to abortions (Art. 219-20), maltreatment of minors and incompetent (Art. 223b), violation of fiduciary (*Untreue*) relations (Art. 266), and prostitution (Art. 361, n° 6) of the statute of 26 May 1933.
2. Misuse of automatic fare-collection devices (Art. 265a), forest fires (Art. 310a), and the failure to give assistance in an emergency (Art. 330c) of the statute of 28 June 1935.

iii. *Changes in the criminal code necessitated by the war*. Those changes made in the criminal system for war purposes (see above p. 000 ff.) are not in harmony with the military requirement of the occupant and should therefore be abrogated.

It is therefore recommended that Military Government abrogate the following status and decrees:

Decree of 17 August 1938 and 26 August 1939—*RGB1.*, I, 1455;
Decree of 9 September 1939 (extraordinary measures in the field of broadcasting)—*RGB1.*, I, 1683;
Decree of 15 September 1939 (enemies of the people)—*RGB1.*, I, 1679;
Decree of 16 September 1939 (changes of procedure, court martial, and criminal code) *RGB1.*, I, 1841;
Decree of 25 November 1939 (supplementary protection of war potential)—*RGB1.*, I, 2319;
Decree of 5 December 1939 (perpetrators of crimes of violence)—*RGB1.*, I, 2378;
Decree of 11 May 1940 (relations with war prisoners)—*RGB1.*, I, 769;
Decree of 10 October 1940 (new version of military penal code)—*RGB1.*, I, 1347;
Statute of 4 September 1941 (change of penal code)—*RGB1.*, I, 549 (except par. 3);
Decree of 23 December 1941 (winter clothing collection)—*RGB1.*, I, 797;
Decree of 20 September 1942 (larceny in the fields)—*RGB1.*, I, 558;
Paragraphs 5 and 8 of the decree of 9 March 1943 (protection of the family)—*RGB1.*, I, 140.
Arts. 9-10 of decree of 29 May 1943 (slander, duress)—*RGB1.*, I, 339.

*iv. Penalties*. One of the chief devices by which the Nazi regime forced conformity to its policies was the manipulation of the penalties decreed for various crimes.

It is recommended that Military Government abrogate the provisions as to the penalty of castration contained in paragraphs 42a and 42k of the penal code. It is suggested that the abolition of the security measures of which this penalty is a part is a question for the German people and not for Military Government, and that in this respect Military Government has discharged its obligations when it restores the procedural guarantees surrounding its application.

It is further recommended that Military Government by proclamation confine the imposition of the death penalty to those instances in which it was used before February 1933, and that the method of execution be that used prior to the same date.[51]

As it is neither feasible nor advisable for Military Government to revise the bulk of German criminal legislation, Military Government may find it advisable to permit the courts, when reopened, to deviate from the scale of punishment imposed by the Nazis in those cases in which Military Government has decided to retain the crime as defined by the Nazis or in pre-existing German law. If Military Government should so decide, it is suggested that Military Government consider the advisability of vesting in the judge a broad discretion to depart from the standards of minimum penalty fixed in Nazi legislation which is otherwise retained. Military Government may well bear in mind that uniformity in this matter has been secured in practice through exercise of the state's right to appeal in criminal cases.

*v. Juvenile cases.* While opinion may be divided on the innovations made by the Third Reich in the jurisdiction over juveniles, there seems no urgent need for revision. It is therefore recommended that the Youth Correction Act of 6 November 1943[52] be retained, except for Nazi features contained in certain paragraphs.[53] The law should thus be made applicable not only to German youth but to all youths coming within the jurisdiction of the German courts. It should also revert to the pre-Hitler rule that children under 14 are not criminally responsible for their acts, and that the juvenile courts have exclusive jurisdiction of offenses by children under 18 years of age.

## C. Procedural Law

1. **Preventive detention.** –In view of Nazi practices, Military Government will desire for political and psychological reasons, to make it clear that the use of preventive detention is to be held to the irreducible minimum and that the accused is free to request an oral hearing on the necessity of maintaining such an order. Release on bail is permissible under German law.

The solution thus lies in the return to an adequate system of protection against arbitrary detention orders.

It is therefore recommended that the guarantees contained in the pre-Nazi codes be restored. This will require abrogation of the appropriate sections of the statute of 24 April 1943[54] and that of 28 June 1935.[55]

2. **Right to representation.** The question of the restoration of the right to representation is a delicate one. If the criminal courts are reopened before the bar has been completely purged, there may be a tendency on the part of some lawyers to indulge in political obstruction. In such instances, neither the methods nor the ends of the Anglo-American "con-

tempt" proceedings would constitute an adequate remedy. The issue for Military Government hinges, therefore, upon its willingness to continue a highly restricted right to representation.

It is recommended that, if the bar has been completely purged when the courts are reopened, there be no restriction of the right to representation and that the mandatory representation provisions of the pro-Nazi period be restored.

If, on the other hand, the bar has not been completely purged, Military Government may decide to control the admission to practice before the criminal courts. In this case, it may establish its own tests for admission to practice. In addition it may vest in the presiding judge the right at any stage of the proceedings to remove a defense attorney and to permit the defendant to choose a successor. If Military Government should elect to give the presiding judge this right, it is suggested that an appeal from his decision be given to the highest zonal administrative agency dealing with judicial affairs.

3. **Right to introduce evidence**. It is recommended that Nazi provisions giving all criminals courts the discretionary right to refuse or admit evidence should be abrogated. As, however, Art. 3, par. 1 of the presidential decree of 14 June 1932[56] remains in force, criminal courts dealing with less important cases will retain the right to exercise full discretion in the admission of evidence.

It is further recommended that all barriers to securing evidence, such as the rule established by the statute of 1 December 1936,[57] that Nazi officials and Party members could not be called, without special permission, to give evidence as to Party matters, be abrogated.

4. **Right to appeal and to ask a new trial**. It is recommended that the right to appeal or to ask a new trial, whether exercised by the state or by the defendant, be restored in the form which it had before 1 February 1933.

It is further recommended that the state's right within one year to appeal from a final decision be abrogated.[58]

5. **Basis of decision**. It is recommended that Military Government take whatever action, over and above the purge of judicial personnel, it deems necessary to restore to the German criminal courts a genuinely independent decision. On the other hand, Military Government will have little or no interest in abolishing such procedural rules as the rule that, when several laws seem applicable to a particular factual situation, the judge may elect to apply the milder in fixing guilt and punishment rather than acquit the defendant,[59] or the rule that the Supreme Court is free to depart from precedents.[60]

## D. Problems of Jurisdiction

It is recommended that all special courts established after 1 February 1933 be closed and that all jurisdictional changes made after 1 February 1933 whose retention is not specially recommended in this Guide be abrogated.

The abolition of courts created by the Nazis requires no comment in justification. The abolition of the special military courts may be thought to require justification on different grounds. The Weimar Constitution did not allow the existence of any military tribunals in peacetime except for personnel on board warships. While in theory only the peace treaty can restore full peace in Germany warranting the restoration of this Weimar rule, certain other factors may well enter into consideration. The restoration of military courts was one of the first acts of the Third Reich. Experience has shown that the granting of special exemptions from general court jurisdiction effectively protects military organizations against outside control. During the period of demobilization, it will be important not to encourage the formation or maintenance of nuclei of possible political resistance. It would seem advisable, therefore, for Military Government to couple military courts with special Nazi courts, to abrogate the statutes authorizing their existence, and to revert to pre-Nazi jurisdictions.

It is recommended that Military Government, in order to effect the necessary changes in criminal procedure and criminal jurisdiction, abolish the following statutes, decrees, and provisions. This list mentions only rarely important executive or other decrees based on enabling clauses of laws and decrees. Therefore Military Government proclamation of abrogation should be drawn to include all executive decrees as well as decrees implementing or amending prior legislation.

Decree of 21 March 1933 (formation of special courts)—*RGB1.*, I, 136.

Statute of 12 May 1933 (reestab1ishment of military courts)—*RGB1.*, I, 264.

Statute of 24 April 1934 (procedural changes)—*RGB1.*, I, 844.

Statute of 28 June 1934 with the exception of Art. 1, sec. 2, secs. 4a, 4b ; Mt. 2 ; Art. 4, sec. 2 ; Art. 6 (changes in criminal procedure and jurisdiction). The exceptions concern convictions on alternative grounds, admissibility of changes in sentences to the defendant's disadvantage even in cases of the defendant's own appeal, restrictions of preliminary judicial investigation, free discretion of the state's attorney to ask for trial or to *nolle pros'* in cases involving blackmail, proceedings against fugitives from justice—*RGB1.*, I, 844.

Statute of 26 June 1936 (reestablishment of Supreme Court martial)—*RGB1.*, I, 517.

Statute of 18 April 1936 (People's Court)—*RGB1.*, I, 369.

Statutes of 19 September 1936 (new version of code of criminal procedure for court martials)—*RGB1.*, I, 751, 756.

Statute of 1 December 1936 (examination of NSDAP members in civil courts)—*RGB1.*, I, 994.

Decree of 17 August 1938 and 26 August 1939 (court-martial procedures in wartime and for special duties)—*RGB1.*, 1939, I, 1457.

Decree of 1 September 1939 with the exception of pars. 1-4 and par. 24; (jurisdiction and criminal procedure). Exceptions concern the right of the court president to distribute functions within the court as representative of executive power and discretionary powers granted to the court in regard to the admission of evidence—*RGB1.*, I, 1658.

Statute of 16 September 1939 (criminal procedure, court martial procedure)—*RGB1.*, I, 1841.

Decree of 17 October 1939 (special jurisdiction for members of SS and police formations for special tasks)—*RGB1.*, I, 2107.

Decree of 31 January 1940 (jurisdiction of criminal courts and procedural provisions)—*RGB1.*, I, 405.

Decree of 3 December 1940 (special criminal jurisdictions, for labor service members)—*RGB1.*, I, 485.

Decree of 6 May 1940 (territorial extension of German criminal law)—*RGB1.*, I, 754.

Edict of the Führer of 21 March 1942 (simplification of judicial administration) with the exception of par. 1. The exception concerns the abolition of the court's right to reject the state's attorney's request to bring a case to trial—*RGB1.*, I, 139.

Decree of 13 August 1942 (further simplification of the administration of criminal justice) except Art. 1. The exception concerns the same point as was mentioned in the preceding—*RGB1.*, I, 508.

Decree of 29 May 1943 (simplification of criminal procedure and criminal law administration)—*RGB1.*, I, 342.

Decree of 29 May 1943 (further personnel economies in administration of criminal justice)—*RGB1.*, I, 346.

1. **Distribution of functions**. It is suggested that Military Government may find it expedient to retain the decree and laws of 1935, 1937, and 1939[61] which made the distribution of functions within a court a purely administrative function exercised on the order and in behalf of the Min-

istry of Justice. It is further suggested that Military Government should consider the wisdom, during the first phases of occupation, of establishing procedures which would enable the district attorney or prosecutor (or the attorney general in the appeal courts), or the defendant, at any stage of litigation to move for a change of venue, in order that cases which have political significance may be heard by a special chamber. The power to assign judges to special functions, which the president of each court now enjoys, would permit the creation of such special chambers within the framework of existing German procedure. This will put the administration in a position to secure conditions for fair trial for both the state and the defendant.[62]

It is also suggested that the law members of the criminal courts be selected from lists submitted by reliable and representative organizations, and that selection from such lists be made by the Military Government officer supervising court activities, on recommendations from a committee consisting of one member of the local court and six persons appointed by the Military Government officer in question.[63] Both the committee and the personnel of the lists in question should be screened in order that Nazi supporters may be excluded.

2. **Division of jurisdiction between Military Government courts and the German courts.** A considerable part of the German criminal law will be suspended by proclamations issued by Military Government. For example, the enforcement of the treason provisions and the extensive special legislation in the same field will be suspended by Military Government and new regulations enacted for the purposes of occupation. Further, in discharge of its obligations to protect the occupying forces and to maintain law and order, Military Government will be obliged to issue other regulations.

In view of the conditions which may be expected to prevail in Germany, at least during the first phases of occupation, the prosecution of even the politically less important cases to German courts would seem clearly inadvisable.

It is therefore recommended that in the first phase of occupation the prosecution of breaches of Military Government regulation be the exclusive function of Military Government courts and that the shifting of all or any of this function to German courts should not be considered until the German courts have been thoroughly purged and have demonstrated their reliability for a satisfactory period of time.

3. **Jurisdictional conflicts between Military Government courts and the German criminal courts.** Very often cases will arise in which it may be genuinely doubtful whether the case falls within the jurisdiction of German or Military Government courts. It is recommended that Military

Government courts be given exclusive jurisdiction to decide such conflicts of jurisdiction.

It is also recommended that, if there is any question of such conflict of jurisdiction, arising at any stage of litigation, the state's attorney or prosecutor should move for a stay of process. It is further recommended that, while the state's attorney or prosecutor may so act of his own motion, his duty to act and the issuance of the stay of process should be mandatory if a request for such action is forwarded to the state's attorney by the Military Government officer supervising court officers. It is suggested that, if the state's attorney secures the stay of his own motion and forwards the records to the Military Government officer supervising court affairs, that officer be charged with the duty of deciding the issue himself or submitting it within thirty days to the appropriate Military Government court, and that such cases be given precedence on the dockets of Military Government courts.

It is also recommended that the decision rendered by Military Government courts be made binding on German courts and that a judgment entered in any case by a Military Government court preclude consideration by German courts of the same case. This last should be construed as an application of the principle "ne bis in idem"[64] which is the basis of paragraph 264 of the code of criminal procedure. This rule goes beyond the concept of double jeopardy as commonly applied in Anglo-American jurisdictions. It not only prohibits the court from sentencing a defendant for the same offense for which he has already been sentenced or of which he has previously been acquitted, but also prevents the court from considering the case again under a new and somewhat varied legal theory. For example, a defendant who had been acquitted by a Military Government court for having stolen some ration cards could not be brought before a German court for having embezzled the same ration cards. Utilization of this principle, familiar to the German legal world, would remove from the German courts any pretext for assuming jurisdiction in cases in which Military Government had entered judgment.

It is, finally, recommended that Military Government enact regulations defining the personnel over which Military Government courts have exclusive jurisdiction.[65]

## E. Amnesty Problems

1. **Need for action by Military Government**. One of the questions which will confront Military Government even in the earlier phases of occupation will be the treatment of prisoners whose imprisonment was caused primarily by oppressive Nazi practices. The liberation of political prisoners alone will constitute a prime problem. The psychological effect of

the speedy release of political prisoners and the prompt review of other cases cannot be overestimated. The population in occupied areas would find in such measures a harbinger of their right to build a new regime. On the other hand, if Military Government fails to take immediate steps for the release of political prisoners, it is likely that a wave of jail deliveries will take place. Such a development would not only undermine the authority and prestige of Military Government but also lead to an indiscriminate release of all criminals, including those common offenders whose liberation would increase the difficulties of administration for Military Government. It is submitted that this psychological factor alone, without regard to the traditional Anglo-American amnesty practice, would require Military Government to consider to what extent it should first, release prisoners in concentration camps and, second, grant amnesty and the review of oppressive Nazi sentences and to what extent it should leave the correction of these issues to the future German state.

It is suggested that the need for Military Government action should hinge upon the length of the occupation and should recognize that its course of action may differ according to whether the occupation is long or short.

2. **Short-term occupation**. If the period of occupation is short, the time factor will limit to some degree the scope of Military Government's action. However, it seems unquestionable that, in view of the established American tradition and the existing policy statements by the United Nations, even in a short-term occupation, Military Government should immediately provide release for prisoners in concentration camps and a full amnesty for political prisoners as sentenced by courts.

a. *Persons in concentration camps*. Concentration camps are the epitome of all that is shameful in Nazism, and should be immediately investigated and closed. However, Military Government may well bear in mind that, in addition to political opponents, Jews, etc., the Nazi regime may have used such camps to detain certain categories of criminals deemed particularly reprehensible from the Nazi point of view such as "dangerous criminals," black-market operators, those charged with absenteeism in industry, etc. To the extent that the persons found there were detained without trial or have already served their sentences in prison, it is recommended that they be released as in the case of political prisoners, as there would be no legal basis for further detention.

Some of those found in concentration camps may have been sentenced by judicial action but sent there rather than to ordinary prisons. It is recommended that, to the extent that they have not served their terms, they be treated under the amnesty procedure, shortly to be described.

It is further recommended that the persons to whom the amnesty procedure does not apply should be transferred to regular prisons to serve the balance of their terms.

In addition to concentration camps, the Nazi regime has established a number of similar camps for the extra-legal detention of certain categories of persons, such as the "Protective Youth Camps" (*Jugendschutzlager*) for unruly juveniles. These camps should likewise be dissolved and the inmates released.

While this action may be regarded in general as essential, Military Government should bear in mind that probably it will not wish to apply this procedure to all persons found in such camps. It may desire to except from this procedure, first, Nazis, who, although Nazi in sympathy, have opposed the regime in some respect; second, Nazis who have been "planted" in such camps; and, third, Nazis who caused their own detention in an attempt to avoid popular reprisals or Allied punitive measures. The detail of the methods by which Military Government may achieve this purpose will depend upon the conditions existing at the time of occupation, and should therefore be fixed only at that time. It is suggested, however, that Military Government may wish to give the first category some special consideration.

b. *Definition of political crimes.* The difficulty for Military Government will lie not in the determination of the need for such an amnesty but rather in the definition of political crime and of the machinery by which to implement that definition.

The traditional definition of "political crime" includes two distinct categories: First, those which are intrinsically political, such as treason, desertion, sedition, espionage, and the like; and second, those which are ordinarily nonpolitical but become political through political motivation, such as murder committed for political reasons. The problem for Military Government is complicated by the fact that, while the Nazis have by statute widened the content of political crimes, the second category, always more delicate of determination, has been even more vastly increased under the conditions of Nazism. The totalitarian regime has so much suppressed all normal methods of opposition, that, for example, a combination of economic motive and of the desire to revolt against the regime may underline such crimes as "breach of labor contract."

Nor are these positive factors the only difficulties in the definition of a political crime. There are two negative factors which require consideration.

It is essential for psychological reasons that the definition of political crime should be drawn to exclude any implication of amnesty for those Nazis who have taken part in unlawful operations against persons and property and who, for the first time, may be held accountable.

It is no less vital for the success of Military Government administration that the amnesty program should not in any way undermine Military Government's support of such programs as rationing and price control. Deliberate rebellion against Nazi authorities, desire for profit, or simply hunger may all have been factors in such offenses. However, Military Government's interest in such cases should be reviewed and adjustment of arbitrary and unjust punishments rather than automatic amnesty.

The need for immediate action is circumscribed not only by the time factor present in short-term occupation but also by personnel limitations. It would seem inevitable that Military Government draw its definition of political crimes and of the scope of amnesty with these considerations in mind. It is recommended, therefore, that, holding in view in its drafting the two negative factors mentioned above, Military Government should define political offenses as embracing the following: First, offenses traditionally recognized as political; second, those which the Nazis have included in their widened concept of political crimes; and, third, those cases in which the offense was a violation of laws which it is the fixed purpose of the United Nations to abrogate. The third category would include violation of those statutes restricting relations between individuals on account of their race or nationality or their status as foreigners or prisoners of war, as well as those directed against persons exclusively because of their origin and religious affiliation.[66]

c. *Definition of military crimes*. It is suggested that Military Government consider also an amnesty for criminal offenses against the Military Criminal Code as well as for offenses of soldiers coming under the Decree on Wartime Criminal Law of 17 August 1938[67] and of subsequent amending and executive decrees to the latter decree. It seems justifiable to include these offenses under the amnesty since the majority have been committed under the stress of war, and, where they cannot be labeled political crimes proper, they may often have been so motivated that Military Government would not be interested in continuing the punishment.

Two important exceptions, however, present themselves. The first concerns the abuse of authority, e.g., insulting or maltreatment of subordinates or the instigation of a subordinate to commit a crime. The second exception concerns offenses such as marauding, looting, rape, or robbery. Many of the last-mentioned offenses will have their specific war criminal aspect and thus fall outside the scope of amnesty. Insofar as cases coming under the two excepted categories are of little consequence, the proposals for a general amnesty discussed below could be made applicable to them.

d. *Treatment of short-term sentences*. It may be felt that even in the first phase of the occupation Military Government may consider the release of a larger group of persons who have been punished under the Nazi regime. Without doubt the reopening of the German courts will be marked by a flood of petitions for retrial of cases which were not adequately heard because of harsh rules introduced by the Nazis (see above p. 000). The granting of amnesty to most of the persons who received an original sentence of not more than 18 months would go far to stem this tide, since it would remove two-thirds of such petitions. In granting amnesty a clause would be attached to the proclamation stating that the reimprisonment can be ordered for those who have committed serious crimes, but whose sentences have been reduced because of their standing as Nazi Party members (old party fighters, etc.)

e. *Action by Military Government.* In a short-term occupation, Military Government will scarcely have the time or personnel available to devise or sponsor a screening of cases in which cruel and unjust punishments have been inflicted under the Nazi regime. The following recommendations are therefore made:

a) That in these circumstances Military Government confine its action to the liberation of persons convicted of political and military crimes as defined above, and that it treat conviction for such offenses as establishing eligibility for immediate and automatic amnesty. It is suggested that the amnesty for political crimes entail as its logical consequence the expunging of the entry in the criminal register concerning each case. In all other cases Military Government may leave this restoration of full civil rights to the normal German procedure.
b) That an amnesty be given to all offenders on whom an original sentence of not more than 18 months imprisonment or hard labor was imposed and that at the same time the state's attorneys be ordered not to start new proceedings for offences committed before the date of effective military occupation of their district when the expected punishment would not exceed 18 months.
c) That the proclamation establishing this definition make it clear that this is only the preliminary step and does not preclude further action in the field.

This procedure is suggested because it affords a quick method of identifying the person and the offense, without any need to screen evidence or review records, and involves a minimum of personnel for Military Government. However, this action should not preclude the simultaneous establishment of review procedure.

3. **Long-term occupation**. The possibility of long-term occupation requires prompt consideration by Military Government of measures for the review of the cases of victims of Nazi oppression in the courts. Such measures should be considered as an essential part of the de-Nazification program for Germany.

a. *First phase of occupation*. It is suggested that in the first phase of occupation Military Government follow the pattern previously laid down for short-term occupation.

b. *Subsequent action of Military Government*.[68]

c. *Agency to administer program*. While there can be no question of the political and psychological necessity of the liberation of those whose offenses fail within the above-mentioned concept of political and military crimes, grave questions arise in the case of other types of cases, in which review of records is necessary to reveal the political motive in the crime, or in which the adjustment of the penalty would seem to amount to a substantial revision of the German criminal system. If Military Government is obliged to continue to operate as the governing unit in Germany and no indigenous German government grows up to assume the responsibility for such action, it would seem inevitable that Military Government provide some machinery to handle this problem.

As a first step it is recommended that the decree of 11 June 1940[69] be abolished. This decree provides that sentences of hard labor imposed during wartime against any offender should start to run only after the war. This rule also applied to judgments of courts martial, and police or SS courts, if the judgment stipulates the loss of civil rights. The automatic effect of this abrogation would be to release many prisoners whose cases would otherwise have to be considered for review.

Another step of equal importance is the provision of review machinery for sentences of more than 18 months. In this group many political offenders are likely to be found whose cases were not automatically recognized as political crimes. For these cases Military Government should set standards of procedure in order to obtain a minimum of uniformity. Often political questions are involved which make close Military Government control desirable. However, the need for speedy action and the probable shortage of trained Military Government personnel may require the utilization of a German agency.

The office of the state's attorney at the district court in whose area the prisoner was originally sentenced seems to be best equipped for this undertaking. The files of the prisoner are kept in this office and the same agency is entrusted by law with the function of supervising the execution of the punishment. Moreover, some measure of uniformity of procedure and decision will be facilitated by the fact that the district attorney will probably work under Military Government supervision, exercised either at the district or at the appeal court level.

The district attorney should submit to the Military Government delegate a list of cases to which, in the opinion of the district attorney, the amnesty should apply. If, after a lapse of time fixed by Military Government, the delegate raises no objections to the proposed list, the prisoners should be released or their sentences reduced.

However, Military Government may find it practicable to provide at the same time for a board of inquiry in each appeal-court district. Such a board would consider the cases of prisoners who were not included on the district attorney's list for release or partial remittance of sentence, as well as the cases which the Military Government delegate failed to approve.

### F. Prosecution of Nazi Offenders against German Citizens

A problem no less serious in its psychological implication will confront Military Government, in case of long-term occupation, in the treatment of Nazi offenders against German citizens. While a considerable number of Nazi criminals will probably face trial before Allied courts as war criminals, there will remain many who will presumably not be subject to those courts because they committed the offenses in question in German territory against German citizens. These persons have escaped prosecution either because their misdeeds were amnestied by the Nazi Government or because no prosecutor dared to initiate proceedings against them. Because of the failure of prosecution, the statute of limitations may have run in their favor. While some of them may be arrested for interference with Military Government's discharge of its duties or for disturbance of public order, it may be expected that many of this group will escape such detention. Some of the crimes may have been so atrocious and some of the offenders so prominent in public life that popular demand for prosecution may be great.

It may be assumed that, after the courts have been reopened, and the statutes and practices abrogated which formerly protected Nazi offenders, prosecutors will not be afraid to initiate action upon such flagrant offenses. It is recommended that Military Government take whatever steps are in its power to assist and encourage such action.

There will remain, however, a group of offenders of this category who cannot be convicted or prosecuted (a) because the German courts, even if purged, may invoke the doctrine of superior orders, or (b) because the statute of limitations will have run in favor of the defendant, or (c) because a Nazi amnesty or the statute on Measures of State Emergency, of 3 July 1934, may have intervened.[70] The problem of the disposition of this group of offenders is fundamentally a problem for the German people. To open the way for their prosecution in German courts, even during the period of occupation, by abrogation of the statute of limitations as to such offenses or by action on the above measures would be so drastic a change in the system of German criminal law that MG should not take such a step in the absence of a specific directive to that effect from the political authorities.

## G. Problems of Administration

**1. Supervision of German courts.** After Military Government has reopened the German courts, it will be confronted with the problem of how far it should supervise their activities. It is suggested that some degree of supervision is advisable in all phases of occupation but that supervision may be relaxed as the German courts demonstrate their strength and reliability.

In the first period after the reopening of the courts, it seems inevitable that Military Government should set up a system for supervising the operation of the courts. It is recommended that the supervision be centralized in the hands of one Military Government officer, and that he assign his subordinates to every appeal court and to the more important district courts.

The special function of the Military Government officers assigned to the individual courts would be to follow closely criminal proceedings initiated in the German courts. To that end, the prosecutors in the district court should be required to send him two types of reports: First, daily reports on all cases which may directly or indirectly affect the interests of the occupying powers; second, weekly reports on indictments, informations, and notices of appeal in all cases which originally are not brought before a single judge in the local court. They should also report acquittals, sentences, and all written opinions handed down in their courts, as well as cases terminated by nolle pro's (*Einstellungsbeachlüsse*).

This procedure would permit the Military Government officer to keep close watch over the dockets of the criminal courts, and to form judgments as to their strength and independence. It would further enable him to have close contact with the work and personality of the judges and prosecutors. The sum total of this information, evaluated by the Military Government officer in whose hands supervision was centralized, would be valuable evidence to be considered by those officers within Military Government in deciding shifts in personnel or, more vital, continued operation of the German courts.

**2. Executive revision of sentences.** In contradistinction to the Rhineland occupation, where the prerogatives of the executive exercised by the

Ministry of Justice remained in principle in German hands, Military Government should exercise all executive authority. It will have consequently the prerogative of pardon and of commutation of sentences, not only in regard to those cases which come before Military Government tribunals, but also in regard to those cases where German criminal courts will retain jurisdiction.

# 21

Franz Neumann

## *THE PROBLEM OF INFLATION IN GERMANY*

(October 16,1944)

Editor's note: R&A 1657. Neumann's authorship is indicated in a letter dated December 10,1943, from Eugene Anderson to Carl Schorske (RG 226, entry 60, box 1: Projects Committee Correspondence).

The document also indicates the participation of Rudolf Eisenberg, member of the Central European Section and specialist in economic and fiscal policy, in the drafting of the report.

Classification: Confidential

### I. Experience of 1914–1924

#### A. The War Financing and Its Defects

In 1914 the German government based its war finance program on the assumption that the war would be short. No additional taxation was introduced. Loans were considered sufficient to cover the total war expenses.[1] The government obtained the necessary cash by discounting treasury notes with the Reichsbank which, in turn, sold these notes to banks and large business firms. Every six months loans were floated to redeem the treasury notes. The political and fiscal organization of the country made it nearly impossible to raise taxes for war purposes. The states refused to let the Reich collect income taxes, and the Social Democratic party would not consent to the increase of consumption taxes without a simultaneous increase of direct taxes.

Mobilization and initial war expenses, in the summer of 1914, were financed by the issue of two billion marks in Reichsbank notes against treasury notes. The note issue facilities of the Reichsbank were enlarged and special loan offices (*Darlehenskassen*) established to cooperate with the Reichsbank and make credit easily available to local government bodies and private enterprise.[2] The notes of the loan offices were used as cover for bank notes. In order to facilitate the conversion of the economy to war production, the government paid high prices for all deliveries and thus started a general boom. A great liquidity of the money and capital market resulted from the discounting of treasury notes by the Reichsbank, but the expectation that all war expenses could be covered by bond issues was not realized. The amount of loans subscribed to by the public, partly with the help of bank credit, permitted repayment of only a portion of the treasury notes outstanding at the time of the loan issue, and the short-term debt increased steadily[3]. Moreover, the Reichsbank did not succeed in selling much more than one-half of the treasury notes to the public. An inflationary expansion of the note circulation resulted from its growing portfolio of treasury notes. Out of the total war expenditure, some 144 billion marks, the government raised about two-thirds by bond issues and one-third by treasury notes, but no tax receipts were used to cover war expenses.

The issuance of additional paper currency exceeded by far the amount of gold and silver coin withdrawn from circulation. The total amount of currency increased by approximately the same amount which the Reichsbank put at the disposal of the government by discounting treasury notes for its own account (see table on p. 000). Deposits on checking accounts with the Reichsbank also increased considerably. By the end of 1915 the general price level had risen 50 percent. The decreased supply of consumer goods and the increase in private incomes made it necessary to introduce price controls and rationing of various commodities. These measures stabilized prices for some time. The larger war effort of 1917–18, however, caused a new rise of prices,[4] though their increase was not so fast as the expansion of the currency circulation. This was due to the reduced velocity of money circulation, caused by changes in payment habits (especially the use of cash instead of commercial bills), the holding of larger cash reserves by the public, and the hoarding of currency for tax evasion and for use after the war, as well as to the issuance of German currency in occupied territories and speculative purchases of marks by foreigners.

In the foreign exchange market the depreciation of the mark was less pronounced than the reduction of its domestic purchasing power. Foreign exchange controls were operating and the Reichsbank had increased its reserves by withdrawing gold and silver from circulation. The huge deficit in the balance of trade was covered by sales of gold and securities, by foreign credits, and by exportation of German currency.

The following table[5] shows the financing of war expenses and some of its effects. (The figures are cumulative from the beginning of the war to the end of each year).

| | *Loans issued* | *Treasury notes issued* | *Treasury notes held by R.B.* | *Increase in currency circulation*[a] |
|---|---|---|---|---|
| | | *(in billion marks)* | | |
| 1914 | 4.5 | 2.9 | 2.7 | 2.7 |
| 1915 | 25. | 5.7. | 5.2 | 4.1 |
| 1916 | 46. | 12.6 | 8.9 | 6.3 |
| 1917 | 71. | 28.6 | 14.2 | 12.5 |
| 1918 (October) | 96. | 48.2 | 20.4 | 20.7 |

*INDICES*

| *End of year* | *Total currency circulation* | *Wholesale prices official* | *Dollar exchange rate* |
|---|---|---|---|
| 1913=100 | | | |
| 1914 | 143 | 125 | 107 |
| 1915 | 166 | 148 | 123 |
| 1916 | 209 | 151 | 136 |
| 1917 | 304 | 203 | 135 |
| 1918 (October) | 440 | 234 | 157 |

a Compared with the 6 billion RM coin and notes circulating in 1913.

## B. The Post-war Deficit and Reestablishment of Free Prices

The excessive volume of currency held by the public, the large deposits in commercial banks, and holdings of government paper, on the one hand, and the reduced capacity of production and depleted stocks of raw materials and goods, on the other hand, were cause for a much steeper price inflation than had so far developed. Even if the budget had been immediately balanced it would have been a difficult task to stabilize prices and incomes at the level which they had reached during the war and to reestablish a free market.

After the Armistice, however, the expansion of currency circulation proceeded even faster than during the war. The cessation of hostilities did not substantially reduce the expenses of the government, which now included the cost of demobilization, expenses in connection with the

Armistice (especially payments for deliveries to the Allies), cost of provisions purchased for the population, as well as unemployment relief and the deficit of railroads and other public enterprises which had to be covered by the Reich.[6]

The facility with which deficits were financed with the aid of the Reichsbank developed a habit of extravagance in public policy. The fiscal powers of the central government, however, were still inadequate. The coalition government, under Socialist leadership, combined efforts to raise the tax receipts with plans for social reform and in this way increased the opposition of the wealthy classes to proposed income and property taxes.[7] Until the end of 1920, taxes barely covered one-third of the budget expenses. The government every month issued several billion marks of treasury notes, between one-third and one-half of which remained in the portfolio of the Reichsbank. The currency circulation increased steadily and at a more rapid rate than the advances to the government, because the Reichsbank expanded its indirect advances to States and communes as well as the discount of commercial bills. The liberal credit policy of the central bank thus was partly responsible for the inflationary currency expansion. The Reichsbank considered it a duty to supply the economy at all time with the money necessary to perform payments at the actual price level, and it refused to adopt a deflationary policy.[8] This increase in domestic prices was attributed to the external depreciation of the mark for which the reparation payments were blamed.

Wholesale and retail prices remained under government control until the fall of 1919, and the price index did not exceed 300 percent of the 1913 level. After the release of the controls, prices within a few months rose to an average of twelve times the pre-war level, far exceeding the increase in currency circulation. This may have been the result of the smaller supply of goods and the accumulation of the consumers' needs. The scarcity of goods contributed also to the depreciation of the mark on foreign markets, since heavy imports of foodstuffs and raw materials constituted a one-sided burden on the balance of payments.[9] Exports of German goods, especially coal, were credited in part as reparations, and the total export volume was much lower than before the war. The accounts were balanced by gold exports, foreign credits and speculative acquisition of German notes and bank balances by foreigners. It is important to note that until the summer of 1921 Germany had not made cash reparation payments of any size.[10]

The decline of the mark, after the war, was slow until the summer of 1919, when the rate was about half of the pre-war parity. The signing of the peace treaty with its reparation clauses produced a psychological shock and the depreciation accelerated. In February 1920 the dollar in Berlin reached the rate of 100 marks, in contrast to 4.20 marks in 1914.

After a reaction the rate fluctuated for over a year between 40 and 70 marks. During the first six months of 1921 it was fairly stable at about 64 marks. The external and internal depreciation of the mark was then very much the same. The price level reached at the beginning of 1920 remained stable until the summer of 1921, and wages slowly advanced to the same level.

At this stage the inflationary effects of the currency expansion during the war and immediate post-war period might have been considered fully consummated and a stabilization of the currency a possibility. That confidence in the mark had been restored was shown by the sale of foreign currency held by German nationals to the Reichsbank and by purchases of marks by foreigners. The government, however, did not succeed in balancing the budget, being too weak to cut down expenses and increase tax receipts adequately. Even after the tax reform of 1920, revenue did not cover more than 50 percent of the expenses. As indicated in the following table giving data with respect to the Reich budgets for the years 1919 to 1923, only a small part of the deficit during that period was caused by reparation payments.

| *Financial year* | *Income* | *Expenditure* | *Deficit* | *Expenses under Peace Treaty* |
|---|---|---|---|---|
| | | *(in million gold marks)* | | |
| 1919–20 | 2.559 | 8.560 | 5.999 | |
| 1920–21 | 3.178 | 9.329 | 6.054 | 1.851 |
| 1921–22 | 2.927 | 6.651 | 3.676 | 2.810 |
| 1922–23 | 1.488 | 3.951 | 2.442 | 1.137 |
| 1923 (April–Dec.) | | | 6.538 | .742 |

Source: Bresciani-Turoni, *op. cit.*, p. 93 and 436–7.

Except in 1921–22, the budget would have shown large deficits even without payment of reparations. The continuous financing of the deficit by note-printing undermined currency stability, but the Reichsbank and the high bureaucracy maintained an attitude of distinct complacency towards the depreciation of the mark. The decline in the mark's value was accepted as proof that the burden of the peace treaty was intolerably high. Reactionary groups, representing industry and agriculture, welcomed the development for selfish reasons, because the inflation brought them high profits and reduced the burden of their indebtedness. Industry was specifically favored by the time lag in the adaptation of wages and other cost items to rising sales receipts in domestic and export markets.[11]

The adjustment of domestic prices and of foreign exchange rates to the increase of currency in circulation, after the price controls had been lifted, is shown in the following table:[12]

| | *December 1918 (in percent of 1913)* | *May 1921* |
|---|---|---|
| Wholesale prices | 245 | 1308 |
| Dollar rate | 197 | 1483 |
| Currency circulation | 550 | 1370 |
| Deposits with Reichsbank | 1300 | 1400 |
| Deposits with Berlin banks | 400 | 1200[a] |
| Deposits with all banks | [b] | 840[a] |

a December 1920.
b Not available.

## C. Final Depreciation of the Mark

The period from the summer of 1921 until the summer of 1922 was the only one in which sizeable cash payments on the reparations account were made. During this time the total of reparation payments was high enough to account for the greater part of the budget deficit. In June 1921, the dollar rate in Berlin slowly began to rise, owing probably to purchases of foreign exchange by the Reichsbank for use in payment of the one billion gold marks reparations due 31 August 1921.[13] After the partition of Upper Silesia a wave of economic pessimism spread over Germany,[14] and the decline of the currency, accentuated by domestic and foreign speculation, developed into full-fledged flight from the mark. Purchases of foreign exchange by German speculators reached enormous proportions; large foreign holdings of paper marks were thrown on the market; the dollar rate in Berlin rose to 295 in November 1921, later receding to 180, which however was three times higher than the rate in May. These developments shook the confidence of the German public in the stability of the currency. To prevent losses from rising costs, industrial and trade groups increased their sale prices at once when the dollar moved up, whereas lower dollar rates did not affect the price level immediately.

Until July 1922, several smaller cash payments were made on the reparations account. Then cash payments were stopped. During 1922, the trade balance was in equilibrium, and the external value of the mark therefore was under no pressure except that of the flow of capital from Germany and of foreign speculation.[15] The speculation and panic were instrumental in the depreciation of the mark. Budget deficits and increased private credits of the Reichsbank and commercial banks made the price inflation technically possible. The government had to raise most of its payments in keeping with the inflated price level, but tax receipts reacted slowly to the fall of the mark, especially taxes based on income in the preceding tax period. The greater part of the budget deficit was financed directly by the printing of notes, inasmuch as the public was reluctant to invest in government paper. Nevertheless, a determined effort of the government to halt the inflation would have been successful; during each of the occasional periods of temporary stability the budget situation improved noticeably.[16] As it developed, the increase of note-circulation was not prevented, and speculation could be resumed with the aid of the Reichsbank, which greatly increased its advances on commercial bills.

The depreciation of the mark made great progress during the latter half of 1922, although no payments were made to the Allies. The decline was officially explained in terms of vanishing confidence in any improvement of governmental finances and currency, as a result of the mere existence of the peace treaty.[17] The occupation of the Ruhr in January 1923 gave a new impulse toward depreciation. Enormous amounts were spent by the government to finance the "passive resistance" in the occupied territory. Part of this money was sold at once by the recipients (industrial firms) against foreign currency.[18] The increased credit volume of the Reichsbank also served to finance speculation against the mark.

Since foreign exchange rates developed without any relation to economic factors, and prices automatically followed the dollar rate, it soon proved nearly impossible to print the amount of money necessary to perform all commercial and financial transactions at the inflated prices. There was a serious shortage of currency, and only the use of auxiliary money, of foreign currency and especially an enormous increase in the velocity of circulation made the price inflation possible.[19] Wages were paid daily and everybody tried to rid himself of currency and other forms of paper money as quickly as possible. Some kind of "stable money" was increasingly resorted to for actual payments, or at least for accounting purposes, and prices and wages were fixed on an index basis. The Reichsbank, nevertheless, until late in 1923 gave credit in paper marks and accepted repayment in devaluated currency, which made it highly profitable for its customers to go into debt.

The depreciation of the mark progressed so fast that both the gold value and the domestic purchasing power of the money in circulation were reduced to a fraction. On 7 August 1923, for example, this value was only 20 million dollars.[20] If the amount of currency in circulation had not been increased at once, the speculation would have broken down and prices would have declined to a level more in line with the volume of money.[21] But the supply of marks was virtually limitless. In the books of the Reichsbank, especially, the inflation could progress without any difficulties of a technical nature. Deposits with the Reichsbank increased during the last months of 1923 so much that they exceeded the circulation of Reichsbank notes by 30 percent, whereas before the war they reached only one-sixth of the note issue.

Eventually the mark was almost entirely abandoned as a means of payment. The public was eager to accept a new currency which appeared to be based on "stable value." The dollar increased from 200 marks in February 1922 to 7,500 marks in December 1922, and to 4,200,000,000,000 marks in November 1923. In effect, the mark unit had disappeared.

The amount of currency in circulation and the assets upon which it was issued are shown in Table 1 on the following page<~?~PE: note>.

## D. Stabilization of the Currency

The dollar was quoted in Berlin at 160,000 marks on 3 July 1923; at 13,000,000 marks on 4 September; at 5,000,000,000 marks on 11 October and on 20 November 1923 it reached 4,200,000,000,000 marks. At this time it was decided arbitrarily to stabilize the currency because the paper mark was worth an even one-trillionth part of its pre-war value, one-billionth in the European nomenclature. However, the dollar rose even higher; in occupied Cologne it rose to eleven trillion marks. But by energetic measures the rate was brought down to the stabilization level and held there. Stabilization measures consisted mainly in keeping down the circulation of mark notes and preventing speculators from operating with the new money, the Rentenmark.[22] The gold value of the total paper mark circulation, on 15 November 1923, was only 150,000,000 Goldmarks; in addition, some 1,169,000,000 Goldmarks of emergency money were circulating. An unknown part of the foreign exchange hoards of the population was also used as a means of payment. Most of the emergency money had no cover whatsoever, but the lack of confidence in the paper mark was so marked that the population preferred almost any medium to the legal currency. This situation enabled the government to put the Rentenmark into circulation.

The Rentenmark, issued after 15 November 1923, by the newly formed Rentenbank, was not declared to be legal tender. It circulated alongside the paper mark at a legal conversion rate of one Rentenmark to one trillion paper marks. The total circulation was restricted by law to 2,400,000,000 Rentenmark, of which one-half was placed at the disposal of the government to cover its immediate needs, and the remaining half was to be used to finance agriculture and business. The Rentenmark had no metallic cover. It was redeemable in bonds which represented a lien imposed on all German agricultural and industrial property. Because its issue was limited and there was a relation to a stable value, the public accepted it eagerly. The rejection by the Rentenbank management of the government's request for an increase of advances, in December 1923, further strengthened this confidence.[23]

TABLE 1. GERMAN CURRENCY IN CIRCULATION, ASSETS ON WHICH IT WAS ISSUED, AND INFLATION INDICES, 1921–23

| | *Treasury notes* | | *Reichsbank and Loan Office* | | |
|---|---|---|---|---|---|
| *End of* | *Total issued* | *Held by Reichsbank* | *Bills and advances* | *Currency in circulation* | *Deposits on clearing accounts* |
| | | | *(in billion marks)* | | |
| 1920 | 153 | 58 | 35[a] | 81 | 22 |
| 1921 | 247 | 132 | 16[a] | 122 | 33 |
| 1922 | 1495 | 1185 | 675 | 1293 | 530 |
| | | | *(in billion marks)* | | |
| June 1923 | 22020 | 18338 | 9970 | 17303 | 9953 |
| | | | *(in billion of billion mark)* | | |
| Nov. 15 1923 | 192 | 190 | 42 | 93 | 129 |

*Relative Progress of Inflation*

| *Date* | *Dollar rate* | *Wholesale prices* | *Cost of Living* | *Wages Laborer* | *Currency Circulation* |
|---|---|---|---|---|---|
| | | | *Index based on 1913=1* | | |
| May 1921 | 14.8 | 13.1 | 11.2 | 11.4 | 13.5 |
| May 1922 | 69.1 | 64.6 | 38. | 28. | 26.8 |
| Nov. 1922 | 1,711. | 1,151. | 446. | 333. | 80. |
| June 1923 | 26,202. | 19,385. | 7,650. | 6,002. | 2,865. |
| | | | *(billions)* | | |
| Dec. 1923 | 1,000. | 1,262. | 1,247. | 790. | 82. |

a Mostly credits advanced by Loan Offices to States and Communes

Source: Statistisches Reichsamt, *op. cit., passim.*

The total circulation of currency in Germany more than doubled from November 1923 to April 1924. Emergency money was replaced by paper marks issued by the Reichsbank against bills and foreign currency and balances. The gold and foreign exchange holdings of the Reichsbank increased from 500 million to one billion Goldmarks within one year, notwithstanding the large excess of imports over exports, which necessitated payments. It was estimated that outside of the Reichsbank, in 1923, over three billion Goldmarks of foreign values had been held.[24] The depreciation of the mark had wiped out the great amounts of German currency and bank deposits held by foreigners derived from speculative purchases. It also destroyed credits extended to Germany during and after the war.

The stability of the mark once more was threatened early in 1924. After November 1923 the Reichsbank resumed the extension of liberal credit to German business because it believed the country needed more money to operate. Within four months the private advances of the Reichsbank increased from 364 million to 1915 million Goldmarks. This enabled speculators to buy foreign exchange. Domestic prices began to rise and the mark rate in New York decreased by 15 percent. Thereupon the Reichsbank reduced its credits, causing many exporters and hoarders to sell their holdings of foreign currency in order to get liquid money necessary for their business. In brief, the exchange situation was relieved and the mark again reached the stabilization parity.[25] On 11 October 1924, the new Reichsmark replaced the paper currency in circulation at the conversion rate of one trillion paper marks for one Reichsmark. The larger part of the outstanding Rentenmark currency was retired within a few years, the Reichsbank taking over the advances of the Rentenbank to private debtors, while the advances to the government were successively amortized.

The exchange had been stabilized before the budget was balanced, but in November 1923, expenses were drastically reduced. In particular, the payments for "passive resistance," the main cause of the deficit, were stopped. The railroad deficit disappeared when the rates were collected on a revalued basis: the funded public debt had been wiped out in the inflation. Tax receipts increased soon after stabilization of the mark. In January 1924, for the first time since 1914, budget receipts equaled expenses.

The credit extended by the Rentenbank to the government had no inflationary effects because the increase in currency circulation which it caused was compensated for by a decrease in the velocity of the money turnover. The newly printed notes simply went into the pockets of the public and increased the total volume of money in circulation to an amount more adequate to meet the inflated prices. The development of currency circulation between November 1923 and April 1924 is indicated in the following table:

| *Kind of Currency* | *Amount in Circulation* | |
|---|---|---|
| | *15 November 1923* | *7 April 1924* |
| | *(in million Goldmarks)* | |
| Reichsbank and similar notes | 155 | 684 |
| Rentenbanknotes | 0 | 1722 |
| Gold loan and similar paper | 176 | 210 |
| Emergency issues | 988 | 266 |
| Coins | 0 | 63 |
| Total | 1319 | 2945 |

Source: Wagemann, *op. cit.*, p. 50.

## E. Recapitulation and Political Background

The basic cause of the inflation in Germany, in 1914–1923, was the budget deficit. Though to a certain extent an unavoidable result of war and defeat, the deficit and the effects of its financing on the currency were largely aggravated by the mistakes and weaknesses of the government's financial policy. The inflation was greatly facilitated by the liberal credit policy of the Reichsbank, especially during periods of external depreciation of the currency. Excessive imports of foreign goods and substantial payments of foreign exchange on account of reparations resulted at certain periods in a disequilibrium of the balance of payments, and depressed the foreign value of the mark. The public confidence in the national currency, already badly shaken by the progressing internal and external depreciation, was undermined further by national and international political events. An extensive flight from, and speculation against, the mark reduced its foreign value rapidly, whereas the fear that domestic prices would rise contributed to their rise in line with the external depreciation of the currency. The velocity of the circulation of money was increased and thus made hyper-inflation possible. The vicious circle was broken when the firm intention of the government to stabilize the currency was demonstrated, and the Reichsbank abstained from continuously increasing the volume of currency in response to requests of government and public. The stabilization took place after the value of the currency unit had been reduced to virtually zero, but it is certain that it could have been achieved much earlier. Granted that stabilization would have been difficult immediately after the war, when a drastic reduction of the currency circulation would have been necessary, it might have been achieved in 1920 at the latest. At that time, price controls had been abolished; the general price level had reached a temporary stability in equilibrium with the volume of circulating currency and the foreign value of the mark.

To understand the inertia of official circles in the face of the depreciation of the currency, it must be borne in mind that Germany was endeavoring to achieve a reduction of the financial obligations imposed by the Allies, asserting that the burden could not be covered by taxation. The government was anxious to demonstrate the catastrophic effects of the payments on the German economy. In financial circles the theory prevailed, and in Nazi Germany is still officially maintained,[26] that the external depreciation of the currency was caused by the excessive burdens placed on Germany, and that inflation and budget deficits were a consequence of this depreciation. German and foreign economists have since proved that the argument of reparation greatly exaggerated the facts, and that only during a short period in 1921 was the payment of reparations a governing factor in the budget deficit and the disequilibrium in the balance of payments. The reparation policy of the Allies, however, supplied an excellent opportunity for the inflation-minded industrial leaders of Germany to realize their plans. These men also had the political power to prevent the government from drastically reorganizing the budget, and the economic power to disregard any regulations against flight of capital.

In post-war Germany the government consisted of frequently changing coalitions of heterogeneous political parties. This condition resulted in unstable political conditions and greatly reduced the power of the government. The parties of the right, representing "big industry" and agriculture, and those of the left, seldom participated in the government; but they exercised a strong influence on the policies of the moderate parties. The Social Democrats were obliged to respect the viewpoints of the radical left, whereas the Catholic Center and the Democrats combined in economic matters with the rightist parties. The Socialists reached the height of their power immediately after the revolution, in 1918, without taking full advantage of it; after 1919 the political power of the bourgeois parties increased steadily, whereas the economic power of the reactionary groups had never been diminished. Nearly every government between 1919 and 1923 made serious efforts to increase the tax receipts and to balance at least the ordinary budget, but all reforms, beginning with Erzberger's plan in 1919[27] and ending with Hilferding's plan in 1923[28], proved failures because of the opposition of the rightist parties.

The conservatives were in general opposed to the Weimar Republic and to the fulfillment of the peace treaty and did not hesitate to use any political or economic weapon calculated to weaken the government and discredit its peace policy. They were aided in this by the higher bureaucracy of the government and by the Reichsbank. The Reichsbank, under Havenstein[29], lent itself wholeheartedly to the purposes of powerful industrialists such as Stinnes, Voegler and others. Havenstein openly fought against the treaty fulfillment policy and deferred the decision to stabilize the currency as long as possible. The inflation, which was disastrous to wage-earners and the middle classes, enabled the owners of big industry to obtain for a nominal consideration all the money they desired for modernizing their plants and extending their economic domains. Only when the danger of a social revolution became imminent, in the autumn of 1923, after the inflation had reduced to zero the debts of agricultural and industrial interests, did the parties representing moneyed interests consent to a stabilization of the currency. This time a stabilization plan succeeded; it met the approval of industry and agriculture and was put into effect with their backing. The noticeable social effects of the inflation were the rapid accumulation of large fortunes, the extravagance and ostentation of inflation profiteers, the expropriation of small capital owners and rentiers, and the poverty of large parts of the population. For the majority of the German people the inflation left a memory of horror. The experience suffered after the last war has led them to give willing assistance to the efforts of the Nazi regime to combat the inflationary effects of the present war financing. In a work published in 1940,[30] Ernst Wagemann lays the blame for the inflation of 1923 on the reparation policy of the Allies and the "impudent" speculative forces inherent in a liberal economy. It may be assumed that this is the general opinion in today's Germany.

## II. Finances of Nazi Germany 1933–1943

### A. Work Creation and Rearmament

During the six years from ascension to power until the beginning of the war, the Nazi regime succeeded in putting six million unemployed persons back to work, and in spending ninety billion-RM for armaments[31] without causing a price inflation. Until 1935 the economic policy of the government was directed toward reemployment. Restrictions on foreign exchange operations made the German currency and credit system largely independent of foreign influences and of the withdrawal of capital funds. The "work creation" programs initiated by the pre-Hitler governments were considerably increased in scope and volume, and were supplemented by tax reductions favoring entrepreneurs specifically and by grants made to home owners to assist them in rebuilding their property.

Within two years, the Reich spent five billion RM[32] for work creation. The greater part was financed outside of the budget, by issue of "work creation bills" for 2.6 billion RM and of tax remission notes for 1.6 billion RM, valid for tax payments in future years.[33]

To prevent the flotation of issues that would obstruct the credit needs of the Reich, organized capital markets in 1933 were placed under the control of a committee headed by the president of the Reichsbank. The Reichsbank law was amended to permit the purchase of Reich bonds, and in 1934 a law was issued reorganizing the banking system. Government paper was made the foremost liquid asset of commercial and savings banks, which opened a new source of financing for the Reich. To reduce the amount of dividends paid and to make the investment in stocks less attractive, corporations were ordered in 1934 to invest in government bonds an amount equal to their declared profits in excess of six percent of the capital. As a result, industrial corporations accumulated undistributed profits, which enabled them to finance their investment internally.

The "work creation" policy was successful in stimulating a general revival of business activity. However, prices also showed a rising trend following the increased demand for domestic and even more for foreign raw materials, the import of which had to be restricted owing to Germany's unfavorable exchange position. Since stability of prices and wages was considered necessary to prevent the rearmament program from being hampered by rising costs and shortages of materials, prices and wages were put under control, and supervisory boards were set up to control the importation and distribution of raw materials.

After 1935, the armament program made it necessary to limit private investment activities and eventually private consumption. By direct government regulation house-building and industrial construction were restricted or brought into line with the government's armament program. The financial needs of the government were given a virtual monopoly on the savings of the nation. The embargo on private issues as a rule was suspended only to permit financing of industrial corporations engaged in the manufacture of armaments. The government extended financial guarantees to encourage banks to finance expansion of such industries. In some instances it ordered industrial corporations to expand their activities into new fields or to join with other enterprises to finance new production (gasoline, artificial fibre, etc.).

Rising tax receipts (17.7 billion RM in 1938–39 as against 6.6 billion RM in 1932–33) made it possible for the Reich to cover more than half of the armament expenditure out of current revenue. Taking advantage of the liquidity of money and capital markets, the government reduced the interest rate on public and mortgage bonds to 4½ percent, and issued yearly increasing amounts of medium and long-term paper. The methods of intermediary financing of government orders were changed repeatedly, but short-term paper could never be dispensed with and the total of outstanding short-term paper steadily increased. From 1935 until 1939 over thirteen billion RM in special bills were issued.[34] Since the banks did not buy these bills at a satisfactory rate, the Reichsbank had its own subsidiary, the Gold Discount Bank, issue promissory notes (Sole bills), to skim off the liquid funds of the banks and invest the proceeds in special bills.

In the spring of 1939, when the amount of the undisclosed short-term debt had become alarming, a short-lived "New Financial Plan" was designed. Its main point was the issue of new tax remission notes which anticipated future tax receipts. The notes were used in payment of government orders up to 40 percent of the total, and had the same legal tender quality if used by the contractor for payment of deliveries and services. Their total issue which amounted to 4.6 billion RM ceased shortly after the outbreak of the war.

Until August 1939 the Nazi government increased the medium and long-term debts of the Reich by 16.6 billion RM, the declared short-term debt by 7.6 billion RM, and incurred an undisclosed short-term debt of 13 billion RM, totalling 37.2 billion RM, apart from the issue of several billion RM tax remission notes. The greater part (approximately 30 billion RM) of the new government debt was taken over by credit and insurance institutions. The compilation of bank credits in Table 2 below, completed by figures for the monthly reporting institutions for the year 1938,[35] shows an increase in the following items:

| | |
|---|---|
| Treasury bills | 4,100,000,000 RM |
| Bills | 11,500,000,000 RM |
| Bonds | 12,900,000,000 RM |
| Total | 28,500,000,000 RM |

In view of the decrease in commercial credits during the same period, the rise in bills must be attributable exclusively to the discount of special bills, of which the Reichsbank alone had 12–13 billion RM in 1938.[36]

From 1933 to 1938, labor incomes increased by 64 percent and the total national income by 70 percent, but the output of consumption goods by only 30 percent. The expansion of money and credit was not out of line with the increase in national income. The currency circulation rose from 5.5 billion RM in 1933 to 10.7 billion RM in April 1939; but in view of the fact that 1.1 billion RM in currency had been issued in exchange for Austrian and Czech currency in the annexed territories,[37] the increase amounted to only 76 percent.

The index of wholesale prices increased by 17 percent from April 1933 to April 1939. The rise was not uniform; prices of agricultural products increased by 30 percent, those of industrial raw materials by 9 percent, and those of finished products used for consumption by 24 percent. On the other hand, prices of manufactured goods for industrial use decreased by 1 percent. The index of living cost increased by 9 percent. This index does not allow for deterioration in the quality of certain commodities. According to some estimates, the index understated the actual price movement by 10 percent.[38]

It clearly appears that the Nazis succeeded in financing all of their pre-war armament expenditures (about 15–20 billion RM per year, or 20–25 percent of the national income) by taxation and out of the savings of the population, without inflation of the price structure. They achieved these results with a rigid tax policy, general price and wage control, systematic restriction of private spending and investment activity, and monopolization of accumulated savings for government use.

The official gold parity of the Reichsmark was unchanged. In most international transactions, however, a depreciation had developed which was acknowledged officially by the payment of premiums to German exporters. The disparity between the domestic purchasing power of the mark and its official foreign value was estimated by the *Reichskreditgesellschaft*[39] at 38–40 percent in April 1939. Deterioration in the quality of some German goods and shortages in the available supply are not taken into account, the comparison being based on the official price index. The increase in credits to the Reich found its counterpart in higher deposits and currency circulation.

TABLE 2. SELECTED GERMAN INCOME AND CREDITS FIGURES, 1913–37

*A. Claims expressed in money (billion Reichsmark)*

| | *1913* | *1929* | *1935* | *August 1939* |
|---|---|---|---|---|
| Currency | 6.6 | 6.6 | 6.4 | 10.8 |
| Current account deposits | 12.3 | 15.5 | 12.5 | 18.5 |
| Savings deposits | 23.3 | 14.8 | 18.5 | 26.0 |
| Insurance | 8.2 | 5.9 | 10.0 | 15.1 |
| Total | 50.4 | 42.8 | 47.4 | 70.4 |
| Held by public: | | | | |
| bonds | 40.5 | 13.6 | 14.6 | 18.1 |
| mortgages | 25.0 | 6.5 | 6.5 | — |

Sources: 1913–35: *Probleme des Deutschen Wirtschaftslebens*, Berlin, 1937. p. 600. Figures for 1939 calculated according to *Frankfurter Zeitung*, 1 Jan. 1943.

*B. National income in Germany, old territory*[a] *(billion Reichsmark)*

| | *1938* | |
|---|---|---|
| Agriculture | | 5.8 |
| Trade and industry, professional services | | 14.8 |
| Wages and salaries: | | |
| Industrial | 16.8 | |
| Other | 16.8 | |
| Large salaries | 9.1 | 42.7 |
| Capital income | | 3.0 |
| Rent | | 1.1 |
| Pensions and relief payments | | 7.6 |
| Private income | 75.0 | |

| *1938* | | |
|---|---|---|
| Undistributed corporation income | 3.4 | |
| Public enterprises | 1.5 | |
| Indirect taxes and social contrib. | 5.2 | |
| less deferred income (public source) | – 5.4 | 79.7 |

a *Wirtschaft und Statistik*, 1930, p. 706.

*C. Credit extended by types of institutions*[a] *(in billion Reichsmark)*

| | *1932* | *1937* |
|---|---|---|
| Central banks | 3.9 | 6.6 |
| Postal agency | 0.4 | 0.8 |
| Commercial banks | 15.6 | 20.3 |
| Savings banks | 12.7 | 16.1 |
| Cooperatives | 4.5 | 5.2 |
| Mortgage banks | 13.9 | 18.2 |
| Insurance | 7.2 | 11.9 |
| Conversion office | 0.0 | 0.5 |
| Total | 58.2 | 79.6 |

a According to *German Statistical Handbook, 1938.*

*D. Credit extended by type of credit*

| | *1932* | *1937* |
|---|---|---|
| Agricultural mortgages | 5.4 | 6.3 |
| Other mortgages | 15.7 | 18.2 |
| Municipal credit | 8.6 | 9.9 |
| Current acct. advances | 11.2 | 9.6 |
| Bills | 4.3 | 13.6 |
| Treasury bills | 1.3 | 2.2 |
| Advances on merchandise and securities | 2.5 | 1.4 |
| Securities | 6.4 | 15.4 |
| Other credits | 2.4 | 1.3 |
| Total | 57.8 | 77.9 |

The total Reich debt, including the undisclosed part, amounted in August 1939 to 53 billion Reichsmark, about 65 percent of the national income in 1938, as compared with over 160 percent in England and France at the same time. If compared with tax receipts, the government debt in Germany reached then only 300 percent of the yearly tax revenue, as compared with 800 percent in England and France. In the United States the debt amounted to only 60 percent of the national income, but to over 700 percent of the tax revenue. The relevant figures are presented in the following table.

| | *1938–1939 Government debt* | *National income* | *Tax receipts* |
|---|---|---|---|
| Germany (billion RM) | 53 | 82 | 17.7 |
| France (billion Fr.) | 414 | 250 | 54 |
| United Kingdom (billion Ł) | 7.2 | 4.4 | 0.9 |
| United States (billion $) | 40.4 | 67.5 | 5.5 |

Source: L.N. *World Ec. Survey 1939–41*, pp. 80, 94.

In 1933 the German national debt had amounted to only 25 percent of the national income, a fact accounted for by the drastic reduction consequent to the inflation. The financing of rearmament in Germany was thus made much easier.

## B. Principles of War Financing

At the outset of the war the government initiated a deflation experiment involving general reductions of wages and the transfer to the Reich of amounts saved by industry. The transfer was accomplished by means of price-reductions on war supplies sold to the government and direct payments into the treasury of a portion of the amount realized from sale of other goods. Later the experiment was abandoned, and thereafter no efforts were made to reduce incomes sufficiently at the source to bring them into line with the restricted supply of consumer goods.

Production and distribution of all goods are controlled so thoroughly that the state has no difficulty in obtaining whatever portion of the national output is desired. Reduced consumption facilities constitute an effective compulsion to save, and government regulations bar any investment possibilities other than in government paper or through bank deposits. Though the individual has retained a certain freedom in handling his unspent income, the state enjoys a virtual monopoly over savings from its control of banking. The government has consistently refrained from openly restricting this freedom further by additional taxation or the institution of forced savings. Reliance has been placed upon strict and comprehensive economic controls to prevent the inflation which otherwise would inevitably result from the discrepancy between supply of goods and volume of money expressing demand.

Their technique of war financing is described by the Germans as silent financing, because it abstains from public campaigns for the direct purchase of Reich bonds. Liquid funds and savings accumulating with credit institutions are fully invested in government paper, though mostly of the short-term type. This results in a high percentage of floating debt. The government admittedly would prefer to sell Reich bonds directly to the investor in order to prevent the cash surplus of the nation from increasing rapidly and to facilitate post-war consolidation of the debt. However, it is considered undesirable to evoke the memories of the 1914–18 war loan drives, and the government restricts its propaganda to the advocation of saving in deposit accounts and the discouragement of currency hoarding.

So far, price inflation has been avoided; but the government has not been successful in preventing an inflation of means of payment, especially currency circulation. The German citizen has not been persuaded to deposit all of his non-spendable income with credit institutions; instead he has persisted in hoarding a sizeable and increasing part of it in the form of cash. This accumulation of cash and deposits in the hands of the public, for which no goods can be bought in legal markets, increases the pressure on price and distribution controls. The result has been a lack of confidence in the value of money among certain groups of the population which threatens the stability of the whole economic system. At the end of 1942, the government tried to reduce the surplus money stocks by a number of measures, such as discontinuation of advance payments on war contracts, sale of armament works to private enterprise, and collection of the house rent tax for several years in advance. The results were not satisfactory, however, because the formation of savings deposits was retarded, and large bank-and-mortgage-credits were taken up by the persons affected by the scheme. The consequence was that the treasury felt obliged to discontinue for some time the issue of Reich bonds.

Various other measures to skim off the excess money, such as capitalization of the industrial assessment tax, and especially increased direct and indirect taxation, were discussed at the time. These, however, were never put into effect. The main reason for this inactive attitude of the government is the fear that increased taxation of workers' and farmers' incomes might impair their productivity, and that increased taxation of industrial profits would encounter opposition from "big business."

The rising total of currency and deposits is matched only by the rapid increase in the national debt. This development, coming at a time of large-scale destruction of the national wealth through bombing and other effects of the war, has occasioned increasing concern among the public. Confidence in the future value of the Reichsmark is at a low point and there is considerable doubt as to the security of savings deposits. It is widely believed that only confiscation of savings of inflation will be able to solve the problem of the Reich debt.

## C. Price Controls

Over-all stability of prices and wages has always been one of the principles of the Nazi economic policy. There was built up before the beginning of the war a control organization which covered all but the prices of non-essential consumption goods. Control was reinforced by the price-stop order of September 1939. The imposition of a general rationing scheme and allocation of raw materials and industrial products has thus far prevented any significant upward movement of the official price index. The attempt in September 1939 to lower the cost of war contracts by reduction of wages had to be abandoned, but the government effected reductions of war-contract costs by a reform in the winter 1941–42, which substituted for cost-plus prices a set of uniform target-prices based on the cost of an efficient producer. Production cost is controlled by the aid of uniform book-keeping and cost accounting systems, and excess profits, variously defined, are subject to confiscation by the Price Commissioner. Since 1941 a uniform excess-profits tax is applied which does not prevent industry from making "efficiency" profits.[40] Ersatz and new products also are subject to price control. In order to strengthen the confidence in the value of money a few industrial consumer goods were reduced in price in 1942 by means of direct pressure on cartels.[41] A number of civilian articles had increased very much in price in the period immediately preceding. In 1943 price control was extended to used articles.

Though excess profits are no longer confiscated, the general rule of the war economy decree still applies, under which price reductions may be enforced if certain profits or cost items are not justified according to the principles of economy pledged to the war effort. The development of prices from 1939 to 1943 is indicated in the following table:

| | *Sept. 1939* | *Sept. 1943* | *Increase in percent of 1939 prices* |
|---|---|---|---|
| *Index: 1914 = 100* | | | |
| Wholesale prices | | | |
| Agricultural products | 107.6 | 118.9 | 10.5 |
| Industrial materials | 95.3 | 102.3 | 7.2 |
| Manufactured goods: | | | |
| For industrial use | 112.8 | 113.6 | 0.7 |
| For consumption | 136.2 | 152.4 | 11.9 |
| General index | 106.9 | 116.3 | 9.0 |

| | *Sept. 1939* | *Sept. 1943* | *Increase in percent of 1939 prices* |
|---|---|---|---|
| Living cost | | | |
| Food retail prices | 121.7 | 132.8 | 9.1 |
| Clothing retail prices | 133.7 | 179.1 | 34.0 |
| Heat, light, etc. | 124.2 | 122.0 | decrease 1.8 |
| Rent | 121.2 | 121.2 | 0.0 |
| Miscellaneous | 142.0 | 150.4 | 6.0 |
| General index | 125.7 | 137.9 | 10.0 |

Latest available price index figures (for February 1944) do not show any substantial changes as compared with September 1943.

The pressure on armament prices kept down the index of manufactured products for industrial use, but industry was very often permitted to raise the prices of civilian goods to compensate for reduced receipts out of war contracts. The official explanation refers to higher costs of imported raw materials and domestic substitutes, as well as higher freight charges owing to the transfer of factories. Prices of textile and leather products rose the highest, followed by prices of foodstuffs, which were raised to induce higher reduction. The Reich Statistical Office acknowledged that the consumer spends more for articles of daily use than is shown by the increase in the index because he has to buy more expensive goods, as his usual choice is either unavailable or rationed. It was stated specifically that savings in the expenditure for meat, fat, coffee, cocoa, and soap are more than compensated for by higher expenditure for potatoes, vegetables, ersatz coffee, and nonessential foodstuff.

In view of the widespread shortages in all but the most essential consumer goods, the figures of the price index are representative only for the few basic commodities still available for general consumption, and for the cost of war materials.

### D. Wages and Salaries

At the beginning of the war an order was issued freezing wages and salaries at their pre-war level. In order to reduce production costs, an attempt was made to reduce wage rates to the level of 1936 and to abolish overtime pay. The measure encountered so much opposition[42] that the former rates had to be restored. In October 1942 the wage stop was abandoned[43] in order to increase the efficiency of labor. By labor reclassification and similar measures the earnings of the worker were increased. Owing to the greater number of women and foreign workers who as a rule do not receive the same wage as the German worker, *average* earnings did not increase correspondingly. The following table 3 indicates the gross earnings of industrial workers[44] in 1939 and 1943:

| | *Sept 1939* | *March 1943* | *Increase in percent of 1939* |
|---|---|---|---|
| *Index: 1935 = 100* | | | |
| Hourly earnings | 108.5 | 120.7 | 11 |
| Weekly earnings | 113.4 | 129.6 | 14 |
| Index of living cost | 101.0 | 110.5 | 9 |

For the individual worker whose earnings have followed the general trend the increased cost of living and higher taxation offset the higher earnings. In many cases, however, the income of the family expanded from the simultaneous employment of several of its members. In terms of money the German worker is doing better than before the war, a fact further indicated by the increase in deposits with savings banks, which largely represent the savings of working classes.

### E. Industrial Profits

The war economy decree of 1939 subjected excessive profits to confiscation (called "surrendering") by the Price Commissioner. In 1941 a 25–30 percent surtax was substituted for the surrendering. The surtax was levied on profits exceeding the pre-war level by more than 50 percent (since 1943 by more than 20 percent). Dividends distributed by corporations are taxed very highly if the dividend rate exceeds 6 percent of the stock capital. In consequence, corporations do not pay higher dividends and accumulate the additional profits without publishing the amount. Self-financing of the industry has been favored by this tax provision. Some indication as to the amount of profits accumulated by the German corporations was given during 1942–43 when 1147 corporations, in order to secure the benefits of the decree limiting profit disbursement, increased their stock capital by a total of RM 3,900,000,000 by the issuance of stock dividends out of such profits.[45]

### F. Restrictions on Consumption

A rigorous scheme of direct rationing was imposed at the outbreak of the war on practically all foodstuffs and on a number of other articles of popular consumption. The sale of various other articles was made subject to the surrender of purchase certificates issued on stringent conditions in each individual case. Most of the non-essential goods not subject to rationing disappeared from the market as their manufacture stopped and existing stocks were sold out. The manufacture of goods for civilian needs was further curtailed in 1941, and again in 1943. Various household items have been reserved for air-raid victims, who receive special purchase certificates; but in many instances no goods are available even to these buyers. New industrial production of consumer goods is expected to cover only most urgent civilian needs.[46] Total civilian consumption is at present below the pre-war level, the reduction being much greater, of course, in the supply of industrial products than in foodstuffs.

## G. Control of Capital Markets

The restrictions imposed on investment activities for civilian needs were further tightened when the war broke out. The accumulation of unusable funds and the fear of inflation induced the German public and especially industry to invest heavily in shares. As a result, stock market quotations rose by 50 percent and more until the beginning of 1942. This boom was considered extremely objectionable on psychological grounds, and the government determined to stop it. First it decreed the compulsory declaration of all shares acquired after the outbreak of the war (except for small holdings), then authorized the Reichsbank to take over such shares at the prices quoted on 31 December 1941, in exchange for blocked government paper. Eventually stock market prices were placed under a stop-order perpetuating the quotations of 25 January 1943. This drastically reduced the volume of market transactions because no one was willing to sell his shares at prices considered out of line with the estimated value. A few transactions take place at the Bourse whenever the Reichsbank sells stocks out of its manipulations funds, but the quotations are without real significance Small stockholders are thus deprived of the opportunity of selling their shares at adequate prices, while controlling stockholders are protected against intruders.

Dealing in shares not officially quoted have not yet been put under stop-order, but the authorities have advised the banks not to participate in transactions at excessive prices and have threatened to confiscate newly acquired non-quoted shares. The suspension of stockholders' meetings in 1944 and the restrictions imposed on publicity of corporations also reduced small stockholders' rights. The following Table presents data on shares quoted on the Berlin Bourse:[47]

| Date | *Total of capital corporations listed* | *Dividends paid* | *Total market value of shares* | *Average quotation in percent of par value* | *Average yield in percent of market value* |
|---|---|---|---|---|---|
| | | | *(Million RM)* | | |
| June 1939 | 7.850 | 509 | 9.650 | 123 | 5.3 |
| June 1941 | 7.650 | 506 | 14.460 | 189 | 3.5 |
| June 1943 | 10.330 | 542 | 16.440 | 159 | 3.3 |

The nominal value of German stock capital increased in 1942/43 because many corporations revalued their assets to benefit from a change in tax law. During the war the amount of industrial bond issues increased from 513 million RM in 1939 to 1125 million RM in 1943, the proceeds being destined to finance armament investments. The total of new and junior share issues fell off considerably in 1942/43, the corporations evidently preferring to sell bonds instead of stock and thus to increase the equity value of the shares. Though industrial, mortgage and municipal bonds have no equity value the public is buying them in preference to Reich bonds. In the event of inflation the holders expect to get a higher revalorization quota than would be likely for government paper or deposits. Stop-prices are now being enforced, by voluntary agreement of the banks, at 102.5 percent for mortage bonds and 110 percent for industrial bonds. This is very high since new issues may not be sold to the first buyer above 102 percent and the bonds are mostly redeemable at par after a few years. The irregularity of the market is shown by the fact that 3.5 percent Reich bonds are quoted at 99¼ yielding 3.6 percent, whereas 3.5 percent Bavarian bonds and Reichsbahn bonds are quoted at 103 percent, and rarely available.

### H. Iron Savings and Business Deposits with Treasury

The so-called "iron-saving" system is one of the few cases in which the government tried to bind purchasing power by a direct agreement with the income-recipient. Wage and salary earners of German nationality may arrange for a certain amount, not over 39 RM per month, to be deducted from their payroll. No taxes are paid on the amount saved, but the savings are blocked until after the war. Since only 4 million persons are saving in this way, the scheme seems to be voluntary. An amount of 70–80 million RM per month is saved, which adds up to less than 1 billion RM per year. A great part of the iron savings is deposited with the big banks, the balance with savings banks.

The promise of tax privileges induced industrial firms to deposit, with the government, funds accumulated for renewals which had to be postponed until after the war. No interest is paid by the treasury on these

*Betriebsanlageguthaben* which total 587.6 million RM. A similar deposit constitutes the *Warenbeschaffungsguthaben* amounting to 177 million RM. Such deposits are no longer accepted.

### I. Foreign Trade and Exploitation of Controlled Countries

Government control of foreign trade and exchange before the war had reached such a stage of perfection that no changes in the organization were necessary when the war began. On the contrary, official controls were somewhat liberalized because semi-official organizations were given a monopoly in most trade relations. By its military successes Germany, apart from the enormous war booty amassed at the very beginning also was enabled to impose a system of trade equivalent to outspoken exploitation of the defeated nations.

German "purchases" first of all were favored by overvaluation of the Reichsmark. Secondly they were financed by occupation levies and by credits in the form either of balances in clearing accounts or of sales of German government paper to local banks. German currency was not put into circulation in occupied territories. Instead, a new currency was issued, the *Reichskreditkassenscheine*, covered by an obligation of the Reich. The yearly total of occupation levies was estimated at 14 billion RM for 1942, and at higher figures for 1943 and 1944, because of increased French and the new Italian payments. The total German debts in clearing accounts were estimated by various sources at about 10 billion RM at the end of 1942. These increased further in 1943, when more war contracts were placed outside of Germany and more foreign workers were employed inside the Reich. The remittances of the latter are never paid actually by the Reich. Sales of German government paper to Dutch and Czech banks totalled 1.5 billion RM in 1942.[48] Occupation currency, circulating mostly in the Eastern districts, amounted to a total of 2.9 billion RM at the end of 1943. In addition the *Reichskreditkassen* owed 6–7 billion RM to central and other banks in occupied territories.[49]

Contributions and credits received from other nations are indicated in the following table:

| *According to League of Nations Memo PEF 9, of March 1943:* | *1940* | *1941* | *1942* |
|---|---|---|---|
| | *(in billion Reichsmarks)* | | |
| Occupation cost and similar payments | 6–7 | 11–12 | 13–14 |
| Increase of clearing balances | 1 | 4–5 | 6–7 |
| *According to Bankwirtschaft of June 1943:* | | | |
| Advances of *Reichskreditkassen*: | 1.5 | 3.0 | 1.5 |
| Clearing balances and sales of Reich paper to foreign banks | 1.5 | 6.0 | 7.0 |

In this way the Reich financed the greater part of its imports and the local expenditure of its armies and other organizations. To pay for that part of the imports coming from neutral sources and to maintain the economy of the satellite nations, a certain volume of exports had to be kept up. According to Funk, this volume is near the prewar level.

Before the war, premiums at varying rates were paid to German exporters to allow them to compete on world markets. The rates of exchange established by the German government between the local currency of an occupied territory and the Reichsmark resulted generally in an overvaluation of the latter. In some cases, especially Austria and the Sudetenland, the value of the mark was reduced somewhat as compared with the previous legal rate, but as a rule the legal value of the Reichmark was increased in the case of France by 14 percent, for example, which resulted in an overvaluation of the Reichsmark by 100 percent.[50] Similarly, the former discount of the Reichsmark in the trade with Rumania, Yugoslavia, etc., was reduced during the war.

The enormous amount of German purchases in all occupied and satellite countries brought about such a price inflation that local prices in those countries are at present as high or even higher than in Germany, calculated at the legal exchange rate. In France, the wheat price in 1939 was 197 frcs. per 100 kg., about 34 percent below the German price for wheat. By 1943 the French price had increased to 410 frcs., roughly equivalent to the German price, notwithstanding the devaluation of the franc. The same applies to Slovakia, Hungary, and Rumania. In Greece prices increased so much that Germany had to depreciate the local currency by charging a premium for German goods and using the proceeds to reduce the cost of German imports. In contrast to the prewar situation, prices inside Germany are now lower than prices in the neighbor countries and German importation is hampered by this development. To prevent the domestic price level from being influenced by higher prices of imported goods, various devices are used in Germany, such as subsidies paid to importers or transfer of the increased cost to the price of other goods. Prices of imported goods were subjected to official regulation by the decree of 15 July 1937. Export prices are determined according to the country of destination, in order to offset the higher cost of merchandise imported from there.

### J. Budget Expenditure and Revenue, 1939–43

Publication of full budget figures was stopped by the Reich as early as 1934. Occasionally, however, official spokesmen announced the total of government expenditure for a particular year. These figures can be brought into line with the regularly published total receipts of taxes and customs, and the increase in the public debt, as indicated in the following table, covering the fiscal years 1 April to 31 March:

| *Period* | *Total expenditure* | *Ordinary revenue* | *Borrowing* |
|---|---|---|---|
| | *(in billion Reichsmarks)* | | |
| 1939/40 | 48.7 | 27.5 | 21.2 |
| 1940/41 | 74.8 | 37.2 | 37.6 |
| 1941/42 | 98.4 | 46.0 | 52.4 |
| 1942/43 | 124.3 | 68.7 | 55.6 |
| 1943/44 estimates | 136.0 | 60.0 | 76.0 |

Source: *Berliner Boersenzeitung*, 1 January 1944

The figures for the last two years are not fully comparable with those of the preceding years, because they include various special recurrent and non-recurrent revenue items which formerly were not reported. The previous years show expenditure and revenue figures higher by several billion RM each. In 1942/43, the revenue figure included 8 billion RM advance payment on the rent tax. Ordinary revenue includes also contributions of occupied countries; for details see above, page 000.

K. Ordinary Revenue of the Reich

| | *Taxes and customs (published)* | *Foreign contributions (estimates)* |
|---|---|---|
| | *(in billion Reichsmarks)* | |
| 1939/40 | 23.4 | 1.0 |
| 1940/41 | 27.2 | 7.0 |
| 1941/42 | 31.9 | 12.0 |
| 1942/43 | 34.7 | 15.0 |
| 1943 April–Sept. | 17.7 | 8.0 |

Recurrent domestic revenue from other sources than taxes and customs amounted to 5–10 billion RM yearly. In contrast to the situation experienced in 1914, the German fiscal system in 1939 was fully adequate to the task of financing a sizable part of the war cost from tax receipts. The only new taxes were a 50 percent war supplement on the rates of the income tax, and supplements to the tobacco tax and beer tax. Further, provincial governments and municipalities were ordered to pay a war contribution to the Reich yielding about 2 billion RM yearly. In 1941, the corporation tax was increased. The gross figure of Reich borrowings includes foreign credits totalling roughly 25 billion RM at the end of 1943 (see above p. 000). On the other hand, the repayment of the hidden pre-war debt (special bills), at the rate of approximately 3 billion RM yearly, does not appear in the above statement. There are, of course, various now hidden debts, especially the army finance certificates, guarantees given by the Reich to banks in connection with unpaid contracts and contracts in progress, and armament orders. Their total amount is not known; the estimate of a Swiss paper (100–150 billion RM)[51] seems to be exaggerated.

## L. Public Debt

The published Reich debt increased as follows from 1939 to 1943 (in billion RM):

| | *August 1939* | *December 1943* | *Increase* |
|---|---|---|---|
| Pre–1924 debt | 3.2 | 2.4 | dec. 0.8 |
| Long and medium term | 20.6 | 107.2 | 86.6 |
| Short term | 9.1 | 142.3 | 133.2 |
| Foreign debt | 1.2 | 1.2 | 0.0 |
| Total debt | 34.1 | 253.0 | 218.9 |
| Tax remission notes | 3.1 | 1.0 | dec. 2.1 |

During 1943, more than one-third of the new debt was in the form of short-term paper since the government was unable to increase its sales of bonds, although total credit needs expanded because of the intensified war effort and the air-raids. The yearly increase in the debt is indicated in the following table: (*in billion RM*).

| | *1940* | *1941* | *1942* | *1943* |
|---|---|---|---|---|
| Long-term debt | 16.1 | 21.2 | 23.4 | 23.3 |
| Short-term debt | 18.7 | 27.8 | 53.4 | 46.3 |

The floating debt is now increasing by 5 billion RM monthly; the long-term debt by 2 billion RM. Reich bonds are issued, in two types, yielding 3.5 percent interest. The regular Treasury certificates, repayable within 22 years, are sold at 99.25 percent to insurance institutions, business firms and private investors. The other type, called LI-loans (liquidity loans), repayable within 30 years, are sold to savings banks and insurance institutions for which they constitute an investment which is obligatory to some extent. Recently LI-loans have been issued in form of a limited term annuity loan of 6 percent which covers interest and redemption. No bonds are printed to represent Reich loans, but the investors receive credit in the Reich Debt Register.

To finance war expenditure the Reich began to issue rediscountable Treasury bills in November 1939 when the issue of tax remission notes became impracticable. In 1940 the Reichsbank lowered its discount rate to 3.5 percent as a first step towards a systematic cheap money policy designed to lighten the burden of war financing. The interest rate of government paper was reduced. Short-term paper is now issued in the form of Reich bills due after 3 months and of "non-interest-bearing" treasury notes due after 6 to 18 months, sold at a discount to yield 2 1/8 to 2 7/8 percent interest. A special form of short-term debt is the advance granted to the Reich by the main office of the *Reichskreditkassen* (9 billion RM, at the end of 1943) and the temporary credits of the Reichsbank, usually less than 1 billion RM. The Reichsbank extends most of its government credit by purchasing Reich bills. Reich bonds are purchased only if this is necessary to uphold market quotations.

The average maturity of the floating debt is six months. Thus, over 20 billion RM fall due for repayment every month, and new paper is placed with the holders of maturing notes. There is no doubt that in event of difficulties of prolongation the Reichsbank would be used to finance repayment.

The total debts of municipalities can be estimated at 10 billion RM; the debts of states and provinces at 2 billion RM.

## M. Inflation Potential

The total of private incomes after tax deductions considerably exceeds the amount of goods available for civilian consumption at prevailing prices. In addition, industry and trade accumulate money reserves out of the liquidation of stocks and the postponing of repairs and renewals, the cost of which is included in the price of their products. The total of these voluntary and involuntary savings was estimated at 60–65 billion RM in 1943, as against 50–55 billion RM in 1942 and 11 billion RM in 1938.[52] Those amounts invested in Reich bonds can be considered permanently bound; in the form of savings deposits they are temporarily sterilized but after the war again will become active purchasing power; in the form of currency and checking (current account) deposits they constitute the "inflation potential" which is only prevented from affecting prices and the distribution of goods by the working of official controls.

From this point of view the Nazi method of war financing is not satisfactory, because currency and current-account deposits represent a high percentage of the total increase in money claims held by the public. The small amount of bonds sold directly to the investor indicates one of the flaws in the system.[53]

## N. Accumulation of Money Claims

Though national income increased and private spendings were restricted from 1940 to 1943, the issue of Reich bonds did not expand much until 1942. As a result of the air-raids the general tendency to accumulate liquid funds was strengthened during 1943, and currency circulation and bank deposits other than savings deposits accounted for a much greater part of the "saved" amounts than before. The annual increases in various categories from 1940 to 1943 is indicated in the following table:

| *Yearly increase in* | *1940* | *1941* | *1942* | *1943* |
|---|---|---|---|---|
| | *(In billion Reichsmarks)* | | | |
| Savings deposits | 9.2 | 14.5 | 20.0 | 23.3 |
| Long-term debt | 16.1 | 21.2 | 23.4 | 23.2 |
| Currency circulation | 2.3 | 5.5 | 5.0 | 9.7 |
| Current account deposits | 8.7 | 8.1[a] | 5.6[a] | 9.0 |
| Short-term debt | 18.7 | 27.8 | 35.4 | 46.3 |
| Reichsbank credit | 4.1 | 6.3 | 7.6 | 12.1 |

a Excluding foreign balances.

Estimates of the accumulated money claims at the end of 1938 and 1943 are indicated in the following table:

| | *End of 1938* | *End of 1943* |
|---|---|---|
| | *(in billion RM)* | |
| Currency | 10.4 | 37. |
| Balances with Reichsbank | 1.5 | 8.2 |
| Current account deposits | *18.5* | *52.0* |
| of which with six commercial banks | 5.8 | 18.0 |
| Saving banks | *2.9* | *11.6* |
| Savings deposits | *26.0* | *95.5* |
| of which with commercial banks | 1.5 | 8.0 |
| Savings banks | 19.7 | 65.5 |
| Credit cooperatives[a] | 6.0 | 21.0 |

a Includes current account deposits.

According to *Deutsche Volkswirtschaft* of 3 November 1943 bonded claims were as follows:

| | | |
|---|---|---|
| Reich loans | 100.0[a] | billion RM |
| Mortgage and communal bonds issued by banks | 16.1 | billion RM |
| Industrial bonds | 4.0 | billion RM |
| Provincial bonds | 1.75 | billion RM |
| Municipal bonds | 0.6 | billion RM |
| *Reichsbahn* and *Reichspost* bonds | 3.0 | billion RM |
| Total | 125.0 | billion RM |

a Of which only 4 billion RM in stock form, the balance in form of entry in Reich debt book

## O. The Role of Credit Institutions in War Financing

According to independent German and American estimates, purchases of Reich bonds and treasury paper by individual investors and business firms other than credit institutions account for less than 10 percent of the debt contracts during 1939–1942.[54] These purchases decreased in 1943.

Prior to the end of 1943, credit and insurance institutions financed approximately 95 percent of the public credit needs out of foreign funds, domestic savings, and by increase of the money volume. According to types of credit institutions, credit was supplied as follows:

1) *Out of Foreign Funds:*

The *Reichskreditkasse* advanced to the Reich, in the form of short-term credit, approximately 9–10 billion RM until December 1943, as the countervalue of 2.9 billion RM occupation money in circulation and over 6 billion RM deposits received from banks in occupied territories.

The *Verrechnungskasse* (Clearing Office) purchased treasury paper for an estimated 12–15 billion RM, the countervalue of foreign claims for goods and services purchased by Germany in excess of her own exports and the contributions exacted.

Prior to the end of 1942, the *Konversionskasse* (Conversion Office) purchased Reich paper for 200 million RM out of blocked payments in favor of foreign creditors.

*Dutch and Czech Protectorate banks* acquired Reich paper for over 5 billion RM until the end of 1943. German currency is legal tender in both countries. The central banks, instead of accumulating clearing account balances, are entitled to buy government paper.

2) *Out of Domestic Savings and By Increase of Money Circulation:* German credit institutions and other German investors acquired long term government bonds for the following amounts:

| | 1940 | 1941 | 1942 | 1943 |
|---|---|---|---|---|
| | | *(in billion RM)* | | |
| savings banks | 6.1 | 7.5 | 10.4 | 12.9 |
| credit cooperatives | 1.5 | 1.9 | 2.4 | 3.0 |
| banks | 2.7 | 2.0 | sold 0.7 | sold 0.9 (est.) |
| all credit institutions | 10.3 | 11.4 | 12.1 | 15.0 (est.) |
| insurance companies and other investors | 6.3 | 9.6 | 12.0 | 8.2 (est.) |
| Total bond purchases | 16.8 | 21.0 | 24.1 | 23.2 |
| of which LI-bonds | 8.3 | 7.9 | 9.0 | 12.0 |
| regular bonds | 8.5 | 13.1 | 15.1 | 11.2 |

The above figures are estimates of the *Bankwirtschaft*, quoted in the *Berliner Boersenzeitung* of 1 January 1944, and completed by estimates for 1943, based on figures published in the same paper on 9 February 1944.

Savings banks and other credit institutions do not purchase Reich bonds for the full amount of the savings deposits received, instead they increase their cash reserves in the form of deposits with clearing banks and the Reichsbank. Savings banks, for example, acquired 38 billion RM bonds and increased their balances by 19 billion RM, during 1939–1943. The clearing banks and the Reichsbank invest the funds held entirely in short-term government paper.

Out of the total short-term debt of 142 billion RM at the end of 1943, foreign funds had financed 25 to 30 billion RM leaving some 115 billion RM for domestic funds. The Reichsbank held 41 billion RM, commercial banks and the savings banks system over 20 billion RM each, cooperative banks 6—8 billion RM, a similar amount was held by the Postal system and the balance by other investors. Part of these holdings were financed by savings deposits, part by increased currency circulation and checking deposits. (See page 000 for the respective figures.)

*The share of Reich paper* among all credits and investments of German financial institutions can be estimated at 75 percent at the end of 1943 as against 40 percent in 1938. The figures vary, of course, for each group of institutions.

*Savings banks* directly and indirectly held 66 billion RM Reich paper, over 85 percent of the 77 billion RM deposits. Other assets, mostly mortgage loans, amounted to 11 billion RM.

*The Postal checking and savings system* with roughly 8 billion RM deposits held government paper exclusively.

The five largest Berlin banks held 12 billion RM Reich paper, over 60 percent of the roughly 19 billion RM deposits. Other assets can be estimated at 7 billion RM. The Reichsbank held virtually nothing but government paper.

## P. Credit Policies of Banks

The restrictions on private investment activities and the accumulation of cash among all groups of the population deprived the German credit institutions of any investment possibilities except financing of armament manufacture and war expenditure. German agriculture is reducing its debts slowly, and mortgages on houses in cities also are being repaid. German municipalities and provinces were not allowed to contract new debts. Early in 1944 municipalities were authorized to take long-term credits from savings banks to finance public works necessary for prevention or removal of emergency conditions caused by the war, such as improved air-raid and fire protection, construction of emergency and replacement dwellings, clearing up of destroyed areas, etc.[55] The Allied air-raids also increased the credit needs of industry, which formerly had been able to finance a great part of its expansion from accumulating profits and by issuance of bonds. The German banks finance the reconstruction of damaged plants before compensation is received from the Reich. They also financed the considerable cost of plant relocation. New credits also are being extended for the adaptation of armament production to the changing war requirements, and to finance monopolistic trade organizations as well as the *Reichsstellen*, which set up stock piles of materials. Nevertheless, commercial and industrial credits account for a smaller part of the credit total than before the war, whereas Reich paper has increased very much, tenfold for the large Berlin banks. Much of the industrial credit is investment credit, but the banks were able to safeguard their liquidity by the Reichsbank's promise to rediscount bills which the banks are authorized to draw for the purpose of mobilizing such credits. The security of the advance is reinforced by Reich guarantees, particularly to factories manufacturing new materials and credits for enterprises in occupied territories. To increase their liquidity, the large banks reduced their holdings of Reich bonds during 1942/43, acquiring short-term paper for their new funds, especially the three-month Reich bills rediscountable with the Reichsbank. They have also accumulated large deposits with the Reichsbank, in order to cope with actual and possible repercussions of the air-raids. As a result of this liquidity policy the Berlin banks will be able to convert at least 50 percent of their assets into cash on short notice. These enormous amounts doubtless will be put into action by the banks and their customers when the opportunity arises, i.e., when price, distribution, and investment controls are abolished.

### Q. Circulation of Currency

During the war small copper and nickel coins were replaced by aluminum and paper money. Silver coins are being hoarded. It appears that the public in the main refused to part with its holdings of 1 and 2 pfennig copper coins (originally issued for 19 million RM), remembering that this type of coin had been fully revalued after the inflation of 1923.

At present the Reichsbank is issuing notes for RM 5 and higher; the Rentenbank, notes for RM 1 and 2; and subsidiary coin is issued directly for the account of the Reich. The following table indicates circulation of currency at the end of the respective years:

| | *1938* | *1939* | *1940* | *1941* | *1942* | *1943* |
|---|---|---|---|---|---|---|
| Notes: | | | *(in billion RM)* | | | |
| Reichsbank | 8.2 | 11.8 | 14.0 | 19.3 | 24.4 | 33.7 |
| Rentenbank | 0.4 | 1.0 | 1.1 | 1.3 | 1.3 | 1.5 |
| Coin | 1.8 | 1.7 | 1.6 | 1.7 | 1.7 | 1.8 |
| Total | 10.4 | 14.5 | 16.7 | 22.3 | 27.4 | 37.0 |
| National income | 88 | 95. | 100 | 115 | 122 | 130 |
| Currency circulation in percent of national income | 12 | 15 | 17 | 19.5 | 22.5 | 28.5 |

At the end of 1943 the German public held cash for more than one-fourth of the yearly income, in contrast to one-tenth in 1937. Officially the increase is ascribed to the expansion of territory, increase in the number of wage earners, increased earnings of many workers, and payment of allowances to soldiers' families, veterans, air-raid victims, and others.[56] Allowance is made for most of these factors in the comparison of currency circulation with the national income.

The increase in the circulation, apart from a few billion RM, necessary for the larger turnover and the higher prices and incomes, is a result of hoarding and desire of the public to hold liquid assets. The Allied air-raids have increased this desire. In a sense the additional circulation is filling the genuine need for liquidity felt by workers and business firms affected or threatened by air-raids and evacuation. However, the money volume is excessive and liable to affect the price and income structure unless countermeasures are taken. If the same percentage of circulation is applied to national income for the year 1943 as existed before the fall of 1938, viz. 10 percent, the result is a "normal" circulation of 13 billion RM and an "excess" circulation of 24 billion RM.

## R. Checking (Current Account) Deposits

Until the end of 1942 the increase in currency circulation was paralleled by an expansion of deposits in drawing or current accounts, with commercial, saving and cooperative banks, as illustrated in the following table:

| | *August 1939* | *December* | | *Increase in percent of August 1939* | |
|---|---|---|---|---|---|
| | | *1942* | *1943* | *1942* | *1943* |
| | *(in billion RM)* | | | | |
| Currency circulation | 10.8 | 27.3 | 37.0 | 153 | 240 |
| Deposits in current accounts | 18.5 | 42.9 | 52.0 | 132 | 180 |

During 1943 current account deposits did not increase so fast as the circulation of currency. The volume of such deposits is not fully indicative of the amount of bank money available to the public, however because in Germany payments without cash[57] are not limited to the amount of the party's credit balance on the bank's books but often are permitted in excess of this balance and thus bring the account into the red. The volume of bank transfers, of course, is limited by the amount of liquid reserves held by the banks as a whole, and these reserves have increased during the war, especially in 1943. The reserves are held primarily in the form of deposits with the Reichsbank; secondarily in the form of rediscountable bills like Reich bills, "Dego-bills" (issued by the *Golddiscountbank*), and "Mefo-certificates" (issued by the Reichsbank to represent "special bills"). In addition, the banks have rediscount promises of the Reichsbank for credits granted to finance armament projects.

Deposits with the Reichsbank not only constitute cash reserves for the banking system but compose the funds circulating in the Reichsbank clearing system. The turnover in these accounts more than trebled from 1938 to 1943, but the average turnover per 1 RM deposit decreased greatly. The same applies to the four other clearing systems existing in Germany, namely the system of the commercial banks, the system of the savings banks (called "Spargiro"), the system of the credit cooperatives, and the postal Giro system. All of these systems operate along the lines outlined above, namely by executing money transfer orders of customers by book entries without use of cash. Owing to the expansion of deposits on current accounts, from 1938 until 1942, the average turnover decreased in the *Deutsche Bank* by 40 percent, and in the savings banks system by 33 percent.

## S. Purchasing Power of the Reichsmark

The *Reichskreditgesellschaft*, a leading German bank, in the fall of 1940 calculated the domestic purchasing power of 1 RM as equivalent to 24 cents in the United States.

The comparison was based on the assumption that the relation of price levels in the two countries in 1929 was correctly expressed by the then official exchange rates. The nominal parity of the Reichsmark was, and still is, 40 cents. Its real purchasing power was, therefore, 40 percent below the parity. Because of the increase of American prices, compared with the stability of German official prices, the disparity is smaller at present. This comparison, of course, is not entirely conclusive because of the basic shortages and quality deterioration in the German supply; but it might be representative of a number of goods in the wholesale trade and especially of the great part of the German production of goods which go into the war effort.

The German people do not have much confidence in the stability of the value of that part of their money which cannot be spent within the ration quotas. The disregard for this money that has developed among the population is shown by the extremely high prices paid for non-rationed goods, black market operations, excessive spending for pleasure on the part of the wealthy, and the unreasonable amounts often verging on bribery given as tips. Though afraid to contravene regulations, openly, everyone is trying to amass as much goods and "real values" as possible. Prosecutions for infringement of price regulations are frequent. The control of distribution however is still efficient enough to prevent withdrawals of large quantities of goods from regular trade channels. The present turnover in black market operations, according to all indications, is not very great.

## T. Barter

The shortage of durable and semi-durable consumer goods caused barter operations to spread. For some time it seemed probable that barter would become instrumental in breaking the price and distribution controls. The government at first tried to prohibit all barter trading but it soon recognized that barter of non-rationed goods, such as household articles and used clothing, would be helpful in mobilizing, for immediate use, the reserves of semi-durable goods held by the population.

To prevent black-market operations from being conducted in the form of barter and to bring this type of trade under government control, special barter halls were established, mostly by the municipalities in former pawnshops. In other cases retail shops were designated as authorized barter centers. There official appraisers establish the price at which each article is to be exchanged against another.[58] It was recently stated that 23 barter shops were opened in Berlin, which seems to prove that these barter markets do not have much importance in the total dealings with consumer goods. Barter in rationed goods and especially barter between dealers and manufacturers is strictly forbidden because it is equivalent to an infringement of distribution controls.

## U. "Real Values"

German papers criticize in strong terms the desire of some people to acquire "real values," such as shares and landed property. They advocate special taxes on such assets acquired after the beginning of the war so that the buyers will not be better off than those investors who put their savings in banks or bonds.[59] It is difficult at present to find any investment in Germany other than currency, bank deposit, or government paper. Building activities have been restricted for a long time, and transactions in real estate are subject to license, making sales at high prices impossible. Foreign exchange operations are under strict control. Stock market dealings are limited by the price stop-order and the threatened confiscation of larger blocks of shares acquired after 1939. Antiques, objects of art, paintings, rare postage stamps, and similar objects are the only "real values" which give the owner a certain chance of safeguarding his property in event of inflation. The prices of these items have risen beyond all limit. According to some reports, it is planned to extend price control on rare postage stamps to stop this kind of speculation. Since transactions in collectors' items do not reduce the amount of money seeking investment the competitive bidding rarely can be stopped.

It is evident the German public is trying by every possible means to escape the threatening depreciation of money and money claims, and that the government in turn is taking various steps to make such action impossible or impotent. As yet there are no indications of a repudiation of the currency.

### V. Foreign Quotations for German Currency

The prices paid for German coin and banknotes in neutral countries cannot be taken as a measure of the real value of the German currency. Some German money is still brought out of the country (illegally), and it is known that the German government has sold its own paper money in foreign markets to acquire international claims. Price movements are overemphasized by speculation circles which especially in Switzerland are very active. Swiss quotations of German currency show silver coin 21–23 Swiss francs for 100 RM, paper marks 12–14 Swiss francs for 100 RM, traveling checks 85 Swiss francs for 100 RM, in contrast to a legal parity of 172.5 Swiss francs for 100 RM.[60] But these figures do not begin to show the extent to which the German military outlook is discounted in Switzerland, the claim of one information source notwithstanding.[61] If the Reichsmark notes are at present only 7 Swiss francs for 100 RM against 13 Swiss francs a few weeks earlier, it simply means that oversupply and speculation pushed the price down that far, and possibly also that some people (the buyers) do not expect the depreciation of the Reichsmark after the war to go below that rate, which is equivalent to $1.60 for 100 RM, or 4 percent of the pre-war value.

The following transactions will illustrate this statement: A 100-RM banknote, bought in Zurich for 7 Swiss francs is worth 2000 French francs in France. This amount if smuggled out of France can be sold in Zurich for 30 Swiss francs, at the rate of Swiss francs 1.5 per French francs 100. Similar, but more profitable transactions were possible as long as *Reichskreditkassenscheine* were legal tender in France, because their Zurich value was lower than that of the regular German currency.

## III. The Inflation Problem after Defeat of Germany

### A. Present Equilibrium

The German price and income system can be expected to remain in its present unstable equilibrium either until the political system breaks down or until the distributive system is thrown into permanent disorder by some strong cause. Until then, the consistent and comprehensive government controls will prevent inherent inflationary tendencies from becoming active. To all practical purposes, there is at present no price inflation in Germany, because (1) the supply of food is sufficient to cover basic needs, and is distributed equally at official prices; (2) prices of rationed goods, rents, and services are stable; (3) only a small part of all transactions is carried out at inflated prices. On the other hand, there is an inflation potential, which consists of the following factors: (1) private consumption has been reduced, whereas private incomes have increased owing to intensified production for war purposes; (2) taxation covers only a part of the war cost; (3) unspent incomes and proceeds from liquidated stocks are not invested in government bonds but in currency and bank deposits; other investment possibilities do not exist; (4) there is a great lack in the supply of durable and semi-durable consumers' goods; (5) prices of second-hand goods, collectors' articles, and the few items available on black markets have increased considerably.

Money without a purchasing certificate has no purchasing power and is unspendable. Comprehensive market controls prevent it from influencing price levels and the distribution of goods. The inflation danger remains however, for this surplus money has not been completely neutralized, in spite of the efforts of the government to effect this.

## B. German Post-war Plans

It still would be technically possible to re-establish a free market on the present price level, or at least to reduce controls and expand supplies at official prices. But to dispose permanently of the threat of inflation, the surplus cash reserves must be reduced. German economists are confident that once their country has won the war it will be able to expand production of civilian goods rapidly, to supply the domestic populations and even to export great quantities of goods at pre-war prices. But they consider the inflation potential represented by surplus cash reserves an urgent problem which must be solved if the war economy is eventually to be transformed into the normal, i.e., free, system.[62] Lately the German economic press has published a number of articles and studies in which the methods of post-war adjustment of currency, prices and the government debt are discussed. The ideas advanced by these professional economists parallel some of the alternative solutions discussed in this paper.

In case Allied fiscal policy calls for the prevention of inflation, an Allied program may be put into force either directly through MG or indirectly through the national government. The policies suggested below are presented without reference to the executive authority which may put them into effect.

## C. Dangers of Moderate Inflation

It is sometimes urged that a controlled, "moderate" inflation of prices would be desirable in order to bring the total of currency and deposits into a mere normal relation with the nominal national income. The excessive circulation of money would thereby be reduced. The difficulty, of course, lies in stopping inflation at a predetermined level.

Once prices and wages have begun to spiral upward, with cause and effect interacting, there is great danger that the movement will become uncontrollable. In addition to the accumulated money reserves, new credit would expand the currency circulation and the velocity of turnover would also increase.

An equally serious difficulty is that inflation disrupts the price and income system and consequently the social pattern. Prices never rise in a uniform manner. Some products go up in price rapidly; others show only a moderate increase, depending on the particular market situation. Living costs increase less than wholesale prices or even retail prices. On the whole, wages trail rising living costs, but workers in a few industries might be able to bargain successfully for adequate pay. Speculators and business men as a class make large and easy profits. Even after stabilization of the over-all price level following inflation, the price and wage system remains highly unstable. Continuous adjustments are necessary. Due to numerous changes in property relations, annihilation of small savings and alterations in the tax system during the period of inflation make the distribution of national income and the tax burden much more unequal than before the inflation. Social frictions and political unrest are thereby increased.

A runaway inflation in Germany would be attended by grave social consequences. Any government therefore will have to use all means to prevent a repetition of the 1919–23 experience. Encouragement of moderate inflation would only further increase the risk of runaway developments. A depreciation of the mark to a fraction of its present value would be undesirable because of the opportunity this presents for speculators and because of the danger of the concentration of wealth in a few hands, and the annihilation of small savings.

### D. Provisional Exchange Value of the Mark

The Allied governments from the outset will face the problem of the future mark exchange parity, although for some time to come no strictly commercial transactions can be expected between Germany and other countries. The German public will be anxious to discover whether the government intends to depreciate the German currency and to what extent. Few, if any, expect the mark to retain its former value. The exchange value of the mark against the dollar, the pound, or the currency used by the occupation army will be taken as an indication of its future value. If the value of the mark is set low, prices immediately will tend to increase to a fictitious parity with American and British prices. It should be noted, however, that this tendency will probably be supported only by the force of speculative investment in merchandise stock. Commercial exports stimulated by a low mark rate will probably be made impossible by Allied control of foreign trade.

The value of the mark as set up for conversion of soldiers' pay will influence its domestic purchasing power. Another factor will be the price at which foreign supplies are sold. Both rates must be carefully established if speculative elements are not to find support.

Comparison between the official German price level and American prices reveals that the overvaluation of the mark, estimated before the war at 40 percent has been reduced as a result of the increase in our prices. At official prices 1 mark buys roughly as much as 30 cents in the US, against 40 cents legal parity. Based on wholesale prices the difference may be even smaller. This comparison, however, does not take into account the lower quality of many German products.

The inflationary elements in the German economic system might prove too strong to assure that a parity based on comparison of official prices can be held in the long run. To some extent this applies also to a parity which takes a moderate price increase into account, as would, for example, the rate of 25 cents for 1 RM, which is close to the parity of the two currencies before devaluation of the dollar. German prices would have to increase by approximately 20 percent to reach actual parity with our prices.

A dangerous possibility would be to adopt a very high rate of depreciation for the mark; for example, a rate based on the price paid for German banknotes in Zurich (7 centimes, equivalent to 1.6 US cents, for 1 RM), Lisbon, Stockholm, or the prices paid on German black markets for dollar or Swedish kronen-notes, gold, or rare articles. None of these prices is indicative of the future price level in Germany, but it is evident that by establishing a high rate for the dollar and the pound issued by the occupation armies the inflationary tendencies will be strengthened.

It is important to recognize that since private commercial transactions in both goods and claims will probably be forbidden at first by Allied authorities, the significance of the initial foreign exchange value assigned the mark is almost wholly psychological. Heavy weight in the choice of a rate should therefore be given to the probable impact of the rate on internal tendencies to merchandise speculation in Germany.

### E. Control of the Spending of the Occupation Force

The funds spent by an occupying force have, as a rule, an inflationary effect. The possible dangers are twofold: first the expansion of the currency circulation; second, the introduction of a subsidiary currency in the form of occupation money. The following safeguards should be noted:

1) By using regular German currency for all local payments the public would be prevented from having a yardstick for the depreciation of the mark and thus a means of speculation. Soldiers might possibly receive part of their pay in marks and the balance in a currency which could not be used by the German public. It would be similar to the German *"Wehrmachtsbehelfsgeld,"* which has full value in army canteens and can be sent home to the soldier's family, but in the occupied country has only one-tenth value. This makes it possible to regulate the local spendings of soldiers.
2) If occupation currency is issued, the local value of the soldiers' pay should be kept low to prevent inflationary effects as long as the supply situation is binding. The German public should be discouraged from efforts to use the occupation currency as a bridge to Allied currencies. This could be achieved by announcing an early withdrawal of the occupation money at the same rate as that at which it was circulated initially. If local prices rise so greatly that soldiers' purchasing power must be increased, it would be possible to do so by increasing the pay in local money instead of adjusting the rate of the occupation currency.

### F. Breakdown of the Distributive System

An anti-inflation policy without continuance of some system of price control and rationing is unlikely to succeed. When government controls are transferred to the new authority, at least temporary interruptions of the regular distribution of consumers' goods may be anticipated. Probably the military defeat will be considered a signal for the end of the control system and a start of the price race. Insufficient supplies might cause a breakdown of the rationing system; transactions; without stamps, coupons, etc., might become the rule, money being then the only instrument of distribution. Prices would rise quickly.

Price inflation is always focused in the cost of foodstuffs. The prices of utilities, rents, and the few industrial products, such as coal, which are available for civilians, are easier to control and will remain at the official price level longer than agricultural goods. The events leading to and accompanying the defeat and military occupation probably will disturb the delivery of foodstuffs to the legitimate markets. But the new government nevertheless might succeed, without long delay, in making larger supplies available for the legitimate trade by using German or

Allied stocks and by inducing farmers to resume their deliveries in exchange for fertilizers or other industrial products, at higher prices if necessary. For this purpose, premium certificates entitling the farmer to purchase scarce material, issued in addition to the price of delivered goods could be employed. Or there might be employed large-scale barter operations between consumers' and workers' cooperative organizations on the one hand, and agricultural cooperatives on the other. If necessary, consumers' cooperatives, etc., could be assisted by the government through adequate allocation of industrial products. The success of these measures would depend on various factors, such as the season of the year, the volume of stocks available from the last harvest, and transportation facilities. As soon as the distribution of rationed goods is resumed with a sufficient volume of supplies, black market prices will decline speedily, and it might even be possible to reestablish former prices.

If, however, controlled distribution of foodstuffs and of a minimum of industrial products were disrupted for a longer period and price controls became ineffective, the accumulated money reserves would be released unless drastic measures were taken; prices would rise at a speed varying according to local conditions and the supply and demand situation of the merchandise in question. In view of the experience of 1919–23, the German people's reaction will be quick. The situation might be aggravated by political conditions, such as lack of confidence in the stability of the economic and political system or inability of the government to organize distribution, collect taxes, and finance its expenditure without printing notes.

## G. Stabilization of the Price and Income Level

Once an inflationary situation has developed, it may be attacked from two sides: by an increase in the supply of food and consumers' goods and by a restriction of the money in circulation. It can be expected, moreover, that the authorities after a time will regain control over prices and more or less stabilize the cost of living. However, the price system will have become thoroughly disorganized, and far reaching adjustments will be necessary. It seems advisable to make these adjustments at once and to bring all prices into uniformity by reestablishing at least the present price relations, if it is impossible to hold present prices. All prices, wages, and rents might be increased by a uniform percentage fixed by the authorities, as from a specific date. The present prices are fairly well in line with the inherent price and cost relations between products made of the same raw material. Having been in force over a long period, these prices are well known to everybody, and control could resume where the present system leaves off. A rapid and uniform adjustment would be possible, and the whole economy would be likely to regain much more quickly the stable basis which it needs for successful reconstruction. Moreover it would be easier to hold the new price level and to combat the inflationary tendencies which will always reappear. Various price changes may be necessary, especially for agricultural products, but for a certain period it would be important to hold to the new prices rather rigidly in order to reestablish public confidence in the stability of the currency.

In deciding on the stabilization level, consideration has to be given to various factors, such as food prices, wages etc., To secure delivery of farm products without much coercion, it might be advisable to take the cost of foodstuffs on the farm as a yardstick of the depreciation of the mark and the necessary advancement of the general price level. Wages probably will not rise as fast as food prices, but profiteering and black market operations may bring higher food prices in towns than would correspond to the increase in producers' sales proceeds. There will be great differences between prices in the various regions of the country. Under such circumstances decisions would have to be reached speedily and backed up with all the force and variety of means at the disposal of the government, since the stability of the price level will be short-lived as long as the inequalities of the increase are not leveled. General confidence would be greatly strengthened by announcing a comprehensive financial and economic program and by demonstrating the government's willingness to carry it through against opposition.

### H. Volume of National Income

Discontinuance of war production will reduce the national gross income flow by at least 50 percent. Other factors, however, for some time might overcompensate the deflationary effects of the end of the war:

1) Public relief and discharge payments to workers, demobilized soldiers, etc.;
2) Government payments for war damages;
3) Government payments to industry for unfinished contracts;
4) Financing of public expenditure by printing of notes;
5) Reconversion of industrial plants to peacetime production financed by accumulated funds and new credits, with a resultant price competition for available materials;
6) Payments for production for export on relief, rehabilitation, and reparation accounts.

In these circumstances, the various alternative policies described below would be more or less useful in achieving the general objective.

## I. Currency and Bank Deposits

In 1938, within the Germany of that period, there was estimated a national income of 80 billion RM and a currency circulation of approximately 8 billion RM. At present the circulation amounts to 35–37 billion RM, and it certainly will increase further before and after the occupation. If present prices are retained, the circulation must be reduced roughly by 80 percent to bring it down to the normal figure based on a pre-war national income. If prices are doubled, the desirable restriction would amount to 60 percent, and so on. A circulation of 40 billion RM would be sufficient to carry the pre-war income at five times increased prices. However, after stabilization of the price level the public might still have habits of holding more money than before the war. A less drastic reduction than that based on the above calculation might be sufficient to block inflationary tendencies. On the other hand, production and national income will not reach the pre-war level at once.

The forcible reduction of currency circulation could be effected before the price level is stabilized, as one of the measures to bring about stabilization. Therefore its objective would be rather to stop inflation than to bring currency circulation into the right relation with the national income.

Currency circulation could be reduced by impounding a part of all personal cash holdings at the occasion of an exchange of all currency against new notes. Against the part retained by the government, a non-transferable receipt would be issued. At the same time, the corresponding part of all bank and savings deposits, which total at present well over 150 billion RM, would need to be transferred to a special account, to be used in the same way as the currency withheld:

1) For exchange against Reich bonds at present held by the Reichsbank and the other credit institutions; or
2) For use in payment of the individual's obligations for capital levy, war-profit, or similar extraordinary taxes.

Exchange of the present German currency for new notes in any case might be desirable in view of possible territorial changes and also to prevent the financing of Nazi underground movements out of currency hoards established by the Nazis before their downfall. The program outlined above would result in:

1) Reduction of the German money reserves to a figure in normal proportion to the price and income level;
2) Release of the banks from their excessive holdings of government paper and the placement of these bonds in the hands of the saving public, or their withdrawal against tax duty.

To block an important source of inflation, extension of credit by the banks could be restricted to that necessary to finance reconversion and increase in the production of consumer and export goods. Control of bank credits, therefore, might well be intensified. The big banks hold various titles which enable them to draw cash from the Reichsbank: Treasury-bills, "Dego-bills," "Mefo-certificates," rediscount promises of the Reichsbank, and also guarantees of the Reich. Unless the use of these titles is made subject to the general restrictions imposed on the Reichsbank, currency circulation is likely to expand dangerously, since all banks will show a great desire for liquidity. If the bank holdings of Reich paper are reduced, the public soon will regain confidence in banking.

Currency conversion and the partial blocking of present currency and deposit holdings are operations which should, if possible, not be carried out more than once. It would probably be wise, therefore, to delay their execution until the magnitude of the problem is fairly clear, lest inadequate measures be taken. The technical difficulties of arranging these operations also argue for a delay of several months.

## J. The Budget

Ordinary Reich expenditures amounted to 5.6 billion RM in 1933/34 (latest available figure). The League of Nations' World Economic Survey estimated non-military expenditure during 1941/42 at 10 billion RM. The increase was due to the higher burden of the Reich debt. (Yearly interest payments may be estimated at 6 billion RM on a Reich debt of 240 billion RM.) Pensions and family allowances for soldiers were estimated at 12 billion RM yearly. By reducing civilian expenditure to its former level, and saving a great part of the interest burden by reduction of the debt, the ordinary budget expenditure would sink to approximately 8 billion RM yearly, plus whatever will be spent for unemployment relief, occupation costs and pensions. This, however, would require either adjustment of interest payments or extraordinary taxation in the nature of a capital levy.

In case of a general price rise, expenditure with the exception of interest on the debt, will increase accordingly. Subsidies paid to reduce food prices easily cause large budget deficits; it might be preferable instead to discontinue payment of subsidies and increase agricultural prices. Tax revenue in 1938/39 with business going full blast amounted to 17.7 billion RM.

Apart from the ordinary budget and dependent on special measures will be the financing of public works, especially the rebuilding of war-damaged areas, and the financing of reparation and other non-commercial export production. It would perhaps be advisable to continue collecting the various war surtaxes and perhaps even temporarily to increase some tax rates. Further, to adapt the tax system to changes in the price level, various changes would have to be made, such as an increase in fixed rates (that is in marks) and in railroad fares, change of progressive tax rates, etc. Delay in adopting these measures might have detrimental effects on the situation of the Reich treasury.

For psychological reasons war pensions might be transferred to a special budget fund and covered out of special taxes. On the other hand indemnities for air-raid and other war damages cannot be paid out in cash without inflationary effects. In many cases the person suffering the damage could be given compensation by the restoration of his property in kind. For example, destroyed houses could be rebuilt. The balance of any claims would be paid in government bonds. A special tax on undamaged property might be assessed to cover these indemnities.

Pending final settlement the government might temporarily interrupt payment of interest and redemption of the Reich debt. The short-term debt might then be transformed by unilateral act into a long-term debt.

If a capital levy were imposed, a large part of the debt could be withdrawn and the balance coverted into a uniform debt with postponed maturity. Reduction of the interest rates (now 3½ percent) would have undesirable effects, since it would reduce the cash value of the bonds, prevent savings banks from paying attractive interest on deposits, and influence unfavorably the operations of insurance institutions.

## K. Repudiation of the Reich Debt

Repudiation of the Reich debt is sometimes advocated as a means of solving the budget problem by a simple and effective measure, and of demonstrating to the German people the extent to which the Nazi regime had destroyed public wealth. Inasmuch as some 95 percent of the debt is held by credit institutions, it would be necessary to declare void a high percentage of all deposits, perhaps 75 percent. The repudiation scheme therefore would encounter great technical difficulties. The percentage of Reich paper held by credit institutions is far from uniform; complicated methods of accounting would be necessary to assure equal distribution of the burden among the institutions. Moreover, if a part of the deposits were to be declared void, additional measures would have to be taken to prevent an inequitable distribution of the burden upon the individual investor. Many small depositors would probably have to be compensated for a part of their loss, and to find the necessary means for this, a new debt or a special tax would have to be established. Additional measures would be desirable to offset the onesided benefits gained by the industrialist and the farmer as well as the shrewd investor who acquired shares and land, etc.

All the desired effects of the repudiation could be achieved by a capital levy imposed on real and nominal values held by any person. The rate could be differentiated to prevent socially undesirable effects. By distributing the government paper held by the banks among their depositors, and legalizing the use of this paper for payment of the levy, the Reich debt could be reduced or even nullified, according to the rate of the capital tax adopted.

A capital levy is widely expected by the German public, which considers it necessary to offset the disparity between nominal and real wealth caused by the war. Various, though for political reasons ineffective, attempts in this direction were made after 1918.

## L. The Capital Levy

The capital levy or tax on increase in value of property is an effective technique of preventing the holders of "stable values" from making great and unjustified profits out of the depreciation of the currency. The German tax system includes a regular property tax, based on the value of personal property as ascertained every five years. In 1935, the total value of property declared, excluding property under 5,000 RM, amounted to 70 billion RM. In addition, corporations reported a net property of 25 billion RM. Part of this included claims in terms of money, cash, deposits, etc. These increased during the war by at least four times. The other assets are stable values which, unless destroyed, have to be revalued. This applies also to agricultural property which always has been apprized very low (based on fictitious yields).

By assuming a multiple of the pre-war or book value of stable assets, and adding money deposits claims after subtracting debts at face value, the new value of the property can be established easily and could be made subject to a levy or tax. The scheme might be completed by a tax on war profits, since during the war industrial profits have not been taxed so as to prevent formation of new fortunes or the increase of existing ones.

The capital levy and war profits tax should be assessed and collected in a short time. If they are not, they would seriously hamper economic recovery without securing the desired effect on currency and prices. The payment of these taxes, would be made chiefly in the form of the blocked deposits and impounded currency, or of government bonds. The levy might operate to reduce the economic power of big business, since the greater part of savings deposits are in the hands of small and middle class investors. Industrial firms possibly may be short of money or claims which they could use for payment of the tax. To cover the deficit, corporations would have to issue new shares or bonds, or ask the banks for credit. This would provide the government with an unusual opportunity for influencing the composition of German industrial ownership.

It is important to realize, however, that serious criticism from the point of view of the Allies can be advanced against the proposal of a capital levy:

1) Assuming that an adequate scheme for the control of currency and bank deposits is adopted, the levy on capital can accomplish nothing that a high income tax or other usual type of tax could not achieve.
2) The administration of a capital levy is extremely complicated;
3) Its chief significance is in the redistribution of national wealth and income which it accomplishes, and such measures of long-term social reforms are probably best avoided by the occupying forces.

### M. Reparations

Payment of reparations will aggravate the inflation danger by affecting the budget and the balance of international payments. If the German government is obliged to spend sizable amounts domestically because of reparations, e.g., in payment of goods bodily transferred to the Allies or wages for workers engaged in reparation work, it may be necessary to discourage the government from printing notes for such payments, and to insist on adequate taxation. If external payments are requested, care should be taken that the stability of the currency is not impaired more than is unavoidable. If exports are not sufficient to cover the desired payments, imports and other debit items could be reduced.

### N. Public Works

Reemployment policies could be centered around building of homes and rebuilding of railroads and utilities. To reduce the burden on the Reich budget, plans will probably have to be devised to enable the states, municipalities, private tenants and homeowners to share in the financing. The public will be more easily induced to finance a great part of the cost if there is a direct relationship between the loan and the use of the money, such as financing house-building in the vicinity. Private capital could be supplied in the form of deposits with cooperative building associations and of municipal bonds issued with a Reich guarantee. The system of intermediary financing through banks, employed by Germany in the thirties, may be adopted to great advantage. Funds of savings banks and credit cooperatives could be used as soon as deposits start to increase again. Private building of homes may have to be subsidized out of public funds and by public guarantee for mortgages.

### O. Foreign Trade and Exchange

Controls of foreign exchange dealings should continue in force. Exportation of capital and speculation in German currency in particular should be prevented. Regimentation of foreign trade is likely to be necessary to assure that German trade fits into the desired pattern of international exchange of goods. Domestic prices should not be influenced by foreign trade developments. It might be advisable, therefore, to establish an official import-export agency which would have a monopoly on German foreign trade and would purchase and sell import and export goods inside and outside of Germany. This also would prevent Germany from using dumping and other unfair competitive practices. As soon as prices and exchange rates are stabilized, the desired degree of freedom could be restored to German foreign trade.

German clearing debts and Reich securities or currency, especially *Reichskreditkassenscheine*, held by foreign countries could be declared void and the claims of the creditor nations settled as part of the reparations problem. As a result, the specific form under which German looting took place would not influence the right of the nation damaged to claim an indemnity, or its amount.

## P. Conclusion

The economic, social and political dangers, from the Allied point of view, of an unchecked inflation in Germany are generally recognized. In the end, however, many experts have tended either to minimize the possibility that a small inflation might develop into one of the runaway type, or else to consider the available means of combating the inflation as insufficient. The problem is thus declared either nonexistent or insolvable.

The present paper attempts to show that, if the inflationary elements in the German economic structure are to be overcome, it will be necessary to adopt a comprehensive anti-inflation policy consisting of monetary and fiscal measures, such as reduction of currency circulation and of bank deposits, capital levy or some other provision for extraordinary taxation, together with price and wage control securing rapid adjustment of all prices and incomes to a level at which stability can reasonably be expected. It also will be necessary to provide the population with a regular supply of consumer goods at official prices to cover their basic needs. A decisive and fully implemented stabilization attempt, backed by a strong government, might reasonably be expected to succeed in bringing price and income levels and the volume of money into equilibrium, thereby laying the foundation for a stable economic system.

# Part V

# A NEW GERMANY IN A NEW EUROPE

# 22

Franz Neumann and Paul Sweezy

# *THE ADAPTATION OF CENTRALIZED EUROPEAN CONTROLS OF RAW MATERIALS, INDUSTRY, AND TRANSPORT*

(October 30,1903)

Editor's note: R&A 1450. On October 23, 1943, Eugene Anderson asked for authorization from the Projects Committee to realize, as requested by UNRRA (United Nations Relief and Rehabilitation Administration), a study by the Central European Section on the desirability of retaining certain centralized European economic controls and mechanism, whose description and catalog number perfectly correspond to the report published here. The information is confirmed even on the cover of this report, described as a memorandum for the UNRRA's founding conference, held in Washington, DC, on November 9, 1943. Anderson's letter also indicates Franz Neumann and Paul Sweezy as the two drafters of the report (RG 226, entry 60, box 1: Projects Committee Correspondence).

Classification: Restricted

## Introduction

a) German economic controls over occupied Europe aim at the utilization of all resources of occupied Europe, manpower, raw materials, machines and machine tools, railroads and other vehicles, industrial capacities, etc., for the German war effort. To achieve this, the Germans have applied two methods:

1. centralized machinery—in the bureaucratic and self-governing field—operating from Berlin has been established;
2. indigenous economic institutions have been transformed so as to correspond to the German control patterns.

Since the German control machinery is, in turn, composed of two sectors, a bureaucratic and a self-governing one, the adaptation of indigenous institutions affected equally the self-governing and the bureaucratic institutions of each country under German domination.

As a consequence, each occupied country possesses raw materials allocations agencies after the German model in France, e.g. the *Comité Central de Repartition des Matières Premières*, with approximately 14 sections, and each country has transformed its trade associations into compulsory organizations, in France, e.g. the Central Organizing Committee comprising 190 functional organizations.

b) Some of the major German agencies regularly operating in occupied Europe are:

1. The Ministry of Armaments and Armament Production operated in occupied Europe through the following agencies:
   a. those formerly under the office for War Economy and Armaments in the Supreme Command of the Armed Forces, namely
      1. armament inspections in
         Prague
         Government General
         Ostland
         Ukraine
         Netherlands
         Belgium
      2. war economy staff in
         Denmark
         Norway
      3. the war economy and armament staff in France comprising the three armament inspections Paris, Amiens and Dijon.
      4. war economy offices at
         Saloniki
         Agren
         Roumania
         Slovakia
         Transmistria
         Finland
         (also in neutral countries)
   b. its own, newly created regional organization for each Armament Inspection, namely:
      1. *Wehrkreisbeauftragte* (corps area deputies);
      2. Transport deputies under the Ministry's office for transport Organization (*Dienststelle fuer Transportordnung*);

3. Power engineers subject to Speer as Inspector General for Water and Power;
4. Building Construction Deputies (*Baubevollmaechtigte*) subject to Speer as Commissioner General for Building Construction and as Minister for Armaments;
5. Field Offices (*Aussenstellen*) of the Ministry's Department for the Expansion of Armament Production (*Amt fuer Ruestungsausbau*);
6. Occasionally Armament Commissions, the coordinating agencies in the regional level for all agencies engaged in the production of armaments, directed by the armament inspectors.

c. The Main Committees (*Hauptausschuesse*) maintain representatives in occupied Europe for the technical coordination of indigenous industries with German requirements.

2. German Purchasing Commissions for the Armed Forces under the Supreme Command of the Armed Forces.
3. The organization of the Ministry of Economic Affairs is represented abroad by agents of
   a. the National Economic Chamber;
   b. National Group Industry;
   c. Most of the Economic Groups;
   d. The five *Reichsvereinigungen* for Coal, Synthetic Fibers, Iron, Hemp, and Textile Finishing have either field offices or agents.
4. The Speer Ministry and the Ministry of Economics jointly maintain the Central Order Agencies (*Zentralauftragsstellen*) in occupied Europe.
5. The Commissioner General for Labor Supply maintains agents, as do the *Reichbahn*, *Reichspost*, and *Reichsbank*.
6. To these must, of course, be added the occupation authorities proper, namely the *Reichs Kommissars* and Military Commissars, the *Reichs Protector* and Governor General, each of them having one or several departments dealing with economic, financial and social operations.

## A. The Centralized Controls

1) *Auftrageverlagerung*, or the shifting of orders from German private firms or German government purchasing agencies to business firms in occupied Europe plays a considerable role in the German war economy. *Auftrageverlagerung* is intended (a) to effect an improvement in the social position of the occupied countries by giving them employment, (b) to secure additional industrial capacity for the German war economy.

Though the first aim is usually exaggerated in German statements, it must in no way be underestimated. There is no question that the Germans actually seek to provide employment and, of course, the best way to achieve this is to incorporate the indigenous economies into the German war economy. At first the shifting of orders was more or less unplanned, though definitely encouraged. German business agents visited factories and placed their orders with them. Government purchasing agencies did the same. Fairs were arranged by the Germans. The purpose was not to sell German goods but to stimulate production by indigenous businesses according to German patterns and with German substitute materials.

This rather irregular procedure was abandoned by a Goering decree of August 26, 1940, entitled "On the Planned Exploitation of the Economy of Western territories for the German War Economy." Goering is in charge of the economic exploitation of all occupied territories as Hitler's delegate for the Four-Years-Plan. The above mentioned decree provides for the establishment of *Zentralauftragestellen* (abbreviated ZAST) that is, of Central Order Agencies. The following exist today:

1) For Belgium and northern France—ZAST Brussels.
2) For France—Paris, at the military commander's office.
3) For the Netherlands—the Hague, at the office of the Reichskommissar.
4) Norway—Oslo, at the office of the Reichskommissar.
5) Serbia—Belgrade, at the office of the General Deputy for the Economy.
6) Denmark—Copenhagen, at the office of the War Economy Staff.

All orders exceeding 5000 marks have to be registered with the ZAST, which explores the possibility of placing orders. A second decree exhorts the National Group Industry to scrutinize all orders as to whether they are capable of being shifted while the Minister of Economics in the ruling of October 18, 1940, insisted that all German agencies engaged in the allocation of iron and metals should resort as much as possible to *Auftrageverlagerung*. A list of the most important plants engaged in the manufacture of armament orders with a priority [*illegible word*] was attached.

A decree of April 30, 1941, issued jointly by the Supreme Command of the Armed Forces and the Minister of Economics, set up the machinery and the methods. The ZASTs are independent agencies subject to the orders of the Armament Inspectors (in France to those of the Chief of the War Economy and Armament Staff) and of the Chiefs of the Economic Departments in the Administration Staff of the Military Commanders. In this way, cooperation is achieved between the agencies engaged in the control of the civilian and the military sectors. The chief of the ZAST is now appointed by the Speer Ministry while his deputy is appointed by the Ministry of Economics.

The methods to be employed by the ZASTs are the following. Each order which is to be placed abroad has to be registered with the ZAST if:

a) its price is above 5000 marks,
b) more than 500 kilograms of iron or steel, or more than 100 kilograms of non-ferrous metals, or spinning yarns or thread, or more than 25 kilograms of rubber are required for its execution.

It is prohibited to shift German orders abroad without the ZAST's consent.

The decree also provides for the selection of indigenous business firms. If a German corporation has business dealing with a foreign firm, it may directly establish contact. If this is not the case, the German firm has to solicit support from its Economic Group.

2) To facilitate the foregoing progress, the German Economic Groups maintain representatives abroad. In France, for instance, ten Economic Groups have delegations, namely:

1. Building industry
2. Clothing
3. Iron, steel and metal sheet
4. Electro-technical
5. Vehicles
6. Castings
7. Timber processing
8. Aircraft
9. Machine building
10. Raw material finishing and related iron industry branches.

The National Group Trade equally maintains representatives abroad.

If an order is to be placed by the armed forces, the competent Armament Inspector or his subordinate, the chief of the Armament Command, has to be approached. In addition German business firms may directly approach the ZAST. The negotiations between the German and foreign firms have to be conducted directly without the cooperation of the ZAST though the economic Group or the armament inspector have to be first informed.

However, recently no such direct negotiations between German and indigenous firms are taking place since in all occupied countries indigenous trade associations have been remodeled along lines of the German trade associations. *Auftrageverlagerung* is thus today made on the basis of negotiations between the representatives of the German Groups abroad and the leaders of indigenous associations who in turn distribute the orders among the members of their Groups. All contracts must be concluded subject to the consent of the ZAST.

3) While the ZAST was originally concerned only with the shifting of orders it had soon to concern itself with raw material control. Raw material stocks in occupied countries may not be sufficient to meet demands. Or if they should be adequate they may be urgently needed in Germany for production there. As a consequence, the Germans soon integrated their system of *Auftrageverlagerung* into their raw material control apparatus. This integration was begun early in 1942 and found its expression in a series of rulings of the various national boards engaged in raw material controls. The essence of these rulings is the following. The ZASTs have assumed jurisdiction over raw material control for the following cases:

1. The delivery of raw material from Germany to occupied Europe;
2. the delivery of raw material from occupied Europe to Germany;
3. raw material transactions among occupied countries;
4. raw material transactions between occupied countries and foreign countries.

The allocation of raw material therefore rests fully with the ZASTs which have the ultimate authority to determine whether raw materials (including machinery) should be imported from Germany into occupied Europe or should be exported from occupied Europe into Germany, and whether occupied France should supply, for instance, coal to Holland. The technicalities of the procedures are omitted here; they can be fully understood only if the German system of raw material allocation is fully explained.

The transfer of raw material from Germany to occupied Europe, and from occupied Europe to Germany, is facilitated by the abolition of tariffs as of December 1, 1942, resulting in a considerable simplification and cheapening of production.

4) While the ZASTs have ultimate jurisdiction over raw material allocation and shifting of German orders, the Main Committee of the German Ministry for Armament and Armament Production have assumed full control over the technical aspects of production not only in Germany but also in occupied Europe. Each Main Committee has its representatives in occupied Europe. The Main Committees are composed exclu-

sively of engineers and construction men from the larger industrial Groups of Germany. They are today the supreme organizations for the rationalization of production. They determine

a. The methods of production
b. The kind of raw material to be used
c. The most efficient plan to be selected.

It is, therefore, their decision that ultimately decides upon whether or not a plant can obtain machinery, raw material and labor. For certain industries, especially for the building construction industries, all German agencies in occupied countries are coordinated in one single agency. In France it is called the "Verbindungstelle der deutschen Bauwirtschaft fuer die besetzen Westgebiete" (Liaison Office of the German Building Industries for the Occupied Western Territories).

The various German National Boards are also engaged in rationalization by prohibiting the use of certain materials, ordering the use of other materials, or prohibiting the production of certain products. Since December 1, 1942, all these restrictions upon production in Germany have been declared applicable to occupied Europe, especially to Western Europe.

A major role in the control of production is played by the *Reichsvereinigungen*, especially those for Iron and Synthetic Fibers. These national compulsory peak cartels do not include as members the industrial firms in occupied Europe. But the latter are, in turn, organized in similar cartels which have entered, or have been compelled to enter, into agreements with the *Reichsvereinigungen*, imposing all regulations concerned with rationalization and standardization upon the indigenous businesses.[1]

In the fields where no *Reichvereinigungen* exist, a similar role is played by the groups or regular cartels. The Economic Groups in Germany have been, since the spring of 1943, authorized to engage in marketing (cartel) activities, and have entered into agreements with the corresponding compulsory trade associations in Belgium, Holland, France, Norway, which impose their will upon the latter.

5) Control of raw material (especially of bulky goods) leads necessarily to even tighter control over transportation facilities.

a) *Control of motor vehicle transportation* is already implied in the prohibition on the use of gasoline and tires. Remaining motor vehicles (especially tractors, trucks, and stationary engines) have been made subject to all orders of the Speer Ministry aiming at the transformation of liquid-driven into producer-gas engines. The distribution network is controlled by the *Fest-*

*kraftstoff AG* and the *Generatorkraft AG*, corporations in the Speer Ministry and under the direction of the Four Year Plan's Central Office for Generators (*Zentralstelle fuer Generatoren*). This office determines whether coal, lignite, briquettes or peat is to be used and the number and location of filling stations.

b) German measures standardizing inland shipping are applicable in all occupied Europe.

c) Rail transport is integrated with the Reichsbahn. In the territories annexed by the Reich, the railroads have simply become part of the German System. Railroads in the Government General form a branch of the Reichsbahn, the so-called *Ostbahn*. In Western Europe, they continue to be run by their indigenous administrations subject, however, to German orders. Most of the countries had to deliver rolling stock to Germany. In some cases (esp. 1941 in the Protectorate and in Holland) vehicle pools were established, and the indigenous railroad administrations were obliged to surrender rolling stock to Germany.

The construction of locomotives and railroad cars is fully controlled by the Speer Main Committee *Schienenbahnen* which maintains representatives in those parts of occupied Europe where German manufacturers are unable to do so.

The ultimate coordination of all transportation facilities in Germany and occupied Europe (except in theaters of military operations and rear areas) now rests with the *Dienstelle fuer Transportordunung* in the Speer Ministry, established in 1942 jointly by the Ministry of Transportation, Economics and Armaments. Affiliated with it is an *Arbeitsstab*, a research organization which presents charts and graphs for the rational organization of the most important communication channels.

6) Raw material and production control necessarily involves control of labor supply. German labor control comprises today:

1. the control of the native labor in the occupied territory;
2. the recruitment of foreign workers for Germany;
3. the control of German workers employed in occupied Europe.

The controls are exercised by indigenous Employment Exchanges (Holland, Belgium, France, Norway and Denmark); while in the occupied Eastern territories, German Employment Offices have been established. The Employment Offices establish priorities for the allocation of native labor and are also concerned with the regulation of wages and labor conditions.

These offices operate under the general supervision of agents of the German Commissioner General for Labor Supply who is authorized to "issue directions to the supreme Reich authorities, the offices under them, as well as the offices of the Party and its formations and affiliated organizations, to the Reich Protector, the Governor General, the Military Commanders and the Chiefs of Civil Administration."

Sauckel has made the Gauleiters in Germany and certain officials in occupied territory (like Ritterbusch in the Reichcommissariat Holland) his agent for the coordination at the regional level of all labor problems in German-occupied Europe.

Neither the German Labor Front nor the indigenous Fascist labor organizations play any role in the administration of labor supply and in the control of wages or labor conditions. They are "educational" institutions designed to indoctrinate and terrorize the working class.

### B. Their Adaptation

1) Europe may be faced at the end of the war with problems that can only be solved on a continent-wide basis—at least for a transitional period. In judging whether the existing centralized machinery should be retained, the interests of those United Nations which continue to wage war against Japan (Great Britain, the USA, and possibly liberated Holland and France) should be considered. Those continuing commitments necessitate the utmost economy in shipping space and will, therefore, limit for some time to come the supply of food, fertilizers, raw material, machines and finished products which can be sent to liberated and occupied countries.

This in turn must lead to the fullest utilization of European resources for the satisfaction of the basic needs of the European continent and, possibly, for supplying allied armed forces with certain equipments.

From this follows:

a. continued control of oil.
b. continued control of non-ferrous metal, especially of copper and tin.
c. increase or, at least, maintenance of coal and lignite production in Europe.
d. increase or, at least, maintenance of agricultural production.
e. increase or, at least, maintenance of synthetic fiber production.
f. utilization of German stocks of agricultural products, iron, steel, and non-ferrous metals, machinery and machine tools and rolling stocks for the civilian purposes and for the liberated countries.

2) There are two ways in which the utilization of European capacities for these purposes can be achieved.

a) The above-described centralized controls may be abolished. Full sovereignty may be restored to liberated countries, while sovereignty over Germany would be exercised by Military Government officials.
b) Or the German controls over Europe may be fully or partly retained, and transformed from organs for the spoliation of occupied Europe into agents for its rehabilitation.

3) In the first case, the utilization of European resources and capabilities could be achieved by international agreement obligating the German and Austrian MG authorities to surrender stocks, machinery, etc., while liberated countries would be obliged to perform certain functions for those United Nations still engaged in the war against Japan. It is highly likely that such agreements would not work. Excuses for evading responsibilities are numerous and cannot be excluded beforehand. Neither can an agreement concretize sufficiently the duties that partners are to perform. It would inevitably have to be couched in abstract and general terms, the implementation of which would then be left to understandings for each specific case. Such a situation is ideal for evasion and blackmail.

It must also be understood that continental jurisprudence (not only German) has no such rigid interpretation of "pacta sunt servanda" as has Anglo-American jurisprudence. The *clausula rebus sic stantibus* and similar formula make it fairly easy to evade obligations that are deemed inconvenient.

There may even be good and substantial reasons for not honoring obligations. Each government-in-exile or each government that exercises sovereign power in a liberated country must be anxious to please its people, and will thus want to resume as fast as possible the production of consumer goods. Each country will also try to improve its competitive position. It will attempt to seize as much property in Germany as possible. It will desire to increase at once its rolling stock, machinery, tools, and raw materials. In this way it will try to stimulate industrial production regardless of the needs of its neighbors and the commitments of Great Britain and the USA in the war against Japan.

There would be competition for oil, coal, lignite, machinery, iron, steel, non-ferrous metal, fertilizers, and it might very well happen that while one country succeeds, another is left behind and becomes fully dependent upon supplies from Great Britain and the USA.

4) The second case—retention and adaptation of centralized European controls—promises better results. It could at once make available in a planned manner all German stockpiles, especially of food-stuffs, fertilizers, textiles and clothing. It could organize the transportation system on a European scale thus considerably diminishing demands on Great Britain and the USA.

If this basic idea is accepted, the following methods appear feasible:

a) The German control system of labor supply should be destroyed. The Commissioner General for Labor Supply, even if his functions should be retained for MG over Germany, should not operate in liberated countries through MG agents. The hatred engendered by the deportation of labor is too powerful and cannot be disregarded. Labor control should consist of:
   a. the return of foreign workers to Germany,
   b. their rehabilitation in their home countries and, if this should not be feasible for a transitional period, their temporary rehabilitation in Germany,
   c. control of German labor proper by MG authorities.

b) The key German office for the economic control of Europe is Speer's Ministry for Armaments and Armament Production. All of its top officials and all regional representatives should be replaced by civil affairs officers. The top of the Speer Ministry should be controlled by a United Nation Committee, composed of all or some of the United Nations. This Ministry has been, since September 3, 1943, responsible for practically all production in Europe and has full authority over the raw material control agencies, namely the National Board, the *Reichsvereinigungen*, the Groups and the cartels as *Bewirtschaftungsstellen* (raw material control agencies) and *Auftragslenkungsstellen* (order distribution agencies), over transportation, gas and electricity. It has assumed that it would be sufficient to staff each of their departments in the Speer Ministry with two United Nations officials, and to replace the regional agents by one United Nations official.

   That would require for Germany 20 top officials, 85 regional officials and a much smaller number for each liberated zone.

c) The Ministry of Economics is today concerned mainly with the rationing of consumer goods, foreign trade (in cooperation with the Ministry of Foreign Affairs) and currency and banking control. But it still retains the administrative supervision of the Groups, *Reichsvereinigungen*, and the cartels. As a consequence, the Ministry of Economics held and still holds key positions for the spoliation of occupied Europe. The control by MG of the United Nations authority should be envisaged.

d) The control of both ministries gives MG also control of the *Zentralauftragsstellen* which, for executive purposes, are the key agencies for a planned utilization of European resources. Care should be taken not to appoint a Frenchman to direct the ZAST, Paris, or a Belgian to direct that at Brussels, etc., but to appoint officials who are not likely to accede to pressure from the local national government. The entire German personnel of the ZASTs has to be discharged and replaced by indigenous officials.

e) The German Ministry of Transportation should come under MG control, as well as the remaining ministries, especially that for Agriculture.

f) Due to the integration of business and self-government control, the mere replacement of German government officials by MG officials will not be effective unless the Self-Governing Organs of Industry are coordinated. Their dissolution is impracticable. Though one may dislike cartels, and definitely abandon the idea of controlling the international market by international cartels, indigenous cartels and groups are today primarily administrative organs of the state which have even lost the right to agree upon production and sales quotas. The power of the state over them is legally unlimited. Without them, economic controls could not be exercised by MG unless MG administration develops into a huge bureaucratic machinery. It is precisely to avoid overbureaucratization that the Nazis have encouraged compulsory organization of business. It is therefore recommended that the following be retained:

The National Groups (7)
The 31 Economic Groups in the National Groups Industry
The 6 National Transportation Groups
The 5 Reichsvereinigungen
The other cartels—of which only 220 remain in Germany, according to a statement by Hans Kehrl[2] of the Ministry of Economics on August 31, 1943.

It may safely be assumed that at least two MG officials will be necessary to operate each one of these organs; that means a minimum of 540 officials.

The compulsory trade associations in occupied Europe should be retained and put under reliable businessmen or United Nations representatives. The personnel required will be considerably lower than that of Germany.

The major organizations in occupied Europe are:
in Belgium: Le Comité Central Industriel
in Holland: Council for Industrial Organizations
in France: General Organizing Committee for Commerce with its functional Organizing Committee.

1. Among the 190 compulsory committees in France, only about ten can be considered as important, namely those for
   steel and iron
   coal
   public utilities and electric equipment
   general committee for textiles
   motorvehicles
   building construction
   chemicals
   iron and ferrous metals

g) Similar considerations apply to agriculture. The German Food Estate since 1939, and still more so since 1942, has been a mere administrative agency of the government. Besides, its major section comprises the *Hauptvereinigungen*, the national compulsory vertical cartels, which include all agricultural producers and distributors, and the regional *Wirtschaftsvereinigungen* under them.

Similar compulsory organizations have been established in occupied Europe as follows:
in Belgium: Corporation Nationale de l'Agriculture et de l'Alimentation;
in Holland: De Landstand;
in France: Office Interprofessionel.

2. It is self-understood that the raw material allocation agencies in liberated countries be retained.

h) Large stocks of food, clothing, and raw materials will be held by the German armed forces. MG officials, or the occupation army, should take these over.

5) If these suggestions are adopted, the following steps should be envisaged.

a) All stocks of food, clothing, consumers goods, raw materials, machinery and finished products should be attached and all disposition of these prohibited. Such an order could easily be formulated after the model of a German attachment decree frequently issued by National Boards. In order to simplify procedures, foodstuff below, say, 200 marks current value and other goods below, say, 500 marks current value could be exempt.

b) Registration of stock with civil affairs officials may prove unnecessary if records kept by the armed forces, the National Boards, etc., could be procured. If they are destroyed, the German registration forms of the Food Estate and the National Boards could be used for registration with MG authorities.
c) All agricultural delivery quotas imposed by the Food Estate should be maintained.
d) These preliminary steps done, the whole machinery outlined above could be put into motion. The ZASTs could transfer raw materials from Germany to occupied Europe. Deliveries would be made to the compulsory trade associations and cartels for allocation among their members.
e) Machinery and goods which the Germans have transferred from occupied Europe could be restored without engendering a competitive and unregulated run by government or individuals.
f) Orders for armament goods, etc., could be given by the Allied Powers to industries in occupied Europe through the compulsory trade associations and cartels while Germany's Group and *Reichsvereinigungen* and cartels could be obliged to supply the raw materials and machinery to the corresponding associations in occupied Europe.
g) Rolling stock should be pooled and the Speer Ministry's existing organization should be used to allocate it rationally to the various countries.

## Conclusion

This paper has been limited to a consideration of technical and administrative problems involved in immediate post-war control over the European economy. No attention has been paid to the even more difficult political problems which will be involved. In conclusion, however, it must be pointed out that there will necessarily exist a close connection between administrative and political issues. The maintenance of centralized control as it has been established by the Nazis without at the same time continuing in force the Nazi system of political oppression and domination assumes the prior consent of the governments of the liberated territories. It is possible that such agreements can be reached with the present government in exile (including the French National Committee), but it must not be overlooked that some or all of these governments may never actually succeed in re-establishing themselves in their homelands after the war. In this case agreements with them would be of small value, and the occupying powers would be faced with the necessity of coming to new agreements with the *de facto* governing authorities of the liberated territories, or of establishing direct MG if this should prove impossible. It should be pointed out that the latter procedure would be contrary to the professed objectives of the United Nations and would be looked upon by the people of Europe as little more than a continuation of the Nazi regime's new auspices. From this consideration the conclusion may be drawn that no system of control should be forced either directly or by economic blockade and boycott upon any territory unwilling to accept it. A scheme of centralized control can be justified only on the basis of the greater benefits which it promises to provide. It should therefore be flexible enough to permit any country which remains unconvinced of these benefits to remain outside without incurring penalties in the form of economic strangulations.

# 23

Franz Neumann

# *THE REVIVAL OF GERMAN POLITICAL AND CONSTITUTIONAL LIFE UNDER MILITARY GOVERNMENT*

(September 18,1944)

Editor's note: R&A 2076. Neumann's authorship is indicated in various documents, including two letters from Neumann himself (May 11 and October 11, 1944, respectively) to Chandler Morse and to Gordon Stewart and Felix Gilbert (RG 226, entry 146, box 84, folder 98: Neumann Franz L). A prospectus on works in progress from the Civil Affairs Guide also includes this report with the catalog number R&A 1655.31. However, there is also a handwritten annotation on the side that says: "To be made into another sort of paper." The report, in fact, no longer appears in successive lists from the Civil Affairs Guides. This probably explains its different catalog number and why, despite being approved by the Editorial Committee, the report wasn't included in the War Department Pamphlets like the other guides.

Classification: Secret

## I. American Interest in a Three Power Agreement for the Revival of German Political Life

It is assumed that American interests demand policies of MG designed to maximize the cooperation of the US, UK, and USSR. The suggestions made in this paper with respect to the revival of German political life are formulated with a view to providing an environment in which such cooperation is possible. An agreement on the following questions, therefore, will be required:

1. The dismissal or retention of an existing German government;
2. The appointment of a temporary central German authority by MG;

3. The political, social, and economic policies to be pursued in Germany;
4. The time and conditions under which local and national elections are to be held;
5. The time and method of the disestablishment of MG.

Uniformity can best be achieved by concentrating as much power as possible in the Allied Central Council for Germany and by reducing the authority of the zonal commanders to that of executive agents of the ACC.[1]

The policy of the Three Powers toward Germany will not only put to a test their own cooperation but will deeply affect the strength and direction of the democratic forces. Uniformity is vital in order to avoid the division of Germany, under MG, into spheres of influence. Basic differences in the occupation policy are likely to create such spheres of influence, since Germany has always been pulled to either the East or the West.

If the Western Powers cooperate with the traditional ruling groups, if they try to maintain Germany's social structure and frown upon basic social changes, the democratic forces are likely to look to the USSR, even if the USSR should have a policy not very different from that of the Western Powers. If, on the other hand, the USSR should expropriate small holdings, openly side with the German Communist Party, and terrorize Social Democrats, Catholics, and liberals, the democratic forces will then orient themselves toward the West.

The USA has a greater interest in arriving at a tripartite agreement on military government over Germany with the USSR and UK than the USSR. The military position of the USSR in Central Europe will be superior to that of any other power. No combination of European powers (if allowed to emerge) can even approximately equal it. Such superior military power will attract many who are not used, either ideologically or socially, to having anything in common with the USSR. Her military superiority is, moreover, enhanced by the political strength which she derives from the aspirations of the European masses as well as from the political skill of the USSR. Large groups of workers and the impoverished social groups in Germany will look to the USSR for aid in achieving their social liberation. They, and other groups, can more easily be organized by the USSR, which possesses a high potential of manipulative skill. There are thousands of reliable and fanatical communists, German and foreign, ready to infiltrate every group and organization in order to swing them over to the USSR or at least to influence them for other purposes.

Great Britain if she so desires will be able to limit the influence of the USSR only if she is able either to organize the Western Powers under her hegemony or if she is fully backed, now and in the future, by the USA. Both possibilities seem uncertain, while the actual and potential strength of the USSR is a reality and the USA cannot expect to exert direct military influence in Central Europe. At the same time USA will have an interest in preventing Germany from being politically drawn into USSR's orbit or from becoming legally absorbed by her.

It is thus to the interest of the USA to bind the policy of the USSR by agreements covering as many aspects of policy toward Germany as can possibly be foreseen.

It is believed that the policies outlined below will provide the maximum opportunity for the reconstruction of a German society which will constitute the smallest possible threat to a lasting agreement among the Three Powers. Such a society must of necessity embrace elements from both Anglo-American and Soviet social structure and practice. Germany under this conception would be a democracy with competing political parties, civil liberties and protection for small property holders. At the same time, it would have such socialistic features as the nationalization of key industries, banks, and insurance institutions and the break-up of large estates.

## II. The Legal Continuity of a German Government Existing at the Time of Occupation

The Three Powers, at the time of occupation, may be faced with a German Government already organized or German groups may attempt to establish a government during the process of occupation. While the political advisability of retaining such a government will be discussed below its legality should not be recognized as derivative from either the Nazi state or the Weimar Constitution.

There is no present or past constitutional pattern that can be used to establish a government in Germany. German constitutional life has become shapeless. As a result of the leadership principle, there is no supreme institution apart from Hitler. The Reich Cabinet is not a policy-making body. The Privy Cabinet Council has no function. The Ministerial Council for the Defense of the Reich does not even represent the major holders of power; Speer and Goebbels, for instance, are not members. The *Reichstag* is composed of Party officials appointed by the Deputy leader of the Party.

There is, furthermore, no institutionalized body within the Party. There are *Reichsleiter* in charge of the various functional departments and *Gauleiter* in charge of the major regional divisions of the Party. But there is no supreme Party institution apart from Hitler himself. He has preferred to deal with specific leaders on specific problems, to call in any individual, from either the Party or industry, at his pleasure and to discuss with them whenever he felt such discussion was necessary.

The shapelessness of German political institutions constitutes a marked difference between German National Socialism and Italian Fascism. In Italy the monarchy existed to supply continuity and the Grand Council of Fascism, itself, was the place where the overthrow of Fascism was engineered. The existence of the monarchy permitted a transition, without a break in the legal continuity, from the Fascist regime to what may now be called a semi-parliamentary government.

The legal basis of the Nazi government could, moreover, be questioned. The law from which the Nazi state derives its legal continuity is the Enabling Act of 24 March 1933 for "Relieving the Distress of Nation and State." It granted to the Reich Cabinet almost unlimited legislative power, including the power to deviate from constitutional limits. The Act was to expire on 1 April 1937. It has, as a matter of fact, been extended twice, the last time without time limit by an Edict of the Führer of 10 May 1943. Hitler, however, reserved for himself the right to convoke the *Reichstag* for "confirmation" of the powers of the national cabinet.

The constitutionality of the Act is, however, questionable. The Communist deputies who were in prison, concentration camps or hiding, were not "invited" to the *Reichstag* meeting by *Reichstag* President Göring. Some of the Socialist deputies could not attend the sessions because of danger to their lives. The absence of these legally-elected members, therefore, was due to the threats or strong-arm methods of the Nazis.

The act granted the powers to the "present national cabinet," which was then composed of three Nazis and nine non-Nazis. This particular clause was inserted at the behest of Hindenburg, who hoped to prevent Hitler from throwing out von Papen and Hugenberg. Nevertheless Hitler carried out his intentions toward these men shortly afterwards.

To base the authority of a government on a constitutional instrument of such doubtful validity as the Act of 24 March 1933 would thus be inadvisable. The *Reichstag* is a pure Nazi instrument and must be dissolved along with the other high agencies. Consequently there is no Nazi constitutional statute from which any future German government can derive its powers.

It should be made equally clear that it is impossible to invoke the Weimar Constitution. Although no Nazi act abrogated it formally, Nazis effectively destroyed the entire institutional structure of the Weimar Republic.

The offices of Reich President and Reich Chancellor have not only been merged but have even been amalgamated with that of the Party leader. The *Reichstag* consists of appointees of the Party. The *Länder* are no longer autonomous units and Prussia, in particular, has cased to exist as a *Land*. The initiative of the people has been abolished and the Nazi referendum has no binding effect upon the government.

No German government can thus claim allegiance either by virtue of its succeeding the Nazi government or by invoking the Weimar Constitution.

## III. The Policy of Military Government toward a German Government

The Three Powers should not accept the legality of the Nazi state and of a government deriving its powers from it. Nor should they recognize a government claiming authority for the Weimar Constitution. As a consequence, a legal vacuum will exist unless a revolutionary government has been established prior to occupation.

Any government can, however, derive its authority solely from the occupying powers which are thus confronted with the following political problems:

1. Should a German government be recognized?
2. If not, what other institutional arrangements should be made?

The decision may be influenced by the composition of a government that may exist at the time of occupation or may arise during the process of Germany's collapse.

It is most likely that at the end of the hostilities, central German authority will have vanished. It is improbable that forces from below could overthrow the regime and establish a revolutionary government before the occupation. These forces could come to the fore only if sections of the ruling groups could overthrow the Nazis in a *coup d'état*. Such a political blow is not likely to happen because the leadership of the opposition among the ruling groups appears to have been eliminated, after the attempt upon Hitler's life on 20 July 1944. Field commanders may surrender without central orders and a state of chaos may prevail. This chaotic state of affairs will become more marked if military operations have to be carried out on German soil.

It is nevertheless necessary to discuss MG's attitude toward the alternative types of government presented since the future cannot be predicted with accuracy.

### A. MG and Nazi and Rightist Governments

The clear commitments of the United Nations will not permit MG to deal with a Nazi government. Such a government will be ousted and its members detained.

A rightist government may be installed by the Nazi Party or, at least, by a powerful group within the Party. The Party, or elements within it, may hope that such a government would provide it with some kind of protection against internal and external reprisals.

A rightist government may also come into power by means of a *coup d'état*, which would unquestionably find support among the traditional ruling groups (industrialists, bankers, owners of great estates, high civil servants) which have in the past served as the political advisers of the military.

The traditional ruling groups may, moreover, decide to enlarge the basis of their government by including certain pre-Nazi political figures of the type of the Catholic trade union leader, Adam Stegerwald;[2] the prelate, Kaas; the nationalist, Schlange-Schöningen; or, even a Social Democrat like the former Reichstag president, Paul Löbe.[3]

Should an attempt along these lines fail, and the ruling groups refuse to assume the sole political responsibility, they may well decide to appoint an outwardly non-political cabinet, composed of administrative technicians such as Secretaries of State, court presidents, and others. Any such government will, however, be merely the prelude to profound social change.

MG should not retain such a government for the following reasons:

Such a government would, though outwardly cooperating with MG, concentrate on strengthening its powers to take over after the expiration of MG. It would prevent a wholesale purge of the administrative machinery, would sabotage any social and economic transformations affecting its privileges, and stifle the revival of democracy.

It might be argued that such an unpopular government, burdened with the execution of hard peace terms, should be kept in power in order to discredit the very forces which created it. However, psychological imponderables, arising from a seeming alliance of the United Nations with German reaction, would outweigh these considerations. Moreover, the reactionary groups would surely seek to draw in moderate left wingers or, if they failed to achieve this, they would be likely to break with MG over a crucial issue and represent themselves as the defenders of popular and national rights. If they saw their way clear, the reactionaries would lay the foundations for a neo-Fascist regime.

These considerations make it paramount for MG not to have dealings with a rightist government composed of or representing generals, bankers, industrialists, owners of large estates and civil servants, even if representatives of pre-Nazi parties are included. Such a government could merely be asked to accept the surrender terms and then be dissolved.

### B. MG and German Regional Governments

It is quite possible that separatist tendencies may become active during the period of collapse. Local governments may arise in Bavaria, Württemberg, Baden, the Rhineland and the Saar, and they may even declare their independence of Germany. They will undoubtedly beseech the occupying powers for support. Such support would probably be needed to maintain such governments, for separatist tendencies are weak in Germany. However, support should only be given them if American policy aims at the partition of Germany. This problem, as has been stated before, is beyond the scope of this paper.[4]

### C. MG and a Council Movement

The moment the Nazi leaders give up or are overthrown, the whole social and political system of Nazi Germany will be in jeopardy. It is Hitler himself who holds German society together. No other Nazi or non-Nazi leader has the peculiar ability, the special endowment (what the Germans call "charisma") to hold German society together in its present form. As a consequence, the collapse of his government may be the signal for revolutionary outbursts from below, for strikes, for acts of bloodshed and violence.

It is most likely that the institutional form of these tendencies will be the council. Workers Councils, Soldiers and Sailors Councils, Peasants Councils, or Popular Councils embracing various functional councils on local levels will probably arise. These councils will aim at concentrating all powers (legislative, executive, and judicial) in their hands. They may not be hostile to the political parties which may be fully represented in them, but the councils are likely to strive for rapid national consolidation before other authorities install themselves.

It is most likely that the issue "central government versus councils" will be undecided at the time of occupation. Germany may be dotted with hundreds, perhaps thousands, of such revolutionary organs; there will not have been time for these to have established themselves as the national government. Indeed, there may be again a Dual State of the type Trotsky described as existing in Russia in the period following Kerensky's appointment.[5]

If the council movement is allowed to proceed, it may be ultimately successful. To dissolve the councils would be dangerous. It would imply the destruction of the very organs which spontaneously express the abhorrence of Nazism and the longing for a new society. On the other hand, it is impossible to retain such revolutionary organs with all powers concentrated in their hands.

It might be advisable, therefore, to accept councils wherever they are found and to treat them as the interim legitimate representation of the municipality or of the functional group which they claim to represent. This would involve the following considerations:

a. If, in a city or rural county, a Peoples Council (*Volksrat*) or a Soldiers, Workers and Peasants Council has been formed and has assumed the governmental power in this locality, the Council rather than the existing municipal or county administration should be accepted by MG. This would solve at one stroke the problem of de-Nazification on the level of local administration. It has been recommended that a rigid policy of de-Nazification in regard to mayor, city councillors, and rural councillors (*Landräte*) be followed,[6] but the acceptance of the rival councils as the legitimate local authority would provide an immediate solution and be equally acceptable to the purposes of MG.

Acceptance, however, raises at once an important question: does the council legitimately represent the people? In view of the fact that all authorities under the Nazi regime share the taint of unconstitutionality with the Nazi government, there need not be any legalistic scruples about rejecting such authorities and turning to new ones. But political doubts may quite legitimately arise. It is true that only minorities can, in the initial stage, be expected to be politically active, but ultimately their claim to represent the majority must be put to the test. Elections should thus be held as soon as military security permits. Campaigning is a prerequisite for such elections and a considerable amount of political freedom should prevail prior to such elections.[7]

b. A quite different problem is created by purely functional councils especially by Workers and Peasants Councils. If they are revolutionary organs, they will undoubtedly try to transform the property structure of German society. Workers Councils will try to expropriate owners and to operate factories. Peasant Councils will divide up states.

It is the problem of Workers Councils that will present MG with the most delicate issue. If the emergence of the trade unions is delayed the importance of the councils will be proportionately higher as organs of labor activity. The complete destruction of the unions by the Nazis, the old age of the surviving union leadership, the ambiguous role played by these leaders in the last stage of the Weimar Republic, the overbureaucratization of the trade union movement—all these factors will present service obstacles to a rapid revival and national organization of the unions without outside assistance. The desirability of outside assistance has been frequently urged.[8] In view of the problem attendant upon the rise of the trade unions, the importance of Workers Councils will increase and astute trade unionists readily recognize this.[9] It may be that out of these Councils alone trade unions and a new political labor movement will emerge. Nevertheless, recognition seems impossible under MG. The acceptance of the Workers Councils as and where they are would give sanction to a high degree of political and economic chaos; in some cases factories would be operated by councils, some by their old owners, and in other instances a mixed regime of councils and owners might prevail. Such far-reaching changes should be made only in a uniform manner, applying to the whole of Germany. Consequently, measures undertaken by councils will have to be undone, unless uniformity has already been achieved prior to the establishment of MG.

If MG should order the rescinding of such expropriation measures, the proclamation should take care not to restore the *status quo*, that is, not simply to return the property to previous owners. Owners and managers of factories occupied by Councils should be investigated as to their Nazi activities and sympathies and should not be reinstated if they are proved to be Nazis.[10] In such instances, MG should appoint temporary managers from among the council members or other non-Nazi personnel.

In addition, the status of the Workers Councils should be legalized by MG proclamation as grievance committees[11] similar to those provided for in the Works Council Act of 1920,[12] but endowed with powers giving them a voice in all management matters. The proclamation should provide for democratic elections of Workers Councils as soon as considerations of military security permit.

Such a policy toward governmental and functional councils will not solve the basic problems. It is suggested as the best interim approach to the most delicate problem with which MG will probably be confronted.

## IV. The Establishment of a Central German Administrative Authority

The above analysis indicates that the occupying powers may find politically acceptable governmental organs only on the local level. MG will be confronted with two alternative courses to carry out its administrative tasks: it may either channel its orders to the various German authorities directly, or operate through a central German administrative authority which would have to be established.

The Army and Navy Field Manual states that the policies of MG shall be determined exclusively by MG and not by or in consultation with "local political personalities or organized political groups".[13] At the same time, MG officers are advised to supervise, rather than to administer.

The task of governing Germany is tremendous. No outside agency can possibly perform the job without reliance on native personnel. There are two ways in which German personnel can be utilized. It can be used within and through German institutional arrangements after the Nazis have been purged, or entirely through the organization of MG. The first type presupposes the continued existence of the major non-Nazi German agencies, the second their dissolution or suspension.

It is the first way that alone promises success, although in some marginal cases, such as public safety organization, MG may be compelled by circumstances to suspend completely German police agencies and to incorporate into the MG organization such German personnel as is retained or newly appointed.

The need for retaining the frame of the German agencies is demonstrated by the experiences of German Military Government in Europe. Germany dispensed with native administrative agencies only where she wanted to transform occupied territory into colonies,[14] namely Poland and occupied Russia. This attempt was unsuccessful; Germany was able only to occupy cities and strategic points and never extended her control over whole territories. In other countries, Germany not only utilized native personnel through native administrative channels, but was eager to retain native cabinets. Where this was impossible (as in Belgium and the Netherlands) the permanent Secretaries of State in various ministries were organized into Councils of Administration which had, for all practical purposes, the position of a cabinet, operating through decree-laws.

This German practice in military government is all the more remarkable because German policy was aimed at the despoliation of the occupied countries. It was little concerned with international limitations upon the powers of an occupying force. Moreover, this German practice was adhered to in spite of two advantages the Germans possessed as compared to the United Nations:

1. German personnel was more numerous than Allied personnel is likely to be and was, moreover, better acquainted with the occupied countries. Germany had prepared long in advance for the control of Europe and could avail herself of large numbers of *Volksdeutsche*.
2. Germany had the advantage of taking over countries in which the physical damage was not great and where the administrative structure still survived; only in the USSR was the opposite true.

In spite of these factors, German observers admit that the task of their MG could not have been carried out without a division of labor between German and native agencies.

Consequently, Allied MG for reasons of efficiency will have to rely considerably upon indigenous personnel working through national indigenous agencies. These should be headed by German administrators under MG control and the chiefs of German central agencies should form a Council of Administrators (*Ausschuss der Staatssekretäre*, i.e., committee of secretaries of state) through which the central MG agency should operate. This government would be a committee of technicians rather than a sovereign government. It should be endowed with little or no political significance. All policy decisions in regard to Germany should thus be made by the occupying powers, and the Council should merely execute them.

Its personnel should be carefully chosen. The members should be neutral, should not have been members of the Nazi Party or of a reactionary party, and should not have played an active political role.

Such a Council should be appointed by MG at a very early moment and the proclamation should make it clear that the functions of the Council derive from MG and not from German laws. Orders to German agencies should, as a rule, be routed through this Council which would be responsible to MG for the efficient performance of the agencies. At the proper time, the Council should be charged with the preparation of such elections as may be ordered.

## V. Basic Issues in German Politics under Military Government

### A. The Revival of Political Parties[15]

German political life should be revived through a process of democratic evolution from below. Such a process will probably bring to the surface many of the political traditions of the pre-Nazi period. In spite of the annihilation of all political parties and of trade unions by the Nazis, the revival of the traditional party and trade union system can be expected. The Italian experience has clearly demonstrated the endurance of the European party pattern. Its revival is almost certain in view of the fact that political parties in Europe are not arbitrary creations but spring from a definite social stratification and specific social philosophies. The Social Democrats, Communist, and Catholic Center parties will thus be reorganized, probably under their old names, within a very short period after the collapse of Nazi controls. The so-called bourgeois parties will also revive, although they may assume different names.

It is likely that the weight of the left-wing parties (Communists, Socialists, and left Catholics) will be greater than at any time during the Weimar period. This is the consequence of the changed social structure of the German people which is now composed of approximately 60 percent workers, salaried employees, and peasants, about 15 percent of persons without occupation, 6–7 percent of civil servants, about 8–10 percent of unpaid family workers, and about 6 percent of owners and managers.

It must, however, not be assumed that the large masses of the population will become at once politically active and articulate. The contrary is most likely to be true. Political apathy combined with intense preoccupation with daily domestic problems will be the outstanding factors determining mass psychology.

Apathy of the masses, however, in no way eases the political problem. Rather, it intensifies it, for it leaves the political field to determined minorities which may or may not reflect the unconscious demands of the masses. It seems probable that political parties will be confined to minorities. However, mass movements might develop once the oppressive burden of immediate problems has been lifted or the urgency of immediate problems drives the masses into political action. The crucial problems around which political action will center, will probably be:

a. the purge of the Nazis;
b. the foreign policy (partition and territorial changes);
c. the problem of full employment and its relation to socialization;
d. the effect of reparations.

Although the de-Nazification and socialization issues may unite Communists, Socialists, and left Catholics, it is quite possible that the foreign policy issues may deeply divide them, especially if the Communists accept and support far reaching territorial changes at the expense of Germany and if certain influential Catholics should support separatism.

It is equally possible that a powerful National Bolshevist movement may come to the fore in post-war Germany supported by the nationalist youth, left-wing communists, and radical socialists and that they may combine the desire for revenge with that for a social revolution. Such factors would militate against the revival of the traditional left parties.

## B. The Purge of Nazis

The main political issue after the cessation of hostilities will be the purge of Nazis from public and social life. It would be wrong to believe that being a Nazi was the privilege of any one social class. The conflict between Nazis and anti-Nazis cuts across all social groups. It would be equally wrong to assume that Nazis in higher administrative and social positions are more hated and more ruthless than those on lower levels. Quite the contrary is frequently true. Popular wrath will be directed against the local farm and peasant leader, the street block leader, the member of the plant brigade, etc., as the most concrete and visible manifestations of the Nazi regime. While all this is possible there are nevertheless specific social connotations of Nazism that may have already become predominant during the collapse period. There are more Nazis among businessmen, peasants, and the middle classes than among workers. This may not always indicate a stronger infiltration of Nazi doctrines into these social strata (except the middle classes): it may merely express the fact that the industrialist, because he counts more, has been subject to greater pressure and would have had to risk more than the worker. The industrial leadership has, however, benefited from Nazism and has reaped the spoils from "aryanization," Germanization, and concentration of capital. The greater numerical representation of the wealthier classes in the Nazi Party and their participation in spoliation is likely to transform the antagonism between Nazis and non-Nazis into a social conflict which may challenge the very class division of German society.

With the de-Nazification of government and society, moreover, goes a still more far-reaching political issue, namely, the eradication, along with the Nazis, of the roots of imperialism and aggression.

## C. The Foreign Policy

Problems of foreign relations will vie with the purge of Nazism for first place among the concerns of the German people.

First in importance will be the problem of separatist movements. If separatist movements should emerge, they may very well give rise to violent dissension in Germany, for the desire for national unity clearly permeates all social classes. Yet the issue may become loaded with religious and social antagonisms. If Catholic regions should be in favor of separatism, the dormant resentment against political Catholicism, so frequently utilized by the Nazis, may again come to the fore. The "ultramontane" policy of some German Catholic groups may give rise to a hatred of Catholicism. Social aspects of the conflict over separatism will also appear. It is conceivable that some groups of industrialists especially in the Rhineland, hoping to fare better in separate states may support separatist movements. They may fear that a unified Germany would turn socialist. Should this happen, Socialists and Communists may unite behind a nationalist and socialist program against industry.

More real, however, is the question of the annexation of German territory such as East Prussia, German Upper Silesia and even Lower Silesia. Should this be decided upon, it is the national question which will assume paramount importance. It will, however, not be merely a political but a tremendous social and economic problem.

The loss of largely German territories to Poland may deeply affect German political life; it may play a predominant role in labor politics. Socialists of all shades may be opposed to annexation; Communists may acquiesce in it if annexation is approved by the USSR.[16] In this case the struggle between Communists and Socialists in Germany may assume more serious proportions than under the Weimar Republic and nationalist groups may thus be strengthened.

## D. The Problem of Employment

The economic deterioration will aggravate the political situation. One of the key issues in the struggle of the political parties for power is likely to be the problem of employment. It must be borne in mind that the Great Depression and the Nazi regime have radically altered the approach of the Germans toward economic problems. Unemployment is no longer regarded as something that cannot be altered, as something inherent in the nature of the economy. Such matters, Germans feel, are capable of being changed by the conscious effort of men. There is good evidence to indicate that the Germans do *not* consider the Nazis' "socialism" a fake or mere propaganda but as a reality because they identify socialism with full employment. These profound changes in the ideology and psychology of the common man will produce pressure on any government to promote a full employment policy.

It is, however, difficult to see how private initiative can provide employment. It is questionable that German private capitalists will have any investment incentive without guarantee of an adequate return. They may be willing to enter into some risk (although monopolistic aggregations of economic power try to avoid exactly this) but they will almost certainly refuse to invest unless they feel sure that their properties will not be expropriated at the end of MG. Such guarantees are not likely to be forthcoming, so that industrialists will possibly liquidate their investments and either hoard or export their cash holdings. Such an investors strike is likely to deepen the antagonism between capital and labor.

## E. The Problems Raised by Reparations

The problem of employment is intrinsically connected with the problem of reparations. Three different types of reparations may be demanded: payments in labor, in capital equipment, and in land.

The creation of labor battalions for work abroad will undoubtedly create deep resentment, if uniformly applied, but may find support if confined to Nazis.

Transfer of capital equipment will aggravate unemployment. Payments in kind will affect the standard of living, prices, and taxes. The main issue will be who has to pay the costs and will thus determine Germany's fiscal policy. Taxation, the size of social insurance and public welfare payments, and internal reconstruction will be largely determined by the distribution of the weight of reparations. These factors, in turn, will affect the value of German savings in bonds and deposits. For it might become necessary to devaluate government bonds and deposits in order to make possible the financing of any program of employment and reparation. This, in turn, will lead to widespread dissatisfaction among the investing public, especially among the middle classes, and the reparations issue might again, as in the past, become political dynamite. The distribution of the weight of reparations may again become a crucial issue in the struggle between the left and right.

### F. The Fact of Military Government

The presence of foreign troops will probably stimulate an aggressive nationalism. This does not mean that the population, particularly workers, Catholics, and liberal elements will not be cooperative. They may be and are likely to be so. But the readiness to cooperate with MG is in no way a measure of their democratic convictions. Many will cooperate for selfish reasons: Nazis and pro-Nazis to save themselves from popular wrath, business men in order to continue doing business, civil servants to keep their positions, etc.

### G. The Day-to-Day Problems

All these nation-wide problems will be reflected in the day-to-day problems of the Germans. The reuniting of families, reconstruction of dwellings, the rationing of food and consumers' goods, the maintenance of some kind of price control and, above all, the effort to make an adequate income in a period of rising prices, growing black markets, and decline of earning facilities will require tremendous efforts by every individual. Demoralization and destitution may be expected.

The day-to-day problems will be aggravated by the destruction of the administrative machinery. The situation is already (August 1944) difficult, for regular administration has broken down to a considerable extent under the impact of air warfare and the tremendous shortage of personnel. The gaps have been filled by the Party and its auxiliaries, but the Party will be dissolved by MG if it is not already in complete disintegration prior to the occupation. With no Party and no adequate civil service machinery, the efforts of the individual and any new voluntary associations must increase tremendously.

The difficulties of daily life will be blamed variously on the Nazis, the owning classes, the occupying forces, competing political parties, the punitive terms, reparations, the Jews, the Poles, etc. The broad political issues may thus frequently be confused, and may not immediately become apparent.

## VI. The Policy of Military Government

### A. The Need for a Positive Policy

It is often asserted that MG should "stand by" and not interfere with the political development in Germany. If this is done, so it is claimed, the democratic forces would inevitably rise to power and themselves eliminate Nazi and pro-Nazi movements and trends. This would be true only if a transfer of power to the democratic forces would take place in Germany before occupation or were allowed to take place under MG.

If such a transfer does not occur or if it should begin and then be frozen by MG, a policy of political nonintervention is impossible. Talleyrand once said (with regard to foreign relations) that there is no difference between intervention and nonintervention because nonintervention is, in reality, an intervention in favor of the strong. This view is fully valid for Germany after hostilities. The forces of Nazism, reaction and aggression are deeply entrenched in Germany. They are to be found not only in the Nazi Party; they are in agriculture, business, the civil service, the officer corps, and among intellectuals. Camouflaged as "democratic" or "anti-Bolshevik" movements these forces will go underground. Reactionaries (represented now by the Nazis and pro-Nazis) will, as these elements did in 1918 and 1919, permeate the civil service, sports clubs, and business concerns and organizations and thus try again to constitute a state within a state.

"De-Nazification"[17] would still leave the forces of reaction and aggression entrenched in Germany's social and political structure. Nonintervention would thus actually preserve their power. As a consequence, if it is desired to strengthen democratic forces, it is necessary for MG to adopt a positive policy.

Such a policy, however, faces one serious difficulty. The establishment of a democratic government by the occupying powers is likely to compromise the latter to such a degree that the forces of nationalism and reaction may very well receive popular support. It is for this reason that it has already been recommended not to appoint or recognize a democratic government which would be required to execute highly unpopular policies.

Between the two extremes—nonintervention and establishment of a democratic government—a way must be found to strengthen the democratic forces without seriously compromising them. The solution cannot be abstractly formulated but must be envisaged in terms of the concrete problems with which Germany will be faced in the post-hostilities period.

## B. MG's De-Nazification Policy

In order to strengthen democracy, a most radical de-Nazification policy should be executed. While this sounds obvious, such a policy is likely to encounter serious obstacles. A radical purge policy may very well complicate the administrative problems which MG will normally encounter in tackling the machinery of government and business. It may very well happen that MG will be faced initially with a choice between cooperation with the Nazis or administrative chaos. It should be the established policy of MG to solve this dilemma always and at the earliest opportunity by choosing to carry out a far reaching purge rather than to insist upon orderly administration.

There are two spheres where this principle should be adhered to as rigidly as possible: interior administration, especially the police, and business.

The policy of cautious purge pursued in Italy need not be followed because of two factors: Germany, after surrender, will not be a battle zone, so that strategic considerations will not apply; and the potential number of substitutes for dismissed or detained Nazis is large. There are in Germany thousands of laymen who are not tainted by cooperation with Nazis, and who are able to assume many administrative positions. The extensive participation of laymen in local, provincial, and state administration, the thousands of lay judges of labor law courts, the tens of thousands of former members of work councils, all discharged by the Nazis, possess a range of administrative skills which surpasses anything known in Italy.

## C. The Disposition of Nazis

The second point is the disposition of Nazis after they have been removed. Here the emphasis should be upon the punishment of Nazi criminals and the formation of labor battalions composed of active Nazis. Germans who have committed criminal acts as defined in the Moscow Statement on atrocities, may be expected to be seized by the occupation troops. But the Moscow statement does not cover crimes committed by Nazis in Germany against Germans. It is here that swift action is indispensable. These men must either be handed over to reconstituted German courts or, if these are suspended,[18] detained by the occupation troops and tried. Labor battalions for work in Germany and liberated countries should be formed from the SS, SA, the Nazi Party leadership and other active Nazis.

## D. The Selection of Administrative Personnel

The third point is the selection of officials for German administration. This follows already from the first point—the de-Nazification policy. Every effort should be made to appoint (temporarily) democratic persons to administrative positions. The choice of officials will determine the attitude of the democratic Germans not only toward MG but equally toward democracy.

It is obvious that this step involves serious administrative problems. It might be said that there will not be enough trained civil servants from these ranks. This should, however, not be a deterrent The role of the trained civil servant in the operation of modern administration is quite frequently exaggerated. Two historical experiences demonstrate this: the one is the Weimar Republic, the other Nazism. In the Weimar Republic, a considerable number of laymen were active in administration. Major fields of administration (especially labor and welfare) were controlled by laymen in all administrative echelons. The success of this experiment has never been questioned. For its own reasons Nazism has done away, especially in the last war year, with thousands of administrators and replaced them by Party members without administrative experience. The Nazi administrative machine has, however, not broken down but has continued to function adequately.

Two alternative factors are responsible for the expendability of administrative technicians: the devotion of laymen to the cause; a consistent direction of the machine by a determined political will. In the Weimer Republic, the laymen were genuinely devoted to the jobs they had to perform; under Nazism, the Party leadership provided the political direction. Generally, human capabilities are much greater, especially in times of duress, than is generally expected, and the number of laymen who were active during the Weimar Republic in administrative and semi-administrative positions ran into several hundred thousand.

It is, therefore, possible to have an operating administrative machinery with a minimum of trained civil servants, supplemented by a much larger number of laymen drawn from the democratic forces described above.

Such a personnel policy is also necessary to break the *esprit de corps* among the German civil service. The spirit of solidarity among judges and bureaucrats was, under the Weimar Republic, one of the greatest obstacles to the penetration of democratic elements into the judicial and administrative bureaucracies.

This *esprit de corps* can be broken by determined backing of the new appointees by MG and the ruthless elimination of those who engage in these forms of sabotage.

## E. Demilitarization and Auxiliary Police

The ramifications of a pro-democratic personnel policy extend to the questions of de-Nazification and demilitarization in Germany, for MG must see that Nazi elements do not continue in or filter into military, semi-military, or police agencies. If democratic elements instead are installed in what protective devices are established, additional support for MG is assured.

Demilitarization, moreover, implies not only the disestablishment of Germany's armed forces and an industrial disarmament, but necessitates among other things: the total prohibition of para-military organizations; effective prohibition of the use of sport and cultural associations for secret rearmament and clandestine Nazi activities; the cessation of pan-German racist and annexationist indoctrination through such institutions.

MG may be faced with the same situation that prevailed after World War I when the establishment of the Free Corps was tolerated by the Allied Powers and encouraged by the Social Democratic leadership in order to fight internal and external bolshevism. This experience should serve as a warning. Under no circumstances should the German police unless it is radically purged or German Army formations or semi-military installations be allowed to restore order. This task will devolve upon the occupying powers.

One important exception to this rule must be made. The future strength of the democratic forces will be determined not only by the mass support they can attract, but also by the amount of force at their command. Arms count as much as mass support and ideology. It may therefore be advisable for MG to deputize as auxiliary police carefully chosen democratic groups in Germany and equip them with light arms, so that they will be in a position to break up such remnants of the Nazi movement as are likely to exist and may openly emerge as soon as the occupation ends. It is fully realized that MG cannot hope to police Germany without the participation of German police forces.[19] But it is exceedingly doubtful that even a minor sector of the existing German police forces can be trusted to use its power to break up the forces of Nazism and reaction. Even the so-called "non-political" police officers are likely to side against the democratic elements, as the term "non-political" was, under the Weimar Republic, synonymous with reaction.

### F. MG's Economic Policies

Many of the policies of MG in the field of economics will affect considerably the strength of the democratic forces. In dealing with the problem of inflation, care must be taken to avoid developments similar to those of 1922–23, when a few accumulated riches and the masses were impoverished.[20] If prices are stabilized, care should be taken to prevent stabilization from being confined to wages and from ending with wage stabilization. If the currency is devaluated, the devaluation should be equitable and should place heavier burdens on the rich than on the poor.

In executing reparations policies, care should be taken to avoid curtailment of vital social services. It is preferable for expenditures to be met by means of heavy taxation of the upper income groups and corporations.

If MG should decide to become custodian of public property or private corporations, these should not be put under the management of private enterprises. They should be handed over to the new German government unless it is decided to dispose of the enterprises in favor of the United Nations, in order to satisfy demands for restitution.

This by no means exhausts the economic problems. But the general principles that should underlie the solution of these problems can readily be perceived. Burdens should not be shifted primarily to the lower strata in society, nor should the demand for nationalization of key industries, though MG itself cannot fulfill it, be impeded or forestalled by MG's economic policies.

## VII. The Problem Of Elections

The strength and character of the democratic movement must be put ultimately to the test of elections. The holding of elections implies the risk that the forces of reaction may show themselves much more powerful than might be imagined before the election, and that the conditions imposed on Germany may make the democratic force protagonists of an aggressive nationalism.

These risks must and can be minimized, though they cannot be eliminated. If they should continue to exist, MG may have to reconsider the advisability of holding elections.

### A. Disfranchisement of the Nazis

The most important measure to be enacted is the disfranchisement of the Nazis, for the first elections, on the local and national levels. All

Germans who were members of the Nazi Party on a certain date (a date prior to the unconditional surrender, say 1 August 1944) or at the date of surrender, should be disfranchised. This would apply to approximately 10 percent of the total population and possibly to a lesser percentage of the population entitled to vote, in view of the high prevalence of Party membership among the younger generation. Disfranchisement of certain groups in society is altogether compatible with the idea of civil rights. The ultimate aim of constitutional civil rights has never been merely to protect all kinds of political activities, but to provide the basis for the formation of a political will. Political activity which is directed primarily against the very democracy it is supposed to create has never been protected by militant democracies.

The disfranchisement of the Nazis is a prerequisite to the restoration of democracy and minimizes the risk inherent in elections.

## B. Local Elections

Elections can be held only if the media of communication are functioning, if political activity in the form of discussions, meetings, and organizations has functioned for some time and if large-scale violence has subsided. There should thus be, at the earliest opportunity, a considerable amount of political freedom. Germans should be free to assemble, print, speak, and even demonstrate unless this freedom is clearly incompatible with military security. The printing presses, the offices, the halls, etc., owned by the Nazi Party and its affiliates, should be leased by MG or the Public Property Officer to the political parties and organizations. But no such freedom should be granted to Nazi or similar organizations.[21] Violence will occur, anti-Nazis will attack Nazis, and take justice in their own hands. MG will be compelled to suppress outbreaks, but should be as lenient as compatible with its dignity and military security, so as not to be pushed into a position where it appears to be the guardian of the Nazis.

It would, however, be advisable to begin with local elections, rather than with elections to a national assembly. If the popular councils should prevail, these, rather than the traditional mayoral organization (mayor, municipal dist.) should be put to the test of elections. It may, however, not be preferable to hold elections for the whole Reich territory at the same time, but rather to stagger them according to the progress made in de-Nazifying and pacifying parts of the Reich territory. The territory selected for the first local elections should however, under no circumstances, be geographically identical with the occupation zone of one of the three powers. If it is confined to one zone, the impression will inevitably arise that the occupant of one zone follows policies different from those in the other two zones. In other words, if it is decided to confine elections to one part of Germany, this portion should include sections of all three occupation zones.

Since the risks involved in elections are great, no matter when they are held, local elections should be arranged "at the earliest possible moment."[22] Local elections are likely to provide a political barometer of the political attitude because the issues on which elections will be fought are likely to be national rather than local in scope.

## C. Election Methods

For the first election, all decisions pertaining to the election methods should be made by MG. It is advisable to use the system prevailing before 1933. Under that system local assemblies were elected by men and women over 20 years of age, voting according to the principle of universal and equal suffrage, employing the secret ballot, and selecting candidates on the basis of proportional representation. The only restriction in local elections were certain residence requirements, usually 6 months. In view of the large shifts of population in Germany, a briefer period of residence may be required.

Two principles of the election law may deserve discussion: the low voting age and proportional representation.

Quite frequently it is urged that the voting age be raised from 20 to 25 or even to 30 years because, so it is said, Nazi indoctrination has been most successful in the lower age groups. Available intelligence does not bear out this view. It is likely that those age groups which were indoctrinated by the Party in its "fighting period," that is, from 1924–1932, will show the strongest indoctrination. That would comprise the age groups from 25 to 40 years. Only those Germans 40 years and over seem to show more resistance to Nazism. Since it is impossible to confine the right to vote to the older generation, it is suggested that no change be made in the age requirement.

The objections to the system of proportional representation are more serious. This system, it is maintained, favors the party bureaucrat at the expense of the independent politician and, even more serious, splits the vote by giving undue representation to small parties (so-called splinter parties), thus making difficult, if not impossible, the evolution of a two-party system with clear majorities. Some attribute the rise of Hitler to this very election system. None of the objections can be said to have validity in the post-hostilities period. The ratio of party functionaries among the elected functionaries has been relatively stable in Germany since 1910. It was the large parties which dominated the elections under the Empire and under the Republic, regardless of the electoral system. It is true that small parties are favored under the system of proportional representation, but this evil, if it is one, can easily be remedied by setting the required minimum at a point higher than that required under the Weimar Republic.

The advantages of proportional representation in the post-hostilities period are, moreover, such as to outweigh all the disadvantages. If it is the aim of MG to achieve internal stability in Germany, in order to prevent the ascendancy of more demagogues and to minimize the danger that secret Nazis and other agents will infiltrate all political groups, the organized political parties should have every opportunity to dominate the field. The parties can control the electorate and their candidates. Proportional representation allows the organized parties to achieve a predominant position in politics and thus favors rationality of political relations.

### D. Elections to State and Provincial Diets

As soon as the first local elections are completed, a decision has to be reached whether state (*Länder*) elections are to be held. The answer will be determined by the policy toward centralization of the German Reich. It is suggested that the question is a secondary one and that it has been given an undue share of attention. Major questions regarding Germany after the cessation of hostilities are of national character; none of these can be solved by a regional solution. There may, however, be rather strong so-called "particularist" trends, especially in southern Germany, and there is no reason why these developments should not be able to find adequate legal expression. It is, therefore, advisable to allow elections to state diets, under the election methods outlined previously.

This, however, should not be permitted in the State of Prussia. Prussia has ceased to exist as a state though it still exists as a legal entity. The Prussian provinces are today no longer political divisions of Prussia but of the Reich and thus have a status equal to that of the states. There is no need for MG to resuscitate Prussia as a state, and further, the occupation zones are likely to cut across Prussia. As a consequence, the provincial diets of Prussia should take the place which the diets in the *Länder* have, and the provincial president should be elected in the same way as the *Länder* diets elect their governments. The elevation of the Prussian provinces to political divisions of the Reich will thus complete the process of Prussia's dissolution, although the significance of the step dwindles before the real political and economic problems discussed above.

### E. National Elections

1. to establish a genuine government;
2. to permit the disestablishment of MG.

It is impossible to predict when national elections for a constituent assembly should be permitted. Certain prerequisites can, however, be stated. United Nations' policy toward Germany should be crystallized before elections are permitted. This implies:

1. The border questions should be settled.
2. The amount of reparations should be fixed.
3. Clarity should exist whether, to what extent, and what kind of international supervision is to be maintained over Germany after the cessation of MG, how long it is to last, and under what conditions it is to be changed or abrogated.
4. It should have been decided whether, and under what conditions, Germany is to be admitted into an international security organization.

If these four questions are settled (no matter whether in the form of terms imposed upon Germany or arrived at in an agreement with her), political opinion in Germany can really be formed. As long as there is uncertainty what the political and economic future of Germany is going to be, the uncertainty will necessarily distort public opinion.

Moreover, it is desirable that restitution and a considerable part of the reparation program be already executed before national elections are permitted so that the democratic forces are not compelled to assume too great responsibilities for the future and thus become the target of the reactionary and nationalistic groups for carrying on a new "fulfillment" policy.

MG will then have to determine whether the time is ripe for national elections, whether, above all, the victory of the democratic forces can be reasonably expected.

All principles developed for local and state elections should be made applicable to the national election, and the Council of Administrators should be charged with the responsibility for their preparation.

If the arrangements are compatible with the unconditional surrender instrument and such terms as have been imposed upon Germany, MG should give definite assurances that the outcome of the election will be accepted and that the Constituent Assembly is free to organize Germany in any way it thinks best. It must be especially free to enact expropriation and socialization measures and to provide for far reaching legislative acts intended to eliminate aggressive elements from German society.

# 24

FRANZ NEUMANN

## *THE TREATMENT OF GERMANY*

(OCTOBER 11, 1944)

Editor's note: R&A 2564. Among the materials of the Research and Analysis Branch preserved at the National Archives and Records Administration, there is a folder titled "Treatment of Germany" (RG 226, entry 37, box 1). Inside, together with a draft of the report published here, there is a momorandum from Neumann dated September 10, 1944, and titled "How to Weaken Germany." As Neumann himself explains in an October 31, 1944, letter to Gordon Stewart and Felix Gilbert (RG 226, entry 146, box 84, folder 98: Neumann Franz L.), the text was thought of as a personal contribution to an internal debate at R&A sparked by the memorandum "The Treatment of Germany" by Emil Despres, head of the Economics Division of the OSS and member of the Joint Intelligence Committee of the Joint Chiefs of Staff. In the same letter, Neumann explains that both his memorandum as well as Despres's were rejected by the Joint Intelligence Committee, although making it clear that from his own point of view his text was questionable and that he had written it for merely "tactical" internal reasons. However, Neumann also affirms having presented a second version of the memorandum that undoubtably corresponds to the text published here: the structure, the object, and ample passages of "How to Weaken Germany" are included; in addition, the following note also appears on the cover: "This dociment was presented to the Chief's Committee for approval or disapproval of the general principles that it expresses. It is not intended to circulate outside of the Research and Analysis Branch. Rather, it is hoped that it can serve to stimulate discussion for a new version that can satisfy all people involved." After a meeting of the committee in which Neumann and Marcuse also participated, this version was again rejected in favor of a series of "more concrete" reports on the problem of the partition of Germany, the problem of the demilitarization of Germany, the treatment of Junkers, and how to break the power of the German industrial class; the effective realization of these reports, however, lacks certainty.

Classification: Secret Control (not to be shown outside OSS)

## I. Methods of Treating Germany

1. The main objective of the United Nations in the treatment of Germany is to prevent that country from ever again becoming a threat to the security of the world. The problem of securing this objective could be approached through any one of the following means:

a. The destruction of Germany's industrial potential.
b. The destruction of Germany as a political entity.
c. The removal from German society of the causes of aggression.

2. This paper seeks to demonstrate that the first two solutions should be deferred until it is clear that the third alternative proves unworkable. In other words the United States should aim at eliminating the causes of aggressiveness in German society. To achieve this objective temporary and long-term disabilities should be imposed upon Germany.

3. The deferment of the first two solutions is preferable for the following reasons:

a. It is most compatible with the stated policy of the US that Europe should not be divided into spheres of influence.
b. It will best eliminate obstacles to cooperation among the US, UK, and USSR.
c. It may reduce the military commitment of the US in Europe.

4. Only 20 percent of Germany's working population are engaged in agriculture while 40 percent are employed in industry and handicrafts. The destruction of Germany's industry would thus create social and economic tensions which would lead to social convulsions and would require the investment of a considerable force for a long period. It would, moreover, take Germany less than 20 years to rebuild her industrial machinery. If this is to be prevented, the continued cooperation of the Three Powers over an indefinite period must be assured. This, however, cannot be taken for granted. The disappearance of Germany as an industrial nation might also have adverse effects upon the European economy. As a producer and as a consumer Germany's disappearance might leave such deep gaps in the pattern of Europe's economy that the economic

rehabilitation and continued prosperity of Europe might be seriously threatened.

The effects of de-industrialization of Germany are, at present, unforeseeable, though it is safe to assume that the effects upon Germany would be such as to make integration into the USSR economy the most attractive solution for the large majority of Germans.

5. The destruction of Germany as a political entity after her reduction to the 1937 frontiers could be achieved by:

a. The cession of German territories to neighboring states.
b. The partition of Germany into two or more sovereign states.
c. The permanent internationalization of certain German regions.

Since Germany's 1937 political and ethnic boundaries pretty well coincide, transfers of territories, beyond mere boundary rectifications, would be justified only if they promote the European security system. According to US conceptions, two prerequisites must be met: spheres of influence of Great Powers should not be established, and the desire for territorial changes must be expressed by freely elected and popularly supported governments of the claimant countries. In light of these considerations, no decision as to territorial changes should be made now. They should be postponed until the alignment of political forces has become clear. This in turn requires that the states which are to benefit from territorial changes possess fully representative governments; the sentiments of the French, Dutch, Belgian, and Danish peoples have not yet been expressed, nor does available intelligence indicate prevailing sentiments for or against the acquisition of German territory. In the case of Poland, the two competing governments appear to have quite different attitudes; while the Communist-dominated Polish Committee of National Liberation desires to make Poland beholden to and dependent upon the USSR by proposing the transfer of large stretches of Germany, members of the Polish Government-in-exile in London have, for opposite reasons, evinced considerable skepticism about such transfers.

The problem of Germany's eastern boundaries may, however, have to be settled now, for the refusal of the US to act in this matter may jeopardize the continued cooperation of the USSR with the Western Powers. In this case, the US should acquiesce in the cession of East Prussia and Upper Silesia to Poland but should not consent to more far reaching demands. The transfer of Pomerania and the eastern part of Lower Silesia, with the expulsion of the German population, would considerably aggravate Germany's domestic problems.

The US should not now consent to the partition of Germany. Separatist feelings do not enjoy popular support in Germany and are unlikely to develop. But such feelings may, however, be promoted by certain groups which will see in partition the best protection of a part of Germany against what they will call "bolshevization." To promote partition, the Allied Powers would have to give support to the very groups which have been and are sure to be inimical to democracy.

Partition, besides, would have to be maintained by force. While it may be that the USSR will see no obstacle to a permanent investment of force, it is uncertain that domestic conditions in the US and the UK will permit this for any length of time. The consequence would be that the control over the policing of Germany would fall to the USSR.

In view of the high degree of economic integration in Germany, the new states would, moreover, be unable to exist separately. They would inevitably be driven to seek support from and alliance with each other or with stronger neighbors. The consequence might be the creation of spheres of influence in Germany, a development incompatible with declared US policy.

Partition should be considered only if no stable, genuinely democratic government arises.

No permanent international sphere (such as one composed of the Saar, Rhine, and Ruhr areas) should be created, for such an international arrangement would be tantamount to partition.

It is conceivable, however, that United Nations rule over this and similar areas should be maintained for some time after the disestablishment of MG and that those areas should be returned to German sovereignty if and when stable, non-aggressive, and democratic government has emerged.

## II. The Causes of German Aggression

1. A policy aiming at removing the causes of aggression in German society may prove more successful in arriving at the stated objectives of US policy. It does not preclude the destruction of Germany as a political entity or as an industrial power if this should prove necessary. It is, moreover, a solution that might contribute to the post-war economic recovery of Europe and lead to the pacification of Europe. Such policy, however, must be combined with impositions upon Germany which would give the United Nations full power to change their policies towards Germany any time they become sure that Germany's domestic development or the constellation of forces in Europe make it necessary to destroy German economic or political strength.

2. The elimination of the causes of German aggressiveness must be carried out by the victorious powers and by the German people. The paper will attempt to show how this division of labor can best be organized. It presupposes, however, an understanding of the causes of German aggressiveness.

3. German imperialism is not solely the product of the Nazi Party. If this were the case, the dissolution of the Party and the elimination of Nazis from political, economic, and cultural life would be adequate. Germany's aggressiveness, however, antedates the rise of Nazism, which is merely the current manifestation of the reaction to the defeat suffered by Germany's aggressive forces in 1918. These forces were then composed of the Junkers, the industrial and financial leadership, the German Officers Corps and the high bureaucracy, all of which formed the German ruling class. The four groups were united by bonds of marriage and material interests. They were actively supported by the majority of the petty bourgeoisie and were during the First World War upheld by the larger part of German labor which, however, turned against the ruling groups after 1917.

These four groups helped Nazism into power; its most important financial and industrial corporations prepared rearmament and financed the Party; the Junkers placed their estates and manpower at the disposal of racialist and paramilitary organizations for use as training grounds; the Officers Corps encouraged and led reactionary, racialists, and Nazi groups as auxiliaries for the fight against Germany's democratic forces and to facilitate the rearming of Germany; highly placed bureaucrats and judges protected the anti-democratic forces in their efforts to undermine the forces of democracy.

The democratic forces, composed of the labor movement and an ever-declining Democratic Party, lacked militancy, and were, besides, weakened by the irresponsible policy of the Communist Party. The lack of militancy may be due to the fact that Germany has never experienced a revolution comparable to the English, French, American, or Russian revolutions. The ruling groups have never been dispossessed and the social structure of Germany has never been radically altered. In spite of its weakness, however, democracy was considered a serious threat by Germany's imperialist groups and was therefore completely annihilated when Nazism came to power.

The stratification of the traditional ruling groups was not basically altered under Nazism. Many new elements, it is true, mostly Nazi leaders and Nazi businessmen, have entered it, and some of the members of the traditional classes, especially Junkers, have either lost power or have been eliminated during the war and the purges. For obviously opportunistic reasons, the remainder of the traditional elements is now likely to be opposed to the Nazis in its midst and to Nazism.

Years of indoctrination by the Nazi Party and by previous nationalistic groups and the material benefits which the masses of the people derived from rearmament and spoliation have, however, created a nationalistic and aggressive spirit which is by no means confined to the ruling groups and the middle classes. The elimination of the Nazi Party, and of the power of militaristic Junkers, industrialists, and bankers will thus not automatically transform the masses of the German people into peace-loving and democratically-minded people. Many years of education under an operating democracy will be necessary to demilitarize the spirit of the masses.

The forces of democracy can, however, not be set free without a radical change in the social structure of Germany which would deprive these groups of the economic basis of their social and political power.

## III. US Policy toward Germany

1. The United Nations have, however, no certainty that during or after the collapse of Nazism democratic forces will emerge and will be able to establish themselves. It is possible that Nazism has not only destroyed the democratic organizations (parties and trade unions) but has exterminated the active and most of the potential leaders and killed the democratic spirit in Germany for some time to come.

Any democratic government, therefore, that emerges in Germany must demonstrate unequivocally its stability as well as its ability to purge Germany's social structure of its aggressive elements. Declarations and protestations of this intent will not be enough.

2. Reasons of political morality further require that the German people must share the responsibility for Nazism and its train of aggressiveness and atrocities. No matter how many Germans have rejected the works and ideology of Hitlerism, restitution and reparations become undoubtedly the political responsibility of Germany as a political entity. Measures must be devised, therefore, which will impose upon Germany certain liabilities and responsibilities to be borne by the German people.

3. The responsibility for bringing an end to German aggression is shared by the United States, United Kingdom, and USSR.

It is to be hoped that they will accomplish this end by working together, either within or without the framework of an international security organization. It is to the interest of the US that the policy toward Germany should be formulated in terms that will promote the greatest cooperation among the Three Powers. At the same time, the US must not be required to make too heavy or too long an investment of military force in Europe.

4. The policies aimed at removing the causes of German aggressiveness may be summarized as follows:

a. Short-term measures designed to destroy Nazism and the military forces, punish war criminals, assure restitution of looted property, and repatriate displaced persons.

b. Conditional measures to be imposed upon Germany at once, which can be abrogated or relaxed according to the development of Germany's democratic forces.
c. Permanent measures designed to impose long-term disabilities upon Germany.

5. Three instruments are at the disposal of the United Nations for the execution of these policies:

a. Military government and military occupation.
b. Allied supervisory commissions operating during and after MG with or without military occupation.
c. An international security organization.

Since it is of the utmost importance that the three instruments work along the lines of a consistent policy, their measures should be integrated into an over-all policy toward Germany.

## IV. Short-Term Measures during the Period of Military Government

1. The occupation of Germany by Allied military forces is indispensable for the consolidation of our victory and for the complete elimination of the organized forces which have made war against us. Occupation will, at the same time, bring home to the German people the full realization that they have suffered a decisive military defeat.

2. The elimination of the hostile organized forces required not only military occupation but the establishment of military government over Germany. MG's principal objectives are both positive and negative in character.

The negative objectives are:

a. The destruction of Nazism;
b. The destruction of Germany's armed forces;
c. The trial of war criminals and the disposition of Nazis.

The positive objectives are:

a. The restitution of looted property;
b. The repatriation of displaced persons;
c. The preparation for the formation of a German national government, democratic and non-aggressive in character;
d. The execution of such economic and financial terms as may be delegated to MG.

3. All seven objectives should be carried out as speedily as is compatible with military occupation. A long occupation could bring with it a tendency toward the assumption by military government of responsibility for the public welfare of Germany. If MG anticipates, moreover, a long period of responsibility, it may of necessity place its requirements

of order and efficiency ahead of the vigorous purging of German institutions. Utilization of Nazi officials, even with the intent to remove them subsequently, will create a situation militating against their later elimination. Even though the attainment of the primary objective of denazification will entail serious disruption of normal governmental functions and the orderly conduct of German life, MG has no other alternative than to prosecute this policy.

4. The denazification of Germany should be carried out regardless of the consequences to the functioning of the administrative and economic machinery. Ruthless application of this policy will, in turn, strengthen the democratic forces, psychologically as well as organizationally, and will provide a better foundation for the establishment of a national government.

5. Denazification should be applied to all social strata and institutions. It includes the following steps:

- a. The dissolution of the Nazi Party, its formations, affiliates and supervised organizations, and of such governmental agencies as have been created by the Nazis for the execution of their policies (Four-Year Plan Office, Commissioner Generals, Inspector Generals, etc.). The properties of the Party organization should be seized and disposed of for the purposes of rehabilitation, indemnification, and reparations.
- b. The removal and detention of:
  1. all officeholders in the Nazi Party, its formations and affiliated organizations;
  2. all members of the SS, the Security Service of the SS, and the Gestapo;
  3. major officeholders in government, administration, and cultural institutions;
  4. major officeholders in business and agricultural corporations and organizations.

  The properties of these individuals should be seized.
- c. The removal and detention of all Germans who have participated in the crimes and persecutions of the Nazis, or have directly benefited from the "Germanization" of occupied Europe and the "aryanization" of Jewish property. The possessions of these individuals should also be seized.

6. The destruction of Germany's armed forces requires:

a. The complete dissolution of all military and para-military organizations and the imprisonment of all or parts (officers corps) of the armed forces and their auxiliaries;

b. The seizure of all war materials;

c. The immediate dismantling of all armament factories not convertible to peacetime use.

d. The dissolution of all police agencies on the national and regional levels and the purge of the remaining local police agencies.

7. The trial and execution of war criminals should be extended beyond the limits defined in the Moscow Statement on Atrocities. It should also include individuals who have committed crimes in Germany against Germans. If Allied military courts should be unable or unwilling to try such cases, the perpetrators should be handed over to reconstituted German courts.

8. The detention of certain Nazis and the execution of others does not solve the problem of how to dispose of the Nazis generally. The following program, therefore, should be carried out:

a. All persons defined above in section 5, sub-heads *b* and *c*, should be organized into labor battalions and employed in the reconstruction of devastated areas in liberated areas if they are desired by the respective countries.

b. All members of the Nazi Party and those defined above in section 5, sub-head *c*, should be disfranchised and declared unfit to hold elective or appointive positions.

The positive objectives of MG should be also carried out with the utmost despatch.

9. The restitution of looted and transferred property should be speedily effected. Wherever the original property has been destroyed or rendered useless, substitute property should be taken. Unless Germany is threatened by starvation, disadvantageous consequences for the German economy should not be taken into consideration.

10. German industry and agriculture should be operated primarily for the benefit of rehabilitating the liberated areas. Profits derived from their operation should not be distributed among German owners but should be used for reparation and rehabilitation. Large estates, especially those of the Junkers, should be sequestrated by MG until such time as a German democratic government is capable of dividing them up.

11. The repatriation of displaced persons should be carried out with the utmost speed in agreement with the receiving countries. The consequences to German economy should not be considered even where the transfer of persons leaves gaps in industry, agriculture, transportation, and utilities. In cases where the gaps must be filled to meet the needs of the occupation authorities, MG should compel Germans, regardless of their social status, to fill these gaps.

12. Once these tasks have been accomplished and a democratic, nonaggressive German authority has been established, MG in Germany should come to an end. This central German authority assumes all the obligations arising from the terms imposed upon Germany. Elections will have to be held under MG, if such a German authority is to have

relative stability and is to represent popular anti-Nazi forces. Elections should first be held for local authorities as soon as possible; elections for state (*Länder*) assemblies (except in Prussia where provincial diets should be elected) should follow: national elections will mark the final phases of the political preparations. The success of the anti-Nazi forces in these elections will depend to a considerable extent upon the policy of MG, especially its denazification policy.

## V. Conditional Measures during the Probationary Period

1. The disestablishment of MG is not identical with the withdrawal of the Allied occupation forces, nor does it imply the termination of Allied control of Germany. Strategic points in Germany should be occupied and an Allied control machinery should be established to insure the fulfillment of such terms as will be imposed upon Germany. The occupation troops may be withdrawn and part of the Allied control machinery be disestablished when:

a. A fairly stable and fully acceptable government must have arisen.

b. This government must have furnished adequate proof that it has seriously undertaken the elimination of aggressive elements from German society. This should include:

a) Special disabilities upon former officers of the professional army and upon Nazis;

b) Far reaching purge of the bureaucracy and the judiciary of sympathizers with reaction and aggression;

c) The destruction of the economic power of the Junkers by an appropriate land policy;

d) The elimination of the power of big business from economic, social, and political life, even to the extent of nationalizing the most powerful industrial and financial corporations.

2. It should be made clear to the German people that the character and severity of the long-term disabilities laid upon Germany will depend upon the nature and policies of their government and the fulfillment of the terms imposed upon Germany.

3. These terms will include heavy reparations payments. Although the US has little direct interest as a reparation claimant, it is of interest to the US that the resources of Germany be speedily and effectively devoted to the relief and rehabilitation of liberated Europe. Reparations payments should start as early as possible, even during the period of MG. The payments should include raw materials, capital equipment, labor

services, and finished goods (if desired), and should be required regardless of the consequences to the German economy, the limit being only the maintenance of bare subsistence for the German people. The relaxation of payments or their cessation should be made dependent upon the fulfillment of the conditions stated in the first section of this chapter.

4. Allied commissions should be instituted for the attainment of the following objectives:

a. for the political supervision of the German government, especially for the vetoing of such German legislation which is considered incompatible with the execution of the terms imposed upon Germany;
b. the collection of reparations;
c. the control of Germany's foreign trade;
d. the supervision of Germany's industrial and political disarmament.

5. Compliance of the German government with the demands made by the Allied Supervisory Commission will be assured by the continued military occupation of strategic points and by such sanctions as may be imposed by them upon the German government.

## VI. Permanent Impositions upon Germany

### A. Absolute Impositions

1. It has already been stated that, no matter what protestations a German government may make and no matter what its actions, certain disqualifications upon the government should be imposed at an early date.

2. Germany should never be permitted to maintain armed forces. It should be permitted merely to maintain an adequate but unmilitarized police force. Consequently, the production of armaments should be completely prohibited, even for export. The controls in this matter should be shifted from the Allied Supervisory Commission (as defined in Chapter V, section 4, d.) to the international security organization (ISO) as soon as this body has begun to function. The relaxation of these prohibitions should be made dependent upon the approval of the ISO.

3. Certain ocean ports and waterways should be internationalized and Germany should be prohibited from fixing discriminatory freight port and hauling rates for those European countries which are, by their location, compelled to use German facilities. This would apply especially to the Netherlands, Czechoslovakia, Poland, and Austria. Any change in status of ports and waterways should be made contingent upon the consent of the beneficiaries and approval by the ISO.

4. Germany should not be allowed to build or acquire civilian aircraft during the probationary period. In the succeeding period, the construction of such aircraft should be under the supervision of the ISO.

5. Germany should be forbidden from uniting with Austria, and no customs union should be permitted without the approval of the ISO. Germany should be compelled to submit to the ISO for approval all international arrangements made with Austria.

6. Germany's customs and tariff legislation should be submitted to the ISO for approval, until such time as ISO abrogates this disability.

7. Treaties which Germany desires to conclude with other countries should be submitted to the ISO.

8. The relations of Germany to German citizens abroad or non-German citizens of German descent should be subject to Allied control. This would cover:

a. financial support granted Germany by Germans abroad;
b. cultural and financial support by Germany to Germans abroad.

The ISO may at any time change its decisions and reintroduce abrogated disabilities or impose new ones, if the domestic situation in Germany requires such action.

### B. Deferrable Impositions

1. If the elimination of the causes of the aggressiveness from German society has not taken place, or if the new German government is neither capable nor willing to execute the terms imposed upon Germany, the destruction of Germany as a political and economic power should be considered.

The deferment of these decisions will allow a crystallization of public opinion in the United Nations which is needed for the support of a truly stable settlement.

It may be argued that partition can best be carried through while war emotions are still uppermost in world opinion. Since partition will involve continued public support for its enforcement by the responsible governments, however, it would be dangerous to embark upon such a policy until the permanence of such support is manifest.

During the probationary period, stable governments with broad public support will have arisen in the liberated countries. They will be able to express not only the desires of their peoples but will also be able to assess the character of the new German state.

Part VI

# TOWARD NUREMBERG

# 25

Otto Kirchheimer and John Herz

## *THE "STATEMENT ON ATROCITIES" OF THE MOSCOW TRIPARTITE CONFERENCE*

(December 10, 1943)

Editor's note: R&A 1482. On October 30, 1943, in Moscow, the governments of the United States, Great Britian, and the Soviet Union jointly signed the Declaration of the Four Nations on General Security and divided it into four parts—the Joint Four-Nation Declaration (together with China), the Declaration Regarding Italy, the Declaration Regarding Austria, and the Statement on Atrocity—the latter establishing a series of criteria for the persecution of Nazi Germany for war crimes after the end of hostilities.

The authors are indicated in R&A 113.33, *Political Intelligence Report*, n. 33, 1.3.

John H. Herz (born Hans Hermann Herz, 1908–2005), was a German intellectual, naturalized in the United States, who specialized in international law and relations. After obtaining a PhD in 1938 at the Institut de hautes études internationales et du développement at the University of Geneva, Herz, under the psyeudonym Eduard Bristler, published a study titled *The National-Socialist Doctrine of International Law*. Later, after being forced to seek refuge in the United States, Herz found a position at the Institute of Advanced Studies at Princeton before being hired in 1941 by the Department of Political Science at Howard University. In 1943 he joined the staff of the Central European Section, seconding Kirchheimer as an expert on legal and administrative questions, and he was part of R&A's delegation at the Nuremberg Trials. After the end of World War II, he worked as a political analyst for the State Department until 1948, when he returned to Howard University, remaining there until 1952, when he transferred to City College in New

York. His works include *Political Realism and Political Idealism* (1951) and *International Politics in the Atomic Age* (1962). His ties with Kirchheimer are also described in the long biographic profile of Kirchheimer that Herz wrote together with Erich Hula as an introduction to a collection of Kirchheimer's writings, *Politics, Law, & Social Change* (ed. F. S. Burin and K. L. Shell [New York: Columbia University Press, 1969]).

Classification: Restricted

The "Statement on Atrocities," issued by the Tripartite Conference over the signatures of President Roosevelt, Prime Minister Churchill, and Premier Stalin contains a joint declaration concerning war crimes and war criminals. This Declaration, while reiterating earlier pronouncements on the subject, is important because it clarifies certain hitherto doubtful points, and, above all, because it constitutes the first *common* announcement of intentions on the part of all three major powers. Earlier statements, while often parallel and of similar wordings, nevertheless could be interpreted as reflecting certain divergences, in particular between the United States and Britain, on the one hand, and the Soviet Union, on the other hand.

1) Parallel statements of October 25, 1941, by the President of the United States and the Prime Minister of Great Britain drew the attention of the world to the shooting of hostages and announced that retribution would be exacted from the guilty. On January 12, 1942, the governments of the smaller countries overrun by the Axis emphasized their determination to punish "through the channel of organized justice," those in any way responsible for war crimes. On August 22, 1942, President Roosevelt announced that it was the purpose of the United Nations to bring the perpetrators of war crimes before "courts of law" when victory was won. This declaration was reiterated on October 7, 1942, when the President added that "the successful close of the war" should "include surrender to the United Nations of war criminals" and that a commission for the investigation of war crimes would be established. The Soviet Government, apparently disagreeing with the procedure thus envisaged, on October 14, 1942, came forth with a strong statement which, in particular, insisted upon the immediate trial of any war criminal who was already in the hands of the powers fighting the Axis, thus referring to Rudolf Hess. On December 16, 1942, there followed a joint declaration of eleven countries, including the United States, Britain, and Russia, which condemned the extermination of Jews and promised in very general terms that those responsible would not escape responsibility. On July 29, 1943, Roosevelt and Churchill made parallel statements warning neutral coun-

tries against any attempt to help war criminals to escape their just desert. Finally, parallel American and British declarations, dealing with crimes committed against the population of certain districts of Poland and reaffirming the resolution to punish the perpetrators of these acts, were issued on August 29, 1943.

2) The Moscow Declaration contains the first agreement of the three major powers regarding the procedures to be applied in the treatment of war criminals. It thus eliminates the fear that divergences of opinion among them might later endanger the practical application of the principle. In many respects it seems to constitute a victory for those who, led by Russia, as one of the main direct victims of German atrocities, had insisted upon uncompromising prosecution and concrete procedures. On the other hand, Russia appears to have dropped its previous demand for the trial of war criminals *durante bello*. The agreement thus achieved shows the world that the three major powers, "speaking in the interests of the thirty-two United Nations," are at one in their resolution to punish war criminals according to existing codes of criminal law and procedure.

The Moscow Declaration refers to the renewed and increased danger that more and more ruthless cruelties will be committed by the "Hitlerites and Huns" under the impact of enforced retreat and defeat. It solemnly reiterates the statement that those responsible for any of these acts shall be brought to justice. The fact that the statement refers mainly to Germany and Germane would not exclude the prosecution of other Axis powers and satellites, in particular since the Declaration Regarding Italy contains the stipulation that Fascist war criminals shall be brought to justice. In addition to the restatement of the general principle, however, the Declaration contains a number of important procedural as well as substantive policies.

3) First of all, the statement makes it bluntly clear that surrender of war criminals will be exacted as soon as an *armistice* is granted, and that no procrastination on the part of any German government will be tolerated. Thus the unfortunate experiences after the last war with respect to the surrender and prosecution of war criminals will not be repeated. In another respect, too, the declaration seeks to prevent situations under which war criminals might evade prosecution: in case the German government should not be able to hand over criminals who have become fugitives, the three powers announce their intention to "pursue them to the uttermost ends of the earth." This means not only that these fugitives from justice will not be allowed to hide anywhere in Germany proper or any satellite country but also that they will not be protected by any "asylum" in neutral countries. This situation had already been envisaged in the American-British declaration of July 29, 1943, warning neutrals not to shelter prospective war criminals. Since the reactions of some of

the neutral countries were not entirely favorable, and the possibility that they might protect such fugitives under the principle of non-extradition of political criminals thus seemed not excluded, the statement reiterates in even stronger terms that the traditional right of offering asylum to political criminals will not be recognized as covering the war criminals of this war.

4) The Moscow Declaration furthermore clarifies the procedure by which war criminals, once they have been apprehended, will be brought to trial. For the first time a definite procedure is outlined for those persons whose acts are "localized" in one of the Allied countries. They will be handed over to the authorities of countries where their crimes have been committed in order to be judged according to the laws of these countries by indigenous courts. While these courts will operate on the basis of their respective municipal laws, it does not seem excluded that they may also apply certain rules of international law (e.g., those contained in the Hague Convention on Land Warfare). This provision will doubtless simplify and accelerate prosecution as municipal courts can be quickly reorganized and doubts about the law and procedure applicable will be kept to a minimum. Also it avoids the problems which would arise if an international court should decide such cases on the basis of new legislation which would be given retroactive force.

One may assume that punishment is also contemplated for offenders against Allied nationals (such as war workers or prisoners of war) on enemy territory, as well as for non-German war criminals (such as "Quislings")[1] who may be found outside their respective countries, e.g., in Germany.

5) The statement mentions cases in which the lack of "geographical localization" raises questions with regard to the procedure to follow. These cases apparently involve persons who from German territory have directed measures of oppression against one or several Allied governments or their nationals. It would also appear to apply to war criminals, who have successively committed atrocities on territory of several Allied countries. Since such persons might be wanted by several governments simultaneously for trial, the declaration avoids competition by entrusting the disposition of these cases to the "joint decision" of the allied governments. While the Declaration does not indicate whether the decision will follow a political or a strictly juridical pattern, it emphasizes at least that for these cases, which will probably comprise the most important criminals, the Allied governments will act in common. The question arises whether the statement refers also to those members of the German and Italian governments whose crimes were directed against the German and Italian people. In so far as they at the same time have committed crimes against one or more Allied nations they will be dealt with by joint decision of the Allied governments. But in so far as their activities were re-

stricted to national affairs, they seem not to come under Allied jurisdiction under the terms of the Moscow Declaration. This interpretation follows not only from the fact that the statement speaks only of atrocities directed against Allied nations, but also, more directly, from point 7 of the Declaration Regarding Italy, which refers to "fascist chiefs and army generals known or suspected to be war criminals."

6) Regarding the question of the effect of the Declaration on Germany and the use which can be made of it in PW operations, two points must be emphasized. First, the Declaration makes it clearer than did any of the previous war crime declarations that the governments of the four main Allied powers are serious with respect to the prosecution and punishment of war criminals. This intention is clad for the first time in the form not of statements on the part of individual statesmen or governments but in that of a joint declaration issued as a result of one of the most important conferences of these powers. It should be emphasized that this declaration thus shares in the "solemn" and "official" character of the Four-Power declarations and eliminates any doubt as to the agreement which prevails among the major powers in this respect. The firmness of the Allies' intention to bring war criminals to court is also evidenced by the fact that the new declaration is much more detailed and specific as to procedures than was any prior statement, and that its specifications are of a nature to guarantee success. The intention of requiring war criminals to be handed over under the armistice agreement and of bringing them to justice either in the liberated countries or according to a decision by the Allied powers ensures that there will be no repetition of what happened after the last war—the delay and open sabotaging of the Allied demands by Germany, together with the sham trials of Leipzig.[2] As long as the war continues and the guilty are not yet in the hands of the Allies, the announcement of the envisaged measures and procedures is probably the strongest effort which can be made to deter Germany or Germans from continuing atrocities. The rather broad definition of responsibility, holding guilty all who commit, or consent to atrocities, may also induce many Germans to dissociate themselves from the demands or orders of their superiors. The more German morale deteriorates under the impact of retreat and defeat, the stronger the influence of the threat of retribution can be expected to become.

If the Declaration can thus be used as a means of deterrence, it can also be utilized to reassure the main part of the non-Nazi German population with respect to the post-war intentions of the victorious Allies. At this time many Germans, having become aware of the number as well as the severity of the misdeeds committed by the regime in occupied territories, are likely to be very much concerned about the possible consequences in case of defeat. In particular, the picture of a wholesale and indiscriminate revenge, visited upon all Germans irrespective of guilt, cannot but be constantly before their eyes; this fear has actually been exploited by Nazi propaganda in order to make every German an "associate" in the crimes committed by the regime. The assurance that war crimes will be dealt with on the basis of law and the principle of individual rather than collective responsibility can be used to allay fears of the German people and to turn them against those who have tried to make them accomplices. In this respect the Declaration should be read in conjunction with President Roosevelt's statement on October 7, 1942, in which he said that "it is not the intention of this government or of the governments associated with us to resort to mass reprisals. It is our intention that just and sure punishment shall be meted out to the ringleaders for the organized murder of thousands of innocent persons and the commission of atrocities which have violated every tenet of the Christian faith."

# 26

## Franz Neumann

# *PROBLEMS CONCERNING THE TREATMENT OF WAR CRIMINALS*

(September 25,1944)

Editor's note: R&A 2577.1. On the cover of the report is the following annotation: "Unrevised. Do not give out." Beside the classification level there is a second annotation that declares the report "suppressed." As explained in a letter dated May 22, 1945, from Richard Hartshorne to Sherman Kent, the report was in fact replaced by a new one titled *The Trial of War Criminals*, which Hartshorne attributes to Neumann and Phoebe Morrison of the Central European Section (RG 226, entry 1, box 2, folder: War Crimes). This is also confirmed in a letter written on March 8, 1945, by Neumann himself to Morrison, in which Neumann comments on, and points out additions to be made to, a temporary draft of a memorandum on war crimes written by Morrison. On this occasion, Neumann is referring to report R&A 2577 as being his (RG 226, entry 146, box 84, folder 98: Neumann Franz L.). Both the first and second reports were considered suppressed by the Project Committee after notification of an official position by the United States on war crimes.

In the introductory description of the report published here, an appendix is mentioned with a provisional list of Germans to be treated as war criminals on the basis of the criteria established in the report. This appendix, however, has not been found.

Classification: Secret

The United Nations have announced as one of their major war aims the prosecution and punishment of war criminals. The Moscow "Statement on Atrocities," following upon numerous official utterances of Allied leaders, has outlined certain procedures. However, additional steps will be necessary to enable the Allied powers to implement the Moscow Statement and to coordinate their war criminal policy.

I. First, it is necessary to determine which of the manifold Axis policies and activities should be singled out as "war crimes."[1] The main criterion in making this selection is to be found in national codes and/or in the established principles of international law. On this basis the following main groups can be distinguished:

a) Shooting of hostage;
b) Forcible deportation of civilian populations;
c) Spoliation of civilian population (expropriations, pillage, etc.);
d) Maltreatment of prisoners of war or civilian internees;
e) Collective reprisals (killing of inhabitants of a town or other groups, who are made collectively responsible for an individual hostile act; burning down of villages for same reason: Lidice[2]);
f) Atrocities against whole groups in pursuance of a general program of "annihilation," e.g., massacres of Jews; maltreatment of special categories of persons because of political or religious convictions (Communists, Socialists, Pacifists, Jehovah's Witnesses) or because of their standing in the community (intellectuals, etc.).

II. A large number of persons have been directly or indirectly involved in such crimes. Declarations hitherto issued do not sufficiently indicate the principles according to which responsibility of such individuals shall be established.

a) In cases of massacre of Jews in a concentration camp may all hierarchical superiors of the executing Gestapo squad, from the district Gestapo chief up to Himmler as Reich Leader SS and Chief of the German Police, be held responsible, even when no specific order for the commitment of the act can be found? In case of shooting of hostages, may superior officers up to the Army High Command be held responsible, though no specific confirmation of the order is found?

Under traditional legal procedure the establishment of individual responsibility is required. The Moscow Statement, by referring to persons who "have been responsible for or have taken a consenting part in" war crimes, suggests a broader interpretation of the concept of "responsibility" than it has traditionally received. According to the peculiar structure of Nazi organization and to the "leadership principle" which under the Nazi regime everywhere rules the relationship between members of official organizations, the hierarchical superior is responsible for whatever happens within the functional and territorial sphere of his jurisdiction [without legal limitations].[3]

Fundamental policies are laid down centrally by Hitler or his associates, with full latitude for the execution of policies being delegated to the sub-leaders in the various fields and regions. To this broad power corresponds broad responsibility. Since there exists an unbroken chain of command and corresponding obedience from the highest policy-making level down to the lowest level, every act executed at the lower level must be attributed to each of the hierarchical superiors. Since each of them has a share in the elaboration and execution of a policy in a given field, the plea cannot be accepted that he had no knowledge of a specific act of the details of its execution or that he did not order it himself. In other countries such an excuse is usually valid, because acts of officials would be lawful only if authorized by the law of the land; consequently, any excess is attributable to the individual official and not to his hierarchical superiors. Under the Nazis, however, various agencies and organizations, such as the SS have been exempted from legal limitations so that whatever is done within the broad framework of the Nazi program must be presumed to have official authorization. Under these circumstances, the only admissible excuse would consist in the proof that the incriminated person did all in his power to prevent the act or that, having been unable to prevent it, he resigned immediately after the commission of the act.

b) It may be desirable to bring to justice not only the instigators of a crime but also those who took part in its immediate execution. The latter, however, may be expected to raise the exception of having acted under binding orders. Such a plea cannot be considered in the case of those who in executing a policy have a certain amount of discretion. It might, however, be pressed by persons who acted under specific orders which left no individual choice. The plea of superior orders has been widely discussed in connection with military orders, but little agreement has been achieved. While many army manuals, among them the American,[4] admit the plea without exception, others favor its admission only under narrowly defined conditions, if at all. It would therefore be desirable to have a policy of statement clearly defining the attitude to be taken in this respect.

Since the authoritarian structure of the Nazi regime makes individual resistance against orders more dangerous and consequently less to be expected than elsewhere, a general prohibition of the plea does not seem warranted. The individual member of an army firing-squad detailed to shoot hostages may very well risk his life if he refuses to obey. While the same justification would apply to members of Party formations such as the SS, the policy statement should take into consideration whether or not such a person had joined the organization voluntarily. If he did so, he must be assumed to have had full knowledge of the practices and functions of the organization and can therefore not avoid his share of responsibility.

Policy statements covering these points are desirable for two reasons. They would provide the prosecuting agencies with a criterion concerning the categories of persons against whom proceedings should be initiated. Second, they would facilitate reaching some measure of conformity on the part of the various national or international trial agencies who might otherwise arrive at divergent conclusions.

III. No less important problems will occur in connection with the apprehension or extradition of war criminals. In this respect, a distinction has to be made between persons who at the moment of surrender are in Axis territory and those who may have succeeded in escaping to neutral countries.

a. Legally the most practical procedure of ensuring the delivery of criminals would be to include in the instrument of surrender a clause according to which the German (or other Axis) authority then in power is obliged to hand over to the Allies any persons wanted by them for prosecuting as a "war criminal." This obligation should not only comprise those who may at that time be specified by name, but also those who may be specified later. Any municipal rule that forbids extradition of nationals to foreign powers then in force in an Axis country should explicitly be ruled out by the insertion in the instrument of surrender of a clause invalidating municipal law in contradiction to that instrument.

In case there is no instrument of surrender because of the lack of any central Axis authority, military or civil, criminals will be apprehended by Allied authorities in their capacity as occupants of Axis territory. As such the Allied authorities exercise police power which includes the power to arrest criminals. If the criminals are to be tried in Axis territory, either by indigenous courts or Allied military courts,[5] the legality of the procedure is beyond doubt. If they are to be handed over to authorities outside Axis territory (courts of one of the United Nations, or some international body), this would legally constitute extradition and therefore have to be based on German (Axis) extradition law and procedure. In case there are no extradition treaties, the procedure can be validated only by an Allied order based between the apprehending Allied authorities and the respective Allied countries.

b. Since the apprehension of criminals who have escaped to neutral countries may meet with difficulties, it will be important to close all avenues of escape. A number of neutral countries have already expressed their intention not to grant asylum to such elements.[6] This has been somewhat difficult in the case of countries such as Switzerland and Sweden, which have a liberal tradition of granting asylum to political fugitives. These countries, however, have recently officially emphasized that most of the so-called "war crimes" committed by the Axis in this war are in reality common crimes for which asylum was never traditionally extended.[7] In order to strengthen their willingness to cooperate in these matters and also to induce other neutrals to be cooperative, it is desirable that in all discussions and official utterances the character of so-called "war criminals" as common criminals be stressed.

If certain individuals should nevertheless succeed in reaching neutral territory, their extradition would be facilitated by the recognition of their deeds as common crimes. Difficulties might still arise. E.g., countries which do not have the death penalty might refuse extradition unless assured that such penalty would not be applied.[8] Other countries adhere to the rule that no extradition is granted for trials before special courts.[9]

IV. The questions where, by whom, and how criminals shall be prosecuted and tried have not been fully answered by the Moscow Statement.[10] This Statement discusses only two kinds of crimes: those committed in Axis-occupied territories and major crimes which have no particular geographical localization. For the first, the Statement recommends trial by the respective national courts according to their municipal laws. If not found in the country of trial, the accused will have to be apprehended and brought to that country according to procedures of apprehension and extradition discussed above.[11] The second kind concerns those "central planners" who are responsible for over-all programs of atrocities and persecutions, for which the Moscow Statement provide punishment "by joint decision of the Allies."

The Statement, however, omits to provide procedures for a number of cases: crimes have been committed in Axis territory, and a criminal not belonging to the group of the "central planners" may have committed crimes in different countries. For these cases, too, it is desirable to have clear policy statements.

Crimes committed in Axis territory may concern Allied nationals (e.g., foreign workers, prisoners of war, or foreign Jews or political opponents). Alternative legal procedures are possible: establish jurisdiction of the country of the victim, or try the perpetrator in the Axis territory. The latter procedure appears preferable because the penal codes of the various countries usually do not provide for punishment of the acts committed abroad. If the crimes are to be tried in Axis territory, the question arises as to which courts should be given jurisdiction. Whatever the disposition of reconstituted German courts, the Allied powers can not well be expected to entrust the vindication of their nationals to German courts, especially after the experiences made with war crime trials before the German *Reichsgericht* after the last war. There remains the possibility of dealing with these cases by military courts established by the occupying powers. It is generally recognized that such courts can deal with cases that antedate occupation. They will mainly apply international law concerning "war crimes," which, since it has been substantially incorporated into German law, would seem to be applicable to German defendants.

It has recently been asserted that crimes such as the persecution of Jews or political opponents, committed in execution of the general Nazi programs, are to be considered as "war crimes" even if committed against Axis nationals or stateless persons in Axis territory. It may not appear feasible for Allied municipal courts or military courts established by the occupants to try such cases. Such cases could most advantageously be brought before reconstituted German courts.[12] Punishment of Nazi crimes by German courts would go far to prove to the German people and the whole world that Germany repudiates the crimes of its former leaders.

V. In certain cases there remains the necessity of establishing some international agency for dealing with "war criminals." The Moscow Statement considers punishment of "major criminals whose offenses have no particular geographical localization" by "joint decision of the governments of the Allies." While this seems to cover the "central planners" whose programs have been put into practice wherever the Axis became predominant, some international or inter-Allied institution should also be established for determining "priority" in those cases where criminals are wanted by several countries.

All these cases might be brought before an inter-Allied or international court. But political expediency would appear to make it advisable to choose instead a political agency. Such procedure would avoid that the intricate and difficult question of what law should be applied in the treatment of such criminals—a question which would become paramount in case of an international court—comes up. In this way it would also be easier to take care of the case of Hitler if it should ever arise. A genuine court would have to deal with the objection—frequently raised in connection with the intended trial of William II—that Hitler enjoys immunity as "head of state." Any such objection would be avoided by making his "punishment" a matter of political decision and not of judicial trial, as has also recently been recommended with reference to the precedent set in the case of Napoleon I.[13]

An international or inter-Allied political body could apply generally recognized principles and standards of criminal law without being obliged to follow any particular system. Such a political body could either consist of members of Allied governments themselves or be a specially appointed commission. In both cases full discretion could be exercised as to the measures to be applied. Setting-up of a special body would seem preferable in view of the fact that it will not only have to deal with the major criminals, but have to decide the question of priorities to be established among the claims of different countries for the trial of the same war criminal.

From the foregoing it would appear that a number of points concerning the treatment of "war criminals" should be clarified in official declarations. There should be:

a. an official enumeration of the major groups of incriminated acts;
b. a policy statement establishing the principle of functional responsibility of superiors and delimiting the scope of application of the plea "respondeat superior";
c. a statement to the effect that "war crimes" committed in Axis territory come also under Allied jurisdiction, simultaneously delimiting the jurisdictions of the following three types of agencies: Allied municipal courts; Allied military courts established in Axis territory; and an international or inter-Allied agency;
d. the character, composition, and envisaged jurisdiction of any international or inter-Allied agency.

# 27

Otto Kirchheimer and John Herz

## *LEADERSHIP PRINCIPLE AND CRIMINAL RESPONSIBILITY*

(July 18, 1945)

Editor's note: R&A 3110. Among the documents preserved at the National Archives and Records Administration, it was not possible to determine with certainty the author of this report. In his *Zur Archäologie der Demokratie in Deutschland*, Söllner attributes the report to Kirchheimer, in spite of the fact that, in the interview published in the second volume of the same work, John Herz claims authorship, although explicitly recognizing Kirchheimer's participation in its drafting. It is therefore probable that, as in other reports, the text was a joint effort on the part of these two authors.

Classification: Secret

### Introduction

The purpose of this paper is to illustrate the general theory of responsibility of a superior for the acts of his subordinates under the Nazi hierarchical organization.

The structure and function of the Nazi State was such that, while all power and authority was theoretically vested in Hitler, as Fuehrer, nevertheless a great range of discretionary power was exercised by regional "sub-leaders," who, rather than being mere automatons of Hitler and other high officials of the Nazi hierarchy, were considered collaborators in the Nazi scheme, and as such were responsible for the formulating of broad policies within the particular sphere of their jurisdiction. The more such policies involved a political aspect, the freer they were from any form of legal restraint, and the less likelihood was there that any specific orders would be handed down from the policy making leaders to their executory subordinates. Because of this frequent absence of direct orders, and often an absence of any knowledge on the part of these policy making leaders as to the actual methods used in carrying out their policies, considerable difficulty might be encountered in incriminating such leaders on established legal principles. For instance, the Law of Conspiracy requires an intentional participation in the criminal design by the co-conspirator; and under the doctrine of principal and accessory there must be a specific enticement or encouragement to commit some specific criminal act, mere assent or acquiescence being insufficient. But under the Nazi theory of responsibility, a leader is responsible for the acts of his subordinates despite the fact that he may not have ordered or acquiesced in the particular action of such subordinate. By drawing an analogy to the "leadership" theory of responsibility as developed by the Nazis themselves, a theory of incrimination in connection with war crimes might be developed which could be applied to fit the special circumstances arising under the Nazi hierarchy, and which might be much more comprehensible to an incriminated member of the Nazi party or State than any technical established rule of law which might otherwise be followed.

## I

According to Nazi theory, the German political community, built upon three basic pillars consisting of the Nazi Party, the state machine, and the military, is organized as an "order of leadership" (*Führungsordnung*).[1] This implies that power and authority is always exercised by one "leader," who, although supported by the alleged confidence and allegiance of his "followers," is supreme within his particular sphere and is completely unhampered by any parliamentary or otherwise representative or democratic devices.[2]

Thus at the top of the entire structure, Hitler as *Führer*[3] concentrates in his person all political power, unrestricted by any group or institution, whether of state, Party, or otherwise, and responsible, according to Nazi theory, only to his "conscience" and the "judgment of history."[4] Under him, the leadership principle permeates the whole structure of Nazi society: "Leadership is the general structural element in the public life of the Reich. It determines not only certain specific realms but dominates all organizations, institutions, and associations which participate in the communal life of the people. State institutions—above all administration, armed forces, and labor service—as well as the orders of estates—economic and cultural estates, Labor Front, enterprise communities—are governed by the leadership principle."[5] It implies, for instance, in the realm of state administration, that there are no longer any councils or representative bodies which have any share in policy-making or decision (although they may still exist as allegedly "advisory" bodies), and the "collegiate principle" has been replaced by one-man decision throughout the bureaucracy, one man always having complete authority over those beneath him and exclusive responsibility toward his superiors.[6] It is true that there has been a good deal of heated discussion in Nazi literature about whether administrative chiefs are real "leaders" in the Nazi sense, possessing, as some authors profess, a specific and intimate "loyalty relationship" with a closely-knit "followership," which allegedly is characteristic of leader-followership relations in the Party.[7] The argument does not, however, affect the decisive structural element of the leadership principle, as outlined above, which is its authoritarianism.[8]

Spheres of "sub-leadership" have been carefully established by Nazi theorists on the basis of the new leadership-pyramid set up in the various fields of public life.[9] Thus in the realm of state government, the various ministers are the main collaborators of the *Führer*. These are real "subleaders": "The Führer uses the Reich ministers not as subordinate executive organs," as a mere technical apparatus, but as "collaborators . . . who within their jurisdiction are able to act in a creative fashion . . . responsible co-creators of the *Führer*, who under the *Führer*'s guidance administer their offices independently."[10] Their co-signature of laws and decrees symbolizes the fact that the minister "is more than a mere technical instrument of the Führer, that he rather performs independent substantial services"; his signature implies his assuming responsibility toward the *Führer*.[11] Similarly, and on the same level, such top officials as the chief of the German Police or the Reich Labor Leader of the Labor Service are immediate "sub-leaders" under the *Führer*.[12]

While the Reich government thus constitutes the "supreme leadership council" (*Oberster Führerrat*), the main sub-leaders in the state bureaucracy, with their own autonomous sphere of jurisdiction, are, for instance, the Reich Governors, Provincial Presidents, District Presidents, and *Landrate*. The Lord Mayors and mayors of the municipalities, large and small, are likewise generally recognized as leaders of their communities since all representative institutions of local self-government were abolished[13]. "Today, each German municipality is headed by a community leader who bears sole responsibility for the whole administration, and thus has become the central figure in a completely different way from the former municipal heads."[14]

Similarly, economy has become "leadership economy" (*Führungswirtschaft*), headed at the top by Göring as Four-Year-Plan Commissioner and under him led by the leaders of the various organizations of so-called economic self-administration, *Wehrwirt schaftsführer,* etc.[15] There are the leaders and sub-leaders of the other "estates" organizations such as the Reich Food Estate, the Labor Front, the leaders of handicraft and artisans' guilds.[16] In the field of labor not only the Reich Labor Trustees but also each "leader of the enterprise" has been conceded such leadership functions.[17] In the realms of the army and the Party, of course, the principle has found its most conspicuous expression. As far as the latter is concerned, under the Führer and his deputy, the corps of the *Reichsleiter* constitute the supreme leadership council of the Party, under which there are the various regional and functional officials (*Hoheitstrager*) of Party and Party organizations.[18]

## II

Considering this very clear-cut order of jurisdictions in the Nazi leadership hierarchy it would appear as if there would be a similarly clear-cut system of responsibilities, based upon the individual directions and orders given by the various leaders and sub-leaders in their respective areas and fields of jurisdiction. This is however not the case. It would be the case in a non-totalitarian system where jurisdictions and their limits are based upon a well-defined law and where holders of authority or of official functions can be assumed to act within these limits. Under such systems, actions exceeding legal limitations are thus attributable to the individual office-holder who has acted or given orders to act in a specific instance, and not to his superiors. On the other hand, besides the leadership principle, the Nazi totalitarian system is characterized by a somewhat far-reaching exemption from legal restriction which the various agencies and organizations possess, and which gives their "leaders" not only unlimited authority but also practically unlimited latitude of action. This means that in general a leader or sub-leader does not rely so much on giving direct orders, but rather on formulating certain fundamental principles and policies, while delegating a large amount of discretion for carrying them out to their subordinates in the various fields and regions. One of the reasons why the Nazi system has relied more on the execution of implied policies than on outspoken orders lies in the very illegality or immorality of a great many of its policies. For instance, it would have been inadvisable, for security reasons as well as reasons of internal and external propaganda, to clad the policy of extermination of Jews, including its "technical" details (system of deportation, erection of gas chambers, removal and utilization of bodies, etc., etc.), into written directives handed down and crystalized from the policy-making top to the executive machine at the bottom. Therefore, at the top broad policies would be formulated, and the sub-leaders would be relied upon for carrying out these policies without their receiving any specific orders.

This is why the Nazi theory of leadership has stressed again and again that "leaders" (including sub-leaders) are on the one hand free from "formalistic" and "nomistic" legal restrictions, while on the other hand each one of them is strictly bound to observe the fundamental Nazi principles in all his actions, and to act in each specific instance "in the spirit of National Socialism." Thus according to Huber,[19] "the essence of each administrative act consists in the realization of the will of the Führer as supreme holder of political power." This however does not imply being bound to formal legality. The aim is not "to put administration under abstract norms, as in the liberal *Rechtsstaat* where the principle of the legality of administration meant that each executive act should be exactly predetermined by law . . . but rather, under the leadership state, not to limit the executive by specialized laws . . . Administrative action is intended to implement and crystalize the living law of the people, not a formal norm embodied in statutes. This is why the authorities may possibly act even without express legal basis, namely, whenever the unwritten living law of the people requires such action." Another Nazi theorist[20] similarly states that in the leadership state "as a matter of principle the official is put into a position of personal responsibility, without being able to hide behind given legal orders . . . The new state, in order to safeguard the leadership character of administration, tends to avoid too much regulation by law."

It must be said, however, that this latitude in devising and implementing policies without regard to limitations of law depended largely on the extent that the matter governed by a particular policy contained a "political" aspect. The greater the political aspect of the action concerned, the less it would be subject to legal restrictions. On the other hand, the more the action concerned itself with a purely "technical" field, the more it would be subject to express regulation. It is, of course, true that in the Nazi system everything, even the apparently most "neutral" or "technical" field, assumes a political character, since everything is liable to be judged in the light of its agreement or disagreement with Nazi *Weltanschauung* and policies. Moreover, even the activities of the most "technical" agencies may become auxiliary activities to some highly "political" action, for instance, where the President of a Railway Directorate is put in charge of providing for the transportation necessary to import foreign slave labor into the Reich, or to deport Jews to extermination camps. Nevertheless, it is possible to draw a general distinction between agencies and activities which are usually political and those which are not[21]. To the former belong, above all, the police, which, in the Nazi sense, has functions much broader than the mere safeguarding of security and order. It is likened to the armed forces in its overall function to defend the internal structure of state and society against any disturbance,[22] and its most important branch, the Political Police (Gestapo), is in reality all-powerful, since in the Nazi state the *Kompetenz-Kompetenz*, i.e., the right to decide about jurisdictions, lies with the political authority.

In the realm of the police, therefore, Nazi theory has most frankly recognized the principle of the basically "lawless" action of public authorities. The general "task" presumed to have been given to the police in the Nazi state—that of safeguarding the state and regime against any disturbance—implies the supremacy of any of its actions (whether in the form of decree, directive, internal instruction, or pure action) over any existing law: "The activity of the police is neither lawless nor illegal, . . . if it deviates from former police law, it creates new police law. In whatever form . . . it may appear, it changes the existing police law—even if the latter has the form of a statute—in a legally valid manner."[23] For the police is said to differ from all the other branches of public administration, "which work in solid and stable legal forms"; "it is solely the armed forces with their function to fight the external enemy and the Political Police in its fight against state-hostile tendencies which must be free from such restrictions in order to be able to fulfill their tasks."[24] One Nazi author,[25] in order to show the practically unlimited discretion of the police, has evolved a theory according to which "the police is the irrational and indefinite residuary portion of state sovereignty remaining after deducting all of the particular realms of sovereignty. Since the sovereignty of the National Socialist state cannot be rationally delimited, there has to be this ultimate and undefinable substance within the state . . . There is no positive statute which conveys jurisdiction to the police today. The police draws its legal competences merely from the essence of state sovereignty and its implementation by the Führer . . . The police touches and penetrates the liberty of the individual in an irregular fashion. . . . Any legal authorization here remains a fancy." Thus, police becomes "a function whose activities are determined solely through what is politically necessary," and the only "law" applicable to the police is the body of regulations which "distributes this political task among the different police authorities."

This means that the police as such can do whatever it deems necessary, without being restrained by legal limitations. The only legal restrictions necessary even under the Nazi system are those of an internal jurisdictional nature, telling this or that part of the police organization what it may do or may not do, i.e., delimiting functional and regional jurisdiction. As to means and measures there has been no limit: "The legal means at the disposal of the Political Police have not been regulated. They cannot be legally regulated, because the Political Police has to have a free hand in the choice of the measures which may become necessary . . . Since the essence of the Political Police lies in its function to combat all state-hostile tendencies, it has the right to have resort to any measure necessary for this task, as long as there are no laws expressly forbidding it . . . It has already been shown that after the issuing of the decree on the Protection of Nation and State of February 28, 1933, and the change from the liberal to the National Socialist concept of state and law such limits do no longer exist." There is therefore the "largest imaginable scale of legally permissible means."[26]

In veiled though sufficiently clear language one Nazi author, who apparently was not quite in agreement with this radical theory and practice,[27] has described how in the development of police law under Nazism legal limitation had to give way to complete lawlessness and arbitrariness. "Functions and jurisdiction of the Gestapo, as they are developed today, are by no means adequately described through the legal regulations which have been issued concerning them . . . The new structure was built with an accent on organization, not on substantive law. What was necessary and opportune at the moment had precedence over any intention to build up a system of well-defined laws. Thus, substantive police law has been of secondary importance only. . . . The concepts of security, order, and danger proved to be sufficiently elastic to justify any and every police action which purported to protect the community, the national wealth, and the order of societal life."[28]

## III

Considering the hierarchical structure of the Nazi leadership organization on the one hand, and the wide and indefinite realm of discretion given to each leader in the implementation of fundamental policies on the other hand, it appears possible to develop a new concept of responsibility for actions committed under the Nazi program. A system under which broad policies are devised at a certain level of leadership but where the execution of such policies takes place at lower levels, without the issuance of formal or written orders, and without the imposition of legal restrictions upon the lower state, would seem to place responsibility for whatever happens in the fulfillment of such policies, within the functional and regional realms of jurisdiction, upon the particular leaders who controlled such realms, whether or not they can be proved to have given any specific orders or even to have known of the particular methods used in carrying out the general policies. For example: If a general policy adopted on the highest level of leadership has been to the effect to "eliminate all Jews from European life once and for all," and if in pursuance of such policy a large part of the Jewish population under Nazi rule has actually been exterminated, the acts of physical extermination may be attributed to all leaders and sub-leaders who, under the highest leadership, had functional and regional jurisdiction in connection with the implementation of the Jewish policies of the Nazi regime. All of them can be presumed to have known the Nazi program and the Nazi policies in this respect, all of them have used their positions to implement them, and all of them have known that in the execution of policy directives no legal restrictions would be observed. Whether or not under such conditions, they have been aware of the particular details of execution in specific cases, appears immaterial.

The Nazis themselves have admitted to this interpretation of responsibility of "leaders." Hitler has said:[29] "Whoever wants to be a leader has with the highest and unlimited authority also the ultimate and heaviest responsibility." Nazi authors have repeatedly stressed this "responsibility" angle of Hitler's power.[30] Since under the Nazi system the responsibility of the top leaders was practically unenforceable, the reason for this emphasis on responsibility was, therefore, obviously propagandistic: it was meant to show that, unlike "tyrannical" or "dictatorial" regimes, the Nazi regime was not one of arbitrariness and lack of responsibility.[31] It has however been stressed with equal forcefulness for the sub-leaders, where responsibility might mean actual answering for one's actions and behavior to one's superiors. It is claimed that only under the leadership principle can there be genuine responsibility: "The responsibility here imposed is clear and unequivocal, nobody can dodge it in favor of an anonymous majority, it is undodgeable (*unabwätzbar*)."[32] This leader-responsibility has been defined by Nazi theorists in a much broader way than criminal responsibility is usually defined. According to Nazi theory, the leader has to answer for what those entrusted to his leadership do, even if, in some particular case, they have acted against instructions and without any concurring guilt (intent or negligence) on the part of the leader: "There is a deeper meaning in the fact that an officer can under no circumstances use the excuse that his men have failed . . . The genuine leader regards the guilt of his followership as his own and accepts it, even if, as the case may be, he has been really without guilt himself. He himself may make responsible those who have actually failed, but toward his superiors he alone is the guilty one. Only thus one can understand the principle of authority over those below, responsibility to those above in all its profound meaning."[33]

There may indeed be a "deeper meaning" and a more profound justification in holding responsible those who under the Nazi system have occupied positions of higher leadership. In a system based upon terror, on the one hand, and propaganda (opinion monopoly) on the other, "followers" on the lower levels of the leadership pyramid can be said to have almost been deprived of their capacity to act freely. They have become more or less automatons through physical or psychological influence, and their actions should legally be attributed to those who have used these means of influence.

In Nazi theory, actions referred to as "failures" and for which the leaders should answer are, of course, actions which are *not* in accordance with the Party program and Party policies. In reversing these standards and in making the Nazi leaders responsible for what *we* consider as war crimes, they would indeed have to answer for what has actually been done in accordance with their own standards and policies. The "law" according to which the Nazi leaders have acted was in reality the absence of any legal limitation and since their actions have been in contradiction to what an over-whelming majority of peoples and nations consider as fundamental standards of law and decency,[34] the application of these standards to them seems to imply not the absence of but the vindication of justice.

## Appendix I

In the following, a few examples are given for the implementation of the leadership principle in various fields of public life by way of legislation. It must be kept in mind that, while in some fields this principle was introduced by express statutory or decree provisions, it was never expressly introduced into others, where it was simply implied.

a) Into the Reich Government itself the leadership principle was introduced by implication only.[35] Führer and government have become free from any control by the *Reichstag*.[36] The law on the Abolition of the *Reichsrat* (Federal Council)[37] freed the government from control formerly exercised by that body.

b) Leadership principle in the political sub-divisions of the Reich was implemented by

i. the abolition of the legislative assemblies of the States;[38]
ii. the Second Law for the Coordination of the States with the Reich of April 7, 1933[39] and the Law on Reich Governors of January 30, 1935,[40] establishing the Reich Governors as regional leaders in the non-Prussian parts of the Reich;
iii. the Second Decree concerning the Reconstruction of the Reich of November 27, 1934,[41] conferring a similar leadership position upon the Provincial Presidents in the Prussian Provinces.

c) The German Municipal Code of January 30, 1935[42] introduced the leadership principle into local government of cities, towns, and villages, by expressly endowing the mayor with leadership powers (art. 32) and providing for merely advisory functions of municipal councils (art. 48).

d) In the field of labor law, the leadership principle was embodied in the basic Law concerning the Organization of National Labor of January 20, 1934.[43] Art. 1 established the entrepreneur as leader of the enterprise, art. 2 conferred all powers of decision upon this leader in his relations with the employees as "followership," and art. 5 declared that the Councils of Trust, established by the law, had only advisory functions.

e) In the field of economic controls the Decree concerning the Four Year Plan of October 18, 1936[44] provided for the appointment of Goering as leader of the setup and conferred broadest leadership powers upon him. In other fields of economic organization, the leadership principle was more implied, as, for instance, in the First Decree concerning the Execution of the Law on the Preparation of the Organic Structure of German Economy of November 27, 1934[45], where the principle is implied in the organization of the various economic "Groups" and "Chambers."

f) In the field of agricultural controls, the major agency dealing with these matters, the Reich Food Estate, was created on the basis of the leadership principle, the Reich Peasant Leader being established as leader of the Food Estate: First Decree concerning the Provisional Structure of the Reich Food Estate of December 8, 1933, issued by the Reich Minister of Food and Agriculture.

g) Finally, there may be mentioned two organizations somewhere in the middle between state and Party organizations. The Law on the Reich Labor Service of July 26, 1935[46] established the Reich Labor Leader of the Labor Service as leader of the Labor Service (art. 8). The Law concerning the Hitler Youth of December 1, 1936[47] gave corresponding leadership powers to the Reich Youth Leader (art. 9).

## Appendix II

### Evaluation of Sources Referred to in the Paper

In the following, authors are referred to in the sequence in which their writings appear in the footnotes of the paper.

H.B. *Brausse*: Young Nazi student of political science and public law, specialist in theory of "leadership."

Hitler: *Mein Kampf*: This book, under Nazism, was recognized as a kind of source of law, in authority taking precedence even over official laws and decrees.

E.R. *Huber*: One of the three or four foremost Nazi authorities on theory of the state and on public law, notably constitutional law. Foremost protagonist of the "new Nazi concepts and doctrines" which Nazi theoreticians opposed to "old liberal thought."

Hans *Frank*: In addition to his other leadership functions (Reich Minister, Governor General of Poland), official "leader" of German (Nazi) lawyers. His statements, therefore, have quasi-official character.—The periodical *Deutsches Recht* was the official publication of the Nazi Lawyers Association (NSRB).

Otto *Koellreutter*: Professor of public law at the University of Munich. Prior to 1933 a German Nationalist, he turned Nazi in 1933, and defended the principal Nazi tenets and doctrines although, from time to time, trying to preserve some remnants of pre-Nazi thinking and concepts in the face of the more radical theorists.

C.H. *Ule*: One of the younger Nazi students of public law, student of E.R. Huber.—The periodical *Verwaltungsarchiv* is an old German public law periodical which, of course, was Nazified after 1933.

Reinhard *Hoehn*: One of the few foremost Nazi theoreticians of public law and political science. Like Huber tried to create new "Nazi" concepts for this science.

Theodor *Maunz*: Nazi author specializing in administrative law. His writings contain certain remnants of pre-Nazi doctrine.

*Zeitschrift fuer die gesamte Staatsreichtswissenschaft*: Old and renowned German political science review. Nazified after 1933.

Arnold *Koettgen*: Authority on administrative law. Became outwardly, but otherwise not too thoroughly, Nazified after 1933.

Johannes *Weidemann*: Nazi specialist in municipal government.

Hans *Frank* (editor): *Deutsches Verwaltungsrecht* (1937): The volume contains contributions by several of the most authoritative Nazi authors on public law and administration and can thus be considered as quasi-official.

Sigmund *Dannbeck*: Attorney-at-law, author on topics of administrative law.

W. *Laforet*: Professor of public law. Belonged to Center Party prior to 1933, not particularly thoroughly Nazified after 1933.

Ernst *Fraenkel*: German lawyer and political scientist now living in this country. His *Dual State* is one of the best treaties on the Nazi legal and political structure, abundant in source material.

Werner *Best*: Nazi of the old guard, became legal advisor to the Gestapo after 1933 and one of the Nazis' foremost experts on police law and police—in particular Gestapo—practice.

*Deutsche Verwaltung*: A Nazi periodical dealing with questions of public law.

Walter *Hamel*: One of the younger Nazi theorists of political science and public law.

# 28

## Herbert Marcuse

## *NAZI PLANS FOR DOMINATING GERMANY AND EUROPE: THE NAZI MASTER PLAN*

(August 7, 1945)

Editor's note: R&A 3114. In a letter from Franz Neumann to George Demos, dated June 13, 1945, in which are listed the members of the Central European Section involved in the research on war crimes, Marcuse is indicated as the general manager of project R&A 3114, "Nazi Plans to Dominate Europe" (RG 226, entry 37, box 2, folder: Central European Section). In addition, in a list of reports to be realized in the project "Nazi Plans for Dominating Germany and Europe," Marcuse is noted as the author of the general outlining text on the Nazi master plan (RG 226, entry 146, box 38, folder 534: Miscellaneous Washington Files).

The text is accompanied by eight appendixes, not included here, containing criteria for classifying the main sources cited; electoral statistics; a speech made by Hitler on January 30, 1944; extracts from the Civil Affairs Handbook *Communications and Control of Public Opinion*; the founding program of the National Socialist Party; a Nazi bibliography; Wehrmacht personnel in Nazi companies; and the summary of a conversation held in the Reich's offices on November 4, 1937.

Classification: Secret

### I. Introduction

This paper attempts to demonstrate the existence of a comprehensive Nazi plan for aggression, conquest, and domination in Europe and even beyond Europe. The plan was conceived and developed chiefly by the National Socialist German Workers' Party (NSDAP) with its affiliated and supervised organizations, in conjunction with certain influential circles among the German armed forces, the high civil service, and the industrial leadership of Germany. The scope, details, and instruments of the plan were developed in several stages, which may roughly be defined as (1) from 1920 to 1933, the year in which the Nazis seized power in Germany; (2) 1933 to 1934, in which year they completed the establishment of totalitarian control over Germany; (3) 1934 to 1939, during which period they carried out their total preparation for the war of aggression; (4) 1939 to 1944, in which years they executed their policy of domination throughout the occupied parts of Europe. On all four stages, the execution of the plan involved the use of unlawful means.

## II. The Role of the Party in the Nazi Plan for Domination

### A. The NSDAP, Its Origins and Early Development

The chief actor in the Nazi plan for domination was the NSDAP. According to Hitler's own account in *Mein Kampf*, and according to authoritative Nazi publications,[1] the first organizational nucleus of the NSDAP was the German Workers' Party, founded in January 1919 in Munich by Anton Drexler. In the same year, Adolf Hitler, then still a soldier in the Reichswehr, contacted the German Workers' Party, in his own words, "on superior orders" by the military authorities. He participated in the discussions of the Party, which, in the following year (1920), assumed the name of National Socialist German Workers' Party, and he acquired a Party organ of his own, the *Völkische Beobachter*. The first major public meeting of the NSDAP took place in Munich on 24 February 1920, with Hitler as speaker. At this meeting, Hitler publicly announced the program of the Party. On 1 August 1921, Hitler was elected "Leader" of the Party. The first Party Congress took place on 27 January 1923.

Whereas the original group reportedly consisted of only seven members, the Party membership rose, according to the official Party statistics,[2] to 849,009 in January 1933, prior to the installation of the Nazi Government. In 1935, the Party counted 2,493,890 members, 5.2 per cent of whom had joined prior to 14 September 1930, and 28.8 per cent from 14 September 1930 to 30 January 1933, the day of the establishment of the Nazi Government. The Party participated for the first time in the Reichstag elections in 1924, when it obtained 32 seats or 6.5 per cent of the total vote; in 1932, in the last free election, it obtained 196 seats or 33.1 per cent of the total vote.

Beginning in 1921 with the establishment of the *Sturm Abteilungen* (SA), the Party founded numerous formations and affiliated and supervised organizations[3] which, after the seizure of power, covered all fields of public life (political, economic, cultural, military, etc.).

Prior to 1933, the most active of these organizations were the SA (established in 1921) and the SS (established 1923 and reorganized in 1925), para-military organizations which were the chief instruments in the terroristic activity of the NSDAP.[4]

After the seizure of power on 30 January 1933, the NSDAP was made the sole political party in Germany and "the sole bearer of the German state idea."[5] At the same time, personal identity was established between the Party leadership and holders of key positions in the Government; Hitler as the Leader of the Party became Chancellor of the Reich; General von Blomberg, Divisional Commander of the *Reichswehr*, joined the Hitler government as War Minister, and the Party established control over all spheres of business, culture and education. Totalitarian control over all media of public opinion and communication was centralized in the Reich Ministry of Propaganda and Popular Enlightenment, headed by Goebbels. From 1933–34 onward, totalitarian amalgamation between the NSDAP and the Government prevailed throughout the territory of the Reich.[6]

## B. The Key Figures

The persons who, during the time of the formulation of the Party program, and during the building up of the basic organizational structure (roughly 1920–23), played the decisive part in the NSDAP were, in addition to Hitler:[7]

- Hermann Esser, chief editor of the *Völkische Beobachter*, (VB) in 1920
- Dietrich Eckart, chief editor of the VB in 1921 (together with Alfred Rosenberg)
- Rudolf Hess, who joined the NSDAP in June 1920
- Alfred Rosenberg, chief editor of the VB 1921 (together with Dietrich Eckart)
- Max Amann, *Geschaftsführer* of the NSDAP in 1921
- Gottfried Feder, political lecturer in 1919–20, and official commentator of the Party program
- Wilhelm Frick, Hitler's protector in the Munich Police Directorate in 1920–23

This group of key party men was later joined by others who became Hitler's close advisers and collaborators—notably Göring, Goebbels, Himmler, Bormann, Ribbentrop, etc.

After the seizure of power, it may be said that aside from Hitler, members of the following groups were mainly responsible for the formulation and execution of Party policy:[8]

- the *Reichsleiter* of the NSDAP
- the heads of the *Reichsdienststellen* of the NSDAP
- the *Gauleiter*

the heads of the formations, and affiliated and supervised organizations

This paper does not attempt to fasten responsibility for the instigation and execution of specific war crimes on any specific individuals, groups, or organizations. However, the fact that the objectives of the NSDAP were publicly stated, and that every Party member was obligated to know and to fight for the realization of these objectives (see II D 1 and 2 below), makes every member of the NSDAP who voluntarily joined the Party co-responsible. The same holds true for the affiliated and supervised organizations.

After the seizure of power and the complete amalgamation between NSDAP and Government (see V C below) under Nazi control, the objectives of the NSDAP became also those of the German Government.

From this time onward, therefore, the leading government authorities share responsibility with the Nazi Party.

## C. Objectives

The objectives of the NSDAP are to be found in the following sources:

1. The program of the NSDAP, the so-called 25 Points (1920). The program was declared "unchangeable" (*unabänderlich*) by the General Meeting of Party program on 22 May 1926.[9]

   After the seizure of power, the official *Nationalsozialistisches Jahrbuch* called the Party program the "fundamental political law of the state."[10]
2. Hitler's book *Mein Kampf*, written in 1924.
3. Books, pamphlets, articles, and speeches by leading persons in the NSDAP and its affiliated organizations, such as the persons mentioned above.
4. Articles in the press of the NSDAP, chiefly the *Völkische Beobachter* and its subsidiaries; also the *Angriff*, and the *Stürmer*.
5. The evidence brought forth in the trials for high treason against Hitler and others in 1924 and 1930.[11]

   The Program of the NSDAP (1920) contained the chief elements of the Nazi plan for domination and conquest:

   a. Incorporation of all Germans into a Greater German Reich (point 1).
   b. Abolition of the peace treaties of Versailles and St. Germain (point 2).
   c. Demand for "land and soil" (colonies) (point 3)[12].
   d. Racial discrimination and anti-Semitism (point 4).

e. Fight against the democratic-parliamentary system (point 6).
f. Rearmament (point 22).

In point of fact, the objectives of the NSDAP were much more far-reaching than the brief and careful formulations of the Program indicate. This becomes clear if they are taken in conjunction with the other sources enumerated in II C above. Viewed in this context, and in the light of the activities of the NSDAP from 1920 to the seizure of power, the objectives may be described as follows:

a. Overthrow of the established democratic-parliamentary government of Germany by all means, legal and illegal.
b. Establishment of a totalitarian Nazi dictatorship with complete elimination of all political, ideological, religious, racial and other opposition, and with the abolition of civil rights and liberties.
c. Full-fledged rearmament of Germany and systematic preparation for war in all fields of social, economic, and cultural life.
d. Use of the new military force for incorporating foreign territory into the German Reich and occupying more territory for the German "living space."

The fact that the NSDAP had these objectives, and that they were systematically executed through the use of force, violence, and other unlawful means, will be demonstrated in the following chapters.

### D. Special Characteristics

#### 1. The Leadership Principle

The NSDAP was organized according to the "leadership principle": "The *Führer* idea is the basis for the organization of the Party."[13] This meant that the Party was governed and administered by the authority of the *Führer*, whose decrees, orders, and decisions were the supreme law of the Party simply by virtue of the fact that they emanated from him. As it was officially stated: "The will of the *Führer* is the supreme law in the Party."[14] The will of the *Führer* involves not only absolute authority, which had to be obeyed unquestioningly, but also infallibility. "The *Führer* is always right" said the first of the Commandments for the National Socialist.[15] The Party Program, given by the *Führer*, had, for every member, the authority of a dogma: "The Program shall be a dogma to you: it demands of you the utmost devotion to the Movement."[16]

While the leadership principle assured the binding nature of Hitler's statements and declarations for the aims and policies of the entire Party and, through it, for the entire movement, the same principle established the full responsibility of all individual "sub-leaders" within the province and jurisdiction of their office or position.[17] For the leadership principle applied not only to Hitler as the supreme leader, but also to all the various sub-leaders under him, and thus permeated the entire Nazi hierarchy. The various *Hoheitsträger* of the Party were, in their respective provinces, themselves *Führer*: every Political Leader (*Politischer Leiter*) was a "political Führer"[18] and the entire Party was an Order of Leaders (*Führerorden*).[19] The National Socialist idea of leadership presupposed a "full feeling of responsibility"[20] in every leader. By the same token, every leader was vested with full authority in his province (*Hoheitsgebiet*):

> "The Hoheitsträger, for example, is superior (*Vorgesetzter*) to all Political Leaders in his *Hoheits*-gebiet. He possesses in every respect unconditional authority (*unbedingte Anordnungsgewalt*) with regard to them."[21]

However, this does not free the sub-leaders from the obligation of unconditional obedience to the *Führer*:

> "All Political Leaders are to be considered (*gelten*) as appointed by the *Führer* and are responsible to him."[22]
>
> but:
>
> "They enjoy *full authority* over those below."[23]

## 2. Advocacy of Direct Action

The NSDAP differed from most political parties by the fact that it bound its members much more closely to the principles and objectives of the Party, and that it was in all its parts geared to direct action, endorsing illegal and unlawful action whenever such was deemed necessary to promote the Party's goals.

As to the first, Hitler's *Mein Kampf*, in laying down the organizational principles of the NSDAP,[24] contrasted it with the "bourgeois parties" in that all members of the NSDAP were bound to fight actively for the aims of the Party, to "stand up for them and to spread them," to "exchange the slogan of a weak and cowardly defense with the battle cry of courageous and brutal attack." Accordingly, Hitler distinguished sharply between mere "followers" and actual "members," and reserved membership only for the most valuable and reliable candidates. By the same token, membership in the Party was, at least up to 1933–1934, entirely voluntary (as it was for the SA and SS), and the members formed "a definitely limited, tightly organized political community of believers and fighters, uniform in spirit and will power. . . ."[25]

That the NSDAP was a party of direct action follows almost inevitably from its fundamental opposition to the democratic-parliamentary system.[26] The party did not recognize the democratic processes as binding and used them only as an instrument for boring from within and for enhancing its opportunities for Nazi propaganda.[27] For the same reason, the Party leadership openly endorsed the illegal struggle against the established government, and made extensive use of unlawful means.[28]

## E. Early Supporters

### 1. The Reichswehr

That Hitler worked as a political agent of the *Reichswehr* as early as 1919 is demonstrated by his own account in *Mein Kampf*. There he relates that in May 1919, while doing service in the *Reichswehr*, he "was summoned to join a commission for the examination of the events of the revolution in the Second Infantry Regiment."[29] He was reportedly instrumental in singling out the "red" soldiers for execution. A little later, he says that:

> "One day I received orders from my headquarters (*von der mir vorgesetzten Dienststelle*) to find out what was behind an apparently political society which, under the name of 'German Workers' Party', intended to hold a meeting on one of the following days . . ."[30]

This is confirmed by the short biographical note on Hitler in Cuno Horkenbach's *Das Deutsche Reich von 1918 bis Heute*, edited with the help of "Reich and State Authorities" in 1935; which describes him as

> "until 1920 in the *Reichswehr*, entrusted with the functions of a *Bildungsoffizier*" (officer for political training).[31]

From that time on until 1933, the relations between the Army and the NSDAP were veiled in secrecy; and after 1923 the *Reichswehr* withdrew officially from politics, and its open reunion with the Nazi movement took place only after Hitler's seizure of power.[32]

### 2. The Free Corps

The Free Corps were para-military organizations which sprang up at the end of the First World War. They did not recognize the stipulations of the Treaty of Versailles and fought a private war on their own in order to retain the old German frontiers, especially in the East. They were, moreover, violently opposed to the democratic government of the Weimar Republic and engaged in a bitter terroristic campaign against its supporters.[33] The Free Corps were thus in their basic objectives in agreement with those of the early Nazi movement; many of the Free Corps leaders, indeed, later became prominent in the Party.[34]

3. The Industrialists

The point at which influential industrial circles started to support the NSDAP is still unclear. By 1923, however, contact between the Party and one of the most important industrial combines of Germany had already been established, and financial contributions were forthcoming. This is the testimony of the magnate, Fritz Thyssen. He relates that, in 1923, he met General Ludendorff, who told him that the NSDAP was the only party capable of accomplishing "national recovery." Thyssen writes:

> "I followed his advice. I attended several public meetings organized by Hitler. It was then that I realized his oratorical gifts and his ability to lead the masses. What impressed me most, however, was the order that reigned in his meetings, the almost military discipline of his followers."[35]

A few days later, Thyssen met Hitler personally in the presence of Ludendorff:

> "Ludendorff and Hitler agreed to undertake a military expedition against Saxony in order to depose the Communist government of Dr. Zeigner.[36] The ultimate aim of the proposed expedition was to overthrow the Weimar democracy, whose weakness was leading Germany into anarchy.
>
> Funds were lacking. . . . He (Ludendorff) had already solicited and obtained the help of several industrialists, particularly that of Herr Minnoux of the Stinnes firm. For my part, I gave him about one hundred thousand gold marks. This was my first contribution to the National Socialist Party."[37]

This testimony of Thyssen's also confirms the fact that the overthrow of the established democratic government by force was the avowed aim of the NSDAP, and that certain industrialists actively supported this aim. That financial support by heavy industry continued during the following years and that contact was maintained between the NSDAP and the Rhenish-Westphalian Coal Syndicate is indicated in another statement by Fritz Thyssen. According to Thyssen, in 1928 Rudolf Hess approached him

> "on the initiative of old Geheimrat Kirdorf, for many years the director general of the Rhenish-Westphalian Coal Syndicate, with whom I was on friendly terms. Hess explained to me that the Nazis had bought the Brown House and had great difficulty in paying for it. I placed Hess in possession of the required funds on conditions which, however, he has never fulfilled."[38]

It is noteworthy that, in 1928, Thyssen was Chairman of the Board of *Vereinigte Stahlwerke*, the greatest German steel combine. Thyssen furthermore states that "Kirdorf had been a member of the National Socialist Party long before me."[39]

Contributions on a large scale by German industry to the NSDAP, however, were probably not made before 1932; they are discussed in IV B below.

## III. The Master Plan and the Stages of Its Execution

The execution of the Nazi program necessitated the development of a comprehensive plan covering domestic as well as foreign policy, activities in Germany as well as in foreign countries.

When the Nazis began their activity shortly after the end of the first World War, they were faced with a parliamentary-democratic German government committed to the fulfillment of the Treaty of Versailles. The majority of the German population, moreover, supported the Government and was set against a foreign policy of aggressive expansion. Consequently, in order to be able to achieve their goal, the Nazis had to begin by overthrowing the democratic-parliamentary government of the Weimar Republic. Moreover, since a great part of the German population remained opposed to the Nazi program, and since the realization of the program required the *total* mobilization of Germany, the Nazis had to strive for the establishment of a totalitarian dictatorship. The struggle against the democratic-parliamentary government and the fight for a totalitarian dictatorship were therefore the first stage of the execution of the Nazi master plan. This stage was completed in 1933. After the Nazi Government had been installed in power in 1933, it had to establish totalitarian control over all spheres of public and private life, for the preservation of democratic rights and liberties was incompatible with its authoritarian philosophy and with its determination to stay in power. This stage of the master plan involved the elimination of the entire political, ideological, racial, and religious opposition, unlimited control over all media of communication, over education and welfare, over the entire machinery of administration, etc. This task was carried out during the first years of the Nazi regime.

With the establishment of totalitarian control over Germany and the elimination of all opposition, the Nazis concentrated on "all-out" preparation for the war of aggression. This preparation took place on at least three levels:

a. ideologically: the development of the conception of *Lebensraum* and of the racial superiority of the Germans;
b. militarily: the building up of the German *Wehrmacht* in all its branches, and the transformation of the entire national economy into a war economy;

c. politically, economically, culturally, infiltration and Fifth Column activity in foreign countries.

Germany's new war potential was then systematically tested by open military action: in the Rhineland occupation, Spain, Austria, Czechoslovakia.

After these tests had proved successful, the Nazi Government in 1939 launched the European war. The master plan reached its final stage with the conquest of the greatest part of the European *Lebensraum* for Germany; the conquered territories were transformed into parts of the German living space and ruthlessly exploited and despoiled for the benefit of the German war machine and in the interests of permanent German domination of the continent.

In one of his surveys of the history of the Nazi movement, Hitler himself described the above outlined four stages of the Master plan as the four great tasks of the Nazi regime:[40]

"*Task No. 1*—By the solution of social problems, the Reich had again to acquire its lost internal social peace; that is, the elements of class cleavage– the bourgeoisie and the proletariat–had to be eliminated in all their manifestations, and in their place a national community set up. The appeal to reason had to be supplemented with a *ruthless elimination of the viciously resisting elements in all camps*.

"*Task No. 2*—The social-political unity of the Nation was to be supplemented by national-political unity; that is, in place of the Reich body rent asunder not only politically but also in its statehood, *the National Socialist unified State had to arise*, with a structure and with a leadership equipped to face and withstand even the greatest trials of attack and pressure.

"*Task No. 3*—The unified State built upon national and political foundations had the task of *immediately creating that Wehrmacht* which in its intellectual outlook and moral attitude, its numerical strength, and in its material armament could serve as a satisfactory instrument in the tasks of self-assertion. After the rest of the world had rejected all German offers for the limitation of armaments, the Reich had to fashion its own *armament* accordingly.

"*Task No. 4*—In order to be able at all to maintain her position in Europe with a chance of success, there was necessary the *incorporation of all those countries which are populated by Germans or which constitute areas belonging to the German Reich* for more than a thousand years and which are territories indispensable nationally and economically, for the preservation of the Reich, that is, for its political and military defense."

The execution of the master plan involved on all stages the use of force, violence, and other unlawful means. This followed in a general way from the principles of Nazi philosophy, which rejected pacifism, humanitarianism, and democratic values as decadent cowardice, and which proclaimed the natural right of the strong and of the sword. The use of force and other unlawful means was furthermore necessitated by:

1. The outspoken aim of the Nazi movement of replacing the democratic-parliamentary system by a Nazi *dictatorship* (documentation below in Ch. IV);
2. The outspoken aim of eliminating all opposition ruthlessly and with all available means (documentation below in Ch. V, A.);
3. The outspoken aim of disregarding "artificial" national frontiers and of carrying out Nazi propaganda and activities in foreign countries (documentation below Ch. VI, B.);
4. The declared Nazi policy of treating occupied territories as parts of the German *Lebensraum* and of mobilizing them totally for the German war machine (documentation below, Ch. VII.).

There are, moreover, numerous statements by responsible Nazi leaders explicitly endorsing the use of force and other unlawful means (quoted below, *passim*).

## IV. The Overthrow of the Democratic-Parliamentary German Government and the Fight for the Establishment of a Nazi Dictatorship

In order to conquer new German living space, the Nazis had first to seize power in Germany and to prepare Germany for the event of war:

> "For oppressed countries will not be brought back into the bosom of the common Reich by means of fiery protests, but by a mighty sword. To forge this sword is the task of the domestic political leadership of a people; to guard the work of forging and to seek comrades in arms is the task of the foreign policy leadership."[41]

The domestic policy of the Nazis was thus the first stage in their foreign policy of aggression and conquest. This policy involved the overthrow of the established democratic-parliamentary government of the Weimar Republic by a Nazi dictatorship.

### A. Political Terror against the Democratic Government

The German state as it was established after the downfall of the monarchy was a parliamentary democracy. Within the framework of this democracy, preparation for the establishment of German supremacy over Europe was impossible because of opposition from the democratic parties, which were committed to a policy of peaceful international cooperation, and to fulfillment of the Versailles Treaty or its revision by legal and peaceful means. As the election figures from 1919 to Hitler's rise to power show, the anti-militarist and anti-expansionist parties were consistently backed by the majority of the population.

Under these circumstances, the removal of the democratic-parliamentary government was the precondition for the attainment of the goals of Nazism.

> "From the very first day the watchword was: unlimited struggle against Berlin. . . . One thing was certain: Lossow, Kahr, and Seisser had the same goal that we had:[42] to get rid of the Reich government with its present international and parliamentary position and to replace it by an anti-parliamentary government."[43]

That destruction of the Weimar Constitution and of the parliamentary system was the goal of the Nazi movement[44] was established by the People's Court of Munich, District 1, on 1 April 1924, after reviewing the evidence produced at the trial of the Nazi leaders for the unsuccessful Hitler putsch of November 1923. After the putsch, the goal remained the same.

In 1927, for example, Wilhelm Frick declared that:

> "our next goal still remains the conquest of the political power of the state; it is the prerequisite for the realization of our ideals."[45]

The "unlimited" struggle of the Nazis was directed against the democratic-parliamentary system as such, because this system everywhere stood in the way of the dictatorial leadership and control which was the aim of the Nazi movement:

> "The character of the parliament . . . obstructs this unifying leadership . . . so the first act of annihilation must be directed against the Jewish-democratic parliamentarism."[46]

> "The parliamentary system is nothing more than a state-sanctioned nuisance and a Jewish racket. Do you know the difference between the parliamentarian system and the skin of a sausage? Both are only fit for a cat."[47]

Gottfried Feder, the official interpreter of the Nazi Party program, stated that:

> "the nuisance of the parliamentarian-democratic right to vote will be swept away."[48]

> "The National Socialists long for the day when the well-known lieutenant with his ten men will put an inglorious but well-deserved end to this infernal sham (the parliament) and will open the way for a racial dictatorship."[49]

In his booklet *Der Nazi-Sozi*, Goebbels openly claimed the right of the Nazi movement to seize the state power and to shape the state by dictatorial force:

> "History is replete with examples showing that a young and determined minority has always been able to overthrow the rule of a corrupt and disintegrated majority . . . Thus it will be with us. Once we have conquered the state, the state is ours. Then shall we, and we alone, be responsible bearers of the state. . . . Then, by dictatorial force, we will reshape the state according to our principles."[50]

The Nazi party units were to be trained systematically "in the nature of dictatorship" for the day of the seizure of power. For example, in the official collection of organizational circulars published by the *Gau* Headquarters of Greater Berlin, there appears the following statement:

> "The Party, or rather its units, must be the school through which he (the National Socialist) must pass to obtain practical training in the nature of the dictatorship, so that he can begin the real work on the day that power is won."[51]

Hitler's emphasis on the "unlimited character" of the struggle against the established form of government indicates the endorsement of force and other unlawful means. Such endorsement was repeatedly proclaimed by the Nazi leadership:

> "We are not afraid to engage in political activities, though we be condemned as illegal."[52]

> "Should the Party be prohibited, then we shall continue to work illegally."[53]

> "to prepare the downfall of this order and to overthrow it by all available means."[54]

> "Just as Mussolini exterminated the Marxists in Italy, so must we also succeed in accomplishing the same through dictatorship and terror."[55]

> "Fight daily and, if it be necessary, on the barricades. This fight will be fought with machine guns, mines, and grenades."[56]

"Adolph Hitler does not leave us the least bit of uncertainty when he says—In this fight heads will roll in the sand, either theirs or ours. Therefore we must see that it is the heads of others that roll . . ."[57]

After the failure of the Hitler putsch of 1923, the Nazi leadership officially abandoned the endorsement of illegal means and oriented the strategy and tactics of the movement on legality. However, the Nazi leadership openly declared that they would use the legal rights and liberties granted to the opposition by the democratic state only in order to undermine and destroy this state. This was brought out specifically when the Nazis decided to enter parliament and to work as a parliamentary party:

"We enter parliament in order to supply ourselves, in the arsenal of democracy, with its own weapons. We become members of the Reichstag in order to paralyze the Weimar sentiment with its own assistance. If democracy is so stupid as to give us free tickets and *per diem* for this "blockade" (*Barendienst*), that is its own affair."[58]

"We do not come as friends, nor even as neutrals. We come as enemies: As the wolf bursts into the flock, so we come."[59]

Actually, the terroristic struggle waged by the Nazi Party continued throughout the period of the Weimar Republic (see documentation below, V). It should be noted that the statements on the use of violence and terroristic means quoted above refer to the period after 1923. And as late as 1932 Hitler declared:

"If the present regime does not make way for us, we will remove it."[60]

Indeed, the history of the Nazi movement was, from its inception, a chronicle of all forms of terror: murders, street battles, assaults, blackmail, etc.[61] It waged its terroristic fight chiefly with organized bands of the Nazi Party and its affiliated para-military organizations. The first reservoir of the Nazi movement was the so-called Free Corps, armed organizations which sprang up immediately after the end of the first World War and which fought a brutal war of their own, not only against the frontier regulations of the Treaty of Versailles but also against the democratic forces in Germany. The criminal history of the Nazi movement begins with the *Feme* murders committed by these Free Corps;[62] many of the persons involved in these murders subsequently became prominent Nazi leaders, and the ratio of former Free Corps leaders in the Nazi hierarchy was very high.

On 3 August 1921, Hitler established the first of his own para-military organizations, the *SA*. Its avowed task was to make the NSDAP "the master of the street:"[63]

> "Possession of the street is the key to the state power—that was what the *SA* marched and fought for."

In 1923, the *SA* was reorganized into a military unit (*Wehrverband*), to be mobilized for "active resistance against foreign domination" (in the Ruhr territory, then occupied by the French).[64] After the Hitler *putsch* of November 1923, the Reich Commissar for Bavaria, Von Kahr, prohibited the *SA*, but it continued to exist illegally."[65]

Pfeffer von Salomon, then the Supreme Leader of the *SA*, defined the organization in 1928 as follows:

> "The *SA* is the militant force of the Movement; it is the personification of the will to power of a political organization."[66]

The famous line of the Horst Wessel Song, the official Party anthem—"Clear the street for the Brown Battalions"—epitomizes the function of the *SA* as the terroristic shock troops in the fight for the establishment of the Nazi dictatorship. The same function for the *SA* is indicated in the statement of Curt von Ulrich, its Inspector General, to the effect that the present rulers will disappear overnight

> "when our day comes: free the streets for the Brown Battalions, free the streets for the Storm Troopers."[67]

The other chief terroristic organization of the Nazi movement was the *SS*. Its nucleus was the *Stosstrupp Hitler* (Assault Troop Hitler),[68] founded in 1923; its designation indicates its function. Prohibited in 1923, the *SS* was reestablished in 1925 as *Schutz Staffeln* (Protective Guards);[69] together with the *SA*, it "protected" Nazi meetings and demonstrations during the following years. Official Nazi sources described the *SS* as an "ever-reliable troop, an elite troop of the Party," as an "instrument of unconditional utilization (*Einsatzmöglichkeit*) for the *Führer*,"[70] and as the "political ideological fighting league (*weltanschauliche Kampfbund*) of the Party."[71] According to the same sources, the first task of the *SS* was

> "the protection of the *Führer* and of the speakers of the Party from bodily attacks by political enemies."[72]

After Hitler's rise to power, the *SS* developed as the leading and privileged elite organization of the Party and was everywhere, inside and outside the Reich, entrusted with the ruthless execution of Nazi terroristic policies.[73]

That the Nazis actually carried out their terroristic fight against the democratic-parliamentary government, and that they actually used in this fight violence, murder, assault, and other unlawful means, is established by:

1. the court findings in the trial before the Munich People's Court against Hitler and others for high treason (1924);

2. the court findings in the trial before the *Reichsgericht* against the Ulm Reichswehr officers (1930, file 12 J 10.1930);
3. the court findings in the trials against various individual Nazis, some of which are quoted in R&A Report No. 3114.1, "the Attitude of the NSDAP toward Political Terror";
4. German press reports quoted in the same report.

### B. Propaganda for Aggressive Expansion and Acquisition of New Living Space.

The terroristic fight against the established parliamentary-democratic government in Germany was explicitly tied up by the Nazis with the struggle against the Treaty of Versailles, against "internationalism" and "humanitarianism" everywhere, and with the propagation of a "fanatical nationalism" which was to provide the "spiritual" ground for the policy of rearmament and aggressive expansion. The link between the Nazis' domestic and foreign policy becomes clear in Hitler's own words:

> "In the first place, our people must be delivered from the hopeless confusion of international convictions and educated consciously and systematically to fanatical nationalism. . . . Second, insofar as we educate our people to fight against the delirium of democracy and bring it again to the recognition of authority and of leadership, we tear it away from the nonsense of parliamentarianism . . . Third, insofar as we deliver the people from the atmosphere of pitiable belief in possibilities which lie outside the bounds of one's own strength–such as the belief in reconciliation, understanding, world peace, the League of Nations, and international solidarity–we destroy these ideas. There is only one right in the world and this right is one's own strength."[74]

Hitler openly declared that: "My program was to abolish the Treaty of Versailles."[75] He declared that he was resolved to use illegal means for the attainment of this goal in the trial against the Reichswehr officers at Ulm in 1930. He stated in reply to questions as to the methods he advocated for the revision of the peace treaty:

> "I presume here that we have triumphed. Then we shall fight against the treaties with all means, including those which, in the view of the world, are illegal."[76]

Hitler, moreover, made it clear that abolition of the Treaty of Versailles would be only the first step in the implementation of a plan for expansion beyond the German frontiers of 1914:

> "The frontiers of 1914 signify nothing at all for the future of the German nation. They neither embodied a protection in the past,

nor would they embody strength for the future. The German nation will neither maintain its internal integrity through them, nor will its sustenance be guaranteed by them, nor do these frontiers appear appropriate or even satisfactory from a military viewpoint . . ."[77]

The limits of German expansion were only vaguely defined by the *Lebensraum* to which the Nazis felt the German race was entitled. Alfred Rosenberg defined the goal of Nazi foreign policy as follows:

"To create . . . room for the coming hundred million Germans is the objective of National Socialist foreign policy."[78]

The geographical extent to which the new *Lebensraum* was to be expanded was left open. However, it was made clear that the living space claimed as German or Germanic would go beyond the frontiers of 1914 (see Hitler's statement quoted above), that it was to be

"a Nordic Europe, with a German Central Europe,"[79]

and that in the

"great struggle for existence, for honor, freedom, and bread on the part of such a creative nation as Germany, no account can be taken of Poles, Czechs, etc., who are as impotent as they are devoid of values and presumptuous. They must be pushed towards the East, so that the soil may become free for cultivation by Teutonic peasant hands."[80]

To these definitions of the German living space must be added the demands of the Party Program:

The union of all Germans into a Greater German Reich (point 1), and colonies (point 3).

According to Gottfried Feder's official interpretation, this meant the

"establishment of a closed (*geschlossenen*) national state which comprises all German tribes (*Stämme*)," including the Germans in the Sudetenland, Alsace-Lorraine, Poland, Austria, and the Austrian succession states.[81]

In 1927, Alfred Rosenberg, Chief of the Department for Foreign Policy of the NSDAP, published a pamphlet *Der Zukunftsweg einer deutschen Aussenpolitik* (*The Future Road of German Foreign Policy*). This pamphlet, in conjunction with the statements quoted on the preceding pages and with Werner Daitz' writings discussed in VII below, demonstrates how closely the actual expansion and aggression of Nazi Germany followed preconceived programs and ideas. Here is the translation of a few pertinent paragraphs:[82]

"The German awakening must affirm (*bejahen*) folkish imperialism for the German people insofar as living space is necessary to make possible a healthy, strong existence for the German people. In accordance with geographic conditions this folkish imperialism must take care that this living space is immediately connected with the motherland and does not suffer the same fate as the power efforts (*Machtbestrebunjen*) of the German Middle Ages and the time of the Migration.

"With this recognition that the German people, if it does not want to perish in the true meaning of the word, needs for itself and for its offspring land and soil of its own, and with the second sober understanding that this soil can no longer be conquered in Africa, but must be opened up in Europe and primarily in the east, with this recognition the organic direction of a German foreign policy is established for centuries to come."[83]

"Formulated in a few words, the program is: the British take over the protection of the white race in Africa, in India, and in Australia; North America undertakes the protection of the white race on the American continent, Germany in the whole of Central Europe, in closest alliance with Italy, which receives supervision over the Western Mediterranean and the rule of the Adriatic, in order to isolate France and defeat the French attempts to lead black Africa against white Europe."[84]

"If we have understood that the abolition of the Polish State is Germany's first desideratum, an alliance between Kiev and Berlin and the establishment of a common frontier becomes a folkish and political necessity for a future German policy."[85]

"From the point of view of internal policy, an alliance with the rich southern Ukraine would yield great opportunities for exporting German industrial and chemical products. . . . It suffices if the goals are envisaged by a German politician; then ways and means will be found, to support or to prepare the national Ukrainian revolution against Bolshevik Moscow, in order to create conditions which guarantee Germany space, liberty, and bread."[86]

Propaganda for abolition of the Treaty of Versailles, for rearmament, and for acquisition of new living space was perhaps the chief appeal in the Nazi bid for dictatorial power. The Nazi leadership openly declared, as early as the 1920's, that their aims would involve the use of force and the waging of war:

"The goal of foreign policy is the preservation of a people's means of subsistence; it is nothing else than the preservation of the life of a nation. The path to this goal will, in the final analysis, always be war. The means will be the might of the nation as it is set up in its military organization, plus clever political leadership, which chooses the course of policy wisely and then employs the means ingeniously. Any foreign policy, therefore, is linked up with the power constituted in the nation; and a resourceful organization of this power, namely, the military.

"It is impossible in the long run to carry out our foreign policy without building up the army. If this is not done, the result will always be negative. It is the function of domestic policy to build up the army as a means by which foreign policy can attain its ultimate goals. Domestic policy must follow lines which make possible the creation of powerful armed forces."[87]

Nazi foreign policy, in short, like its domestic program, was from the beginning predicated upon the use of force and aggression:

"There is no distinction between war and peace. Struggle is ever present . . . The final decision lies with the sword. In the power of the sword lies the vital strength of a nation. There is, therefore, no difference between domestic and foreign policy."[88]

Hitler professed again and again his awareness of the fact that the aims of the Nazi movement would involve the use of force and violence against other nations:

"If this earth really has room enough for all to live in, then one should give up the space that we need for living. One will certainly not like to do this. Then, however, the right of self-preservation comes into effect; and what has been denied to kindness will have to be taken with the fist."[89]

"One had to make it clear to oneself that this goal (the acquisition of land in Europe) could be reached only through fighting, and quietly to face the passage at arms."[90]

." . . the new Reich would again have to start marching along the road of the Knights of the Order of former times to give, with the help of the German sword, soil to the plow and daily bread to the nation."[91]

The entire conception was summed up by Goebbels as follows:

"The only instrument with which one can conduct foreign policy is alone and exclusively the sword."[92]

Thus, even prior to 1933, the building up of a powerful army became the cornerstone of Nazi policy–an army which, in its organization and strength would go far beyond the defensive force which could be built up within the framework of the Versailles Treaty:

"We admit freely and openly that, if our movement is victorious, we will be concerned day and night with the question of how to produce the armed forces which are forbidden us by the peace treaty. We solemnly confess that we consider everyone a scoundrel who does not try day and night to figure out a way to violate this treaty, for we have never recognized this treaty.

"We admit, therefore, that as far as we are concerned the German Army in its present form is not permanent. For us it will serve only as a great cadre army, that is, as a source of sergeants and officers. And in the meantime we will be continuously at work filling in the ranks. We will take every step which strengthens our arms, which augments the number of our forces, and which increases the strength of our people.

"We confess further that we will dash anyone to pieces who should dare to hinder us in this undertaking. . . . Our rights will be protected only when the German Reich is again supported by the point of the German dagger."[93]

The power of this army, and not any legal rights or international agreements, was to be the means by which the expansion of German soil was to be accomplished:

"When nations are in need, they do not ask about legal rights. There is then only one question. Does a people have the power to acquire the soil and territory which it needs?"[94]

"If you do not give us space on this earth then we ourselves will take this space. That is why we are National Socialists."[95]

In 1928, Hitler reiterated his earlier statement that the acquisition of new soil is to go far beyond any "revision of frontiers" and declared that he would have "enough energy" to lead Germany to war for this goal:

"We admit that for us the future of Germany does not lie in a mechanical revision of frontiers. In such a case we would again be forced to rely upon world trade, which in turn would make up competitors of four or five other states. That is no future. The National Socialist movement extends far beyond the deceitful level of such a philistine conception. It is the champion of that idea which claims that if we do not acquire more soil then we shall some day perish. We pursue no policy which will not secure the existence of the people for all time. . . . *I believe that I have enough energy to lead our people to war*, and not for the revision of frontiers, but for the deliverance of our people in the most distant future, *so that our people acquire so much territory that the sacrifice in blood can be returned to posterity in fourfold measure*."[96]

One year before his accession to power, Hitler made his famous speech at the Industry Club in Düsseldorf (27 January 1932). This speech, which was arranged by Fritz Thyssen, brought about, according to Thyssen's own testimony, "the connection between Hitler and the entire body of Rhenish-Westphalian industrialists."[97] The speech established one of the most important links in the Nazi master plan: it won over the leaders of German heavy industry to the Nazi program by demonstrating to their satisfaction that the only solution for Germany's economic and social troubles was the restoration of her power position in the world, and that this could be accomplished not by peaceful economic competition but only by aggressive political and military means:

> ." . . it was not German business which conquered the world and then came the development of German power, but in our case, too, it was the power state (*Machtstaat*) which created for the business world the general conditions for its subsequent prosperity. In my view it is to put the cart before the horse when today people believe that by business methods they can, for instance, recover Germany's power-position instead of realizing that the power-position is also the condition for the improvement of the economic situation. . . . there can be no economic life unless behind this economic life there stands the determined political will of the nation absolutely ready to strike–and to strike hard."[98]

The Düsseldorf speech helped greatly to convince the industrial leadership of Germany that the Nazi movement was willing and capable of restoring and enhancing their economic and political power. Thyssen reports that:

> "it was during the last years preceding the Nazi seizure of power that the big industrial corporations began to make their contributions."[99]

This was the beginning of the full-fledged cooperation of German industry with the Nazi regime.

## V. The Elimination of All Opposition and the Establishment of Totalitarian Control over Germany

### A. Eradication of the Opposition

The first acts of the Hitler government in 1933 were to abolish civil liberties and to eliminate political, ideological, racial, and religious opposition. The elimination of the opposition was prepared long beforehand as an act of ruthless and totalitarian revenge. This is demonstrated not only by the Nazi leaders' numerous statements that they would erect a racial dictatorship,[100] but also by their many exhortations, prior to the seizure of power, that the Nazis should store up hatred and revenge until all power was concentrated in the Nazi movement. In doing so, the Nazi leadership declared, they would be able to strike the deadly blow with the greatest effectiveness and the least risk. For example, Goebbels said in 1929:

> "To know how to wait is now essential, both for the leaders and the led. . . . To creep upon the enemy cooly, to feel him out, and ascertain where his most vulnerable spot is, and to throw the spear calmly and with careful aim, so that it will pierce this weakness, and then perhaps to smile pleasantly and say: 'pardon me, neighbor, I cannot do otherwise,' is a dish of vengeance which is enjoyed in cold blood."[101]

The anxious waiting for the "day of reckoning," the "night of the long knives" runs like a *Leitmotif* through the Nazi utterances prior to 1933. The *Ten Commandments for Every SA Man* contain the following statement:

> "If nothing else is possible, submit yourself to the state's power. But console yourself: our day of reckoning will come."[102]

*Gauleiter* Terboven, later Nazi Commissioner in Norway, announced in a meeting at Essen on 7 October 1929:

> "Then the people will awaken, then the National Socialists will come to power, and then there will not be enough lampposts in Germany. The present representatives of the German Government will have to answer with their heads to the German people, and particularly to the National Socialists, for their actions in the past"[103].

The late Manfred von Killinger, former German Consul General in San Francisco, German Minister to Rumania, and SA *Obergruppenführer*, stated in a meeting on 10 November 1929:

> "But take care that some day we do not throw down the gauntlet to you and not, to quote Danton, in the form of a guillotined king's head, but rather with the cut-off heads of your highest politicians."[104]

Finally, Goebbels, in relating a propaganda tour through Berlin in January 1932, remarks at the sight of the "red mob" on the streets:

> "This *Gesindel* (scum) must one day be exterminated like rats."[105]

Once in power, the Nazi Government proceeded at once to carry out its threat. A number of authoritarian decrees provided the official basis.[106]

The *Verordnung des Reichspraesidenten zum Schutz von Volk und Staat* of 28 February 1933 suspended articles 114, 115, 117, 118, 123, 124, and 153 of the Constitution of 1918, which guaranteed basic civil rights and liberties. An order of 9 May 1933 confiscated all property of the Social Democratic Party and of its newspapers, as well as of the *Reichsbanner* (the SPD's para-military formation) and its press. The law of 26 May 1933 confiscated the property of the Communist Party. The decree of the Prussian Prime Minister (Hermann Göring) of 23 June 1933 prohibited all activities of the Social Democratic Party. Finally, the Law against the Formation of Parties of 14 July 1933 made the National Socialist Party the only political party in Germany and outlawed all attempts to maintain the old parties or to form new parties.

Abolition of the trade unions was carried through without even a semblance of legality. On 2 May 1933, *SA*, *SS*, and members of the National Socialist Plant Organization occupied the trade union buildings, removed or arrested the officials, and installed their own "commissars." The funds and property of the trade unions were confiscated and given in "trusteeship" to Robert Ley, leader of the Nazi Labor Front.

The same months saw the first wave of wholesale arrests, internments, and executions of political opponents. They were chiefly carried out by the Secret State Police (Gestapo),[107] which at that time was being organized by Hermann Göring and entrusted to Ministerial Councilor Rudolf Diels.[108] Göring himself assumed personal responsibility for the acts committed by the police:

> "I declared at that time before thousands of racial comrades: every bullet which now comes out of the barrel of a police gun is my bullet. If one calls this murder, then I have murdered. I have ordered all this, I back it up, I bear the responsibility. . . ."[109]

The Gestapo was also given jurisdiction over the concentration camps, which were established during the same period. Göring himself explains the establishment of concentration camps by the need for liquidating the political opposition:

> "Thus the concentration camps originated, where we sent at first thousands of functionaries of the Communist and Social Democratic Parties. Certainly, in the beginning, excesses did occur. Certainly, here and there, innocents were affected. . . ."[110]

Authorization for the indefinite detention of persons without trial and without sentence was derived from the "Law for the Protection of People and State,"[111] which abolished civil liberties, from Section 42 (a) of the

Nazi Criminal Code (Law of 24 November 1933),[112] and from the decrees of the Prussian Prime Minister of 30 November 1933 and 10 February 1936.[113]

The persecution and elimination of the political opposition was from the beginning conceived as a war of extermination beyond the limits set by the law and by legal procedures. This was openly announced by Hermann Göring, then the chief of the Prussian Secret State Police:[114]

> "The gentlemen must understand one thing: I do not think of waging merely a defensive war, in a bourgeois manner and with bourgeois hesitancy. No, I am going to give the signal to launch the offensive on the entire line.
>
> "Racial comrades, my measures will not be sicklied over by any juristic scruples. My measures will not be sicklied over by any bureaucracy. Here, I do not have to carry our justice, I have only to destroy and exterminate—nothing else. This struggle, my racial comrades, will be a struggle against chaos, and I do not wage such a struggle simply with the police (*mit polizeilichen Machtmitteln*). A bourgeois state may have done so. Certainly, I shall also use the powers of the state and of the police to the utmost, lest you draw any wrong conclusions, my Communist gentlemen. But the death struggle I shall wage with those here below, with the Brown Shirts."[115]

Naturally, no reliable figures are available for the number of political, religious, or racial opponents killed by the Nazis or interned in prisons and concentration camps. However, enough evidence has been accumulated to show that, in most cases without trial, without any legal protection, and without the possibility of appeal for the victims:

1) practically the entire leadership of the Communist Party was exterminated or imprisoned—with the exception of those who could flee from Germany;
2) many leaders of the Social Democratic Party and of the trade unions were exterminated or imprisoned;
3) many militant clergymen, Catholic and Protestant, were imprisoned;
4) uncounted numbers of the rank and file of the political, religious, and ideological opposition were exterminated or imprisoned.

In some instances, the criminal terror also hit dissidents in the Nazi Party itself, and prominent persons in the rightist camp—the so-called Röhm putsch of 1934 is the most notorious example.

In all these cases, treatment of opponents went far beyond the legal limits set by the Nazi Government itself. Not only the commanders of concentration camps and the Gestapo officials, but also every *SA* and *SS* man had practically unlimited discretion in the arrest and treatment of the victims. The instances of torture, starvation, and all kinds of maltreatment are uncountable. Some of them are documented in the various reports on the Nazi concentration and internment camps. A large amount of material has been collected by the World Committee for the Victims of German Fascism, by the German Social Democratic Party, and by other labor organizations, and additional evidence can be supplied by the now liberated inmates of the camps.

### B. Extermination of the Jews.[116]

Nazi anti-Semitism is distinguished from other forms of anti-Semitism by the fact that it aims at the very extermination of the Jews. To the Nazi mind, the Jew is the racial, political, religious, ideological, and economic arch-enemy: he is the embodiment of everything that, by its very nature, is hostile to Nazism. Reconciliation is therefore impossible: Jewry and Nazism cannot coexist; the war between them is a life and death struggle all over the world.

In the Nazi plan for conquest, this anti-Semitism played from the beginning an essential part:

1) The Jew was the weakest enemy of Nazism; the attack on him therefore was the most promising and the least risky one.
2) The Jew was the one enemy against whom the Nazis could hope to unite otherwise divergent masses of supporters.
3) The elimination of the Jew, as a competitor, would be most profitable to the petty bourgeoisie, which furnished the largest mass support for the Nazi movement.
4) The Jew was found in all countries; Nazi anti-Semitism was therefore a convenient means for mobilizing potential Nazi allies in foreign countries, and for stirring up unrest and disorder in foreign countries.
5) The ubiquity of the Jew as arch-enemy provided the Nazis with a justification for carrying the struggle for power beyond the frontiers of the Reich, for the attack on "Jewish-Bolshevist Russia," for the war with the "Jewish-plutocratic democracies," etc.

For these reasons, anti-Semitism was one of the most effective instruments for the world-wide infiltration and expansion of Nazism. The decisive importance of anti-Semitism in this context is testified to by the fact that anti-Semitism is one of the very few elements of Nazi philosophy which have been unmitigatedly maintained throughout the history of Nazism. Anti-Semitic propaganda, indeed, increased in violence after the outbreak of war, and it remained one of Goebbels' chief weapons for winning adherents and sympathizers for the Nazi cause in the enemy countries.

The Jews were subjected to the same kind of unlawful treatment as the other opposition groups (see above); but, since they were considered the arch-enemy of the Nazi movement, with whom no reconciliation whatsoever was possible, their persecution was even more brutal and inhuman than that of the other opposition groups. In the concentration camps, the Jews belonged to the prisoner groups which were singled out for special maltreatment and torture. By the same token, the number of Jews murdered by the Nazis surpasses the number of all other categories of victims.[117]

## C. Establishment of Totalitarian Control over Germany

The avowed aim of the Nazi movement was the establishment of the Nazi dictatorship. This implied that, after the destruction of the democratic-parliamentary system in Germany, the Nazi Movement, through the Party and its affiliated organizations, would seize complete control over the state, all branches of the administration, and all spheres of public life.[118]

The Nazis' aim was accomplished during the years 1933 and 1934. In his speech before the Prussian State Council on 15 September 1933 Göring declared that the goal had been attained: he referred with scorn to the "system of parliamentarism and pacifism" that had been destroyed by the National Socialist revolution. The official *Nationalsozialistische Jahrbuch* described the events of 1933 as follows:

> "the taking over of leadership by the NSDAP in 1933 brought about the seizure of all power instruments (*Machtmittel*) and institutions of the state by National Socialism.";[119] and the official *Organisationsbuch der NSDAP* confirms that the NSDAP "dominates the entire public life."[120]

The foundation for the complete control over the state was the Law for the Safeguarding of the Unity between Party and State of 1 December 1933.[121] According to this law:

> "the NSDAP is the bearer of the German state idea (*Staatsgedankens*) and is indissolubly joined with the state."

The same law made the Deputy of the *Führer* and the Chief of Staff of the *SA* members of the Reich Government, "in order to guarantee the closest collaboration between the offices of the Party and *SA* on the one hand and the public authorities on the other."

At the very top, Nazi control over the government was solidly anchored in the personal identity of Hitler as *Führer* of the Party and as Reich Chancellor, and through the vesting of the Chief of the Party Chancellory with the authority of a Reich Minister.[122] The system of personnel identity extended from the top down through the entire administrative pyramid: identity between *Reichsleiter* of the Party and Reich Governors, between *Gauleiter* of the Party and heads of provincial or state governments, etc. The *Reichsführer SS* was at the same time Chief of the German Police and later on Minister of the Interior. Party members were placed in key positions in the Reich and *Länder* Ministries and in all important departments of the national, regional, and local administration.[123] The government agencies controlling the organization of business and labor were in the hands of trusted Nazis. The Reich Food Estate, which controlled the whole of German agriculture, was a mixed Party and Reich organization.[124]

No less complete was the Nazis' control over public opinion, especially the press, radio, and the other principal means of communication and propaganda. The cornerstone of the legislation establishing this control was the Editorial Law of 4 October 1933.[125] This law made professional journalistic activity throughout the territory of the Reich "a public task" (*öffentliche Aufgabe*) "regulated (*geregelt*) by the state." All journalists had to be registered and approved by the *Reichsverband der Deutschen Presse* (Reich Press Association). Its President was appointed by the Reich Minister for Enlightenment and Propaganda (Goebbels). Wilhelm Weiss, president throughout the period of the Nazi regime, was at the same time chief editor of the *Völkische Beobachter*. The Reich Press Association was a corporate member of the Press Chamber, whose President, Max Amann, was NSDAP *Reichsleiter* of the Press and chief of the Party's Central Publishing House. The Press Chamber in turn was part of the Reich Chamber of Culture, a subordinate agency of the Reich Propaganda Ministry. This dual channel of Reich and Party controls secured the complete coordination of policy as well as personnel with the Reich and Party authorities.[126]

The controls were centralized in the Reich Propaganda Ministry, operating through its three press divisions: Home Press, Foreign Press, and Periodical Literature. The head of all three of them was Otto Dietrich, Under Secretary of State in charge of press. Since he was at the same time Reich Press Chief and Chief of the Party Press, complete coordination of government and Party controls was fully insured.

Legally, there was no censorship, but the Propaganda Ministry issued daily directives covering the entire policy of the press.[127] The daily contents of the papers, method of treatment of certain news items, preference or omissions, and setting up of headlines were all prescribed in these directives. The papers were held responsible for strictly following these directives. This "remote control" eliminated the necessity of pre-censorship, while the journalists' compulsory membership in the Reich and Party organizations described above (loss of which made further exercise of the profession impossible) functioned as post-censorship.[128]

In addition to the controls centralized in the Propaganda Ministry, a complete set of Party controls proper existed. They were exercised through the Press Political Division of the NSDAP (headquarters Berlin) and the Press Personnel Division (headquarters Munich), both functioning under Otto Dietrich. The regional organization of these controls was centralized in the *Gau* Press Office, whose chief was at the same time the *ex officio* delegate of the Home Press Division of the Reich Propaganda Ministry and of the Reich Press Chamber in the respective Party *Gau*. Complete coordination between Reich and Party controls was thus also insured in the regional organization.[129]

A similar system of controls was set up for the entire field of education. The Law on the Hitler Youth of 1 December 1936[130] organized "the entire German youth within the territory of the Reich" in the Hitler Youth, in order to "educate it physically, mentally, and morally in the spirit of National Socialism." The Reich Youth *Führer* of the NSDAP was made Youth *Führer* of the German Reich and given the position of a Supreme Reich Authority. Subsequent decrees on the execution of this law were promulgated by the *Führer*. The second of these decrees, issued on 25 March 1939,[131] made service in the Hitler Youth obligatory for all youths from the age of 10 to 18, and subjected them to the "*öffentlich-rechtliche Erziehungsgewalt* (Public Legal Educational Authority) in accordance with the decrees of the *Führer* and Reich Chancellor."

As to the schools, all elementary and secondary school teachers were organized in the NS Teachers League, which, in 1936, also took over the "property rights" of the pre-Hitler teachers associations.[132] The university professors were incorporated into the *NS Dozentenbund*, which was reorganized as a formation of the NSDAP on 24 July 1935.[133]

Control over the entire student body was exercised chiefly through the NS Students League (*Studentenschaft*). In July 1934, the Deputy of the *Führer* (then Rudolf Hess) made this organization the exclusive organ responsible "for the ideological, political, and physical training" of the students.[134] An order of 18 April 1936 made active service in one of the formations of the NSDAP obligatory for all members of the NS Students League.[135]

In general, Nazi controls over education show a pattern similar to those over public opinion. Controls were centralized in the Reich Ministry of Education, a creation of the Nazis. Three Party agencies cooperated with the Ministry on the preparation and censorship of textbooks and other educational material: the Party Official Examination Committee for NS Literature, the Reich Office for School and Instructional Literature, and an attached Reich Committee. The first of these agencies published a monthly bibliography (*Nationalsozialistisches Bibliographie*),[136] listing approved books and pamphlets in all fields of literature.

Through the Party (in the sense described above), the Nazi leadership thus exercised unlimited control over all spheres of public life:

> "In the NSDAP, the *Führer* has created for himself an instrument which, built up, developed, and geared to action by him, sets the goal and direction for the entire German people."[137]

> "The taking over of leadership by the NSDAP in 1933 brought about the seizure of all power instruments (*Machtmittel*) and institutions of the state by National Socialism in order to mobilize these (instruments and institutions) for the intellectual and psychological preparation of the people for the complete removal of the oppressing treaties and of the humiliating situation of the Reich."[138]

The dictatorial and totalitarian control exercised by the Nazi Party was so complete that, eventually, it comprised not only the public but also the private life of the entire population:

> "The organization of the Party is so strong and so thoroughly developed that today it embraces (*erfasst*) all homes (*Haushalte*) of all *Volksgenossen* in the territory of the Reich, including the territories added in the years 1938 and 1939."[139]

The Nazi Party not only established control over the entire machinery of the state (government and general administration) but also integrated the armed forces into the total organization and mobilization of Germany for the execution of the Nazi program. The integration of the armed forces into the Nazi scheme was based on the active support of the Nazi movement by the Army Command, a support which was opposed by only a few individuals, who never became active until Hitler's failure to win the war had become obvious. Collaboration between the Hitler movement and the armed forces dates back to the years immediately after the end of the First World War, when Hitler worked as an agent of the Reichswehr (see IIE above). During the later period of the Weimar Republic, the High Command of the Reichswehr preserved an official neutrality toward the Nazi movement. In January 1933, however, General Werner von Blomberg, divisional commander of the Reichswehr, joined the Hitler government, and from then on the armed forces developed as one of the chief exponents and followers of Nazi ideology and policy, systematically preparing for the war of aggression.

"Four and a half years after the proclamation of universal conscription (*Wehrfreiheit*), which restored the right of every German to fight with the weapon in his hand for the vital rights of his country, the German Wehrmacht was mobilized for the preservation of the Greater German *Lebensraum*. The Wehrmacht was prepared for this battle . . ."[140]

Numerous declarations of loyalty and support for the Nazi leadership came from the High Command of the Armed Forces. Werner von Blomberg himself, then Colonel General and Reichswehr Minister, declared in 1935:

"The Wehrmacht protects the German people and its living space. It serves the *Führer* with unconditional (*rückhaltloses*) confidence and obedience . . ."[141]

Moreover, many high army officers joined top Nazi agencies and enterprises (Reich as well as business) in leading positions and as liaison men, for example, in the Four Year Plan Office, the Reich Ministry of Economics, and the Speer organizations[142]. Wilhelm Keitel, the Chief of the Supreme Command of the Armed Forces, was a member of the Ministerial Council for the Defense of the Reich, while the Armament Council, operating under the Speer Ministry, was made up of leading industrialists and army officers.

## VI. Rearmament and Preparation for the War of Aggression

### A. Rearmament

The elimination of the opposition and the establishment of totalitarian control over Germany fulfilled the precondition for the execution of the aggressive and expansionist foreign policy of the Nazis. After the seizure of power, the Nazi leadership devoted all its efforts to the building up of the armed forces without which the acquisition of new living space was impossible. Hitler himself testified to this effect:

"The second (condition for our success) was national armament, to which I have fanatically devoted my energies for nearly six years" (1938)[143].

"Now I can proudly admit: we did then certainly complete an armament such as the world has never yet seen. . . . I have in fact armed in these five years. I have spent milliards on this armament: that the German people must now know! I have seen to it that a new army should be provided with the most modern arma-

> ment known. I have given to my friend Göring the order: Make me now an air-arm which can protect Germany in the face of any conceivable attack. Thus we have built up a military force (*Wehrmacht*) of which to-day the German people can be proud and which the world will respect if at any time it makes its appearance."[144]

On 16 March 1935, the Nazi government decreed the reestablishment of universal military conscription. This was the beginning of the period of open rearmament. The Nazi rearmament took place according to a preconceived plan, which provided for various stages of rearmament in such a way that the world would not be provoked too much by Germany's violation of the Versailles Treaty, and that at every stage willingness of the world to accept the *fait accompli* could be tested. This was first revealed in Goebbel's speech at Cologne on 24 January 1936, one and a half months before the occupation of the Rhineland by the new Nazi army:

> "Our program is not yet complete. I can only say what I have said to show you what is coming. We are now playing the overture, and it is one with many leitmotifs. One only takes the world into one's confidence when one has a *fait accompli* to show. Had we revealed the story of our army prematurely, other armies might have marched in. We worked, and nobody was able to pry."[145]

However, the method of gradual rearmament was abandoned in favor of full-scale rearmament where an entirely new force had to be created. This was the case of the air force. As early as 1935, Göring declared in a statement to the Berlin Foreign Press Association:

> " . . . the air force was so strong that any power attacking them would have to face a 'very, very hard struggle in the air.' He added that there was not a single old aeroplane or old engine in the fleet. He continued by saying that he had followed entirely new methods, rejecting a policy of slow and gradual arming, because there would have been a danger of not having the fleet ready 'in the event of difficult moments.' What he had done was to expand technical and industrial capacity to the limit, so that he could create the air arm at a single blow. Aeroplanes had not, before that, been concealed in forests or in the ground; they simply had not been there."[146]

The new Wehrmacht was from the very beginning conceived as an essential factor in the expansionist foreign policy; the Nazi Leadership was fully aware of the fact that this policy involved the risk of war, and they were willing to bear that risk. On 5 November 1937, a meeting is said to have been held in the Reich Chancellery at which Hitler, the War Minister (von Blomberg), the Foreign Minister (von Neurath), and the chiefs of the three branches of the armed forces (von Fritsch, von Raeder, Göring) participated.[147] Hitler declared that:

> "in order to solve the German problem, there exists only the way of force, which way is never without risk."

He then outlined the different situations in which force could be applied with the least risk for Germany. Hitler furthermore declared that he was resolved to take action against Czechoslovakia and Austria, and that he was interested in the continuance of the civil war in Spain.

Corroboration of this report may be seen in the *ex-post facto* statements of other Nazi leaders to the effect that Germany had been willing and ready to use its armed forces if the Munich agreement had not been reached. Thus, with reference to the Sudetenland, Ribbentrop stated before the Foreign Press Association in Berlin on 7 November 1938:

> "In this connection I wish to state that Germany was very much in earnest during this period and that if a solution had not been found in Munich at the eleventh hour the *Führer* would have freed the Sudetenland by force of arms."[148]

On 1 March 1939 Göring declared that in September 1938 peace had been saved and Germany's right recognized because the world knew that the German armed forces would otherwise have solved the question by other methods. He added:

> "And it was known abroad that we were not bluffing. In those days we were ready. One command—and a hell, an inferno, would have been made for the enemy; a short blow, but his destruction would have been complete."[149]

## B. Intervention in Foreign Countries

The rearmament of Germany was accompanied and supplemented by a series of military and political interventions in foreign countries. This policy was part of the comprehensive plan for expansion and war. Evidence for this is provided by the authoritative statements of responsible Nazi spokesmen that they had vital interests in these countries. Austria was regarded as belonging to the Reich; in the case of Czechoslovakia and Poland, the alleged maltreatment of German national minorities was evoked as justification; and in Spain, Germany made itself the champion in "Europe's struggle against Bolshevism."

These interventions took place on two levels: military and political-economic (Fifth Column activities, business penetration, etc.).

## 1. Military Intervention

German military interference in foreign countries fulfilled the three-fold purpose of testing the Nazi war potential, testing the degree of opposition on the part of the violated countries and on the part of the great powers, and securing the necessary operational bases for Germany in the event of war.

### *A. Spain*

There is no available record of any admission by Nazi leaders of military intervention during the actual operations. However, the Nazi Government confirmed that German "volunteers" fought with the Franco troops,[150] and Hitler has openly declared and sought to justify the contention that Germany could not remain "neutral" in the Spanish civil war:

> "In July 1936 I had just determined to answer the call for help which this man (Franco) sent to me: I would help him to the extent that and so long as the rest of the world should give its support to the domestic foes of Spain.
>
> "From that time National Socialist Germany began to take an active part, under the leadership of this man, in the struggle for the restoration of a national and independent Spain."[151]

Hitler gave as justification for his interference in the Spanish civil war two main reasons: the danger of the spread of "Bolshevism" and the threat to Germany's economic interests in Spain. As regards the latter point, he declared:

> "Germany needs to import ore. That is why we want a Nationalist Government in Spain, so that we may be able to buy Spanish ore."[152]

Further, in his speech before the soldiers of the Condor Legion on their return from the Spanish war, Hitler professed his official sponsorship of their participation on France's side:

> "For I sent you out to help a country in misfortune, to support a heroic man. . . . You have now returned, having bravely executed my commission. . . .
>
> "It was painful for us all to have to keep silence on your fight year after year, but from the first I had the intention, after the end of this war, to give you in the homeland the reception which brave, victorious soldiers deserve . . ."[153]

And in his telegram to Franco of 9 June 1939 Hitler spoke of

> "the battle which we have waged in common against Bolshevism . . ."[154]

After the termination of the military operations, the German papers came out with specific statements on the fact and extent of German military intervention:

On 30 May 1939, the German press published many articles on the exploits in Spain of the Condor Legion. Among the details given was the statement that in July 1936, Hitler had decided that he must stand by General Franco in his fight against Bolshevism. On 31 July the first detachment of 85 volunteers, traveling as tourists, left for Cadiz in the liner Usamoro, taking six Heinkel pursuit planes. Simultaneously twenty Junkers transport planes were flown from Berlin to Morocco, and within a few weeks 15,000 men, as well as heavy weapons, had been carried across from Africa. In August, more aircraft, anti-aircraft guns, and tanks were sent, and in November, the Condor Legion left for Spain, under General Sperrle.

The Legion took part in nearly every great action of the war, while German instructors and equipment were sent to organize and conduct artillery, tank, engineer, infantry, and other schools in which 56,000 young Spaniards received instruction.[155]

In addition to strictly military intervention, the Nazis conducted extensive propaganda and Fifth Column activities in Spain.[156]

*B. Austria*

From the early days of the Nazi movement, Austria was considered one of the primary objects of Nazi policy. The reunion of Austria with the Reich was on the Nazi program from the beginning. In the first chapter of *Mein Kampf*, Hitler wrote:

> "German Austria must again come back to the great German motherland. . . . even if this reunion, from an economic point of view, were immaterial; yes, even if it were harmful, it must nonethe-less take place. The same blood belongs in a common Reich."

Hitler also confessed that actual intervention was planned long before it was carried out:

> "I myself, as a son of the *Ostmark*, was filled with a sacred wish to solve this problem and thus lead my homeland back to the Reich. In January 1938, I finally resolved that in the course of that year, in one way or another, I would fight for and win the right of self-determination for the 6,500,000 Germans in Austria.")[157]

Goebbels confirmed that the annexation of Austria had been for a long time in the Nazis' mind as a preconceived plan:

> "We have solved many of our problems by waiting for a good opportunity. Then we have jumped at it. We could not tell in ad-

vance at what time we would annex Austria or occupy the Rhineland or introduce conscription. The real art is to scatch such a thing when the stake is as small as possible and the profit as high as possible. The colonial question will be solved in the same way."[158]

Protests by the Austrian Government against systematic Nazi subversion in Austria were rejected on the ground that the Nazis did not consider such activity as taking place in a foreign country. For example, the head of the Austrian desk in the German Foreign Office stated to the Austrian ambassador, Tauschitz, on 1 August 1934:

"The NSDAP does not consider Austria to be foreign territory and its propaganda could not step in front of these illegal frontiers. The Party takes the position that this act does not constitute interference with the internal affairs of a foreign state . . ."[159]

That the Nazis did not rely on the effect of more propaganda nor on claims to the "right to self-determination," is reported by Neville Henderson. He stated, on the basis of his conversation with Hitler, that the latter did not intend to rely on the result of a plebiscite in Austria unless such plebiscite were to be held under his own auspices.[160]

The incessant propaganda and Fifth Column activities of the Nazis in Austria started in the early 1920's. They are discussed in VI B2c below.

*C. Czechoslovakia*

As with Austria, the incorporation of Czechoslovakia into the German living space was one of the earliest objectives of Nazi policy. This is indicated in the statements quoted in IV B above; it is furthermore expressed in Alfred Rosenberg's authoritative exposition of Nazi foreign policy, made as early as 1927 (see IV B above). Additional confirmation may be found in the interrogation of Karl Hermann Frank, former German State Minister for Bohemia and Moravia, especially the report of an interview with Hitler by an American journalist on 16 January 1935. During this interview, Hitler is said to have stated that

"Czechoslovakia is an unnatural creation of the treaty of Versailles, a dangerous springboard and aircraft carrier for the Soviets. According to the report of the American journalist, Hitler used then for the first time the word 'Protectorate' when speaking of the relation between Germany and Czechoslovakia."[161]

After the military occupation of Czechoslovakia, Hitler declared openly that

"this territory has lain in the living space of the German people for a thousand years . . ."[162]

and that, in occupying the country, he only reasserted

> "the ancient German right and reunited what through its History, its geographical position, and all the rules of reason had to be united."[163]

Monrad Henlein, the Nazi Gauleiter and Reich Governor for Sudentenland, admitted in a public lecture given at Vienna on 4 March 1941 that

> "as far back as 1933–1934 he founded his Nazi party in Czechoslovakia in agreement with Berlin and with the only aim of destroying the whole Czechoslovak republic."[164]

Officially, military intervention by the Nazis was usually justified by the allegation of mistreatment of German nationals in the respective countries, and violence and terror on the part of the non-German population or governments.[165] The extent to which such incidents were either instigated by the Nazis or simply fabricated may be ascertained by interrogations of members of the anti-Nazi population or of non-German nationals in the respective border regions. In the case of Poland, evidence is available which shows the carefully planned fabrication and staging of border incidents on the part of the Nazis. This evidence consists in part of the testimony[166] of one Alfred Naujocks, who worked as an agent of Reinhardt Heydrich, then chief of the German Security Police. He stated that:

> "On 10 August 1939, N. was told by Reydrich that Hitler was planning to attack Poland within a month and therefore it would be necessary to stage some 'frontier incidents' to persuade the world that the Poles made the first aggressive move, not the Germans. In this way Naujecks believes Hitler prepared for Germany's unprovoked attack on Poland, being able in his September 1, 1939 speech to express his anger at the 'Polish frontier outrages' and assure his audience that such insults could only be answered by the sword.
>
> "The first step in this nefarious scheme was to pick selected life-term prisoners from the concentration camps, kill them by means of hypodermic injections, dress them in Polish army uniforms, and after riddling their bodies with bullets, place them in carefully chosen positions in German frontier villages of Upper Silesia. The casual observer would then think that small parties of Polish troops had been carrying out abortive raids on Reich territory.
>
> "The bodies were forwarded to specified villages in packing cases labelled 'preserves'. Some of the victims arrived at their

destination only half dead, having received inadequate dosage and had to be killed before they could be used.

"In order to substantiate their 'frontier incidents,' Heydrich and his cohorts decided to publish a story to the effect that the Gleiwitz broadcasting station had been attacked by Polish insurgents.

"On orders from Heydrich, Naujocks went to that town with five or six men. On his arrival he arranged for a Polish speaking German to take possession of the microphone by 'force' and to broadcast an appeal to his 'countrymen', urging them to rise up against the Germans. The broadcast was then broken off, shots were fired and finally a corpse provided by Naujocks, was left on the floor, riddled with bullets."

## 2. Political Infiltration

Nazi military intervention in foreign countries was systematically prepared and supplemented by large-scale Nazi infiltration long before the actual assault. Much of the basic evidence has been collected in *National Socialism*, ed. Raymond E. Murphy and others, US Department of State, Washington 1943. The Nazis employed several methods for such infiltration, all of which were centrally directed and supervised by the respective Nazi Party or government agencies. The chief methods used by the Nazis were:

1) Working through German nationals in foreign countries.
2) Working through indigenous pre-Nazi groups and individuals in foreign countries.
3) Working through apparently unpolitical and peaceful business connections.
4) Working through especially trained agents.
5) Use of "cultural cooperation" for Nazi propaganda.
6) Acquisition of interests in the foreign press and in other means of communication and propaganda.

These Nazi activities were designed to weaken or overthrow the established governments in foreign countries which were likely to resist Nazi aggression.[167] This aim was to be attained by creating disorder and terror and by winning over to the Nazi cause powerful groups in the respective countries. These groups later became the nuclei of Nazi collaboration in government and business.

The Nazis used an entire network of agencies and organizations for implementing their infiltration tactics in foreign countries. The first official Nazi Party organization designed for work in foreign countries was the *Auslandsorganisation der Reichsleitung der NSDAP* (established as Foreign Section of the Reich Directorate of the NSDAP in 1931, reorganized as Foreign Organization of the NSDAP in 1934). In 1937, Ernst Wilhelm Bohle, then the head of the organization, was transferred to the Ministry of Foreign Affairs, an arrangement which demonstrated the official link between the foreign propaganda agency of the Nazi Party and the Nazi Reich government.[168]

In addition to the *Auslandsorganisation*, the Nazis used many other agencies and organizations, among them such institutions of long pre-Nazi standing as the *Verein für Deutschtum im Ausland*, and the *Deutsche Auslands Institut* (League for Germandom in Foreign Countries) and the German Foreign Institute.

Wherever Nazi parties existed in foreign countries (as in Austria and Czechoslovakia), they were systematically employed as spearheads of Nazi penetration and as central terror agencies directed against foreign democratic governments. Everywhere, the Nazi Fifth Column promoted and fostered anti-Semitic tendencies with the object of creating unrest and disunity in foreign countries.

As early as 1934, the *Völkischer Beobachter* boasted that, through the *Auslandsorganization*, Nazism had extended its tentacles all ever the world:

> "The influence of the Nazi Party in foreign countries extends literally around the entire globe. 'My sphere is the whole world' might aptly be placed over our headquarters in Hamburg. This Foreign Organization . . . comprises today more than 350 national branches and fulcrum points of the Nazi Party everywhere. . . . The Nazi Party will develop even further in an effort to transplant to all foreign countries the objectives of the National Socialist Reich."[169]

By virtue of the incorporation of all foreign Nazi parties and groups into the Foreign Organization of the NSDAP, the activities of these parties and groups were centrally supervised and directed by the German Party and government authorities.

### A. Spain

Material on the organization and activities of the Nazi Party and its agents in Spain has been collected (together with photostats of documents) in: *The Nazi Conspiracy in Spain,* by the editor of the *Brown Book of the Hitler Terror*, London 1937.

### B. Austria

The Nazi movement in Austria dates back to the early 1920's. In 1926, the Austrian Nazi Party was made a *Gau* of the NSDAP. From then on, all political, cultural, and military organizations of the Nazi Party in

Austria were integral organizational parts of the NSDAP. The *Nationalsozialistisches Jahrbuch* for 1934 lists on pp. 139–141 the then (33) *Gauleitunger* of the NSDAP and, as the last of them, the *Landesleitung Oesterreich*.

The Nazi Party in Austria committed a series of criminal acts (including murder, arson, assault, etc.) directed against the legally established Austrian Government and its supporters and culminating in the putsch of July 1934, which led to the murder of Chancellor Dollfuss.[170]

3. Economic Penetration

One of the most effective methods of Nazi penetration in foreign countries was to work through normal business channels. Clever utilization and expansion of international business connections played a decisive part in the Nazi plan for the domination of Europe and prepared, accompanied, and supplemented military intervention and occupation. The foundation for this policy was laid in Hitler's speech before the Industry Club at Düsseldorf (quoted above, IVB), which tried to demonstrate that the future of German business was intrinsically tied up with an aggressive and expansionist German foreign policy, backed by the power of the sword. Actually, German business followed upon the heels of the German Wehrmacht and incorporated the occupied territories into a vast industrial and financial empire, ruled by the key German enterprises. (This phase of Nazi domination is dealt with in a separate war crimes paper.)[171]

How effectively German business was prepared for the job may be illustrated by one example:

> "On the very day of the occupation of Prague (15 March 1939), representatives of the *Deutsche Bank* presented themselves at the Bohemian Union Bank in Prague and proposed to "protect" the interests of the Bohemian Bank, threatening that the Bank would be considered a "Jewish enterprise" subject to confiscation if their offer was rejected."[172]

The *Deutsche Bank* had also ready a whole series of monographs (*Oesterreich im Deutschen Wirtschaftsraum; Das Sudetenland im Deutschen Wirtschaftsraum; Bohmen und Mahren im Deutschen Wirtschaftsraum*) which contained a detailed analysis of the business facilities and opportunities in these countries.[173]

This method was predicated upon full-scale collaboration of the German industrialists, whose enterprises and holdings provided the nuclei of expansion. Many of the most powerful German industrialists had supported the Nazi movement prior to Hitler's rise to power, others followed suit, and, by the beginning of the war, the Nazification of German industry had been completed. The Nazi political leadership was instrumental in the formulation and implementation of German economic policy in all branches of the war economy. Top Nazis were sitting on the boards of the most important industrial and commercial enterprises, just as top industrialists occupied leading positions in the Nazi organization of the economy. Close liaison existed between industry and the High Command of the Wehrmacht.[174]

This amalgamation between the Nazi political hierarchy and the industrial leadership was the basis for the German exploitation and spoliation of occupied territories. After the German armies had conquered these territories, the Nazi leadership turned over to the German industrialists vast properties and labor power as reward for their collaboration.

## VII. The Concept of *Lebensraum* and *Grossraumordnung*

The Nazi occupation policy was the logical development and the realization of the Nazi concept of *Lebensraum*. In its basic principles, this policy was thus not fabricated *ad hoc*, but conceived beforehand as part of the Nazi master plan for the domination of Europe.

To show this, it is necessary to follow the development of the Nazi idea of living space in its later phases.

Around 1940 the German concept of *Lebensraum* assumed more definite shape and emerged as meaning the domination of Europe by Nazi Germany. With the success of the first war year, the language of the Nazis became even less inhibited and blunter. On 14 July 1940, the *Frankfurter Zeitung* declared that the first phase of the "European revolution" was completed under the instrumentality of German arms.

> "For the first time in history the task of the whole continent from its center was conceived as a politically membered entity, not from the standpoint of obsolete rivalries but in order to organize the needs of nations on the *Führer* principle. The nucleus of the new order was not changes of frontiers, but the union of the whole continent under German and Italian leadership, with a clear demarcation and graduation of the responsibilities of its members."[175]

One day later, a Foreign Office spokesman told the foreign press in Berlin that:

> "Nobody now contests that Germany and Italy are predestined to reorganize Europe on a new basis." He further declared that "National Socialist values are of a super-state significance and the expression of the demands of the 20th Century, while it is of determinative significance that the reorganization of Europe

should be carried out pre-eminently under the leadership of the best and most successful organizing people."[176]

On 20 July 1940, it was announced in Berlin that Schacht[177] had completed the task entrusted to him by Hitler of preparing a plan for the post-war economic co-ordination of the whole of Europe, to be ready for use in the near future. His plan was embodied in a memorandum consisting of three parts: (1) general principles for the reorganization of Europe; (2) specific proposals on currency questions; (3) a program of colonial development.[178]

On 1 August 1940, the *Berliner Borsenzeitung* wrote that the German people must now rise to its European mission. Only a nation conscious of its European responsibilities had the right to a part in historically constructive work. Hence, both France, contaminated by Judaism, and Plutocratic England were not entitled to lead. The paper added that "leader-peoples" bore the responsibility not only for their own national destiny but for the smaller peoples belonging to the same *Lebensraum*.[179]

The whole concept is summed up in *Das Reich*, which declared on 23 October 1940 that:

> "Our people are destined to be the pivot and leaders of the new European order. They must always fight against the temptation to devote their energies to the good of others. That temptation was never as great as now."[180]

This "new European order" which was soon taking form under the Nazi occupation policy was further defined and organized under the concept of *Grossraumordnung* (large space order). The conception was most fully developed in the years 1938–1940 by Werner Daitz, Reich Commissar of the Economic-Political Office of the *Reichsleitung* of the NSDAP, and member of the Reich Economic Council of the *Reichsleitung* of the NSDAP. Daitz defined the European *Grossraum* economy emerging under Adolf Hitler as:

> "the Reich of the *Hanse,* which established an economic, operational, and cultural order (*Wirtschafts-*, *Arbeits-* und *Kulturkreis*) extending from the Black Sea over Danube, Main, Rhine, Flanders, North Sea, Baltic Sea, Ilmen Lake, Djnepr, Black Sea, and uniting all peoples comprised in this *Verkehrszirkel* (operational circle) or bordering on it, into one European *Grossraum* economy."[181]

He stated explicitly that "the European continent must reemerge there where, around 1500, the Hanseatic *Grossraum* economy came to an end."[182]

This whole European *Grossraum* was to be divided between German and Italian leadership. The Greater German Reich had its geopolitical basis in the *Nordostseeraum* (space of the North and Baltic Sea) with the *Ostraum* belonging to its "living and economic space," while Fascist Italy dominated the Mediterranean space.[183]

In his article of 1932, which was reprinted in 1938 (see VII above), Daitz made it perfectly clear that the economic integration into *Grossraum* spaces was at the same time to be a political integration since:

> "It is necessary for every nation that its space of economic autarchy, that is, everything that it needs for the maintenance of its economic and state-political independence, lie within its political frontiers."[184]

The same article outlined the direction of the German *Ostraum* policy as the:

> "activation of the entire belt of states from Latvia down to the Black Sea."[185]

and demanded the building up of a strong navy for the protection of this *Ostraum* policy:

> "Under no circumstances can Germany neglect building up its navy so that it can at any time bar (*sperren*) the Sound, the Straits, and the North Sea-Baltic Canal, the gates to Germany's future living and economic space, the *Ostraum*."[186]

While thus proclaiming their "mission" to dominate Europe, the Nazis did not neglect to continue their preparations for the incorporation of "adjacent" African territory into the European *Grossraum*. On 29 April 1941, the appointment of General von Epp as Minister for Colonies was announced. On the same day, a Government spokesman stated that Germany had for years been making the most systematic preparations for the administration of a vast African empire as an adjunct to Europe.[187]

Some statements by the Nazi leaders indicate that, in their mind, the German "mission" had assumed the form, not only of European, but even of world leadership. For example, in an address to students in Berlin, Goebbels claimed as early as 14 June 1939 that "not Great Britain but Germany should rule the world."[188]

Hans Frank, the Governor General of Poland, declared on 21 December 1941 in Cracow that

> "It is the greatest gift of heaven to be able to call oneself a German, and we are proud to master the world as Germans. Today Adolf Hitler is called upon to be the leader of the world—unhampered by anyone."[189]

The idea of a European *Grossraumordnung* under German domination became an established fact of Nazi policy, and the Nazis announced that the fact was meant to stay. For example, in 1940, the *Deutsche Auslandswissenschaftliche Institut* (Institute for Research on Foreign Countries) arranged a series of lectures on *Probleme des Europaischen Grosswirtschaftsraumes*. The Institute was the nucleus of Office VII of the Security Service of the *Reichsfuhrer SS*, headed by Franz Alfred Six, who was at the same time the head of the *Kulturpolitische Abteilung* in the Foreign Office. The lectures were published in 1943 in a series edited by Six. They contain the following statements:

> "Within its new frontiers Greater Germany which, after the victory of its arms, is entitled to the political, economic, and cultural leadership in the European space together with its Axis partner, must militarily, military-economically (*wehrwirtschaftlich*), and morally be and remain so strong that any attempt to change this state of affairs through intra- or extra European forces is *a priori* without a chance of success."[190]

> "The Central European Space, essentially the Greater German Reich with at present 880,000 square kilometers and 112 million inhabitants, is not only geographically and politically, but also economically the natural center of gravity for continental Europe . . . A stable foundation for the economic reorganization of Europe is first provided chiefly by the cooperation of the Central and South Eastern European space which is to a great extent independent of Great Britain and Overseas and which is economically stable with South Europe. From this foundation can then be undertaken a cautious incorporation (*Einbau*) into the new order of the North and West European spaces (*Teilraume*), which are strongly sensitive to crises."[191]

These statements—and the quotations from Werner Daitz—also show that the idea of the New Order as *Grossraumerdnung* contained from the very beginning the Nazi policy of economic expansion and integration as it developed under the Nazi occupation.[192]

## VIII. Unlawful Elements of Nazi Occupation Policy

### A. General

Daitz' exposition reveals the chief elements which become basic for the Nazi occupation policy: the idea of the "leading nation" (the Greater German Reich) with the mission of "organizing" the European *Grossraum* on the economic, political, and cultural levels; and the division of the

*Grossraum* into (a) the leading nation's own autarkic living space, (b) this nation's economic living space, which, after acquisition from without, is to be included in its national frontiers, and (c) the territories bordering on the national and economic living space. This conception was explicitly tied up with Nazi occupation policy by Werner Best,[193] who also played an important part in its execution. (He was chief of the Civil Administration in occupied France, and German Plenipotentiary in Denmark.) From this concept was derived the idea of differential treatment for the different peoples in the *Grossraum*: the population in the "racial core" of the living space of the "leading nation" was to receive better treatment and, accordingly, a higher form of administration, granting them rights of self-government which were withheld from the population in the more remote parts of the *Grossraum*. This required a variety of types of administration of the occupied territories, ranging all the way from an "alliance administration" with a certain amount of independence for the administered country, down to a "colonial administration," which concentrated all powers in the hands of the Nazi Government.[194]

According to Werner Best, the German people was called upon to rule (*walten*) not only over "its own folkish order but also over the manifold parts of a growing "*Grossraumordnung*." This tremendous task did not allow of any "division or splitting-up" of administrative functions: to the ruled peoples, the ruling power of the German nation had rather to demonstrate itself as a unified and centralized power.[195] The "leading nation" would exercise power over all spheres of public life and possess "total leadership" (*Totalität der Führung*), which includes administration as well as *politische Menschenführung*.[196]

Stripped of its metaphysical terminology, this meant that the "leading nation" had the right, even the "mission," to use all material and human resources within the scope of its *Grossraum* for the preservation of its own dominant position. The entire political, cultural, and economic life of the "ruled peoples" had to be geared to the requirements of the "leading nation." If this nation were at war, the entire population of the *Grossraum* would have to work for its war effort:

> "The task of *Grossraumwirtschaft*, which is coming into its stride, is to mobilize all the people in this space. It must be expressly pointed out that none of the countries belonging to this space will be allowed to stay aside."[197]

This mobilization is to be carried through without "obsolete" considerations for the standard of living of the population in these countries:

> "The obsolete views concerning the maintenance of the present standard of living, which are held, for instance, in the countries

of western and northern Europe, are no longer of importance and cannot be recognized by us. The necessity of mobilizing all efforts for the war dominates the present hour."[198]

The Nazis recognized neither international nor national limitations upon the forcible, compulsory incorporation of the occupied territories into the German war machine. The degree of terror and compulsion applied in the implementation of the Nazi measures varied with the degree of native cooperation and resistance. However, the following illegal and criminal measures were applied everywhere in pursuance of the Nazi occupation policy:

1) Forcible eviction and deportation of the native population beyond "military necessity." In many cases, the land and the property of the evicted were awarded to Nazis or to Nazi sympathizers in the occupied countries.
2) Wholesale confiscation of property (state as well as private).
3) Spoliation and exploitation of the occupied countries beyond "military necessity" in favor of German business, Nazi Party and government officials, Nazi collaborationists, etc.
4) Punitive measures against the civilian population of the occupied countries: indiscriminate killings, shooting of hostages, burning down of houses and villages, internment, torturing, starvation, etc.
5) Unlawful treatment of military personnel belonging to the occupied countries.

Documentation on the criminal character of the Nazi occupation policy is provided in the war crimes paper *Criminal Responsibilities in Connection with Planning and Execution of Occupation Policy*, R&A Report No. 3113. Criminal methods were used in all forms of Nazi administration of occupied countries, but they were made the very principle of administration in the form described by Best as "colonial administration" (see above) and applied chiefly to the occupied Eastern European territories. Best described the principles of this form of administration as follows:

> "The law of the colonial administration is posited without limitations by the government of the leading nation or its colonial authorities as the immediate right of the leading nation. . . . As regards the preservation of the natives (*Eingeborene*), it should be noted that according to experience, they react against *lebensfeindliche* (life-destroying) measures of the colonial administration by dying out (*Aussterben*), since they are unable to offer resistance."[199]

## B. Political Controls

The Nazi occupation policy was geared not only to full administrative but also to full political control.[200] Direct control by the Nazi Party and its affiliates over the occupied territories was achieved through the establishment of *Arbeitsbereiche* (Activity Spheres) or, in the incorporated areas, *Gaue* of the NSDAP. The first of these Activity Spheres was established in the Government General on 6 May 1940.[201]

The administrative setup in the occupied territories shows that the terroristic machine was from the beginning conceived as an integral part of the administration. This is demonstrated by the fact that the Higher SS authorities were superimposed upon the general administration, responsible directly to Himmler.[202] In most cases, the Higher SS and Police leaders also held the office of Public Safety in the central administrative machinery of the respective countries. As early as 1939, the Higher SS and Police Leaders were made responsible for Germanization in all territories already annexed or to be annexed, and in the same year Himmler himself was appointed *Reichskommissar für die Festigung des Deutschen Volkstums* (Reich Commissar for the Strengthening of German Folkdom).[203] This agency conducted to a great extent the policy of Germanization of the occupied countries.

One of the chief instruments of Germanization was the *Deutsche Volksliste* (German Racial Register), which established in the occupied territories four categories of candidates for German citizenship, with varying privileges and duties. The Racial Register was determined by the *Reichsführer SS* in his capacity as Reich Commissar for the Strengthening of German Folkdom, and by the Reich Minister of the Interior.[204] For details of the Germanization procedures, see war crimes paper on "Criminal Responsibilities in Connection with Planning and Execution of Occupation Policies," R & A Report No. 3113.

## C. Economic Exploitation

Terroristic political controls over the occupied territories were supplemented by a tight net of economic controls, adapted to and even integrated into the pattern of control that prevailed in Germany. These controls were exercised through close cooperation and coordination of agencies of the Nazi Government and of the self-government system of business which was set up in 1943. Within this framework of organization, the entire economy of the occupied countries was compulsorily organized and made the organ of Nazi spoliation and exploitation. The large German industrial and commercial enterprises were the chief beneficiaries of these activities: the *Reichsvereinigungen*, the German compulsory peak cartels, were entrusted with the task of "organizing" European resources, and innumerable German firms operated in the occupied countries, either directly or through branches and subsidiaries.

The policy of economic spoliation and exploitation was determined by central German agencies. The most important ones were:

1) Delegate for the Four Year Plan (Göring). Authorization was given, or assumed, among others, in the "Decree on the Planned Utilization of the Occupied Western Territories for the German War Economy" (26 August 1940)[205] and in the "Decree on the Utilization of the Occupied Eastern Territories for the German War Economy" (29 July 1941).[206]
2) Speer's Ministry for Armament and War Production, operating mainly through Armament Inspectors.
3) Several Reich Commissioners and Inspectors, directly responsible to Hitler or Göring.

# 29

Otto Kirchheimer

# *NAZI PLANS FOR DOMINATING GERMANY AND EUROPE: DOMESTIC CRIMES*

(August 13, 1945)

Editor's note: R&A 3114.2. In the June 13, 1945, letter from Franz Neumann to George Demos in which the members of the Central European Section involved in research on war crimes are listed, Kirchheimer is indicated as the general manager overseeing reports of the internal crimes committed by the Nazi regime (RG 226, entry 37, box 2, folder: Central European Section). The same letter, in listing the reports to be realized in the project "Nazi Plans for Dominating Germany and Europe," names Marcuse as the author of the text for generally framing the Nazi master plan and attributes the part dedicated to domestic crimes to Kirchheimer (RG 226, entry 146, box 38, folder 534: Miscellaneous Washington Files). The same document indicates Kirchheimer as the author of a report, *Nazi Changes in Criminal Procedure* (R&A 3081, July 10, 1945), to which there is also a reference in the report here. A note on the cover says: "Approved by the Prosecution Review Board," and there is also a summary "prepared by a member of the Prosecution Review Board" in the report that is not included here.

The report is correlated to a shorter one (R&A 3114.2APP), which has not been published here and which contains six appendixes: documents to be used as evidence (Runderlass by Goering February 17, 1933; newspapers seized or forbidden by Nazis, February 1943; covering letter and text of order of seizure of assets of the Social Democratic Party; list of organizations whose property has been confiscated under the Law for the Confiscation of Property of Groups Hostile to the State and the People, 14 July 1933; "List of People Confiscated"; "List of Periodicals and Papers Quoted."

Classification: Secret

## Introduction

The following paper consists of two parts. Part I discusses the criminal responsibility of the Nazis for their violations of Domestic German law. Part II concerns the violations themselves—the suppression of labor organizations and political parties, the muzzling of the press, the illegal passage of enabling legislation, etc.

The principal problem which the Part I confronts and attempts to solve is the expected plea by the Nazi Defense that the acts of which the prisoners are accused were in fact authorized by the laws of the Third Reich. While it would be possible to demonstrate that the Nazi regime itself was not the legal successor to the Weimar Republic, the Nazis could fall back upon the claim that as a frankly revolutionary government its constitutionality rested on its long and uncontested exercise of power. This, it is suggested, can only be countered by insistence upon the traditional view that a government's constitutionality depends upon how representative it is of its people and how wide an allegiance it is able to evoke from its citizenry.

On the other hand, it is pointed out, even after the Third Reich's unconstitutionality is established, it will not necessarily be wise to consider retroactively invalid all of its legislation. Rather, the principle of "selective retroactivity" should be applied, and those policy measures, amnesties, and other laws especially protecting Nazis from the consequences of their crimes be specifically rescinded. That there are ample precedents for such a practice can quickly be demonstrated. It will be necessary, in any event, to go beyond this invalidation of laws: one must also reject those Nazi interpretations of their own laws which, if accepted, would render the Party virtually "beyond the law." This is the more important in that the Nazis—as far as the letter of the law was concerned—never legally sanctioned the great majority of the types of violence in which they engaged and, consequently, can without difficulty be brought to book for them, once their immunity is removed.

In Part II it is demonstrated how—and under what pretexts—the Nazis went about the organization of their system of terror. The police were converted into an instrument of repression; the opposition parties were driven underground; the elections were rigged; and the trade unions were taken over. In this the Nazis worked through two types of agencies—the "legal terror," which operated by way of the courts and the application of Nazi laws, and the police and organizational terror, which applied force directly. Responsibility for this methodical violence lies with various agencies, of which the most culpable are the Ministry of Justice, the Ministry of Interior, the top Party authorities, and the courts.

## Crimes Committed in Violation of Domestic German Law

### I. Legal Basis of Criminality

If Germans are to be made responsible for offenses committed in Germany against German citizens, the question arises as to which body of law should be considered applicable. From 1933 to 1945 Nazi law was the law of Germany. Should it form the basis for the indictments, should the defendants be allowed to invoke it in their favor, or should the court refuse to recognize it at all?

#### A. Is the Nazi Regime Constitutional?

The position might be taken that none of the legal acts of the Nazi government are valid, since the regime itself was not constitutionally established, that is, that when it was formed the constitutional rules of the Weimar Constitution were disregarded. The National Socialist regime has, of course, insisted that it did come into power according to the rules of the Weimar constitution, that Hitler was called to the office of Reich Chancellor according to the forms of the Weimar Constitution, and, that his popular mandate was confirmed by the election of 1 March 1933. Furthermore, National Socialism has asserted that the Third Reich's legislative activity, as well as the whole framework of its new constitutional organization, rest on a duly enacted enabling act.[1] This enabling act of 24 March 1933 was at first restricted to four years, and then extended three times, twice by the Reichstag for a definite period,[2] and the last time by an edict of the Führer for an indefinite period.[3]

This claim of the Nazis, however, is scarcely tenable. First, the Reichstag which voted the enabling act did so without the participation of the eighty-one members of the Communist Party, who had been forcibly prevented from taking their seats.[4] Moreover, the two-thirds majority necessary for the voting of the enabling act was reached only through heavy extra-parliamentary pressure in the form of threats on the Center Party. In addition, the Government did not conform to the terms of the enabling act, which had restricted its lifetime to that of the current Reich government—the Nationalist-Nazi coalition. With the departure from the cabinet of Alfred Hugenberg, leader of the Nationalist Party, on 29 June 1933, the legal basis for the enabling act ceased to exist.[5]

If the Nazi regime's claim to constitutionality, then, rested only on its having preserved the constitutional forms of the Weimar Republic, its plea would appear more than doubtful. In fact, however, it bases its case on quite different grounds. The official utterances of Nazi politicians as well as of Nazi constitutional lawyers stress the fact that the National Socialist regime was a revolutionary one.[6] Formal continuity with the Weimar Constitution was used merely as a ruse to facilitate the Nazis' rise to power, assuring the sometimes questionable loyalty of the military, judicial, and technical groups. The regime's real claim to constitutionality rests on its uncontested exercise of power for a prolonged period. But such an interpretation should conform to the traditional view,[7] which makes the constitutionality of a government dependent on its character as representative of the people and its ability to command the loyalty of the citizenry, rather than on its having originated in conformity with the constitutional rules of the preceding regime.[8]

If it were concluded that the Nazi regime was established by constitutional processes and operated within the constitutional framework, all laws and orders under it would remain valid. If, on the other hand, it were decided that the regime has been unconstitutional, all its legal acts would be retroactively invalidated. As the Nazi regime lasted over thirteen years and as a great body of legislation was introduced during this period, a great number of legal acts and transactions would now be open to challenge.

### B. Precedents Dealing with Retroactive Revision of the Legislation of a Defunct Regime

Such radical conclusions have, however, rarely been drawn in comparable situations in history. The practice, although never uniform and governed by political rather than legal considerations, has been to adopt a kind of "selective retroactivity." In order to preserve the essential elements of social stability, it has shown a tendency to leave undisturbed legislative, administrative, and judicial acts pertaining to the private affairs of the citizens, concentrating instead on the political acts of the former regime. This is strongly apparent in the decisions of the Supreme Court of the United States dealing with the Confederate Legislation. It ruled that acts necessary to peace and good order among citizens—such as acts sanctioning and protecting marriage and domestic relations, governing the course of descents, regulating the conveyance and transfer of property, real and personal, and providing remedies for injuries to persons and estates, and other acts which would be valid when emanating from a lawful government—must be regarded in general as valid when preceding from an actual, though unlawful, government; but that acts in furtherance or support of rebellion against the United States or intended to defeat the just rights of citizens, and other acts of like nature, must in general, be regarded as invalid and void.[9]

An analogous example presents itself in international law, in which the question has often arisen: What recognition should a returning sovereign give to the acts of the occupant? There exists no uniformity of opinion on this problem.[10] Yet, a tendency is noticeable to recognize only those acts which would find justification in the international law of occupation. Acts of the occupant in regard to technical matters and to strictly private relations have generally a better chance of finding recognition than acts having a political connotation, however small it may be.

This situation differs somewhat from the one we have to deal with insofar as international law offers certain rules by which the validity of occupation acts can be measured.[11] Whereas there exists, unfortunately, no such yardstick in positive law to apply to the acts of a native sovereign. His constitutional powers are subject only to those limitations which he is himself willing to recognize or to establish. But, in spite of this difference, it remains significant that both the returning sovereign and the succeeding regime tend to differentiate between, on the one hand, purely technical acts and acts regulating relations between private parties, and, on the other hand, acts carrying political implications.

This principle finds contemporary illustration in the Italian decree on "Sanctions against Fascism" of 27 July 1944.[12] This, it is true, with a sweeping gesture abolishes retroactively all criminal laws "passed for the protection of Fascist institutions and political organs." In establishing the criminal responsibility of members of the Fascist government and hierarchy for the abrogation of political liberties and constitutional guarantees and for the creation of the Fascist regime, it denies implicitly that the Fascist regime ever exercised constitutional powers. But whereas the decree orders the application of certain paragraphs of the earlier penal code to some political acts, it does not abrogate the new Fascist penal code *en bloc*. In other words, although treating the Fascist regime as a usurpation of power, it stops short of assuming the invalidity of all its legal acts and sticks to the principle we have noted: "selective retroactivity."

France, too, affords an example of this differentiation. The ordinance of 9 April 1944[13] "Concerning the Re-establishment of Republican Legality" starts by branding the constitutional legislation and executive acts of the Vichy regime as illegal. But this illegality is laid down only "in principle." Article Seven explicitly states that for "*considerations d'interet pratique*" all those acts of the *de facto* government, the invalidity of which have not been expressly declared in the ordinance, are maintained. And even insofar as the small number of abrogated ordinances is concerned the invalidation is not, in the majority of cases, given retroactive force.

Only in thirty-nine cases, most of them in the field of labor and propaganda, was retroactive invalidation ordered.[14]

In Denmark, the criminal code has just been retroactively amended as of 9 April 1940; membership in the various German corps and other acts of treason may be punished by death and imprisonment. The law, the lifetime of which is restricted to one year, thus introduces the death penalty, hitherto unknown in Danish law, to crimes committed during the occupation.[15]

### C. The Use of Existing Legislation for the Prosecution of War Criminals

If German laws still on the books at the time of the Nazi collapse are to be used as a basis for criminal prosecution, it will be necessary first to exclude certain specific Nazi interpretations of them.

According to the Nazi doctrine, for example, the Party and its organizations constituted independent bodies fully equal to and sometimes set above the state apparatus. They were not subject to the orders of the state and insofar as legal rules governing their inter-relationship existed, they only concerned a few areas of possible conflict:[16] they did not establish or predicate the application of state law to any kind of Party activities.

In other words, the Party lived according to its own laws. Its concepts were different from the prevailing concepts applied to actions of ordinary citizens. For this reason, special jurisdictions had to be instituted for certain categories and actions of Party members, and care was taken to exclude such acts from adjudication by the regular law courts.[17] The Party, indeed, exercised political power at the same level as the state organs.[18] The Party organs attributed to themselves the same position in the fight against internal enemies as the army did in regard to external enemies in times of war. They assumed not only the right, but the duty, of destruction.

Clearly, if such a doctrine were recognized, many if not most of the offenses committed by the Nazis would enjoy immunity and the rules of the criminal law would be inoperative, for such acts would be covered by the unwritten law arising out of the National Socialist philosophy. Such an interpretation would obviously be quite unacceptable, the more so because of the divergences of treatment it would necessitate between Nazis who committed offenses in connection with internal German politics and Nazis active in foreign territory or occupied with the affairs of foreigners in Germany, who could be punished according to international law.

The following should therefore be disregarded in the interpretation of German laws by the court:

a. General National Socialist concepts calling for the application of the regular law only to acts of the ordinary citizen, and reserving a separate system of rules governing certain special functionaires of the Party.[19]

b. The preamble of National Socialist laws, which to a large extent took the place of actual legislative intent.

c. Clauses inserted into a great number of laws giving an interpretation in conformity with the National Socialist philosophy.

The necessity of stripping away the Nazi interpretation of their own laws can be seen even more easily when it is understood that no Nazi legislation has ever expressly abrogated the protection granted by the criminal law against attacks on the life and bodily integrity of any individual. For instance, the police decree of July 1, 1943[20] which shut Jews off from access to regular law courts and transferred jurisdiction in Jewish cases to the police, did not create new substantive law. It did not transfer to the Party and police organs the right to kill or inflict bodily harm on Jews. It shifted jurisdiction, but not the right to commit acts which, by the existing rules of criminal law, were considered murder or assault.

In the realm of administrative law such exemptions from judicial control were often introduced by special laws and decrees,[21] while in criminal law the same result was usually reached through the inability or unwillingness of the state attorney to bring Nazi offenders to trial.

But in any case even the German constitutional writers, when developing the theory of the so-called "*justizlose*" *Hoheitsacte* (acts of the sovereign not subject to judicial review), did not pretend that the mere fact of withdrawing an action from judicial scrutiny would make it "lawful."[22]

The Nazi Government, indeed, has attempted in only one instance to justify specifically a series of political murders: after the purge of July 1934 the Fuehrer issued a special law[23] upholding the acts committed on 1 and 2 July on the grounds of the existence of an emergency. Some Nazi interpretations to the contrary, it seems fairly obvious that the Nazi regime would not have issued such a strange and extraordinary law if the majority of the German people had been willing to accept the theory that public authorities are free to kill their political enemies and competitors without benefit of trial. The issuance of such a law is, in fact, to be considered as confirmation of the thesis that the substantive rules of criminal law, including those pertaining to murder, were never revoked under the Nazi regime, even though they were never enforced when politically inconvenient.

A word might be said, however, concerning this "whitewashing" law of July 1934 which, if valid, would erase criminal responsibility for the murders committed during the Röhm revolt. Some doubts may arise as to which of the murders were the "authorized" ones and which would come under the category of "unprivileged" murders. That not all of them were duly authorized may be concluded from the fact that the Fuehrer issued a proclamation decreeing that whoever acted without authorization would be put at the disposal of the state attorney, and in the same proclamation declared that all measures necessary to overcome the Röhm revolt had been taken during the night of 1 July 1934.[24] This assertion would seem to establish a presumption that any murders committed after that date were not duly authorized.

However that may be, such a law obviously cannot be given recognition. The merger of administrative action and an individual legislative measure, the retroactive vindication of this action and the anticipation of the outcome of a judicial investigation by the elevating of crimes to the rank of lawful acts may be justifiable from the viewpoint of the National Socialist doctrine,[25] and to members of the Party and its organizations the murders may seem excusable in that the victims were bound by a special loyalty and subject to a special discipline. But any interpretation which follows normal constitutional concepts must necessarily reject such theories. A jurisdictional shift which makes the perpetrator of an act the judge of its guilt or innocence is invalid. Even if it were construed as a measure of amnesty, it would be exposed, like other Nazi amnesties, to the objection that the authorities who proclaimed it are the main beneficiaries.

While this 1934 statute would probably be invoked by the defense in connection only with the Röhm murders, the Prussian statute on the Secret State Police of 10 February 1936,[26] which applied to the whole Reich, might prove of much wider importance in the strategy of the defense. By this statute the secret state police were explicitly entrusted with the task of "battling against all movements dangerous to the state."

This statute has to be read in connection with the emergency decree of 28 February 1933[27] abrogating constitutional guarantees and permitting specific restrictions of personal freedom. The decree of February 1933 allows arrest and detention without trial.[28] But would both laws taken together justify willful murder and assault? Does their explicit mentioning of an officially approved aim, the fight against enemies of the state, authorize the application of means not sanctioned by the law of the land? It does not. Neither implicitly nor explicitly do these statutes legalize any means which contravene the penal code or which would be sanctioned only in a number of very narrowly defined circumstances (such as resistance to arrest or attempted fights). Such special circumstances, moreover, would have to be proven by the party invoking them, the defendant.

Support for this line of argument can be found in utterances by Dr. Best, former general counsel of the SS administration. In discussing the legal means of coercion at the disposal of the police when fulfilling their task of combatting dangerous political movements, Best described a scale of interference with personal freedom ranging from the mildest admonition to the most severe—protective custody—mentioning restrictions of movement and forced domicile as intermediary weapons.[29] Since Best was speaking explicitly of legal means, it is obvious that he must have considered all other means utilized by the police as not being covered or protected by the law.

In this connection it may be worth mentioning that the German Civil Service Act of 1937[30] explicitly established the principle that any state employee was responsible for the conformity of his acts with existing law (par. 7). He had to follow the orders of his superiors, but if it became clear to him that their execution would constitute a violation of existing criminal law, he was to defy them.[31]

No act of violence against political opponents or complicity in such an act had any sanction in criminal law. In cases of willful homicide, then, the conflict between an order by a superior and the boundaries set to official action by the criminal law can be assumed to have been clearly discernible to the individual. It can further be assumed that he acted with full knowledge that no protection would be afforded to him in German law.

There are some borderline homicide and assault cases which may need further theoretical clarification. It is obvious that no hereditary health legislation can be evoked to justify the killing of old, sick, and helpless people in rest homes, old age homes, etc. The perpetrators of such acts, whether principals or accessories, are guilty of murder. But the question arises whether or not the "Law for the Prevention of Hereditarily Diseased Offspring" of 14 July 1933[32] could be invoked as a defense in numerous cases of medical "operations" resulting in death or permanent bodily harm to the victims. Insofar as such operations have been carried through in conformity with and are covered by the terms of this law, which restricts sterilization to nine categories of cases, the law might constitute a valid defense. But any other operations not covered by these categories—such as operations on politically undesirable elements—would, if resulting in death, be treated as murder or manslaughter,[33] and otherwise as an aggravated assault.[34]

### D. The Necessity for Retroactive Rescission of Nazi Laws

This example of the "Law for the Prevention of Hereditarily Diseased Offspring" shows the limits to the usefulness of existing criminal legislation for the prosecution of domestic offenders. It is useful for the prosecution of criminal acts insofar as they are not protected by legislation enacted by the Nazis. It cannot be used to prosecute those responsible for the inauguration or execution of reprehensible policies, if these policies were carried through by means of duly enacted laws and decrees.

The fact that a law or decree was duly enacted does not, of course, mean that its purposes were not reprehensible. Even where, as in the case of the sterilization laws mentioned above, the ostensible aim may not seem objectionable, its actual intent becomes more clear when seen in the context of the Nazis' whole policy or when its avowed legislative aims are compared with actual administrative practices.[35] In other cases there may not even be a question that a law—no matter how proper in form and enactment—cannot stand.

In this latter category belongs the so-called racial legislation proper, especially the "Law for the Protection of German Blood and Honor"[36] and various decrees reducing the status of the Jews to that of mere slaves. If this legislation is to be considered void only from the day of the Military Government Proclamations, most of those responsible for the inauguration and the execution of this policy would escape punishment, so long as they had avoided direct participation in murder or assault. No state attorney or judicial official could be held criminally responsible for his share in the enforcement of sanctions against "race defilement." To be sure, not all officials who participated in the enforcement of such a law will be held criminally responsible in any event. Many may be able to prove that they applied it *contre-coeur*, tried to use delaying tactics, or to help in other ways the victims of this legislation. Yet it remains true that as long as the law is considered valid law until it was officially rescinded, the prosecution will be unable to make out a case against the small nucleus of persons principally responsible for its being put on the statute book and enforced.

The same considerations would generally apply to the activities of members of official repressive agencies such as the People's Court,[37] the various special courts, and the Party and army jurisdictions.[38] If the laws on which their judgments and sentences rested were not to be retroactively invalidated, a prosecution could be based only on par. 336 of the German Criminal Code. According to this article, an official may be held criminally responsible if he has broken the law in favor, or to the disadvantage of, one party. Due to the almost unlimited discretion left to the court by the Nazi rules of procedure,[39] however, it would be a next to impossible task to establish an intentional disregard of procedural rules to the disadvantage of the defendant. As regards the substantive law, indeed, the very Nazi judges who are to be made responsible for a policy of systematic terrorism are the ones who can most effectively pretend to have strictly adhered to the spirit as well as to the letter of the new laws. If criminal prosecution of state attorneys and members of Nazi courts is contemplated, the laws on which their main activities rested[40] will have to be voided.

If such retroactive rescission is decided upon, it can be handled in either of two ways:

a. A list can be promulgated rescinding a number of specifically enumerated laws and decrees with retroactive force.
b. The laws and decrees to be rescinded can be defined in a general way—e.g., "all criminal laws enacted for the protection of National Socialist Domination and institutions." Interpretation as to which criminal laws and which penal provisions of other laws would come under that definition would be left to the court.

### E. The Statute of Limitation

Will it be necessary to set aside temporarily the statute of limitation in order to carry through the prosecution of war criminals for the violation of domestic offenses?

As it now stands, the statute of limitations operates after the lapse of 20 years in regard to offenses punishable by death or hard labor for life; after 15 years for offenses punishable by up to 10 years of hard labor; and after 10 years in the case of offenses punished by lesser sentences. (par. 67, penal code).

Due to the premature end of the Nazi regime, most major Nazi criminals will have no opportunity to benefit from this statute, especially as Nazi legislation itself has in many instances retroactively increased the scale of punishments.

However, because a few Nazis might still be able to claim immunity under this statute, it might be advisable to take advantage of the legal proviso which allows cancellation of limitations for periods in which there has been a complete breakdown of criminal justice.[41] Judicial administration under the Nazis could certainly be so characterized. A directive to the court, then, could be issued ordering that the statute be disregarded for offenses committed between 1932 and 1938. There would be no need to extend this period beyond 1938: the earliest date thereafter at which the statute would again begin to operate would be 1948; and it should certainly be possible to bring these criminals to book by then.

### F. Nazi Amnesties

In sharp contrast to practices prevailing under the Weimar Republic, the Third Reich issued a great number of amnesties. Such general amnesties were issued in 1933,[42] 1934,[43] 1936,[44] 1938,[45] and at the beginning of the war in 1939.[46] They were accompanied by a number of special amnesties for the populations of newly annexed territories and by various amnesties for breaches of discipline in a great number of professions. The general amnesties cover the following offenses:

a. Minor offenses of all types covering between one to six months imprisonment and fines.
b. Minor offenses by political enemies of the regime covering defamation and similar offenses generally resulting in prison terms up to six months.
c. All types of offenses and sentences of "overzealous" political adherents to the new regime. Whereas the 1933 and 1938 decrees (the latter insofar as acts in Austria's "Freedom fight" are concerned) give amnesty for *any* Nazi act, the other amnesties stop short of forgiving willful murder.

These amnesties become all the more important in that they extended not only to final sentences and pending trials, but also to cases still under investigation by police and state attorneys and cases which had not yet even come to the attention of the authorities. If the offenses in question fell before the date on which the amnesty went into effect, they were covered by it.[47]

Most Nazis under indictment can doubtless be prosecuted regardless of these Nazi amnesties. But a few of them might be able to claim immunity under the clause excusing "over-zealous adherents." In the 1934 and 1936 amnesties, it is true, this clause was qualified by a proviso that it was not to apply "if the manner of execution of their deed or their motives give proof of a depraved mentality." No such reservation, however, exists in either the 1933 or 1938 amnesties. Thus, those responsible for the Reichstag fire of 1933 might be able to invoke the amnesty of that year which excused the "overzealous." Consequently, it would be advantageous to the prosecution if the court were directed to disregard all amnesties which especially benefit "overzealous adherents."

## Domestic Crimes

### II. The Organization of Terrorism

#### A. The Rise of the System

The Nazis have never left any doubt that once in power they would not stick to "legality." Insofar as the Nazis professed to adhere to constitutional and legal methods, their statements were for the record only. In fact, the word "legality" when used by the Nazis acquired a quite different meaning. It did not mean that their orders would keep within the constitutional framework, but that once in power they would have the right to do as they pleased. A Party newspaper put the Nazis' position very succinctly;

> It is our supreme task to save the German nation. Everything is legal which will effect the salvation of the German nation. We are

> legal. You are legal. Your legality means the destruction of the national opposition. But our (Nazi) legality will start at the very moment when your (Republican) legality is on the way out. At that moment we will use our legality to destroy yours.[48]

This intention of doing away with the Weimar Constitution and its guarantees of free political activity by all lawful organizations and of replacing it with the dictatorship of the Nazi Party was openly professed in the oral propaganda of the Nazi agitators, and even in the written documents of the Party it was only thinly veiled. As justification, Nazi propaganda used to refer to a hypothetical Communist putsch for which these emergency measures ostensibly were prepared.[49]

Immediately following the Nazis' seizure of power, the campaign of terror against their political enemies began. Its first object was the Communist Party. In the official declaration of the incoming government the victory over the "Communistic decomposition of Germany" had been called "the decisive act for the rebirth of Germany."[50] The Communist Party was deprived of the right to hold meetings, and its headquarters in Berlin were occupied by the police. An official report was put out indicating that a search of the headquarters had produced material proving the imminence of a Communist revolt.

The police were promptly reorganized with a view to making them a reliable instrument for terroristic activities. The truncheon was replaced by heavy arms. Scores of SA and SS men were recruited, and old "unreliable" police officials were dismissed. The police were ordered to establish the friendliest relations with SA, SS, and the Stahlhelm organization of veterans of the first World War. At the same time the most vigorous measures were ordered against the Communists. A circular by Hermann Goering to all police authorities on 17 February 1933 stated: "Hostile attitudes toward persecution of SA, SS, Stahlhelm, and of nationalist parties must be avoided. I expect all police authorities to establish the best relations with these organizations, which contain the most important elements for the reconstruction of the state. In addition, every activity for national purposes and nationalist propaganda should be vigorously supported. Only in the most urgent cases may police restrictions be applied to their activities. . . . The most stringent measures are to be used against Communist terror acts. Police officials who in the exercise of their duty make use of their firearms will be protected by me without regard to the consequences of their use. Every official should always keep in mind that the omission of a measure will weigh much more heavily against him than faults committed in the exercise of his duty."

The same attitude characterizes the address made by the new Berlin police president, Admiral von Levetzow, to officers of the *Schutzpolizei*. "We do not forget the great services of the National Socialist Party, of its valiant SA and SS . . . and thus I ask every one of you, please, do see in them your loyal allies, your most trustworthy helpers for the suppression of revolts and riots."[51] This order to treat the National Socialist and nationalist organizations as the favorite sons of the police seemingly did not go far enough, for within a short time the SA, SS, and Stahlhelm were, first in Prussia, and later in the other states, elevated to the rank of auxiliary police.[52] This measure allowed the SA and SS to assault and intimidate their political enemies under the cover of legality. Persons suspected of wavering politically were to be impressed by the official coordination of the Nazis' private army and its close cooperation with the state police.

A few days after the SA and SS had been elevated to the rank of auxiliary police the Reichstag fire broke out (27 February 1933). The fire, which was immediately attributed to the Communists and Socialists, served as a pretext to start a wave of systematic prosecutions of political enemies. The arrest of 4,000 Communist Party functionaries and the closing down of the Communist and Socialist press was ordered.[53]

A pseudo-legal basis for some of these measures was found in an emergency decree of the President "for the protection of the German people" of 4 February 1933,[54] issued at the instigation and pressure of the National Socialist members of the cabinet. This decree gave the police wide powers to prohibit and control political meetings and, in reduced degree, to seize newspapers as well as to forbid their appearance for a period of four weeks. The pretext that Marinus van der Lubbe, the presumptive arsonist, had supposedly confessed to being associated with the Social Democratic Party was used to close down Social Democratic newspapers. Even Center Party newspapers did not escape the same fate, although measures taken against them were mitigated somewhat after some petitioning by high-placed Catholic political figures.[55]

These exceptional measures taken against the Communist, the Social Democratic, and to a lesser degree the Center Party were not related to any emergency, but were part of a carefully laid plan to stamp out opposition, particularly left-wing movements, as quickly as possible, and especially to eliminate the possibility of their putting up a fight of any consequence in the national elections of 5 March. The terror served also to show the German people that the left wing parties, although still formally appearing on the election lists, were doomed. Insofar as the Communists were concerned, this fact was made officially clear before the election. Thus, for instance, Goering in a broadcast on 1 March declared: "We not only want to defend ourselves against the Communist danger, but it is our most important task to vanquish Communism and to extirpate it from Germany."[56]

The political terror exercised under the shield of state authority by National Socialist organizations was, however, by no means restricted to the extreme left. It was also extended to the Center Party, especially in those regions where this party had a large following in working-class circles. This fact may be seen from the message of protest sent to Goering by the chairman of the Center Party in Krefeld: "The Center Party Krefeld had been assembled in a closed Party meeting in the town hall. The meeting was broken up by the National Socialists according to plans made in advance. A National Socialist contingent, part of which had gained admission by false tickets, and part of which had forced their way into the hall, threw a bomb at the speakers' platform. One of the contingent struck Stegerwald with the butt of a revolver."[57]

To a certain extent this policy of terrorism had been legalized by the decree of the Reich President "for the protection of the people and state," issued immediately after the Reichstag fire.[58] The decree had suspended the most important fundamental rights guaranteed by the Weimar constitution. It allowed, among other things, search, seizure, and arrest without any legal limitations. In addition, paragraph 2 gave the Reich government the right to take over the functions of those state governments which would not comply with the orders issued by the Reich Government. It thus gave the National Socialist government additional legal weapons to force into line recalcitrant state governments which were loathe to carry through the policy of terror.

With all legal hurdles thus cleared, the National Socialists started immediately to establish concentration camps so that the more dangerous political enemies would be safely out of the way during election week. Goering himself has admitted that from the beginning thousands of Communist and Socialist functionaries were put into these concentration camps. "Thus the concentration camps were set up, in which we had to put for the time being thousand of functionaries of the Communist and Socialist Party. It goes without saying that here and there some innocent people were hit. It goes equally without saying that beatings have occurred here and there and that acts of brutality have been committed. But measured by the past and by the magnitude of the event, the German revolution has been the least bloody and the most disciplined of all revolutions."[59]

The elections which took place on 5 March in an atmosphere of terror although without open Nazi interference—at least in the urban areas—gave the National Socialists neither a simple majority for their own Party nor together with the other nationalist parties the two-thirds majority necessary for constitutional changes. The parliamentary difficulties resulting from this situation were circumvented by the simple device of barring the Communists from attendance in the Reichstag. This step proved to be rather simple since those Communists who had not already gone into hiding or fled the country had been put into concentration camps before the election. This action of the government was officially legalized one week after the decisive Reichstag session in which a two-thirds majority for the passage of the Enabling Act was achieved through the exclusion of the Communists.[60]

Immediately after the Reichstag elections the Nazi Party started to take over power from the remaining non-nationalist state governments. Whenever these governments did not give way voluntarily, SA troops occupied the respective government buildings.[61]

### B. The Suppression of Trade Unions, Political Parties, and Other Organizations

All trade unions, whatever their political complexion, tried to reach an agreement with the Nazi government. By offering to renounce any kind of political activity they hoped to be able to continue in their trade union functions. Their position in this attempt to reach a compromise with the Nazis seemed favorable. The work councils elections, which had taken place in February and March 1933, had ended with a resounding victory for the old established unions.

The representatives of the established unions had received 81.6 percent of the vote, the National Socialist lists only 11.7 percent, the Communists 4.9, and various splinter groups 1.8 percent.[62] Dismayed by the result, the Nazis suspended further elections to work councils on 4 April 1933.[63]

Meanwhile, the most important Socialist trade unions had shown their willingness to reach a compromise with the Nazis not only by renouncing any further relation with the Socialist Party, but, more positively, by publicly welcoming the proclamation of 1 May as a national holiday. They took this gesture of the Hitler government as proof of the German workers' full acceptance by the national community.

The Nazis, however, had decided not to enter into any compromise with the existing unions. As early as the beginning of April 1933 Dr. Robert Ley had been secretly appointed head of "a National Socialist committee for the protection of German labor." On 21 April[64] the directive for taking over the German General Trade Union Federation (*Allgemeiner Deutscher Gewerkschaftsbund*—ADGB) and of the General Free Union of Salaried Employees (*Allgemeiner Freier Angestellbenbund*—AFA) had been issued. These directives laid down that SA and SS men were to be employed for the seizure of the buildings as well as for the taking into custody of the presidents and regional secretaries of the organizations as well as of the branch directors of the *Bank der Arbeit*.[65]

The action was carried through as provided in the directive. According to an order of the Attorney General at the Berlin District Court of 12 May 1933, the assets of the trade unions were seized. By an order of the same authority of 9 May 1933 the assets of the Social Democratic newspapers, and the Defense League of the Weimar coalition forces (*Reichsbanner Schwarz-Rot-Gold*, were also seized. Officially, the orders were issued in connection with the inquiry against the trade union leader Leipart, who was charged with embezzlement. Nothing was ever heard of this judicial investigation, and neither he nor any other prominent labor leader was ever tried for these fictitious embezzlements.

The Christian trade unions, a group of unions which had close relation with the Center Party were granted a somewhat more extended lease of life. Their representatives were even allowed to attend the June conference of the International Labor Office in Geneva so as to prove the existence of independent trade unions. Yet in spite of the appearance of the Christian trade unionists, the German delegation, led by Dr. Ley, was given a hostile reception. The usefulness of the independent Christian trade unions within the framework of the Nazi state had obviously come to an end. Therefore on 21 June 1933 the Christian trade union offices were seized by the *Nationalsozialistische Betrieb szellen-Organisation* (*NSBO*) according to the pattern evolved for the seizure of the trade unions.[66]

With the trade unions gone, the political parties remained to be taken care of. Most of them had not functioned since April. But, insofar as their legal position was concerned, only the Communist Party was outlawed. Members of the other parties still continued as members of town councils, etc. Therefore, by an order of the Prussian Ministry of the Interior of 25 June 1933, the Social Democratic Party was declared to be a party hostile to the state. Members were barred from any participation in parliaments, city councils, and other elected bodies. As noted above, the property of the organization previously had been taken over under an injunction issued by the Attorney General of the Berlin District Court of 9 May. This action was now extended to the whole territory, by an order of Göring.[67] But since he exercised jurisdiction only insofar as Prussia was concerned, his order was "regularized" by a decree of the Reich Ministry of the Interior of 7 July 1933, which also invalidated the Reichstag seats of the Democratic Party.[68]

At the same time, the middle class parties were "invited" to disband. In the case of the Center Party and the Bavarian People's Party, this invitation was effectively supported by a search of the premises of the organizations as well as by the arrest of prominent Party members. Under this dispensation, the following parties disbanded "voluntarily": German State Party (*Deutsche Staatspartei*) as of 28 June 1933; Center Party (*Zentrum*) as of 3 July 1933; Bavarian People's Party (*Bayerische Volkspartei*) as of 4 July 1933; German Hanoverian Party (*Die Deutsch-Hannoverische Partei*) as of 1 July 1933; the Christian Social People's Service (*Die Reichs leitung des Christlich-Sozialen Volksdienstes*) as of 1 July 1933; the German People's Party (*Deutsche Volkspartei*) as of 4 July 1933.[69]

The German Nationalist Party or, as it had called itself since May, the "German Nationalist Front," had been associated with National Socialists in the Reich Government since 30 January. It did not, however, fare any better. Its organization, especially the Nationalist *Kampfringe*, had proved themselves the most skillful and most serious opponents of the Nazi organizations. Therefore, their disappearance was mandatory from the viewpoint of the Nazi Party. In consequence, on 21 June 1933 these formations were prohibited on the basis of the decree of 28 February 1933 issued against Communist terrorists dangerous to the existence of the state. The Nationalist Front headquarters were seized and occupied by the police and SA. However, it proved difficult to disband this nationalist organization. Although Franz Seldte, the leader of the Stahlhelm and Reichs Minister of Labor, had abandoned the nationalist organizations to their fate, they were powerful enough to continue resistance for sometime before the SA with the help of the police was able to get rid of this dangerous competitor. The members of the nationalist Reichstag group were allowed to join the National Socialist Reichstag group en bloc.[70]

The final blow to competing parties was in the making, and on 14 July the prohibition and dissolution of the individual organizations was followed by a general law forbidding the formation of new parties.[71] The funds and other assets of any kind of organization in disagreement or competing with the Nazi organizations, insofar as they had not been seized before by individual measures or orders, were seized in accordance with the law concerning the confiscation of Communist property of 26 May 1933.[72] This law was extended to embrace any organization hostile to or in competition with the National Socialists. Later on, a second law officially enlarged the basis for confiscation. This law "concerning the confiscation of funds and assets of those elements inimical to the existence of state and people" explicitly mentioned property and rights belonging to the Social Democratic Party, but also included any other property and assets used for the furtherance of Marxist or any other activities and movements endangering the security of state and people. The Reich Minister of the Interior decided on the application of the law and no legal remedy was provided against his decision.[73] According to two decrees the head of the Reich Food Estate was empowered to incorporate or to abolish various agricultural organizations.[74]

Long before these confiscatory laws were issued, however, National Socialist "commissars" had infiltrated into all kinds of cultural, social, and economic organizations, as well as into individual business concerns. Sometimes these commissars were appointed by local Nazi organizations. In many cases, the self-styled "commissars" extorted great sums from individuals and organizations by promising to protect them against more far-reaching Party demands. Eventually their activities became so obnoxious that these "commissars" whose existence had never been recognized by law had to be officially withdrawn by order of Reich Minister of Interior Frick of 6 July 1933.[75] According to the order the last "commissars" were to disappear as of 1 October 1933. The order was implemented by a circular of the Prussian Minister of Justice to the state attorneys ordering them to prosecute cases of extortion and illegal assumption of public office. However, while the decree may have granted some relief to business enterprises and individual businessmen faced with extortionate demands no such relief was in sight for the thousands of voluntary organizations and associations which were either forcibly brought into line (*gleichgeschaltet*) or simply shut down and their properties confiscated.

### C. The Legalized Forms of Political Terror

The terroristic program of the National Socialists was put into effect through two types of agencies: (a) the legalized terror which worked through the courts and the application of National Socialist legislation; (b) the police and organizational terror which applied force and violence directly to political enemies without the intervention of legal agencies.[76]

These forms of terroristic activities were not mutually exclusive and sometimes overlapped in practice, as the following discussion will show:

a) Prisoners handed over to the legal authorities were often maltreated and "prepared" before they were put at the disposal of the legal authorities. Even after a prisoner had been turned over to the legal authorities, he might be "released" to the Gestapo for further interrogation when intervening circumstances made it imperative for the Gestapo to withdraw the case from the legal authorities. In many of these cases the prisoner died while being further investigated by the Gestapo.[77]
b) Political prisoners who had served a sentence or who had been acquitted by the court were nevertheless put into concentration camps for "educational" purposes.[78] Any secret police official as well as any concentration camp officer can testify to this practice. Moreover, the concentration camp files of individual prisoners will contain material on this point. The most famous case in point was that of Martin Niemoeller.

In some instances, moreover, the "revision" of an "inadequate" court sentence was carried through by local Party organizations without going through the formality of putting the political prisoner into a concentration camp. He was either beaten or killed.

Legalized political terror was effected by means of special legislation enacted by the Nazis. The first penal sanctions against opposition groups were laid down in the decree for the protection of the German people of 4 February 1933.[79] The decree increased the maximum punishment for an attempted public incitement to acts of violence from one year to five years imprisonment. The same decree contained certain administrative restrictions on public assemblies, and determined the legal conditions required for suspending the publication of periodicals. Breaches of these regulations and prohibitions were made criminal offenses.

But the real cornerstone of the Nazi dictatorship was formed by the above mentioned decree for the "protection" of the people and the state of 28 February 1933, issued in connection with the Reichstag fire. From then on, resistance to orders issued in the interest of public security was punishable by sentence to hard labor and confiscation of property and even with capital punishment if a death occurred as a result of the contravention. Moreover, the application of the death penalty for political offenses was greatly increased.[80]

At the beginning of April, profiting from the artificially-created Communist scare, the scope of the death penalty was again enlarged in the "law for the defense against acts of political terror."[81] The above-mentioned law of 14 July 1933 made punishable any attempt to form new political parties or to keep up organizational activities of old political organizations.[82] The law for the maintenance of the public peace and the legal order of 13 October 1933[83] introduced the death penalty for attempts on the life of state employees and Party functionaries; it provided the same penalty for any attempt to smuggle anti-Nazi literature into Germany.

Whereas these laws and decrees were directed against any attempt to revive organizational activities directed against the new regime, the law of 20 December 1934 against surreptitious attacks upon State and Party[84] concerned itself mainly with individuals who persisted in making disrespectful remarks about the regime. It penalized slanderous utterances against the German nation, the Government, the Nazi Party, and its leading personalities. Even private malicious utterances against leading personalities were punishable if the author should have known that his words might receive publicity. The truth of the remark was no defense if the statement was liable to endanger the authority or the good name of the Government or of the Party. The law against secret radio transmitters, dated 24 November 1937,[85] made unlicensed broadcasting a crime punishable even if committed by negligence.

To these special political laws must be added the changes brought about in Sections 80–87 of the German Penal Code dealing with treason (*Hochverrat*). German law distinguishes between two kinds of treasonable crimes: High treason (*Hochverrat*), which is directed against the internal security of the state and treason (*Landesverrat*), which concerns the external security of the state in relation to other powers. High treason is the attempt to alter the constitution by violence. It comprises also an undertaking to sever territories from the Reich (Section 80). Even the pre-Nazi law of high treason went far in penalizing preparatory and conspiratory acts. To the general conception used heretofore, the Nazis added detailed provisions referring to particular crimes, namely, duress directed against the Reich President or members of the government (Section 81), the training of armed forces or the abuse of public authority (Section 82), and a number of remote acts which were preliminary to preparatory acts. Such acts were those tending to establish or maintain organized contacts for the preparation of high treason, or tending to influence the masses by publications or other means of communication, or preparatory acts committed outside Germany or by the importation of publications or other means of spreading propaganda (Section 83). The printing, distributing, or keeping for distribution of printed matter containing treasonable writings was punishable if the person committing any of these acts was in a position to realize the treasonable character of the contents after careful investigation (Section 85). All cases of treasonable undertakings and conspiracies, and the particular preparatory acts mentioned above, were made capital offenses. The Nazis further introduced fines without a statutory maximum and replaced the seizure of property belonging to principals and ringleaders by outright confiscation of their property.

These laws and decrees formed the main legal tools with which the legalized terror operated until the beginning of the war. After the war began new penal legislation was introduced. One of the new decrees dealt with "extraordinary measures in the field of broadcasting" and subjected to severe punishment listening to foreign broadcasts.[86]

Of great significance was the decree on "special wartime crimes" which, interestingly enough, bore the date of 17 August 1938, but which was published only after the beginning of the war in September 1942.[87] Under paragraph 5, it ordered the death penalty for whoever publicly tries to "undermine the will to resist of the German people or their allies." The loose wording of this section covered almost any form of political resistance and thus became the cornerstone for political prosecutions during the war. There were also numerous other penal laws which by their loose wording could be utilized against any form of political opposition. These laws are not specifically discussed here, but are included in the list below, inasmuch as they make the death penalty either mandatory or permissive.

The following compilation covers the crimes made punishable by death under the pre-Nazi regime and those to which the death penalty was made applicable under Nazi law. In contrast to the three crimes punishable by death before 1933, there appear no less then forty-four under Nazi laws.

A. *Crimes Punishable by the Death Penalty under Pre-Nazi Laws*

1. Murder (Penal Code, Section 211);
2. Homicide through the use of explosives (Section 5, Law against the Criminal and Dangerous Use of Explosives of 9 June 1884—*Gesetz vom 9 June 1884 gegen den verbrecherischen und gemeingefaehrlichen Gebrauch von Sprengstoffen* TRGl. 61);
3. Slave-raiding, involving the loss of human lives (Section 1, Law on the Punishment of Slave Raiders, of July 1895—*Gesetz zur Bestrafung des Sklavenraubes*).

B. *Crimes Punishable by the Death Penalty under Nazi Laws*

1. High treason (Penal Code, Section 80);
2. High treason by means of coercion (Section 81);
3. Conspiracy to commit high treason (Section 82);
4. Certain acts preparatory to committing high treason (Section 85);
5. Undertaking to kill the Reich President (Section 5, no. 1; Presidential decree for the Protection of People and State, of 28 February 1933—*Verordnung des Reichspräsidenten zum Schutz von Volk und Staat*, RGBl. I, 83);
6. Armed riots (Section 5, no. 2, (*ibid.*);
7. Deprivation of liberty for the purpose of taking hostages in political strife (Section 5, no. 3, *ibid.*);
8. Causing the death of a person by violating certain executive security regulations (Section 4, *ibid.*);
9. Terrorizing the populace by committing offenses while wearing a Nazi uniform (Section 3, Law against Vicious Attacks Directed against State and Party and for the Protection of Party Uniforms, of 20 December 1934—*Gesetz gegen heimtückische Angriffe auf Staat und Partei und zum Schutz der Parteiuniformen*; (RGBL. I, 1269).
10. Posing as a member of the police or of the Armed Forces while committing a crime (Section 1, decree on the Extension of Criminal Protection against False Assumption of Public Authority, of 9 April 1942—*Verordnung zur Erweiterung und Verschärfung des strafrechtlichen Schutzes gegen Amtsanmassung* (RGBl. I, 174);
11. Causing danger to life and property by the use of explosives; (Section 1, no. 1, Law for the Defense against acts of Political Terror, of 4 April 1933—*Gesetz zur Abwehr politischer Gewelttaten, (*RGBl. 162)
12. Arson or explosion of a public building in order to intimidate the populace (Section 1, no. 2, *ibid*);

13. Causing a public danger by the use of poison, or by inundation (Section 1, no. 3, *ibid.*);
14. Spreading news from foreign broadcasts (Section 2, decree on Extraordinary Measures concerning Broadcasting, of 1 September 1939—*Verordnung über ausserordentliche Rundfunkmassnahmen* RGBl. I, 1683);
15. Undertaking to betray state secrets (Section 89);
16. Undertaking to obtain state secrets with the intent to betray (Section 90);
17. Disloyal conduct of diplomatic affairs (Section 90g);
a. Contacting a foreign government with intent to seriously injure the Reich (Section 91, I)
b. Contacting a foreign government with intent seriously to injure a Reich National (Section 91, II)
18. Serving with enemy forces during time of war (Section 91a);
19. Aiding and abetting the enemy (Section 91b);
20. Causing a grave danger to German reputation by untrue statements (Section 90f, II);
21. Espionage (Section 2, decree of Special Wartime Criminal Law, of 17 August 1938—*Kriegssonderstrafrechtsverordnung* RGBl., 1939, I, 1455, 2131);
22. Illegal guerrilla warfare (Section 3, *ibid.*);
23. Undermining of military strength by incitement to disobedience or desertion, or by self-mutilation, and certain other means (Section 5, *ibid.*);
24. Any offense, intentional or negligent, involving a serious danger or disadvantage to the war effort or to the security of the Reich, whenever "the sound instincts of the people" indicate that the regular penalty would not be a sufficient retribution for the act committed (Section 5a, *ibid.*, as amended by the Fifth decree to supplement the decree on Special Wartime Criminal Law, of 5 May 1944—*Fünfte Verordnung zur Ergänzung der Kriegssonderstrafrechtsverordnung*, RGBl. I, 115);
25. Persistent acts of injuring the vitality of the German people through abortion (Section 218);
26. Serious cases of failure to report certain impending capital crimes (Section 139 II);
27. Sabotage of military equipment, defense installations, or pertinent raw materials (Section 143a);
28. Sabotage of vital supply plants (Section 2, decree on the Protection of the War Potential of the German People, of 25 November 1939—*Verordnung zur Erganzung der*

*Strafvorschriften zum Schutz der Wehrkraft des deutschen Volkes*, RGBl. I, 2319);

29. The offense committed by a German national of transferring to, or holding in, another country any private property to the detriment of the German economy (Law against Economic Sabotage, of 1 December 1936—*Gesetz gegen Wirtschaftssabotage* RGBl. I, 999);
30. Setting roadblocks with intent to rob (Law against Highway-robbery through Use of Roadblocks, of 22 June 1938—*Gesetz gegen Strassenraub mittels Autofallen*, RGBl. I, 651);
31. Kidnaping of children with the intent of extortion (Section 239a);
32 Intentionally endangering rail, water, or air transportation (Section 315);
33. Destruction, concealment, or retention of necessary raw materials or products, or concealment or falsification of pertinent coupons and certificates (Section 1, Ordinance on War Economy, of 4 September 1939—*Kriegswirtsschaftsverordnung*, RGBl. I, 1609; and of 25 March 1942, RGBl. I, 147);
34. Misappropriation of objects gathered through the public metal collection (Ordinance on the Protection of the Metal Collection of 29 March 1940—*Verordnung zum Schutz der Metallsammlungs*, RGBl. I, 565);
35. Misappropriation of objects gathered in the collection of winter garments (Ordinance of the Führer on the Protection of Collection of Winter Garments for the Front, of 23 December 1941—*Verordnung des Führers zum Schutz der Sammling von Wintersachen für die Front*, RGBl. I, 797);
36. Making untrue statements about the demand or amount of labor or raw materials, products, machines, and tools in the armament industry (Decree of the Führer on the Protection of the Armament Industry, of 21 March 1942—*Verordnung des Fuhrers zum Schutz der Rüstungswirtschaft*, RGBl. I, 165);
37. Looting in evacuated districts (Section 1, Decree against Enemies of the People, of 5 September 1939—*Verordnung gegen Volksschädlinge*, RGBl. I, 1679);
38. Any offense against life, limb or property (not a contravention) committed while taking advantage of air-raid precautions (Section 2, *ibid*);
39. Endangering national resistance by committing arson or other crimes which create dangers to the public (Section 3, *ibid.*);

40. Any criminal offense committed with intention of taking advantage of the exceptional conditions due to the war, provided the "sound instincts of the people" require the death penalty in view of the viciousness of the offense (Section 4, *ibid.*);
41. Any use of arms or of similarly dangerous instruments while committing rape, robbery, or any other act of serious violence, or threatening a person's life or limb with such weapons, or attacking or repelling pursuers with such weapons after committing a crime (Section 1, decree against Violent Criminals, of 5 December 1939—*Verordnung gegen Gewaltverbrecher*, RGBl. I, 2378);
42. A third offense committed by a person regarded as a dangerous habitual criminal, provided the death of the offender is necessary for the protection of the national community or for the sake of a just retribution (Section 1, Law on changes of the Criminal Code, of 4 September 1941—*Gesetz zur Änderung des Strefgesetzbuchs,* RGBl. I, 549);
43. Any further sex offense committed by a person previously sentenced for indecent assault by duress or against children or for rape (Sections 176–178), provided the death of the offender is necessary for the protection of the national community or for the sake of a just retribution (Section 1, *ibid*);
44. Violation, either intentionally or by negligence, of orders issued by certain executive agencies, concerning the organization of total war, provided the violation caused a severe disadvantage or a serious danger to either the conduct of the war or the security of the Reich (Ordinance for Securing a Total War Effort, of 25 August 1944—*Verordnung zur Sicherung des totalen Kriegseinsatzes*, RGBl. I, 184).

In order to understand fully the scope of these new provisions, two other changes in the German criminal law must be taken into account:

1. Attempt, incitement, volunteering, conspiracy, and participation as an accessory were liable to the same penalty as the commission of the consummated offense.
2. Juveniles between the ages of 14 and 18 were no longer exempt from capital punishment.

Of equal importance with the building up of penal legislation giving the National Socialists the legal weapons to suppress their enemies was the Nazis' policy of denying and depriving the victims of the regime's terrorism of any legal protection. This policy of non-intervention was carried through on the legislative as well as the administrative levels. On the legislative level there were a number of amnesty laws which barred the courts and prosecuting authorities from taking cognizance of any criminal acts committed by "overzealous adherents of the Nazi Party."[88] On the administrative level this policy meant that the Ministry of Justice was completely disinterested in having the prosecuting authorities follow up the numerous crimes committed by the Nazi organizations. It also meant that the Ministry disregarded reports on atrocities committed by those organizations and gave neither encouragement nor orders to start official inquiries.

In addition, the right of terminating pending legal procedures by fiat of the sovereign (right of Abolition or *Niederschlagungsrecht*) was misused to cover up intended or already executed murders by Nazis. If some Nazi authorities prepared a murder, they made such murders "legal" by using blanks signed by Hitler or Goering, and renouncing the State's right to order inquiry and to bring the culprit to trial[89].

### D. The Responsibility of Various Agencies

The basic legal and administrative patterns of oppression were worked out in theory and practice by a number of top German agencies. Any differences in policies thus elaborated in these various Reich agencies were afterwards ironed out by the Reich Chancellery headed by Reich Minister Heinrich Lammers. After the outbreak of war, this task was carried out by the Ministerial Council for the defense of the Reich, of which Lammers in his position as head of the Reich Chancellery was the secretary.[90]

The main ministries and other high authorities involved in these procedures included the following:

1. *The Ministry of Justice*

   This Ministry was responsible for the framing of legislation. Even if a piece of legislation originated in another ministry, the Ministry of Justice participated in the elaboration of the new legislation, particularly if it was criminal legislation.

   At the same time, the Ministry assumed the highest administrative responsibility in the field of the administration of criminal justice, for it could order the state attorneys either to prosecute or not to prosecute specified cases. The responsibility for never having ordered any inquiry into the countless political murders committed by the National Socialist regime rests entirely with this Ministry.

   From 1933 to January 1941 the Ministry was headed by Dr. Franz Gürtner. After his death in 1941, the ministry was provisionally headed by the Secretary of State, Franz Schlegelberger. In 1943 Georg Thierack, the former president of the

People's Court, was appointed Minister and remained in office until the end of the regime. The two Secretaries of State in the Ministry were Dr. Roland Freisler and Schlegelberger. After Freisler's appointment as head of of the People's Court, H. Klemm was appointed Secretary of State. The sections of the Ministry most responsible for the framing and execution of the terroristic policies were the section on Criminal Legislation, headed by E. Schäfer, and the section on Criminal Prosecution, Criminal Procedure, and Prisons, headed by Dr. Vollmer.

2. *The Ministry of Interior*

   The Ministry of Interior was chiefly instrumental in the elaboration of political legislation properly so-called. It was chiefly responsible for the issuance of the emergency decree of 28 February 1933 and of the enabling act of 24 March 1933, by which Nazi rule was substituted for the legislative process as provided by the Weimar Constitution. It was equally responsible for all legislative as well as administrative measures aiming at the suppression of independent and social organizations and the confiscation of their assets.

   The Ministry of Interior was headed by Dr. Wilhelm Frick up to 1943, then by Heinrich Himmler. The Secretaries of State were Dr. Hans Pfundtner and Dr. Wilhelm Stuckart; after 1943 Dr. Stuckart served alone. The head of the Section for Constitution and Legislation responsible for the working out of terroristic legislation was Dr. Werner Hoche.

3. *The Highest Party Authorities*

   The Party authorities were not supposed to bring pressure to bear upon those officials and agencies entrusted with the administration of criminal justice. This principle, however, was never seriously adhered to, as can be seen from the repeated attempts to enforce some measure of orderly procedure upon Party personnel so far as such interventions into the course of justice were concerned. The following extract from an order of the Party Chancellery of 19 October 1944 may be taken as evidence:

"According to paragraph 3 of the circular of 2 December 1942 (*Reichsverfugungsblatt, Ausgabe* A, *Folge* 50/42) direct interventions in pending judicial procedures are not allowed. The opinion sometimes advanced that this circular concerns itself with civil law cases only is incorrect. The principle that all Party officers have to refrain from an illicit and inadmissible pressure on judicial proceedings also extends to criminal trials.

"If a Party office deems it imperative to make the court familiar with the political position of the Party concerning an individual criminal case, the Party Chancellery has to be informed, so as to take the necessary steps with the Reich Minister of Justice. Direct negotiations with the courts are not admissible."[91]

The responsibility for participation in acts of judicial terrorism on the higher level rested therefore with the Party Chancellery. This fact, however, does not exclude the possibility that individual Party organizations exercised pressure on the respective district attorneys' offices and the local courts in order to effect their terroristic aims.

4. *The Courts*

While the agencies mentioned above were responsible for the framing of legislative policies, it was the courts having jurisdiction over political crimes which gave administrative directives, exercised political pressure in general, and assumed direct responsibilities for carrying through the legalized terrorism. The most important courts involved were the following:

a. *The People's Court and the Supreme Reich Attorney at the Court*

The People's Court was established in June 1934[92] to handle cases of high treason. The jurisdiction of the People's Court was extended several times and at the end of the regime was almost all-embracing. The different sections of the court travelled throughout the country, each one composed of two professional judges and three members appointed by Hitler from the SS and Party ranks "on account of their special knowledge of defense against subversive activities, or because they are intimately connected with the political trend of the nation."[93]

Up to 1943, the President of the People's Court was Dr. Georg Thierack, who became the last Nazi Minister of Justice. Roland Freisler then succeeded to the Court Presidency. Supreme Attorney General of the People's Court was Lautz.

b. *The Appeal Courts and the Attorney General at the Courts*

The Appeal Courts handled only minor treason cases transferred to their jurisdiction by the Supreme Reich Attorney General of the People's Court.

c. *The Special Courts*

After 1933 political cases, insofar as they were not handled by the People's Court, were handled by the Special Courts set up at the various district courts.[94] In the earlier period of the regime, these courts were especially active in convicting members of left-wing parties who had tried to keep contacts with members of their former organizations.

d. *The Hauptamt-SS Tribunal in München-Starnberg as well as the SS Courts*

The lower SS courts handled political cases insofar as they concerned members of the Higher SS staffs, of the SS Troops for Special Tasks (SS-*Verfügungstruppe*), of the SS Deaths-head Formations (*SS-Totenkopfverbände*)[95] and of the police forces for special operation.

e. *The Military Courts*

The Supreme Military Tribunal (*Reichskriegsgericht*), the Military Courts of Appeal, and the Lower Military Court handled political cases involving members of the Armed Forces. According to reports emanating from French sources, the members of the Supreme Military Tribunal showed supreme disregard of the most elementary rights of the defendants, in cases of Germans as well as foreigners, who were tried before that court.[96]

In 1944 many of the functions of the military courts were transferred to an Army Central Court (*Zentralgericht des Heeres*) sitting in Berlin. This Army Central Court took cognizance of all political offenses committed by members of the Armed Forces, insofar as the People's Court did not take jurisdiction.[97]

## E. The Problem of Statistics and Records

No statistical information is available to OSS at this time which would give an adequate picture of the results of political terror in Germany between 1933 and 1945. No complete list of persons murdered for political reasons is presently available; nor is there available any complete record of the number of persons kept in concentration camps or otherwise mistreated by the Nazis. Notwithstanding the lack of full statistical data, it is possible to differentiate among a number of categories of political murder committed by Nazi agencies, organizations, or individual Nazis and to present pertinent cases under each heading. It may also be recognized that in the majority of instances the murders were carried through "administratively," but in some cases political murders were carried through by more or less formalized proceedings before the courts. The categories of political murders are the following:

A. *Political Opponents*

1) Communists (Thälmann)

2) Social Democrats (Hilferding)
3) Trade Unionists (L. Erdmann)
4) Other Leftists (H. Litten)
5) Nationalists (Oberfohren)
6) Military Leaders (Von Witzleben)

b. *Members of Religious Opposition Groups*
1) Catholics
2) Protestants
3) Sects

c. *Jews and Gypsies*
d. Persons killed out of personal revenge (Von Kahr)
e. Persons killed on account of special knowledge of facts which had to be kept secret in the interests of National Socialists (Rall)
f. Persons killed as a result of mistaken identity (Willi Schmidt)

Such statistical records as are available will be found in one of several places. The nature of these sources and their respective value are examined briefly in the following pages.

*I. Judicial Records*

German criminal statistics have been published up to the year 1939. These statistics do not, however, cover the work of the People's Court, in which a steadily increasing number of political crimes were handled, nor do they include the cases coming before SS and Police Courts and Military Courts.

These statistics have been published in abbreviated form up to 1940 in *Wirtschaft und Statistik*. The full results are regularly published in *Kriminalstatistik*, which forms part of the *Statistik des deutschen Reichs*; the largest criminal statistics are those for 1933 and 1934 which appear in the *Statistik des deutschen Reichs*, volumes 478 and 507. But these statistics are not very revealing due to the shifts in the system of repression, the adding of numerous new criminal offenses and the virtual disappearance of some old ones, and the absence of figures for the activities of the People's Court. It was pointed out above that the Nazi law provided the death penalty for a great variety of crimes. How many persons suffered this penalty is suggested by an article published by Georg Thierack, Minister of Justice, on 23 August 1944, in which are given the figures for the growth of the number of death sentences during the 1940–43 period. These figures seem to include death sentences handed down by all courts coming under the jurisdiction of the Ministry of Justice (including the People's Court, but not the Military and SS Courts):

| *Year* | *Number of Death Sentences* |
|---|---|
| 1940 | 926 |
| 1941 | 1,292 |
| 1942 | 3,660 |
| 1943 | 5,336 |

A breakdown of the death sentences handed down in 1943 is drawn in the following table:[98]

| *Crimes* | *Number Sentenced* |
|---|---|
| High treason | 1,747 |
| Crimes against the broadcasting laws | 11 |
| Undermining the people's will to resistance | 108 |
| Crimes against the occupying power | 282 |
| Sabotage and insubordination by foreign workers | 138 |
| Retention of arms by citizens of the Protectorate | 39 |
| Retention of arms by Poles | 2 |
| Sabotage in the Protectorate | 66 |
| Murder, attempted murder, and violent crimes | 250 |
| Refusal to help air raid victims | 3 |
| Arson | 35 |
| Dangerous habitual criminals (theft, fraud, taking advantage of the blackout and of war-time conditions) | 938 |
| Thefts from the railways | 122 |
| Thefts of field post parcels | 136 |
| Abortion | 1 |
| Looting in bomb-damaged houses | 182 |
| Crimes against the war economy | 236 |
| Sexual crimes | 114 |
| Embezzlement of NSV funds intended for bomb victims | 2 |
| Defrauding soldiers on front service | 2 |
| Desertion | 19 |
| Crimes against the decree for the protection of the *Winterhilfwork* | 3 |
| *Rassenschande* ("race pollution") | 4 |
| Other crimes | 6 |
| Death sentences from the occupied eastern territories | 894 |
| Total | 5,336 |

Of the 5,336 death sentences reported for 1943, 1,747 concerned political offenses of German citizens, 527 political offenses of foreign nationals. A certain number, however, of the remaining 2,943 death sentences probably involved cases with a definite political complexion.

### *II. Police Records*

No police records were published showing the number of arrests made by the different branches of the police and the ultimate disposal of these cases. However, such records exist for internal consumption and some of these records concerning the first half of the year 1944 are known. They concern the number of arrests reported to the various *Staatspolizeileitstellen*, as the table on the following page shows.

### *III. Concentration Camp Records*

Files and statistics concerning each case of internment in a concentration camp were kept in the Central Registry of the central Gestapo Office (which was part of the Reich Main Security Office). In each case of an internment order, the original of the order, made in the Gestapo Office, was sent to the respective camp commander, while the office retained a copy. Thus in addition to the files in the central Gestapo Office, files concerning each camp inmate should also be found in the various concentration camps concerned. An exception to this rule is the case of the mass deportation, internment, and extermination of Jews. In these cases, no records were kept about the individual persons in the central agency, nor were those registered who were killed immediately upon arrival in an extermination camp.

### *IV. Party Records*

It is not to be expected that any records are in existence relating to arrests, detention, and murders carried through by organizations and individuals belonging to the NS Party as distinct from State authorities.

*Total Number of Arrests Reported by Staatspolizeileitstellen*[99]

| | *January–June 1944* | | | | | | | | |
|---|---|---|---|---|---|---|---|---|---|
| | *January 1944 Total*[a] | *February 1944 Total* | *March 1944 Total*[a] | *April 1944 Total*[a] | *Number of foreigners* | *May 1944 Total* | *Number of Foreigners* | *June 1944 Total* | *Number of Foreigners* |
| Communism, Marxism | 1,340 | 1,877 | 1,283 | 1,387 | 906 | 2,188 | 1,558 | 1,478 | 865 |
| Reaction, Opposition | 2,079 | 2,154 | 2,322 | 529 | 235 | 567 | 246 | 723 | 324 |
| Resistance Movement | 2,128 | 2,470 | 2,371 | 1,781 | 1,288 | 41 | 17 | 37 | 17 |
| Catholic | 27 | 54 | 76 | 71 | 42 | 6 | 1 | 7 | – |
| Evangelical Church | 7 | 12 | 9 | 5 | – | 63 | 9 | 78 | 27 |
| Sects Movement | 118 | 178 | 68 | 147 | 49 | 3,166 | 2,494 | 3,593 | 3,021 |
| Jewish Matters | 1,711 | 436 | 402 | 453 | 137 | 331 | 92 | 533 | 148 |
| Treachery | –– | –– | –– | 1,665 | 628 | 1,913 | 709 | 2,498 | 913 |

a. No breakdown into foreigners and native Germans is given for January–April.

Part VII

# A NEW ENEMY

# 30

Herbert Marcuse

## *STATUS AND PROSPECTS OF GERMAN TRADE-UNIONS AND WORKS COUNCILS*

(May 27, 1946)

Editor's note: OIR Report 3381. This report was realized by the Office of Intelligence Research, the division in the State Department where, after the dissolution of the OSS, many analysts from the Research and Analysis Branch ended up, including Herbert Marcuse. In his *Description of Three Major Projects*, Marcuse claims authorship for this report, specifying having been the manager for planning, coordinating, and drafting the entire report, with the exception of a few parts relative to the Soviet Zone that he, however, revised.

The original text is accompanied by two appendixes, here omitted, containing a list of the main figures of the new German labor movment and the units of Freie Deutsche Gewerkschaftsbund in the Soviet Zone.

Classification: Confidential

### I. Introduction

#### A. Pre-Hitler Trade-Unionism

The German trade-union movement has developed in a different direction from American unionism. The German union represented a definite political philosophy and, although theoretically independent, it was actually affiliated with a particular political party: the Free Trade-Unions, whose membership constituted more than 65 percent of organized labor prior to the Nazi regime, with the Social Democratic Party; the Christian-National Trade-Unions (about 18 percent of the total organized labor) with the Center Party and the German National People's Party; the German Trade Associations (*Hirsch-Duncker*) with the Democratic Party. In addition, there were a number of unaffiliated (peaceful, yellow) company unions, and the Communists maintained a small Red Trade-Union Organization (RGO). Consequently, the traditional trade-union functions (collective bargaining, welfare and relief, pressure for social legislation) were carried out within a political framework and with political aims.

The Free Trade-Unions, the most powerful and most nearly representative section of German trade-unionism, were politically identified as part of the Social Democratic movement. The Stuttgart Trade-Union Congress (1902) heard it declared that the trade-unions and the Social Democratic Party were merely two different routes leading to socialism, and the Mannheim Congress (1906) resolved that the trade-unions and the political movement were on an equal footing, and that the central executives of the two organizations should agree on all important decisions.[1] However, although the Free Trade-Unions continued to adhere to socialism as an ideal, their day-to-day policy was, increasingly, that of asserting the interests of their members within the framework of the existing capitalist-democratic state. Under the Weimar Republic, their aim was the gradual democratization of the economy through widening governmental control over the large monopolistic enterprises, strengthened labor participation in economic and political affairs, and extended social legislation. The antirevolutionary and anti-Communist attitude of the trade-unions, moreover, encouraged the gradualism of the Social Democratic Party, and on more than one occasion the trade-union chiefs influenced the party leadership against militant political action in opposition to the Nationalist, and, later, the National Socialist reaction.

Although the Trade-Union Congress held at Nürnberg (1919) emphatically reaffirmed the socialist character of the movement by declaring that "the trade-unions should not limit themselves to representing the job interests of their members, but should rather become the focal point of the class interests of the proletariat in order to aid the victorious struggle for socialism,"[2] the Free Trade-Unions increasingly concentrated on their independent occupational functions. At the same time, the trade-unions sought to assert the interests of their members through class collaboration rather than the class struggle. This policy found theoretical expression in the principle of economic democracy (*Wirtschaftsdemokratie*) promulgated by the Trade-Union Congress at Hamburg (1928), according to which the capitalist system can be "bent" in the interest of the working class.[3] The socialization of the economy can be started within a capitalist framework by the gradual democratization of the economy, the strengthening of government control, and increasing the participation of organized labor in administration.

The policy of economic democracy widened the gap between the practice of labor movement and its socialist goal. The trade-union principle of neutrality toward the political parties—originally intended to unite all workers, regardless of party affiliation, in the fight for the emancipation of the proletariat from exploitation—became an expression of the primarily economic character of the unions and of their organizational independence. The implications of this principle were revealed when, in the spring of 1933, the trade-union leadership, seeking to save their organization, tried in vain to compromise with the Hitler regime. However, the vast majority of Social Democratic trade-unionists remained anti-Nazi, and many of them continued their opposition activity underground after the entire trade-union organization had been dissolved.

## B. The Spontaneous Revival of Trade-Unionism after the Collapse of the Nazi Regime

With the collapse of the Nazi system, organized labor reemerged—in the words of a high US military authority—as the "most democratic class of the population."[4] Trade-union committees and shop councils were among the first anti-Nazi organizations to spring into being as the Nazi regime finally disintegrated. They were chiefly composed of old trade-unionists and new militant antifascists from among the working population. The great majority of them were Social Democrats or Communists; a few were Christian trade-unionists. They started to organize the workers and employees in these plants and shops which were still functioning, taking in all enterprises within a town or city, and striving for an even closer regional integration. In most cases, the initial trade-union committees derived their authority not from elections but from the record and resolution of their leaders, who, in the vacuum left by the sudden collapse of the Nazi system, took matters into their own hands.[5]

In spite of their spontaneous character and their local variety, the new trade-union organizations had a number of significant features in common. The idea of a united trade-union movement organized on an industry basis was accepted "practically without exception."[6] The pre-Hitler trade-union movement, as mentioned above, had been split into at least three main groups, and the new trade-union movement strove from the very beginning to avoid such a cleavage. The formula "one shop, one union" was accepted in principle, although opinions differed on the degree to which the various industrial unions should be centralized and integrated into a single overall peak union. The drive for a unified trade-union organization implied the principle of neutrality toward the various political parties, and all the new trade-union committees except some on the extreme Right accepted it.[7]

One of the most violently debated questions was that of elective versus appointive officials—an issue which revealed the fact that political differences still existed within the trade-union movement beneath the harmonious surface. At the same time, the issue foreshadowed the divergence between the western and eastern zones as regards trade-union development. The old Social Democratic trade-unionists, conservative in their political complexion and distrustful of the Communists, feared that the immediate election of officials from below would radicalize the movement, and endanger the centralization of leadership in their hands. In contrast, the demand for elective officials was widespread among the younger and more militant trade-unionists.[8] The issue was finally settled in the US and British Zones by the Anglo-American policy of gradual democratization, which gave the old leadership time to consolidate their position and influence.[9]

In the Soviet Zone, most of the officials—self-appointed and appointive alike—were from the beginning either Communists or Social Democrats in favor of a more radical trade-union policy; and insofar as this was the case, retention and centralization of their leadership was in the interest of the occupation authorities and of their Communist supporters. Elections were introduced only under pressure from the Western Powers, and after the pro-Soviet leadership had consolidated its position.

The trade-union organizations concentrated in the first instance on the urgent tasks of de-Nazification and reconstruction of the necessary services. However, under the prevailing conditions, their activity with regard to de-Nazification assumed a highly political significance. The trade-union committees were demanding a thoroughly democratic reconstruction of the German economy. The Nazis had based their totalitarian economy on support from industrial leadership and total subjection of labor. The trade-union movement insisted that—as a precondition for the democratic reconstruction of Germany—the compromised industrial leaders be removed and the rights and liberties of labor be restored. Although the trade-union committees were prepared to bide their time with respect to general social legislation embodying the rights and liberties in question, they insisted—in conjunction with the Antifascist Committees (Antifa) which had emerged throughout Germany during the disintegration of the Nazi regime—on immediate and radical de-Nazification measures. These measures frequently led to wholesale arrests of Nazis, Nazi supporters, and reactionaries, to confiscation of their property, to the setting up of provisional antifascist managements in plants and offices, and to the establishment of German antifascist local administrations.

In Hamburg, for example, the aims of the Socialist Free Trade-Union extended to the expropriation of business and large estates and the virtual control of practically all the civilian affairs of Hamburg. The workers, who had formed the union shortly after the British occupation of the city, had been motivated in large part by political aims of this character.[10] Similar developments occurred in Hanover and Brunswick, where the union program openly embodied the principle of the class struggle.[11]

The new trade-union movement was bound to clash at this point not only with military government, as the new bearer of sovereignty,[12] but also with the old ruling groups in Germany. The latter still held their strategic positions in the economy. Employers frequently refused to recognize the trade-union and works council representatives, and in some cases went so far as to confiscate union dues.[13]

As the old social and political struggle was resumed in this way, a traditional conflict reappeared within the labor movement itself. The antifascist trade-union committees and works councils were to a large extent directed by new men, more radical and more socialist than the pre-Hitler trade-union leaders; and with them in their militant attitude stood the Communists. The representatives of the old-trade-union bureaucracy, mostly right-wing Social Democrats, fought shy of the revolutionary implications of the antifascist labor movement, and within about two months after the formation of the new trade-union committees, the differences between them and the old leadership became acute.[14]

In this situation each of the occupation authorities could either: (a) endorse the radical political activity and composition of the new labor movement, and let it expand under its direction, or (b) replace it with a new organization oriented toward a different policy. The Russians took the first course, the Western Powers the second. Thus as the spontaneous antifascist trade-union movement was subordinated to divergent occupation policies, the movement subsequently developed in different ways in the various zones.

## C. Beginning of Divergent Developments

In the western zones, the occupation authorities on numerous occasions took the position that the radical political activity of the new trade-unions infringed upon their sovereignty and threatened to undermine administrative and economic continuity. Consequently, most of the trade-union committees were dissolved,[15] and gradually replaced by an "unpolitical" type of organization—especially in the British Zone, where the prevalence of Communists in the trade-union committees may have been an additional motive for their dissolution.[16] In contrast, the Soviet occupation authorities initiated the first authorized post-Nazi trade-union organization, and made it into a powerful political instrument.[17]

Anglo-American Military Government objected to the new trade-union committees chiefly on the ground that they had not been democratically elected by the rank and file. It insisted that the trade-unions be built from below on the basis of elections in the individual shops. Moreover, it was Anglo-American policy to confine the original scope of trade-union organization to individual enterprises, and to permit it to spread only gradually to the local and regional levels.

Soviet policy, on the other hand, fostered the development of trade-unionism from above, and gave it wide authority.[18] In the east the centralized union organization was consistently used by the occupying power as the spokesman for far-reaching social and economic demands, which were tantamount to an insistence on revolutionary change. In the western zones, where no such change was introduced or promoted, trade-union activity was largely restricted to the field of industrial welfare and to local policies.

This difference in policy led to a completely divergent development of trade-unionism in the western and eastern zones, and was of the utmost importance in the evolution of post-Nazi Germany. At present, trade-union policy is still being determined by the respective zone commanders,[19] although a draft of an inter-Allied law on trade-unions was discussed at the meetings of the Control Council in October and November 1945.[20] This draft attempted to reconcile the divergent Anglo-American and Soviet conceptions by retaining the insistence on democratic organization of the unions from below, while at the same time extending the scope of trade-union activities and permitting amalgamation. Its acceptance was blocked by the French delegate's veto.

## D. The Fundamental Issues

On the surface, the essential difference in trade-union policy in the western and eastern zones seems to involve two main issues:

1. The democratic organization of the trade-unions and the degree to which they are to be centralized and integrated;
2. The political neutrality of the trade-union movement.

Behind these issues, however, lie fundamentally different conceptions of antifascist policy for post-Nazi Germany. These divergent conceptions determine trade-union policy in the Anglo-American and Soviet Zones. The French authorities, with few exceptions, have followed the general pattern of the Anglo-American Zone. Within this pattern, differences prevail between the development in the British and in the American Zones, but they do not lessen the fundamental contrast between the western and eastern conceptions.

1. *MG Policy Conception in the Anglo-American Zone.* The fundamental conception in the US and British Zones is the gradual introduction of democratic forms from below, without revolutionary changes in the traditional social structure. This conception implies—except for the Nazis and Nazi sympathizers—the participation of all social and political groups, equally and without special preference, in the process of democratic reconstruction, this process being based on the free, secret election of representative bodies on the local level.[21] Local and regional bodies are granted far-reaching autonomy in order to prevent undemocratic centralization that might reopen avenues for authoritarian tendencies.

The conception further implies that labor organizations, like all other organizations, shall function within the framework of existing property relations pending a change in these relationships by general democratic vote. Moreover, the Anglo-American conception of trade-unionism as a primarily economic (non-political) movement has been applied to the reconstruction of German trade-unionism.

This Anglo-American conception had far-reaching consequences as regards the reconstruction of the German trade-unions. In at least two aspects it ran counter to their tradition. The German trade-union movement had been a highly centralized organization whose power and influence, because of the unequal distribution of the industrial centers in Germany, had depended to a large extent on nation-wide centralization. Moreover, as has been pointed out above, the German trade-union movement had been largely political in character; its largest group had been closely affiliated with the Social Democratic Party, and the trade-unions frequently had determined the policy not only of this party but also of the government during periods of Social Democratic leadership. The trade-unions, therefore, had played an important part in the struggles that marked the history of the Social Democratic Party under the Weimar Republic: the political fight for extended social legislation and increasing labor participation in the direction of the economy, and the two-front battle against the nationalist-militarist reaction on the one hand and the Communists on the other.

Because of the tradition and record of the German trade-union movement, its leaders have been reluctant to accept the Anglo-American policy on trade-unionism. They strongly object to the restrictions upon the scope of labor organization and upon trade-union political activity. With regard to the restrictions on scope, the trade-unionists assert that the prevailing tendency toward centralization of economic life under government control calls for a corresponding centralization of the trade-union movement.[22] They argue that this becomes increasingly imperative as the reactionary forces of business leadership became more active. Lack of integration, it is claimed, would seriously weaken the effectiveness of labor's resistance to these forces. Similar reasoning lies behind the objection to the political restrictions imposed by military government.[23] The trade-unionists hold that the final liquidation of Nazism and militarism cannot be achieved without the nationalization of key industrial enterprises. This argument is based on the theory that the very structure of German industry under private ownership makes for an aggressive and expansionist economic policy. Under these circumstances, they reason, the mere removal of certain top industrialists cannot possibly accomplish the final elimination of German aggression, a goal which could best be achieved by activating labor, the greatest democratic force in Germany. They contend that labor, most effectively represented by the trade-unions, should have a share in management, in the over-all planning for peacetime production, and in the transfer of key enterprises to the municipal and state governments;[24] in addition, the right to bargain collectively on wages and hours should be restored to the trade-unions at the earliest possible moment.

According to these German trade-unionist critics, the outwardly technical and organizational problems of the reconstruction of the trade-unions actually involve problems of a highly political character. The restrictions which Anglo-American policy implies are considered tantamount to an atomization of labor, which in turn weakens the position of the democratic forces in their struggle against entrenched reactionary interests in big industry. In the prevailing situation, even the Anglo-American insistence on building up the trade-unions from below on the basis of elections in the individual plants, is felt to work to the disadvantage of labor.[25] The cumbersome process inevitably slows down the establishment of an effective integrated trade-union organization, especially since communication among the various regions is extremely difficult, and since local Military Government practice differs widely within the zones.

On the issue of democracy within the trade-union organization the criticism voiced by the trade-unionists in the western zones approaches that implied in the Soviet conception and policy.

2. *MG Policy Conception in the Soviet Zone*. The basic conception underlying Soviet policy toward the German trade-union movement is that, after twelve years of Nazi totalitarianism, the German masses by themselves cannot develop democratic forms of life capable of rendering impossible a revival of militarist expansionism. Pro-Nazi and reactionary forces, the protagonists of this conception argue, are still active throughout the country, and large sectors of the masses, who were cut off from the rest of the world and subjected to thorough Nazi indoctrination for over a decade, might easily, in free elections, endorse policies and personalities which were playing the game of reaction. With respect to the situation of the trade-unions themselves, these spokesmen point out that the German labor movement, split as it was into two antagonistic camps, had been unable to prevent the rise of Nazism. The bulk of the movement followed the Social Democratic leadership, which, it is claimed, was chiefly responsible for the weakness of the Weimar Republic. The Soviets attach importance to the fact that this anti-Communist and anti-Soviet leadership was predominant in the trade-unions, and seems to have retained its influence over the rank and file.

Under these circumstances the democratic reconstruction of the trade-unions from below would, it is felt, probably lead to a restoration of the old Social Democratic bureaucracy. All indications are that the Social Democratic leadership would again follow their traditional line, which the Communists and the Soviets consider as appeasement of the "big bourgeoisie" and Western capitalism, while they themselves see in the liquidation of the economic and political power of the big bourgeoisie a necessary first step toward the democratization of Germany.[26] They conclude that the free play of democratic processes in present-day Germany would work to the advantage of groups whose inability to defend the labor movement against reactionary forces is a matter of record.

In this situation, according to the Soviet conception, the liquidation of the reactionary and anti-democratic forces in Germany calls first of all for the creation of a powerful centralized organization whose political reliability is beyond question and which is capable of imposing upon the German masses the antifascist measures which they are not able to carry out by themselves. For the reasons outlined in the preceding paragraphs such an organization must, it is felt, be created and maintained from above so long as the reactionary forces continue to exert their influence over the rank and file. This is, in essence, the old Leninist idea of the dictatorship of the "*avant-garde*" over the still unprepared masses. In this conception, not only are democracy and dictatorship not contradictory, but the former depends upon the latter at a certain stage of its development: the establishment of a genuine democracy must be preceded by the radical destruction of all groups and interests which, by virtue of their social position, are set against the establishment of such a democracy.

In pursuance of their policy, the Soviet occupation authorities directed the trade-union movement into a highly centralized organization (the *Freier Deutscher Gewerkschaftsbund*) which, from its seat in Berlin,[27] claimed authority over the entire Soviet Zone and, beyond that, over the entire Reich.[28] On almost all levels officials were appointed whose foremost characteristics were experience in unionism and readiness to collaborate with the Soviets. As far as centralization is concerned, this policy was able to revive and utilize the tradition of the pre-Hitler trade-union movement. For its leadership, however, the authorities had to rely heavily on Communists, who had always been a small minority in the German trade-unions. In order to make up for the numerical weakness of the Communists among the rank and file, the Soviet authorities gave vigorous support to the drive for a unified trade-union organization which would absorb the former Social Democratic, Christian, and Democratic unions.[29]

Under the policy conception that obtains in the Soviet Zone, then, the trade-union movement is avowedly being built up as a highly political instrument for the liquidation of the imperialistic, anti-Communist, and anti-Soviet forces in Germany. The economic functions of the trade-unions are, at present, being subordinated to this goal, and both their political and their economic functions integrated into the framework of social changes being introduced in the Soviet Zone. The Soviet conception assumes that only fundamental changes in existing property relations can guarantee the development of Germany along non-aggressive democratic lines, and that this presupposes the destruction of the economic position of the big bourgeoisie and of the Junkers. The trade-union movement has therefore become an instrument for use in connection with the program of land reform and nationalization. Trade-union representatives in the plants, for example, took the initiative in demanding the abolition of cartels and trusts, and the replacement of Nazified managements by reliable anti-Nazis or by government ownership and control. In most cases, the trade-unions are represented in the new managements. Moreover, they have been incorporated into the planning machinery being set up in the Soviet Zone.[30]

## II. Trade-Union Development in the Western Zones

### A. The American Zone

The US Government directive issued to General Eisenhower in April 1945 instructed him to

> "permit free collective bargaining between employees and employers regarding wage, hour, and working conditions, and the establishment of machinery for the settlement of industrial disputes. Collective bargaining shall be subject to such wage, hour, and other controls, if any, as may be instituted or revived by your direction."

The controls authorized by this directive were invoked by Military Government. Wages were generally frozen at the pre-occupation level. Moreover, in view of the totally disrupted state of the German economy, Military Government did not allow any bargaining on hours, and placed severe restrictions on the workers' freedom of movement. German labor offices were designated to maintain control over wages.[31] New wage rates were authorized when, because of a change of product, because of a change in materials used, or for other reasons of a similar character, the previously established wages were no longer appropriate. However, it was directed that "the introduction of new systems of rates of pay for labor must not increase average wages," and must meet with the approval of the German labor offices.[32] As to working hours, it was declared that "existing regulations concerning hours and other labor standards, except as modified herein, will be maintained until further notice".[33] In December 1945 the unions were also authorized to bargain collectively on special allowances for rent, age, length of service, or number of dependents, as well as sex differentials in identical work, again with the proviso that the average level of wages not be altered by such agreements.[34] In point of fact General MacSherry, Director of Manpower Division, US Military Government, declared in February 1946 that "trade-unions are not allowed to negotiate with the authorities about wages and working hours," although they may discuss working conditions and production problems.[35]

Under these conditions, the activities of the trade-unions could hardly extend beyond discussion of grievances and industrial problems and advice on de-Nazification. This limitation is stressed in the general directive to the Commanding Generals of the various Military Districts issued in July 1945:[36]

> "You will permit the self-organization of employees to provide for the selection by secret ballot of stewards to represent the employees in a plant or trade within a plant. The stewards may negotiate with employers concerning grievances. Request for the formation of trade-unions for other purposes will be submitted to this Headquarters with your recommendation."

The directive restricts each trade-union organization to an individual plant or to a single trade within one individual plant.

A November 1945 directive set forth regulations governing the procedure for setting up trade-unions. Implementing the stipulation in the Potsdam Declaration that "subject . . . to the maintenance of military security, the formation of free trade-unions shall be permitted," the new directive specified the establishment of "initial trade-union organizations,"[37] which were defined as those "which unite the workers of either one and the same industrial or commercial enterprise or institution according to their profession, or employees of several small enterprises or scattered professions and some others, within the limits of a small regional administrative district."

Formation of the "initial" trade-union organizations must, under the directive, proceed according to a democratic expression of will and initiative, on the part of the workers; a collective statement in this sense must be submitted to the respective military authorities. The workers must designate representatives competent to assume responsibility for the election procedure, in accordance with which a general meeting of the workers and employees of an individual plant or town borough elects the officials of the local union. The same meeting also elects the delegates to the district conference of the local unions. Amalgamation or merger of several local unions may be permitted "when appropriate," but this requires the consent of the military authorities and involves a complicated procedure. It must, for instance, be established that the amalgamation is approved by the membership of the various unions concerned.[38]

Under these directives, the unions were required to develop first within the limits of "small regional administrative districts," but the way to gradual integration and centralization was at least thrown open. On April 14, 1946, Military Government announced the authorization for the formation of trade-unions on a *Land* basis,[39] and Order #31 of the Allied Control Council, dated June 3, 1946, permitted the establishment of trade-union associations on a zonal basis.[40] Article 1 of this order stipulates that

> "in accordance with the conditions stated in Article 2 of this order, the Supreme Commanders of the various zones are to give permission, first, for the setting-up of trade-union associations of the industries in each zone so that the local trade-unions of every individual industrial branch can be concentrated; secondly, for the joint organization of the trade-union associations on a zonal basis so that representatives of all trade-unions within the zone can meet regularly at conferences in order to settle questions of organization and activity of the trade-unions."

Article 2 of the same order reiterates the stipulation that the trade-unions must be formed and organized on a democratic basis, and that the form of the organization must be the result of the free choice of the membership.

The general framework within which the unions were to operate was established by the policy statement of March 1946, which contains the following chief points:[41]

1. Trade-unions may bargain collectively with employers or employers' associations concerning wages, hours, and working conditions, within the framework of the social and economic policies established by military government.
2. Charters of trade-unions should provide for annual elections of trade-union officials by the membership.
3. The publication of at least one trade-union periodical should be permitted in the US Zone.
4. Trade-unions should receive preference in the allocation on a custodial basis of certain non-industrial property essential to their normal functions (such as meeting halls, office space, etc.).
5. Trade-unions may also act on behalf of the professional economic or social interests of their members; and to this end military government should seek the cooperation of the unions in such matters as de-Nazification, elimination of militarism, education in democracy, execution of Allied policy regarding the elimination of monopolistic practices and types of business or-

ganization, reconstruction, and development of a peaceful German economy.

6. Trade-unions should be invited to participate jointly with employers and German authorities in (a) the administration of Labor Offices and in the administration with other interested groups of social insurance institutions on all levels; and (b) the discussion of and planning for de-Nazification of enterprises, price control measures; rehabilitation of industry, trade, transportation, communications, agriculture, and housing policies.
7. Insofar as the German administrative organs do not deal with the problems cited in (6), the trade-unions should be consulted directly.
8. Trade-unions should be given equal representation or consultative powers with any other economic groups before the Secretariat of the Council of Minister Presidents (of the various *Länder*).

Since the "social and economic policies established by military government" include the freezing of wages, collective bargaining was excluded as a major function of the new trade-unions, and the main weight of their activity fell into the other fields opened to them by Military Government: assisting in de-Nazification and in the elimination of militarism, promoting education in democracy, and cooperating in the execution of Allied policies regarding the elimination of monopolistic practices and cartels.[42] In exercising these functions, the trade-union representatives are acting as advisers to the military authorities or, to an increasing extent, to designated German authorities. Trade-union activity is thus chiefly concerned with questions of personnel (de-Nazification of management and administration) and of labor conditions in individual enterprises.

A directive of the Allied Control Council dated January 26, 1946 introduced a norm of an eight hour day and a forty-eight hour week for all workers. Both Military Government and the designated German authorities are empowered to establish exceptions. Within the framework of these stipulations, trade-unions and other recognized representatives of the workers are permitted to negotiate concerning "the correctness of the working hours as laid down by the directive," but no changes can be introduced without the consent of the German authorities.[43]

Trade-union leaders are striving for the lifting of the restrictions placed on union activity, especially on the collective bargaining for wages. A resolution adopted by the zonal trade-union conference at Frankfurt on April 14, 1946 declares that, in view of the rising prices and the shortening of working hours, the freezing of the wage level is "intolerable for the working population." The resolution goes on to suggest the following measures:[44]

1. Reform of the currency.
2. Reexamination of the price system.
3. Participation of trade-unionists in price fixing and price control.
4. Abolition of the existing Chambers of Industry, Commerce and Handicraft; establishment of Economic Chambers with equal participation of employers and employees, which can serve as agencies for collective bargaining.

The unions also complain of the slow pace and narrow scope of de-Nazification. In Frankfurt am Main, for example, the union representatives withdrew from the de-Nazification committee in protest against what they termed the passive antifascist policy being pursued there.[45] The complaints of the trade-unions were found justified by the Commission of the World Federation of Trade-Unions to Investigate Conditions in Germany. The preliminary report of this commission, which was in Germany from January 30 to February 19, 1946, stated that de-Nazification, especially in industry, was still lagging, and that many Nazis and Nazi supporters were holding important positions in management. Although a policy directive explicitly declared that indispensability should not be considered as a criterion for the retention of persons otherwise subject to dismissal, the report found that this directive has "far too often been ignored by the officers of military government charged with its implementation."

At present, the state of union organization in the American Zone is roughly as follows:

The great majority of all unions are functional (industrial or craft) unions. The rest (probably less than 25 percent), not having reached the stage of subdivision into functional unions, are still area (general) unions and include all workers and employees in a specific area regardless of their trade or occupation.[46] The area originally covered by a union is usually all or part of a district (*Kreis*), generally a city or town. The various functional unions within a district are allowed to form an *Ortskartell* (Local Labor Committee), which may in turn associate with other committees into regional organizations. As of February 1946, only one such larger regional organization was reported: the *Württembergische Gewerkschaftsbund*, covering all of North Württemberg.[47] Under the June 3 ACC order permitting zonal organization, the integration of local and regional unions may be expected to progress fairly rapidly. The zonal trade-union conference held at Frankfurt on April 14 elected a committee of nine to coordinate union activities in the three *Länder* of the American Zone, and to prepare for eventual organization on a zone-wide basis.[48] The same conference suggested combining the various local and regional unions throughout the American Zone into 15 functional zonal unions.[49]

As of May 1946, total union membership in the American Zone was approximately 600,000. Military Government spokesmen think that this figure will probably be doubled in the course of the next four to five months.[50] Württemberg-Baden shows the highest degree of unionization (over 220,000), with Greater Hesse in second and Bavaria in third place. Membership is naturally concentrated in the large cities: Frankfurt and Stuttgart are leading (with approximately 55,000 as of April 1946).

The degree of unionization is very high. As of April 1946, the total of wage and salary earners employed in the American Zone was 3,259,300.[51] On the basis of this figure, approximately 20 percent of the employed wage and salary earners would be unionized.

Although the political neutrality of the trade-union movement has been strongly emphasized in the American Zone, it is to a large extent Social Democratic in character, and old Social Democratic trade-unionists are predominant in its leadership. There are several reasons for this. The vast majority of experienced trade-unionists in the pre-Hitler period were Social Democrats, and the complete liquidation of trade-union activity under the Nazi regime prevented the rise of new and younger leadership. Moreover, the policy of reorganizing the trade-unions from below on the local level worked to the advantage of the Social Democratic functionaries, because the Communists did not have any important local trade-union tradition to support their attempts at organization. The overall occupation policy of refraining from fundamental changes in the social and economic structure further strengthened the Social Democrats against the more radical Communist position. However, among the rank and file, Communist strength seems to be greater than before 1933, and the new Communist trade-union leaders show a high degree of initiative and activity.

The Christian trade-unions, which were not particularly strong in the regions that comprise the American Zone, have accepted the prevailing conception of a unified trade-union movement barring the old ideological differences. Recently, however, at least parts of the Christian trade-union movement have again been striving for an independent organization. In Bavaria "confessional elements" among the trade-unionists are reported to have formed an organization called *Ketteler Werk*[52] (named after the Bishop of Mainz, who was the leading Catholic protagonist of social legislation in the second half of the nineteenth century). The new organization is said to have strong Catholic Church backing, and has, it is reported, been legalized by Military Government.

Opposition against a unified trade-union organization on the part of the Christian unions was also voiced at the Congress of the International Christian Trade-Union Federation, held at Amsterdam on June 4–6, 1946.

Various speakers protested the policy of "forcing workers to organize in a single trade-union federation."[53]

A comparison of typical trade-union programs at different stages of development shows a gradual extension of their scope and political emphasis. The first programs of the Bavarian trade-unions drafted under Military Government direction (June–August 1945) stressed the political and religious neutrality of trade-unionism. ("This federation is strictly neutral as regards religion and party politics."[54] "The trade-union will steer clear of party politics, political aims, and political discussions. . . . All religious organizations will be respected. . . ."[55])The programs asserted that the chief aim of the unions is "to safeguard and further the economic, social, and cultural interests" of their members.[56] The unions promised to strive for an early restoration of full collective bargaining and democratic labor legislation. All reference to Marxist principles was omitted.

In March 1946, however, the demands of the Bavarian trade-unions became more outspoken and political. Political neutrality is no longer stressed. The program drafted at this time declares that "the trade-unions reject the restoration of a capitalist economy and demand the reconstruction of the economy in a democratic-socialist form."[57]

However, this statement is followed up only by such demands as that for trade-union participation, on an equal footing, in economic reconstruction, that for creation of economic chambers on a basis of parity, that for the restoration of full collective bargaining along with thorough de-Nazification. Actually, the program remains focused on the strictly economic and welfare activities of trade-unionism, although the desire for more radical political and economic activity is clearly recognizable. When the program was under discussion, demands were voiced for the 40 hour, five day week, and for the transformation of capitalistic production into a planned economy oriented toward the needs of the consumer. Hermann Schlimme, as delegate of the trade-unions in the Soviet Zone, emphasized the role of the unions in the liberation of the working class.[58] This suggests that the development of trade-unionism in the Soviet Zone is exerting its influence on the western labor leaders.

The demand for nationalization has also been included in the program of the Darmstadt trade-unions, which asks for the socialization of the mines, fuel and power plants, banks and insurance companies, heavy industry, and transport.[59]

## B. British Zone

In the British Zone, the pressure exerted by the occupation authorities on behalf of decentralization and localization is, in accordance with the tradition of British trade-unionism, very strong. In November 1945, a delegation of British trade-unionists visited the British occupation Zone and discussed the question of organization with German trade-union leaders. The delegation summarized its findings in a report to British Military Government. A part of German trade-unionism has accepted the British conception and come out in favor of "independent individual unions"; but the German trade-unionists emphasize that such unions should be united "on the principal issues." This decentralistic conception was advanced most outspokenly by the Hamburg trade-unionists,[60] who adopted a resolution calling for "independent trade-unions exercising administrative and financial autonomy, based on the principle of industrial organization." Accordingly, the Hamburg trade-unions were organized in 13 independent unions.[61] On the other hand, the representatives of the Rhine Province, the Ruhr, and Berlin advocated a strong, centralized peak organization, grouped, in line with the tradition of the German trade-union movement,[62] into professional subdivisions. The organization plan drawn up by the Ruhr trade-unionists contained the following statement:[63]

> "The structure of the collective trade-union is one of a single, general trade-union and is not, therefore, of a Federation of autonomous unions. . . . A division of the single general trade-union into seventeen specialist groups is envisaged. This number will increase to eighteen if the majority of workers from the railway and postal services form a special trade group."

This form of organization, which is widely supported by German trade-unionists, was sharply criticized by the British trade-union delegation. The chief objections were that all effective power would ultimately reside with a small group of men at the top, and that this would result in a situation very similar to that existing when the Nazis took power. Instead, the British delegation recommended that a confederation be formed, in which autonomous independent unions would exercise complete authority over their own affairs.[64]

However, the tendency toward centralization successfully resisted this strong external pressure. At the first zonal conference of the trade-unions in the British Zone, held at Hanover March 12–14, 1946, the representative of British Military Government declared that the occupation authorities now leave it entirely to the German trade-unions to decide on their form of organization. The meeting thereupon passed a resolution stating that the trade-unions could adequately perform their functions only through "strictest organizational coordination and unification."[65] Another resolution demanded trade-union participation, on an equal footing with management, in the peak organizations of the economy, and the promulgation of a new Works Council Law establishing the right of the works councils to share in the direction of production and in the distribution of profits.

At present, the prevalent form of union organization, very similar to that in the American Zone, is the functional (industrial or trade) organization on the local level. Some smaller unions are organized on the provincial level (for example, the following unions include the whole North Rhine Province: chemicals, paper, glass, printing and graphics, lumber, and food); the larger unions are organized on the district (*Bozirk*) level.[66] Moreover, in several cases the district unions are combined into "general" unions, comprising all professional unions within one district. The General Trade-Union Association of Hanover, for example, with 22,000 members, is subdivided into 15 industrial groups.[67] The organization plan for the Trade-Union League of the North Rhine Province provides for a subdivision into 14 industrial and trade groups.[68]

Total union membership in the British zone is reported as about equal to that in the American Zone (600,000). Particularly strong is the unionization in Hamburg and in the Ruhr region. Hamburg alone reported an aggregate union membership of about 120,000 as of December 1945. The leading groups were the General Transport Workers' Union with 21,500, and the Metal Workers' Union with 20,000 members.[69] According to the same report, the presidents of all Hamburg unions were old-line Social Democrats.

The political restrictions placed upon trade-union activity seem to be extremely narrow, even in the field of de-Nazification. At a meeting of local trade-unionists in Hamburg in February 1946, it was stated that union organizations were not allowed to take part in de-Nazification, and that loyal trade-unionists hesitated to make reports against Nazis still in key positions because they feared that they might lose their jobs.[70] Beyond the field of welfare and working conditions, the unions are confined to advisory functions. Two representatives from the trade-unions are included in the German Advisory Council which has recently been established in the British Zone.[71] Recently, with the cut in the food rations, the question of a change in the working time has again become acute. British Military Government has left the shortening of working hours "to free agreement between the workers and the employers."[72]

As in the American Zone, the new trade-union movement in the British Zone is largely dominated by the old Social Democratic leadership. In the Ruhr region, however, there is a large contingent of Communists, and the Christian trade-unions, whose strength has always been in the territory now included in the British Zone, are trying to regain and extend their influence.

### C. French Zone

Information on the trade-union movement in the French Zone is extremely scarce. The isolated reports available indicate that the development has been extremely slow, and that the pressure for localization and de-politicalization is greater than in the other western zones. According to a report from Mainz, trade-union activity was still considered illegal as late as September 1945.[73] The chief of the French police there is said to have informed the German trade-unionists that any attempt at organization would be suppressed. From the Saar region, trade-union activity was reported as early as July 1945, but here, apparently, the movement was infiltrated very soon by Francophile separatists.[74]

In October 1945, a decree was issued permitting the resumption of trade-union organization on a local basis for the "protection of occupational interests." All other union activities were prohibited, especially collective bargaining.[75] Authorization was made dependent on the approval of the local mayor. More recently, a meeting of trade-unionists of South Württemberg and Hohenzollern took place at Tübingen (February 8, 1946). The representative of French Military Government declared that his Government favored the reorganization of the trade-unions on a democratic basis, "unpolitical, and free from religious ties." He added that the trade-unions could participate in the work of reconstruction only if they were "representatives of purely occupational interests."[76]

The authorization to form trade-unions contains more restrictive stipulations than in any other zone. As of April 1946, the associations of functional (industrial) unions into federations or alliances was still prohibited, although permission for such associations was promised for the future. It is furthermore stipulated that union members must be at least 18 years of age, and all administrative officers at least 30 years of age. The French Military Government refuses to grant authorization to form a union unless the industrial activity in question has been reactivated.[77]

## III. Trade-Union Development in the Eastern Zone

### A. The Revival of Trade-Unions

A few weeks after the Russians completed the occupation of Eastern Germany, Marshal Zhukov published an order granting the workers the right to form trade-unions. These unions were to act as collective bargaining agencies, but they also were to perform more far-reaching social and political functions. In pursuance of this order, trade-union committees were established in the different states and provinces and in Greater Berlin to supersede the local trade-union committees and antifascist committees which had formed spontaneously before the arrival of the Russian troops.

The proclamation announcing the formation of the most important of these committees, "the preparatory trade-union committee of Greater Berlin,"[78] was signed by two well-known Social Democratic trade-unionists, Bernard Göring and Hermann Schlimme, by Ernst Lemmer and Jacob Kaiser, *Hirsch-Dunker* and Christian trade-unionists, respectively, by Otto Brass, former left-wing Socialist who had recently joined the Communist Party, and by three old-line KPD functionaries, Paul Walter, Roman Chwalek, and Hans Jendretsky.

The program formulated by the Berlin preparatory trade-union committee and published on June 17 emphasizes the political tasks of the trade-unions rather than their purely labor functions. It stresses the principle which is the theme of Russian-sponsored political activity: the unity of all antifascist democratic forces. Of the four main tasks allotted to the trade-unions, one has to do with the battle against Nazism and militarism, and another with the education of the working class in the spirit of democratic progress. A third emphasizes the role of the working class in the speedy reestablishment of the productive machinery. Only one of the four program points is devoted to the traditional trade-union functions: the representation of workers in the conclusion of collective agreements, the organization of labor protection and employment services, and the reconstruction of a democratically organized social insurance system. However, even this last point is restricted by the stipulation that these rights and functions must be exercised within the framework of "the orders given by the occupying powers."

The importance of this early resumption of union activities lay mainly in the political sphere. It tended to counteract the moral bewilderment caused by the behavior of the Russian occupation forces and, especially, by the policy of machinery removal, which was bitterly resented by all workers irrespective of their political preferences.

From the beginning of the occupation, the Communists, though careful to allow to the old SPD trade-union functionaries their full share in the union revival, set the tone of the unions. The most skillful Communist organizers were detailed to the trade-unions, in order to work through this favorable medium for the immediate Communist objective: the establishment of working-class unity through the merger of the SPD and KPD. The initial trade-union meetings were attended almost exclusively by former trade-unionists; but the manifold functions which the unions almost immediately assumed, and the ostentatious support they received from the new authorities, led very soon to a sharp increase in membership figures. Many thousands joined before they had work, in the hope, often justified, that union membership might help them to find a job. In Leipzig, for example, the membership grew from 4,644 in August to 69,000 in October and 131,000 in January 1946.[79]

Although complete figures on union memberships are lacking, some indication of their present strength has appeared in statements of various regional trade-union leaders in their reports to a zonal conference held February 9–11:[80]

| | |
|---|---|
| Thuringia | 340,000 |
| Berlin | 329,000 |
| Province Saxony | 580,000 |
| State Saxony | 800,000 |
| Brandenburg | 123,000 |
| Mecklenburg-Vorpommern | 80,000 |
| | 2,252,000 |

These figures seen to be somewhat exaggerated: Hans Jendretzky, the zonal union president, on the same occasion estimated the total membership at 1,600,000.[81] In any event, new increases have certainly taken place since the conference.[82] There are few statistics available for the membership of individual functional unions. However, the following figures represent the distribution of the 329,000 Berlin members among the various industrial unions.[83]

| | |
|---|---|
| Public Services | 67,000 |
| Commercial employees | 53,000 |
| Metal workers | 52,000 |
| Railway, post, and telegraph | 40,000 |
| Construction workers | 31,000 |
| Food industry workers | 16,000 |
| Technical employees and foremen | 12,000 |
| Graphic arts | 6,000 |
| Factory workers | 6,000 |
| Teachers | 6,000 |
| Amusement workers | 5,000 |
| Textile workers | 4,000 |
| Total | 292,000[84] |

In the absence of comparable employment records for the majority of industries and professions, no definite conclusion can be drawn concerning the extent to which membership in the unions and total employment coincide. However, in some regions and for some trades, a virtual identity exists between employment and union membership figures. For example, the Thuringian representative reported to the Trade-Union Congress that 1,400 factories had been fully organized. Of 350,000 gainfully employed workers, he asserted that 340,640 belonged to the union.[85] In Berlin, the comparatively high figure for the public services and the employee organizations, as compared with the industrial unions, is partly explained by the fact that the resumption of industrial production has not kept up with the public services and administrative activity, and partly by the much tighter party and union control over public and semi-public professions. Berlin reports 100 percent unionization of the police, 90 percent among the railway workers, and 80 percent in the post offices.[86] On the other hand, not much progress has been made among the 260,000–280,000 workers in Berlin's artisan shops.[87]

### B. Elections to the Trade-Union Congress

Although the Berlin preparatory trade-union committee could not pretend that it had received a mandate from the German workers, it did desire to prove that it was a genuinely representative organization. The KPD leadership, however, realized that elections might lead to open opposition between the KPD and the SPD, and that this might endanger the merger policy. This consideration was the more important because the elections were to take place on all levels: every union member was to cast a ballot, the individual members in the plants voting for the district conference, which in turn selected the delegates to the regional conventions, which, finally, were to send delegates to the zonal conference. In order to suppress party competition, the trade-union executive got the SPD and KPD committees to agree to the omission from the ballots of the individual candidates' party affiliation. However, since the party affiliations of the candidates were known in most cases, the voting on all levels was conducted largely on a party basis. The following table illustrates the preponderance of Communist delegates elected in some representative districts of the zone:[88]

| | *Berlin* | *Thuringia* | *Land Saxony* |
|---|---|---|---|
| Communists | 312 | 103 | 247 |
| Social Democrats | 226 | 61 | 69 |
| Christian Democrats | 3 | 1 | } |
| Liberal Democrats | 1 | - | 11} Distribution among the three groups not stated. |
| Non-party | 17 | 4 | } |

A number of irregularities apparently occurred, mostly to the disadvantage of the Social Democrats. The Communist success may be partially ascribed to the better organization of the KPD propaganda apparatus in the factories. The Communists, however, were eager to avoid the impression that they had packed the convention with their adherents, because this might diminish the value and authority of the convention's decisions. They therefore proposed to grant voting rights to an additional 180 Social Democrats and 30 Christian Democrats, thereby balancing the Communist majority. The rationale of this decision as explained by Wilhelm Pieck, the leader of the Communist Party, was that the Communists wanted "the establishment of parity among the friends of working-class unity."[89] In other words, the issue was no longer between Social Democrats and Communists, but between Social Democratic trade-union officials who were prepared to offer no resistance to the Communist policy of immediate merger of the KPD and SPD, and those who were openly hostile to it. In consequence, despite the majorities which Communist delegates received in local elections, the trade-union executive committees in the zone were constituted as follows:

| | *Whole Russian Zone* | *Greater Berlin* | *Thuringia* | *Saxony* |
|---|---|---|---|---|
| Communists | 19 | 14 | 16 | 15 |
| Social Democrats | 18 | 13 | 6 | 10 |
| Christian Democrats | 4 | 3 | 1 | - |
| Liberal Democrats | - | - | 1 | - |
| Non-party | 4 | - | 2 | - |

Hans Jendretzky (Communist) was elected first president of the zonal executive; B Göring, the Social Democratic representative of the former white-collar organizations, became second president; and the Christian Democrat Ernst Lemmer was made third president. Jacob Kaiser, the Christian trade-unionist, who had refused to be a candidate, was made a consultative member.

The Berlin executive, elected on February 3, has a similar composition. The first chairman is Chwalek, a Communist; Schlimme, a Social Democrat, is second chairman; and Lemmer serves as third chairman.

Some procedural difficulties have arisen from the fact that the Berlin trade-unions are formally under the authority of the four-power *Kommandantura*. Therefore both the formal subjection of the Berlin trade-unions to the zonal union executive and the election of Berlin trade-union officials like Lemmer, Jendretzky, and Göring to positions within the zonal union executive would have required prior authorization by the *Kommandantura*. However, the fact that neither *Kommandantura* nor the Allied Control Council has been able to agree on this point has not prevented the inclusion of the Berlin trade-unions in the Soviet Zonal union system, although the Berlin delegates have refrained from voting in the zonal conference up to the present time.

### C. The New Union Structure

The pre-Hitler Free Trade-Unions were dominated by a politically self-perpetuating Social Democratic leadership, which was rarely disturbed by the appearance of more radical and dynamic personalities. By the end of the war, although few of these leaders remained, a great many of their lieutenants were available, and had good anti-Nazi records. Their cooperation was eagerly sought by the politically dominant KPD, which needed their experience and reputation in reviving the unions. Consequently, the important union jobs have always been divided about equally between Social Democratic union functionaries and the new KPD personnel.

The new union organization is a unified association for all workers and employees, to the exclusion of any rival unions. For this reason, a small number of former officials in the Christian and *Hirsch-Duncker* unions, such as Jacob Kaiser and Ernst Lemmer, were associated with the Social Democrats and Communists in executive functions.

Although the Social Democrats were give a full share in the union administration, the KPD set the tone of the new organization. The Communist leadership inside and outside the union has condemned the record of the pre-1933 union leadership, and particularly its unsuccessful attempt to compromise with Hitler in the spring of 1933. Only former leaders who, like the metal workers' president Wilhelm Dissmann, struggled in vain again the reformists, are honored in the *Freie Deutsche Gewerkschaftsbund* (Free German Trade-Union Association).[90]

The *Freie Deutsche Gewerkschaftsbund* has replaced the craft unions with 18 industrial unions. This fact alone tends to diminish the influence of the former right-wing functionaries, who were especially strong in the smaller craft unions. In many of the new industrial unions, a Communist alternates with a Social Democrat in the performance of executive functions. Moreover, the constituent unions occupy a less important position than formerly: there is constant pressure for unified political and social action, and, in addition, the individual unions have lost their financial independence. Schlimme, the Social Democratic member of the executive, has defended this policy of financial centralization with the argument that it is necessary to prevent competition among the constituent unions.[91]

At another point, however, traditional union policy has been upheld. The KPD slogan of "one shop—one union" involves not only the replacement of craft unions by industrial unions, but also the disappearance of separate unions for white-collar workers. However, the argument that the interests of this group are sometimes in conflict with those of other workers has been accepted, and paragraph 4 of the provisional trade-union statutes allows for the formation of special trade-unions for the white-collar group. Two of these unions have been authorized within the *Freie Deutsche Gewerkschaftsbund*. However, it has been announced that no special Civil Service union will be tolerated: civil servants will be included in the 18 existing industrial unions.

The preliminary trade-union statute is to be binding until the meeting of a new union assembly, scheduled to be held before September 1946. The union program, as formulated in paragraph 1 of the provisional statute, is sufficiently flexible to allow full freedom for the execution of union strategy. Since it is the program of a trade-union organization rather than a political party, it does not specifically refer to socialization, although recent events have made the union's affirmative position on this issue completely clear. The liquidation and transfer to public authorities combines, cartels, and trusts is already being carried out, together with the elimination of all fascists, war criminals, and their supporters from commerce and industry. This makes a formal statement in support of socialization largely superfluous.

Trade-union action is now being directed toward the development of a unified plan for the whole economy, and the definition of union rights within it. During the February conferences, it became clear that the efforts of the executive did not meet with the full approval of the union delegates in either respect.

The lack of a unified plan has been criticized mainly by Social Democratic delegates such as Dr. Otto Suhr and Dr. Hans Acker,[92] who believe that the trade-unions should assume leadership in the economy. However, neither the KPD leadership nor the majority of the SPD officeholders were willing to go to such an extreme. The Communist leaders, Walter Ulbricht in particular, were careful to emphasize that capitalism has by no means disappeared.[93] Although this may be true for the western zones, it is an obviously incorrect description of the situation in the Russian-occupied area. Since the KPD leadership looks forward to an early unification of the trade-unions throughout Germany, it is interested in avoiding over-emphasis upon the structural differences between west and east.

The old-line Social Democratic union officials do not support complete identification of trade-unions with the economic administration, because they take the position that the greater the official union responsibility for the management of the total economy, the smaller the possibility for the unions to act as representatives of specific worker interests. A considerable proportion of union effort is already being directed toward raising the morale of the workers and combatting absenteeism,[94] which is very common as a result of the scarcity of consumer goods, which makes it seem useless for a man to work more than the time necessary to obtain the official rations. Continued concentration on the function of raising productivity levels would, on the other hand, decrease the confidence of the workers in the union organizations. (The trade-union leadership has already been forced to combat a recent tendency among the members to take a dim view of the union's present usefulness from the standpoint of immediate material advantages to be gained.)[95] Therefore, as the situation stands now, the trade-unions, although closely associated with the economic administration on all levels, are not identical with it. Certainly there is no limit set to the trade-unions' right to propose and stimulate the setting of production schedules with the goal of increasing or planning a more coherent output. But the responsibility, even in the enterprises which are taken over by the local administration, rests with the appointed director, even where his appointment has been made on the initiative of the workers themselves.[96] It has been authoritatively stated that the director alone is responsible for the administration of the factory, and that the trade-unions and works councils, having no direct right of interference and command, exert influence only through addressing themselves to the regular organs of control.[97] On a higher level, production is directed by the provincial administration, in which representatives of the trade-unions participate at least theoretically.[98]

Under Weimar, the organization and functioning of the trade-unions was keyed to the existence of powerful employer organizations, identical with the entrepreneurial associations which became semiofficial organs under the Third Reich. In contrast to the western occupation authorities, particularly the British, the Russians have blocked all attempts to reestablish entrepreneurial organizations. Therefore, since no private organization exists to resume the exercise of the collective bargaining functions of the former employer organizations, these functions revert to the individual factories. This development has not been uniformly favorable to the workers, especially in the smaller enterprises[99]. Workers sometimes accepted wages which were even below the Nazi levels, which had continued to govern wage rates in accordance with the official freezing orders of the Soviet military authorities. Any modifications in the freezing orders had to be approved by the administration. The general clamor for wage increases, which was one of the main concerns of the various district and zonal trade-union conferences, could not continue without receiving some measure of satisfaction. At the same time, the question of fixing shorter working hours was again being debated among workers dissatisfied with the continuation of "voluntary" extension of hours.

Even Ulbricht announced a request for a basic eight hour working day and a 45 hour week.[100]

Yet it would have been neither politic nor technically feasible to trust the various administrations with the establishment of new wage contracts, replacing the present arrangements based on the freezing orders. Such a move would have jeopardized the very existence of the unions, because it would have completely revoked their right of collective bargaining. No definite solution has yet been found for the problem of replacing the former employer organizations. However, the trade-unions, the KPD, and the SPD appear to have reached an agreement recently on a possible substitute to which the collective bargaining function might be entrusted. This agency is to be the completely revamped chamber of trade and commerce.[101] It is planned to staff it with one-third union representatives, one-third employer representatives to be appointed by the employer in agreement with the economic department, and one-third representatives of the department of labor and welfare. Collective agreements could then be concluded through the medium of this agency, with the labor and welfare department as an arbiter. Under present arrangements, however, the labor administration would still have to validate the collective agreement before it entered into force. Thus the labor administration would appear in the double role of a voluntary arbiter and an administrative agency with the final decision over any agreement concluded under its auspices.

It is fairly obvious that in the newly emerging social system, from which the private entrepreneur is being gradually eliminated, neither the function of the trade-unions in the determination of wages and labor conditions nor the role of the administration has been definitely settled. The same uncertainty exists with respect to the workers' right to strike. No formal prohibition seems to exist and small strikes are known to have taken place in a number of enterprises under private management. But there is no record of a strike in one of the enterprises under the management of the administrative authorities. Since a number of private enterprises will continue to exist for some time, it is likely that the trade-unions will make use of the strike not only to achieve social gains, but as a political weapon against the remnants of private capitalism. Eventually, however, continuing changes in the social structure will inevitably produce radical revision of many traditional trade-union functions.

## IV. The Works Councils

The reorganization of the trade-unions was accompanied—frequently preceded—by revival of the works councils or shop stewards (*Betriebsräte*) movement. The works councils originally appeared, during the November 1918 revolution, under the domination of radical leftist elements. Later, by the Works Council Act of 1920, they were institutionalized to represent labor in the individual plants. They included non-unionized as well as unionized workers and employees. Chiefly advisory and educational organs, without direct participation in management (although ineffectually represented on the boards of directors), their main practical function arose from their right to carry any worker's dismissal before the labor courts. Both legally and organizationally they were distinct from the trade-unions. In most cases, however, the trade-unions were able to establish control over the councils, and, by extending this control, to make them their executive organs. But in some regions the more radical labor elements were able at times, to use the councils as levers against union domination in their attempt to revive the revolutionary tradition of the councils.

## A. The Western Zones

As the Nazi regime was disintegrating, workers' committees spontaneously appeared, frequently with the same radical political tendencies as the Antifascist Committees and in conjunction, with them. Unlike those in the eastern zone, the western zone committees were promptly dissolved. Subsequently, the works councils in the western zones were largely dominated by the old-line trade-union officials. In the Essen and Duisburg area, for example, the old-line union leaders controlled the selection of works councils after the reopening of the mines and plants. They chose candidates from among their own ranks, and drew up the lists for the first elections.[102] Similarly, in Bavaria, the first post-Nazi trade-union organization tried to build up the works councils within its own organizational framework, as the "first representatives of the union membership."[103]

In most cases, military government insisted on new elections, to take place three months after the original election. An exception was Württemberg-Baden, where new elections were to be held only if at least 25 percent of the represented employees petitioned for them.[104]

In November 1945, with the approval of military government, the mayors throughout the US Zone issued a proclamation concerning the election of works councils.[105] Its chief provisions were the following: Employees of a factory or of a commercial, financial, or other business establishment or public office, or of an individual department or trade group within such an establishment, are permitted to elect by secret ballot, for a period of three months, representatives who will lay their grievances before the employers. Application for an election must be submitted to military government by at least 25 percent of the employees.

Election of former officials of the German Labor Front, members of the Nazi Party, Nazi followers, and militarists is forbidden. Wages and working hours cannot be the subject of collective negotiations at present. With respect to the relation between works councils and trade-unions, the proclamation states only that the above regulations do not prevent employees from joining approved trade-unions, which in any case are said to be provisional, constituting only the first step toward a restoration of free and democratic trade-unions.

A parallel proclamation was issued in the British Zone in December 1945.[106] It defines the function of the works councils as the negotiation with the management of labor issues as they arise within the individual enterprise. Otherwise, the proclamation contains stipulations similar to these in the American decree; but it is silent, on the relation between works councils and trade-unions.

A total of 1,991 shop steward elections are reported to have been held as of December 1945 in the American Zone. These elections represented approximately 266,000 employees.[107] Information on the political composition of the works councils is extremely scarce, and only isolated figures are available. Most reports from the western zone indicate a strong Social Democratic majority, with the Communists second and the other parties far behind. The most recent results reported were from the I.G. Farben works at Leverkusen, where 70 percent of the workers and 83 percent of the office employees voted. They elected ten Social Democrats, six Communists, four Christian Democrats, and three "independents."[108] Communist majorities are reported from the coal mines and other industrial establishments in the Rhineland and in the Ruhr, with the Social Democrats a strong second.[109] The following are the results of works council elections in 44 mines in the Ruhr area:[110]

| | |
|---|---|
| Communists: | 23,977 |
| Social Democrats: | 14,665 |
| Christian Democrats: | 10,239 |
| Others: | 8,056 |
| Total: | 56,937 |

About 70,000 persons were eligible to vote in the elections.[111]

Politically, the works councils are traditionally more radical than the trade-unions. At a meeting of 165 works councils of the Industrial Group Mining of the Trade-Union League Greater Hesse, resolutions were adopted embodying the following demands:[112]

1. Unification of anti-fascist democratic Germany, which must also comprise the Ruhr.

2. Liquidation of cartels, trusts, latifundia, and large banks, and their transfer into the hands of the provincial or *Länder* administration.
3. Full participation (*volles Mitbestimmungsrecht*) by works councils in the management of the trade-unions and of the economy.
4. An eight hour day and a forty-five hour week; a seven hour day for the miners.

The conference also advocated the fusion of the Social Democratic and Communist Parties.

### B. The Eastern Zone

In the eastern zone, the workers' committees and the closely related antifascist committees continued to function after the occupation had begun. In the few factories where production was continued, works councils elected from proven antifascist workers often discharged supervisory personnel, and maintained a close watch upon the legal owners to prevent their transferring or hiding their assets. At the beginning of the autumn, when the workers in many places had asked that a system of works councils be established,[113] the need became apparent for a fuller definition of the functions of these councils. Any notions that future works councils would run their respective enterprises were now discouraged.[114] The administration of those factories whose proprietors had fled or been dispossessed was, at least for the time being, put into the hands of the local authorities, the remaining industrial and commercial properties being temporarily left under the control of their proprietors or directors. This temporary solution allowed the works councils to concentrate on representing the workers' interests with management, rather than fusing their functions with those of the employers.

In October, after a conference of works councils in Erfurt, the first works council law was passed in the state of Thuringia.[115] It gave voting rights to every worker in the shop over 16 years of age, and provided for works councils to be elected in each enterprise having more than 20 workers. Smaller plants were to elect a workers' representative only.

The list of functions of these works councils was greatly enlarged over those contained in the old works council law of the Weimar Republic. In formulating these functions, the law closely follows the action program of the preparatory trade-union committee of June 1945. Political tasks and the increase of production are emphasized, along with the traditional duty of representing the workers' interest with the management.

Works council representatives are to be selected to participate in all meetings of the board of directors and, in a very important new concession, it is stipulated that the assent of the workers is a precondition for dismissal action against any employee. The bill requires close collaboration between works councils and employers, and between works councils and union representatives, who are granted the right to take part in all negotiations conducted by the council.

At first it was expected that following the pattern of the agrarian reform, corresponding laws would be immediately issued in the other provinces and states of the Russian Zone. However, no such step was taken, apparently because the occupation authorities considered it necessary to clarify the relation between works councils and trade-unions. After the German defeat, the policy of the eastern zone political parties toward the councils had not been altogether clear. Although the Social Democrats and the old trade-unionists favored re-establishing the dependency relation between council and unions, the line of the KPD was more opportunistic. For a while, the Communists apparently considered using the works councils as a weapon against the old union leadership. They were confronted, however, with somewhat intractable works councils which loudly protested the removal of their most precious machines and instruments by the occupation forces. Therefore, when the process of Communist infiltration into the unions seemed to have progressed satisfactorily, the KPD largely returned to the old policy of asserting the superiority of the trade-unions over the works councils.[116]

It now became one of the chief tenets of official trade-union policy that the works councils were to be subjected to union control. For this purpose, special work committees (or, in small enterprises, a workers' representative) have been established, to be elected by all union members within an enterprise. Their functions have been defined in paragraph 6 of the new trade-union statutes adopted at the Berlin zonal congress in February 1946:

> "In all problems the works committee should represent the interests of the union members toward the entrepreneur or the management. The committee is to supervise the carrying out of the collective agreements concluded by the trade-unions. In agreement with the works council, it negotiates the working regulations for the enterprise and supervises carrying them out. The works committee together with the works council cooperates with the management in the production program of the enterprise in the framework of the general trade-union policy. One of its tasks is increasing the trade-union influence by the gaining of new members."

Thus, the functions of the works committee elected by the union members and those of the works council elected by all the employees overlap to a great extent.[117] It may be expected that there will be identity of personnel between the membership of the council and the membership of the committees. However, in cases in which the works council might come under the control of political dissidents, the existence of the committee would give the union management a lever with which to dislodge the council. At the same time, the existence of the committees, which are pure union organs, will facilitate the implementation of the union directives within the enterprise.[118] In short, the old union policy of subordinating the works councils to union directives has been revived, with the difference, however, that the works councils, instead of serving as the executive organs of the reformists, will represent a trade-union bureaucracy with a strong Communist influence.

### C. The ACC Works Council Law

Organized labor in all occupation zones has been clamoring for a new comprehensive works council law institutionalizing the participation of labor in the democratic reconstruction of the economy. In February 1946, the Berlin trade-union conference for the Soviet Zone asked for such a law, and recommended a draft to the zonal authorities for speedy enactment.[119] A meeting of plant representatives of the Munich trade-unions, held in March 1946, advocated re-issuing the law of 1920,[120] and the zonal trade-union conference held in the same month at Hanover favored a new law which would grant the works councils the right to participate in decisions on production and on the distribution of profits.[121]

The Works Council Law enacted by the Allied Control Council on April 10, 1946 hardly fulfills these expectations.[122] Its 13 short paragraphs are written in very general language. The law is rather explicit on only one of the controversial points. It affirms the principle of close collaboration between trade-unions and works councils, authorizing the unions to participate in the establishment of preparatory committees, in the organization of elections, and in the selection of candidates. The law is not specific about election procedures, and only insists on the application of "democratic principles" and secret balloting. The list of works council functions corresponds to a large degree to the old works council law. It emphatically does not extend the rights of the works councils to participate or collaborate in management functions, even omitting to affirm the management's duty of keeping the councils {informed on the progress and activities of the enterprise, and the councils' right to send representatives to the meetings of the board of directors. It contains no provisions regarding the most vital function of the old works councils: their right to bring action before the labor court against workers' dismissals. Many clauses of the law, as it stands now, require implementation in the form of decrees by the various zonal authorities before they can become effective. Questions will inevitably arise over whether the law constitutes a maximum program, or whether additional functions may be added, as long as they do not conflict with the text of the law. The trade-unions can be expected to emphasize the second interpretation. They will demand new legislation similar to the much more far-reaching provisions of the draft, recommended by the Berlin trade-union conference, with respect to collaboration both in personnel policy and in management functions.

## V. Conclusion

The divergence in policy conceptions between the eastern and western zones makes for divergence in structure and strategy within the trade-union movement. Owing to the movements' dependence on occupation policy, and because of the social and economic pattern shaped by this policy, the "political neutrality" of the trade-union movement has become a fiction. In the west, most of the trade-unions tend to remain Social Democratic, which means *de facto* acceptance of the existing form of society, the focus of union activity on representing the interests of the workers within the framework of this society, and thus continued adherence to a strategy of class collaboration rather than class struggle.

So long as the disruption of economic life and the requirements of military government exclude such important trade-union functions as free collective bargaining for wages and hours, a primarily "economic" trade-unionism can be effective and vital only within narrow limits. With the progress of political self-administration and economic reconstruction, in which Social Democrats and Christian Democrats are likely to play the leading part in the western zones, such a trade-union movement would be connected politically with an administration endeavoring to incorporate the working class into a democratic capitalistic system. The situation of the trade-unions would thus be similar to that existing under the Weimer Republic. The Social Democratic conception of trade-unionism would direct union strategy to the gradual democratization of existing economic institutions and relations through increased government control over the economy, nationalization on a limited scale, and participation of labor in management.

In the Soviet Zone, the conception of the "political neutrality" of the trade-union movement has been explicitly rejected:

> "How can one talk of political neutrality, after more than twelve years of fascist domination, during which the poison of fascist ideology has penetrated deep into the ranks of the working class? It is no accident that bourgeois circles too advocate political neutrality. . . . Such circles would like to confine the activities of the

> trade-unions to the smallest every-day problems, and prevent the power of the trade-unions from being mobilized for . . . guaranteeing the rights of the working class in the plant, the economy, and the State."[123]

The trade-unions, therefore, are becoming a part of the political labor movement, now represented by the Socialist Unity Party (SEPD), which is described as the political vanguard of the working class in the antifascist struggle. The unions and the party both are striving for the establishment of a socialist society. However, in their attempts to achieve the common goal, each of them applies its specific methods, and performs a different function. The SEPD defines the political aims, determines the tactics, and exercises the political leadership. The trade-unions are the organizations of the broad masses of the working people, and seek to include the totality of the working-class population. Their function is not only to educate the working masses along approved lines, but also to fulfill the ordinary needs arising from their employment status.

Therefore, so long as a socialist society is not achieved, the unions form the mass basis for the exercise of the uncontested leadership function of the political party. According to the official thesis, the necessity for this dualism arises from the fact that capitalism still prevails in Germany. Since the unions have essentially the same aims as the SEPD, there is no problem of "political neutrality" for the unions.

It is true that friction exists between the trade-unions as the representatives of the immediate interests of the workers and the long-range policies of the political leadership. Indeed, one of the chief recurrent tasks of the political leadership is to decide whether, at any given moment, the good will of the union membership is more important than the achievement of the production quota. Depending on this political decision, the union leaders will at times have to redouble their efforts at "educating" the membership, while at other times they will be able to remind the workers of the gains achieved with respect to wages and hours. But essentially, however, there is no separate problem of union development distinct from the course taken by the other political and administrative institutions of the Soviet Zone. As an integral part of the new social fabric, the unions move at the same rate as the others in the direction of a centralized socialist society.

# 31

HERBERT MARCUSE

# *THE POTENTIALS OF WORLD COMMUNISM*

(AUGUST 1,1949)

Editor's note: OIR Report 4909. In August 1949 the Office of Intelligence Research produced a lengthy report, 532 pages in six parts, under Marcuse's direction, titled *The Potential of World Communism*. In it are analyzed international Communist agencies (4909.1); the Communist parties in Western and Central Europe (4909.2); the satellite states of the Soviet Union, more specifically, Czechoslovakia (4909.3); the Far and Middle East (4909.4); Asia (4909.5); and Latin America, i.e., Cuba (4909.6). The text published here constitutes the summary report that precedes the six studies. Marcuse's direct authorship is indicated in an interview with Barry Katz by Bernard Morris, who, as an analyst with the Division of International and Functional Intelligence of the State Department, participated in the team coordinated by Marcuse for the realization of the research project (B. Katz, *Herbert Marcuse and the Art of Liberation: An Intellectual Biography* [London–New York: Verso, 1982], p. 132, n. 51).

Classification: Confidential

## Preface

This report is a first approach to a general study of international Communism prepared under the supervision of the OIR inter-divisional Committee on World Communism (CWC). It is neither complete in global coverage nor final as a statement of conclusions, but is intended as a preliminary sketch of analysis to stimulate further thought and investigation.

Particular countries have been selected for detailed study in this report on the basis of their value as representatives of the different areas in which Communism is now a significant factor, with regard to the immediate availability of resources. The introductory chapter is a preliminary effort to develop from these country studies a generalized analysis of strength and weaknesses.

Clearly much work remains to be done. This report will later be reissued, with additional country studies and with a revised introduction based upon review of the present study and other related investigations.

The experiences of the Soviet Union soon provided the operational pattern and theory for the new "people's democracies." In backward countries, the transition from an agrarian to a highly industrialized society "jumps" the various stages of liberalism and proceeds within the framework of a highly centralized planned economy with an authoritarian government that eliminates all oppositional elements and imposes totalitarian regimentation. During this period, the Communist regime depends primarily on the ubiquitous and effective administrative and police controls or military power rather than on popular approval. The "coalition" governments were shortly transformed into outright Communist regimes.

At the war's end, Communist strength in France and Italy was probably sufficiently great to warrant a revolutionary effort to seize power. The Communists were deterred not only by the presence of the Allied armies but also by Soviet interest in avoiding an open break in the wartime alliance. Under such circumstances, they may have decided that they could gain power by operating within the governmental coalition.

The rapid expansion and consolidation of Communist power had an enormous effect on the non-Communist world, which correspondingly changed its policies. The great power of the United States began to be exerted to contain Communist expansion outside the Eastern orbit and to aid in the stabilization of the non-Communist governments of Western Europe. The Communists were forced to adopt new strategy and tactics to meet the changed postwar situation.

This sketch of the evolution of the Communist movement since its inception indicates that the main focus has shifted from the highly advanced countries of the West to the relatively backward area of the Eastern orbit. From an indigenous social movement, deriving its basic dynamism and force from the revolutionary efforts of the working class to reorganize its own society from within, Communism in the Eastern orbit has become primarily a vast political, economic, and military system outside the capitalist world, with central power and direction located in the USSR. The national Communist Parties are used primarily in the interest of this system, and their policies and objectives are adjusted to it.

## I. Introduction

Communism today is an international movement consisting of 60 national Communist Parties claiming an aggregate membership of about 20 million, supplemented by a network of affiliated auxiliary or "front" organizations of both national and international scope. The development of the Communist movement has been accompanied and strengthened by regional concentration. Communism today holds power in one contiguous area stretching from the River Elbe in Germany to the North Pacific. In this vast area, usually called the Eastern orbit, national Communist Parties have formed the governments and organized the society. The international and the national strategy of all the parties within and without the orbit are to a greater or lesser extent coordinated with the foreign and domestic needs of the USSR, the major central unit of strength within the orbit. A common doctrine binds the movement together and produces a sense of comradeship, which is itself a great social force.

Communist doctrine offers a full explanation of the historical evolution of society, a theory of action and organization through which Communism shall work its will upon that society, and an elaborate catalogue of tactical devices for the immediate accomplishment of local aims. Although unitary in its theoretical scope, in practice the doctrine conceals essentially strong centrifugal elements. For example, while doctrine originally laid down the principle that the Communist state would grow out of the most highly developed capitalist economy, in fact Communism has had its greatest successes in relatively backward areas. Complex adjustments in theory, not always thoroughly satisfactory, have therefore been necessary. Again, while the power and leadership of the Kremlin are undoubtedly elements of strength to international Communism, yet the various national parties, in their growth and development and in their striving for local influence and support, must constantly seek to relate their policies to local circumstances. This explains in part the divergent policies that Communists sometimes espouse in different localities. Moreover, there is always the possibility, realized in Yugoslavia, that local needs will be incompatible with the policies laid down by the Soviet leadership.

Even the Kremlin itself, which is generally conceded the right, as the bulwark of Communism, to impose upon the movement the requirements of its own power position, cannot avoid being affected by Communist doctrine, which constitutes the very language of its thinking. By the same token, the lesser parties and groups of the movement must be similarly torn between reality and doctrine. It is, therefore, vital to distinguish between the power and security interests of the USSR, the local strivings of the national Communist Parties elsewhere, and the broad influence of common doctrine and tradition as it affects both the USSR and other Communist elements.

The final evaluation of international Communism must include all the aspects mentioned, but many contributory analyses will be required before such final evaluation may be attempted. As a step toward filling one gap, this report presents a preliminary consideration of the potentials of Communism outside the USSR. It deals with Communist strength and vulnerability apart from Soviet national power, and refers to the USSR only insofar as Soviet influence directly affects the assets and liabilities of the rest of the Communist world.

This Communist world is considered primarily in three main groupings. The first is the Eastern orbit, comprising two main areas, the satellites in Europe and in Asia, which are contiguous to the USSR and under Communist control but differ from the USSR and each other in their stages of political and economic development. The second grouping is South Asia, a region of colonial and semi-colonial countries, where the Communists have, following World War II, markedly increased their strength by virtue of their championing of and participation in the movements for national independence and agrarian revolution of the dependent peoples. The third is the West, where Communism experiences essentially different conditions. In most Western States, the Communist Parties constitute an opposition to a highly developed social, economic, and political system. Except in France and Italy, where they dominate the labor movement, the Communists in the West function generally in a milieu where the labor movement, primarily under Social Democratic leadership, has accepted the established system as the framework for its demands and objectives. In addition, the great power of the United States is being exerted to contain external Communist expansion from the Eastern orbit and to insure the economic and political stability of regimes that face an internal Communist threat.

## II. The Evolution of World Communism

At its inception, the Communist movement promised that, by following its lead, mankind could create a new rational society in which poverty, heavy toil, discrimination, and war would be eliminated. This goal of a better world achieved through a specific plan of human action is still today an essential part of the Communist ideological arsenal, attracting and holding millions of followers. One of the important anomalies that underlie present-day Communist operation is that this goal so obviously has not been reached in the area that for 32 years has devoted itself to realizing the better world. The USSR has fulfilled few of the promises for eliminating the burdens of mankind. The conflict between the professed goal and the incompatible means employed to achieve it is but one reflection of a deeper contrast—that, against all original anticipations of the founders of Communist theory, Communist Parties today held power in an area comprising formerly backward, pre-capitalist, and semicolonial countries. This circumstance has occasioned a complete transformation of the Communist movement.

According to the original Marxian concepts, the locus of the Socialist revolution was to be in the highly industrialized countries of the Western world. There, the "capitalist system" had "matured" and was ready for the next stage of world society—Socialism. Capitalism had developed the technological and productive forces to the highest point possible within its framework and created a politically well-trained, "class-conscious" proletariat embracing the great majority of the working population. Under these circumstances (and only under these circumstances) the Socialist revolution would mark the leap into a materially and culturally higher civilization. Freed from the "fetters of the profit system" the productive forces could be fully utilized for an immediate increase in the standard of living, for the elimination of poverty and want, and for the abolition of repression and injustice. This free and rational Socialist society would produce and distribute in the interest of all its members the immense social wealth created by the existing system. The need for the state as an instrument of repression would disappear.

This concept postulated the full development of all material and intellectual forces basic to a higher culture as the prerequisite for Socialism. When the Bolsheviks, under Lenin's leadership, took power in Russia in 1917, they consequently believed that the success of their revolution would be possible only if it were "saved," that is, guaranteed and expanded by a series of revolutions in the capitalist countries of Europe. This belief was shared by the Communist Parties and the Communist International, which originated in the aftermath of World War I, as the leftist opposition to the European Socialist Parties that had supported the war and had after the war continued to oppose the revolutionary overthrow of the established system. The Communist Parties aimed at the abolition of the "capitalist state and economy" through the revolutionary action of the working classes, the establishment of a "proletarian dictatorship," and the rapid transition to a socialist society. The indigenous social revolution was the primary objective, and the USSR was to support the national Communist Parties in the attainment of this objective, for in this way alone could the Soviet state survive.

The events of the early 1920's brought about a fundamental change in the position of World Communism. The European revolutions were defeated—including Austria and Hungary in 1919, Germany finally in

1923. The desired extension of the Russian Revolution did not occur. The Russian Communists had succeeded in effecting the revolution only in a country whose level of development was far lower than that achieved in the capitalist countries of the West. The promised millenium of the socialist society was far away. A new Stalinist leadership emerged that sought to attain the future goal in a new way.

The "socialist revolution" had succeeded in a country where few of the prerequisites for Socialism existed. Therefore, the prerequisites had to be created after the fact. In a region with a low degree of technology and industrialization, with a small industrial proletariat, with a large backward and hostile peasantry forming the majority of the population, this goal required subjection of the population to the greatest sacrifices, to complete regimentation, to authoritarian rule that exploited and directed all human and natural resources toward the development of large-scale heavy industry and mechanized agriculture. Only such an economy could provide the basis for a lasting increase in the standard of living and the promised socialist freedom from want. This course implied, for a long time to come in backward Russia, continued and even strengthened repression, domination, poverty, toil, the creation of a large and regimented labor force, and the raising of labor productivity by all available means. The Communists were in a situation in which they had to imitate, reproduce, and telescope what they had damned as the worst features of the capitalist system in order to attain in a short time the level of industrial power that capitalism had gradually attained over centuries.

The complete subordination of the national Communist Parties to the foreign and domestic interests of the USSR was the external concomitant of this internal evolution in the Soviet pattern during the period between the two World Wars. This tendency was also reinforced by the failure of the Communist Parties themselves to develop as successful revolutionary instruments. The "great crisis of the capitalist system" terminated not in successful socialist revolution but in the establishment of the Nazi regime in Germany, which put an end to all Communist action, absorbed Austria and Czechoslovakia, and buttressed Italian Fascism. The Spanish civil war ended with the triumph of Franco. The French Popular Front Government, which had stirred Communist hopes, failed. The only intact bulwark of Communism was the USSR.

The continued survival of the USSR from external threat was considered to be a function of its ability to maneuver in a world of hostile "imperialist-capitalist" states. The primary Communist aim was to avoid the development of a combined capitalist "attack" on the "Socialist fatherland." The Communist Parties were used as pawns in the diplomatic game of creating governmental policy favorable to the USSR. This was most clearly seen at the time of the Franco-Soviet pact of 1935, when the

French Communists gave up their opposition to the French military budget. Such use of Communist Parties became a hallmark of Communist policies later during the period of Nazi-Soviet pact and the subsequent World War II period of Allied unity.

The conditions created by World War II provided the Communist movement with new and great opportunities and led to the Eastern orbit's consequent position as the second greatest power in the world. The Germans in overrunning Europe, and the Japanese in displacing the old colonial rulers of the Far East, had radically altered the fabric of prewar political organization. The resistance movements that arose expressed the hope of great numbers of people for a basic change following the successful completion of the war against German Fascism and Japanese Imperialism. There was a general desire in Europe to eliminate those who had collaborated with and made possible the victory of the Nazis. In the Far East, the war gave new stimulus to national independence movements. The Communist Parties, motivated principally by the desire to ensure the defeat of the Nazis and the victory of the USSR, provided active participants and leaders in the resistance movements.

In the underground movements, the Communists had the advantage over their political rivals. They had perfected illegal organization in many areas long before the outbreak of the war. The victories of the Russian Army testified to the enormous progress that the Communists had achieved in creating a strong state and military machine in the USSR and enhanced the prestige of Communists elsewhere. At the war's end, Communists were in positions of power in many regions.

Communist-controlled coalition regimes were established in the Eastern European states in the wake of the Soviet armies and within the reach of Soviet military power. The military division of Europe and Asia marked the outermost limits of this expanded Communist orbit. The political and economic consolidation of this Eastern orbit became the principal Communist goal.

The Communist movement had acquired new characteristics. Emphasis now was laid on the utilization of the existing state machinery through holding key posts, characteristically the Ministries of Interior, National Defense, and Propaganda, in "national union" governments to achieve ultimate Communist control.

## III. The Communist Program

### A. The "Two Camp" Theory

The framework of the "Two Camp" theory, set forth in current Communist doctrine, provides the basis for understanding the present strategy and tactics of the international Communist movement. According to this concept, the present historical period is characterized by the fact that the world is split into two opposing camps; that of "imperialism and monopoly capitalism" on the one hand, and that of "socialism and popular democracy" on the other.

The "aggressive" leadership of the "imperialist anti-democratic camp" is exercised by the United States. Included in the fold are the "British, French and other colonial imperialists in Western Europe, the Middle East, and South American Republics that rely on the American imperialists politically and economically." Conversely, the "peace-loving anti-imperialist democratic camp" follows the lead of the Soviet Union. It comprises the "new democracies" in Eastern Europe, the "liberated areas" of China, the Communist Parties, the "laboring class and people's democratic movement in various countries, and the national emancipation movement in various colonies and vassal states."

Stripped of its propagandistic overtones, the Communist characterization of the Western Powers as "aggressive" indicates recognition of the fact that the initiative and strength in Europe today lies in the hands of the West.

## B. The Present Communist Plan

The principal components of the Communist plan today are:

1. To direct the greatest effort toward matching the power of the West by transforming the Eastern orbit industrially into a highly integrated economic unit. This requires the avoidance of a world military conflict that would jeopardize the existence of the Eastern orbit.
2. To expand Communist power in Asia insofar as this does not involve the danger of an immediate major war.
3. To insure that Western Communism shall operate as an internal opposition force devoted to a program of hampering capitalist economic and political stabilization.

The Communist Parties in the Eastern orbit, in the colonial and semicolonial countries of Asia, and in the advanced Western states are implementing this program in their local planning and activities.

### 1. The Eastern Orbit

a. *The European Soviet Satellites.* Communism in the European Soviet satellites is geared to the technological-economic reconstruction of these countries as effectively functioning parts of an integrated, Soviet-directed, Eastern orbit economy. This program involves, in the predominantly agrarian countries, industrialization and mechanization; in the already industrialized regions (Germany, Czechoslovakia, and to a lesser degree Poland and Hungary), a redirection of the economy toward the needs of the USSR and the orbit as a whole. All the Communist regimes in the Eastern orbit are concentrating on this task. The stability of these regimes depends, apart from the military and police power they possess, on the "neutrality" (as a minimum) and on the active support (as an optimum) of all classes of the working population during the period of technological development of the national economies.

The peasantry, which still forms the great majority of the population in all satellite countries except Czechoslovakia, cannot be antagonized to the extent that it would resort to large-scale sabotage necessitating violent suppression by the authorities. Therefore, collectivization of agriculture, which Communist doctrine regards as indispensable for "socialism," is slowed down until the hostility of the property holders can be overcome by "education" and a tangible increase in their living standards.

In the field of industry, the transition to mechanized and rationalized mass production requires the regimentation and disciplining of the labor force accompanied by improvement of efficiency and speed-up techniques. Toward this end, the trade unions are integrated into the state apparatus and lose their function as instruments for the satisfaction of labor's demands vis-a-vis management and the government. The leading representatives of the trade unions are absorbed into the ruling strata. The prevailing scarcity and the forcible adjustment of the national economies to the requirements of the USSR and the orbit make for further and continued police controls.

Since the economic program of the Communist regimes would be greatly facilitated by the large-scale resumption of East-West trade, the Communists are in favor of re-establishing such trade relations as long as the fundamental drive toward the economic coordination of the orbit is not obstructed. The absence of this trade makes the regimes entirely dependent on internal orbit resources and aggravates the unsatisfactory internal economic situation.

b. *China.* In China, the primary task is the consolidation of the military victories of the Communist armies through the creation of a new government and the complete destruction of the opposing Kuomintang regime. Further, in contrast to the Soviet satellites in Europe, and in accordance with the relatively lower level of industrial development of these areas, the Chinese Communists follow a policy based on the concept of "new democracy." During this stage, the "class struggle" is waged against the relatively small groups of "landlords" and "capitalists" who are the "agents of the foreign imperialists." The Communists softpedal radical agrarian reform, encourage private capital in selected sectors of the economy, and try to broaden the political basis of the regime. They consider trade relations with the "imperialist powers" desirable, and to attain this goal they may give economic concessions as long as they entail no political concessions that would jeopardize Communist control.

This program reflects the fact that the Communists have achieved leadership and won their victories in China on the basis of the promise of agrarian revolution, although their objective is the creation of a "Socialist state," following the model set by the USSR. Their problem is to prevent the development of a series of conflicts that would undermine their control. They seek to reconcile the as yet indispensable bourgeois elements to the requirements of state direction of economic development; to contain the agrarian revolution within limits and by taxation provide for the costs of the administrative machinery; and to restrain the military and subordinate it to the emergent civilian regime. The Communists hope to overcome their difficulties through the building of a national reconstruction front that includes representatives of all classes. At the same time, they emphasize the "urban" and "proletarian" basis of the revolution in order to prepare for the earliest possible transition to the form of "people's democracy" as it exists in the rest of the Eastern orbit. They aim to industrialize China and create a large working class that will serve as a counterweight to the peasantry and insure the stability of the new developing bureaucratically centralized political regime.

### 2. The Colonial and Semi-Colonial Countries of Asia

The Communists are gearing their activities to the changing needs of the movements for national independence and agrarian revolution that provide the basic impetus for change throughout South Asia. They attempt to dominate the movements for national independence and insure the complete severance of ties with the Western powers. They favor guerrilla warfare and engage in civil war, since they calculate that such struggles will remain localized.

Communists identify the interests of the emergent national states with that of the "anti-imperialist democratic camp" and seek to promote good relations between these states and the Eastern orbit through local participation in the various international front organizations. The Communists seek support among all groups and strata of the population in an effort to set the peoples of these areas against the West, and, in particular, against the United States.

### 3. The Western Countries

The main Communist objectives in the Western World at present are: to slow down and sabotage the European Recovery Program and the North Atlantic Pact; to mobilize "anti-war" sentiment through the galaxy of international front organizations; to weaken and possibly replace the present "anti-Soviet" and "anti-labor" governments by more "progressive" and "pro-Soviet" governments; and to defeat the Social Democratic

Party and anti-Communist trade-union leaderships, which the Communists regard as their most dangerous enemies.

This program is designed for the present period during which "capitalism" is relatively stable in the West. The persisting high standard of living in the Western World—as compared with the Eastern orbit—results in continued support of the established system by the working classes. The "socialist" orbit does not have the attraction and appeal necessary to give to the home-grown Communists of Western countries the necessary prestige as leaders who will usher in a higher type of society. The Communists bank heavily on a crisis in the Western economic system to provide them with opportunities for leadership. Thus, propaganda about the "forthcoming crisis" looms large in present Communist tactics.

The Communists renounce the violent "seizure of power." Instead they strive for the formation of broad coalition governments that would implement Communist objectives. They recognize thereby that forceful attempts would find insufficient support among the population of countries which accept the democratic process and in which the Communists cannot count on the police, the military, and the proximity of the Soviet Army to influence events in their favor.

Only in the event of a major economic crisis that completely disrupts the Western powers and leads to a corresponding growth in Communist strength and influence may the Communists be expected to attempt the seizure of power by forceful means.

## IV. Assets and Liabilities of World Communism

### A. General

The major appeal of Communism stems from the paradoxical situation of the coexistence of immense social wealth, technological mastery of the productive forces, and widespread want, toil, and injustice. Communism offers both a doctrine and instrumentality through which the structure of world society can allegedly be altered to solve this paradox. Communism's relatively rapid expansion together with the status of the orbit as a great regional world power, lends weight to the claims of the Communists and infuses their followers with dogmatic faith in the inevitability of their success. This Communist asset is further reinforced by the quality of the Communist leadership and the hierarchic military character of the movement itself, which gives a machine-like air of efficiency to its operations.

In evaluating the strength and weakness of Communism in the Eastern orbit, it is necessary to distinguish between overt Communist power, as expressed in control over the administration, the police, and military and para-military organizations, and Communist popular support.

Today in the Eastern orbit, there is a marked disproportion between overt power and popular support. While in many of the regions where Communists are now in control the Communist regime followed a long period of semi-dictatorial rule and foreign occupation against which the Communists fought with resulting popular credit, they have come to power wholly or partly from the outside, in the wake of the Soviet Army. The system of dictatorship that they have set up does not register the popular will, and in some of these areas popular following is reported to be virtually non-existent. The continued domination by the Soviet Union promotes nationalist feeling directed against the local regimes, which are considered little more than puppets.

However, Communist efforts directed toward the industrial development of these areas constitute an important asset of Communist strength that must be adequately considered in any reasonable evaluation. The fact that the many differing peoples within the orbit are given an opportunity to learn the techniques of an industrialized society has had an enormous impact on these peoples and on the dependent and semi-dependent areas of the world outside of the orbit.

This impact has been particularly great in vast regions of Asia where the Communists have succeeded in linking their program with the satisfaction of the material wants of the underprivileged mass. In China, the Communists are leading a combined movement of national reconstruction and agrarian revolution. In Indochina and throughout South Asia, Communism benefits from a similar union of national and social desires. The authoritarian character of the Communist movement finds reinforcement in the structure of native society itself. Communists are regarded as effective leaders who will show the way to an industrial system with all its attendant benefits.

By the same token, the dependent and semi-dependent areas of the Near East would offer favorable prospects for Communist development, but here the potentialities of the Communists are limited by Western influence, by conflicting loyalties of racial, religious, and national groups, by a relative lack of political consciousness and organization, and by effective methods of governmental domination. Latin America is politically and economically an integral part of the Western system and therefore can be expected to offer adequate resistance to Communist progress.

There are also effects attendant upon the regional concentration of Communist power in the Eastern orbit that condition the Communist "wave of the future." In its impact on the Western world, a liability of Communism is the fact that it has become a great *outside* political and military power rather than an indigenous social force. The "socialist reconstruction" of the orbit, accompanied as it is by the most highly developed methods of state coercion, political terror, low standard of living, and regimentation, creates a type of society that is regarded as a threat to the progress already made by the peoples of the West.

The most serious vulnerability of Communism is the fact that the Western world remains a viable social organization backed up by the resources and power of the United States. The extent to which the West through non-Communist methods provides its own answers to popular needs is a deterrent to internal Communist activity and a threat to the Communist regimes.

These general considerations provide a framework within which Communist assets and liabilities can be investigated concretely in the following three-fold division of the world: the Eastern orbit, the colonial and semi-colonial countries of South Asia, and the Western countries.

## B. The Eastern Orbit

1. *The European Soviet Satellites.* The economic development of the European Soviet satellites is based on agrarian reform and nationalization of industry. These measures were, however, introduced not in the course of indigenous revolutionary action, but principally as a result of military operations. The old ruling groups—the landed aristocracy and industrial leadership—were overthrown. The native working classes were yet to be won to the support of the new regimes.

The fundamental present weakness of satellite Communism lies in the fact that, while it requires the support of the working population to aid in the rapid transformation of the economy, the process of transformation itself requires intensified exploitation of both the industrial and agricultural populations.

a. *Political considerations.* The political form under which the Communists rule, the "people's democracy," is more than a mere facade. The Communists, while retaining all the key positions of control, have "taken in" a variety of front organizations and non-Communist political and professional groups and have made concessions to the desires of varying elements of the population such as the middle classes, the small and medium peasants, intellectuals, technicians and specialists, and the managerial bureaucracy. A whole new social stratum is created that buttresses the regime in power. This is particularly true where the regime allows for a relatively great measure of socio-economic participation by hitherto backward and semi-dependent peoples. The "people's democracy" thus is flexible enough to permit the form of the state to adjust to the changes accompanying economic development.

b. *The agricultural sector.* In the predominantly agrarian countries of satellite Europe, agrarian reform was instituted by the new Communist regimes in an effort to win popular support and destroy the large landowners and their political influence. A policy of confiscating estates over

50 hectares in size was designed to win for the regime the support of large numbers of the peasant population. However, such agrarian reform conflicts with the nationalization aims of the new state. Rapid industrialization calls for a corresponding mechanization and rationalization of agriculture, and the latter is in turn incompatible with the maintenance of small peasant holdings. Final collectivization of agriculture is an indispensable objective, but one that meets with bitter hostility on the part of the old and the newly established small agrarian property holders. Moreover, the low level of agricultural production, the lack of equipment and facilities, and the need for an uninterrupted flow of food supplies make any large-scale attempts at collectivization an extremely dangerous undertaking. The Communist regime is forced to give in to these adverse conditions. Such steps as are taken are slow and precarious. Heavy taxation and state interference in production and sales also contribute to peasant resentment, already aroused by the threat of eventual collectivization.

c. *The industrial sector*. The Communist regimes began with a decline rather than an improvement in the status of the industrial worker. This was due primarily to war destruction, reparations, and the redirection of industrial production. The anti-Communist sentiment of the large majority of the peasant population was not offset by a sufficiently strong pro-Communist attitude among the working class. Moreover, except in Czechoslovakia and eastern Germany, the industrial working class is numerically weak. Yet, such popular strength as the Communists have is concentrated in the trade unions, which have become—practically if not officially—government organs and the most important parts of the administrative machine.

The Communists have achieved a measure of success in their continued propaganda campaign to win the worker support for the "socialist aims" of the new regimes. This appeal is furthered by the promise of comprehensive social security schemes, the use of preferential price policies, and other devices designed to raise the workers' economic and political status.

However, here too the requirements of the Communist plan for national development generally conflict with the occupational interests and demands of the workers. These requirements include the raising of the standards of productivity of labor by all available means: longer working hours, strict discipline, efficiency wages, speedup techniques, practical outlawing of strikes, and resistance to wage demands. The "transition to socialism" by way of rapid technological progress means that the workers must forego their most-cherished traditional trade-union objectives; they have to work longer and harder without acquiring tangible benefits of better and freer living. Outside the cadres of the militant Communist functionaries, the majority of the industrial workers feel that, despite the change in government, there is as much, and perhaps more, exploitation than previously. This is especially true in the more advanced industrial regions, where economic development under the aegis of Communist regimes has been accompanied by a marked deterioration in the standard of living.

It may be assumed that the Communists are aware of this situation and are taking a calculated risk. Communists believe that, if their ambitious reconstruction plans succeed and the Eastern European satellites develop industrially as parts of an integrated economic unit, it will be possible to raise the standard of living. They then anticipate that the anti-Communist sentiment of the population will change. This is a long-range objective, but the Communists hope, through their monopoly of power, to maintain themselves until such time.

d. *The development of "Titoism."* A serious obstacle to the Soviet plan for development of the Eastern orbit as an integrated economic unit is the disparate economic structure of the satellite countries. Immediate economic interests of individual satellites are often sacrificed, thus creating tensions within the orbit that promote tendencies toward "nationalist deviations." The monolithic structure of the orbit is weakened. The native regimes, anxious to improve their home situation, tend to look outside the orbit for trade to satisfy some of their needs.

In the Eastern orbit, the case of Yugoslavia provides a unique example of an open break with the USSR by a Communist regime unwilling to subordinate its national interests to those of the USSR. This development has focused attention on the prospect that international Communism may prove vulnerable by virtue of the conflicting national interests of the various Communist regimes. Hitherto, in the international movement, local Communist Parties have generally subordinated their particular national needs to the requirements established by the Stalinist leadership. Since their energies have been directed primarily toward acquiring power in the non-Communist state in which they operate, the local parties have had neither the strength nor the leadership for a successful struggle against Soviet controls. The advantages inherent in adhering to a powerful disciplined international organization backed by the Soviet Union have outweighed any local difficulties arising out of such control. Those independent Communists who have broken away have been able to build little more than small splinter groups.

The conflict between Yugoslavia and the USSR arose over the discriminatory subjection of Yugoslav trade and industry to Soviet needs, coupled with Soviet inability to mediate the difficulties that had arisen for fear that the disciplined character of the Communist movement, and its own central leadership would be weakened. The Yugoslav regime has been successful so far in opposing the USSR because it alone among the European satellites has a strong independent political and military apparatus and indigenous prestige and support. In all other aspects of its rule, it is a typical "people's democracy."

The absence of similar conditions in the other satellites (with the possible exception of Albania, which may be loyal to Moscow because of its own national conflict with Yugoslavia) may preclude further defections. However, Tito's success in withstanding the strong pressure of the USSR and his corresponding ability to find external aid lend weight to his own efforts to promote defection by similarly minded Communists. The basis exists for conflict that would exacerbate all the internal difficulties of the Communist movement now held in check and weaken the hitherto centralized direction of International Communism. Possibility of defection exists in China, where the Communist Party also has a broad popular base and its own military forces and, because of the extremely underdeveloped character of the national economy, must pursue a careful policy of national planning.

2. *China*. The nature of the Communist movement in China has been conditioned by the fact that its major successes stem from the agrarian base it created during the period following its defeat as a movement in the industrial and commercial centers. The original impetus provided by agrarian revolution within China was further strengthened by the failure of the Kuomintang regime to answer the desire for national reconstruction. Nevertheless, during the recent period, Chinese Communism has developed primarily as a military rather than a social movement. The Communist armies are not composed of Communist workers and peasants fighting for a revolutionary program. They are simply armies, and anti-Communist Kuomintang divisions are included wholesale after brief indoctrination.

Insofar as the Chinese Communists combine the national aspirations of various sectors of Chinese society with the material interests of the underprivileged masses, their popular basis is far larger and stronger than that of Communism in the European Soviet satellites, including important sections of the native middle and upper classes. However, this community of interests is precarious. The Communists will soon be faced with the choice of deciding for their own revolutionary program as against a more moderate policy. As the movement succeeds in consolidating large areas and conquering the commercial and industrial centers, the requirements of effective administration and economic reconstruction come into conflict with the original program for fundamental social and economic changes. The Communists inherit a bankrupt and devastated economy marked everywhere by scarcity and want bordering on famine. The uninterrupted functioning of the administrative and economic apparatus, increased productivity and production, and maintenance of foreign trade and credit become vital for the survival of the regime. Private capital, free enterprise and the incentive of profit must be enlisted to keep the economy operating.

In addition, rigid centralization is imposed by the Communist leadership. The controls are most binding on the peasantry and the small number of industrial workers. These classes are exhorted to work harder, since they are now working for their "own" state, and to abandon demands for improvement of their lot. If the Soviet Union should prove incapable of furnishing needed goods, machines, and raw materials and the national economy were forced to depend on help from the "capitalist world," Communist difficulties would multiply and faith in their promises would be weakened.

The very factors that provided the Communist movement with an impetus would then militate against it. In a country as vast as China with its relatively undeveloped means of communication, its provincialism, and its tradition of hostility to central authority, all the tendencies would combine to produce renewed movements of social unrest directed chiefly against the payment of taxes and for land division.

The emergent Chinese Communist regime is also faced with the problem of reconciling its own national needs with the interests of the Soviet Union in the Far East. The large northern areas have not been under centralized Chinese authority for long periods. The Soviet Union has tried to orient these areas toward the adjoining Soviet territory in terms of trade and economic development. Their inclusion in China is not only a matter of national pride but also vital to the economic future of Communist China itself. Under such circumstances, the subordination of Chinese Communism to the international movement and the direction of the USSR may well conflict with Chinese national interest.

### C. The Colonial and Semi-Colonial Countries of Asia

It is predominantly in South Asia that the Communists have, in the period following World War II, been successful among dependent peoples in building up effective organizations capable of conducting large-scale guerrilla warfare. The motive force that the Communists exploit stems from the twin desire for national independence and agrarian reform. The primary asset of the Communists has been the reluctance, and in some cases the refusal, of the metropolitan powers to recognize the vitality of this movement and bestow the rights of self-government.

While independence is still to be won, nationalist and Communist leaders work together. Communists are afforded the opportunity to assume a large measure of control of the nationalist movement. Once a considerable degree of self government has been achieved, however, a process of differentiation takes place; the nationalists part with their

Communist allies on domestic and international problems. The degree to which Communism remains a force is dependent upon the ability of the Communists to exploit such local difficulties as are not dealt with effectively by the nationalists. In Indochina, the Communists dominate the leadership of the Vietnam Democratic Republic because of French inability to meet nationalist demands. In India and the Philippines, the Communists are only aggressive minorities exploiting peasant and labor dissatisfaction with the more conservative nationalists who have achieved control of the new governments following the grant of independence.

The chief weakness of Communism in such areas is that the traditional pattern of native society operates against the acceptance of Communist objectives by nationalist collaborators once nationalist aspirations are satisfied. The Communist movements themselves are small and composed primarily of Western-educated leaders and members recruited from the small urbanized population. They have yet to win a following among the mass of the peasant population living in the villages.

A major asset of Communism in the area is the success of the Chinese Communists. Not only do the local Communists gain in prestige but also they can be expected to gain support from the change in loyalty of the appreciably large Chinese minorities in Southeast Asia. Moreover, many nationalist politicians can be expected to "accommodate" themselves to the new balance of power that will be established following the consolidation of a Chinese Communist regime. This factor is only partially offset by the natives' traditional fear of domination by China and animosity toward the Chinese minorities because of their economic power throughout South Asia.

A vulnerability is the form and extent of continued interest in the area by the Western powers concerned. The dependent areas are particularly sensitive to political change based on world power relationships. Active collaboration with and encouragement of nationalism have in such areas served as a counterweight to the organized Communist drive to align these areas with the "anti-imperialist camp."

### D. The Western Countries

Communism in the Western countries is generally a small oppositional force directed against "capitalist stabilization." Exceptions are France and Italy, where its organizations are important and powerful political parties. Generally, the major asset of Communism is the fact that as a force acting as the "militant representative" of labor's rights, it has retained, in spite of all the Soviet control and direction, some reputation as an independent political movement. Western European Communism is not yet stigmatized in the eyes of the working classes by that sacrifice of traditional working class demands which is characteristic of Communism in the Eastern orbit. In the West, the Communists do not have to fight for longer and harder working conditions, for regimentation of labor, against strikes and slowdowns, and for strengthening the authority of management. On the contrary, they can assume the role of champions of the "best interests of the working class" in opposition to "the established political and economic system."

The strength or weakness of Communism is related directly to the economic situation in the West and varies directly with the existence of effective social democratic labor parties or effective non-Communist trade union leadership. The spectacular growth of Communism in France and Italy would appear to be due to special conditions operating in each country. In Italy, the combined effects of Fascist rule and defeat in war produced a political vacuum that was exploited by an extremely competent and effective Communist leadership. Moreover, there was a lack of differentiation between the Communist and Socialist movements, which had survived common persecution by the Mussolini regime. In this atmosphere, Communists could utilize "working class unity" to promote their program.

In France, the decline of the Socialist Party and the change in its composition (it had become a party of predominantly lower middle class elements), linked with the great prestige that accrued to the Communists as protagonists of the resistance against German occupation, combined to produce a situation in which the Communists emerged as the principal political representative of the working class.

Subsequently in France and Italy, Communist political objectives have been skillfully tied up with economic demands that non-Communist labor leaders can hardly refuse to endorse. In addition, the two Communist Parties have advanced their program as spokesmen for the "national interest" against "foreign imperialism," as a continuation of their role during and immediately following the war. Consequently, they have effectively drawn to themselves many elements that have traditionally been alien to Communism. Their support stems from factors such as the fear of a rebuilt Germany, the hostility of small business and agricultural elements to the "monopolists," the fear of a new war, and the restoration of national pride.

The same program is generally implemented wherever the Communists operate in the Western countries. The united front with non-Communist groups and the representation of labor interests in terms of the "national interest" are the principal Communist tactics. Propaganda that underscores the threat of American domination through the guise of economic and military aid programs is a restatement of this "national line." This propaganda, coupled with the general apprehension arising from the prospect of an East-West war, is the most effective Communist weapon.

However, the success of the efforts of the West to promote substantial and lasting recovery has gone far to dissipate the effects of Communist propaganda and weaken the support that Communists have found outside the ranks of their own militants.

# NOTES

## Introduction

1. D. Giacchetti, "June 1969: The 'Hot' Italian Days of Herbert Marcuse," *Il Protagora*, no. 4 (July–December 2004). Available online at: http://www.marcuse.org/herbert/booksabout/00s/69ItalyLecturesDGiachetti04z.htm.

2. "Marcuse: Cop-out or Cop?," *Progressive Labor* 6 (1969): 61–66; L. L. Mathias, "Schwere Vorwürfe gegen Herbert Marcuse,," *Bulletin des Fränkischen Kreises*, 4 June 1969.

3. On the OSS see B. F. Smith, *The Shadow Warriors: OSS and the Origins of the CIA* (New York: Basic Books, 1983); also R. H. Smith, *OSS. The Secret History of America's First Central Intelligence Agency* (Guilford, Conn.: Lyons Press, 2005).

4. Herbert Marcuse, Juergen Habermas, Heinz Lubasz, and Telman Spengler, "Theory and Politics: A Discussion," *Telos*, December 21, 1978, 124–53.

5. B. Katz, *Foreign Intelligence: Research and Analysis Branch in the Office of Strategic Services 1942–1945* (Cambridge, Mass.: Harvard University Press, 1989). See also R. Wink, *Cloak and Gown: Scholars in the Secret War, 1939–1961* (New York: Morrow, 1987), esp. chapter 2.

6. Alfons Söllner, *Zur Archäologie der Demokratie in Deutschland*, 2 vols. (Frankfurt am Main: Fischer Verlag, 1986), 1:25.

7. W. Langer, "The Research and Analysis Branch,," memoir sent to Kermit Roosevelt, March 5, 1947, RG 226, entry 146, box 48, folder 666, US National Archives at College Park, Md. (hereafter cited as USNA).

8. "Joint Psychological Warfare Committee, Functions of the OSS,," in *War Report of the OSS*, 2 vols.(New York: Walker and Co., 1976), 2:348.

9. E. M. Earle, *Rentless War* (New York: Columbia University Press [Columbia Home Front Warbooks], 1942), p. 5, n. 3.

10. H. Marcuse, letter to M. Horkheimer, 11 November 1942, in H. Marcuse, *Technology, War and Fascism*, ed. D. Kellner (London: Routledge, 1998), p. 234. On the OWI, see A. Winkler, *The Politics of Propaganda: The Office of War Information 1942–1945* (New Haven, Conn.: Yale University Press, 1978).

11. *History of the Central European Section during the Incumbency of Eugene N. Anderson as Chief*, 17 February 1945, USNA, RG 226, entry 37, box 5, p. 1.

12. A. R. L. Gurland, O. Kirchheimer, and F. Neumann, *The Fate of Small Business in Nazi Germany* (Honolulu: University Press of the Pacific, 2003). Information on Neumann's and Marcuse's contracts can be found in USNA, esp. RG 226, entry 38, box 3, and RG 226, entry 145, box 4, folder 43: Personnel of the Research and Analysis Branch. Kirchheimer's contacts are, instead, in RG 226, entry 146, box 86, file 1335. On Neumann's and Kirchheimer's intellectual ca-

reers, see W. E. Scheuerman, *Between the Norm and the Exception: The Frankfurt School and the Rule of Law* (Cambridge, Mass.: MIT Press, 1994).

13. R. Wiggershaus, *The Frankfurt School: Its History, Theory and Political Significance* (Cambridge, Mass.: MIT Press, 1995).

14. M. Horkheimer, "Traditional and Critical Theory," (1937) in M. Horkheimer, *Critical Theory: Selected Essays* (New York: Continuum Publishing Corporation, 1975), pp. 188–243; H. Marcuse, "Philosophy and Critical Theory," (1937) in H. Marcuse, *Negations: Essays in Critical Theory* (Boston: Beacon Press, 1969), pp. 134–58.

15. H. Marcuse, letter to M. Horkheimer, November 15, 1942, in Marcuse, *Technology, War and Fascism*, p. 237.

16. Wiggershaus, *Frankfurt School,* pp. 303–7.

17. Ibid., p. 305.

18. M. Horkheimer and T. W. Adorno, "Soziologische Exkurse," *Frankfurter Beitrage Zur Soziologie* 4 (Frankfurt am Main: Europaische Verlag, 1956 [our translation]).

19. F. Pollock, "State Capitalism: Its Possibilities and Limitations," *Studies in Philosophy and Social Science* 9, (1941).

20. F. Pollock, "Is National Socialism a New Order?" ibid. On Pollock, see C. Campani, *Pianificazione e teoria critica. L'opera di Friedrich Pollock dal 1923 al 1943* (Naples: Liguori, 1992).

21. J. Burnham, *The Managerial Revolution: What is Happening in the World* (New York: John Day Co., 1941). On "Tatkreis," see G. Marramao, "Pluralismo corporativo, democrazia di massa, Stato autoritario," in F. De Felice, G. Marramao, M. Tronti, and L. Villari, *Stato e capitalismo negli anni Trenta* (Rome: Editori Riuniti, 1979).

22. M. Horkheimer, "The Authoritarian State" (1942), in A. Arato and E. Gebhardt, *The Essential Frankfurt School Reader* (New York: Continuum, 1982), pp. 95–117. For a reconstruction of Horkheimer's essay in the wider context of the German debate on the "total state," see C. Galli, "Strategie della totalità. Stato autoritario, Stato totale, totalitarismo nella Germania degli anni Trenta," *Filosofia politica* 1: (1997): 27–61.

23. F. Neumann, *Behemoth: The Structure and Practice of National Socialism, 1933–1944* (Chicago: Ivan R. Dee, 2009), p. 430.

24. E. Lederer, *State of the Masses: The Threat of the Classless Society* (New York: W. W. Norton, 1940), p. 18.

25. O. Kirchheimer, "Changes in the Structure of Political Compromise," *Studies in Philosophy and Social Science* 9 (1941): 456.; H. Marcuse, "State and Individual under National Socialism," in Marcuse, *Technology, War and Fascism,* p. 69–87.

26. H. Marcuse, "State and Individual under National Socialism," p. 77.

27. Katz, *Foreign Intelligence*, p. 9.

28. See Neumann's report from September 25, 1942, *German Social Democracy in the United States and Great Britain,* preceded by Neumann's brief autobiography and a note from an OSS official to Ambassador John C. Whiley that warns of the "highly personal and critical" positions expressed in the document by virtue of Neumann's past as general counsel of the German Social-Democratic party but that, for the same reason, also endowed him with an "intimate knowledge of the facts."

29. F. Neumann, letter to Chandler Morse and Gordon Stewart, August 3, 1944, USNA, RG 226, entry 146, box 84, folder: Neumann, F.L.

30. N. West, *Venona: The Greatest Secret of the Cold War* (London: HarperCollins, 1999), 252, 339; A. Weinstein and A. Vassiliev, *The Haunted Wood: Soviet Espionage in America* (New York: Modern Library, 2001), esp. pp. 249–51. On the American intellligence and counterintelligence system, see also P. Deery and M. Del Pero, *Spiare e tradire. Dietro le quinte della guerra fredda* (Milan: Feltrinelli, 2011).

31. This is, for example, the interpretation of Henry Stuart Hughes, head of the Central European Section from 1945, although acknowledging of having been "directed" de facto by Neumann and Marcuse who both enjoyed an "extraordinarily elevated individual prestige" in the structure (A. Söllner, *Zur Archäologie der Demokratie*, 2:47).

32. See, e.g., *The Problem of Objectivity in R&A Reporting,* USNA, RG 226, entry 37, box 5.

33. R. Hartshorne, *Draft of Proposed Guide to the Preparation of Political Reports*, USNA, RG 226, entry 37, box 5; *Style Sheet for Use in the Research and Analysis Branch*, USNA, RG 226, entry 99, box 104, folder 97303.

34. This was the case with Marcuse's report *The Social Democratic Party of Germany*, published in this volume, approved only in September 1944 after a long internal debate. See letter from R. Hartshorne to S. Kent and C. Schorske, July 14, 1945, and the following memo to W. Langer, July 23, 1945, USNA, RG 226, entry 1, box 3.

35. See pp. 76–91. However, in this case there were also criticisms from the Project Committee for having "reduced people to statistical 'automatons' whose attitudes and actions are determined by their socioeconomic position" (Katz, *Foreign Intelligence,* p. 43).

36. *History of the Central European Section,* pp. 1–2.

37. H. Marcuse, letter to M. Horkheimer, April 18, 1943, in Marcuse, *Technology, War and Fascism*, p. 243.

38. Katz, *Foreign Intellligence*, p. 12.

39. J. Herz, *Vom Ueberleben: Wie ein Weltbild entstand: Autobiographie* (Dusseldorf: Droste Verlag, 1984, p. 136 [our translation]).

40. P. 107.

41. P. 101.

42. P. 100.

43. P. 96.

44. P. 131.

45. P. 101.

46. P. Viereck, *Metapolitics: From the Romantics to Hitler* (New York: Knopf, 1941).

47. P. 69.

48. H. Marcuse, "The New German Mentality," in Marcuse, *Technology, War and Fascism*, pp. 139–90.

49. P. 68.

50. P. 58.

51. Pp. 136–137.

52. P. 134.

53. P. 110.

54. P. 131.

55. P. 439.
56. P. 420.
57. P. 230.
58. P. 285.
59. P. 302.
60. Pp. 314–315.
61. Pp. 397–411.
62. P. 441.
63. Pp. 253–263.
64. *Dissolution of the Nazi Party and Its Affiliated Organizations: De-Nazification of Important Business Concern in Germany*, R&A 1655.5, March 1945.
65. P. 280.
66. P. 299.
67. *Some Criteria for the Identification of Anti-Nazis in Germany*, R&A 2189, November 15, 1944.
68. P. 286.
69. Pp. 309 and 429.
70. P. 105, but see also unknown author, *The Underground Movement in Germany*, R&A 992, September 27, 1943.
71. P. 299.
72. *Labor Relations and Military Government*, R&A 1655.28, p. 7.
73. MG Law n. 5, in *Documents on Germany Under Occupation, 1945–1954*, ed. B. Ruhm von Oppen (Oxford: Oxford University Press, 1955).
74. P. 295.
75. H. Marcuse, *One-Dimensional Man: Studies in the Ideology of Advanced Industrial Society* (Boston: Beacon Press, 1991), p. 1.
76. J. H. Herz, "The Fiasco of Denazification," *Political Science Quarterly* 4 (1948): 569.
77. B. Smith, *The American Road to Nuremberg: The Documentary Record 1944–1945* (Stanford: Hoover Institution Press, 1982), p. 58.
78. Pp. 451–456.
79. P. 460.
80. On the category of the "objective enemy," see C. Galli, "Sulla guerra e il nemico," in *Paranoia e politica*, ed. S. Forti and M. Revelli (Turin: Bollati Boringhieri, 2007), 21–42.
81. Pp. 471–472.
82. E.g., *Problems Concerning the Treatment of War Criminals: List of Potential War Criminals Under Proposed US Policy Directives*, R&A 2577.2, September 30, 1944.
83. As acting chief, Neumann inaugurated a profound internal restructuring of the Central European Section that, however, would remain largely unconsummated. Marcuse was charged with coordinating the studies on the American occupation zone, and Kirchheimer assumed responsibility for the French sector. See F. Neumann, "Plan for the Reorganization of the German and Austrian Unit of the Central European Section," May 3, 1945.
84. For a wider treatment on the OSS's contribution to the Nuremberg Trials, see M. Salter, *Nazi War Crimes: US Intelligence and Selective Prosecution at Nuremberg. Controversies Regarding the Role of the Office of Strategic Services* (London–New York: Routledge, 2007), esp. pp. 307–444.

85. C. Schorske, "R&A Contribution to the War Crimes Program," July 9,1945, document held at USNA and cited in M. Salter, *US Intelligence, the Holocaust and the Nuremberg Trials: Seeking Accountability for Genocide and Cultural Plunder*, 2 vols. (Leiden–Boston: Martinus Nijhoff Publishers, 2009), 2:605–606.

86. J. Donovan, "Progress Report on Preparation of Prosecution," n.d., Jackson Papers, Cornell University, box 101, reel 7.

87. Jackson Papers, Cornell University, vol. 19.

88. Pp. 475–526. See also International Military Tribunal, Indictment, 6 October 1945, in *The Nuremberg War Crimes Trial, 1945–1946. A Documentary History*, ed. M. R. Marrus (Boston–New York: Bedford, 1970, pp. 57–70.

89. Pp. 522–554.

90. See, e.g., S. Aronson, "Preparations for the Nuremberg Trial: The O.S.S., Charles Dwork, and the Holocaust," in *Holocaust and Genocide Studies* 2 (1998): 257–81.

91. Pp. 27–28.

92. Neumann, *Behemoth.*

93. L. Löwenthal, letter to H. Marcuse, June 29, 1943, in *Das Utopische soll Funken Schlagen. Zum 100. Geburtstag von Leo Löwenthal*, ed. P.-E. Jansen (Frankfurt am Main: Klostermann, 2000), pp. 101–14.

94. H. Marcuse, Letter to M. Horkheimer on 28 July 1943, in Marcuse, *Technology, War and Fascism*, pp. 244–45.

95. *Nazi Plans for Dominating Germany and Europe: The Criminal Conspiracy against the Jews*, R&A 3114.2, August 13, 1945, p. 1. http://www.trumanlibrary.org/whistlestop/study_collections/nuremberg/documents/index.php?documentdate=1945-00-00&documentid=C192-2-2&studycollectionid=&pagenumber=1.

96. Opening remarks by Judge Jackson, 21 November 1945, cited in Salter, *US Intelligence*, pp. 584–85. Also available online at http://fcit.usf.edu/holocaust/resource/document/DocJac06.htm.

97. This, e.g., is Aronson's thesis: "OSS had very valuable documentation, but which did not reach its 'Jewish expert,' Charles Dwork, on time, or rather was simply never used. But for the time being it was OSS's Franz Neumann who, having developed his own opinions about the Holocaust years before, seems to have played the major role in London, at least in preparation for the International Military Tribunal" (Aronson, "Preparations for the Nurenberg Trial," p. 269).

98. A. Schlesinger, *A Life in the Twentieth Century: Innocent Beginnings, 1917–1950* (Boston: Houghton-Mifflin, 2000), p. 307.

99. B. Katz, "The Holocaust and American Intelligence," in *The Jewish Legacy and the German Conscience*, ed. M. Rischin and R. Asher (Berkeley, Calif.: Judah L. Magnes Museum, 1991), p. 297.

100. *Nazi Plans for Dominating Germany and Europe: The Criminal Conspiracy against the Jews, Exhibit A: Statistics on Jewish Casualties' During Axis Domination*, R&A 3114.2, n.d. For a wider vision of the Frankfurt contribution to defining the Holocaust in the Nuremberg Trials, see Salter, *US Intelligence*, 2:572–636.

101. *Allied Military Government and the Jewish Problem*, R&A 1655.23 report, April 29, 1944, drafted by E. Johnson under the supervision of Neumann and with the participation of Marcuse and Kirchheimer.

102. T. Taylor, *The Anatomy of the Nurember Trials: A Personal Memoir* (New York: Knopf, 1992), p. 90.

103. *Sixty-Five Leading German Businessmen*, 28 June 1945, R&A 3020, USNA, RG 153, entry 135, box 14.

104. Marcuse et al.,"Theory and Politics: A Discussion," p. 131. In past years there had been a strong controversy over the real support of German big business to the Nazi regime. In his book *The Collapse of the Weimar Republic* (Princeton, N.J.: Princeton University Press, 1981), David Abraham mantained that big business had major responsibilities for Hitler's rise to power. The thesis was strongly criticized by several American scholars, one being Henry Ashby Turner, who argued that German business support had been much exaggerated (*German Big Business and the Rise of Hitler*: [New York–Oxford: Oxford University Press, 1985]). However, several scholars coming from the Central European Section, such as Arno J. Mayer and Carl Schorske, defended Abraham's position.

105. H. Marcuse, letter to M. Horkheimer, April 6, 1946, in Marcuse, *Technology, War and Fascism*, p. 251.

106. Smith, *OSS*, p. 343.

107. Marcuse stayed in the "limbo" of the State Department until the death of his wife in 1951, when he obtained a contract at the Russian Institute of Columbia University and then the Russian Research Center of Harvard for research that culminated in his 1958 book on Soviet communism (*Soviet Marxism* [New York: Columbia University Press, 1985]). As for Kirchheimer, he stayed in Washington until 1955 before assuming the directorship of the Political Science Department at the New School for Social Research.

108. D. Kellner, *Introduction* to Marcuse, *Technology, War, and Fascism*, 25–27.

109. Pp. 591–610.

110. *Anti-Semitism in the American Zone,* document from March 3, 1947, preserved in the Herbert Marcuse Archive, Stadt- und Universitäts Bibliothek, Frankfurt am Main, although no precise information is available on it.

111. O. Kirchheimer, *Political Justice. The Use of Legal Procedure for Political Ends* (Princeton: Princeton University Press, 1961), p. 3.

112. Marcuse, *One-Dimensional Man.* On the importance of the OSS years in the development of Marcuse's postwar critical analysis of advanced industrial society, see T. B. Müller, *Krieger and Gelehrte. Herbert Marcuse und die Denkesysteme in Kalten Krieg* (Hamburg: Hamburger Edition, 2010).

## 1: Anti-Semitism: Spearhead of Universal Terror

1. On April 1, 1933, the SA organized the first national action against the Jews, promoting a national boycott day against the economic and professional activities of citizens of Jewish origin, painting the star of David on the shop windows and doors of thousands of buildings while chanting slogans like "Don't buy from the Jews" or "The Jews will ruin us." During the demonstration there were numerous episodes of provocations and threats and even a few sporadic episodes of racial violence. The boycott marked the beginning of the Nazi party's campaign against the Jews. In fact, a few days later, on April 7, 1933, the first descriminatory law against the Jewish people was passed. The law, *Gesetz zur Wiederherstellung des Berufsbeamtentums* (Law for Reestablishing Professional Civil

Service) restricted employment in public services to those with clear "Aryan descent." [ed. note]

2. Hjalmar Schacht (1877–1970), banker and German politician. After having contributed in a decisive way to bringing the German industrial world closer to the Nazi Party, from August 1934 to November 1934 he was the minister of economy for the Nazi government while maintaining the position of president of the Reichsbankuntil 1939. Despite adopting openly anti-Semitic positions, he publicly declared himself contrary to all "illegal activity" against the Jews. Having fallen into disgrace for his critical positions against massive investments in arms production, he was deported in 1944 to the Dachau concentration camp, accused of participating in the assassination attempt against Hitler in July of that year. Although he was acquitted at the Nuremberg Trials, he was sentenced to eight years by the German government on other charges. He was released in September 1948, founded his own bank, and became an economic adviser for various foreign governments, including that of Gamal Nasser in Egypt. [ed. note]

3. Ernst Edward von Rath (1909–1938), German diplomat. His assassination in Paris by a young Jew of Polish origin sparked the so-called Kristallnacht (Crystal Night) on November 9, 1938, during which around 400 Jews were killed and over 30,000 others were deported to various concentration camps. [ed. note]

4. A system of fortifications realized for Germany's military reorganization, promoted by the Nazi government through reviving the Siegfried Line created during World War I. [ed. note]

5. Werner Best (1903–1989), jurist and Nazi politician. He held various positions in the Nazi government, incuding head of the Administration of France under occupation, where he earned the name "Butcher of Paris," and then as plenipotentiary of the Third Reich in Denmark. Previously, he had contributed to the construction of a legal base for the racial policies of the Third Reich as Heinrich Himmler's close collaborator. [ed. note]

## 2: Possible Political Changes in Nazi Germany in the Near Future

1. Andrey Andreyevich Vlassov (1900–1946), General of the Soviet Army. After the German invasion of the USSR in 1941, he distinguished himself as the commander of the armies that defended Moscow and Kiev. After his army was defeated by the Germans in June 1942, he promoted the constitution of the nationalist Committee of Liberation of the People of Russia and the Russian Army of Liberation that would fight side by side with the Nazis against the Soviets. [ed. note]

2. FCO Berlin (Press in German to Europe, August 7, 1943), and *Washington Post*, August 9, 1943.

3. There is abundant evidence for that in Ps/W interrogations; see i.e. Secret 561/2/4, August 9, 1943; information obtained in the USA between 29 and 31 July 1943; and, Roundups (Central European) no. 19, p. 12; no. 18, pp. 11 and 14; no. 16, p. 13.

4. See the decree of August 26, 1940, "On the Planned Exploitation of the Economy of the Occupied Western Territories for the German War Economy"

in *Die Reichsverteidigungsgesetzgebung*, vol. II, *Auftragsverlagerung* IV, pp. 1–7; also the text of the decree of August 15, 1941, which gave Goering authority "For the Exploitation of the Occupied Eastern Territories for the German War Economy" published in *Heeresverordnungsblatt*, vol. 23 no. 50, September 5, 1941, Part C.

5. See the memorandum of the Central European Section, "Some Remarks about the Ruling Class in Germany," II, 2, and Franz Neumann, *Behemoth: The Structure and Practice of National Socialism*, New York 1943, pp. 396–398.

6. *New York Times*, August 9, 1943.

7. Three exceptions have to be made. The death of Fritz Todt has paved the way for the rise of Albert Speer; Himmler's power has increased; and Ribbentrop has outdistanced Rosenberg in the field of foreign policy.

8. See Neumann, op. cit., pp. 41–61, pp. 62–71, and pp. 83–85.

9. *Der Beutsche Ordenstaat*, Munich, 1934.

10. Text from *Neue Zuericher Zeitung*, May 17, 1943.

11. See Neumann, op. cit., p. 66.

12. See the memorandum of the Central European Section, "The Free Germany Manifesto and the German People," August 6, 1943, IV, 3 [ pp. 149–166].

## 3: Changes in the Reich Government

1. Berlin, in German to Europe, August 24, 1943.

2. See the Appendix.

3. [See pp. 41–42.]

4. [pp. 31–37].

5. Carlo Scorza (1897–1988), Italian politician. He adhered to Fascism early on, from the March on Rome. He was national secretary of the National Fascist Party from April 19, 1943, until the fall of Mussolini. [ed. note]

6. Here the author is referring to the Sudeten German Party, founded in 1937 by Konrad Henlein (1898–1945), a Czecholosvakian politician and leader of the Sudeten German separatists who, after the Nazi annexation of Bohemia, became Gauleiter of the region. [ed. note]

## 4: Speer's Appointment as Dictator of the German Economy

1. Transocean in English to North America, September 8, 1943. FCC Daily, September 9, 1943.

2. Berlin (Press) in German, September 8, 1943.

3. Plain from Bern, September 7, 1943.

4. Plain, Bern, September 6, 1943.

5. "Some Remarks about the Ruling Class in Nazi Germany"—see *PW Weekly* no. 12, p. 16, and *Weekly Roundup* (Central Europe) no. 20, p. 5.

6. *Europakabel*, January 8, 1943.

7. *Das Reich*, July 20, 1943.

8. Established in the spring of 1943; see *Hamburger Fremdenblatt*, April 2, 1943.

9. *Frankfurter Zeitung*, July 21, 1943; created in cooperation with the Ministry of Economics.

10. *Neues Wiener Tagblatt*, February 5, 1943.

11. OSS dispatch from London, May 26, 1943.

12. Stockholm, Plain, July 19, 1943, quoting the *Ostsee Zeitung*, June 29, 1943.
13. *Der Deutsche Volkswirt*, October 3, 1942.
14. *Das Reich*, November 22, 1942.
15. *Frankfurter Zeitung*, May 10, 1942.
16. *Das Reich*, April 19, 1942. Microfilm no. 19.
17. See Office of Strategic Services, "Banks, Industry and the Nazi Party."

## 5: The Significance of Prussian Militarism for Nazi Imperialism: Potential Tensions in United Nations Psychological Warfare

1. This citation is from Winston Churchill's speech to the English Parliament on September 21, 1943, later published in *Vital Speeches of the Day* 9 (1943): 743–54. [ed. note]

2. Stockholm wire, September 23, 1943.

3. The landed aristocracy of the East-Elbian territories were, by virtue of their economic position, a pre-capitalistic, semi-feudal class. Their power depended, not on expansion, but on the maintenance of their dominion, and on its protection from international capitalistic competition. "The large estates East of the Elbe are by no means mere economic units, but they are local political centers of domination. According to the Prussian tradition, they were supposed to provide the material basis for a stratum of the population which the State had entrusted with the exercise of political power. . . . The members of the landed aristocracy were qualified for this trusteeship . . . because they were "economically saturated," with relatively undeveloped acquisitive instincts and an economic intelligence below average. Moreover, they are not inclined to a purely business-like exploitation of their political position, or at least they are not dependent on it." — (Max Weber, *Entwicklungstendenzen in der Lage der ostelpischen Landarbeiter, gesammelte Aufsatze zur Sozial- und Wirtschaftsgeschichte*, 1924, p. 471.) Weber argues on the basis of these facts, the large estates of the Prussian nobility constituted an "effective counter-balance" against the political monopoly of the industrial bourgeoisie.

4. Here the authors are referring to the German multinational corporation IG Farben, commonly called German Dye Trust in the United States. [ed. note]

5. Public funding provided by the German government beginning in 1929 to support the bankrupt agricultural activities in Eastern Prussia. At the end of 1932, this political measure was at the center of a scandal (*Osthilfeskandal*), in which the family of the president of the Republic, Paul von Hindenburg, was involved, it having been discovered that in many cases the funding provided by the government to support the regional economy was being used by the Junkers to acquire luxury items for themselves. [ed. note]

6. Alfred Hugenberg (1865–1951), politician and German industrialist. He was one of the main German industrialists in communications in the years before the war. Head of the German National People's Party, he was Minister of the Economy and Agriculture in Hitler's first cabinet. However, he was forced to give his resignation after only a few months, following which he suffered a progressive economic and political decline, culminating in the concession of all his businesses in the communications sector. [ed. note]

7. *Kadavergehorsam*, literally "corpse obedience." This term of Latin origin with Jesuit roots, coined by Ignazio da Loyola, is used to indicate perfect Christian obedience. It began circulating in Germany during the Reformation with a controversial anti-Jesuit meaning. However, it was only really affirmed in the second half of the nineteenth century during the *Kulturkampft* debates, to describe the typical Prussian and German military mentality. The term was then popularized in the 1960s by Hannah Arendt to describe the behavoir of Nazi hierarchs in the execution of the Final Solution in her work *Eichmann in Jerusalem: A Report on the Banality of Evil.* [ed. note]

8. *Reichserbhofgesetz*, law passed in September 1933 that established the possibility of hereditary transmission of an agricultural good only for farmers of pure German blood. [ed. note]

9. Broadcast of August 26, 1943. This broadcast was, perhaps significantly, beamed to Great Britain in English.

## 6: German Social Stratification

1. *Tatsachen und Zahlen über Deutschland*, ed. by Wilhelm Bauer and Peter Dehen, 1941, p. 13.

2. The generals of the Waffen SS are included among group 1(e).

3. *Die Soziale Schichtung des Deutschen Volkes*, 1932, p. 82.

4. *The Fate of Small Business in Nazi Germany*. Senate Committee Print no. 14, 78 Congress, I. Session, 1943, p. 135.

5. *Statistisches Jahrbuch für des Deutsche Reich*, 1973, p. 79.

6. *Neues Bauerntum*, December 1942.

7. OSS Report, R and A no. 1194, pp. 7 and 11.

8. Ibid., p. 11.

9. OSS., Political Intelligence Report, no. 21, Central Europe, pp. 6–7.

10. Figures are based on Julius Theodor Geiger's *Die Soziale Schichtung des Deutschen Volkes* (Stuttgart, 1932) with only partly legible numbers. Geiger's source is the census of 1925. [ed. note]

11. Small Business Report, loc. cit., p. 133.

12. Ibid. p. 140–141.

13. *Statistisches Jahrbuch für des Deutsche Reich*, 1937, p. [*illegible number*].

14. *Small Business Report*, op. cit., p. 115 f.

15. *Small Business Report*, p. 125

16. *Statistisches Jahrbuch* 1937, p. 25.

17. *Small Business Report*, pp. 132–3.

18. *Statistische Jahrbuch* 1937, p. 25

19. *Sonderbeilage: Wirtschaft und Statistik*, 1941, no. 19, p. 10.

20. *Small Business Report*, pp. 132–3.

21. *Statistisches Jahrbuch*, 1937, p. 78.

22. *Statistisches Jahrbuch*, 1937, p. 79.

| | |
|---|---|
| Bavaria | 286,165 enterprises under 20 ha (1933) |
| Rhine Province | " 87,651 |
| Württemberg | " 72,960 |
| Brandenburg | " 61,086 |
| Westphalia | " 47,511 |

| | |
|---|---|
| Baden | " 23,110 |
| Hannover | " 37,757 |

23. *N.S. Landpost*, August 13, 1943.

## 7: German Morale after Tunisia

1. The expression *Festung Europa* (Fortress Europe) was used by English military propaganda during World War II to identify the areas of continental Europe under Nazi control. Nazi propaganda used it as well, to indicate the plans to prevent an English invasion of the occupied zones of Europe, including the so-called Atlantic Wall," an imposing system of fortifications built by the Nazi regime between 1942 and 1944 along the entire western coastline of Europe. [ed. note]

2. T. N. Kaufman, *Germany Must Perish!* (Newark, N.J.: Argyle Press, 1941); R. G. Vansittart, *Black Record: Germans Past and Present* (London: Hamilton, 1941); H. K. Smith, *Last Train from Berlin: An Eye-Witness Account of Germany at War* (New York: Knopf, 1942). [ed. note]

## 8: Morale in Germany

1. Kilgour Cable quoting *Muehlhauser Tageblatt*, July 18, 1943.
2. *Salzburger Landeszeitung*, July 10, 1943 (ND #1191).
3. *Hakenkreuzbanner*, August 15, 1943 (ND #1221).
4. July 31, 1943, from eyewitness account of German and foreign workers reaction to the fall of Mussolini.
5. For detailed information see OSS Special Report on "Interrogations of Prisoners of War: Opposition to Nazis."
6. Allied Forces Headquarters, August 10, 1943.
7. See OSS Special Report #1130, "Changes in the Reich Government," August 26, 1943 [pp. 38–47].
8. See OSS Special Report #1194, September 13, 1943 [pp. 48–60].
9. Weekly Roundup no. 21, Central Europe, August 10–16, 1943.
10. See OSS Report #1034, "Possible Political Changes in Nazi Germany," August 10, 1943 [pp. 31–37].
11. Weekly Roundup #25, Central Europe, September 7–13, 1943.
12. *Stockholm Tidningen*; August 29, 1943 (ND #1226).
13. See OSS Report on Air Raid Morale [This is most likely Franz Neumann's report "The Social and Political Effects of Air Raids on the German People," pp. 118–132; ed. note].
14. Stockholm wire #2260 quoting *Hamburger Fremdenblatt*.

## 9: Possible Patterns of German Collapse

1. Ludwig Kaas (1881–1952), Catholic priest and German politician. From September 1928, he was head of the Zentrum [center] Party in the German Parliament and was one of the main supporters of negotiations between the Vatican

and the Nazi government that resulted in the accords of July 20, 1933. In exchange, the Zentrum Party voted in favor of the Enabling Act, giving Hitler plenary power. [ed. note]

2. Friedrich Gustav Emil Martin Niemöller (1892–1984), German theologist. Although he was a national conservative and initially a supporter of Adolf Hitler, he became one of the founders of the Confessional Church, which opposed the nazification of German Protestant churches. For his opposition to the Nazis' state control of the churches, Niemöller was imprisoned in Sachsenhausen and Dachau concentration camps from 1937 to 1945. From the 1950s on, he was a vocal pacifist and antiwar activist, and vice-chair of War Resisters International from 1966 to 1972. [ed. note]

3. Hans von Seeckt (1866–1936), German general. From 1920 to 1926 he was head of the German army as *Chef der Heeresleitung*. During those years, unbeknownst to the Weimar government, he started the so-called *Schwarze Reichswehr* (Black Army), a secret anti-Polish military alliance with the Soviet Union. [ed. note]

4. Ulrich von Brockdorff-Rantzau (1869–1928), German diplomat, the first foreign minister of the Weimar Republic and German ambassador to the USSR from 1919 until his death [ed. note].

5. Max Hoffmann (1869–1927), German military officer and diplomat. He was a general on the Eastern Front during WWI and participated in armistice negotiations with Russia. [ed. note]

6. Gustav Stresemann (1878–1929), German politician, who served as chancellor and foreign minister during the Weimar Republic. He was co-laureate of the Nobel Peace Prize in 1926 for having drafted the Locarno Treaties (1925), definitively ending the conflict between Germany and France. [ed. note]

7. Interessen-Gemeinschaft Farbenindustrie AG, German industrial conglomerate in the chemical sector. Under Nazism it was the financial heart of the regime. In 1941 it built the biggest chemical industry of the time at Auschwitz, using the workforce of the nearby concentration camp and also making ample use of prisoners as gunea pigs for chemical and medicinal experiments. It was also the producer and supplier of Zyklon-B, the lethal substance used in the gas chambers and prisons. In 1941 an American investigation revealed the existence of an agreement with Rockefeller's Standard Oil Co. and, more generally, deep ties with American industrial and military establishments. See C. Higham, *Trading with the Enemy* (New York: Delacorte Press, 1983); A. C. Sutton, *Wall Street and the Rise of Hitler*, 2000; J. Borkin, *The Crime and Punishment of I. G. Farben* (New York: Free Press, 1978); R. Sasuly, *I. G. Farben* (New York: Boni & Gear, 1947). [ed. note]

8. A handwritten note on the report. [ed. note]

## 10: The Social and Political Effects of Air Raids on the German People: A Preliminary Survey

1. *New York Times*, 24 March 1944.

2. Based on data supplied by Economic Capabilities Subdivision, 1 January 1944.

3. Based on data supplied by Economic Capabilities Subdivision, 1 May 1944.

4. Based on data supplied by Economic Capabilities Subdivision, 1 January 1944.

5. Air Raid Precautions. [ed. note]

6. *The Size, Organization and Function of German Civil Defense . . . ,* R&A 1071.

7. British Handbook, "Civil Defense" (1853-HBC–Part II).

8. Anti-aircraft. [ed. note]

9. FCC: Daily Report, 24 April 1944.

10. *Hamburger Tageblatt*, 9 December 1943 (*News Digest* # 1320).

11. FCC: *Weekly Analysis*, 6 November 1943.

12. *Der Führer*, Karlsruhe, 23 September 1943 (*News Digest* # 1254).

13. Construction company created by Fritz Todt, Minister of Armaments of the Third Reich that, during World War II, built fundamental civil and military infrastructures, like the Atlantic Wall, in close collaboration with the high command. [ed. note]

14. "The Size, Organization and Function of Civil Defense." R&A 1071.

15. *Die Deutsche Volkswirtschaft*, 1943, no. 26, p. 795.

16. "The German Housing Position, 1939–43," R&A 1426.

17. Decree concerning Conversion of Dwellings (*Die Verordnung über die Zweckentfremdung von Wohnung*) 14 August 1942, RGB1., I 545; Decree concerning Renting of Dwellings about to be Vacated (*Die Verordnung über die Vermietung freiwerdender Wohnungen*) 5 October 1942, RGB1., 573; decree of 9 October 1942, RGB1. X, 586, empowering municipalities to take possession of dwellings on behalf of families with many children, war wounded and widows and orphans of war victims; decree concerning Administration of Dwellings (*Die Verordnung zur Wohnraumlenkung*) 27 February 1943, RGB1., I 127.

18. *Berliner Börsen-Zeitung*, 18 February 1944; Decree of September 1943 "Deutsche Wohnungshilfwerk."

19. OSS # 31637, 18 April 1944.

20. Vestmapläns *Tidning*, 28 April 1944 (Press Intell. Cable).

21. Berne Cable, 4 September 1943.

22. Reichstheaterkammer, professional organization of theater workers. [ed. note]

23. *Hamburger Tageblatt*, 5 October 1943, quoting "Artistenwelt."

24. "Changes in the German Plan for the Distribution of Air Raid Evacuees," R&A 1159.

25. Nazionalsozialistische Volkswohlfahrt, organization created by the Third Reich to provide social assistance to the German people. [ed. note]

26. FCC: *Central European Analysis*, 30 December 1943, 3 March 1944.

27. FCC: *Central European Analysis*, 2 September 1943.

28. *Reichsgesetzblatt*, 26 October 1943.

29. *Leipziger Neuste Nachrichten*, 21 December 1943 (*News Digest* # 1329).

30. *Sie und Er*, quoted in OSS A-25526-a, 19 April 1944.

31. OSS A-23915, 31 March 1944.

32. "Faced with imminent peril the German people instinctively rally round anything that represents the idea of authority and are grateful to their leaders for not losing their heads and acting and thinking in their stead."(*Feuille d'Avis*, Neuchâtel, 15 April 1944; *News Digest* 1425, B23.)

33. A former German worker who was with the revolutionaries in 1918/1919, writes to his emigré son:

> the situation is quite different from what it was in 1918. Today we are really fighting against enemies who want to annihilate us. Under those circumstances all our points of dissension disappear. (OSS, CID # 65652, 6 March 1944.)
>
> Out of fear for the future everyone will fight on, and the workers are prepared to produce even greater results than in the past (same source).

## 11: The Attempt on Hitler's Life and Its Consequences

1. *The Ruling Class in Nazi Germany, PW Weekly*, 23 July 1943.
2. See also OSS Source # 34017, 25 July 1944.
3. Quoted from H. Rosinsky, *The German Army*, Washington, 1944.
4. Date of the Allied landing in Normandy. [ed. note]
5. OSS # 35739, 19 July 1944.
6. OSS # 36770, 19 July 1944.
7. OSS Source S, 18 July 1944.
8. OSS # 35770, 19 July 1944.
9. OSS # 35919, 22 July 1944.
10. OSS # 35739, 19 July 1944.
11. OSS Daily, 18 July 1944.
12. A probable reference to Daniel 5:5. [ed. note]
13. OSS Source # 33696, 21 July 1944.
14. The Germans asserted, however, on 27 July 1944, that Beck committed suicide. (See below.)
15. According to Hitler, 21 July 1944.
16. FCC *Daily Report*, 21 July 1944, p. CCA 3.
17. FCC *Daily Report*, 22 July 1944, p. CCC 6.
18. *New York Times*, 24 July 1944.
19. *New York Times*, 27 July 1944.
20. The German radio identified today (27 July 1944) the following conspirators:

Col. Gen. Ludwig Beck is said to have committed suicide.

Col. Gen. Erich Höpner is awaiting trial. Höpner, who was Chief of Staff to Field Marshal v. Rundstedt, was retired in 1942.

General Friedrich Olbricht, Chief of the General Army, office was court-martialled and shot.

21. OSS Source #33934, 24 July 1944, differs from this interpretation.
22. Both appendixes have been omitted in this volume. [ed. note]
23. FCC *Daily Report*, 21 July 1944, p. CCC 5.
24. OSS Source #33934, 24 July 1944.
25. All quotations from *The Morale of the German Ruling Class*, *PW Weekly*, 21 April 1944, pp. 11–18.
26. QES Source 33896, 21 July 1944.
27. For details see *The Free Germany Committee and the German People*, OSS, 6 August 1943, pp. 12–14 [pp. 149–166].

28. *New York Times*, 27 July 1944.
29. Italicized by the author.
30. There are already reports of the execution of Schacht, von Neurath, and members of the Stauffenberg family.
31. Names and rank in *Order of Battle of the German Army*, February 1944 (MID), pp. 35–49.
32. *New York Times*, 20 July 1944.
33. *Seydlitztruppen*, German military troops organized by the Red Army and using prisoners from the Battle of Stalingrad and sent to Germany to fight the Nazis. The name is derived from General Walther Kurt von Seydlitz-Kurzbach (1888–1976), founder of the League of German Officials and, later, the National Committee for a Free Germany. [ed. note]
34. FCC Daily Report, 26 July 1944, p. 4.
35. Emphasis supplied.
36. Text in *New York Times*, 26 July 1944.
37. *New York Times*, 27 July 1944.
38. *The Ruling Class in Germany*, op. cit.
39. FCC Daily Report, 28 July 1944, pp. CCB 3/4.
40. *The Process of German Collapse* R & A no. 7477, 4 December 1943.
41. For details see *The Free Germany Manifesto and the German People*, R & A, 6 August 1943, pp. 6–12 [pp. 149–166].

## 12: The Free Germany Manifesto and the German People

1. Full, apparently authentic text in *New York Times*, August 1, 1943.
2. The *Pravda* has accepted the manifesto, see Plain Moscow Aug. 2, 1943. This backing may be temporary and may be withdrawn as has been pointed out in report, *The Soviet Union and Free Germany*, submitted jointly by the U.R.S.S. Division and Central Euroepan Section. This possibility will be discarded here.
3. See especially Hitler: A Survey of P/W Opinion Secret B370 July 29, 1943.
4. See *Die Internationale*, vol. I, no. 11/12, pp. 244 seq.
5. *Die Internationale*, vol. I, no. 4, pp. 3 seq.
6. See Arnold Struthahn, "Die Auswaertige Politik des deutschen Kommunismus und der Hamburger Nationals Bolschevismus" in *Die Internationale*, vol. I, nos. 17 and 18, p. 340.
7. See Rakosi in "Jahrbuch fuer Wirtschaft, Politik und Arbeiterbewegung" 1923–24 (official publication of the CP), Hamburg, 1924, pp. 17, and Thalheimer, op. cit. p. 601.
8. Accord signed April 16, 1922, between Germany and Soviet Russia in which the two governments renounced their respective territorial and financial claims made at the end of World War I. [ed. note]
9. See *Russian Information Review*, vol. 2, 1922–23, p. 244.
10. Minutes of the Party Congress of 1927, p. 303.
11. Thalheimer in "Jahrbuch fuer Wirtschaft, Politik und Arbeiterbewegung," 1923–24, p. 598.

12. "Jahrbuch fuer Wirtschaft, Politik und Arbeiterbewegung," 1923–24, p. 26.

13. Albert Leo Schlageter (1894–1923), German military officer. After having participated in World War I, he enrolled in the University of Freiburg and became a member of an extreme right-wing Catholic group. Shortly after he joined the *Freikorps*, he took part in the *Kapp Putsch* and other paramilitary actions against Communist political organizations. In 1922, his *Freikorps* unit joined the Nazi party. The next year, during the Ruhr occupation, he led a clandestine paramilitary in various actions of sabotage against the occupying French forces. Arrested by the French, he was put to death on May 26, 1923, becoming a symbol for all German national-socialist groups. [ed. note]

14. Quoted by Georg Schwarz, *Voelker, Hoeret, die Zentrale. KPD Bankrott*, Berlin, 1933, p. 91.

15. See Schwarz, op. cit., p. 92.

16. *Die Internationale*, vol. 14, p. 492.

17. Resolution of the Twelfth Ekki Plenum in *Die Internationale*, vol. 15, p. 384.

18. Schwarz, op. cit., p. 206.

19. He is now one of the main members of the Free Germany movement in Mexico. He is an outstanding novelist and writer on military affairs. Renn is a pen name. He belongs to the German nobility.

20. See Peter Maslowski, *Thaelmann*, Leipzig, 1932, p. 77.

21. Maslowski, op. cit., p. 88.

22. *Die Internationale*, vol. 13, p. 584.

23. Maslowski, op. cit. p. 79.

24. *Stahlhelm, Bund der Frontsoldaten*. Founded in 1918 in Magdeburg by Franz Seldte, its name was taken from a newspaper published by Hans-Jurgen von Blumenthal, who would later take part in the assassination attempt against Hitler on July 20, 1944. In 1930 it had 500,000 members, becoming the most important Freikorps group. [ed. note]

25. Remmele has been executed by the G.P.U. in Russia together with Heinz Neumann.

26. See Thaelmann in *Die Internationale*, vol. 15, p. 386.

27. Franz Neumann, *Behemoth: The Structure and Practice of National Socialism*, New York, 1942, pp. 41 and 42.

28. Konrad Heiden, *Geschichte des Nationalsozialismus*, Berlin, 1933, pp. 202, 203.

29. Published in Mommsen and Franz, *Die deutschen Parteiprogramme*, vol. III, Leipzig, 1931, pp. 116–117.

30. Otto Strasser, *Aufbau des Deutschen Sozialismus*, 2nd edition, Prague, 1936, pp. 88–89.

31. 1919, especially p. 101.

32. *Der Arbeiter, Herrachaft und Gestalt*, 2nd edition, Hamburg, 1932.

33. See also Franz Neumann, op. cit., pp. 139 to 199.

34. Pyotr Andreyevich Shuvalov (1827–1889), Russian politician and close collaborator with Alexander II. He participated in writing the Berlin Treaty of 1878. [ed. note]

35. Text in Pribram, *The Secret Treaties of Austria and Hungary*, vol. I, p. 275.

36. See on his doctrine Franz Neumann, op. cit., pp. 105–106.
37. Nowak (ed.), *Die Aufzeichmungen des Generals Max Hoffmann* (1929).
38. Especially vol. II, pp. 365–367.
39. *Deutschland zwischen West und Ost*, 1933, especially pp. 31–41.
40. See especially Wheeler-Bennett, "From Brest-Litovsk to Brest-Litovsk" in *Foreign Affairs*, 1939–1940, p. 196.
41. *Thoughts on Germany*, 1932, pp. 310 and 311.
42. *Der Kontinentalblock* (1941), pp. 15–16.
43. *Vermaechtnis*, vol. II, pp. 93–94.
44. "Deutschlands Aussenpolitik in der Nachkriegazeit," in Harms (ed.), *Volk und Reich der Deutschen*, vol. 3 (1929), pp. 182–183.
45. See the discussion in Franz Neumann, op. cit., pp. 203–210.
46. Walter Rist, "Der Weg der KPD" in *Neue Blaetter Fuer den Sozialismus*, vol. III 1932, pp. 79–91.
47. This figure is questionable. It is quoted by Pjatnitzki, *Internationale Presse-Korrespondenz*, 1932, no. 32.
48. 1,008,953 in 1931 see *Jahrbuch der Deutschen Sozialdemokratie*, 1931, Berlin, 1932, p. 109.
49. 1931: 4,700,000 members.
50. *Jahrbuch der Deutschen Sozialdemokratie*, 1930.
51. Neumann, op. cit., pp. 413–414.
52. There are but a few exceptions, mostly from the ADGB, the Federation of Socialist Unions, and then not leaders but employees, and from the white collar unions, also employees.
53. Rotfrontkämpferbund, paramilitary organization of the German Communist Party founded on July 18, 1924. [ed. note]
54. See i.e. OSS document L 13297 and the study of the Central European Section of the OSS, July 20, 1943, *Report on Prisoner of War Interrogations: Opposition to the Nazis*.
55. See sources on preceding page.
56. See OSS Central European Section "The Nazi Defeat in Tunisia, the Coming Invasion of Europe and our PW."
57. See F. Neumann, op. cit. p. 412/3.
58. See the above mentioned Ps/W interrogations.

## 13: The German Communist Party

1. The attitudes and policies of the Social Democrats will be discussed more fully in the forthcoming report on the Social Democratic Party [pp. 199–225).
2. Figures on KPD membership are given in Walter Rist, "Der Weg der KPD," *Neue Blätter für den Sozialismus*, III, 81:

1919—90,000
1920—50,000 (March)
1920—78,000 (October)
1921—359,000
1922—180,000
1923—267,000

1924—180,000
1927—150,000
1928—130,000
1930—120,000
1931—200,000
1932—320,000

The increase in membership in 1921 is due to the affiliation of the left-wing of the Independent Social Democratic Party (USPD) with the KPD in 1920. In 1932, only 260,000 of the 320,000 members could be classed as dues-paying members. Franz Borkenau, *The Communist International*, p. 363.

3. Walter Rist, *Neue Blätter für den Sozialismus*, 1931, no. 9; Ossip Piatnitzky, *The Organization of a World Party*, p. 25. Between 1923 and 1925, the KPD issued 54,219 membership cards in the Berlin-Brandenburg district; but in 1926, the total membership was 17,219. In three years, 37,000 people had passed through the party organization.

4. Sigmund Neumann, *Die deutschen Parteien*, pp. 90–91.

5. Borkenau. pp. 361–2. In 1931 there were 5,888 street cells and 1,802 factory cells in Germany (*Rote Fahne*, 1 January 1932). The large number of street cells may be explained by the extent of unemployment.

6. Piatnitzky, op. cit., pp. 39–40. The size of the factory cells in Germany as a whole in the years 1926–8 is as follows:

| *Number of members* | *Number of factories* |
|---|---|
| 15 or under | 1,000 |
| 16–50 | 374 |
| 50 or more | 36 |

7. The percentage of party members employed in factories is as follows:

1928—62.3%
1929—51.6
1930—32.2
1931—22.0

*International Press Correspondence*, 1931, no. 36, p. 679.

8. At the high point of its development in 1924 the RGI had 120,000 members. *Jahrbuch für Politik, Wirtschaft, Arbeiterbewegung*, 1925–6.

9. There were 180 factory cells of the KJVD in 1930. Many of these cells published their own newspapers, such as *Der A–E–G–Stift*.

10. H. Siemering in *Die deutsche Jugendverbände*, 1931. The RFB was for youths between the ages of 16 and 21. Those under 16 were organized into *Pioniere*, engaging in sports and elementary training in party doctrines. The RJF newspaper was called *Die junge Garde* and the periodical of the *Pioniere* was *Die Trommel*.

11. Ernst Posse, *Die politische Kämpfbünde Deutschlands*, pp. 68–71.

12. *Sperlings Zeitschrift und Zeitungs Addressbuch*, 1931. A list of the KPD papers included in the Appendix III.

13. The KPD vote surpassed that of the Social Democrats in Berlin in 1930 and after. In the Berlin districts, the Communists traditionally controlled Wedding, and had a strong position in Berlin Mitte, Tiergarten, Kreuzberg, Pren-

zlauer Berg and Friedrichshain. In Potsdam I (*Wahlkreis 4*) the KPD strength was centered in Charlottenburg, Neuköln, Köpenik and Teltow. In Potsdam II (*Wahlkreis 3*) the party was strong in Spandau, Lichtenberg and Wersensee.

14. The material in this section is derived from official statements in *International Press Correspondence* and *Communist International*; also Rosenberg, *History of Bolshevism*; Borkenau, *Communist International* and Sturmthal, *The Tragedy of European Labor*.

15. Based on Erich Müller, *Nationalbolshewismus*; and R & A *The Free German Manifesto and the German People* [pp. 149–166].

16. The Locarno Treaties were seven agreements negotiated at Locarno, Switzerland, on October 5 –16, 1925, and formally signed in London on December 3. The main treaty, called the Rhineland Pact, agreed that Germany recognize the French and Belgian borders established in the Treaty of Versailles. As a result, strongly pushed by England, France would gradually abandon the *Cordon sanitaire* with Poland and Czechoslovakia, leaving Germany free in the management of political relations with Eastern European countries. A brief period of calm between European powers followed, marked by the 1926 entrance of Germany into the League of Nations. On the other hand, the Soviet Union feared further diplomatic isolation as a result of this relative peace among the Allied powers so, in 1922, it tried to remedy the situation by signing the Treaty of Rapallo with Germany. [ed. note]

17. *International Press Correspondence*, 14 January 1932, p. 23.

18. *International Press Correspondence*, 17 January 1931, p. 63.

19. Ibid., 14 January 1932, p. 23.

20. Ibid., 6 July 1931, p. 674.

21. Salomon, *Die deutsche Parteiprogramme*, III, 119–121.

22. *International Press Correspondence*, 30 June 1931.

23. Ibid., 19 September 1932, p. 883.

24. Ibid., 26 February 1932, pp. 207–208.

25. R&A no. 992, *The Underground in Germany*; Otto Bauer, *Die Illegale Partei* (Paris, 1939).

26. CID 61464-C, 14 February 1944.

27. Many prisoners of war who had formerly been arrested for Communist activity reveal in their interrogations that they engaged in the underground work through family influences.

28. *Die Nation* (Berne), 4 March 1944, in *News Digest* 1386; *St. Galler Tageblatt*, 25 March 1944 (Press Intell Cable).

29. OSS #31330, 11 April 1944.

30. Bauer, *Die illegale Partei*, p. 103 ff.

31. *Pravda*, 16 October 1941, quoted in CID 44338.

32. *Communist International*, 1941, no. 6.

33. May Day Manifesto of the KPD, 1943. The same argument was used in the German Communist leaflet distributed to the occupation troops in Belgium on May Day 1943.

34. FNB, no. 110, 4 March 1943; London *Left News*, no. 84, June 1943; New York *Daily Worker*, 10, 11, 24 January 1943; Soviet International News (ICN), 31 December 1942. The meeting was mentioned in a Bern dispatch to the *New York*

*Times*, 22 Dec. 1942. One prisoner-of-war, a former member of the KPD, says that he heard of the meeting in Germany.

35. The manifesto contained a formula for the composition of the "National Front" to consist of "the supporters of the old big parties of the Center, the German National People's Party, the Communist Party, the Social Democratic Party, members of the former Christian and Free trade unions, members of former cooperative and sports movements, the old members of the SA, and even those who were formerly affiliated with the Nazi organizations..

36. CID 49876-C.

37. Examples of the expression of this viewpoint may be found in the following reports: CID 64319-S, 25 March 1944; CID 61695-S, 9 March 1944; CID 63057-S; 63059-S.

38. CID 54293-C, 11 December 1943.

39. *New York Times*, 26 March, 12 April 1944. This group may have been the subject of the Swiss report of the arrest of Communists who were attempting to unite various opposition groups into an "European Union."

40. Stockholm wire, 2024, 4 August 1943; FCC: Special Report #98, "The Free German Movement as Psychological Warfare."

41. FCC: Eastern European Analysis, 26 January 1944.

42. CID 49796-S, 20 October 1943; CID-47683; CID-48164.

43. CID 51724-S, 27 December 1943; CID 29250-S, 16 November 43; CID-54393, 15 January 1944; Press Intell Cable, 21 January 1944.

44. CID 51724-S, 27 December 1943.

45. Paul Merker, "Die Erklarung von Teheran und die Freien Deutschen," in *Freies Deutschland* (Mexico City), 24 January 1944, III, 6–7; also the telegram of Siegbert Kahn, Secretary of the London Committee to President Benes.

46. The Hitler clique was blamed for the war in the Free German broadcast 11 June 1944. FCC: Eastern European Survey, 17 June 1944.

47. Paul Merker, "Wir müssen auf dem Wort 'Respektabel' bestehen," in *Freies Deutschland* (Mexico City), February, 1944, 9–10.

48. A report from Switzerland coming from a "former member of the National Bolshevist Movement" states that the Free Germans advocate a series of "putsches" to overthrow Hitler and already have men in the arsenals and munitions plants. CID 77582–S, 8 June 1944.

49. *Freies Deutschland* (Mexico City) January 1944, p. 18; FCC: Eastern European Analysis, 12 January 1944.

50. Several copies of these papers have been furnished by OSS sources. A reprint of one may be found in CID 59506-S. One leaflet picked up in France is entitled "Freies Deutschland. Organ im Sinne des National Komittees Freies Deutschland."

51. OSS Source B, T 164.

52. Based on *Kader-Information*, reported in a Socialist report as being the official paper of the KPD in Germany.

53. The author is referring here to the December 30, 1812, Convention of Tauroggen, which, in ratifying the armistice between the Prussian and Russian troops, became the first step toward the Treaty of Kalisz, to be signed February 28, 1813, between Russia and Prussia against Napoleon I. [ed. note]

54. CID 62494-R, 5 March 1944.

55. CID 62765-R, 18 March 1944.
56. OSS #27306, 18 January 1944; OSS #27313, 13 January 1944.

## 14: The Social Democratic Party of Germany

1. *Die Sozialdemokratischen Parteien*, Hamburg, 1926, pp. 44–46.
2. Ibid., pp. 45–46.
3. Statistical appendix to Senate Committee Report: *The Fate of Small Business in Nazi Germany*, Washington, 1943, pp. 124–5.
4. *Jahrbuch der Deutschen Sozialdemokratie* 1928, p. 140, and 1931, p. 109.
5. R&A 1550, *The German Communist Party*, p. 7 [p. 167–198].
6. *Internationales Handwörterbuch des Gewerkschaftswesens*, 1930, pp. 26–27.
7. *Jahrbuch der deutschen Sozialdemokratie*, 1929, p. 364.
8. *Jahrbuch der deutschen Sozialdemokratie*, 1929, p. 364.
9. Ibid., pp. 166 ff., 492 ff.
10. Felix Salomon, ed. *Die deutschen Parteiprogramme*, Leipzig, 1931–1932, vol. II, p. 41.
11. Ibid., passim.
12. The Erfurt program of 1891 repeats this sentence verbatim.
13. *Die deutschen Parteiprogramme*, vol. III, p. 1.
14. See below, p. 207.
15. *Sozialdemokratischer Parteitag in Kiel. Protokoll*, Berlin, 1927, p. 178.
16. *Die deutschen Partei programme*, loc. cit., vol. 3, pp. 5–6.
17. Friedrich Stampfer, *Die vierzehn Jahre der ersten deutschen Republik*, Karlsbad, 1936, p. 87.
18. The so-called Kapp Putsch was an attempt by extreme right-wing activists to overthrow the Weimar Republic. On March 13, 1920, led by Wolfgang Kapp (1858–1922), an East Prussian officer and founder of the Patriot Party, activist forces marched on Berlin and proceeded to set up a government. Faced with the army's refusal to repress the coup, the legitimate government, led by Gustav Bauer, was forced to flee to Stockard, where it then called for a general strike. The massive adhesion to the general strike and limited support for the putsch by conservative groups forced Kapp to escape to Switzerland on March 17, allowing for the reestablishment of the Weimar government and democratic normality. [ed. note]
19. *Handwörterbuch des Gewerkschaftswesens, loc. cit.*, p. 1608.
20. Complete table in *Civil Affairs Handbook: Germany*, M 356–9, p. 22.
21. *Die Gesellschaft*, January 1933, pp. 4, 7.
22. Program of Gorlitz, 1921.
23. *Deutscher Geschichtskalender, Die Deutsche Revolution*, 1919, II, 22.
24. *Deutscher Geschichtskalender, Die Deutsche Revolution*, 1919, II, pp. 9 f.
25. Ibid., p. 23.
26. Ibid., p. 146.
27. Fritz Naphtali, *Protokoll des Gewrkschaftskongresses*, Hamburg, 1928, p. 177 ff.
28. *Protokoll des Kieler Parteitages*, Berlin, 1927, p. 168 ff.
29. *Händworterbuch des Gewerkschaftswesens,* loc. cit., p. 2088 ff.

30. Frederick Schuman, *The Nazi Dictatorship*, New York, 1939, p. 232; Franz Neumann, *Behemoth*, 1942, p. 413 ff.; Text in Willy Müller, *Das soziale Leben im neuen Deutschenland*, Berlin, 1938, p. 39.,

31. Harry R. Rudin, *Armistice 1918*. New Haven, 1944, p. 264.

32. Scheidemann, *Memoiren*, 313 ff.; Rudin, op. cit., p. 359.

33. Scheidemann, *Memoiren*, 313 ff.; Rudin, op. cit., p. 359.

34. Neumann, *Behemoth*, p. 11.

35. *Protokoll of the Kiel Congress, loc. cit.*, p. 182 f.

36. *Jahrbuch der Deutschen Sozialdemokratie*, 1928, p. 12 ff.

37. *Ibid.*, 1931, p. 12 ff.

38. *Ibid.*, 1929, p. 21.

39. Hermann Brill had been appointed head of the Thuringian administration by American Military Government. He was later on removed by the Russians. His pronounced western orientation may have played a part in his removal.

40. "Suggestions for a Programme of Immediate Action in the Transitory Period, by the Union of German Socialists in Great Britain," 18 September 1944.

41. R&A Report no. 1113.119. 14 July 1945.

42. OSS source S, 17 May 1945.

43. OSS source S, 21 September 1945.

44. In the western zone they were usually suppressed as violating the ban on political activity. Their present program and activity does not in most cases go beyond exposure of the Nazis and demands for a strong purge policy. These planks have evidently not proved a sufficient program to hold the "Antifa" organizations together; they have tended to dissolve into their political party components (R&A Report no. 1115.125).

45. "Die Wirtschaft im Spiegel des Parteiaufrufes," *Das Volk*, 13 July 1945.

46. *Das Volk*, 8 July 1945.

47. *Das Volk*, 13 July 1945.

48. Ibid., 13 July 1945.

49. Otto Grotewhol (1894–1964) then became one of the founders of the SED and the first minister of the German Democratic Republic, a position he held from 1949 until his death. [ed. note]

50. *Deutsche Volkszeitung*, KPD paper in Berlin, 14 June 1945.

51. *Das Volk*, 18 July 1945.

52. See for example OSS source S–R, 8 August 1945.

53. See R&A Report no. 1113.125.

54. *Das Volk*, 7 August 1945.

55. OSS source S, 7 September 1945.

56. At the present writing, this development appears to have occurred in Bremen, for example; see Situation Report: CENTRAL EUROPE, 7 September 1945.

57. *Das Volk*, 13 July 1945. This rejection was reiterated by Otto Grotewohl in a broadcast of 20 September 1945: FCC: *Daily*, 22 September 1945.

58. OSS source S, 7 September 1945.

59. OSS source S, 7 September 1945.

60. See, for example, OSS source S-R, 22 September 1945.

61. OSS source S, 4 August and 7 September 1945.

62. FCC: *Daily*, 22 September 1945.

## 15: The Abrogation of Nazi Laws in the Early Period of MG

1. This problem is dealt with in the special Guide on Press, Radio and Control of Public Opinion.

2. Concerning details of MG control in this field, see the Guides on Adaptation of German Propaganda Organization.

3. This constitutes only a summary of the detailed discussion of the amnesty problem in the guide on criminal law [probably a reference to Kirchheimer's report *Administration of German Criminal Justice under Military Government*, published in this volume (pp. 318–344); ed. note].

4. Page numbers refer to *Reichsgesetzblatt*, Part I. If not specifically indicated, the volume number corresponds with the year in which the law was issued.

## 16: Dissolution of the Nazi Party and Its Affiliated Organizations

1. See CA Guide *Policy toward Revival of Old Parties and Establishment of New Parties.* [pp. 285–300].

2. Not legally a formation of the Party.

3. Closed down as a result of total mobilization in 1946.

4. Operated only on local levels.

5. For details on the method of dissolution of these mixed organizations, see CA Guides: *Organization of Labor Supply in Germany, Police and Public Safety in Germany, Food Administration for Germany during the Period of Occupation*. The dissolution of the mixed organizations does not imply the abrogation of the statutes and decrees through which these organizations were established.

6. On the procedure with respect to the NS Welfare Organization (NSV), see the CA Guide *Public and Private Welfare in Germany*.

7. Both bodies consist exclusively of prominent Nazis. The members of the *Preussische Staatsrat* were appointed by Göring.

8. On the appointment of the *Wehrwirtschaftsführer* see *Mitteilungsblatt des Wehrwirtschafts- und Rüstungsamtes* vol. 1, no. 7, 10 Apr. 1942.

9. The rank and file of the SS and SA are covered by the categories on pp. 257–258.

10. These institutions are discussed in the CAD Guides on Administration, Labor, etc.

11. See also the CA Guide *General Principles of Administration and Civil Service* [pp. 301–317].

## 17: German Cartels and Cartel-Like Organizations

1. Temporary National Economic Commission: an investigative commission, activated by the United States Congress in 1938 on request of President Roosevelt to monitor the process of monopolistic economic concentration in the United States military but that would soon extend its investigations until it became a veritable forum on fiscal policy. Similarly, on April 15, 1926, the Parlia-

ment of the Weimar Republic activated a investigative commission on the German economy (*Ausschuss zur Untersuchung der Erzeugungs- und Absatzbedingungen der deutschen Wirtschaft*), also known as the *Enquête-Ausschuss*. [ed. note]

2. The cartel tribunal was abolished in 1938. The functions are now being exercised by a senate in the Reich Economic Tribunal (*Reichswirtschaftsgericht*).

3. Six separate national transportation groups have been set up under the Ministry of Transportation, namely, ocean shipping, inland navigation, motor transportation, private railroads, shipping and warehousing, and auxiliary transportation services.

## 18: Policy toward Revival of Old Parties and Establishment of New Parties in Germany

1. "Occupation Government in the Rhineland—1–18–1928." *Institute of World Affairs Research Project on Germany's Position in European Postwar Reconstruction*, pp. 12–18.

## 19: General Principles of Administration and Civil Service in Germany

1. As regards the principles and methods of personnel policy see I. E.

2. *Statistisches Jahrbuch für das deutsche Reich*, vol. 1934, p. 456. This figure does not include civil servants in the post and railway services; they numbered about 500,000 in 1933.

3. See also Appendix B.

4. For a list of "Political Civil Servants" as defined by the Civil Service Act, as well as for an estimate of the higher civil servants to be dismissed, see Appendix C.

5. As to Civil Service problems on the regional and local level see the Guides on local and regional administration.

6. See the Guide on "Elimination of Fundamental Nazi Political Laws."

7. Cf. CA Guide *Elimination of Fundamental Nazi Political Laws*.

8. *RGBl.*, 1, 1937, H. 39, 186.

9. E.g., Preamble; para. 1, 2, and 3; para, 3, 1, and 2; par. 4; par. 26, 3; par. 42, 2 of the Civil Service Act.

10. E.g., par. 31, Civil Service Act: par. 26 of the executory decree of 29 June 1937 (*RGBl.*, I. 669); decree of the Führer of 26 March 1942 (*RGBl.*, I, 1942 H, 153).

11. E.g., par. 2 of Decree Concerning the Training and Career of German Civil Servants, of 28 February 1939 (*RGBl.*, I. 1939, H. 371).

12. E.g., par. 85, Civil Service At: Decree of the Führer Establishing General Principles for the Appointment and Promotion of Civil Servants of the Reich and the Länder of 14 October 1938 (*RGB1.*, I. 893), 4 (3). 8, 12; order of the Reich Minister of the Interior of 4 April 1937 (*RMH1.*i.V., 515); Law Concerning Preferential Treatment and Pensions for the Fighters for the National Revolution, of 27 February 1934 (*RGB1.*, I, 133).

13. E. g., Civil Service Act pars. 5, 25, 59, 72.

## 20: Administration of German Criminal Justice under Military Government

1. The details of this historical development are traced in Civil Affairs Handbook *Germany*, Section 3, "Legal Affairs," pp. 43 ff.

2. For full discussion of these changes in theory, see Civil Affairs Handbook *Germany*, Section 3, "Legal Affairs," pp. 48–49.

3. See, for example, the decree of 4 February 1933, RGB1., 35 and 28 February 1933, *RGB1.*, I, 285, on the protection of the German people and country, the statute of 19 May 1933, *RGB1.*, I, 285, on the protection of the national symbols, and that of 13 October 1933 on the guarantee of internal peace, *RGB1.*, I, 723.

4. Statute of 14 July 1933, *RGB1.*, I, 398.

5. See, for example, the statute of 20 December 1934, *RGB1.*, I, 1269, on surreptitious attacks on the state and the Party and the protection of the Party uniform, and that of 7 April 1937 on the protection of NSDAP labels, *RGB1.*, I, 442.

6. See, for example, the statute of 4 April 1933, *RGB1*, I, 163.

7. The provisions on treason as contained in Criminal Code had been revised by the statute of 24 April 1934, *RGB1*, I, 341, that of 2 July 1936, *RGB1*, I, 532 and that of 16 September 1939, *RGB1.*, I, 1941 and the statute of 22 November 1942 supplementing the provisions on treason, *RGB1.*, I, 668.

8. Statute of 24 November 1933, *RGB1*, I, 995.

9. Statute of 26 May 1933, *RGB1*, I, 295.

10. Statute of 2 July 1936, *RGB1.*, I, 532.

11. Statute of 28 June 1935, *RGB1.*, I, 839.

12. Statute of 22 June 1938, *RGB1.*, I, 651.

13. See, for example, statute of 26 May 1933, *RGB1.*, I, 295.

14. See, for example, statute of 22 June 1938, *RGB1.*, I, supra n. 2.

15. Decree of 15 September 1939, *RGB1.*, I, 1679.

16. Decree of 5 December 1939, *RGB1.*, I, 2378.

17. Decree of 17 August 1938 and 26 August 1939, *RGB1.*, I, 1939, I, 1455.

18. Decree of 25 November 1939, *RGB1.*, I, 2319.

19. Decree of 11 May 1940, *RGB1.*, I, 769.

20. Decree of 23 December 1941, *RGB1.*, I, 797.

21. Statute of 20 September 1942, *RGB1.*, I, 558.

22. Decree of 9 March 1943, *RGB1.*, I, 140.

23. Statute of 24 November 1933, *RGB1.*, I, 995.

24. The details of this tendency are set forth in Civil Affairs Handbook *Germany*, Section 3, "Legal Affairs," pp. 55–56, 60–62.

25. A summary of Nazi action as to juvenile problems is given in Civil Affairs Handbook *Germany*, Section 3, "Legal Affairs," p. 76 et seq.

26. The reference is to Anton Hoefle, minister of the Post Office from 1923 to 1925, who, after a corruption scandal, committed suicide in prison during his preventive detention. [ed. note]

27. *RGB1.*, I, 341.

28. *RGB1.*, I, 844.

29. *RGB1.*, I, 844.

30. A discussion of the nature and function of preliminary judicial investiga-

tion will be found in Civil Affairs Handbook *Germany*, Section 3, "Legal Affairs," pp. 71–72.

31. For description of this function of the judge, see Civil Affairs Handbook *Germany*, Section 3, "Legal Affairs," (M-356-3), pp. 72–73.

32. *RGB1.*, I, 1658.

33. Statute of 1 December 1936, *RGB1.*, I, 994.

34. *RGB1.*, I, 285.

35. *RGB1.*, I, 844.

36. The details of this procedure are given in Civil Affairs Handbook *Germany*, Section 3, "Legal Affairs," pp. 75–76. See the statute of 16 September 1939, *RGB1.*, I, 1841, and the decree of 21 February 1940, *RGB1.*, I, 405.

37. Such courts are: military tribunals, SS and Police Courts, Labor Service Courts. The People's Court has jurisdiction in treason and other political cases.

38. Statute of 29 September 1936, *RGB1.*, I, 756.

39. Decree of 17 August 1938, *RGB1.*, 1939, I, 1457.

40. Decree of 10 October 1940, *RGB1.*, I, 1347.

41. DNB of 5 June 1944.

42. *RGB1.*, I, 754.

43. The functions of this office are described in detail in Civil Affairs Handbook *Germany*, Section 3, "Legal Affairs," pp. 65–68.

44. Decree of 20 March 1935 on Unification of Judicial Organization, *RGB1.*, I, 403; Statute of 24 November 1937 on Organizational Measures for the Courts, *RGB1.*, I, 1268; Decree on Measures in the Field of Jurisdiction and Judicial Organization, 1 September 1939, *RGB1.*, I, 1658.

45. See Feilchenfeld, *The International Economic Law of Belligerent Occupation* (Carnegie Endowment for International Peace, 1942), pp. 90–91; Oppenheim, *International Law* (5th ed., Lauterpacht, 1935), II, 339, 458–59.

46. *RGB1.*, I, 185.

47. *RGB1.*, I, 403.

48. *RGB1.*, I, 548.

49. See condemnation of a similar provision, enacted for the Free City of Danzig, by the Permanent Court of International Justice, Publications of the Permanent Court of International Justice, Series A/B n° 65.

50. Any procedural provision which it is suggested should be retained are discussed infra, p. 25.

51. This requires specific abrogation of the law of 29 March 1933, *RGB1.*, I, 151.

52. *RGB1.*, I, 647.

53. Paragraphs 1 (2), 3 (2), 25 (1), and (2), 35, 60, 76–80.

54. *RGB1.*, I, 341.

55. *RGB1.*, I, 844.

56. *RGB1.*, I, 285.

57. *RGB1.*, I, 994.

58. See statute of 16 September 1939, *RGB1.*, I, 1841.

59. Art. 2b of the statute of 28 June 1935, *RGB1.* I, 839.

60. See Art. 2 of the statute of 28 June 1935, *RGB1.*, I, 844.

61. Decree of 20 March 1935 on Unification of Judicial Organization, *RGB1.*, I, 403; Statute of 25 November 1937 on Organizational Measures, *RGB1.*, I, 1286;

pars. 1–4 of the Decree of 1 September 1939 on Judicial Reorganization, *RGB1.*, I, 1658.

62. See Civil Affairs Guide *Courts and Judicial Administration in Germany*, p. 51 *et seq.*

63. For further details, see Civil Affairs Guide *Courts and Judicial Administration in Germany*, p. 65 *et seq.*

64. Literally, "not twice for the same thing." A legal principle *in vigor* (in effective legal status) for which a judge cannot express two opinions for the same action if it has already been judged. In penal law, this means that someone cannot be tried two times for the same crime. [ed. note]

65. For full discussion of this issue, see Civil Affairs Guide, *Courts and Judicial Administration in Germany*, pp. 58–69.

66. This type of legislation is defined in Civil Affairs Guide *Elimination of Fundamental Nazi Laws.*

67. *RGBl.*, 1939, I, 1457.

68. Part of the original text is missing. [ed. note]

69. *RGB1.*, 1940, 1. 877.

70. *RGB1.*, I, 529. The statute retroactively legalizes murder of political opponents of the Nazis.

## 21: The Problem of Inflation in Germany

1. Bresciani-Turoni, *The Economics of Inflation*, p. 48.
2. Rist, *Les Finances de Guerre de l'Allemagne*, p. 45.
3. Wagemann, *Wo kommt das viele Geld her*, p. 21.
4. Rist, op. cit., p. 73.
5. Based on *Statistisches Reichsamt*, *Zahlen zur Geldentwertung,* passim, and on Rist, op. cit., and Bresciani-Turoni, op. cit., passim.
6. Bresciani-Turoni, op. cit., p. 51.
7. Ibid., p. 55.
8. Ibid., p. 82.
9. Bresciani-Turoni, op. cit., p. 86.
10. Graham, *Hyperinflation*, p. 164.
11. Bresciani-Turoni, op. cit., p. 103.
12. Source: *Statistisches Reichsamt*, op. cit., passim; Rist, op. cit.; Graham, op. cit.
13. Bresciani-Turoni, op. cit., p. 95.
14. Graham, op. cit., p. 166.
15. Bresciani-Turoni, op. cit., p. 87.
16. Ibid., p. 61.
17. Ibid., p. 97.
18. Ibid., p. 106.
19. Graham, op. cit., p. 107.
20. *Statistisches Reichsamt*, op. cit., p. 47.
21. Bresciani-Turoni, op. cit., p. 399.
22. Wagemann, op. cit., p. 53.
23. Bresciani-Turoni, op. cit., p. 348.

24. Ibid., p. 345.
25. Ibid., p. 352.
26. See among others *Probleme des deutschen Wirtschaftslebens* (Berlin 1937), p. 517 and p. 560.
27. Matthias Erzberger (1875–1921), German politician and diplomat. He was head of the German delegation to the Armistice Commission of Compiègne in November 1918. From June 1919 to March 1920 he was vice-chancellor and minister of finances. During that time, he pushed for an economic and fiscal reform plan through higher taxes on luxury goods and war profits, the substitution of all local taxes with a single, centralized, and uniform tax code, and the reduction of fiscal independence of single states. [ed. note]
28. The reference is to a monetary reform promoted by Rudolf Hilferding as the minister of finances of the Weimar Republic (August–October 1923) that, however, was never passed due to Hilferding's premature resignation. [ed. note]
29. Rudolf Emil Albert Havenstein (1857–1923), was president of the Reichsbank from 1908 to 1923. [ed. note]
30. *Wo kommt das viele Geld her?*, Berlin, 1940, p. 38.
31. League of Nations, *World Economic Survey*, 1939–41, p. 29.
32. Karl Schiller, *Arbeitsbeschaffung*, Berlin, 1936, p. 155, p. 177.
33. *Wirtschaft und Statistik*, 1940, p. 157.
34. *Deutsche Volkswirtschaft*, 3 July 1943.
35. *Wirtschaft und Statistik*, 2 July 1939.
36. *Deutsche Volkswirtschaft,* 3 July 1943.
37. *Wirtschaft und Statistik*, 2 July 1939.
38. See *Quarterly Journal of Economics*, May 1942.
39. *Economic Conditions in Germany 1939*, Berlin, 1939.
40. *Deutsche Volkswirtschaft*, November 22, 1943.
41. *Economic Journal*, June 1943.
42. *League of Nations Survey*, 1930–41, p. 29.
43. *Deutsche Volkswirt*, 12 Feb. 1943.
44. *Wirtschaft und Statistik*, Dec. 1943.
45. *Wirtschaft und Statistik,* October 1943.
46. *Deutsche Volkswirtschaft*, June 1943.
47. *Wirtschaft und Statistik*, October 1943.
48. Civil Affairs Handbook, *Germany—Money and Banking*.
49. Dispatch Bern no. 494, 24 January 1944.
50. *League of Nations Survey* 1939/41, p. 154.
51. Dispatch Bern no. 547, 27 January 1944.
52. *Deutsche Boersenzeitung*, 9 February 1944, *Frankfurter Zeitung*, 1 January 1943.
53. *Bankwirtschaft*, December 1943.
54. *Bankwirtschaft*, June 1943, and Civil Affairs Handbook, *Germany—Money and Banking*.
55. Despatches from Bern of 29 February and 7 March 1944.
56. Funk's speech, FCC Daily Report 9 February 1944.
57. Payments without cash are as a rule not made through checks but in the form of transfer orders (called Giro orders). Upon receipt of these orders the bank debits one account and credits the other account or arranges for a credit entry to be made by the bank where the other party has an account.

58. *Frankfurter Zeitung*, 5 August 1943.
59. *Essener Nationalzeitung* quoted in FCC Analysis, 16 December 1943.
60. *Neue Zuricher Zeitung*, 4 January 1944.
61. OSS Report TB-84, 11 February 1944.
62. *Bankwirtschaft*, 1 December 1943.

## 22: The Adaptation of Centralized European Controls of Raw Materials, Industry, and Transport

1. In the field of *rubber*, e.g. there is a rubber agreement between France and Germany of 1941 by which the French Dunlop and Hutchinson firms were obligated to manifacture tires of buna.

In the field of *synthetic fibers*, agreements exist between the France Rayonne and the *Reichsvereinigung* Synthetic Fibers.

In the field of *coal*, agreements have been reached [*between*] the *Reichsvereiningung* Coal and the Belgian and French Coal Syndicates.

In the field of *chemicals*, the agreement is between Francolor and I.G. Farben.

2. Hans Kehrl (1900–1984), Nazi functionary for the Ministry of Armaments, head of the Planning Office. He was sentenced to fifteen years of imprisonment at Nuremburg. [ed. note]

## 23: The Revival of German Political and Constitutional Life under Military Government

1. See CA Guide *General Principles of Administration and Civil Service* [pp. 301–317].

2. Adam Stegerwald (1874–1945), German politician. He was the leader of the leftist wing of the Zentrum Party. In 1921 he became the first prime minister of Prussia and, afterwards, minister of the national governments led by Hermann Müller and Heinrich Brüning. In 1945 he was among the founders of the Social-Christian Union (CSU). [ed. note]

3. Paul Gustav Emil Löbe (1875–1967), German politician. He joined the SPD in 1895 and was president of the Reichstag from 1920 to 1932. He was arrested by the Nazis in 1933 and again in 1944, after the failed putsch on July 20. From 1949 to 1953 he was a prominent member of the Bundestag. [ed. note]

4. See R & A no. 2337, *Particularism and Separatism in Germany*.

5. L. Trotsky, *The History of the Russian Revolution* (New York: Pathfinder, 1980), 1:149–65). [ed. note]

6. See CA Guide, *The Adaptation of Administration on the Local Level*.

7. This subject will be treated at length below, p. 422 ff.

8. See Conference of German Trade Unionists held in Stockholm, 26–27 February 1944, attended by representatives of German, Swedish, Norwegian, and A.F. of L. representatives; Cf. *The Trade Unions in a New Germany*, published by the Trade Union Center. England, 13 February 1944; J.H. Oldenbroek. *The Construction of a New Trade Union Movement in Germany*; OSS A21371, 16 March 1944.

9. For example, J.H. Oldenbroek, Acting General Secretary of the International Federation of Transport Workers.

10. As defined in CA Guide. *Dissolution of the Nazi Party and Affiliated Organizations* [pp. 253–263].

11. See CA Guide *German Labor Relations and MG.*

12. See R & A no. 1723. *Labor Relations in the Weimar Republic.*

13. The Manual (FM 27-5 OPNAV 50E-3 p. 9, sec. 9i) recommends the closing of "unnecessary" offices, the suspension of legislative bodies, the removal of high-ranking political officials from office, and the retention, as far as practicable, of subordinate officials of local governments.

14. Dr. Werner Best, Germany's theorist of Military Government, has admitted this in his articles.

15. For details see the CA guide *Policy toward the Revival of Old Parties and the Establishment of New Parties* [pp. 285–300].

16. There is evidence that the communist members in the various Free Germany Committees, especially in Mexico and London, are already defending the transfer of East Prussia to Poland, while the Socialists and liberals are bitterly opposing the new Communist line.

17. As outlined in the CA Guide *Dissolution of the Nazi Party and Affiliated Organizations* [pp. 253–263].

18. See CA Guide, *Courts and Judicial Administration in Germany.*

19. See CA Guide, *The Police and Public Safety in Germany.*

20. For details see *The Problems of a German Inflation* [pp. 345–394].

21. As outlined in the CA Guide *Policy towards the Revival of Old Parties and the Establishment of New Parties* [pp. 285–300].

22. CA Guide *Adaptation of Administration on the Local Level in Germany.*

## 25: The "Statement On Atrocities" of the Moscow Tripartite Conference

1. Viktor Quisling (1887–1945), head of Norwegian Fascists. After King Haakon fled to London, Quisling served the occupying Nazis. The government he led in 1942 declared the constitution invalid. The deep identification of his name with the Nazi regime's needs made it a synonym for "collaborationist." [ed. note]

2. Trials for war crimes held at the German High Court from May 23 to July 16, 1921, as part of the punitive measures imposed on the German government by the Treaty of Versailles. [ed. note]

## 26: Problems Concerning the Treatment of War Criminals

1. For reasons to be discussed below, the character of many of these crimes as "common crimes" should be emphasized.

2. The reference is to the Czech city Lidice, northwest of Prague and destroyed June 10, 1942, in retaliation by the Nazis following an organized attack by the Czech partisan forces in which Reinhard Heydrich, protector of the Reich in Bohemia and Moravia, was killed. [ed. note]

3. Handwritten addition to the typescript. [ed. note]
4. See Basic Field Manual *Rules of Land Warfare* (FM 27-10, issued 1 Oct. 1940), paragraph 347.
5. See below, under IV.
6. For Switzerland see Situation Report: Central Europe, 5 August 1944; For Sweden ibid., 9 September 1944.
7. See Situation Report: Central Europe, 5 August 1944.
8. See Situation Report: Central Europe, 2 September 1944 (referring to Portugal).
9. See Situation Report: Central Europe, 9 September 1944 (referring to Switzerland).
10. For gaps not discussed in this paper, see R&A no. 1626: *Gaps in the Moscow "Statement on Atrocities."*
11. See above, III.
12. See recommendation contained in CA Guide, *Administration of German Criminal Justice under MG* [pp. 318–344].
13. See letter by Charles Warren to the Editor of *The New York Times*, 7 November 1944.

## 27: Leadership Principle and Criminal Responsibility

1. Cf., for one of the latest and most comprehensive treatments, H. B. Brausse: *Die Führungsordnung des deutschen Volkes* (2nd ed., Hamburg: Hanseatische Verlagsanstalt, 1942).
2. Fundamentally laid down by Hitler, when discussing the leadership organization of the Party, then still legally clad in the form of a private law association: "The Chairman is responsible for the entire leadership of the Movement. He distributes work and power to the members of the committee below him and to other required collaborators. Each of these gentlemen thereby is exclusively responsible for the tasks conferred upon him." (*Mein Kampf*, 424th–428th ed., Munich, Eher-Verlag 1939, p. 661.)
3. The term Führer as such, in Nazi literature, is always reserved to Hitler. Leaders in the various fields and regions below him are referred to as "subleaders" (*Unterführer*).
4. "In the leadership state the unity of state power has been entrusted to the one and sole Führer" (E. R. Huber, "Die deutsche Staatswissenschaft," *Zeitschrift fur die gesamte Staatswissenschaft*, H. Laupp, Tülingen, v. 95, 1934/35, p. 41f.); "In all realms of politics the Führer indicates the aims to be attained, determines the methods to be applied, and makes the basic decisions which become necessary. . . . He has the exclusive ultimate decision in all affairs of the Movement, the Volk, and the Reich, . . . He has not only the totality of executive power but also legislative and judicial power" (E. R. Huber. *Verfassung*, Hamburg: *Hauseatische Verlagsanstalt*, 1937, pp. 114, 121).
5. Ibid., p. 94.
6. Hans Frank, Die Technik des Staates, *Deutsches Recht*, v. 11 (*Deutscher Rechtsverlag*, Berlin, 1941), p. 2626: "Leadership principle in the administration means: always to replace decision by majority by decision on the part of a specific

person with clear jurisdiction and with sole responsibility toward above, and to entrust to his authority the realization of the decision toward below." Cf. also Otto Koellreutter, *Deutsches Verwaltungsrecht* (Berlin: Junker und Dünnhaupt, 1938), p. 8.

7. Survey of the different theories in C. H. Ule, *Herrschaft und Führung im nationalsozialistischen Reich*, *Verwaltungsarchiv* v. 45 (Berlin, C. Heymann 1940), pp. 205ff. Most prominent representative of the theory that administration implies genuine leadership is Huber (see his *Verfassung*, pp. 94, 243f.); his most conspicuous opponents are R. Hoehn and Th. Maunz (cf., e.g., the latter's *Verwaltung* [Hamburg, Hanseatische Verlagsanstalt, 1937], pp. 43f.), who maintain that bureaucracy is a mere machine in the hands of the real leaders.

8. To what an extent everything else is pure ideology is shown by the emphasis put on the right of the sole leader to determine what is the "will" of the "followership" which he supposedly "embodies": "The leader defends the objective idea of the nation, if necessary even against the subjective arbitrariness of a misguided popular opinion (Huber, Die deutsche Staatswissenschaft, *Zeitschrift für die gesamte Staatswissenschaft*, v. 95, 1934/35, p. 41).

9. On some details concerning the realization of the leadership principle in the actual organization of public life in Nazi Germany see *Appendix* I.

10. Huber, *Verfassung*, p. 115ff.

11. Ibid., p. 116f.

12. Koellreutter: *Deutsches Verfassungsrecht* (3rd ed., Berlin: Junker und Dünnhaupt, 1938), p. 139.

13. Huber, *Verfassung*, p. 291.

14. Arnold Kottgen: *Deutsche Verwaltung* (2nd ed., Berlin: Weidmannsche Verlagsbuchhandlung 1937, p. 100. Cf. also Weidemann, *Die Selbstverwaltung der Gemeinden und Gemeindeverbände*, in Frank (ed.): *Deutsches Verwaltungsrecht* (Munich: Eher-Verlag 1937), p. 218: "In contradistinction to the old municipal codes the mayor is no longer able to pass on responsibility to collegiate bodies or assemblies."

15. Huber, *Verfassung*, pp. 294f.; Brausse, op. cit., p. 144; Dannbeck, *Die Amtshaftung*, in Frank: *Deutsches Verwaltungsrecht*, p. 297.

16. Brausse, op. cit., pp. 166ff.; W. Laforet: *Deutsches Verwaltungsrecht* (Munich, *Duncker und Humblot*, 1937), pp. 89f.

17. Brausse, op. cit., pp. 163ff.

18. Brausse, op. cit., pp. 137ff.; Koellreutter: *Deutsches Verfassungsrecht*, p. 154; Dannbeck, loc. cit., p. 297.

19. *Verfassung*, pp. 149 f. See also Huber, „Justiz und Verwaltung," *Deutsches Recht*, 1935, p. 403.

20. Arnold Köttgen: *Deutsche Verwaltung*, pp. 21f., 42.

21. See Ernst Fraenkel: *The Dual State* (New York: Oxford University Press, 1941), with a distinction between the "prerogative" and the "normative" state. The former is the realm of the Gestapo. "The Prerogative State claims that it represents material justice and that it can therefore dispense with formal justice"; its essence, therefore, is "its refusal to accept legal restraint" (p. 46).

22. Werner Best: *Die Deutsche Polizei* (Darmstadt: Wittich Verlag, 1940), pp. 13f.

23. Werner Best, „Volksordnung und Polizei," *Deutsche Verwaltung* (W. Kohlhammer, Stuttgart), 1939, p. 241.

24. Werner Best, *Die Politische Polizei des Dritten Reiches*, in Frank (ed): *Deutsches Verwaltungsrecht*, p. 426.

25. Walter Hamel, „Die Polizei im neuen Reich," *Deutsches Recht*, 1935, pp. 412 ffl, and *Wesen und Rechtsgrundlagen der Polizei im nationalsozialistischen Staate*, in Frank (ed.): *Deutsche Verwaltung* [The reference here is incorrect; the correct title is *Deutsches Verwaltungsrecht*; *Deutsche Verwaltung* is by Werner Best. Ed. note], pp. 381ff.

26. Best, *Die Politische Polizei des Dritten Reiches*, loc. cit., p. 424.

27. Theodor Maunz, *Gestalt and Recht der Polizei*, in *Idee und Ordnung des Reiches* (ed. by E.R. Huber), v. 2 (Hamburg: Hanseatische Verlagsenstalt, 1943).

28. Maunz, loc. cit., pp. 49, 53, 57. See also the same author's „Staatsbegriff und Verwaltung," *Deutsches Recht*, 1935, p. 397.

29. *Mein Kampf*, p. 379.

30. See, e.g., Huber, *Verfassung*, p. 93.

31. See, e.g., Koellreutter, *Deutsches Verfassungsrecht*, p. 147. The leadership state is "not a dictatorship" but "the expression of the popular (*volksverbunden*) guidance of this people and this state by Adolf Hitler."

32. Brausse, „Führung und Verwaltung," *Verwaltungsarchiv*, v. 42 (1937), p. 90.

33. Brausse, *Die Führungsordnung des deutschen Volkes*, p. 92.

34. As a matter of fact, in many cases even in contradiction to what the Nazis, at one time or other, have themselves recognized as legally binding, such as rules of the Hague or Geneva Conventions.

35. See Huber, *Verfassung*, p. 107f.

36. See ibid., p. 101.

37. February 14, 1934 (RGBl I, p. 89).

38. Law on the reconstruction of the Reich, January 30, 1934 (RGBl I, p. 75).

39. RGBl I, p. 173.

40. RGBl I, p. 65.

41. RGBl I, p. 1190.

42. RGBl I, p. 49.

43. RGBl I, p. 45.

44. RGBl I, p. 887.

45. RGBl I, p. 1194.

46. RGBl I, p. 769.

47. RGBl I, p. 993.

## 28: Nazi Plans for Dominating Germany and Europe: The Nazi Master Plan

1. The following account is based primarily on Hitler, *Mein Kampf*, chapters VIII, IX, and XI, and on Johann von Leers, *Kurzgefasste Geschichte des Nationalsozialismus*, published with the approval of the Party official Examination Commission for the Protection of NS Literature, Bielefeld and Leipzig 1933. Additional evidence can be found in the facsimiles of Party posters in the Houghton Mifflin edition of *Mein Kampf*.

2. *Partei Statistik*, ed. *Der Reichsorganisationsleiter de NSDAP*, 1935, vol. 1, p. 12–13.

3. See the War Crimes paper "Principal Nazi Organizations Involved in the Commission of War Crimes," R&A Report no. 3113.

4. See below, sec. IV, A.

5. Law for Safeguarding the Unity of Party and State, 1 December 1933, *Reichsgesetzblatt* 1933, I, p. 523.

6. See V C below.

7. Based chiefly on *Das Deutsche Führerlexikon* 1934–35, and other party-approved biographies; also *Mein Kampf.* Of these persons, Dietrich Eckart died in 1923, and Gottfried Feder receded into the background, but all the others obtained leading positions in the Party or in the Reich Government after the seizure of power.

8. See the War Crimes paper "Principal Nazi Organizations Involved in the Commission of War Crimes," R&A Report #3113.

9. Gottfried Feder, *Das Programm der NSDAP.* Munchen 1933, p. 20.

10. Edited in collaboration with the *Reichsleitung* of the NSDAP by *Reichsleiter* Phillip Beuhler; 1938 ed, p. 146.

11. Files on these trials should be secured in Munich and Leipzig from the courts concerned: People's court of Munich, District One; Decision Rendered on 1 April 1924; and Supreme *Reichsgericht* at Leipzig; File number, 12 V. 10/1930; also to be found in *Die Justiz*, vol. 6, January 1931. Also to be examined are documents published by the Investigating Commission of the Bavarian Diet on the Hitler Putsch, and *Hitler und Vahr, die bayerischen Napoleonsgrossen von 1923*, edited by the *Landesauschusse* of the Social Democratic Party of Bavaria, Munich; part I, 1928; part II, 1928.

12. Though this point did not refer to claims for "land and soil" *in Europe* at the time of the program's formulation, it was later interpreted to mean this. At any rate, point one adequately covered the demand for *Lebensraum.*

13. *Organisationsbuch der NSDAP*, ed. the *Reichsorganisationsleiter der NSDAP. Zentralverlag der NSDAP*, Munich 1943, p. 14.

14. Ibid. p. 146.

15. Ibid. p. 7.

16. Ibid.

17. For a full exposition of the "leadership principle" see the War Crimes paper on "The Leadership Principle, in German-Law and its Significance in Assigning Responsibility for War Crimes," R&A Report no. 3110 [pp. 464–474].

18. *Organisationsbuch der NSDAP,* loc. cit., p. 14.

19. Ibid., p. 86.

20. Ibid. p. 87.

21. Ibid. p. 17.

22. Ibid. p. 14.

23. Ibid.

24. Volume II, chapter I, and passim.

25. Ibid. loc. cit. p. 576 f. Additional evidence is to be found in: Robert M.W. Kempner, *Nazi Subversive Organization, Past and Future*; Studies in Migration and Settlement, no. A-2, 30 October 1943, pp. 17–22.

26. See Chapter III below.

27. See Ibid., IV A.

28. See Ibid., IV A and the war crimes paper "The Attitude of the NSDAP toward Political Terror," R&A Report #3114.1.

29. Loc. cit., p. 279.
30. Ibid., p. 291.
31. Berlin, 1935, p. 958.
32. See V/C below.
33. See below IV A, and the war crimes paper on "The Attitude of the NSDAP Toward Political Terror," R&A Report no. 3114.1, and "The Pattern of Illegal Anti-Democratic Activity in Germany after the last War; the Free Corps," R&A Report 1934.2.
34. Ibid.
35. Fritz Thyssen, *I Paid Hitler*, New York and London, 1941, p. 111.
36. Eric Zeigner (1886–1949), German politician. He was prime minister of Saxony during the Communist insurrection of 1923. After having refused Chancellor Stresemann's ultimatum, on October 27, 1923, he was replaced in his position by President Ebert based on article 48 of the Weimar Constitution, definitively ending his political career. [ed. note]
37. Fritz Thyssen, *I Paid Hitler*, op. cit., p.113–114. In view of the scantiness of information on the relations between heavy industry and the NSDAP during the early period, an interrogation of Fritz Thyssen on this point would be of utmost importance.
38. Ibid., p. 129.
39. Ibid.
40. Speech of 30 January 1944, English translation as broadcast by Berlin on the same date. (FCC: *Daily*, Special Report, 31 January 1944.)
41. Hitler, *Mein Kampf* (Boston: Houghton Mifflin edition, 1939), p. 891.
42. Otto von Lossow (1868–1938), Gustav Ritter von Kahr (1862–1934), and Hans Ritter von Seisser (1874–1973), were members of the Bavarian triumvirate nominated after the 1923 Nazi putsch in Monaco. [ed. note]
43. Hitler's speech before the Munich court, 26 February 1924 (*My New Order*, New York 1941, p. 74, 75).
44. Cited in: Robert M. W. Kempner, *Nazi Subversive Organization—Past and Future*. Studies of Migration and Settlement, no. A-2. Administrative Series, 30 October 1943, p. 73.
45. *Nationalsozialistisches Jahrbuch* 1927, p. 124 (quoted in Kempner, loc. cit., p. 62.)
46. Heinz Haake (Reich Inspector of the NSDAP, SA *Obergruppenführer, Landeshauptmann* Rhineland) *Nationalsozialistisches Jahrbuch* 1925, p. 167 (quoted ibid., p. 61).
47. Albert Roth, *Nazi Reichstag Deputy*, 1929 (quoted ibid., p. 63).
48. *Nationalsozialistische Bibliothek*, Booklet no. 1 (quoted ibid.).
49. Wilhelm Frick at the Nazi Party Convention at Nürnberg1927 (quoted ibid., p. 85).
50. P. 16 (quoted in Kempner, loc. cit., p. 91–92).
51. Quoted ibid., p. 107.
52. *NS Press Korrespondenz* no. 35 (quoted in Kempner, p. 38f.)
53. Ibid.
54. Hitler, *Mein Kampf*, 2nd German edition (quoted ibid., p. 73).
55. Wilhelm Frick (quoted ibid., p. 86).
56. Robert Ley, 1 May 1928 (quoted ibid., p. 101).
57. *Nationalsozialistische Briefe*, vol. 4, 15 May 1929 (quoted ibid., p. 105–6).

58. Goebbels, *Der Angriff: Aufsätze aus der Kampfzeit*, 1936, p. 71.

59. Ibid., p. 73, See also pp. 47–48. Also Wilhelm Frick, *Nationalsozialistisches Jahrbuch*, 1927, p. 124 (Kempner p. 62, 84–85).

60. Munich, 23 January 1932 (*Hitler's Speeches*, ed. Baynes, p. 164).

61. For documentary evidence of the terroristic activity of the Nazi movement during the period of the Weimar Republic, see the War Crimes paper, R&A Report no. 3114: "The Attitude of the NSDAP Toward Political Terror."

62. *Fememord*, a term used in the Weimar Republic to describe the homicides of politicians considered traitors (*Feme*)—such as Kurt Eisner (1919), Matthias Erzberger (1921), and Walther Rathenau (1922)—by German paramilitary organizations. [ed. note]

63. Ernst Bayer, *Die SA*, Berlin 1938, pp. 9, 11.

64. Ibid.

65. Ibid., p. 10.

66. Quoted in Kempner, loc. cit., p. 160.

67. 1929, quoted ibid., p. 164. The *SA* is discussed in detail in the War Crimes paper on the Nazi Party and its Affiliated Organizations (R&A Report 3113.7).

68. Gunter d'Alquen, *Die SS. Geschichte, Aufgabe und Organisation.*, ed. by commission of the *Reichsführer* SS, Berlin 1939, p. 6.

69. Ibid., p. 7.

70. Ibid., pp. 8 and 11.

71. Werner Best, *Die Deutsche Polizei*, Darmstadt 1940, p. 85.

72. Ibid.

73. For a more detailed discussion of the SS see the war crimes paper "*Principal Nazi Organizations Involved in War Crimes and their Policy-making Officials*," R&A Report no. 3113.

74. Hitler, Munich, 22 September 1928; *Völkischer Beobachter*, 23 September 1928 (*Hitler's Words*, edited by Gordon W. Prange, 1944, p. 39 f.).

75. Hitler, Berlin, 30 January 1941; *Deutsche Allgemeine Zeitung*, 1 Feb. 1941 (*Hitler's Words*, ed. Gordon W. Prange, 1944, p. 216).

76. *Frankfurter Zeitung*, 26 September 1930.

77. Hitler, *Mein Kampf*, p. 947.

78. Alfred Rosenberg, *Der Reichsparteitag der NSDAP. Nurnberg* 1927; Munchen 1927, pp. 37–8 (quoted in F. Schuman, *The Nazi Dictatorship*, 1939, p. 56).

79. Alfred Rosenberg, *Der Mythus des 20. Jahrhunderts*, Munich 1933, p. 642.

80. Ibid., 1931, p. 662 (quoted in: *Thus Speaks Germany*, ed. Coole and Potter, New York 1941, p. 261).

81. Gottfried Feder, *Das Programm der NSDAP*, Munich 1933, p. 40.

82. A copy of the pamphlet, which was published by Franz Eher in Munich, is available in the Library of Congress.

83. Pp. 20–21.

84. P. 85.

85. P. 97.

86. P. 38.

87. Hitler, Munich, 22 September 1928; *Voelkischer Beobachter*, 23–24 September 1928 (quoted in *Hitler's Words*, ed. Gordon W. Prange, American Council on Public Affairs, 1944, p. 9 f.

88. Hitler, Munich, 2 May 1928; *Voelkischer Beobachter*, 4 May 1928 (quoted ibid., p. 9).

89. Hitler, *Mein Kampf,* loc. cit., p. 179–180.
90. Ibid., p. 182.
91. Ibid., pp. 182–183.
92. *Der Angriff,* 28 May 1931 (quoted in F. Schuman, *The Nazi Dictatorship*, p. 129).
93. Hitler, Munich, 15 March 1929; *Völkischer Beobachter*, 17 March 1929 (quoted in *Hitler's Words*, p. 11).
94. Hitler, Vilsbiburg, 6 March 1927; *Völkischer Beobachter*, 8 March 1927 (ibid., p. 17).
95. Hitler, Munich, 9 April 1927; *Völkischer Beobachter*, 12 April 1927 (ibid., p. 18).
96. Hitler, Munich 23 May 1928; *Völkischer Beobachter*, 25 May 1928 (ibid., p. 27 f; emphasis supplied.)
97. Fritz Thyssen, *I Paid Hitler*, New York and London, 1941, p. 132.
98. Adolf Hitler, *My New Order*, New York, 1941, p. 111.
99. Thyssen, op. cit., pp. 133–134.
100. See IV A.
101. Goebbels, *Der Angriff,* 18 February 1929.
102. *Nationalsozialistisches Briefe*, no. 24, 15 April 1926 (quoted in: Kempner, op. cit, p. 60).
103. Quoted in Kempner, op. cit, p. 108.
104. Quoted ibid., p. 112.
105. Goebbels, *Vom Kaiserhof zur Reichskanzlei*, Munich, 1937, p. 34.
106. They are discussed in detail in the war crimes paper, R&A Report no. 3113.7, on "Crimes Committed in the Violation of German Domestic Law."
107. See the war crimes paper, R&A Report no. 3152, "Hermann Göring as a War Criminal."
108. Hermann Göring, *Aufbau einer Nation*, Berlin, 1934, pp. 87–88.
109. Ibid., p. 86 f.
110. Ibid., p. 89.
111. *RGBl* I, p. 53.
112. *RGBl* I, p. 995.
113. *Preussische Gesetzsammberg,* 1933, p. 413.
114. *Preussische Gesetzsammberg*, 1936, p. 21.
115. Hermann Göring, 3 March 1933 at Frankfurt a.M., in *Reden und Aufsätze*, Munich, 1942, p. 27.
116. The Nazi anti-Jewish policy is discussed in a separate war crimes paper, "The Criminal Conspiracy Against the Jews," R&A Report no. 3113.11.
117. For documentation see the paper on the Nazi anti-Jewish policy, "The Criminal Conspiracy Against the Jews," R&A Report no. 3113.11.
118. See pp. 13–14.
119. Munich 1941, p. 175.
120. Munich 1943, p. 86.
121. *Reichsgesetzblatt* 1933, I, p. 529.
122. *Organisationsbuch der NSDAP,* loc cit., p. 487.
123. See war crimes paper, R&A Report no. 3113, "Principal Nazi Organizations Involved in the Commission of War Crimes."
124. Ibid.
125. *Reichsgesetzblatt* 1933, I, p. 713.

126. For a detailed description of this setup see R&A Report no. 2500.19, "Propaganda in Occupied Europe"; also: Civil Affairs Handbook on Germany, section 12, *Communications and Control of Public Opinion*.

127. Photostatic copies of these directives are available.

128. Additional evidence of the functioning of these comprehensive controls can be furnished by the interrogation of foreign and German newspaper correspondents, editors, publishers, etc. Some such interrogations are available: see the forthcoming R&A Report no. 2500.19, "Propaganda in Occupied Europe."

129. See Civil Affairs Handbook on Germany: Section 12, *Communications and Control of Public Opinion*.

130. *Reichsgesetzblatt* 1936, I, p. 993.

131. Ibid., 1939, I, p. 709.

132. *Nationalsozialistisches Parteikorrespondenz*, 4 June 1936.

133. *Das Archiv*, ed. Kurt Jahnicke, Ministerial Counselor in the Reich Ministry for Propaganda, July 1935, p. 528.

134. *Das Archiv,* loc. cit., July 1934, pp. 467–468.

135. Ibid., April 1936, p. 11.

136. Copies available. For a detailed discussion of educational controls see: Civil Affairs Handbook: Germany, section 15: *Education*.

137. Fritz Mehnert, Chief of the Main Organization Office of the NSDAP, *Nationalsozialistisches Jahrbuch* 1941, ed. Robert Ley, *Zentralverlag der NSDAP*, Franz Eher, Munich, p. 175.

138. Ibid.

139. Ibid., p. 179.

140. Major Schmidtke, *Nationalsozialistisches Jahrbuch* 1941, p. 168.

141. Prefatory quotation in: Major H. Foertsch, *Die Wehrmacht im Nationalsozialistischen Staat*, Hamburg 1935.

142. Names and details in: Civil Affairs Handbook Germany, Section 2 T: *Economic Controls in Nazi Germany*, February 1944.

143. Saarbrüchen, 9 October 1938; *Frankfurter Zeitung*, 10 October 1938 (*Hitler's Speeches*, ed. Baynos, vol. II, p. 1534).

144. Berlin 26 September 1938, *Völkischer Beobachter*, 28 September 1938 (quoted ibid., p. 1512).

145. Goebbels, cited in *The Bulletin of International News*, vol. XVI, no. 14, p. 572. For complete text see German newspaper of that date—24 January 1936. For other texts, see Royal Institute of International Affairs, London.

146. Göring cited in same publication, vol. XI, no. 23, p. 779.

147. The authenticity of this report is yet to be established.

148. Ribbentrop, cited in *Bulletin of International News*, loc. cit., vol. XV, no. 23, p. 44.

149. Göring, cited ibid., vol. XVI, no. 5, p. 25.

150. Hitler's reply to Franco, *Frankfurter Zeitung*, 24 February 1939 (quoted in: *Hitler's Speeches*, ed. Baynes, p. 1580). Wilhelmshafen April 1939; *Völkischer Beobachter*, 3 April 1939 (ibid., p. 1600).

151. 6 June 1939; *Völkischer Beobachter*, 7 June 1939 (Ibid., p. 1671).

152. Wurzburg, 27 June 1937; *Völkischer Beobachter*, 28 June 1937 (quoted ibid., p. 1355).

153. *Frankfurter Zeitung*, 7 June 1939 (quoted ibid., p. 1673).

154. Ibid., 10 June 1939 (quoted ibid., p. 1675).

155. *Bulletin of International News, loc. cit.*, vol. XVI, no. 12, p. 614.

156. The evidence is collected in: *The Nazi Conspiracy in Spain, by the editors of The Brown Book of the Hitler Terror*, London 1937.

157. Reichstag speech of 30 January 1939 (Hitler, *My New Order*, p. 561).

158. Nurnberg, 7 April 1938 (quoted in *Nazi Guide to Nazism*, ed. Rolf Tell, Washington 1942, p. 76f).

159. *Beiträge zur Geschichte und Vergeschichte der Julirevolte,* ed. on the basis of official sources, *Bundeskommissariat für Heimatdienst*, Vienna, 1934, p. 26.

160. *Hitler's Speeches*, ed. Baynes, p, 1441, note 2.

161. Interrogation by Dr. B. Ecer, 30 May 1945, p. 5 (photostat available).

162. Wilhelmshafen, 1 April 1939; *Völkischer Beobachter*, 3 April 1939 (*Hitler's Speeches,* ed. Baynes, p. 1597).

163. Ibid.

164. Quoted in *Czechoslovak Documents and Sources*, no. 4: *German Imperialism and Czechoslovakia*. Czechoslovak Ministry of Foreign Affairs, Information Service, London 1943, p. 6.

165. See for example Hitler's speeches of 12 and 26 September 1938. Baynes, op. cit., p. 1487 ff and p. 1508 ff.

166. Camp C20 Report, 13 January 1945, OSS X-27S 614–627.

167. For Austria prior to 1933, the documentary evidence has been collected in: *Das Braunbuch. Hakenkreuz gogen Oesterreich.* ed. by the Bundes-Kanzleramt, Vienna, 1933.

168. Emil Ehrich, *Die Auslandsorganization der NSDAP*, Berlin 1937; translation in: *National Socialism*, ed. Raymond E. Murphy and others, Washington 1943, p. 285 ff.

169. *Völkischer Beobachter*, 24 May 1934 (quoted in: Sir John Murray, *The Nazi International.* Friends of Europe Publications no. 69. London, 1938, p. 6).

170. Material on criminal Nazi activities in Austria (together with photostats of documents) has been collected in: *Beiträge zur Vorgeschichte der Julirevolte*, ed. on the basis of official sources, Vienna 1934, *Bundeskommisseriat für Hoimatdienst.*

171. "Nazi Spoliation of Property in Occupied Europe," R&A Report 3113.2.

172. *Czechoslovakia: Money and Banking*. Prepared by the Board of Governors of the Federal Reserve System, May 1945, p. 157.

173. Copies available.

174. The entire organizational structure is described in: Civil Affairs Handbook Germany, section 2T: *Economic Control in Nazi Germany*, 1944.

175. Quoted in *Bulletin of International News*, vol. XVII, no. 15, p. 966.

176. Quoted ibid.

177. Further interrogation of Schacht is indicated here.

178. Quoted ibid., p. 968.

179. Quoted ibid., vol. XVII, no. 16, p. 1036.

180. Quoted ibid., vol. XVII, no. 22, p. 1449 f.

181. "*Das Neue Europa, Deutsches Recht, Ausgabe A,* X, no. 49, 1940, p. 2083.

182. Ibid., p. 2084.

183. Ibid., also Werner Daitz, *"Aussenhandelspolitik und Ostraumpolitik," Der Weg zur voelkischen Wirtschaft und zur Europaeischen Grossraumwirtschaft*, Dresden,

1938., vol.II: *Deutschland und die Europaeische Grossraumwirtschaft*, p. 72 ff. Daitz' article was reprinted from *Nationalsozialistischer Wirtschaftsdienst*, no. 23, 3 October 1932.

184. *"Aussenhandelspolitik und Ostraumpolitik"* op. cit., p. 74.
185. Ibid., p. 73.
186. Ibid., p. 73.
187. *Bulletin of International News.*, vol. XVIII, no. 10, p. 653.
188. Quoted ibid., vol. XVI, no. 13, p. 674.
189. Quoted ibid., vol. XVII, no. 26, p. 1737.
190. *Probleme des Europaischen Grosswirtschaftsraumes*, Berlin, 1943, p. 14.
191. Ibid. pp. 30–31.
192. See next chapter, and the war crimes paper "Criminal Responsibilities in Connection with Planning and Execution of Occupation Policy," R&A Report no. 3113.
193. "*Grossraumordnung und Grossraumverwaltung*," *Zeitschrift für Politik*, 1941; "*Grundlagen einer deutschen Grossraumverwaltung*," in: *Festgabe fur Heinrich Himmler,* Darmstadt,1941, p. 43 ff.
194. Ibid.
195. Werner Best, *Festgabe für Heinrich Himmler,* loc. cit., p. 37.
196. Arthur Seyss-Inquart, "*Die politische Kufgabe des Reichskommissars,*" *Zeitschrift für voilkische Verfassung und Verwaltung*, 1942, vol. VII, p. III.
197. The President of the Hamburg Chamber of Commerce, at a New Year's gathering, 1943. Quoted in: *Germany*: (British) *Basic Handbook*, Part III, p. 3.
198. Ibid.
199. Werner Best, *Festgabe für Heinrich Himmler*, op. cit., p. 58.
200. See VIII A above, especially the statement of Seyss-Inquart.
201. *Das Recht des Generalgouvernements*, Cracow, 1941, p. A 180.
202. See the interrogation of Karl Hermann Frank, quoted above, VI, B l C.
203. *Organisationsbuch der NSDAP*, 1943, p. 314.
204. *Reichsgesetzblatt* 1941, I, pp. 118–120 for the Eastern territories. In the *Reichsgau Wartheland*, the Racial Register was established as early as 1939: *Verordnungsblatt des Reischsstatthalters im Reichsgau Wartheland*, no. 6, 1939, p. 51.
205. *Vierjalnesplan directive* #14395, quoted in *Kommentar fur Wirtschafsgesetzgebung.*
206. Referred to in *The Heilungs Blattdes Wirtsdafts-und Rirsteingsanites* / OKW, 1942, p. 83.

## 29: Nazi Plans for Dominating Germany and Europe: Domestic Crimes

1. Statute concerning the ending of the emergency of people and Reich RGBl. I, 141.
2. Statute of 30 January 1937, RGBl. I, 105; statute of 30 Jan. 1939 RGBl. I, 95.
3. Leader edict of 10 March 1943, RGBl. I, 295.
4. Preliminary statute for the *"Gleichschaltung"* of the states with the Reich,

Par. 10, 1 of 31 March 1933 RGBl. I, 153. These members had been arrested or forced to flee.

5. See the semi-official report of Fritz Poetzsh-Heffter in *Jahrbuch des Offentlichen Rechts* (22) 1935 p. 63, which admits that this question was discussed in various circles, but then abruptly declares that these considerations concerning the doubts of the constitutionality are wrong.

6. Whereas the official manifestations of the Hitler government during the first weeks emphasized for strategic reasons more the idea of the continuity of the old and new Germany, later public utterances took pains to insist on the revolutionary character of the new regime. See, for example, the speeches of Hitler and the official circular of Frick, Minister of Interior, reprinted in *Jahrbuch des Offontlichen Rechts*, vol. 22, 1935, p. 24.

7. Hackworth: *Digest of International Law* I: 178–185.

8. The ability to command obedience and to overcome resistance has been the test accepted by the commentators on the Weimar Constitution as the source of a new constitutional legality. See Anschüetz: *Verfassung des deutschen Reichs*, 3rd ed. 1930 Einl. II, who emphasized the revolutionary origin of the Weimar Constitution.

9. Texas v. White 7 Wallace 700 (1868).

10. Hackworth, op. cit. vol. V, p. 653.

11. E. H. Feilchenfeld: *The International Economic Law of Belligerent Occupation*. Washington, 1942, par. 490–502.

12. *Decreto Legislativo Luogotenenziale #159* (July 27, 1944).

13. *Ordonnance de 9 Aout 1944* (*Retablissement de la Legalite Republicaine*), *Journal Officiel #65*, Aug. 15, 1944, p. 7.

14. In the trials which have taken place so far, of French military figures, officials, and judges, the Court of Justice has consistently evaded the issue of the validity or invalidity of the Vichy legislation. It has invariably based its decision on the concept of treason, and conveying intelligence to the enemy, rather than on constitutional grounds.

15. Situation Report: *Western Europe*, 9 June 1945.

16. Decree of Dec. 28, 1939 (1940 RGBl. I, 45). H. P. Ipsen, *Politik und Justiz*, pp. 240 et seq. Hamburg, 1937. A. Lingg, *Die Verwaltung der NSDAP*, pp. 78 et seq. Munich, 1940.

17. Decree of 1 Nov. 1939, 1940 RGBl. I-2107 Decree of 1 Dec. 1933. 1933 RGBl I-1016

Decree of 17 Oct. 1939. 1940 RGBl. I-2293

Decree of 17 Apr. 1940. 1940 RGBl. I-659.

18. A. Lingg: *Die Verwaltung der Nationalsozialitsischen Deutsche Arbeiterpartei*, Munich 1940, p. 28.

19. Civil Affairs Handbook—Germany, Sec. 3—Legal Affairs, Army Service Force Manual M356-3 (I-C).

20. 1943 RGBl. I-372.

21. CA Handbook M356-3, Sec. V C.

22. H. P. Ipsen, op. cit. p. 239.

23. RGBl. I, 1934 p. 539.

24. *Frankfurter Zeitung*, 4 July 1944.

25. Carl Schmitt, *Der Fuehrer Schutzt das Recht*, in *Deutsche Juristenzeitung*, 1934, p. 945–950.

26. 1936 Pr. G. 521 (*Preussische Gesetzesammlung*).

27. 1933 RGBl. I, 83.

28. Werner Spohr, *Recht der Schutzhaft*, pp. 14, 21 ff. Berlin, 1937.

29. Werner Best: "*Die politische Polizei des dritten Reichs*" in H. Frank: *Deutsches Verwaltungsrecht*, 1937, p. 424. Goering, in a Vienna speech of 26 March 1938 seems also to have subscribed to the preservation of accepted legal forms, when he claimed that "In Germany a human being is only killed if a court has sentenced him to death and the Leader confirms the sentence." Hermann Goering: *Reden und Aufsaetze*, Munich 1942, p. 350.

30. 1937 RGBl. 39.

31. See Goebbels' speech appearing in 28 March 1944 edition of *Völkischer Beobachter*, and Hitler's statement admitting the right of civil disobedience, p. 122 of *Mein Kampf* (Houghton Mifflin edition).

32. 1933 RGBl. I, 529.

33. 212 and 222 ST G B.

34. 224 and 225 ST G B.

35. "Criminal Responsibility in Health and Racial Policy of Nazi Germany" (R&A 3113, forthcoming).

36. 1935 RGBl 1146—law of 15 Sept. 1935.

37. See Part II, this paper.

38. Law of 12 May 1933, RGBl. I, 1264.

39. See R&A paper on criminal procedure.

40. As, for example, the famous par. 5, I, 1 of the special decree on wartime criminal law of 17 August 1938 dealing with "Undermining of the Will to Resist of the German People." (See Part II, this paper).

41. Par. 245, Code of Civil Procedure.

42. Presidential Amnesty Decree of 21 March 1933, RGBl I, 134.

43. Amnesty Law of 7 August 1934, RGBl. I, 769.

44. Amnesty Law of 23 April 1936, RGBl. I, 378.

45. Amnesty Law of 30 April 1938, RGBl. I, 433.

46. *Fuhreredict* on Amnesty of 9 September 1939, RGBl. I, 1753.

47. In regard to numerical importance of these amnesties, see the table in Civil Affairs Handbook–III: Legal Affairs, p. 58.

48. *NSZ Rheinfront* (Mannheim National Socialist newspaper) quoted in a decision of the Fourth Criminal Division of the German Supreme Court of 30 September 1931, *Die Justiz*, vol. 7, 1931–32, p. 159.

49. The argument and its history have been discussed in Wolfgang Heine. "*Staatsgerichtshof und Reichsgericht über das hessische Manifest,*" *Die Justiz*, 1931–32, p. 154.

50. The text of this declaration has been reprinted in Gerd Rüble, *Das Dritte Reich, Dokumentarische Darstellung des Aufbaues der Nation*, 1934, vol. I, 29 (hereafter quoted as Rühle).

51. Quoted from daily Berlin supplement of the *Völkischer Beobachter* of 24 February 1933.

52. Prussian decree of 22 February 1933. See *Rüble*, p. 45, and Hans Volz, *Daten der Geschichteder NSDAP*, 9th edition, 1939, p. 50.

53. Hermann Goering, *Aufbau einer Nation*, Berlin, 1934, p. 92.

54. RGBl. I, 35.

55. See official account in Rüble, p. 46.

56. Fritz Poetzsch-Heffter, "Vom Deutschen Staatsleben" in *Jahrbuch des Offentlichen Rechts*, (1935) vol. 22 p. 15, (hereafter cited as Poetzsch).

57. Quoted in *Frankfurter Zeitung*, 23 February 1933.

58. RGBl. I, 83.

59. Goering, op. cit., p. 89.

60. Preliminary statute for the "Gleichschaltung" of the states with Reich, 31 March 1933, Par. 10, 1, RGBl. I, 153.

61. See, for instance, the proclamation by which General Franz von Epp took over power in Bavaria. The proclamation is reprinted in Axel Friedrichs, ed., *Dokumente der Deutschen Politik,* vol. I, *Die Nationalsozialistische Revolution 1933* (cited hereafter as *Revolution*), 1935, p. 16. Any former Bavarian official, especially Dr. Schaefer (present appointee of the Military Government for it the Bavarian administration), may testify to those matters relating to the taking over of the State Government.

62. *Gewerkschaftszeitung,* 29 April 1933, p. 270.

63. RGBl. I, 161.

64. Ernst Fraenkel, attorney of the Social Democratic Party now employed by Foreign Economic Administration in Washington may be helpful as a witness. For additional witnesses contact officers of re-established Social Democratic Party and Trade Unions.

65. The circular no. 6/33 of 21 April 1933 of the *Oberste Leitung der PO* has been reprinted in W. Müller, *Das Soziale Leben im Neuen Deutschland*, Berlin 1938, p. 51.

66. Müller, *op. cit.*, p. 54.

67. 2. This order, which appeared in *Ministerialblatt für die Preussische innere Verwaltung* I, 1933, S. 749/50, is reprinted in Poetzsch, p. 20.

68. Decree to Assure the Security of State Leadership, RGBl. I, 462.

69. Poetzsch, pp. 21–22.

70. See *Revolution*, I, 44; Poetzsch, p. 22.

71. RGBl. I, 479.

72. RGBl. I, 293.

73. RGBl. I, 479; and decree of 5 August 1933, RGBl. I, 572.

74. Decrees of 8 Dec. 1933, RGBl. I, 1060, and 16 Feb 1934, RGBl. I, 100. See Appendix IV.

75. Poetzsch, p. 24.

76. The question of police terror has been dealt with in a separate study. The present chapter will treat mainly with the political form.

77. See for example the Ali Höhler and the Rall cases reported by Gisevius von der Lubbe volume, p. 147, 151.

78. "When forwarding the dossier concerning the case to the prosecutor for the preparation of the charge in Court, the Gestapo entered a request to the effect that the prisoner was to be handed back to the Gestapo in the case of an acquittal or after he had served his sentence." PW Paper 23, OSS CID 136326.

79. RGBl. I, 135.

80. See the special listing of laws and decrees containing the death penalty as introduced under the Third Reich.
81. Law of 4 April 1933, RGBl. I, 162.
82. RGBl. I, 479.
83. RGBl. I, 723.
84. Law of 20 December 1934, RGBl. I, 1269.
85. RGBl. I, 1298.
86. Decree of 1 September 1939, RGBl, 1683.
87. RGBl. I, 1455.
88. Details are given in Part 1, of this paper. Insofar as the 3 July 1934 law is concerned see "Hermann Goering as a War Criminal." R&A no. 3152.
89. As regards to this procedure see Gisevius; van der Lubbe volume p. 144. Gisevius was an official of the German Consulate in Geneva and former official of Reich Ministry of Interior (to be reached through OSS Bern.) He may testify to the use of the murder blanks.
90. See Lammers' deposition: Seventh Army Interrogation Center, US Army, APO. 358, ref. no. SZIC/32, 29 May 1945.
91. The order 332/44 is printed in *Reichsverfügungsblatt* published by the Party Chancellery of the NS Party, edition C, Munich, 19 October 1944.
92. Law of 24 April 1934, RGBl. I, 341.
93. The activities of the People's Court have been described in PW interrogations 4208, 4373, 4419 by a judge of the Würzburg district court who was a member of the Supreme Reich Attorney's Staff at the People's Court until 1944.
94. See decree of 21 March and 6 May 1933, RGBl. I, 136, 259.
95. Decree of 17 October 1939 and Executive Decree of 1 November 1939, RGBl. I, 2107, 2293; and Decree of 17 April 1940, RGBl. I, 659.
96. GID XL 9277 and 9278 contain a report of 29 April 1945 on the functioning of the Supreme Military Tribunal. The President of the Supreme Military Tribunal was Admiral Bastian, and in the last months General Von Scheele; the Chief Prosecuting Attorney was Colonel Kraell; the Presidents of the different sections were General Barwinski, General Rischer, General Ernst, General Neumann; Admiral Harpst, General Hoffmann, and General Schmautzer.
97. *Allgemeine Heeresmittailungen* no. 326/44, issued 21 June 1944.
98. These figures were published in the Reich Ministry of Propaganda publication, *Die Lage*, 23 August 1944, and are taken from *News Digest*, 21 April 1945, #1740.
99. OSS, CID #129731S.

## 30: Status and Prospects of German Trade-Unions and Works Councils

1. *Internationales Handwörterbuch des Gewerkschaftswesens*, Berlin, 1932, p. 1500 f.
2. *Internationales Handwörterbuch des Gewerkschaftswesens*, Berlin, 1932, p. 1501.
3. Fritz Tarnow, "Wirtschaftsdemokratie und Sozialismus," in *Jahrbuch der deutschen Sozialdemokratie*, Berlin, 1928.
4. General MacSherry, Director of the Manpower Division of US Military

Government, declared in February 1946: "While German industrialists still adhere to nationalistic doctrines and advocate aggressive war, thus failing to show any intention of working for Germany's democratic reconstruction, the German workers are today the most democratic class of the population." German trade-union activity in the last few months, General MacSherry said, had convinced him that they were taking their democratic reconstruction work very seriously. Frankfurt radio, February 8, quoted in (British) *Digest for Germany and Austria*, February 9, 1946.

5. Source N, September 27; OSS R&A Field Intelligence Study no. 16, *Preparations for Trade-Union Activities in Bavaria*, August 8; Field Memorandum no. 892, *Trade-Union Developments in Essen and Adjacent Cities*, September 21, 1946.

6. Source N, September 27, 1945.

7. Some Christian and Democratic trade-unionists dissented. Ibid.

8. Field Intelligence Study no. 16, loc. cit.

9. See D, 1, below.

10. *Manchester Guardian*, October 12, as quoted in PID, *Digest for Germany and Austria*, October 12, 1945.

11. IRIS R&A Report no. 1113.127, October 5, 1945.

12. *Gewerkschafts-Zeitung* (Hamburg), February 1946.

13. REF-097.3/Z640/A-61119.

14. OSS R&A Report no. 1113.125, September 8, 1945.

15. Source N, September 27; *Hochland-Bote* (Garmisch-Partenkirchen), December 22, 1945.

16. OSS/IRIS R&A Reports no. 1113.125, September 3; no. 1113.127, October 5, 1945.

17. OSS R&A Report no. 1113.126, September 21, 1945.

18. Ibid.

19. T-771, March 13, 1946.

20. REF-097.3/Z640/A-28314; 28317.

21. See SHAEF directive of July 7, and OSS R&A Report no. 1113.120, July 21, 1946.

22. REF–P–389, no. 28; *Aachener Nachrichten*, February 12, 1946.

23. See General Eisenhower's proclamation of April 21 in *Die Mitteilungen*, 12th Army Group, April 21, 1945.

24. *Die neue deutsche Gewerkschaftsbewegung: Programmverschläge für einen einheitlichen deutschen Gewerkschaftsbund*, London, 1945.

25. REF-LP/9–1234.

26. See, for example, the preamble to the expropriation decree promulgated by the Saxon state administration in November 1945: "German monopolistic capital bears the chief guilt for Hitler's criminal war policy. . . . The only way to prevent German monopolistic capitalism from plunging the world into the misfortunes of a new war is to deprive the German monopolistic capitalists of their economic power, and to make the productive facilities which are in their hands useful for the benefit and the interests of the entire people." REF-P-390, no. 38.

27. General Berzerin's order of June 14; see *Betrieb und Gewerkschaft* (Berlin), September 1945.

28. FBIS: *Ticker*, March 4, 1946.

29. *Deutsche Volkszeitung* (Berlin), October 26, 1945.

30. FBIS: *Ticker*, March 22, 1946.

31. Allied Control Council Directive no. 14, October 31, 1945, in *Official Gazette of the Control Council for Germany*, no. 3, January 31, 1946.

32. Ibid.

33. Ibid.

34. Monthly Report of Military Governor, US Zone: *Manpower, Trade-Unions, and Working Conditions*, January 20, 1946.

35. Frankfurt Radio, February 11; quoted in (British) *Digest for Germany and Austria*, February 14, 1946.

36. USFET Directive, July 1945, section XV, part 4.

37. Source N, December 3, 1945.

38. Monthly Report of Military Governor, US Zone, January 20, 1946.

39. *Mittelbayerische Zeitung* (Regensburg), April 18, 1946.

40. FBIS: *Daily*, June 5, 1946.

41. REF-P-374, no. 40.

42. Monthly Report of Military Governor, US Zone: *Manpower, Trade-Unions, and Working Conditions*, January 20, 1946.

43. *Der Tagesspiegel* (Berlin), March 16, 1946.

44. *Hessische Nachrichten* (Kassel), May 4, 1946.

45. *Frankfurter Rundschau*, March 23, 1946.

46. Monthly Report of Military Governor US Zone: *Manpower, Trade-Unions, and Working Conditions*, February 20, 1946.

47. *Frankfurter Rundschau*, February 20, 1946.

48. *Die Neue Zeitung* (Munich), April 19, 1946.

49. *Mittelbayerische Zeitung*, April 18, 1946.

50. FBIS: *Daily*, May 7, 1946.

51. Monthly Report of Military Governor US Zone: *Manpower, Trade-Unions, and Working Conditions*, April 20, 1946.

52. REF-097.3/Z640/A-65935. For the parallel development in the British Zone, see II B, below.

53. Department of State Plain Airgram, The Hague, June 7, 1946.

54. OSS R&A Field Intelligence Study no. 16, loc. cit.

55. REF-097.3/Z640/A-55981.

56. OSS R&A Field Intelligence Study no. 16, loc. cit.

57. *Mittelbayerische Zeitung*, March 22, 1946.

58. Ibid.

59. Frankfurt Radio, March 1; quoted in PID Digest, March 6, 1946.

60. *Der Berliner*, December 6, 1945.

61. *Gewerkschafts-Zeitung*, February 1946.

62. *Der Berliner*, December 6, 1945; REF-P-389, no. 28.

63. Source N, February 11, 1946.

64. Source N, February 11, 1946.

65. *Weser Kurier* (Bremen), March 16, 1946.

66. *Neue Rheinische Zeitung* (Düsseldorf), February 9, 1946.

67. Monthly Report of Military Governor, U. S. Zone: *Manpower, Trade-Unions, and Working Conditions*, January 20, 1946.

68. *Neue Rheinische Zeitung*, February 9, According to the *Rheinische Zeitung* of

March 2, 1946, 29 industrial unions were authorized in the North Rhine Province as of that date.

69. REF-097.3/Z640/A-66381.

70. *Daily Herald* (London), February 8, quoted in (British) *Digest for Germany and Austria*, February 9, 1946.

71. REF-P390, no.42.

72. *Osnabrücker Rundschau*, March 23, 1946.

73. REF-097.3/Z640/A-62341.

74. REF-097.3/Z640/A-61626.

75. *Schwarzwälder Post*, quoted in *Neuer Mainzer Anzeiger*, October 26, 1945.

76. *Der Tagesspiegel*, February 9, 1946.

77. Monthly Report of Military Governor U. S. Zone: *Manpower, Trade-Unions, and Working Conditions*, April 20, 1946.

78. Proclamation of the Preparatory Trade-Union Committee for Greater Berlin, June 15, in *Betrieb und Gewerkschaft*, September 1945.

79. *Die Freie Gewerkschaft* (Berlin), March 2, 1946.

80. *Die Freie Gewerkschaft*, February 12, 1946.

81. Hans Jendretzky, "*Nach der Konferenz*," in *Die Freie Gewerkschaft*, February 13, 1946.

82. Membership for Thuringia has been reported at 400,000, and for the state of Saxony, at 1,000,000. *Die Freie Gewerkschaft*, April 6,5, 1946.

83. *Die Freie Gewerkschaft*, March 10: *Das Volk* (Berlin), February 6, 1946.

84. The distribution of the remaining 37,000 workers is unknown.

85. *Die Freie Gewerkschaft*, February 12, 1946.

86. *Die Freie Gewerkschaft*, February 5, 1946.

87. Ibid.

88. ORI Report no. 1113.136, February 6, 1946.

89. *Deutsche Volkszeitung*, February 12, 1946.

90. Walter Ulbricht, *Neue Aufgaben der freien Gewerkschaften, Neue Weg*, Berlin, 1946, pp. 47–68.

91. See Schlimme's report on the District Union Conference of Greater Berlin in *Das Volk*, February 3, 1946.

92. *Das Volk*, February 5, 1946.

93. Ulbricht, *Neue Aufgaben der freien Gewerkschaften*, p. 17, and more recently in his speech before the zonal union's executive committee. *Die Freie Gewerkschaft*, April 7, 1946. See also Paul Walter as quoted in FBIS, *Daily*, October 1, 1945.

94. *Das Volk*, March 23, 1946.

95. Roman Chwalek, "Sind wir ein Unterstützungsverein?" *Die Freie Gewerkschaft*, April 10, 1945.

96. *Deutsche Volkszeitung*, January 29, 1946.

97. Ulbricht in *Die Freie Gewerkschaft*, April 7, 1946.

98. *Das Volk* of February 10, 1946, contains a complaint that the Berlin trade-unions have not as yet been called upon by the Magistrate to discuss the 1946 production plan.

99. *Das Volk*, September 28, 1945.

100. *Deutsche Volkszeitung*, January 29, 1946.

101. *Neuaufbau der deutschen Wirtschaft: Richtlinien der KP zur Wirtschaftspolitik*, *Neuer Weg*, Berlin, p. 23.

102. Field Memorandum no. 892, loc. cit.

103. Field Intelligence Study no. 16, loc. cit.

104. Monthly Report of Military Governor, U. S.Zone: *Manpower, Trade-Unions, and Working Conditions*, February 20, 1946.

105. *Fuldaer Volkszeitung*, November 10; FBIS: *Ticker*, November 8, 1945.

106. *Der Berliner*, December 6, 1945; ORI Report no. 1113.134, January 9, 1946.

107. Monthly Report of Military Governor, U. S. Zone, loc. cit., January 20, 1946.

108. FBIS: *Ticker*, February 21, 1946.

109. Source N, November 25, 1945.

110. *Der Berliner*, March 24; detailed figures in *Deutsche Volkszeitung*, March 23, 1946.

111. As of December 1945, about 342,000 workers were employed in mining in the British Zone. REF-P-64, #22.

112. *Deutsche Volkszeitung*, March 24, 1946.

113. *Deutsche Volkszeitung*, September 12, 1945.

114. *Das Volk*, September 8, 1945.

115. FBIS: *Ticker*, October 23, 1945.

116. *Warum Betriebsräte*, in «Deutsche Volkszeitung», 16 settembre; Chwalek in «Deutsche Volkszeitung», October 25 1945.

117. *Tägliche Rundschau* (Berlin), October 4, 1945.

118. Thus, for instance, the district committee of the Chemnitz trade-unions has addressed requests for the setting up of planning commissions (which will also take charge of machinery exchange and of price formation) to the trade-union committees rather than to the works councils. FBIS: *Daily*, March 23, 1946.

119. Text of the draft in *Grundsätze, Satzungen, Forderungen des Freien Deutschen Gewerkschaftsbundes*.

120. *Mittelbayerische Zeitung*, March 22, 1946.

121. *Weser Kurier*, March 16, 1946.

122. *Tägliche Rundschau*, April 18, 1946.

123. Walter Ulbricht, *Neue Aufgaben der freien Gewerkschaften*, Berlin, 1946.

# INDEX